Lecture Notes in Business Information Processing 335

More information about this series at http://www.springer.com/series/7911

Robert Andrei Buchmann · Dimitris Karagiannis
Marite Kirikova (Eds.)

The Practice of Enterprise Modeling

11th IFIP WG 8.1. Working Conference, PoEM 2018
Vienna, Austria, October 31 – November 2, 2018
Proceedings

 Springer

Editors
Robert Andrei Buchmann (iD)
Babeş-Bolyai University
Cluj-Napoca
Romania

Marite Kirikova (iD)
Riga Technical University
Riga
Latvia

Dimitris Karagiannis
University of Vienna
Vienna
Austria

ISSN 1865-1348   ISSN 1865-1356   (electronic)
Lecture Notes in Business Information Processing
ISBN 978-3-030-02301-0   ISBN 978-3-030-02302-7   (eBook)
https://doi.org/10.1007/978-3-030-02302-7

Library of Congress Control Number: 2018957482

This Springer imprint is published by the registered company Springer Nature Switzerland AG
The registered company address is: Gewerbestrasse 11, 6330 Cham, Switzerland

Preface

The 2018 edition of PoEM (the IFIP WG 8.1 Working Conference on the Practice of Enterprise Modeling) followed an established tradition, being the 11th annual event in this conference series that was initiated in 2008 in Stockholm and has become the main European conference on enterprise modeling. This year, from October 31 to November 2, the conference was hosted by the University of Vienna, organized by the Knowledge Engineering Research Group at the Faculty of Computer Science.

Vienna is Austria's primary cultural, political, and economic center. The University of Vienna is one of the oldest and biggest universities in the German-speaking area, founded in 1365 by Duke Rudolph IV – since then, it has been the academic home of 15 Nobel Prize winners and the origin of highly influential schools of thought. Its Faculty of Computer Science is an important academic hub for the enterprise modeling community, as it hosts the annual NEMO ("Next-Generation Enterprise Modeling") Summer School series.

Enterprise modeling is an established research discipline that was crystallized from technological pillars and methodological enablers emerging from fundamental and applicative research in a diversity of fields – e.g., conceptual modeling, enterprise architecture management, business process management, information systems development, knowledge management systems, and decision support systems. PoEM aims at orchestrating such enablers in coherent methods for capturing multiple perspectives on enterprise systems, to solve practical challenges and to establish a shared understanding of the value of enterprise models and their building blocks. The community fostered by this conference series is interested in enterprise knowledge both for its instrumental value — as a means to an end (e.g., for decision support, information systems development) — and for its intrinsic value, as self-contained knowledge assets coming under the scrutiny of research paradigms such as design science or data science.

Since 2008 when PoEM was initiated with the support of IFIP WG 8.1, the problems raised by this community gained visibility, stimulated the dissemination of roadmaps and experience reports, as well as the development of novel modeling methods addressing various perspectives and requirements. A novel teaching agenda and a practice-oriented roadmap for "enterprise modeling for the masses" are emerging from the community and have taken central place in the recent editions of the conference, evolving in several dedicated workshops.

Two workshops were organized this year at PoEM: the second edition of the practice-oriented workshop PrOse (Practicing Open Enterprise Modeling with OMi-LAB) and the education-focused workshop TLCM (Teaching and Learning Conceptual Modeling). In order to kick start the discussions during the first conference day, a doctoral consortium section was also included, highlighting key research challenges that will set future roadmaps.

We received 64 submissions for the conference, including research papers, experience papers, and short papers. Based on the reviews by members of the Program

Committee, we selected 21 full papers and five short papers (an acceptance rate of 33% for full papers and 40% including short papers). The full papers are grouped in the following topics: Business Process Modeling, Model Derivation, Collaboration Modeling, Reviews and Analyses of Modeling Methods, Semantics and Reasoning, Experience Reports, and Teaching Challenges.

We express our gratitude to the conference Steering Committee, who agreed to have this edition hosted in Vienna and have continuously provided assistance: Prof. Anne Persson, Prof. Janis Stirna, and Prof. Kurt Sandkuhl. An international, widely recognized forum of experts contributed to PoEM 2018, including the notable keynote speakers: Prof. Eric Dubois from Luxembourg Institute of Science and Technology and Prof. Dimitris Kiritsis from École Polytechnique Fédérale de Lausanne. We thank them as well as all the authors who submitted their work and the Program Committee members who ensured a high-quality selection of papers while providing insightful advice for improving the contributions.

We thank IFIP WG 8.1 for allowing this conference series to evolve under its auspices. We also thank the global community of the Open Models Laboratory (OMiLAB, www.omilab.org), which hosts and disseminates results from several enterprise modeling open access projects that have often contributed valuable submissions to PoEM and its workshops. We also thank the Springer team led by Alfred Hofmann and Ralf Gerstner for the technical support regarding the publication of this volume.

Last but not least, we would like to thank the organization team lead by Victoria Döller and Elena Miron for their hard work in ensuring the success of this event.

September 2018   Robert Andrei Buchmann
                                                       Dimitris Karagiannis
                                                       Marite Kirikova

Organization

PoEM 2018 was hosted by the Faculty of Computer Science, University of Vienna, Austria, from October 31 to November 2.

General Chair

Dimitris Karagiannis   University of Vienna, Austria

Program and Publication Co-chairs

Robert Andrei Buchmann   Babeş-Bolyai University of Cluj Napoca, Romania
Mārīte Kirikova   Riga Technical University, Latvia

Local Organizing Chairs

Victoria Döller   University of Vienna, Austria
Elena Miron   University of Vienna, Austria

Steering Committee

Anne Persson   University of Skövde, Sweden
Janis Stirna   University of Stockholm, Sweden
Kurt Sandkuhl   University of Rostock, Germany

Program Committee

Raian Ali   Bournemouth University, UK
Joao Paulo Almeida   Federal University of Espirito Santo, Brazil
Amelia Bădică   University of Craiova, Romania
Judith Barrios Albornoz   University of Los Andes, Colombia
Giuseppe Berio   Université de Bretagne Sud, France
Dominik Bork   University of Vienna, Austria
Robert Andrei Buchmann   Babeş-Bolyai University of Cluj Napoca, Romania
Rimantas Butleris   University of Technology, Lithuania
Tony Clark   Aston University, UK
Sergio de Cesare   University of Westminster, UK
Wolfgang Deiters   Hochschule für Gesundheit, Germany
Michael Fellmann   University of Rostock, Germany
Hans-Georg Fill   University of Bamberg, Germany
Frederik Gailly   Ghent University, Belgium
Marcela Genero   University of Castilla-La Mancha, Spain

Pnina Soffer   University of Haifa, Israel
Janis Stirna   Stockholm University
Darijus Strasunskas   POSC Caesar Association, Norway
Victoria Torres   Universitat Politècnica de València, Spain
Irene Vanderfeesten   Eindhoven University of Technology, The Netherlands
Olegas Vasilecas   Vilnius Technical University, Lithuania
Hans Weigand   Tilburg University, The Netherlands
Robert Woitsch   BOC Asset Management, Austria
Eric Yu   University of Toronto, Canada
Jelena Zdravkovic   Stockholm University, Sweden

Additional Reviewers

Victoria Döller   University of Vienna, Austria
Dominik Huth   Technical University of Munich, Germany
Kestutis Kapocius   Kaunas University of Technology, Lithuania
Martin Kleehaus   Technical University of Munich, Germany
Felix Michel   Technical University of Munich, Germany
Andrea Morichetta   University of Camerino, Italy
Kestutis Normantas   Vilnius Technical University, Lithuania
Ivan S. Razo-Zapata   Luxembourg IST, Luxembourg
Tiago Prince Sales   University of Trento, Italy
Titas Savickas   Vilnius Technical University, Lithuania
Jake Tom   University of Tartu, Estonia
Margus Välja   KTH Royal Institute of Technology, Sweden
Michael Walch   University of Vienna, Austria

Keynotes (Abstracts)

Towards a Megamodel Driven Approach for Regulatory Information Systems

Eric Dubois

Luxembourg Institute of Science and Technology, Luxembourg
`eric.dubois@list.lu`

Abstract. Today, business organizations are more and more facing compliance issues coming from international and national regulatory bodies, from standardisation bodies as well as from recognised professional and/or sectorial associations. Demonstrating compliance to all the requirements included in the different regulations and norms requires huge and costly efforts, in particular regarding the development of information systems supporting the reporting to the supervision bodies. For the supervisory authorities (regulators, auditors, etc.), there are also important challenges in particular regarding the interpretation and the comparison between the reports issued by the different supervised organisations. It is often the case that two business organisations in a completely similar situation (in terms of work practices, infrastructures, etc.) will come with a different reporting due to their interpretation of norms as well as of the nature of evidences that have been collected and compiled for the reporting. An additional complexity comes for business organisations having to report on their compliance to multiple norms.

Where overlapping multi-regulations apply, there is an additional need for a business organisation to use a unique reporting regulatory information system and not to manage several systems with overlapping information. In a world of multi-regulations/multi-regulators, we plead for a standardisation of the reporting for the benefits of regulated entities and of supervisory bodies. This standardisation should apply to the regulatory information systems shared by the different parties. Our proposal is to build these systems on top of conceptual informal models derived from the interpretation of the different norms. Because of the overlap and complementarities of these norms, there is also an important need associated with the management of models derived from them: some common sub-models associated with different norms, more specialised models, different models viewpoints associated with the business organisations and the supervisory bodies, etc. To this end, we are investigating some technological solution based on the concept of megamodel which aims at supporting the management of heterogeneous set of models.

Connecting the Dots in Smart PLM: Preparing Big Industrial Data for Cognitive Analytics and Manufacturing

Dimitris Kiritsis

École Polytechnique Fédérale de Lausanne, Lausanne, Switzerland
dimitris.kiritsis@epfl.ch

Abstract. In the context of Circular Economy, Closed-Loop PLM extends the meaning of PLM in order to close the loop of the information among the different lifecycle phases of a product. Data and information from Middle-of-Life (MOL) such us usage data, maintenance activities, updates etc., could be used at the End-of-Life (EOL) stage to support deciding the most appropriate EOL option (specially to make decisions for re-manufacturing and re-use) and, moreover, combined with EOL data and information it could be used as feedback to the Beginning-of-Life (BOL) phase for improving the new generations of products. Ontologies and associated semantic technologies such as Knowledge Graphs are rapidly becoming popular in various domains and applications to deal with the tremendous increase of available data captured all along the lifecycle of a product. Currently, there is a trend both in converting existing models into ontology-based models, and in creating new ontology-based models from scratch. The aim of this talk is to present the advantages and features provided by the ontologies into PLM models towards achieving Closed-Loop Lifecycle Management.

Contents

Reviews and Analyses of Modeling Methods

Semantics and Reasoning

Experience Reports

Teaching Challenges

Short Papers

Business Process Modeling

Formalising BPMN Service Interaction Patterns

Chiara Muzi[1]([⊠]), Luise Pufahl[2], Lorenzo Rossi[1], Mathias Weske[2], and Francesco Tiezzi[1]

[1] School of Science and Technology, University of Camerino, Camerino, Italy
{chiara.muzi,lorenzo.rossi,francesco.tiezzi}@unicam.it
[2] Hasso-Plattner-Institute, University of Potsdam, Potsdam, Germany
{luise.pufahl,mathias.weske}@hpi.de

Abstract. Business process management is especially challenging when crossing organisational boundaries. Inter-organisational business relationships are considered as a first-class citizen in BPMN collaboration diagrams, where multiple participants interact via messages. Nevertheless, proper carrying out of such interactions may be difficult due to BPMN lack of formal semantics. In particular, no formal studies have been specifically done to cope with complex BPMN interaction scenarios unified under the name of *Service Interaction Patterns*. In this work the depiction of the service interaction patterns in BPMN collaboration diagrams is revisited and fully formalised via a direct semantics for BPMN multi-instance collaborations, thus leaving no room for ambiguity and validating the BPMN semantics. To make the formalisation more accessible, a visualisation of the patterns execution by means of a BPMN model animation tool is provided.

Keywords: BPMN · Collaboration · Service interaction patterns
Formalisation

1 Introduction

The effective and efficient handling of business processes is a primary goal of organisations. Business Process Management (BPM) provides methods and techniques to support these endeavors [17]. Thereby, the main artefacts are business process models which help to document, analyse, improve, and automate organisation processes [13]. To this aim, nowadays BPMN (Business Process Model and Notation) [16] is the modelling notation most widely applied in industry and academia.

For conducting a successful business, an organisation does not act alone, but it is usually involved in collaborations with other organisations. The importance of interactions has been underlined by many authors [1,2,10] and a lot of effort has been done to identify the most common interaction scenarios from

© IFIP International Federation for Information Processing 2018
Published by Springer Nature Switzerland AG 2018. All Rights Reserved
R. A. Buchmann et al. (Eds.): PoEM 2018, LNBIP 335, pp. 3–20, 2018.
https://doi.org/10.1007/978-3-030-02302-7_1

a business perspective, which have been called *Service Interaction Patterns* [3]. Interactions are considered as a first-class citizen in BPMN collaboration diagrams, where multiple participants cooperate by exchanging messages and sharing thereby data. This motivated the use of BPMN to model service interaction patterns [17], initially defined only in terms of textual descriptions. This effort provided a graphical, more intuitive, description of the patterns and allowed to assess the suitability of BPMN to express common interaction scenarios. However, a severe issue in this study is that the precise behaviour of the BPMN models corresponding to some patterns may result unclear, in particular when multiple instances of the interacting participants are involved. This problem is mainly due to the fact that the BPMN standard comes without a formal semantics, which is needed in presence of tricky features, like multiple process instantiation.

In this paper, we then aim at formalising the execution semantics of service interaction patterns specified in BPMN. This is a particularly important challenge in the BPM domain, as a precise semantics of the message exchanges as well as their dependencies is a prerequisite to ensure the appropriate carrying out, in practice, of such interactions. To achieve this goal, we resort to a formal semantics for BPMN collaborations including multiple instances introduced in [6]. The operational semantics is directly defined on BPMN elements in terms of Labelled Transition Systems (LTSs), rather than as an encoding into other formalisms. Specifically, for each service interaction pattern we report the related BPMN collaboration model and provide its formalisation in terms of transitions of the corresponding LTS.

A direct formal characterisation is crucial, as it does not leave any room for ambiguity, and increases the potential for formal reasoning. This is especially important when dealing with multiple instances, whose static and compact BPMN representation hides their complex semantics. Moreover, the BPMN formalisation in [6] enables the use of the MIDA animation tool [7] that provides a visualisation, faithfully following the semantics, of patterns execution. This makes the behaviour of patterns easily understandable also to an audience non-familiar with formal methods. Finally, since the service interaction patterns have been used to evaluate different choreography languages [5], their formalisation allows to validate the BPMN semantics itself, both in terms of the considered BPMN elements and of the expected semantic behaviour.

In the remainder of this paper, we start with the introduction of a motivational example in Sect. 2, followed by an overview of the formalisation of BPMN collaboration diagrams in Sect. 3. In Sect. 4 we provide the representation of the service interaction patterns in BPMN and their formalisation. We present the patterns animation in Sect. 5. Finally, related work is discussed in Sect. 6 and the paper is concluded in Sect. 7.

2   Motivating Scenario

In this section we introduce an order fulfilment scenario to illustrate BPMN 2.0 collaboration diagrams and the depiction of service interaction patterns.

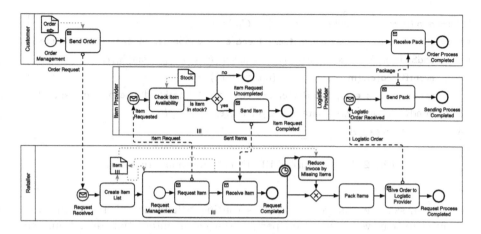

Fig. 1. BPMN collaboration diagram of the order fulfilment scenario.

The considered scenario shows an interaction among a Customer, a Retailer, multiple Item Providers and a Logistic Provider (Fig. 1). The processes of the different interacting partners are represented inside rectangles, called *pools*, and their interaction is given by message edges (dashed connectors) visualising communication flows.

The order fulfilment process is started by the Customer who sends an "Order Request" to the Retailer, via a *send task*. The arrival of this message starts, via a *message start event*, a process instance of the Retailer pool. This latter creates a list of needed items and stores this information in the "Item" *data object collection*. For each item, the Retailer sends out a request to an Item Provider and waits for the response. This interaction is rendered by a *multi-instance sub-process* communicating with the *multi-instance pool* of the Item Provider: each message of the Retailer creates a new process instance of the Item Provider pool. Each Provider checks for items availability and decides either to "Send Item" or not, by following one of the outgoing edges of the *XOR split gateway*, according to the information in the "Stock" data object. In case the item is not available, the Provider does not respond back to the Retailer. Thus, the Retailer rather stops waiting as soon as enough responses have arrived or a given timeout is expired. This latter behaviour is rendered by the *timer event* attached to the sub-process, whose activation produces the execution of task "Reduce Invoice by Missing Items". The Retailer then packs the items and passes the needed information to the Logistic Provider, who is in charge to send the package to the Customer. When the Customer receives the ordered items, via a *receiving task*, its process completes.

In this scenario, already various interaction patterns can be observed, such as *One-to-many send/receive* between the Retailer and the Item Provider(s), or the *Request with Referral* between the Customer, Retailer and Logistic Provider [3]. The service interactions represent different types of dynamic behaviour, ranging from simple message exchanges, to scenarios involving multiple participants and

$$
\begin{aligned}
C ::=\ &\textsf{pool}(\textsf{p}, P) \quad | \quad \textsf{miPool}(\textsf{p}, P) \quad | \quad C_1 \parallel C_2 \\
P ::=\ &\textsf{start}(\textsf{e}_{enb}, \textsf{e}_o) \ | \ \textsf{startRcv}(\textsf{m} : \tilde{\textsf{t}}, \textsf{e}_o) \ | \ \textsf{end}(\textsf{e}_i) \ | \ \textsf{endSnd}(\textsf{e}_i, \textsf{m} : \tilde{\textsf{exp}}) \ | \ \textsf{terminate}(\textsf{e}_i) \\
&| \ \ \textsf{andSplit}(\textsf{e}_i, E_o) \ | \ \textsf{xorSplit}(\textsf{e}_i, G) \ | \ \textsf{andJoin}(E_i, \textsf{e}_o) \ | \ \textsf{xorJoin}(E_i, \textsf{e}_o) \\
&| \ \ \textsf{eventBased}(\textsf{e}_i, (\textsf{m}_1 : \tilde{\textsf{t}}_1, \textsf{e}_{o1}), \ldots, (\textsf{m}_h : \tilde{\textsf{t}}_h, \textsf{e}_{oh})) \\
&| \ \ \textsf{task}(\textsf{e}_i, \textsf{exp}, A, \textsf{e}_o) \ | \ \textsf{taskRcv}(\textsf{e}_i, \textsf{exp}, A, \textsf{m} : \tilde{\textsf{t}}, \textsf{e}_o) \ | \ \textsf{taskSnd}(\textsf{e}_i, \textsf{exp}, A, \textsf{m} : \tilde{\textsf{exp}}, \textsf{e}_o) \\
&| \ \ \textsf{interRcv}(\textsf{e}_i, \textsf{m} : \tilde{\textsf{t}}, \textsf{e}_o) \ | \ \textsf{interSnd}(\textsf{e}_i, \textsf{m} : \tilde{\textsf{exp}}, \textsf{e}_o) \ | \ P_1 \parallel P_2 \\
A ::=\ &\epsilon \ \ | \ \textsf{d.f} ::= \textsf{exp}, A
\end{aligned}
$$

Fig. 2. BNF syntax of BPMN collaboration structures.

multiple message exchanges, as well as routing behaviour, where information is routed to a new collaboration partner during an interaction (e.g. from the Retailer to the Logistic Provider). As the service interaction patterns are textually provided, a visualisation as well as a formalisation is crucial to precisely render the message exchanges between participants, especially because multiple instances are involved. In particular, the interactions between the Retailer sub-process and the Item Provider may result quite intricate, as both generate multiple instances and, in addition, the sub-process is constrained by a timer event. Without a clear understanding of the interplay between these features, formally provided by the operational semantics, different interpretations may easily arise.

3   Background Notions on the BPMN Formalisation

In this section we provide an overview of the formal semantics of BPMN multi-instance collaborations given in [6]. The formalisation relies on a textual representation of the structure of BPMN collaboration models, defined by the Backus-Naur Form (BNF) grammar in Fig. 2. In the proposed grammar, the non-terminal symbols C, P and A represent *Collaboration Structures*, *Process Structures* and *Data Assignments*, respectively. The first two syntactic categories directly refer to the corresponding notions in BPMN, while the latter refers to list of assignments used to specify updating of data objects. The terminal symbols, denoted by the sans serif font, are the typical elements of a BPMN model, i.e. pools, events, tasks and gateways.

Intuitively, a BPMN collaboration model is rendered in this syntax as a collection of pools, each one specifying a process. Formally, a collaboration C is a composition, by means of the $\parallel$ operator, of pools. A pool is either of the form $\textsf{pool}(\textsf{p}, P)$ (for single-instance pools), or $\textsf{miPool}(\textsf{p}, P)$ (for multi-instance pools) where p is the name that uniquely identifies the pool, and P is the enclosed process. At process level, $\textsf{e} \in \mathbb{E}$ uniquely denotes a *sequence edge*, while $E \in 2^{\mathbb{E}}$ is a set of edges. For the convenience of the reader, $\textsf{e}_i$ refers to the edge incoming in an element, while $\textsf{e}_o$ to the outgoing edge, and $\textsf{e}_{enb}$ to the (spurious) edge denoting the enabled status of a start event.

To describe the semantics of collaboration models, we enrich the structural information with a notion of execution state, defined by the state of each process instance and the store of the exchanged messages. We call process configurations and collaboration configurations these stateful descriptions. Formally, a *process configuration* has the form $\langle P, \sigma, \alpha \rangle$, where: P is a process structure; $\sigma : \mathbb{E} \to \mathbb{N}$ is a *sequence edge state function* specifying, for each sequence edge, the current number of tokens marking it ($\mathbb{N}$ is the set of natural numbers); and $\alpha : \mathbb{F} \to \mathbb{V}$ is the *data state function* assigning values (possibly null) to data object fields ($\mathbb{F}$ is the set of data fields and $\mathbb{V}$ the set of values). A *collaboration configuration* has the form $\langle C, \iota, \delta \rangle$, where: C is a collaboration structure, $\iota : \mathbb{P} \to 2^{\mathbb{S}_\sigma \times \mathbb{S}_\alpha}$ is the *instance state function* mapping each pool name ($\mathbb{P}$ is the set of pool names) to a multiset of instance states (ranged over by I and containing pairs of the form $\langle \sigma, \alpha \rangle$), with $\mathbb{S}_\sigma$ and $\mathbb{S}_\alpha$ the sets of edges and data states, and $\delta : \mathbb{M} \to 2^{\mathbb{V}^n}$ is a *message state function* specifying for each message name $\mathsf{m} \in \mathbb{M}$ a multiset of value tuples representing the messages received along the message edge with the label m.

The operational semantics is defined by means of a *labelled transition system* (LTS), whose definition relies on an auxiliary LTS on the behaviour of processes. The latter is a triple $\langle \mathcal{P}, \mathcal{L}, \to \rangle$ where: $\mathcal{P}$ ranged over by $\langle P, \sigma, \alpha \rangle$ is a set of process configurations, $\mathcal{L}$ ranged over by ℓ, is a set of *labels*, and $\to \subseteq \mathcal{P} \times \mathcal{L} \times \mathcal{P}$ is a *transition relation*. We will write $\langle P, \sigma, \alpha \rangle \xrightarrow{\ell} \langle P, \sigma', \alpha' \rangle$ to indicate that $(\langle P, \sigma, \alpha \rangle, \ell, \langle P, \sigma', \alpha' \rangle) \in \to$. Now, the labelled transition relation on collaboration configurations formalises the message exchange and the data update according to the process evolution. The LTS is a triple $\langle \mathcal{C}, \mathcal{L}_c, \to_c \rangle$ where: $\mathcal{C}$, ranged over by $\langle C, \iota, \delta \rangle$, is a set of collaboration configurations; $\mathcal{L}_c$, ranged over by l, is a set of *labels*; and $\to_c \subseteq \mathcal{C} \times \mathcal{L}_c \times \mathcal{C}$ is a *transition relation*.

We refer the interested reader to [6] for a full account of the definition of these relations, while we report in Fig. 3, by way of example, some operational rules. Rule *P-TaskSnd* is used for the execution of send tasks possibly equipped with data objects. These latter are associated to a task by means of a conditional expression, exp', and a list of assignments A, each of which assigns the value of an expression to a data field (the field f of the data object named d is accessed via $\mathsf{d.f}$). Sending tasks also have as argument a pair of the form $\mathsf{m} : \tilde{\mathsf{exp}}$, where m is a message name and $\tilde{\mathsf{exp}}$ is a tuple of expressions. The task is activated only when there is a token in the incoming edge of the task ($\sigma(\mathsf{e}_i) > 0$) and the task's guard exp' is satisfied ($eval(\mathsf{exp}', \alpha, true)$). The effects of the task execution are as follows: the marking σ of the process instance is updated with the movement of one token from e_i to e_o, by means of functions dec and inc, and the message action $!\mathsf{m} : \tilde{v}$ is produced, where the message content $\tilde{v}$ results from the evaluation of the expression tuple $\tilde{\mathsf{exp}}$ ($eval(\tilde{\mathsf{exp}}, \alpha, \tilde{v})$). The produced label is used to deliver the message at the collaboration layer (see rule *C-Deliver*). Rule *P-InterRcv* is similar, but it produces a label corresponding to the reception of a message, which is actually consumed by rule *C-Receive*. Rule *P-XorSplit₁* is applied when a token is available in the incoming edge of a XOR split gateway and a conditional expression of one of its outgoing edges is evaluated to true;

$$\frac{\langle \mathsf{taskSnd}(\mathsf{e}_i, \exp', A, \mathsf{m}\!:\!\tilde{\exp}, \mathsf{e}_o), \sigma, \alpha\rangle \xrightarrow{\;!m:\tilde{v}\;} \begin{array}{l} \sigma(\mathsf{e}_i) > 0, \\ eval(\exp', \alpha, true), \\ upd(\alpha, A, \alpha'), \\ eval(\tilde{\exp}, \alpha, \tilde{v}) \end{array}}{\langle inc(dec(\sigma, \mathsf{e}_i), \mathsf{e}_o), \alpha'\rangle} \quad (P\text{-}TaskSnd)$$

$$\frac{\langle \mathsf{interRcv}(\mathsf{e}_i, \mathsf{m}\!:\!\tilde{t}, \mathsf{e}_o), \sigma, \alpha\rangle \xrightarrow{\;?m:\tilde{et},\epsilon\;} \begin{array}{l} \sigma(\mathsf{e}_i) > 0, \\ eval(\tilde{t}, \alpha, \tilde{et}) \end{array}}{\langle inc(dec(\sigma, \mathsf{e}_i), \mathsf{e}_o), \alpha\rangle} \quad (P\text{-}InterRcv)$$

$$\frac{\langle \mathsf{xorSplit}(\mathsf{e}_i, \{(\mathsf{e}, \exp)\} \cup G), \sigma, \alpha\rangle \xrightarrow{\;\epsilon\;} \begin{array}{l} \sigma(\mathsf{e}_i) > 0, \\ eval(\exp, \alpha, true) \end{array}}{\langle inc(dec(\sigma, \mathsf{e}_i), \mathsf{e}), \alpha\rangle} \quad (P\text{-}XorSplit_1)$$

$$\frac{\langle P_1, \sigma, \alpha\rangle \xrightarrow{\;\ell\;} \langle \sigma', \alpha'\rangle}{\langle P_1 \parallel P_2, \sigma, \alpha\rangle \xrightarrow{\;\ell\;} \langle \sigma', \alpha'\rangle} \quad \ell \neq kill \qquad (P\text{-}Int_1)$$

$$\frac{\iota(\mathsf{p}) = \{\langle \sigma, \alpha\rangle\} \qquad \langle P, \sigma, \alpha\rangle \xrightarrow{\;!m:\tilde{v}\;} \langle \sigma', \alpha'\rangle}{\langle \mathsf{pool}(\mathsf{p}, P), \iota, \delta\rangle \xrightarrow{\;!m:\tilde{v}\;} \langle updI(\iota, \mathsf{p}, \{\langle \sigma', \alpha'\rangle\}), add(\delta, \mathsf{m}, \tilde{v})\rangle} \quad (C\text{-}Deliver)$$

$$\frac{\iota(\mathsf{p}) = \{\langle \sigma, \alpha\rangle\} \qquad \langle P, \sigma, \alpha\rangle \xrightarrow{\;?m:\tilde{et},A\;} \langle \sigma', \alpha'\rangle}{\tilde{v} \in \delta(\mathsf{m}) \qquad match(\tilde{et}, \tilde{v}) = A'}{\langle \mathsf{pool}(\mathsf{p}, P), \iota, \delta\rangle \xrightarrow{\;?m:\tilde{v}\;} \langle updI(\iota, \mathsf{p}, \{\langle \sigma', upd(\alpha', (A', A))\rangle\}), rm(\delta, \mathsf{m}, \tilde{v})\rangle} \quad (C\text{-}Receive)$$

Fig. 3. An excerpt of BPMN semantic rules.

the rule decrements the token in the incoming edge and increments the token in the selected outgoing edge. Finally, rule *P-Int₁* deals with interleaving in a standard way for process elements. More details on these rules are given in the next section, from time to time when they are applied.

4   Patterns Formalisation

In this section we present and formalise the Service Interaction Patterns [3] supported by BPMN. Since BPMN is not specifically tailored to the needs of service interaction patterns, the notation cannot completely support all their features. For instance, while the informal and general description of these patterns leaves it open if in an interaction the counter-party is known at design-time or not, in BPMN it is expected to have a priori knowledge of the interacting partners, i.e. the target pool of a message edge cannot be dynamically selected. On the other hand, in case a message is directed to a multi-instance pool, BPMN supports a form of runtime binding of the message with the correct process instance by means of the correlation mechanism [16, Sect. 8.3.2]. Moreover, it is also possible to dynamically specify other model features, such as the number of involved participants and exchanged messages. Each pattern is presented according to the following structure:

Informal Description. consists of a natural language description, and a graphical representation in terms of a BPMN collaboration fragment.

Textual Specification. provides the textual notation of the BPMN collaboration model.

Formal Semantics. describes the operational rules applied to perform each
execution step, and shows the results in terms of the execution state functions
evolution.

In the following we present first those patterns concerning single transmissions, both bilateral (Sects. 4.1–4.3) and multilateral (Sects. 4.4–4.7), and then
the routing patterns involving multiple transmissions (Sects. 4.8–4.9).

4.1   Send Pattern

Informal Description. A party sends a message
to another one. This pattern can be modelled
as the BPMN collaboration fragment in Fig. 4.
Notably, this is only a way to model it: the send
task could be replaced by an intermediate send
event or by a message end event. However, up to
some technicalities, all cases behave in the same
way, thus we report here only one of them.

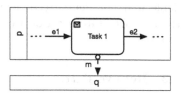

Fig. 4. Send pattern.

Textual Specification. The collaboration fragment in Fig. 4 is repre-
sented in the textual notation as $C = \mathsf{pool}(\mathsf{p}, P) \parallel \mathsf{pool}(\mathsf{q}, Q)$ with $P =$
$\mathsf{taskSnd}(\mathsf{e1}, \exp_1, \epsilon, \mathsf{m}:\tilde{\exp}_2, \mathsf{e2}) \parallel P'$, where p is the sender and q a generic
receiver (represented by a black-box pool in the graphical notation, whose pro-
cess Q is left unspecified in the textual one).

Formal Semantics. According to the form of process P, and the current state
$\langle \sigma, \alpha \rangle$ of pool p's instance, the collaboration can evolve as follows:

– Process P moves by executing Task 1. This execution step takes place
  by applying rule *P-TaskSnd*, which requires the incoming edge e1 of the
  task be marked by at least one token ($\sigma(\mathsf{e1}) > 0$), and the task's guard
  $\exp_1$ be satisfied ($eval(\exp_1, \alpha, true)$). The effects of the task execution
  are as follows: the message action $!\mathsf{m} : \tilde{v}$ is produced, where the message content $\tilde{v}$ results from the evaluation of the expression tuple $\tilde{\exp}_2$
  ($eval(\tilde{\exp}_2, \alpha, \tilde{v})$), and the marking σ of the process instance is updated with
  the movement of one token from e1 to e2, that is $\sigma' = inc(dec(\sigma, \mathsf{e1}), \mathsf{e2})$.
  Therefore, the application of rule *P-TaskSnd* produces the transition
  $\langle \mathsf{taskSnd}(\mathsf{e1}, \exp_1, \epsilon, \mathsf{m}:\tilde{\exp}_2, \mathsf{e2}), \sigma, \alpha \rangle \xrightarrow{!\mathsf{m}:\tilde{v}} \langle \sigma', \alpha \rangle$, where the data state α
  remains unchanged because no data object is connected to Task 1. Hence,
  the overall process P can evolve according to the interleaving rule *P-Int₁*,
  that is $\langle P, \sigma, \alpha \rangle \xrightarrow{!\mathsf{m}:\tilde{v}} \langle \sigma', \alpha \rangle$. Similarly, by applying the rule *C-Deliver*,
  and then the interleaving rule at collaboration level, the execution step of
  the overall collaboration C is represented by the transition $\langle C, \iota, \delta \rangle \xrightarrow{!\mathsf{m}:\tilde{v}}$
  $\langle updI(\iota, \mathsf{p}, \{\langle \sigma', \alpha \rangle\}), add(\delta, \mathsf{m}, \tilde{v}) \rangle$, with $\iota(\mathsf{p}) = \{\langle \sigma, \alpha \rangle\}$. Its effects are: updating the marking in the p's instance ($updI(\iota, \mathsf{p}, \{\langle \sigma', \alpha \rangle\})$), and updating the

message state function $(add(\delta, \mathsf{m}, \tilde{\mathsf{v}}))$ by adding a value tuple $\tilde{\mathsf{v}}$ to the m's message list, in order to be subsequently consumed by the receiving participant q.

- Process P moves by executing an (unspecified) activity of P'. Thus, we have a transition $\langle P', \sigma, \alpha \rangle \xrightarrow{\ell} \langle \sigma', \alpha' \rangle$, from which P can evolve by means of the symmetric rule of $P\text{-}Int_1$, and the overall collaboration can then evolve accordingly. This execution step, anyway, is not relevant for the pattern semantics, and hence is not discussed in more detail.
- Process Q moves by executing an (unspecified) activity. Again this execution step is not relevant for the pattern semantics.

Relying on asynchronous communication, we are able to formalise an unreliable and non-guaranteed delivery. The sending action in fact just updates the message state function by adding a message, without requiring this to be received.

4.2   Receive Pattern

Informal Description. A party receives a message from another party. This pattern can be modelled as the BPMN collaboration fragment shown in Fig. 5. Also here the intermediate receive event could be replaced, in this case by a receive task or by a receiving start event.

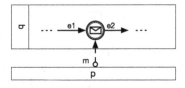

Fig. 5. Receive pattern.

Textual Specification. The textual representation of the collaboration fragment in Fig. 5 has again the form C of the previous pattern, with $Q = \mathsf{interRcv}(\mathsf{e1}, \mathsf{m}\!:\!\tilde{\mathsf{t}}, \mathsf{e2}) \parallel Q'$.

Formal Semantics. Assuming that the intermediate receive event is enabled by a token in e1, the process Q can perform a receiving action, that is the transition $\langle \mathsf{interRcv}(\mathsf{e1}, \mathsf{m}\!:\!\tilde{\mathsf{t}}, \mathsf{e2}), \sigma, \alpha \rangle \xrightarrow{?\mathsf{m}\,:\,\tilde{\mathsf{et}},\epsilon} \langle \mathsf{inc}(\mathsf{dec}(\sigma, \mathsf{e1}), \mathsf{e2}), \alpha \rangle$ is produced by applying rule $P\text{-}InterRcv$. Then, the process Q evolves by means of the interleaving rule $P\text{-}Int_1$. The produced label $?\mathsf{m}\!:\!\tilde{\mathsf{et}}, \epsilon$ indicates the willingness of process Q to consume a message of type m matching the template $\tilde{\mathsf{et}}$. If present, the message is actually consumed by rule $C\text{-}Receive$ at collaboration level. Indeed, this rule requires that there is a message in the m's message queue ($\tilde{\mathsf{v}} \in \delta(\mathsf{m})$) that matches the template $\tilde{\mathsf{et}}$ of the receiving event ($match(\tilde{\mathsf{et}}, \tilde{\mathsf{v}}) = A$); the assignments A produced by this matching are then applied to the data state α of the q's instance, and the message is removed from the queue ($rm(\delta, \mathsf{m}, \tilde{\mathsf{v}})$).

4.3   Send/Receive Pattern

Informal Description. Two parties, p and q, engage in two causally related interactions. In the first interaction, p sends a message (the request) to q, while in the second one p receives a message (the response) from q.

This pattern can be modelled by combining the *Send* and the *Receive* patterns, as shown in Fig. 6.

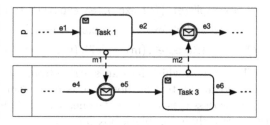

Fig. 6. Send/Receive pattern.

Textual Specification. The textual representation of the collaboration fragment in Fig. 6 has again the form C of the previous patterns, with

$$P = \mathsf{taskSnd}(\mathsf{e1}, \exp_1, \epsilon, \mathsf{m1}: \mathsf{e\tilde{x}p}_2, \mathsf{e2}) \parallel \mathsf{interRcv}(\mathsf{e2}, \mathsf{m2}: \tilde{t}_1, \mathsf{e3}) \parallel P'$$
$$Q = \mathsf{interRcv}(\mathsf{e4}, \mathsf{m1}: \tilde{t}_2, \mathsf{e5}) \parallel \mathsf{taskSnd}(\mathsf{e5}, \exp_3, \epsilon, \mathsf{m2}: \mathsf{e\tilde{x}p}_4, \mathsf{e6}) \parallel Q'$$

Formal Semantics. The execution steps of this pattern are realised by combining the semantic rules for the *Send* and *Receive* patterns. In detail: let us suppose that there is a token in the incoming edge of Task 1 ($\sigma(\mathsf{e1}) > 0$) and the other preconditions of rule *P-TaskSnd* are satisfied; by applying this rule we have that $\langle \mathsf{taskSnd}(\mathsf{e1}, \exp_1, \epsilon, \mathsf{m1}: \mathsf{e\tilde{x}p}_2, \mathsf{e2}), \sigma, \alpha \rangle \xrightarrow{!\mathsf{m1}\,:\,\tilde{v}} \langle inc(dec(\sigma, \mathsf{e1}), \mathsf{e2}), \alpha \rangle$. Then, P evolves by performing a sending action, by means of the interleaving rule *P-Int$_1$*, that is $\langle P, \sigma, \alpha \rangle \xrightarrow{!\mathsf{m1}\,:\,\tilde{v}} \langle \sigma', \alpha \rangle$. At the collaboration layer, by applying rule *C-Deliver*, the message m1 is delivered to q. Now, on the receiving party, assuming that there is a token on e4 and that the template $\tilde{t}_2$ evaluates to $\tilde{et}_2$, by applying rules *P-InterRcv* and *P-Int$_1$*, we have $\langle Q, \sigma_2, \alpha_2 \rangle \xrightarrow{?\mathsf{m1}\,:\,\tilde{et}_2, \epsilon} \langle inc(dec(\sigma_2, \mathsf{e4}), \mathsf{e5}), \alpha_2 \rangle$. The observed label indicates the willingness to receive a message of type m1. Thus, at collaboration level, rule *C-Receive* can be applied to allow process Q to actually consume the sent request message. Now, Task 3 is enabled and, by proceeding in a specular way, Q can send the response message m2 and P can consume it.

4.4 Racing Incoming Messages Pattern

Informal Description. A party expects to receive one among a set of messages. These messages may be structurally different (i.e. different types) and may come from different categories of partners. The way a message is processed depends on its type and/or the category of partner from which it comes.

This pattern can be modelled in BPMN by using in the receiving participant an event-based gateway connected to receiving events. Messages can be expected from one participant (Fig. 7) or they can arrive from different participants (Fig. 8).

Textual Specification. Let us first consider the case in which messages arrive from one participant (Fig. 7). In the textual notation the diagram is rendered as the collaboration of the usual form C, with

$$P = \mathsf{xorSplit}(\mathsf{e1}, \{(\mathsf{e2}, \mathsf{exp}_1), (\mathsf{e3}, \mathsf{exp}_2)\}) \parallel \mathsf{taskSnd}(\mathsf{e2}, \mathsf{exp}_3, \epsilon, \mathsf{m1}\!:\!\tilde{\mathsf{exp}}_4, \mathsf{e4}) \parallel$$
$$\mathsf{taskSnd}(\mathsf{e3}, \mathsf{exp}_5, \epsilon, \mathsf{m2}\!:\!\tilde{\mathsf{exp}}_6, \mathsf{e5}) \parallel P'$$
$$Q = \mathsf{eventBased}(\mathsf{e6}, (\mathsf{m1}\!:\!\tilde{\mathsf{t}}_1, \mathsf{e7}), (\mathsf{m2}\!:\!\tilde{\mathsf{t}}_2, \mathsf{e8})) \parallel Q'$$

The case in which messages arrive from two different participants (Fig. 8) is rendered in the textual notation as $C = \mathsf{pool}(\mathsf{p}, P'') \parallel \mathsf{pool}(\mathsf{r}, R) \parallel \mathsf{pool}(\mathsf{q}, Q)$, where process Q is as the above one, while P'' and R are left unspecified (because they are included in black-box pools).

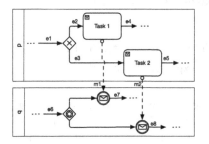

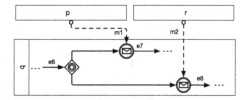

Fig. 7. Racing incoming messages (a).   **Fig. 8.** Racing incoming messages (b).

Formal Semantics. Let us start with the case in which messages arrive from a single participant, and assume that a token is available in the incoming edge of the XOR split gateway of P ($\sigma(\mathsf{e1}) > 0$) and the conditional expression exp_1 is evaluated to *true* ($eval(\mathsf{exp}_1, \alpha, true)$). Thus, rule $P\text{-}XorSplit_1$ can be applied and the token is moved to the edge e2, hence enabling Task 1. Formally, this step corresponds to the transition $\langle P, \sigma, \alpha \rangle \xrightarrow{\epsilon} \langle inc(dec(\sigma, \mathsf{e}_1), \mathsf{e}_2), \alpha \rangle$, where label ϵ denotes the movement of the token internally to the process. The next step corresponds to the execution of Task 1, which is as in the case of the *Send* pattern. Once the message m1 has been sent (hence, there exists a $\tilde{v}$ such that $\tilde{v} \in \delta(\mathsf{m1})$), and assuming that there is a token in e6 ($\sigma(\mathsf{e6}) > 0$), the event-based gateway can evolve by applying the corresponding rule. This corresponds to the transition $\langle \mathsf{eventBased}(\mathsf{e6}, (\mathsf{m}_1\!:\!\tilde{\mathsf{t}}_1, \mathsf{e7}), (\mathsf{m2}\!:\!\tilde{\mathsf{t}}2, \mathsf{e8})), \sigma', \alpha' \rangle \xrightarrow{?\mathsf{m}_1\,:\,\tilde{\mathsf{et}}_1, \epsilon}$ $\langle inc(dec(\sigma', \mathsf{e6}), \mathsf{e7}), \alpha' \rangle$, with template $\tilde{\mathsf{et}}_1$ matching the message $\tilde{v}$. The rule moves the token from the incoming edge to the outgoing edge corresponding to the received message. The produced label enables the application of rule *C-Receive* at collaboration level, which takes care of consuming the message $\tilde{v}$ of type m1 in δ. The case where message m2 is selected to be sent is similar.

In the scenario shown in Fig. 8, even if the transitions produced by the collaboration have the same labels, the pattern semantics is quite different. In fact, in the previous case the organisation p internally decides which message will be sent and only one message will be delivered and consumed, while in this case the organisations p and r act independently from each other and it may occur that both m1 and m2 are sent to q. In such a case, one of the two messages will be consumed, depending on their arrival time, and the other message will be pending forever.

4.5 One-To-Many Send Pattern

Informal Description. A party sends messages to several parties. All messages have the same type (although their contents may be different). The number of parties to whom the message is sent may or may not be known at design time.

In BPMN, this pattern can be modelled as the collaboration fragment in Fig. 9, where each party is represented as an instance of a multi-instance pool and a message is sent to each process instance via a sequential multi-instance send task.

From now on, when a message is sent/ received to/by several parties, we will model these parties as a multiple instance pool. This is the most interesting among various interpretations which are not considered in this work (e.g., representing multiple receiving parties as different single-instance pools). We can have that the number of sent messages is either

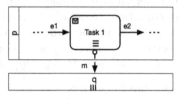

Fig. 9. One-to-many-send.

known at design time (by setting the LoopCardinality attribute of the send task) or it is read from a data object during the process execution.

Textual Specification. Here, to keep the pattern formalisation more manageable, the sequential multi-instance task is rendered as a macro. The macro encloses the task in a FOR-loop expressed by means of a pair of XOR join and split gateways, and an additional data object c_1 for the loop counter. In the textual notation we have $C = \mathsf{pool}(\mathsf{p}, P) \parallel \mathsf{miPool}(\mathsf{q}, Q)$, where process Q is left unspecified and in P the attribute LoopCardinality is set to n:

$$P = \mathsf{xorJoin}(\{\mathsf{e1}, \mathsf{e1'''}\}, \mathsf{e1'}) \parallel \mathsf{taskSnd}(\mathsf{e1'}, c_1.c \neq \mathsf{null}, c_1.c := c_1.c + 1, \mathsf{m} : \widetilde{\mathsf{exp}}_1, \mathsf{e1''})$$
$$\parallel \mathsf{xorSplit}(\mathsf{e1''}, \{(\mathsf{e1'''}, c_1.c \leq \mathsf{n}), (\mathsf{e2}, \mathsf{default})\}) \parallel P'$$

Formal Semantics. The execution steps are realised as in the previous cases, by repeatedly applying the semantic rules of the XOR gateway and the send task. It is worth noticing that at each application of rule *P-TaskSnd* the field c of the data object c_1 is updated with the assignment $c_1.c := c_1.c + 1$. At the end of the pattern execution, the message list $\delta(\mathsf{m})$ contains n sent messages.

4.6 One-From-Many Receive Pattern

Informal Description. A party receives several logically related messages arising from autonomous events occurring at different parties. The arrival of messages must be timely so that they can be correlated as a single logical request. The interaction may complete successfully or not depending on the messages gathered. In this pattern the receiver does not know the number of messages that will arrive, and stops waiting as soon as a certain number of messages have arrived or a timeout occurs.

This pattern can be modelled as the collaboration fragment shown in Fig 10.

Textual Specification. Also in this case, to simplify the formal treatment, we rely on a macro for the multi-instance receive task with a timer. In particular, the multi-instance behaviour is represented by enclosing the receive task in a FOR-loop (as for the sequential multi-instance task). The timer attached to the receive task is instead abstracted via a non-deterministic choice, by resorting to a

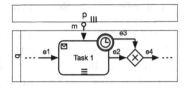

Fig. 10. One-from-many-receive.

race condition. In detail, the receiving party q will get, via an event-based gateway, either a message from a sending party (i.e., an instance of p) or a time-out message from a specific pool t representing the timer. In the textual notation we have $C = \mathsf{miPool}(\mathsf{p}, P) \parallel \mathsf{pool}(\mathsf{q}, Q) \parallel \mathsf{pool}(\mathsf{t}, T)$, where

$$Q = \mathsf{taskSnd}(\mathsf{e1}, \exp_1, \epsilon, \mathsf{m}_{startTimer} : \tilde{\exp}_2, \mathsf{e}') \parallel \mathsf{xorJoin}(\{\mathsf{e}', \mathsf{e}^v\}, \mathsf{e}'') \parallel$$
$$\mathsf{eventBased}(\mathsf{e}'', (\mathsf{m} : \tilde{\mathsf{t}}_1, \mathsf{e}'''), (\mathsf{m}_{timeout} : \tilde{\mathsf{t}}_2, \mathsf{e3})) \parallel$$
$$\mathsf{task}(\mathsf{e}''', \mathsf{c}_1.\mathsf{c} \neq \mathsf{null}, \mathsf{c}_1.\mathsf{c} := \mathsf{c}_1.\mathsf{c} + 1, \mathsf{e}^{iv}) \parallel$$
$$\mathsf{xorSplit}(\mathsf{e}^{iv}, \{(\mathsf{e}^v, \mathsf{c}_1.\mathsf{c} \leq n), (\mathsf{e2}, \mathsf{default})\}) \parallel \mathsf{xorJoin}(\{\mathsf{e2}, \mathsf{e3}\}, \mathsf{e4}) \parallel Q'$$
$$T = \mathsf{startRcv}(\mathsf{m}_{startTimer} : \tilde{\mathsf{t}}_3, \mathsf{e5}) \parallel \mathsf{taskSnd}(\mathsf{e5}, \exp_3, \epsilon, \mathsf{m}_{timeout} : \tilde{\exp}_4, \mathsf{e6}) \parallel \mathsf{end}(\mathsf{e6})$$

Formal Semantics. Once a token arrives at e1 in the process Q, a $\mathsf{m}_{startTimer}$ message is sent to the pool t by means of the send task, in order to activate an instance of the timer process T. This instance will perform a send task, delivering a message $\mathsf{m}_{timeout}$, to signal that the timeout is expired, and then it terminates. As effect of the execution of the send task in Q, a token is moved in e', which enables the looping behaviour regulated by the XOR gateways. At each iteration, the event-based gateway consumes either a message m or $\mathsf{m}_{timeout}$; in the former case the non-communicating task increments the loop counter and the execution of another interaction is evaluated (by means of the XOR split conditions), while in the latter case the edge e3 is followed and the pattern execution completes.

4.7   One-To-Many Send/Receive Pattern

Informal Description. A party sends a request to several other parties. Responses are expected within a given time-frame. However, some responses may not arrive within the time-frame and some parties may even not respond at all.

This pattern can be rendered as the collaboration fragment in Fig. 11. A practical use of this pattern is shown in the scenario in Fig. 1.

Textual Specification. This pattern relies on a multi-instance sub-process with a specific form, i.e. it is characterised by a sequence of a send task and a

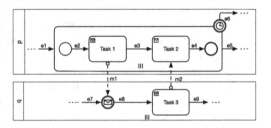

Fig. 11. One-to-many send/receive.

receive task, proceeded and followed by a start and an end event, respectively. As usual, to simplify the formal treatment we resort to a macro. In this case, it consists of a sequential send task followed by a multi-instance receive task with a timer. We have $C = \mathsf{pool}(\mathsf{p}, P) \parallel \mathsf{miPool}(\mathsf{q}, Q)$, where process P is rendered in terms of macros as already shown in the previous patterns (hence, for the sake of presentation, its specification is omitted), while process Q is as follows:

$$Q = \mathsf{interRcv}(\mathsf{e7}, \mathsf{m1}:\tilde{t_1}, \mathsf{e8}) \parallel \mathsf{taskSnd}(\mathsf{e8}, \mathsf{exp}, A, \mathsf{m2}:\tilde{\mathsf{exp}}, \mathsf{e9}) \parallel Q'$$

Formal Semantics. In this pattern we have that process P sends out, by means of rule *P-TaskSnd*, several messages of type m1 that need to be properly correlated with the correct process instance of Q. The content of the messages themselves provides the correlation information. For example, let us assume that two messages of type m1 are sent to q, and that consist of three fields, say $\langle "foo", 5, 1234 \rangle$ and $\langle "foo", 7, 9876 \rangle$. Also, let us consider the case where there are two receiving instances, i.e. $\iota(\mathsf{q}) = \{\langle \sigma_1, \alpha_1 \rangle, \langle \sigma_2, \alpha_2 \rangle\}$, and that template $\tilde{t_1}$ of the intermediate receiving event is defined as $\langle \mathsf{d.f}, \mathsf{d.id}, ?\mathsf{d.code} \rangle$, meaning that the fields f and id of the data object d identify correlation data while code is a formal field. Now, the correlation takes place according to the data states, which we assume to be as follows: $\alpha_1(\mathsf{d.f}) = \alpha_2(\mathsf{d.f}) = "foo"$, $\alpha_1(\mathsf{d.id}) = 7$, and $\alpha_2(\mathsf{d.id}) = 5$. Therefore, the first message is delivered to the second instance, updating α_2 with the assignment d.code $=9876$, while the second message is delivered to the first instance, updating α_1 with the assignment d.code $=1234$.

4.8   Request with Referral Pattern

Informal Description. A party p sends a request to another party q indicating that any follow-up should be sent to another party r. An example of a BPMN collaboration involving the request with referral pattern is shown in Fig. 12, and also in the communication between the Retailer and the Logistic Provider in Fig. 1.

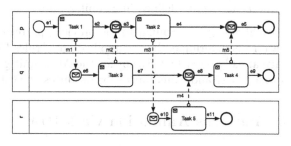

Fig. 12. Request with Referral pattern.

Textual Specification. In the textual specification we have $C = \mathsf{pool}(\mathsf{p}, P) \parallel \mathsf{pool}(\mathsf{q}, Q) \parallel \mathsf{pool}(\mathsf{r}, R)$, where:

$$P = \mathsf{start}(\mathsf{e}_{enb}, \mathsf{e1}) \parallel \mathsf{taskSnd}(\mathsf{e1}, \mathsf{exp}_1, A_1, \mathsf{m1}:\tilde{\mathsf{exp}}_2, \mathsf{e2}) \parallel \mathsf{interRcv}(\mathsf{e2}, \mathsf{m2}:\tilde{t_1}, \mathsf{e3}) \parallel$$
$$\mathsf{taskSnd}(\mathsf{e3}, \mathsf{exp}_3, A_2, \mathsf{m3}:\tilde{\mathsf{exp}}_4, \mathsf{e4}) \parallel \mathsf{interRcv}(\mathsf{e4}, \mathsf{m4}:\tilde{t_2}, \mathsf{e5}) \parallel \mathsf{end}(\mathsf{e5})$$

and Q and R are defined in a similar way.

Formal Semantics. The execution steps and their results are simply realised by applying the semantic rules for the different BPMN elements, as already shown for the previous patterns. It is up to the message sent by pool p to pool r to specify in its content the reference to pool q, whose process waits for the routed message.

4.9   Relayed Request Pattern

Informal Description. A party p makes a request to party q, which delegates the request processing to another party r. This latter party interacts with party p while party q observes a view of the interactions.

This pattern can be rendered as the collaboration fragment in Fig. 13.

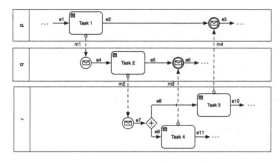

Fig. 13. An example of relayed request pattern.

Textual Specification. In the textual notation the pattern is rendered as follows: $C = \mathsf{pool}(\mathsf{p}, P) \parallel \mathsf{pool}(\mathsf{q}, Q) \parallel \mathsf{pool}(\mathsf{r}, R)$, where:

$$R = \mathsf{startRcv}(\mathsf{m2}\!:\!\tilde{t_1}, \mathsf{e7}) \parallel \mathsf{andSplit}(\mathsf{e7}, \{\mathsf{e8}, \mathsf{e9}\}) \parallel$$
$$\mathsf{taskSnd}(\mathsf{e8}, \mathsf{exp}_1, \epsilon, \mathsf{m4}\!:\!\tilde{\mathsf{exp}}_2, \mathsf{e10}) \parallel \mathsf{taskSnd}(\mathsf{e9}, \mathsf{exp}_3, \epsilon, \mathsf{m3}\!:\!\tilde{\mathsf{exp}}_4, \mathsf{e11}) \parallel R'$$

while P and Q are defined in a similar way.

Formal Semantics. Similar to the previous pattern, the formal semantics of this pattern is determined by the application of rules for sending and receiving message already described, except for the AND split gateway that simply consumes a token in e7 and, simultaneously, produces one token in e8 and one token in e9.

5   Patterns Animation via MIDA

The MIDA (*Multiple Instances and Data Animator*) tool[1] is a web application written in JavaScript, based on the Camunda *bpmn.io* modeller. MIDA, whose graphical interface is shown in Fig. 14, is an animator of collaboration models that can involve multiple instances and data objects. MIDA animates process models by means of the visualisation of tokens flow and data evolution. To correctly enact the collaboration behaviour, the implementation of the tool relies on the formalisation presented in Sect. 3.

---

[1] http://pros.unicam.it/mida.

The core feature of MIDA is the model animation. It results helpful both in educational contexts, for explaining the behaviour of BPMN elements, and in practical modelling activities, for debugging errors. In fact, designers can achieve a precise understanding of the behaviour of processes and collaborations by

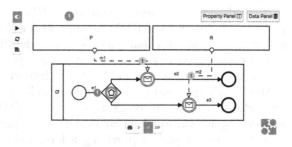

Fig. 14. MIDA tool interface.

means of the visualisation of the model execution.

We have exploited MIDA to model and animate the interaction patterns presented in Sect. 4, providing an intuitive knowledge of their behaviour. We have also used MIDA to animate the motivating example in Fig. 1, thus showing how the tool supports the study of more intricate scenarios resulting from the combination of various patterns. These animations are available from http://pros.unicam.it/service-interaction-patterns/.

6   Related Work

The most common interaction scenarios from a business perspective, named Service Interaction Patterns, have been described in [3,17]. However, they lack of visualisation as well as formal semantics. Since then, effort has been devoted to visualise [1,5,9] and formalise these patterns [2,10,15], as shown in Table 1. This provides a comparison among the state-of-the-art approaches dealing with service interaction patterns with respect to: *(i)* the language used for patterns specification, *(ii)* the main contribution of the work and *(iii)* its limitations. In the following, these works are compared to the contribution of this paper.

Table 1. Review on the service interaction patterns literature.

Paper	Year	Language	Contribution	Limitations
[2]	2005	ASM	Formalisation and extension	No models analysis
[10]	2006	π-calculus	Formalisation	Ambiguities
[15]	2007	CPN	Formalisation and extension	No correlation
[9]	2008	BPMN 2.0	iBPMN: extension for interaction modelling	No formalisation
[1]	2009	Open nets	Overview of services domain challenges	No formalisation
[5]	2014	BPMN 2.0	Extension of BPMN supported patterns	No formalisation

Considering the patterns specified in BPMN, relevant works are [5,9]. Campagna et al. [5] discuss BPMN 2.0 support for the service interaction patterns and propose a set of enhancements to broaden it. However, they do not formalise these patterns and thus, they do not provide formal validation of the proposed solutions. Decker and Barros [9] introduce iBPMN, a set of extensions to the BPMN standard for interaction modelling. They show that most service interaction patterns can be expressed using iBPMN and present an algorithm for deriving interface behaviour models from simple interaction models. However, they do not aim at providing a formal characterisation of the proposed extensions. Both the above works are more interested in overcoming BPMN lacks for supporting interaction patterns rather than clarifying the semantics of the supported patterns, which is instead a major challenge when using BPMN collaborations [8].

Abstract State Machines (ASM) [4], π-calculus [14] and Petri Nets [12] have been proposed as a solid ground to formalise service interaction patterns. The first formalization of the patterns was given by Barros and Börger [2] proposing a compositional framework and interaction flows. They provide ASM for eight service interaction scenarios and illustrate how, by combinations and refinements of them, one can define arbitrarily complex interaction patterns. The ASMs offer an implementation draft of the patterns, but are less suited for the analysis of collaborations. Decker et al. [10] provide a formalisation of service interactions via π-calculus as a first step to analyse collaborations. However, their work shows still some ambiguities. For instance, the *Racing Incoming Messages* pattern allows to receive multiple messages at once, but the work does not clarify how one among the competing messages is chosen for consumption. Moreover, the authors refer to a synchronous communication model, not compliant with the BPMN standard. Mulyar et al. [15] formalise the semantics of the interaction patterns by means of Coloured Petri Nets (CPN). Moreover, they extend the scope of the original service interaction patterns by describing various pattern variants. However, even if Petri Nets provide support for multiple instance patterns, process instances are characterised by their identities, rather than by the values of their data, which are necessary for correlation [11]. Finally, van der Aalst et al. [1] provide an overview of the challenges in the domain of service interaction patterns and they propose to use open nets as a formal framework for addressing these challenges. However, they do not aim at formalising the interaction patterns, of which they only provide a brief description. Differently from the mentioned works, we focus on BPMN by directly defining the semantics of the supported patterns, thus avoiding the mapping to other formalisms equipped with their own semantics.

7 Concluding Remarks

In this work we focus on service interaction patterns, visualising them in BPMN collaborations and providing a comprehensive formalisation by means of a direct formal semantics for BPMN collaboration diagrams. This allows to validate the semantics in [6], as we show it is suitable to cover the interaction patterns expressed in BPMN. Further, the animation tool MIDA has been exploited to model and animate the BPMN collaborations, allowing an intuitive understanding of the patterns execution.

As a future work, we plan to investigate the formalisation of new BPMN interaction patterns where data objects play a more central role.

References

1. van der Aalst, W.M.P., Mooij, A.J., Stahl, C., Wolf, K.: Service interaction: patterns, formalization, and analysis. In: Bernardo, M., Padovani, L., Zavattaro, G. (eds.) SFM 2009. LNCS, vol. 5569, pp. 42–88. Springer, Heidelberg (2009). https://doi.org/10.1007/978-3-642-01918-0_2

2. Barros, A., Börger, E.: A compositional framework for service interaction patterns and interaction flows. In: Lau, K.-K., Banach, R. (eds.) ICFEM 2005. LNCS, vol. 3785, pp. 5–35. Springer, Heidelberg (2005). https://doi.org/10.1007/11576280_2

3. Barros, A., Dumas, M., ter Hofstede, A.H.M.: Service interaction patterns. In: van der Aalst, W.M.P., Benatallah, B., Casati, F., Curbera, F. (eds.) BPM 2005. LNCS, vol. 3649, pp. 302–318. Springer, Heidelberg (2005). https://doi.org/10.1007/11538394_20

4. Börger, E., Thalheim, B.: Modeling workflows, interaction patterns, web services and business processes: the ASM-based approach. In: Börger, E., Butler, M., Bowen, J.P., Boca, P. (eds.) ABZ 2008. LNCS, vol. 5238, pp. 24–38. Springer, Heidelberg (2008). https://doi.org/10.1007/978-3-540-87603-8_3

5. Campagna, D., Kavka, C., Onesti, L.: Enhancing BPMN 2.0 support for service interaction patterns. In: Software Engineering and Applications (ICSOFT-EA) (2014)

6. Corradini, F., Muzi, C., Re, B., Rossi, L., Tiezzi, F.: Animating Multiple Instances in BPMN Collaborations: From Formal Semantics to Tool Support. In: Weske, M., Montali, M., Weber, I., vom Brocke, J. (eds.) BPM 2018. LNCS, vol. 11080, pp. 83–101. Springer, Cham (2018). https://doi.org/10.1007/978-3-319-98648-7_6

7. Corradini, F., Muzi, C., Re, B., Tiezzi, F., Rossi, L.: MIDA: multiple instances and data animator. In: BPM 2018 (Demo). LNCS. Springer (2018, to appear)

8. Cortes-Cornax, M., Dupuy-Chessa, S., Rieu, D.: Choreographies in BPMN 2.0: new challenges and open questions. In: ZEUS, vol. 847, pp. 50–57. CEUR-WS.org (2012)

9. Decker, G., Barros, A.: Interaction modeling using BPMN. In: ter Hofstede, A., Benatallah, B., Paik, H.-Y. (eds.) BPM 2007. LNCS, vol. 4928, pp. 208–219. Springer, Heidelberg (2008). https://doi.org/10.1007/978-3-540-78238-4_22

10. Decker, G., Puhlmann, F., Weske, M.: Formalizing service interactions. In: Dustdar, S., Fiadeiro, J.L., Sheth, A.P. (eds.) BPM 2006. LNCS, vol. 4102, pp. 414–419. Springer, Heidelberg (2006). https://doi.org/10.1007/11841760_32

11. Decker, G., Weske, M.: Instance isolation analysis for service-oriented architectures. In: SCC, vol. 1, pp. 249–256. IEEE (2008)

12. Dijkman, R.M., Dumas, M., Ouyang, C.: Semantics and analysis of business process models in BPMN. Inf. Softw. Technol. **50**(12), 1281–1294 (2008)

13. Dumas, M., La Rosa, M., Mendling, J., Reijers, H.A.: Fundamentals of Business Process Management. Springer, Heidelberg (2013). https://doi.org/10.1007/978-3-642-33143-5

14. Milner, R.: A Calculus of Communicating Systems. Springer, Secaucus, NJ, USA (1980). https://doi.org/10.1007/3-540-10235-3
15. Mulyar, N., van der Aalst, W.M.P., Aldred, L., Russell, N.: Service interaction patterns: a configurable framework. Management **34**, 29 (2007)
16. OMG: Business Process Model and Notation (BPMN V 2.0) (2011)
17. Weske, M.: Business Process Management. Springer, Heidelberg (2012). https://doi.org/10.1007/978-3-642-28409-0

Toward Requirements-Driven Design of Visual Modeling Languages

Jens Gulden[1(✉)] and Eric Yu[2,3]

[1] University of Duisburg-Essen, Essen, Germany
`jensgulden@acm.org`
[2] Faculty of Information, University of Toronto, Toronto, Canada
`eric.yu@utoronto.ca`
[3] Department of Computer Science, University of Toronto, Toronto, Canada

Abstract. The design of a visual modeling language demands for a large number of decisions to be taken, depending on the intended purposes of the language, the domain context, and the goals and requirements of different stakeholders who are the prospective users of the language. Methodical support for the design and choice of visual modeling languages plays an important role in Enterprise Modeling (EM), because EM strongly relies on the use of visual modeling languages for expressing human-understandable abstractions of complex domain contexts. However, existing research primarily discusses individual design aspects of visual modeling languages. The results of these studies partially overlap or contradict each other. The work at hand introduces an approach for systematically identifying and managing trade-offs between competing design recommendations, as well as for gaining an integrated multi-perspective view on requirements towards visual modeling languages. We demonstrate the feasibility of the approach by reconsidering some design decisions taken for the widely used Business Process Modeling and Notation (BPMN) language.

Keywords: Visual notation · Visual modeling languages
Goal modeling · Requirements · Soft-Goals

1 Requirements-Driven Design to Guide Design Decisions for Visual Languages

With the increasing use of modeling techniques in science and practice of Enterprise Modeling and other fields, the demand for advanced visual modeling languages that support modeling tasks more easily and efficiently is increasingly discussed in the literature [13,16,17].

A large amount of research from an Information Systems perspective has been performed already on the use and design of visual modeling languages,

© IFIP International Federation for Information Processing 2018
Published by Springer Nature Switzerland AG 2018. All Rights Reserved
R. A. Buchmann et al. (Eds.): PoEM 2018, LNBIP 335, pp. 21–36, 2018.
https://doi.org/10.1007/978-3-030-02302-7_2

especially on process modeling languages [4,8,21]. This has led to a respectable amount of research questions that have been addressed in the body of literature about individual aspects of visual modeling languages and prescriptive principles suggested for the design of visual modeling languages [2,9,22,24].

While the existing body of research addresses a wide range of isolated design questions, dealing with a set of individual principles does not provide sufficient support for guiding design decisions. This is because in order to develop a visual language as a whole, diverse aspects about the purpose of the language, the prospective users of the language, and their intentions, have to be brought into a coherent balance. Individual recommendations for addressing design principles may contradict each other. The issues they address may also overlap, or there may be blank spots which are not addressed by research yet. In order to apply existing research on visual modeling language design for creating entirely new visual languages, or for extending existing ones in a justified and systematic way, it is thus necessary to have methodical support for discovering contradictions, overlaps, and ambiguities among existing individual design principles, and to have guidance in resolving them.

Especially the fact that many modeling languages are intended to serve as interfaces between different stakeholder groups, e. g., business experts, software developers, or novices to be trained in any of these fields, naturally leads to the situation that in order to fulfill each of these groups' information needs, trade-offs will arise when deciding for the design of a language. Identifying these trade-offs, and resolving conflicts resulting from them, are important tasks in a reflected visual language design process. However, up to now elaborate methodical support for identifying and resolving trade-offs among individual design principles for visual languages, has not been proposed in the modeling literature. As a consequence, the research question addressed in this article is:

How can trade-offs among individual design principles for visual modeling languages be systematically elicited and resolved, to guide justified design decisions during the process of creating, extending, or evaluating visual modeling languages?

In order to provide an answer to this question, we present an approach that treats properties of visual languages and individual design principles as design goals that can systematically be analyzed and made traceable to guide the design choices for a visual language.

The remainder of the article is structured as follows: In Sect. 2 the demand for an integrating perspective on visual modeling language design and systematic support for deriving design decisions from requirements in a justifiable and traceable manner is laid out. Related work is discussed in Sect. 3. In Sect. 4 the proposed approach is elaborated and exemplified on top of the scientific knowledge body of research on visual process modeling languages. The applicability of the approach is evaluated in Sect. 4.4 by using it to reconsider design decisions that had been taken for the BPMN 2.0 language. Section 5 completes the presented considerations with a conclusion and an outlook on future work.

2   Demand for Goal-Guided Design of Visual Modeling Languages

2.1   Principle-Driven Design of Visual Languages is not Enough

The design of a visual modeling language is a complex process which demands designers to find a balance between diverse criteria that a language should adhere to. Among them are the intended capabilities of the language to express concepts of a particular domain, if a domain-specific language is to be developed. Secondly, modeling languages are in most cases used as communication tools among different groups of stakeholders who are the prospective users of the language. They need to be able to apply the modeling language in accordance with their purposes, cognitive skills, and experiences, which may differ strongly depending on the involved types of stakeholders. It may also turn out that a single language is not sufficient for all involved stakeholders, and that multiple visual languages are required which reflect the same underlying semantics. As a third aspect, additional factors such as integration capabilities into a set of other existing languages, or demands for automatic analysis and further processing of models, are likely to play a role and to have influence on the design decisions. As a consequence, the question which is the "right" visual modeling language, and in turn the diverse design questions that come up during the process of specifying a visual modeling language, cannot be answered in the same way for every language.

Existing research has provided a wide variety of detail examinations on individual design principles that play a role for designing visual languages (see Sect. 3). As it is paradigmatically normal for scientific work, every single contribution provides detailed examinations of clearly marked individual research questions. This leads to the situation that most available research is about individual aspects of visual language design, and only a single or few design principles are discussed at a time by each examination.

However, given the strong influence of multiple external criteria such as domain concepts, stakeholder purposes, and language infrastructure demands, a visual language design project has to take into account a high amount of different design aspects. As a consequence, contradictions between proposed design principles will occur, and it will not be possible to follow all existing design principles simultaneously.

For example, when faced with the decision of what symbols to choose for representing concepts in a visual domain-specific language, it may be of help to restrict the symbol design to clearly distinguishable abstract geometrical shapes, in order to provide unique symbols that are easy to recognize for experienced language users. Such a decision would support the design goals of semiotic clarity and perceptual discriminability discussed in [22]. On the other hand, picture-like figurative symbols are likely to be more easily understandable by untrained users, and depending on the domain context, could contribute to a higher level of identification of the users with the visual language and lead to an increased acceptance of the language. Choosing this option would support the design goal of semantic transparency according to [22]. Thus, there is a trade-off between using simple geometrical shapes and speaking pictures as visual symbols, which results from competing and sometimes even contradictory design goals for visual languages.

A method that supports justified visual language design should allow to handle trade-offs of this kind in a way that the choice for a design option can be rationally traced along the criteria that determine a specific language design decision. Especially, diverting demands of heterogeneous stakeholder groups require to resolve multi-criterial design decisions by finding an appropriate balance of trade-offs. Faced with these challenges, the approach presented in this article does not operate on the level of individual design principles, but provides means to systematize multiple design principles in a model-based way, and gives guidance in performing trade-offs and resolving contradictions among them. As a methodical tool for this purpose, the Non-Functional-Requirements (NFR) Framework is employed.

2.2   The NFR Framework

The Non-Functional-Requirements (NFR) Framework provides a methodical approach for reasoning about requirements in terms of goals, decomposed sub-goals, and tasks that are concrete means to fulfill goals [3,5,6]. In the NFR Framework, these elements are represented in a model-based way. Using a lean visual language, requirements can be expressed as ovals that represent goals, while decomposition relationships between the goals are shown as connecting arrows. Fig. 1 shows an example NFR model in the notation used throughout this article, with exemplary goals and tasks from the car design domain.

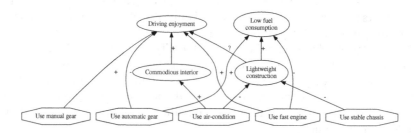

Fig. 1. Example NFR model with language elements used in this article

Relationships between goals can be supportive, in which case the fulfillment of one goal is expected to lead to the fulfillment of another goal, or obstructive, which means fulfilling one goal stands in contrast to fulfilling another goal. Supportive relationships are marked with a '+', obstructive ones with a '-'. Additionally, the relationship between two goals can also be marked as unknown using a '?'.

The bottom row in Fig. 1 contains task elements in octagon shape, which represent possible options to fulfill goals. A decomposition relationship between a goal and associated tasks indicates that if a task is executed, it contributes to the fulfillment of the goal.

All relationships in an NFR model can additionally be attached with claims, which are comments on the decision rationale that has led to the choice for including a particular relationship in the model. Claims provide support in tracing back the chain of justification for design decisions taken, when an NFR model is applied to meet a set of given requirements for the design of a visual modeling language. When included in a diagram, claims are referenced by numbers in round braces that are placed below the '+/-/?' markers of a relationship line.

Figure 2(a) shows a legend of the visual notation for NFR models used in this article. A meta-model that formally describes the abstract syntax of this modeling language is displayed in Fig. 2(b).

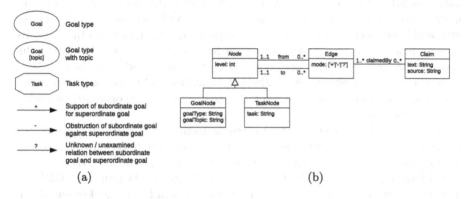

(a)   (b)

Fig. 2. Legend (a) and meta-model (b) of the NFR modeling language used in this article

Creating NFR models involves performing hierarchical refinements from top-level goals to sub-goals, and to identify task candidates as recommendations for how to achieve the respective sub-goals. This way, a justified chain of reasoning gets documented in a complex structure, which would not be possible purely on a textual basis without a dedicated modeling technique. Furthermore, creators and users of NFR models are continuously motivated to question to what extent an NFR model is coherent and complete, which motivates to find a "good" system of goals.

The refinement of goals along the hierarchy in NFR models can be performed in two conceptual directions: One way is to more specifically focus on aspects that constitute a goal, i.e., a superordinate goal such as "Understandability" gets refined into subordinate goals that each are distinct aspects of it, e.g., "Speed of comprehension", "Accuracy of understanding", and "Learnability". The decomposition of a goal in such a way is called *type refinement*. Another way to decompose goals is to distinguish between different objects of interest to which the same goal is applied. E. g., "Understandability" of a modeling language can be demanded for expert users or novice users, or specific syntactic elements of visual modeling languages can be further considered with respect to their understandability, e. g., node-symbols, edges, or layout rules of visual languages. A goal refinement which differentiates between multiple objects of interest to which the same goal is applied is called *topic refinement*. It is indicated by adding the topic name in square braces "[ ]" to the label of the refined sub-goal.

3   Related Work

A wide range of scientific literature has contributed to research on the design of visual modeling languages, particularly by examining characteristics that influence the cognitive handling of visual models [2,9,22]. From this work, a variety of design principles and recommendations for designing visual modeling languages have evolved and been empirically addressed. Especially the principles discussed in [22] have shown a large impact on research activities in the scientific community, and have motivated a variety of subsequent empirical works on the cognitive aspects related to these design principles for visual languages [24,26,30]. Our approach makes use of this profound body of research and suggests to take in an integrative perspective, which allows to identify possible contradictions, overlaps, and unexamined aspects among the existing research contributions and in a systematic way.

The basic idea of incorporating a requirements perspective into visual language design has been introduced by a few research publications. [7] suggests an approach for tailoring a requirements engineering approach for the design of visual languages based on the Goal-oriented Requirements Language GRL [1]. The underlying idea of starting visual language design from a goal-oriented perspective is well motivated, however, the elaboration does not incorporate existing research about characteristics of visual languages to support design decisions.

An empiric survey about requirements towards visual language notations expressed by users is conducted by [28]. The examination is oriented along the design principles of the "Physics of Notation" [22], and is based on interviews of modeling experts about their evaluation of the relevance of each principle. But only a few significant statements from the evaluated answers can be generalized, which may be caused by the fact that [22]'s design principles are not easy to be differentiated from the point of view of a modeling language user. For the purpose of applying existing research to language design tasks, [26] proposes a procedure for the systematic application of [22], which is explicated in the form of a process model for principle-based design of a visual modeling language. This operationalization approach is focused on putting design principles into practice, without explicating language users' requirements and corresponding goals.

Linden et al. [29] reflects on the "inherent difficulty of operationalizing the Physics of Notations" [22]. Continuing this work, [30] proposes a framework for verifying visual notation design as a complementary task to developing a language design method based on existing design principles.

In this article, we refer to the existing body of literature to propose an approach which allows to systematically justify the design decisions that are required to be taken when creating or extending a visual modeling language.

4   Applying Requirements-Driven Design Analysis to BPMN

4.1   An Illustrative Example

Our approach can be used for the design of new visual modeling languages, as well as for creating language extensions and performing justified choices among existing languages to use. To provide a compact demonstration of the approach, we here perform a reconsideration of selected design decisions that have been taken for the Business Process Modeling and Notation (BPMN) 2.0 modeling language [18]. BPMN's visual notation is well established and described in normative documents by the standards organization Object Management Group (OMG). However, the language has grown over time and was compiled from other earlier process modeling languages, without a coherent justification of the appropriateness of each included visual modeling element [14]. This can be demonstrated along an example model issued by the OMG for training and documentation purposes [15] which is shown in Fig. 3. Three areas are marked that reveal examples of possible design deficiencies in the BPMN visual notation, which in larger models have the potential to compromise the comprehensibility and usability of the BPMN language.

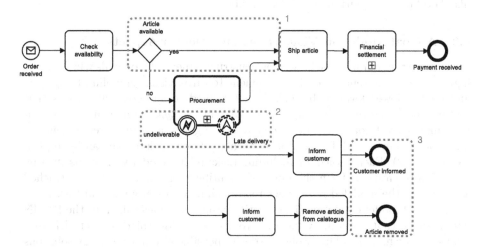

Fig. 3. Order Fulfillment and Procurement example [15] with highlighted problem areas

The area marked with (1) shows a situation where a diverging gateway is used to express the beginning of alternative process flows, but no corresponding converging gateway exists. Instead, the converging merge of the alternative process branches is expressed implicitly by two incoming arrows into the activity "Ship article". While this is syntactically valid in BPMN, there is evidence in the existing body of research that incorporating different notation options for process flows, and especially the combination of a gateway-based and an implicit flow notation, reduces the ease of understanding of BPMN models [20, 24].

In the area marked with (2), two example events "undeliverable" and "late delivery" are shown that can occur during the execution of the "Procurement" task. The visual appearance of the "late delivery" event is composed of the symbol for an escalation event with the shape of an upward arrow head, and a double dashed circular border around the symbol which classifies the event as a non-interrupting event. This means the execution of the task does not stop when the event is thrown. The symbol shape of the upward arrow head is close to the shape of the flash symbol that is used for the error event "undeliverable", and the double dashed border is one out of several possible border styles for events, which can be single solid line, double solid line, single dashed line, double dashed line, or thick solid line. There is evidence in research that the choice of this visual appearance of the example events is inappropriate, as both the symbolic content and the border styles, are neither well distinguishable, nor good to memorize [11, 28].

The area marked with (3) exemplifies that BPMN does not contain strict guidelines for its secondary notation, which is about the choice of how to place elements onto the diagram plane. The two end-events "Customer informed" and "Article removed" are not vertically aligned, which, although not intended, may inadvertently convey additional semantics about the importance or expected likelihood of the occurrence of these events.

4.2   A Goal Model on Visual Language Design Aspects

To demonstrate our approach, we now construct a hierarchy of goals which on the higher levels represent general requirement towards visual modeling languages, and on the lower levels subsequently get refined to sub-goals and tasks that address the issues in the example case. We will use *type* refinements to decompose higher-level goals into more concrete sub-goals, and *topic* refinements to differentiate between different objects of interest to which a goal can be applied (see Sect. 2.2). Each choice for including tasks in the model will be justified by one or more citations from the body of scientific literature, which are attached as claims to the modeled refinement relationships between goals and tasks.

The goal model is then used to identify design decisions taken for the BPMN 2.0 language that potentially have led to the issues identified in Sect. 4.1. In a final step, the model will be applied to derive possible alternative design solutions with respect to the identified issues. We choose BPMN 2.0 as a language that is well known, in order to not mix the demonstration with language details that would distract from the contribution of the goal-based approach. The in-depth analysis of an existing language with our approach widely resembles the considerations that have to be made when creating entirely new visual languages or extensions to existing languages, which is why the demonstration covers the full methodical range of our approach.

With respect to process modeling languages and in particular BPMN, a large body of research is available, parts of which will in the following be structured according to the goal-decomposition approach of the NFR framework. As claims for justification of the constructed goal models, citations from existing principle-based research will be incorporated in the models. We elaborate on the two top-goals "Comprehension" and "Usability" which are are widely addressed in the existing body of research [8].

As a starting point, we decompose the top-goals "Comprehension" and "Usability" into sub-goals which allow to differentiate between different aspects of the general top-goals. These initial decompositions are shown in Fig. 4.

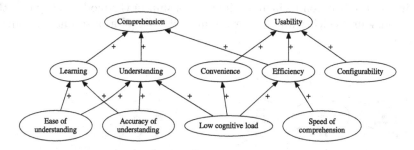

Fig. 4. Goal decompositions that are derived from the top-goals Comprehension and Usability of a visual modeling language

4.3   Comprehension of BPMN

The examination can now drill down to particular sub-goals, in order to relate individual design principles from the body of literature to them. The most common goal investigated by existing research is the effect of visual process modeling languages on the "Comprehension" of models [8]. As a consequence, we focus on refinements of this top-goal in the further examination. Some authors also talk about "cognitive effectiveness" [10,29], which in the context of this article is treated synonymously with comprehensibility. The decomposition of goals that are subsumed under the top-goal of supporting "Comprehension" is shown in Fig. 5.

Ease of Understanding. We will further focus on the decomposition of "Ease of understanding" as one representative sub-goal of "Understanding", and assign to each detail decomposition relationship at least one claim from the scientific literature on visual process model comprehension. The result is a set of concrete design decisions that can be taken when designing visual modeling languages. These are modeled as task elements in the goal model, indicating that they represent means to fulfill the superordinate goals.

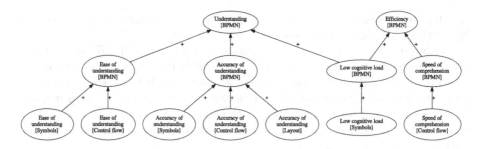

Fig. 5. Decomposition of the top-goal Comprehension

The citations attached to the relationships between goals and tasks are claims that justify the decision to include the relationship in the model. They cite the referenced sources either directly, or are quoted from [8] as a secondary source.

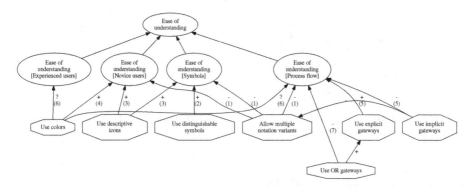

Fig. 6. Decomposition of the goal to ensure ease of understanding into tasks derived from literature references

Figure 6 shows the decomposition hierarchy derived from literature for achieving "Ease of understanding" for visual modeling languages, incorporating a distinction between the topics "BPMN", "Experienced users", "Novice users", "Symbols", and "Process flow". The claims associated with the relationships among the goals are based on the following rationales:

1. *"numerous responses were found that corroborate [the] tendency to require simplicity when dealing with modeling non-experts"* [27]
2. *"the most important requirement [...] is perceptual discriminability"* [28]
3. *"semantic transparency and cognitive fit [...] are indeed vital to ensure non-experts can better understand a visual notation"* [28]
4. *"syntax highlighting with colors for matching gateway pairs is positively related to novices' model comprehension"* [25]
5. *"the use of gateway constructs benefits understanding; implicit representation is often misunderstood"* [20, 24]

6. *"no evidence that syntax highlighting improves experts' performance"* [25]
7. *"avoid OR gateway elements"* [21]

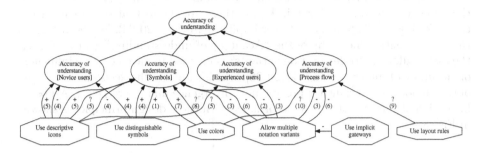

Fig. 7. Decomposition of goals to achieve accuracy of understanding derived from literature references

Accuracy of Understanding. Figure 7 shows the decomposition hierarchy derived from literature for achieving "Accuracy of understanding" for visual modeling languages. The referenced claims are:

1. *"perceptual discriminability deficiencies of symbols in YAWL and demonstrate that these symbols lowered comprehension accuracy"* [11]
2. *"semiotic clarity deficiencies in EPC reduce comprehension accuracy"* [11]
3. *"for modeling with experts semiotic clarity [is] perceived as most important"* [28]
4. *"for modeling with non-experts, perceptual discriminability [...] are perceived as most important"* [28]
5. *"semantic transparency and cognitive fit [...] are indeed vital to ensure non-experts can better understand a visual notation"* [28]
6. *"semiotic clarity deficiencies [...] reduce comprehension accuracy"* [11]
7. *"perceptual pop-out and discriminability show their relevance for comprehension accuracy and perceived cognitive load"* [9,11]
8. *"color had no significant main effect on comprehension accuracy."* [19]
9. *"no evidence of the hypothesized superiority of left-to-right flow direction; model elements [...] were made larger and were repositioned [with] no evidence of an effect on comprehension accuracy"* [12,23]
10. *"colored relevant model elements did not significantly affect comprehension accuracy but lowered time taken."* [23]

4.4 Deriving Design Decisions From the Goal Models

The approach sketched in the previous sections can be applied to systematically consider design decisions of visual modeling languages, in this case the BPMN. Revising the example given in Fig. 3, the three possible design issues that have been identified can now be addressed using the constructed goal model.

Issue (1) in Fig. 3 was identified because of an ambiguous expression of diverging and converging process flow, the first expressed using the visual element of a gateway, the second implicitly by in-going process flow arrows into a following task element. With respect to the goal "Ease of understanding [Process flow]" in the refinement hierarchy shown in Fig. 6, there are claims that suggest favoring the task "Use explicit gateways" over implicit gateways [20,24]. Furthermore, in the decomposition hierarchy of the "Accuracy of understanding" goal in Fig. 7, the task "Allow multiple notation variants" is claimed to have negative influence on accuracy of understanding [11,23,28], which supports the decision to suggest only one notation variant for process flow divergence and convergence. A possible design alternative that is in accordance with these design principles is shown in Fig. 8(b).

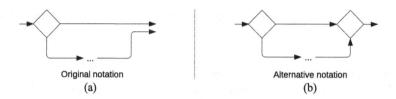

Original notation (a)   Alternative notation (b)

Fig. 8. Original notation (a) and design alternative (b) for issue (1), in accordance with the design principles derived from the goal analysis

With respect to the notation of events, which is addressed by issue (2) marked in Fig. 3, the goal-based analysis reveals that a possible design alternative should consider the tasks "Use distinguishable symbols" and "Use descriptive icons" in the detail models that decompose the "Ease of understanding" and "Accuracy of understanding" goals, since they relate both to the goals "Ease of understanding [Symbols]" and "Accuracy of understanding [Symbols]". These tasks, however, cannot simultaneously be realized, since there is a trade-off between the use of abstract shapes, which are non-descriptive but typically better distinguishable, and the use of picture-like descriptive icons. To resolve this conflict, the relationships of the tasks to their superordinate goals can now be accounted for: In the "Ease of understanding" goal model, both of the tasks "Use distinguishable symbols" and "Use descriptive icons" are almost equally justified by positive claims with respect to the fulfillment of the superordinate goals, with a tendency to "Use descriptive icons" when the goal is to support novice users in achieving "Ease of understanding". The detail model on "Accuracy of understanding", however, unveils that "Use descriptive icons" is only in parts positively associated with its superordinate goals and there are two positive and two negative claims that recommend, respectively advise against, deciding for this task. The "Use distinguishable symbols" task, however, is related to its superordinate goals by supporting relationships only. Given this constellation, a design alternative for the symbols of the error event and the escalation event would take into account to use more simply structured and more clearly distinguishable symbols that are composed of abstract shapes.

An alternative suggestion for a design of the event symbols is shown in Fig. 9(b). This notation provides a higher level of perceptual discriminability, since the "×" and "!" shapes can be better distinguished by the human cognitive apparatus for visual perception, and they still keep up some level of descriptive meaning, because both symbols are more commonly used metaphors for errors and exceptional situations than the symbols from the original notation. The fact that the process flow continues after the escalation event has been thrown, is accounted for by continuing the process flow notation inside the task element instead of operating with different border styles.

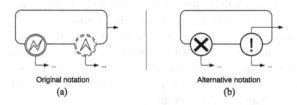

Original notation
(a)

Alternative notation
(b)

Fig. 9. Original notation (a) and design alternative (b) for issue (2) in accordance with the design principles derived from the goal analysis

Reasoning about issue (3) in Fig. 3 with the help of the goal-oriented approach allows the conclusion that with respect to understanding the model, a lack of vertical alignment of the end-event symbols does not provide significant disadvantages. This is explicated in the goal model in Fig. 7 by the unspecified '?'-relationship of the goal "Use layout rules" to its superordinate goal "Accuracy of understanding" [12].

5   Conclusion

With the presented approach, we have demonstrated the applicability of the NFR analysis method to the domain of visual modeling language design, along the example of reconsidering a selection of BPMN 2.0 language design decisions. The demonstrated method adopts a model-based approach for a requirements-driven design, in which decisions and corresponding justifications are explicated with a visual formalism and made traceable through the use of corresponding modeling language constructs. This way, trade-offs between existing design alternatives, and multi-perspective design decisions for different groups of stakeholders and language application scenarios can systematically be taken into consideration. As a model-based approach, it is possible to underpin the suggested method with tooling support that implements the proposed approach as software for guiding modeling language developers.

The approach shows how the NFR analysis method serves as a unifying framework to integrate individual parts of existing research. This makes it possible to form a coherent whole out of individual design principles that formerly have been discussed in an isolated way, and provide model-based means to identify and cope with contradictions or incompleteness among the cited literature. It also allows to justify design decisions using explicit, traceable design rationales in the form of claims.

A number of limitations apply to the current state of the elaboration. At first, for now we have concentrated on design decisions regarding the BPMN language only. However, the analysis of an existing language design with our approach widely resembles the considerations that have to be made when creating new visual languages or providing extensions to existing languages. The results of the demonstration thus can be transferred to the tasks of creating or extending any visual modeling language. Furthermore, the visual notation of NFR models as it is used for now leads to a high degree of fragmentation, due to the high amount of hierarchical branches which both can represent type and topic refinements. More research is required on this, and tooling support with interactive features to navigate between multiple perspectives and levels could provide a solution to cope with the complexity of NFR models.

Future work will extend the presented approach by demonstrating it along a wider range of modeling languages, and further elaborate it to a full-fledged framework that is applicable as prescriptive guidance for the creation of new visual modeling languages.

References

1. User requirements notation (URN) language definition. Recommendation Z.151 (11/08) (2008). http://www.itu.int/rec/T-REC-Z.151/en. Accessed 30 Mar 2018
2. Aranda, J., Ernst, N.A., Horkoff, J., Easterbrook, S.M.: A framework for empirical evaluation of model comprehensibility. In: International Workshop on Modeling in Software Engineering at ICSE, Minneapolis, USA, pp. 7–12. May 2007
3. Boehm, B., In, H.: Identifying quality-requirement conflicts. IEEE Soft. **13**(2), 25–35 (1996)
4. Burattin, A., Kaiser, M., Neurauter, M., Weber, B.: Eye tracking meets the process of process modeling: a visual analytic approach. In: Dumas, M., Fantinato, M. (eds.) BPM 2016. LNBIP, vol. 281, pp. 461–473. Springer, Cham (2017). https://doi.org/10.1007/978-3-319-58457-7_34
5. Chung, L., Nixon, B., Yu, E.: Using non-functional requirements to systematically select among alternatives in architectural design. In: Proceedings of 1st International Workshop on Architectures for Software Systems, pp. 31–43 (1994)
6. Chung, L., Nixon, B.A., Yu, E., Mylopoulos, J.: Non-Functional Requirements in Software Engineering. Springer, Boston (2000)
7. de Kinderen, S., Ma, Q.: Requirements engineering for the design of conceptual modeling languages. Appl. Ontol. **10**(1), 7–24 (2015)
8. Figl, K.: Comprehension of procedural visual business process models. Bus. Inf. Syst. Eng. **59**(1), 41–67 (2017)

9. Figl, K., Mendling, J., Strembeck, M.: The influence of notational deficiencies on process model comprehension. J. Assoc. Inf. Syst. **14**(6), 312–338 (2013)
10. Figl, K., Mendling, J., Strembeck, M., Recker, J.: On the cognitive effectiveness of routing symbols in process modeling languages. In: Abramowicz, W., Tolksdorf, R. (eds.) BIS 2010. LNBIP, vol. 47, pp. 230–241. Springer, Heidelberg (2010). https://doi.org/10.1007/978-3-642-12814-1_20
11. Figl, K., Recker, J., Mendling, J.: A study on the effects of routing symbol design on process model comprehension. Decis. Support Syst. **54**(2), 1104–1118 (2013)
12. Figl , K., Strembeck, M.: Findings from an experiment on flow direction of business process models. In: Proceedings of the 6th International Workshop on Enterprise Modelling and Information Systems Architectures (EMISA), Lecture Notes in Informatics (LNI). GI, vol. 248, pp. 59–73 (2015)
13. Frank, U.: Domain-specific modeling languages: requirements analysis and design guidelines. In: Reinhartz-Berger, I., Sturm, A., Clark, T., Cohen, S., Bettin, J. (eds.) Domain Engineering, pp. 133–157. Springer, Heidelberg (2013). https://doi.org/10.1007/978-3-642-36654-3_6
14. Genon, N., Heymans, P., Amyot, D.: Analysing the cognitive effectiveness of the BPMN 2.0 visual notation. In: Malloy, B., Staab, S., van den Brand, M. (eds.) SLE 2010. LNCS, vol. 6563, pp. 377–396. Springer, Heidelberg (2011). https://doi.org/10.1007/978-3-642-19440-5_25
15. Object Management Group. Bpmn 2.0 by example, version 1.0 (non-normative) (2010). https://www.omg.org/spec/BPMN/2.0/About-BPMN/. Accessed 30 Mar 2018
16. Gulden, J., Reijers, H. A.: Toward advanced visualization techniques for conceptual modeling. In Grabis, J., Sandkuhl, K. (eds.) Proceedings of the CAiSE Forum 2015 Stockholm, Sweden, June 8–12, 2015, pp. 33–40. CEUR Workshop Proceedings. CEUR (2015)
17. Gulden, J., Linden, D., Aysolmaz, B.: A research agenda on visualizations in information systems engineering. In: Proceedings of the 11th International Conference on Evaluation of Novel Software Approaches to Software Engineering (ENASE 2016), pp. 234–240 (2016)
18. Business Process Management Initiative. Business process modeling notation 2.0 (BPMN 2.0) (2011)
19. Kummer, T.F., Recker, J., Mendling, J.: Enhancing understandability of process models through cultural-dependent color adjustments. Decis. Support Syst. **87**(C), 1–12 (2016)
20. Leopold, H., Mendling, J., Gunther, O.: Learning from quality issues of BPMN models from industry. IEEE Softw. **33**(4), 26–33 (2016)
21. Mendling, J., Reijers, H.A., van der Aalst, W.M.P.: Seven process modeling guidelines (7PMG). Inf. Softw. Technol. **52**(2), 127–136 (2010)
22. Moody, D.L.: The "physics" of notations: toward a scientific basis for constructing visual notations in software engineering. IEEE Trans. Softw. Eng. **35**(6), 756–779 (2009)
23. Petrusel, R., Mendling, J., Reijers, H.A.: Task-specific visual cues for improving process model understanding. Inf. Softw. Technol. **79**, 63–78 (2016)
24. Recker, J.: Empirical investigation of the usefulness of gateway constructs in process models. Eur. J. Inf. Syst. **22**(6), 673–689 (2013)
25. Reijers, H.A., Freytag, T., Mendling, J., Eckleder, A.: Syntax highlighting in business process models. Decis. Support Syst. **51**(3), 339–349 (2011)

26. da Silva Teixeira, M.G., Quirino, G.K., Gailly, F., de Almeida Falbo, R., Guizzardi, G., Perini Barcellos, M.: PoN-S: a systematic approach for applying the physics of notation (PoN). In: Schmidt, R., Guédria, W., Bider, I., Guerreiro, S. (eds.) BPMDS/EMMSAD -2016. LNBIP, vol. 248, pp. 432–447. Springer, Cham (2016). https://doi.org/10.1007/978-3-319-39429-9_27

27. van der Linden, D., Hadar, I., Zamansky, A.: On the requirement from practice for meaningful variability in visual notation. In: Reinhartz-Berger, I., Gulden, J., Nurcan, S., Guédria, W., Bera, P. (eds.) BPMDS/EMMSAD -2017. LNBIP, vol. 287, pp. 189–203. Springer, Cham (2017). https://doi.org/10.1007/978-3-319-59466-8_12

28. v. d. Linden, D., Hadar, I., Zamansky, A.: What practitioners really want: requirements for visual notations in conceptual modeling. Softw. Syst. Model. **2**, 1–20 (2018)

29. van der Linden, D., Zamansky, A., Hadar, I.: How cognitively effective is a visual notation? on the inherent difficulty of operationalizing the physics of notations. In: Schmidt, R., Guédria, W., Bider, I., Guerreiro, S. (eds.) BPMDS/EMMSAD -2016. LNBIP, vol. 248, pp. 448–462. Springer, Cham (2016). https://doi.org/10.1007/978-3-319-39429-9_28

30. Linden, D.V.D, Zamansky, A., Hadar, I.: A framework for improving the verifiability of visual notation design grounded in the physics of notations. In: 2017 IEEE 25th International Requirements Engineering Conference (RE), pp. 41–50, Sept 2017

A Method to Enable Ability-Based Human Resource Allocation in Business Process Management Systems

Jonnro Erasmus$^{(\boxtimes)}$, Irene Vanderfeesten, Konstantinos Traganos,
Xavier Jie-A-Looi, Ad Kleingeld, and Paul Grefen

Eindhoven University of Technology, Eindhoven, The Netherlands
{j.erasmus,i.t.p.vanderfeesten,k.traganos,p.a.m.
kleingeld,p.w.p.j.grefen}@tue.nl,
x.e.h.jie-a-looi@alumnus.tue.nl

Abstract. Business process management systems are used to orchestrate the activities in an organization. These information systems allocate resources to perform activities based on information that describes those resources and activities. It is widely recognized that resource allocation can be enhanced by considering resource characteristics during selection. However, little guidance is available that shows how such characteristics should be specified. Human ability is one such characteristic, with the advantage that it is well-defined in the Fleishman Taxonomy of Human Abilities. This paper presents a method that leverages the Fleishman taxonomy to specify activities and human resources. Those specifications are then used to allocate resources to activities during process run-time. We show how ability-based resource allocation can be implemented in a business process management system and evaluate the method in a real-world scenario.

Keywords: Resource allocation · Process management system
Human abilities

1 Introduction

A business process management system (BPMS) coordinates the flow of work between the resources of an organization. An important function of these information systems is to allocate resources to perform activities. This system function is often called *resource allocation* [1], *actor assignment* [2] or *role resolution* [3]. Current resource allocation mechanisms are basic though, because they only consider general organizational information, such as the role, position or business unit of a resource [4]. This proves problematic, because significant variation can be found between resources in the same role, position or business unit [5].

It has been shown that improved resource allocation can lead to improved process performance [6]. More specifically, it is suggested that resource characteristics can be used for advanced resource allocation [7]. Although the potential benefit of more advanced resource allocation based on resource characteristics is generally accepted [8, 9], guidance on the specification of resource characteristics is lacking. We address

R. A. Buchmann et al. (Eds.): PoEM 2018, LNBIP 335, pp. 37–52, 2018.
https://doi.org/10.1007/978-3-030-02302-7_3

this deficiency in the form of a step-by-step method to specify resource characteristics, using a well-established taxonomy of human abilities. We then show how the specifications are used to execute more advanced resource allocation. Figure 1 shows the extension, from basic resource allocation based on role, to a more advanced mechanism making use of abilities in addition to role. Instead of selecting any resource with a certain role, additional information is queried to select a specific resource with that role.

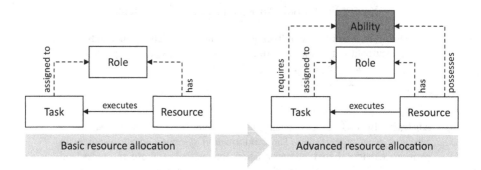

Fig. 1. Introduction of characteristics as additional criteria for resource allocation.

As proof of concept, the extension is used to for run-time allocation of resources based on the specification of tasks and resources in a BPMS. The resource allocation is accomplished in three phases. First, finding all resources that are available and have the appropriate role to perform the task under consideration. Secondly, determine which resources, from the previously found set, are eligible to perform the task, i.e. which resources possess the required abilities to perform the task. Thirdly, selecting a single resource based on a predetermined process objective, e.g. maximize throughput or process flexibility. Figure 2 illustrates the three-phased resource selection approach.

To evaluate the method, we present a case study in a factory. A manufacturing environment is particularly well-suited because manufacturing tasks require a large range of abilities (e.g. physical and sensory abilities, in addition to cognitive abilities).

Fig. 2. Three-phased selection of resource, with an eligibility check and prioritization.

The structure of this paper is as follows: Sect. 2 presents a summary of related work on resource allocation in BPMSs. In Sect. 3 we motivate the use of abilities, as opposed to other human characteristics. In Sect. 4, the method to describe tasks and resources is elaborated and in Sect. 5 we show how the resulting information is used for run-time allocation. In Sect. 6 we discuss the results of the case study and finally in Sect. 7 we reflect on the research and consider next steps.

2 Related Work

BPMSs lead process instances (also called cases) through the activities of a business process according to the process model, by coordinating the resources that execute those activities [7]. A resource, in this context, is any entity that can perform an activity, either alone or in collaboration with other resources, including humans, information systems and cyber-physical systems (such as robots and autonomous guided vehicles). Resources are requested at run-time to perform a work item, towards the objective of a specific activity for a specific process instance [4]. The topic of this research is the matching of a human resource to an activity of a process, i.e. human resource allocation.

Mechanisms for resource allocation in contemporary BPMSs solely consider organizational information of the resource such as role, department or position for this matching. Researchers have identified the need and benefit of more intelligent allocation based on more detailed and complementary resource information [8, 9], but only few studies elaborate on this. Resource allocation essentially consists of two parts: (1) design-time description of resources and activities such that it is possible to determine which resource can perform an activity, and (2) the mechanism that makes use of the descriptions to allocate resources to activities during process run-time [3].

2.1 Description of Resources and Activities

In addition to the standard organizational information, some manual techniques are used to describe resources, in terms of preferences [1] and job experience [10]. Similarly, approaches to describe task requirements [11] and constraints [12] are also proposed. Kumar et al. [13] presents a model to capture compatibilities between resources to improve collaboration between actors in the same workflow. Oberweis and Schuster [14] present a detailed meta-model for the description of resources and their competence, skills and knowledge. While all these studies present compelling arguments to extend resource description, the content of competence, skills, knowledge, etc. is left completely to the user to define. Cabanillas et al. [15] provide a domain specific language called Resource Assignment Language as a complement to BPMN2.0. This language improves the expressiveness of resource description, enabling more advanced resource allocation, but the content is again left entirely open.

To overcome the lack of guidance on resource description, several researchers turn to process mining to discover information about tasks and resources. Liu et al. [16] show how an event log of manual assignment can be used to semi-automate subsequent assignment. Arias et al. [17] extends the concept to allocate a resource to a block of interrelated activities. Huang et al. [18] show how to measure resource behavior in terms of four perspectives, i.e., preference, availability, competence and cooperation, based on process mining. The results of those measurements can then be used to improve resource allocation. Pika et al. [19] expands the allocation criteria by extracting information about the skills, utilization, preferences, productivity, and collaboration patterns of resources from process event logs. Though process mining is used effectively, these studies are still focused on how to retrieve information, instead of what information to retrieve.

More recently, Arias et al. [20] offers a holistic overview of criteria that can be used in human resource allocation. Their taxonomy distinguishes between nine factors, including role and expertise. Although these factors are identified, the taxonomy provides no guidance on how it should be used to describe resources. For example, expertise is defined to include resource capabilities, competences, skills, and knowledge, but those sub-factors are not further elaborated. In fact, clear guidance on the specification of resources and tasks is strikingly absent throughout the literature. The research presented in this paper provides exactly such guidance in the form of a method to specify the abilities possessed by resources and required to perform tasks.

Russell et al. [21] take a different approach, by defining resource management patterns in relation to the lifecycle stages of a work item. 39 workflow resource patterns are catalogued in five categories: creation, push, pull, detour and auto-start patterns. Creation patterns correspond to the "describing" part of resource allocation, while the remaining four categories correspond to the "allocation mechanism" part. Describing resources in terms of abilities, as presented in this paper, aligns well to 'Pattern 8: Capability-based allocation' of the Russell et al. [21] catalogue. This pattern is described as "the ability to offer or allocate instances of a task to resources based on specific capabilities that they possess." They call for a dictionary of capabilities with distinct names and a range of possible values. Our method includes such a dictionary and gives guidance on how to use it to specify resources and activities.

2.2 Resource Allocation Mechanisms

Resource allocation mechanisms vary considerably, ranging from optimization during planning to run-time allocation. Huang et al. [22] combine resource allocation optimization with process mining to develop an approach which improves with data generated during process execution. Shehory and Kraus [23] present several algorithms to optimise allocation by forming coalitions of agents to perform tasks. In physical industries, such as manufacturing, more emphasis is placed on resource scheduling, due to the inherent constraints of physical resources and their location [24, 25]. Havur et al. [26] consider how dependencies defined during design-time affect resource scheduling. Kumar et al. [5] also advocates that balance must be found between quality and performance, by considering the competence of the resources. Koschmider et al. [27] show that changes to resource allocation may affect the process configuration itself.

The research presented in this paper is more concerned with run-time allocation of resources, instead of planning. Zur Muehlen [4] distinguishes between push and pull resource allocation patterns. Push occurs when the system compels a resource to start working on a work item, while pull occurs when a resource requests a work item from the system. The Russell et al. [21] catalogue of resource management patterns recognizes four categories of allocation patterns: push, pull, detour and auto-start patterns. The run-time allocation presented in Sect. 5 of this article adopts push allocation, specifically 'Pattern 14: Distribution by Allocation - Single Resource', because it is better suited to the specific case study. However, using abilities to enhance resource allocation is equally applicable to any of the run-time allocation patterns.

3   Human Characteristics

To elaborate on the eligibility step in the allocation mechanism (illustrated in Fig. 2), we considered the four factors of expertise as defined by Arias et al. [20]: skills, competences, knowledge and capabilities. *Skills* are specific personal attributes that are largely dependent on learning and represent the product of training in particular tasks, i.e. they are practiced acts [27]. *Competences* refer to combinations of knowledge, skills, abilities and other characteristics that are needed for effective performance in a wide range of jobs [28, 29]. The starting point for developing competence models usually lies in the organizational goals and job outcomes, rather than the specific tasks to be carried out. *Knowledge* is the awareness of or familiarity with something, making it specific to a subject or task. *Capability* is difficult to define, because it simply refers to the ability to do something. *Ability* is better defined in industrial psychology, as an enduring attribute of an individual's capability to perform a range of different tasks [30, 31]. For example, whereas 'written expression' is an example of an ability, associated skills could be proficiency in LaTeX functionalities or using in-text citations.

Abilities are more general than *skills* and *knowledge*, but more focused on the actual tasks than *competences*. Thus, a single set of abilities may be applicable to various activities or even different industries. *Skills* and *knowledge* are highly context specific and practically unlimited in number, impeding their universal applicability. Conversely, *competences* are not specific enough to support selection of resources for specific tasks. Additionally, *abilities* have the benefit that they exhibit stability over time, with only gradual improvement with exposure to development stimuli [32].

Various theories and taxonomies are used to describe abilities, mostly related to the cognitive area of human performance [33–36]. The Taxonomy of Human Abilities of Fleishman [37] stands out, as the most comprehensive taxonomy and its validity is established in various studies [38]. It consists of 52 abilities in four categories: *cognitive* (21), *psychomotor* (10), *physical* (9) and *sensory* (12) abilities. *Cognitive* abilities represent the general intellectual capacity of a person. *Psychomotor* abilities combine cognitive and physical traits dealing with issues of coordination, dexterity and reaction time. *Physical* abilities focus solely on the muscular traits of a person. Lastly, *sensory* abilities are the physical functions of vision, hearing, touch, taste, smell and kinesthetic feedback (noticing changes in body position) [39]. Figure 3 shows an extract of the taxonomy of human abilities, with selected abilities in each category. The full list of abilities and their descriptions is available online[1].

---

[1] https://www.onetcenter.org/content.html/1.A?d=1&p=1#cm_1.A.

Although abilities are particularly well-suited for human resource allocation, it does not prohibit the use of additional characteristics, such as skills, knowledge or even resource preference. Such characteristics can also be used to select a resource for a task, but this research aims to provide clear guidance on the specification of human abilities by utilizing the extensive knowledge instilled in the Fleishman Taxonomy of Human Abilities [37].

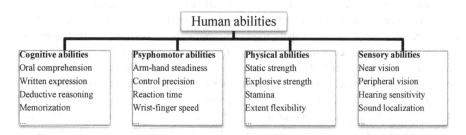

Fig. 3. Extract of the taxonomy of human abilities [37], showing selected abilities in each of the four categories.

The Taxonomy of Human Abilities is accompanied by a tool to determine the ability requirements of various jobs. The Fleishman Job Analysis Survey (F-JAS) guides experts to determine whether an ability is necessary for a job, how important an ability is for a the job, and on what level the ability is required [40]. This can be done for each of the 52 abilities present in the Taxonomy of Human Abilities.

Figure 4 is an extract of F-JAS, showing the scale for a single ability chosen at random (i.e. the written comprehension scale as one of the 21 cognitive abilities). The specific ability and its description is shown at the top, followed by two scales: one to measure the *importance* of the ability (A) and the other to measure the required *level* of an ability (B). The *importance* of an ability is measured on a 5-point Likert scale. By comparing an applicants' abilities with the importance of a required ability, a recruiter can determine whether the applicant is suitable for a job. The *level* follows a 7-point Likert scale to indicate to what extent a certain ability must be possessed by an individual. *Reference anchors* are provided to help the user determine the required level. The full F-JAS can't be shown here, but the rating scales for all 52 abilities are available online[2].

---

[2] https://www.onetcenter.org/dl_files/MS_Word/Abilities.pdf.

A. How <u>important</u> is WRITTEN COMPREHENSION to the performance of *your current job*?

Not Important*	Somewhat Important	Important	Very Important	Extremely Important
①	②	③	④	⑤

* If you marked Not Important, skip LEVEL below and go on to the next activity.

B. What <u>level</u> of WRITTEN COMPREHENSION is needed to perform *your current job*?

Understand signs on the highway ↓   Understand an apartment lease ↓   Understand an instruction book on repairing missile guidance systems ↓

① —— ② —— ③ —— ④ —— ⑤ —— ⑥ —— ⑦

Fig. 4. Measurement scale for one of abilities of the taxonomy of human abilities (https://www.onetcenter.org/dl_files/MS_Word/Abilities.pdf).

The taxonomy and accompanying rating scale are widely used in human performance studies [41, 42] and it is the foundation of the Occupational Information Network (O*NET), the primary job description database of the United States [43]. The reliability and validity of the measurement scales and anchors are confirmed through several studies [38]. In our research, we explore the use of the taxonomy and rating scale to describe human resources and activities to be performed. While this is not its original intention, it is designed to describe humans in relation to business activities.

4 Method to Specify Tasks and Resources in Terms of Abilities

We adopt the Fleishman Taxonomy of Human Abilities (see Sect. 3) to specify task requirements and resource characteristics. Table 1 shows five of the 52 abilities, giving a broad overview of the taxonomy. The identifiers in the first column match those of the Fleishman taxonomy. The full table is available online[3].

Table 1. Extract of the Ability table showing selected abilities of the taxonomy [37].

ID	Ability name	Ability description
1	Oral comprehension	The ability to listen to and understand information and ideas presented through spoken words and sentences
13	Number facility	The ability to add, subtract, multiply, or divide quickly and correctly
25	Control precision	The ability to quickly and repeatedly adjust the controls of a machine or a vehicle to exact positions
32	Static strength	The ability to exert maximum muscle force to lift, push, pull, or carry objects
41	Near vision	The ability to see details at close range (within a few feet of the observer)

---

[3] http://is.ieis.tue.nl/staff/ivanderfeesten/Papers/PoEM2018/.

The proposed method takes a two-sided approach, corresponding to the description of tasks and resources. Figure 5 shows a graphical depiction of method, with three steps each for tasks and resources. To avoid confusion, we use the nomenclature steps, tasks, user and resources. The method is comprised of steps performed by the user. The output of the method are specifications of tasks and resources.

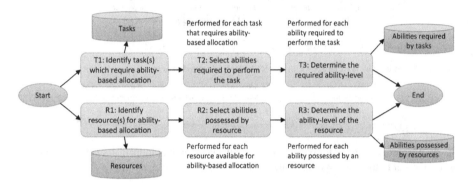

Fig. 5. Depiction of the method to specify tasks and resources in terms of human abilities.

The presented method was evaluated in a manufacturing case study. To make the method more relatable, we use this same case study as a running example. Figure 6 shows the process model of the case study scenario. The description of tasks and resources can be done in any order, but at least one task and two resources must be specified, otherwise resource selection is superfluous.

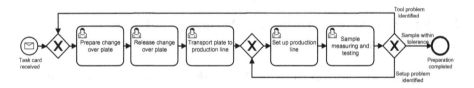

Fig. 6. Case study process with five tasks, used as reference to explain the method.

4.1 Description of Tasks in Terms of Human Abilities

The description of tasks in terms of abilities involves three steps: designating tasks for ability-based allocation, selecting abilities required to perform that task(s), and finally specifying the ability-level required.

Step T1: Identify Task(s) which Require Ability-Based Allocation. Not all tasks will benefit from ability-based allocation. For example, a small factory with a single stamping machine will always allocate stamping tasks to resources operating that machine. During identification, the user needs good understanding of the selected tasks.

Selecting a task implies that the user must be able to determine which abilities are required to perform the task, and at what level those abilities should be rated. This can be particularly problematic if task variations exist in an enterprise. It is essential that the user can identify and scope a task such that its required abilities can be specified for all conditions. Table 2 shows an entry for each task of the process shown in Fig. 6.

Table 2. Tasks that require ability-based allocation for the case study process.

Task name	Description	Role
Prepare change over plate	Tools are placed on the plate for production change over	Tool assembler
Release change over plate	Tool assembly is verified before dispatch	Tool assembler
Transport plate to production line	Assembled plate is moved to appropriate production line	Tool assembler
Set up production line	Tools are placed in the machines in preparation for production	Tool assembler
Sample measuring testing	Machine setup is verified by producing and checking a sample product	Tool assembler

Step T2: Select Abilities Required to Perform the Task. The second step of the method will be performed for each task identified in step T1. The user selects the abilities required to perform the task, because tasks rarely require all 52 abilities listed in the Taxonomy of Human Abilities [37]. This necessitates sufficient knowledge of the task to express its requirements in terms of abilities. Eliminating the unnecessary abilities provides the user with a list of abilities that are required for a specific task and reduces the effort needed for step T3 of the method.

Step T3: Determine Required Abilities Level. F-JAS, as described in Sect. 3, is used to determine the required level of an ability. Step T3 is repeated for each ability selected in step T2. The user uses the references points on the scale to gauge the minimum ability level required and records the result as a value. Table 3 shows the required level of five abilities for the task 'Prepare change over plate'. The task requires the ability 'written comprehension' at level 2, 'memorization' at level 4 and 'problem sensitivity' also at level 2. The remaining fifteen abilities required for this task are shown online[4].

Table 3. Required level of abilities for the first task in the case study process (extract). The full table is available online (http://is.ieis.tue.nl/staff/ivanderfeesten/Papers/PoEM2018/).

Task	Ability	Required level
Prepare change over plate	Written comprehension	2
Prepare change over plate	Memorization	4
Prepare change over plate	Wrist-finger speed	2
Prepare change over plate	Static strength	3
Prepare change over plate	Near vision	4

4.2 Description of Resources in Terms of Human Ability

Description of resources follow similar steps to the description of tasks, except that here we specify possessed abilities. The method again starts with identification of

---

[4] http://is.ieis.tue.nl/staff/ivanderfeesten/Papers/PoEM2018/.

resources and concludes with determination of the level of each ability of each resource.

Step R1: Identify Resource(s) Available for Ability-Based Allocation. Not all resources in an organization will benefit from dynamic allocation. Only resources involved in various tasks should be designated for ability-based specification. In our running example, five resources are authorized (based on their role) to perform all tasks in the process. Table 4 shows the five resources and their roles and statuses. Resource status is updated by the BPMS based on task assignment and completion.

Table 4. Resources included in the case study, involved in the tool assembly process.

Resource name	Role	Status
John	Tool assembler	Idle
Mark	Tool assembler	Idle
Selma	Tool assembler	Idle
Catherine	Tool assembler	Idle
Steven	Tool assembler	Idle

Step R2: Select Abilities Possessed by the Resource. The user determines which of the 52 abilities in the taxonomy are possessed by the resource. This step requires considerably more effort compared to its counterpart in task description, because a resource possesses a wide range of abilities, including those that are not relevant for some tasks. Counsel from someone with knowledge of the employee's abilities is recommended.

Step R3: Determine the Ability Level of the Resource. As with the description of tasks, F-JAS [40] is used to determine the ability levels possessed by resources. Table 5 shows an extract of the ability levels for one of the resources in the case study.

Table 5. Extract of abilities and level possessed by one resource (John) from the case study. The full table is available online (http://is.ieis.tue.nl/staff/ivanderfeesten/Papers/PoEM2018/).

Resource	Ability	Possessed level
John	Written comprehension	3
John	Problem sensitivity	4
John	Wrist-finger speed	4
John	Static strength	5
John	Near vision	5

5   Run-Time Allocation of a Resource Based on Abilities

The information generated by the method presented in Sect. 4 can be used to allocate specific resources to specific tasks, during process run-time. For the purposes of the case study, the information is captured in data tables of a local deployment of PostgreSQL 10. Figure 7 shows database schema used for implementation. Three main tables are used to define tasks, abilities and resources, whereas two intermediate tables, TaskAbility and ResourceAbility, are used to relate abilities to tasks and resources.

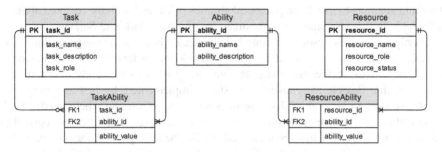

Fig. 7. Data tables used for ability-based algorithm of resource.

Based on the design-time specification of resource characteristics and task requirements, the run-time allocation can be supported with a BPMS. In the case study, the allocation mechanism is implemented in Camunda BPM[5] version 7.8 running on a Wildfly 10 application server. A screencast of the implemented BPMS, accommodating database and operational ability-based allocation is available online[6].

Resource allocation is implemented with a task listener attached to each task designated for ability-based allocation. A task listener triggers a function when a certain event happens in the system. In this case, the event is "task creation", i.e. when the task is instantiated during process execution, and the function is implemented as a Java method. The system passes the "task_id" from the process model to the method and receives a "resource_id" as the assignee. The following pseudo-code illustrates the implemented algorithm:

```
A. SELECT task_abilities AND task_ability_value
       WHERE task_id = 1
B. SELECT candidate_resources WITH resource_role = task_role
C. FOR EACH candidate_resource
       IF ALL resource_ability_value >= task_ability_value
          THEN ADD candidate_resource to eligible_resources
          ELSE EXCLUDE candidate_resource from eligible_resources
D. IF eligible_resources = 1 THEN SELECT assigned_resource
E. ELSE IF eligible_resources > 1 THEN SELECT assigned_resource
       WITH MIN(AVERAGE resource_abilities - task_abilities)
F. ELSE IF eligible_resources = 0 NOTIFY supervisor
G. RETURN resource_id, resource_name FROM assigned_resource
```

The first line of the algorithm (line A) retrieves the required abilities from the TaskAbilities table (Table 3). In this case, the required abilities of task 1 are retrieved. Line B of the algorithm creates a list of candidates with the correct role. In our case

---

[5] https://camunda.org/.

[6] https://youtu.be/1g_Ku1Q2beQ.

study, all resources satisfy this condition. Line C finds eligible resources, by excluding the resources who possess an ability at a lower level than required by the task ("John" posses "written comprehension" at level 4, while the task requires at least 5). The algorithm attempts to match the possessed abilities in Table 5 with the required abilities in Table 3. In the case study two resources are eligible: Mark and Selma.

If only one eligible resource is found, that resource is set as the assignee (line D). If multiple resources are eligible, it is possible to select a preferable resource, based on process objectives. In the case study, the business prioritizes flexibility over throughput. Thus, the 'flexible assignment' heuristic is implemented, by first assigning specialist resources to keep generalist resources available to respond where needed [44]. Generalist in this sense refers to resources with a wider range of abilities, as opposed to specialists who have a narrower focus and usually better equipped for specific tasks. This prioritization is shown in line E. It calculates the average level of abilities possessed by the resource that exceeds what is required by the task. Thus, the calculation determines which resource is better able to perform tasks other than the current task. If no eligible resource is found, the responsible supervisor is informed in line E. Finally, line F returns the "resource_id" and "resource_name" of the assignee to the BPMS.

6   Practical Evaluation of Ability-Based Resource Allocation

The evaluation consists of two parts: (1) application of the method in a real-world scenario and (2) using the data generated by the method to demonstrate resource allocation based on human abilities. The evaluation was done at Thomas Regout International, a medium-sized factory in The Netherlands. The factory uses configurable tools to produce highly customizable metal parts.

Steps T1, T2, and T3 of the method were performed by the operations manager to specify the tasks of the process shown in Fig. 6. This process was selected because all five tasks are performed by human operators and require a wide range of abilities. Afterwards, the operations manager was surveyed and interviewed to evaluate the method itself. The Method Evaluation Model [45] was used as both survey and interview outline. Similarly, the competence manager of the company performed steps R1, R2 and R3 of the method to specify the abilities of five human resources involved in the process. The competence manager was also surveyed and interviewed to evaluate the method from a resource perspective.

The results of the evaluation are not included here due to space limitations, but the full list of questions, responses and discussion points are available online[7]. As a brief overview, only three of the 16 questions received negative responses. All three negative responses were related to ease-of-use as perceived by the operations manager. During the interview it was learned that the operations manager found it difficult to relate to the F-JAS scale to rate the required levels of task abilities. However, he also stated that it became significantly easier with subsequent repetitions of the method for additional

---

[7] http://is.ieis.tue.nl/staff/ivanderfeesten/Papers/PoEM2018/.

tasks. The competence manager was highly enthusiastic about the method and even intends to use it for other purposes, such as recruitment and personnel planning.

Utilization of the generated data was demonstrated with the BPMS. The operations manager and process participants were shown how the BPMS allocates tasks to one of the process participants, based on the ability levels. The attraction of automated allocation was enhanced by rendering selected resources unavailable in the system. If the previously preferred resource is not available, the allocation algorithm selects a different eligible resource, from the available pool.

The case study yielded valuable feedback regarding the execution of the method and it showed that the resulting information can be used for run-time resource allocation. The practical demonstration of the method in the manufacturing industry may affect the effort involved though. Manufacturing tasks require a wide range of abilities relative to more administrative tasks. Application in service industries, such as financial services and insurance may involve less effort. Most of the psychomotor and physical abilities will consistently be excluded from analysis. This is equally true for business functions that are more administrative in nature, even in physical industries. The financial and human resource management functions of any organization will also make use of fewer abilities to sufficiently describe their tasks. Depending on the extent of exclusion of certain abilities, it may be advisable to create tailored taxonomies for specific industries or business functions. Tailoring can also help to make the rating scale more relatable.

7 Conclusion

The objective of this research is to enhance the allocation of human resources during process run-time. Current business process management systems employ basic resource allocation, making use of organizational information to find eligible resources for a task. An activity and a set of resources must be assigned to a specific role to ensure that the correct resource is allocated. Roles are abstracted from the resources or activities of the enterprise, comprising an intersection of the two entities. Thus, if the resources or activities of the enterprise change, it may be necessary to re-evaluate the list of roles.

Abilities, as a set of descriptors, have been shown to be more detached from resources or tasks [31]. When introducing a new activity, the required abilities must be determined, but the list of abilities do not change. Thus, the generalizability of abilities allows for looser coupling between activities and resources. More importantly, abilities are specific and quantifiable, enabling the selection of a preferred resource, instead of any resource with the appropriate role. Indeed, the allocation algorithm, as presented in Sect. 5, finds a single resource from a large set of resources.

The contribution of this work is a step-by-step method that guides the user towards resource and activity descriptions. Although many scholars recognize the importance of additional information to enhance resource allocation [7, 8], this research provides the first clear guidance on how to specify such information. The method leverages the wealth of knowledge instilled in Fleishman Taxonomy of Human Abilities [39, 40], but remains simple to perform. The evaluation, as presented in Sect. 6, shows that the method is understandable and useable by business personnel and that it produces data that can be used for run-time allocation of human resources.

The current research can be extended to introduce additional allocation criteria and more sophisticated prioritization or optimization. For example, risks involved in certain tasks can't be expressed as required abilities or an enterprise may simply want to be more specific, e.g. tasks that require specialized skills. Therefore, the presented method can be expanded to incorporate additional factors, such as skills, experience, preference and authorization. Additionally, more advanced resource scheduling techniques can be introduced to leverage the data produced by the method. Alternatively, the method can be supplemented with a feedback mechanism, where tasks executed by allocated resources generate additional data, such as performance, workload or failure rate.

Acknowledgements. The work described in this paper was part of the HORSE project and has received funding from the European Union's Horizon 2020 research and innovation program under grant agreement No 680734.

References

1. Cabanillas, C., García, J.M., Resinas, M., Ruiz, D., Mendling, J., Ruiz-Cortés, A.: Priority-based human resource allocation in business processes. In: Basu, S., Pautasso, C., Zhang, L., Fu, X. (eds.) ICSOC 2013. LNCS, vol. 8274, pp. 374–388. Springer, Heidelberg (2013). https://doi.org/10.1007/978-3-642-45005-1_26
2. Illibauer, C., Ziebermayr, T., Geist, V.: Towards rigid actor assignment in dynamic workflows. In: Felderer, M., Piazolo, F., Ortner, W., Brehm, L., Hof, H.-J. (eds.) ERP 2015. LNBIP, vol. 245, pp. 62–69. Springer, Cham (2016). https://doi.org/10.1007/978-3-319-32799-0_5
3. Zeng, D.D., Zhao, J.L.: Effective role resolution in workflow management. Inf. J. Comput. **17**, 374–387 (2005)
4. Zur Muehlen, M.: Organizational management in workflow applications – issues and perspectives. Inf. Technol. Manage. **5**, 271–291 (2004)
5. Kumar, A., van der Aalst, W.M.P., Verbeek, E.M.W.: Dynamic work distribution in workflow management systems: how to balance quality and performance. J. Manag. Inf. Syst. **18**, 157–193 (2002)
6. Macris, A., Papadimitriou, E., Vassilacopoulos, G.: An ontology-based competency model for workflow activity assignment policies. J. Knowl. Manag. **12**, 72–88 (2008)
7. Vanderfeesten, I., Grefen, P.: Advanced dynamic role resolution in business processes. In: Persson, A., Stirna, J. (eds.) CAiSE 2015. LNBIP, vol. 215, pp. 87–93. Springer, Cham (2015). https://doi.org/10.1007/978-3-319-19243-7_8
8. Mejía, G., Montoya, C.: Applications of resource assignment and scheduling with Petri Nets and heuristic search. Ann. Oper. Res. **181**, 795–812 (2010)
9. Shen, M., Tzeng, G.-H., Liu, D.-R.: Multi-criteria task assignment in workflow management systems. In: Proceedings of the 36th Annual Hawaii International Conference on System Sciences, p. 9. IEEE, Big Island, HI, USA (2003)
10. Kabicher-Fuchs, S., Rinderle-Ma, S.: Work experience in PAIS – concepts, measurements and potentials. In: Ralyté, J., Franch, X., Brinkkemper, S., Wrycza, S. (eds.) CAiSE 2012. LNCS, vol. 7328, pp. 678–694. Springer, Heidelberg (2012). https://doi.org/10.1007/978-3-642-31095-9_44

11. Ouyang, C., Wynn, M.T., Fidge, C., ter Hofstede, A.H.M. Kuhr, J.-C.: Modelling complex resource requirements in business process management systems. In: ACIS 2010, Brisbane (2010)
12. Senkul, P., Toroslu, I.H.: An architecture for workflow scheduling under resource allocation constraints. Inf. Syst. **30**, 399–422 (2005)
13. Kumar, A., Dijkman, R., Song, M.: Optimal resource assignment in workflows for maximizing cooperation. In: Daniel, F., Wang, J., Weber, B. (eds.) BPM 2013. LNCS, vol. 8094, pp. 235–250. Springer, Heidelberg (2013). https://doi.org/10.1007/978-3-642-40176-3_20
14. Oberweis, A., Schuster, T.: A meta-model based approach to the description of resources and skills. In: Americas Conference on Information Systems 2010, Karlsruhe, Germany, pp. 3677–3688 (2010)
15. Cabanillas, C., Resinas, M., Ruiz-Cortés, A.: RAL: a high-level user-oriented resource assignment language for business processes. In: Daniel, F., Barkaoui, K., Dustdar, S. (eds.) BPM 2011. LNBIP, vol. 99, pp. 50–61. Springer, Heidelberg (2012). https://doi.org/10.1007/978-3-642-28108-2_5
16. Liu, Y., Wang, J., Yang, Y., Sun, J.: A semi-automatic approach for workflow staff assignment. Comput. Ind. **59**, 463–476 (2008)
17. Arias, M., Rojas, E., Munoz-Gama, J., Sepúlveda, M.: A framework for recommending resource allocation based on process mining. In: Reichert, M., Reijers, Hajo A. (eds.) BPM 2015. LNBIP, vol. 256, pp. 458–470. Springer, Cham (2016). https://doi.org/10.1007/978-3-319-42887-1_37
18. Huang, Z., Lu, X., Duan, H.: Resource behavior measure and application in business process management. Expert Syst. Appl. **39**, 6458–6468 (2012)
19. Pika, A., et al.: Mining resource profiles from event logs. ACM Trans. Manag. Inf. Syst. **8** (1), 1 (2017)
20. Arias, M., Munoz-Gama, J., Sepúlveda, M.: Towards a taxonomy of human resource allocation criteria. In: Teniente, E., Weidlich, M. (eds.) BPM 2017. LNBIP, vol. 308, pp. 475–483. Springer, Cham (2018). https://doi.org/10.1007/978-3-319-74030-0_37
21. Russell, N., van der Aalst, Wil M.P., ter Hofstede, Arthur H.M., Edmond, D.: Workflow resource patterns: identification, representation and tool support. In: Pastor, O., Falcão e Cunha, J. (eds.) CAiSE 2005. LNCS, vol. 3520, pp. 216–232. Springer, Heidelberg (2005). https://doi.org/10.1007/11431855_16
22. Huang, Z., van der Aalst, W.M.P., Lu, X., Duan, H.: Reinforcement learning based resource allocation in business process management. Data Knowl. Eng. **70**, 127–145 (2011)
23. Shehory, O., Kraus, S.: Methods for task allocation via agent coalition formation. Artif. Intell. **101**, 165–200 (1998)
24. Altuger, G., Chassapis, C.: Manual assembly line operator scheduling using hierarchical preference aggregation. In: Proceedings - Winter Simulation Conference, pp. 1613–1623. Stevens Institute of Technology, Castle Point on Hudson, Hoboken, NJ 07030, United States (2010)
25. Koltai, T., Tatay, V.: Formulation of workforce skill constraints in assembly line balancing models. Optim. Eng. **14**, 529–545 (2013)
26. Havur, G., Cabanillas, C., Mendling, J., Polleres, A.: Resource allocation with dependencies in business process management systems. In: La Rosa, M., Loos, P., Pastor, O. (eds.) BPM 2016. LNBIP, vol. 260, pp. 3–19. Springer, Cham (2016). https://doi.org/10.1007/978-3-319-45468-9_1
27. Koschmider, A., Yingbo, L., Schuster, T.: Role assignment in business process models. In: Daniel, F., Barkaoui, K., Dustdar, S. (eds.) BPM 2011. LNBIP, vol. 99, pp. 37–49. Springer, Heidelberg (2012). https://doi.org/10.1007/978-3-642-28108-2_4

28. Boyatzis, R.E.: The competent manager: a model for effective performance. Long Range Plan. **16**, 110 (1983)
29. Campion, M.A., Fink, A.A., Ruggeberg, B.J., Carr, L., Phillips, G.M., Odman, R.B.: Doing competencies well: best practices in competency modeling. Pers. Psychol. **64**, 225–262 (2011)
30. Carroll, J.B.: Test theory and the behavioral scaling of test performance. In: Test theory for a new generation of tests, pp. 297–322. Lawrence Erlbaum Associates, Inc., Hillsdale, NJ (1993)
31. Fleishman, E.A.: Systems for describing human tasks. Am. Psychol. **37**, 821–834 (1982)
32. Snow, R.E., Lohman, D.F.: Toward a theory of cognitive aptitude for learning from instruction. J. Educ. Psychol. **76**, 347–376 (1984)
33. Spearman, C.: The abilities of man. Macmillan, Oxford, England (1927)
34. Thurstone, L.L.: Primary mental abilities. University of Chicago Press, Chicago (1938)
35. Guilford, J.P.: The structure of intellect. Psychol. Bull. **53**, 267–293 (1956)
36. Cattell, R.B., Horn, J.L.: A check on the theory of fluid and crystallized intelligence with description of new subtest designs. J. Educ. Meas. **15**, 139–164 (1978)
37. Fleishman, E.A.: Toward a taxonomy of human performance. Am. Psychol. **30**, 1127–1149 (1975)
38. Fleishman, E.A., Mumford, M.D.: Evaluating classifications of job behavior: a construct validation of the ability requirement scales. Pers. Psychol. **44**, 523–575 (1991)
39. Fleishman, E.A., Reilly, M.E.: Handbook of Human Abilities: Definitions, Measurements, and Job Task Requirements. Consulting Psychologists Press, Palo Alto, CA (1992)
40. Fleishman, E.A., Reilly, M.E.: Fleishman Job Analysis Survey (F-JAS). Management Research Institute, Bethesda (1992)
41. Stajkovic, A.D., Luthans, F.: Self-efficacy and work-related performance: a meta-analysis. Psychol. Bull. **124**, 240–261 (1998)
42. Kanfer, R., Ackerman, P.L.: Motivation and cognitive abilities: an integrative/aptitude-treatment interaction approach to skill acquisition. J. Appl. Psychol. **74**, 657–690 (1989)
43. Peterson, N.G., Borman, W.C., Mumford, M.D.: An Occupational Information System for the 21st Century: The Development of O*NET. American Psychological Association, Washington (1999)
44. Reijers, H.A., Mansar, S.L.: Best practices in business process redesign: an overview and qualitative evaluation of successful redesign heuristics. Omega **33**, 283–306 (2005)
45. Moody, D.L.: The method evaluation model: a theoretical model for validating information systems design methods. In: ECIS 2003. Association for Information Systems, Firenze, Italy (2003)

Model Derivation

Grass-Root Enterprise Modeling: Issues and Potentials of Retrieving Models from Powerpoint

Achim Reiz[1], Kurt Sandkuhl[1(✉)], Alexander Smirnov[2], and Nikolay Shilov[3]

[1] Rostock University, Rostock, Germany
[2] ITMO University, St. Petersburg, Russia
[3] St. Petersburg Institute of Informatics and Automation, St. Petersburg, Russia
{achim.reiz,kurt.sandkuhl}@uni-rostock.de,
{smir,nick}@iias.spb.su

Abstract. Enterprise modeling (EM) is an established practice in many organizations, but the majority of stakeholders in organizations who produce content relevant for EM use drawing or presentation tools instead of formalized EM techniques. The model-like content of such drawings or presentations often is very valuable for enterprises which calls for a way of integrating it with "real" models and other structured knowledge sources in organizations. This paper investigates how the model-like content of Powerpoint presentations can be extracted and transformed to EM. The main contributions of the paper are (a) an approach for model extraction from Powerpoint, (b) identification of heterogeneities to be tackled during the extraction process and (c) a prototype implementation demonstrating the approach based on ADO.xx.

Keywords: Enterprise modeling · Grass-root modeling · Information extraction

1 Introduction

Enterprise modeling (EM) is an established practice in many organizations and used for various purposes, such as business model development, visualization of the current situation, strategy development, business and IT alignment, and enterprise architecture management. Many application scenarios and experience reports on the use of EM were published during the last decade, for example in automotive industry [2], manufacturing [1], oil industry [3] or healthcare [4]. However, a number of researchers from the EM community argue that EM is more an "elitist discipline" than common practice [5] because the majority of stakeholders in enterprises who produce content or knowledge suitable for EM use drawing or presentation software (e.g., Visio, Powerpoint, Omnigraffle) instead of EM techniques or tools (e.g., ADO.IT, Troux Architect, ARIS). The model-like content of such drawings or presentations often is very valuable for enterprises which calls for a way of integrating it with "real" models and other structured knowledge sources in organizations.

R. A. Buchmann et al. (Eds.): PoEM 2018, LNBIP 335, pp. 55–70, 2018.
https://doi.org/10.1007/978-3-030-02302-7_4

One result of the debate about how to extend the reach of EM in organizations is a recently published research roadmap [6]. This roadmap includes the topic of grass-root EM which basically describes the vision of people doing EM as part of their daily work, without explicitly noticing formalized modelling approaches and techniques. The general idea of grass-root modelling is related to the concept of natural modelling [26] as flexibility in modeling language or symbols is important in both approaches. One way to implement this idea would be to accept drawings as "local representations" of models for certain stakeholder groups and creating ways of integrating expert modeling and grass-root modeling. This paper aims at contributing to the research roadmap implementation by investigating how the model-like content of Powerpoint presentations can be extracted and transformed, as Powerpoint frequently is used in organizational practice [25]. The main contributions of the paper are (a) an approach for model extraction from Powerpoint, (b) identification of heterogeneities to be tackled during the extraction process and (c) a prototype implementation demonstrating the approach based on ADO.XX.

The rest of the paper is organized as follows. Section 2 gives a theoretical background for understanding diagrams. Section 3 develops these theoretical approaches further to a practical comparing algorithm. This algorithm will be evaluated exemplary in Sect. 4. Section 5 shows current limitations and challenges for the developed approach, Sect. 6 gives a conclusion and an outlook for further research.

2   Background

Diagram theory (Sect. 2.1) and existing work on diagram recognition (Sect. 2.2) form the background for our work and will be discussed in this section. Furthermore, our work is also based on background knowledge from EM. We assume that an enterprise model is captured in an enterprise modeling language with a defined meta-model and a visual notation or diagrammatic representation. More information about EM languages, meta-models and tools is available in textbooks about EM (e.g., [7]).

2.1   Diagram Theory

Visual notations are widely used in enterprise models as diagrams offer significant advantages compared to text: They give overview about a topic with a high level of abstraction, which brings it closer to the problem domain. They also structure and group information together just by the location of concepts and can easily add perceptual inferences, which are easy to understand for humans and are more memorable than text [8]. Further, the dual channel theory states that diagrams (visual content) and text (verbal content) are processed entirely different within the brain and concludes that information that is processed within both layer can generate a more sustainable understanding and learning [10].

A graphical notation consists of semantics and syntax. The visual semantic contains the constructs that are included and their meaning, the syntax how to represent these constructs. The semantic itself is independent from the notation and could also be represented in a mathematical way [12, p. 67]. The syntax though contains the visual variables of the representation: horizontal position (x), vertical position (y), size, brightness, color, texture, shape and orientation [11]. The more these variables are used, the more information a diagram can carry and the readability increases. By using these variables, data gets represented in a notation.

All topics shown above dealt with the so called primary notation: The formal meaning of representations that is described within the semantics. Every attribute of a variable represents a concept. But often, additionally to the formally necessary concepts, other, free variables are used to display informal information to clarify the meaning. This is called the secondary notation. Examples are the color or the placement of objects: If they are close to each other, it may imply a connection between them that is not modelled formal, or the color indicates the affiliation to a group even though from a notational perspective color is not a meaningful attribute.

The analysis of diagrams is not trivial as the reader has to know different aspects to interpret a diagram the right way: The first and most obvious is the notation itself. If it is not clear what the difference between shapes or a straight and dotted line means, the diagram cannot be understood. Also, to understand a complex, detailed diagram, it is necessary to have certain domain knowledge to put the model into a context. At last, a novice reader tends to misunderstand the secondary notation. Even though the formal concepts are understood, the secondary notation might bear knowledge that is important to interpret. As a result to all these preconditions for model understanding, the modeler often has to create more than one diagram for the same construct to fit the target audience, from a novice reader or a management summary to detailed models for fellow colleagues [9, 11 pp. 772–773].

Models are part of the language. Every language is used for communication and consists of meaningful language elements [12, pp. 64–65]. While humans can interpret a language without a formal notation, computers need an underlying fixed concept. But even though people tend to believe that diagrams are less formal than textual language, this is a widely distributed misconception: It just highly depends on the underlying syntax and semantics to ensure a high degree of formality [12, pp. 69–70].

2.2 Methods of Diagram Recognition

Diagram retrieval is not a new topic for the research community. This section gives an overview about existing approaches for the automated model creation on the basis of documents. Many of the approaches originate from image recognition. While there are approaches that consider the transfer from drawings or pictorial representations to modelling languages with the help of human interaction, like the PICTMOD method [24], this section is dedicated to the fully automated document analysis.

The idea of analyzing graphics into a structured, digital representation engaged since the early 1990's to further fill the sensory gap between the real world object and the computational description as well as to fill the semantic gap between the information that a visual data can give a user and the information a computer can retrieve from the given graphics [13, p. 5]. In 1995, Yu et al. already described the need to convert archives of paper based designs and diagrams to an object-oriented format that is easier to access, update, understand and manipulate [14]. To achieve this goal, image recognition uses pattern recognition and image processing techniques like vectorization, symbol recognition, analysis documents with diagrammatic notations like electrical diagrams, architectural plans or maps [15, p. 4]. Further, image recognition interacts with other disciplines like multimedia, machine learning, information retrieval, computer vision, and human-computer interaction to build better recognition systems [13, p. 48]. While image recognition in general covers even more aspects like biometrical face recognition [16], image annotation [17] or even handwriting recognition [18], the following overview is limited to diagram recognition as a technique closer to the research topic.

Blostein [19] developed a process for an image diagram retrieval process. At first in the early processing, all unnecessary objects within the image has to be identified and excluded from the analysis process. In the segmentation phase, the distinction between the different symbols has to occur. This is especially challenging if symbols overlap with each other. The last part of the symbol recognition is the recognition itself. This includes shapes, segments of lines that can belong to the shapes in the form of a relation as well as textual elements. The symbol-arrangement analysis covers the relationship between the identified symbols. While the spatial analysis just depends on the position of the objects, the last two steps align the analyzed picture with knowledge about a formal notation. Flowcharts are especially in the focus of image recognition [14, p. 791, 20, pp. 215–216]. They contain Diagram elements as well as logical relations or associations between them, represented by lines which can be directed or undirected [20, p. 216]. As the image recognition systems are getting more and more advanced, it is now possible to also detect handwritten flow charts [21] or to analyze large engineering drawings [14, p. 794]. In the future, new technologies like Deep neural networks are promising to achieve new breakthroughs in the field of image recognition [22, p. 770].

At the one hand, there are a lot of promising approaches towards the analysis of diagrams out of images. At the other hand, for this kind of work, image recognition lays out an additional layer of complexity: a PowerPoint file itself contains not a picture, but shape objects. Prior to the analysis, it would be necessary to convert the slides to an image file format. This would lead to a loss of information: the.pptx file itself stores attributes like connections in form of start and endpoint of a line and form, color and content of shapes. It is therefore not helpful to drop this information and try to retrieve on an image level, but better to analyze the PowerPoint data structure directly if it is available.

3   Model Extraction from Powerpoint

Our approach for model extraction from Powerpoint followed the principal idea that it should be applicable for all kinds of enterprise models and be suitable for as many variations in Powerpoint slide decks as possible. Applicability for all kinds of EM basically implicates that the target meta-model is not pre-defined but can be loaded dynamically during run-time, including the possibility to check what meta-model(s) would fit best to the content of the slide deck. Suitability for Powerpoint variations means no assumptions are made about presentation styles or slide structures.

This principal idea basically results in the need to transform both, Powerpoint content and EM meta-model, into an internal shape-oriented representation which at the same time serves as intermediate format. "Shape-oriented" in this context means that this internal representation is designed for comparing and matching the shapes included in the Powerpoint content and the shapes making up the visual notation of the EM language. The model extraction process consists of four main steps:

- *Retrieving data from Powerpoint*: Analysis of the Powerpoint document and extraction of diagram data and shape information.
- *Retrieving data from meta-model*: Parsing of the meta-model and retrieving of information about the visual notation.
- *Matching*: Analysis of the content retrieved from Powerpoint and the data retrieved from the meta-model with the purpose to find exact or sufficiently similar matches between shapes in Powerpoint and meta-model. This step includes two sub-steps: (a) Structural analysis what shapes occur in slides and if they fit to the shapes in the EM's visual notation; (b) Semantic analysis if the relationships between the discovered shapes fit to the meta-model of the EM.

The steps introduced above will be elaborated in the next sections.

3.1 Retrieving Information Out of PowerPoint

PowerPoint, the SlideShare Program invented in 1984 was at the time a milestone in communication and is a product and trademark of Microsoft. This section first gives an overview about the development of the diagram-retrieval algorithm from Powerpoint as well as the internal storage of the visual attributes in the software prototype developed. Furthermore, aspects of the implementation are shown.

If a Powerpoint file is loaded into the prototype, each slide is opened individually and searched for a suitable diagram. A diagram is marked as usable if it has shapes that are interconnected with each other by a line. The line has to be connected to two shapes, otherwise a valid relationship is not assumed. If such is found, the analyzer converts the diagram into an internal data representation. This internal representation is programmed for the needs of a further analysis. The internal data representation includes a set of Diagrams. A diagram stores a string with the name of the diagram, extracted from the slide title, as well as sets of the object "shape" and "relation". A shape contains the location and size, as well as the type (e.g. rectangle, ellipse), the stored text – if there is any – and the id. PowerPoint gives each shape a presentation wide unique id which can be used for further identification. A relation contains two shape objects, which maps the start and end point.

Technical Implementation: To retrieve the information out of the.pptx file, the apache POI framework is used with the POI-XLSF component. The XMLSlideShow contains all information from the PowerPoint like the Masterslide-attributes or functions to search for specific data. It contains also a list of slides. The slides are stored in a specific data fragment called XSLFSlide. By iterating over this list, every slide can be accessed. The slide object already provides a lot of function for accessing data as well as altering items. It is possible to create shapes, tables and group items. General information to the used theme, used master slide, layout, title or slide number can be crawled directly. For more information on the content, the item XSLFSlide has a method getShapes() for getting all placeable data. By iterating the shapes with the type XSLFShape, almost all necessary information can be retrieved (e.g. size, type):

```
diagram.addshape(shape.getAnchor().getX(),
shape.getAnchor().getY(),shape.getAnchor().getWidth(),
shape.getAnchor().getHeight(), shape.getShapeType().name(),
shape.getShapeId());
diagram.addShapeTextById(shape.getShapeId(), shape.getText());
```

With these short statements, the shape is stored in the internal diagram representation. At last, the relations between objects have to be set up. In a PowerPoint file, the connector between shapes is not a relationship itself but also a special kind of shape. By validating the type by checking

```
for (XSLFShape sh : slide) {
    if (sh instanceof XSLFConnectorShape) {
        XSLFConnectorShape line = (XSLFConnectorShape) sh;
```

The algorithm identified the specialized object "line". The XSLFConnectorShape contains not all necessary data out of the box. To identify the connectors of the lines, it is obligatory to traverse the inner XML of this data fragment.

```
XSLFConnectorShape line = (XSLFConnectorShape) sh;
XmlObject xml = line.getXmlObject();
```

After creating an Element object with the saxBuilder, XML can be traversed.

```
Namespace ns_a = lineXML.getNamespace("a");
Namespace ns_p = lineXML.getNamespace("p");
Element connectors = lineXML.getChild("nvCxnSpPr", ns_p).
getChild("cNvCxnSpPr", ns_p);
String id =
connectors.getChild("stCxn", ns_a).getAttribute("id").getValue();
```

The node nvCxnSpPr/cNvCxnSpPr contains stCxn and endCxn for the start and end ID of the shapes. As this value is already stored in the internal data representation, the corresponding relationship can be set up.

```
public void addRelation (int idStart, int idEnd) {
    this.relations.add(new Relation(getShapeById(idStart),
    getShapeById(idEnd)));  }
```

The example above shows the creation of a new relation. Giving the individual IDs for the start and end shape, a function crawls all existing shapes and returns the Object "Shape" (getShapeById(id) with the right ID.

If all line shapes are converted to object relations, the line shapes can be deleted:

```
for (XSLFShape sh : slide) {
    if (sh instanceof XSLFConnectorShape)
        diagram.deleteShape(sh.getShapeId());  }
```

If the examined item is a group itself, the algorithm assumes an enclosed meaning within the group and extracts the information by retrieving all shapes and running the algorithm recursive:

```
            "diagrams.addAll(handleDiagrams(diagrams,shape.getShapes(),
"Group-Shape"));"
```

The effect is an own diagram object for the group.

3.2   Using ADOxx Libraries as Meta Models

ADOxx is a meta-modeling tool provided by BOC. ADOxx is not specialized for one modelling language, it just provides the underlying construct for developing any modelling language by creating a meta model. This meta model contains all elements like concepts and the corresponding relations that can be included later in the diagrams. It is also possible to add additional model functionality or validation by programming routines in ADOscript, the proprietary internal script language. With this tool set, it is possible to accurately describe every kind of models like UML, Entity Relationship, BPMN etc. The library containing the meta model is used in this work for diagram analysis. This section shows how ADOxx Libraries can be crawled to retrieve the formal description of the contained Meta Models for further use.

The purpose of the developed software is to be as general as possible. Part of this concept is the idea that every kind of model can be used for analyzing and mapping PowerPoint slides. It is represented in an extensive XML-File, containing all objects with the associated attributes. In the very beginning, the views are identified and internally created. A view is a set of objects that can be put on one diagram type. According to the created view identified by a unique name, the objects are stored internally together with necessary attributes like name and graphical representation. In this state, relations are not yet distinct from objects but a specialized relation object. To separate them, relations within the objects are identified, deleted and the corresponding relation will be stored as a linkage between diagram objects. With this, all necessary information of the meta model is stored and ready for a further analysis.

Technical Implementation: As mentioned above, the meta-model-XML is very detailed and long. While the used example library – a simple Entity Relationship representation – contains already 11555 lines of code, more detailed libraries get even longer: The 4EM-library is stored in 18896 lines of code. The official ADOxx UML library, available in the ADOxx application library[1] is powerful and detailed and has 63854 lines of code in its XML data representation. Even though the size differs strongly, the overall structure of the file does not change. This allows to crawl the documents in a uniformed way. To ensure a convenient and fast document handling, XPATH is used for all queries on the XML-document. First of all, all contained views are identified. In the example case of the ER-diagram, the result is just one item, the "ER diagram". After all views are identified and the internal "view" objects are created, all concepts that belong to a view are crawled. The following exemplary XPATH-Query shows how this is carried out, Fig. 1 illustrates the result:

---

[1] https://www.adoxx.org/live/adoxx-application-library-code-repository.

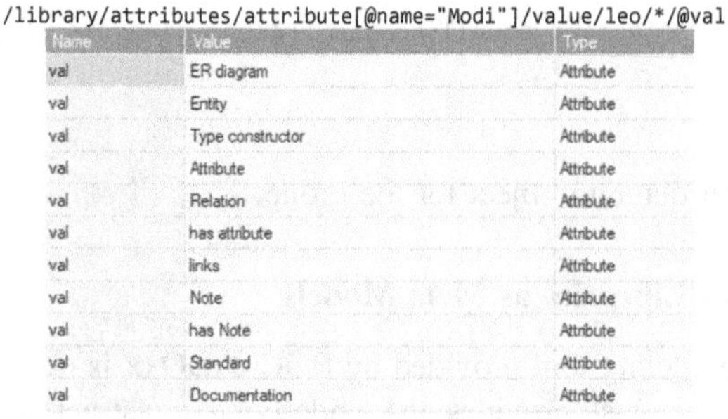

`/library/attributes/attribute[@name="Modi"]/value/leo/*/@val`

Name	Value	Type
val	ER diagram	Attribute
val	Entity	Attribute
val	Type constructor	Attribute
val	Attribute	Attribute
val	Relation	Attribute
val	has attribute	Attribute
val	links	Attribute
val	Note	Attribute
val	has Note	Attribute
val	Standard	Attribute
val	Documentation	Attribute

Fig. 1. XPATH - views and concepts (Screenshot)

If it is known that "ER-Diagram" is a view, all items following this view object have to be the concepts in this view. In this stage, just the concept object with the attribute name is created. Further attributes are added in the next stage. Now that the names of the concepts are known, it is possible to query the XML-document for the specific data. A challenge is the accuracy of the form description. PowerPoint for example provides precise names for shapes – RECT (rectangle), ELLIPSE, ROUND_RECT (round rectangle)", TRAPEZOID, PARALLELOGRAMM, TRIANGLE and RHOMBUS – these are just a few examples. A shape type can be easily accessed. In ADOxx, the amount of shape types is much more limited – just rectangle, round rectangle, ellipse and pie do exist as simple, directly accessible types. Shapes that are not found within these categories have to be built by a "polygon" attribute, an attribute that can represent every different form by modelling lines and curves. Its graphical vocabulary is comparable to the one in the scalable vector graphics format (.svg). For further comparing towards a PowerPoint shape, the mathematical descriptions of the form have to be accessed and analyzed. The example below shows the examination for two graphical forms with 4 coordinates.

```
if (x.get(0) == -1 * x.get(2) && y.get(1) == -1 * y.get(3))
        cm.addUniqueGraphtype("RHOMBUS");
else if (x.get(0) == -1 * x.get(2) && x.get(1) == -1 * x.get(3)
                && y.get(0) == y.get(1) && y.get(2) == y.get(3))
    cm.addUniqueGraphtype("PARALLELOGRAM");
```

These checks – here are just 2 shown, the software itself provides more - assure that complex PowerPoint shapes can be matched to a class stored in the Meta Model. Very complex forms though or those who are not integrated in the checking algorithm trigger a fallback towards a generic "polygon" representation. Every PowerPoint slide has a representational counterpart in the Meta Model analysis. If not and the PowerPoint shape is very complex, the PowerPoint will also be stored as "polygon" within the internal representation. Within a considerable amount of these kind of invalid shapes, the document can still be analyzed and matched.

3.3   Comparing Diagrams and Models

To measure PowerPoint diagrams against a meta models, the diagrams will be checked in two different ways – structural and semantical. While the structural analysis is limited to the form of the shapes, the semantical is more complex and also considers possible interconnections between them. The following Proof of Concept is carried out at the example of an entity relationship diagram. The result will be written to a.csv file for further analysis and testing of the algorithm.

Structural Analysis. Even though the concepts between shapes in PowerPoint and ADOxx are completely different, the similarities regarding to the look of different shapes can be assessed. Figure 2 shows the different representations of shapes. Even though almost all parameters can be altered within a shape, it is normally possible to identify one top level category of a form. In the structural analysis, the software takes these top-level categories and compares if the shape types in the PowerPoint slide are also found within the objects in a view of an meta model.

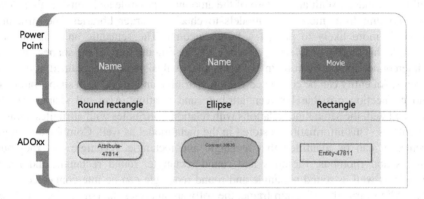

Fig. 2. Shapes in PowerPoint and ADOxx

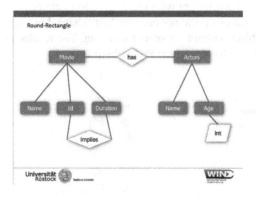

Fig. 3. Slide loaded into structural analysis

In the example of an Entity Relationship diagram, there are 3 important types of forms: An entity (rectangle), a relation (rhombus) and an attribute (round rectangle). The structural analysis now crawls through every diagram and compares if the item contains any form that is not included within the meta model. The output consists of a. csv file that prints out the shapes that do not fit. In Fig. 3, the example slide loaded into the structural analysis is shown. The Entities "Movie" and "Actor" are connected with a relation. Age is wrongfully connected with a parallelogram to outline the data type, but there is a connection between "Id" and "Duration" with a relation as well. This is also not possible in an Entity Relationship diagram.

The algorithm detected that the parallelogram is not a valid content for an ER-diagram. Compared to the goal of an accurate analysis of a diagram fit, it is more and more clear that the focus just on the occurrence of shape forms is not enough. Even though the distinction for forms works properly, the structural analysis does not detect incorrect relationships like the relation between the attributes "ID" and "Duration". The check for relations between shapes is carried out in the semantical analysis.

Semantical Analysis. The structural analysis works especially for a check towards small meta models. With an increase of the amount of possible and considerable shape forms, coming from more meta models to check or larger libraries, the structural analysis is more likely to predict a false outcome. The semantic analysis offers a solution to this kind of problem by not only considering the form of the shapes, but also the interconnection between them. The semantic analysis will be explained at the ER-Example. An entity can be connected with the attribute and the relation shape, but there is no connection possible between attribute and relation. Also, all shapes can be connected with the same kind, relations with relations, attributes with attributes, entities with entities. This information is stored in the meta model as well. Combined with the structure, it can be identified that rectangle and rectangle, rectangle and rhombus, rhombus and rhombus, rhombus and round rectangle, round rectangle and round rectangle as well as round rectangle and round rectangle can be interconnected.

Crawling through a diagram frame, the software analyses the connections between the different forms and counts those, who have a valid connection. While the structural analysis could not find a problem with the connection between the attribute and relation, the semantic analysis does: not only the "int" shape, but also the "implies" shape is identified as an object without the proper meaning. The results are now accurate and provide the right results for the given PowerPoint (Fig. 4).

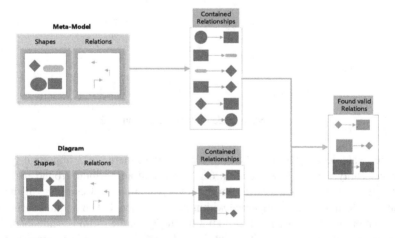

Fig. 4. Structural analysis - comparison between diagram and meta-model relations

4   Experimental Evaluation

We evaluated the software by testing various scenarios containing ambiguities and heterogeneities. This sharpens the understanding of what the algorithm is capable of and where the limitations are. Exemplary, the processing of groupings is included in this section to give an understanding how a minor change for modelling purpose can create major changes in the data structure.

As the grouping implies structure and meaning and also alters the data structure, the processing currently comes with the cost of the loss of information. Figure 5 contains an example for a grouping of shapes. The background shape "Grouped" is just for a better visualization in the example and neither connected nor grouped with the shapes representing the model and gets therefore not analyzed.

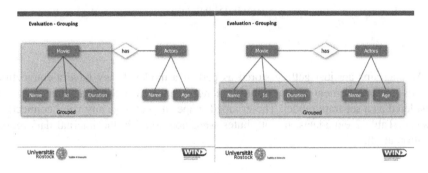

Fig. 5. Grouped shapes – Example 1 (left) and Example 2 (right)

As described in Sect. 3, the retrieving algorithm stores the grouped shapes in a separate data object. As a result, the single slide is represented by two independent data fragments: "Group-Shape" as a representation of the grouped items and "Evaluation-Grouping" containing the rest of the items that are placed directly onto the shape. This example shows the actual problem of grouping: Beside the fact that one relational information is lost (the connection between "Movie" and "has"), the storing of the group is semantically not correct. Even though the group does not contain any semantical information on the visualization perspective, the handling of these kind of shapes is not trivial and can lead to major problems regarding the understanding of diagrams. Figure 5 shows the two examples used in the following.

While in the first example the loss of relational information is still minor, with certain grouping scenarios they can result in a major inability for understanding the diagram. In Table 1, all attributes are grouped. While a semantical meaning could be interpreted, the fact that the grouped shapes are examined separately leads to a misfunction of the algorithm.

Table 1. Grouped shapes – internal data representation – first example

Diagram Name	ShapeType	ShapeText
Group-Shape	RECT	Movie
Group-Shape	ROUND_RECT	Name
Group-Shape	ROUND_RECT	Id
Group-Shape	ROUND_RECT	Duration
Evaluation – Grouping	RECT	Grouped
Evaluation – Grouping	FLOW_CHART_DECISION	has
Evaluation – Grouping	RECT	Actors
Evaluation – Grouping	ROUND_RECT	Name
Evaluation – Grouping	ROUND_RECT	Age

As diagrams are just getting stored as part of a model if they have a connection towards another element and attributes are not connected with each other, they are considered as a separate model. The grouped shapes do not have any valid connection now. As Table 2 elucidates, the attributes were not stored in the internal data representation at all.

Table 2. Grouped shapes – internal data representation – second example

Evaluation – Grouping	RECT	Grouped
Evaluation – Grouping	FLOW_CHART_DECISION	has
Evaluation – Grouping	RECT	Actors
Evaluation – Grouping	RECT	Movie

5   Ambiguities and Heterogeneities in Office Documents

Mukherjee et al. [23] described in their work 6 types of different ambiguities in Office Documents. They can be mapped into two categories: Structural and semantic. Structural ambiguities are the result of an unclear representation, semantic ambiguities origin in a designing process with no formal description language.

All heterogeneities described above in Fig. 6 were discovered and considered in this research project. Furthermore, additional "heterogeneities" were discovered:

Grouping: A normal shape has a connector to a different shape. If a representational object is built out of different shapes and grouped, these connectors often relate to the group, not the individual shape. While it is possible to unbox a group and get all different shapes to store them separately (an approach also used in this application), it is

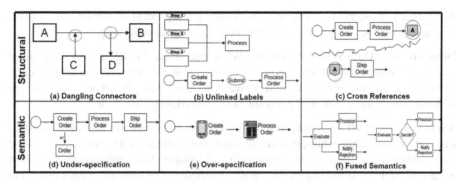

Fig. 6. Semantic and structural ambiguities (adopted from [23])

unclear how the shapes are connected with the rest of the diagram. Storing a whole group just shifts the problem: The group item is not yet unpacked and the contained information not yet ready for further analysis. Groups might contain important explicit information, but it is also realistic that they just contain implicit information, not related to the formal notation. As PowerPoint is primary a design tool, the groups may not contain any knowledge at all and are just used for shifting sizes and positions of a larger amount of shapes. Also, it is possible to create a complex representation out of a group of simple shapes. In that case, just the whole group can be seen as one shape.

Multiple Diagrams in one Slide: The retrieval algorithm searches slide by slide and stores them into the diagram data representation. In the case that two different diagrams are drawn in one slide, they both are stored in one diagram data frame. From a programming perspective, the distinction between diagram parts that belong to each other but have no connection and two different diagrams with different meanings is not possible. Even though no shape or relational information would be lost, the storage of these two diagrams in one data frame is semantically not correct.

One Diagram in Multiple Slides: Opposite to the ambiguity named above, one diagram stored in more than one slide cannot be retrieved properly as well. As the crawler searches slide by slide, this diagram will be stored in multiple diagram data frames, important semantical information will be lost.

Diagram Stored as a Picture: As PowerPoint is just a presentation tool, the diagrams stored in it often come from visualization tools outside of PowerPoint like Microsoft Visio. While a few might be linked to the origin file and stored as an Object, most of the external visualizations are stored as an image. In the first case, it would be possible to analyze the origin language to retrieve the information. But if the diagram is a picture, it is necessary to use advanced image recognition for retrieving the data out of the picture. The methods proposed in this paper cannot applied.

Nested Shapes: Relations between shapes are not necessarily stored via groups or connector shapes. It is possible that shapes are nested in each other to represent e.g. "has" or "is a" relations. While the order and overlap of shape could contain important information, the shape could also be a simple background with no further meaning.

Additionally, these kinds of overlays are mostly not supported by formal visualization languages. For the analysis, it is unclear how to interpret these shapes.

Directed and Undirected Relations: While the Meta Model always contains a direction, the drawing nature of PowerPoint also allows undirected visual representations. On a data perspective though, PowerPoint does store directions – even a line without arrows has a start and endpoint in the underlaying data base.

Microsoft SmartArt: SmartArt and allows the user to build easily complex diagrams like hierarchies, relationships, matrix, pyramids out of predefined visualizations. While the meaning is clear from a visual perspective, the shapes do not use a connector which is easy to analyze. If the shapes are clearly directed and in relation to each other, but apart of the special form used, there is no indication for the relations inside the diagram. Another challenge is the internal data representation of SmartArt. SmartArt is normally not stored like a normal diagram in shapes but uses a special SmartArt-Data representation.

Reading Relation Types: In structured visualization languages, the relation type is stored within a relation object. Yet, Powerpoint does not allow to add text to a connector shape. To describe a relation, a textbox has to be added and placed nearby the connector shape. While it is easily readable for a human interpreter, on a data structure perspective, the textbox and the connector shape are not connected with each other. To bind these two elements, the position of the elements has to be compared to identify if an unconnected textbox is placed near the connector shape.

6 Summary and Conclusions

In this paper, a concept for retrieving models from Powerpoint to the modelling tool ADO.XX was presented. The objective was to investigate possibilities and limits of using office tools, such as Powerpoint, for grass-root EM. We showed how the software prototype retrieves data from slideshows and meta-models from XML representations into an internal data representation. For retrieving PowerPoint data, "Apache POI" was used with additional effort to access information that is not provided by POI. The Meta Model originated of an XML-ADOxx export read by extensive XPATH queries to fetch the overall structure and behavior of the concepts. Two phases of matching were considered, showing an analysis on the level of occurrence of shapes (structural analysis) and with consideration of the relations (semantical analysis). The developed algorithms reach their limits for large meta models. If the notation describes a similar representation for more than one concept, the distinction just on the basis of the appearance is not enough to explicitly identify a model type with the corresponding concepts. Also, the focus of Powerpoint as a drawing tool sets challenges in the occurrence of heterogeneities.

Further research ought to make the software more practically applicable with enabling it to read even inconsistent modelled shapes by solving these heterogeneities. While for the most inconsistencies a way to resolve them is already proposed and requires mainly programming effort, especially the detection of implicit semantic needs more attention in the future and also conceptual research. For further validation of the retrieving algorithm towards different approaches, a comparison between the shown document retrieval methods and the practice of image recognition is recommendable. After the comparison, the possibility of the integration of both methodologies can be assessed. To enable the analysis towards larger Meta Models, further research has to address the limitations of the limited amount of possible optical variables with the identification of further matching criteria. Especially the usage of the (textual) content of a shape could be an additional considerable input.

The possible technical integrations of this kind of algorithms are broad and diverse. On a strategic perspective, the finalized algorithm can not only contribute to a more efficient knowledge management but also help to spread the usage of Enterprise Modelling through the organization without the need for a dedicated training for every modeler. It therefore can be part of a foundation that enables a bottom up grass root modelling.

Acknowledgements. The research was supported partly by projects funded by grants # 18-07-01201 and 18-07-01272 of the Russian Foundation for Basic Research, and by Government of Russian Federation, Grant 08-08.

References

1. Wortmann, J., Hegge, H., Goossenaerts, J.: Understanding enterprise modelling from product modelling. Product. Plann. Control **12**(3) (2001)
2. Lillehagen, F., Krogstie, J.: Active Knowledge Modelling. Springer, Heidelberg (2008)
3. Wesenberg, H.: Enterprise modeling in an agile world. In: Johannesson, P., Krogstie, J., Opdahl, A.L. (eds.) PoEM 2011. LNBIP, vol. 92, pp. 126–130. Springer, Heidelberg (2011). https://doi.org/10.1007/978-3-642-24849-8_10
4. Stirna, J., Persson, A., Sandkuhl, K.: Participative enterprise modeling: experiences and recommendations. In: Krogstie, J., Opdahl, A., Sindre, G. (eds.) International Conference on Advanced Information Systems Engineering. CAiSE 2007. Lecture Notes in Computer Science, vol. 4495, pp. 546–560. Springer, Berlin, Heidelberg (2007)
5. Sandkuhl, K., et al.: Enterprise modelling for the masses – from elitist discipline to common practice. In: Horkoff, J., Jeusfeld, M.A., Persson, A. (eds.) PoEM 2016. LNBIP, vol. 267, pp. 225–240. Springer, Cham (2016). https://doi.org/10.1007/978-3-319-48393-1_16
6. Sandkuhl, K. et al.: From expert discipline to common practice: a vision and research agenda for extending the reach of enterprise modeling. BISE **60**(1), 69–80 (2018)
7. Sandkuhl, K., Stirna, J., Persson, A., Wißotzki, M.: Enterprise modeling – tackling business challenges with the 4EM method. Springer, Heidelberg (2014). ISBN 978-3-662-43724-7S
8. Larkin, J., Simon, H.: Why a diagram is (sometimes) worth ten thousand words. Cognit. Sci. **11**(1), 65–100 (1987)
9. Petre, M.: Why looking isn't always seeing: Readership skills and graphical programming. Commun. ACM **38**(6), 33–44 (1995)
10. Mayer, R.E., Moreno, R.: Nine Ways to reduce cognitive load in mul-timedia learning. Educ. Psychol. **38**(1), 43–52 (2003)
11. Moody, D.: The Physics of Notations. IIEEE Trans. Softw. Eng. **35**(6), 756–779 (2009)
12. Harel, D., Rumpe, B.: Meaningful modeling: what's the semantics of "semantics"? Computer **37**(10), 64–72 (2004)

13. Datta, R., Joshi, D., Li, J., Wang, J.Z.: Image retrieval. ACM Comput. Surv. **40**(2), 1–60 (2008)
14. Yu, Y., Samal, A., Seth, S.: A system for recognizing a large class of engineering drawings - document analysis and recognition. In: Proceedings of the Third International Conference on. IEEE (1995)
15. Lladós, J., Kwon, Y.-B.: LNCS 3088 - Graphics recognition. Recent advances and perspectives
16. Li, S.Z., Jain, A.K.: Encyclopedia of Biometrics. Springer, New York (2009)
17. Ojha, U., Adhikari, U., Singh, D.K.: Image Annotation using Deep Learning: A Review, pp. 1–5
18. Kozielski, M., Doetsch, P., Hamdani, M., Ney, H.: Multilingual off-line handwriting recognition in real-world images. In: 2014 11th IAPR International Workshop on Document Analysis Systems, Tours, France, pp. 121–125 (2014)
19. Blostein, D.: General diagram-recognition methodologies: methods and applications. In: Kasturi, R., Tombre, K. (eds.) Graphics Recognition Methods and Applications. GREC 1995. Lecture Notes in Computer Science. University Park, PA, USA, 1995 Selected Papers, vol. 1072, pp. 106–122 (1996)
20. Sas, J., Markowska-Kaczmar, U.: Logical Structure Recognition of Diagram Images, pp. 215–224 (2015)
21. Lemaitre, A., Mouchère, H., Camillerapp, J., Coüasnon, B.: Interest of syntactic knowledge for on-line flowchart recognition
22. He, K., Zhang, X., Ren, S., Sun, J.: Deep Residual Learning for Image Recognition, pp. 770–778 (2016)
23. Mukherjee, D., Dhoolia, P., Sinha, S., Rembert, A.J., Gowri Nanda, M.: From informal process diagrams to formal process models. In: Hull, R., Mendling, J., Tai, S. (eds.) BPM 2010. LNCS, vol. 6336, pp. 145–161. Springer, Heidelberg (2010). https://doi.org/10.1007/978-3-642-15618-2_12
24. Fill, H.-G.: Bridging pictorial and model-based creation of legal visualizations: the PICTMOD method. IRIS 2015, Jusletter IT, 26 February 2015. ISSN 1664-848X
25. Ciriello, R., Richter, A., Schwabe, G.: PowerPoint use and misuse in digital innovation. In: AIS Electronic Library (2015). http://aisel.aisnet.org/ecis2015_cr/
26. Bjekovic, M., Sottet, J., Favre, J., Proper, H.A.: A framework for natural enterprise modelling. In: 2013 IEEE 15th Conference on Business Informatics, pp. 79–84

A Machine Learning Based Approach
to Application Landscape Documentation

Jörg Landthaler, Ömer Uludağ, Gloria Bondel, Ahmed Elnaggar,
Saasha Nair, and Florian Matthes[✉]

Software Engineering for Business Information Systems, Department of Informatics,
Technical University of Munich, Boltzmannstr. 3,
85748 Garching Bei München, Germany
{joerg.landthaler,oemer.uludag,gloria.bondel,ahmed.elnaggar,
saasha.nair,matthes}@tum.de

Abstract. In the era of digitalization, IT landscapes keep growing along with complexity and dependencies. This amplifies the need to determine the current elements of an IT landscape for the management and planning of IT landscapes as well as for failure analysis. The field of enterprise architecture documentation sought for more than a decade for solutions to minimize the manual effort to build enterprise architecture models or automation. We summarize the approaches presented in the last decade in a literature survey. Moreover, we present a novel, machine-learning based approach to detect and to identify applications in an IT landscape.

Keywords: Software asset management · EAM · Machine learning

1 Introduction

Traditional enterprise architecture management (EAM) uses enterprise architecture (EA) models to support enterprise analysis and planning, in particular in IT-intensive organizations. A standard EA model, e.g. based on the ArchiMate meta-model, comprehensively models many different aspects of an organization from roles via processes through to applications, software components, and IT infrastructure components. The creation of EA models is an error-prone, difficult and labor-intensive manual task [2,10,12]. The field of EA documentation (EAD) seeks to automate the creation of EA models [6]. However, the automated creation of EA models is a challenging task, because not all information is easily available such as the relationship between business processes and software components or due to required high-level semantic information [6].

With the advent of digitalization, IT-landscapes grow in size and complexity [13]. Moreover, elements in the EA become more and more interwoven even across organizational boundaries. As a consequence, another increasingly pressuring challenge is to manage organizational IT-landscapes at runtime, which

R. A. Buchmann et al. (Eds.): PoEM 2018, LNBIP 335, pp. 71–85, 2018.
https://doi.org/10.1007/978-3-030-02302-7_5

requires to capture dynamic aspects such as failures of servers and errors in applications [1]. The question arises whether (automatically generated) EA models can be used to support the operation of large IT-landscapes, for example, to support root cause analysis or business impact analysis. This requires a high-quality of the automatically generated EA models. Fast and automatically generated high-quality EA models could support the initial creation of (as-is) EA models. It could foster the comparison of manually created EA models with the actual EA. Moreover, the progression of the implementation of a target (to-be) EA state could be measured. In the last decade, different approaches to automate EAD have been proposed that vary in their degree of automation and coverage of EA meta-models like ArchiMate. Buschle et al. [2] proposed to use the manually collected information stored in an enterprise service bus and Holm et. al. [10] presented an EAD tool that uses information acquired by network sniffers.

The automated creation of full EA models is a major endeavor that incorporates the detection and identification of many elements of different types and their relationships. In this paper, we focus on the application component elements as defined in the ArchiMate meta-model (application components include applications). In particular, we propose an envisioned approach to automatically document the application landscape of standard software in an organization that is supported by machine learning techniques. Our approach is based on the classification of binary strings of the application executables that are present on a target machine.

Machine learning on application binary strings is used for example in anti-virus software. Our goal is to identify applications, which results in challenges that are very interesting from a machine learning point of view. The machine learning problem has many classes and eventually only few examples. To our surprise, the binary strings of executables vary even for the same application on different devices (with same application version, device type and OS versions). While the problems for the machine learning approach are challenging, we expect the effort to manually create a similar knowledge base solely based on rules to achieve the same goal to be even larger.

Our key contributions for this exploratory paper encompass the presentation of an envisioned approach to EAD based on machine learning, a small literature survey of approaches to EAD proposed so far and the evaluation of the basic technical feasibility of our approach regarding the machine learning aspect using a dataset of applications collected from devices at our research group.

The remainder of this work is organized as follows: In Sect. 2 we present our envisioned approach. We present a literature review of published approaches to automated EAD in Sect. 3. The technical feasibility of our approach is evaluated in Sect. 4, followed by a critical reflection and limitations in Sect. 5. Section 6 concludes the paper with a summary and presents future work.

2   Approach

In this Section, we motivate and describe a machine learning based approach to identify standard software in (possibly large) IT-landscapes and integrate it into a larger picture. The identification of installed or running applications in large IT-landscapes is a major challenge, because many equal, similar and different types of applications are spread over several hardware devices. It is not uncommon that an IT-landscape in a larger company contains several thousand applications. It is desirable to get an overview of all applications present in an IT-landscape to create an inventory (Software Asset Management [5] and License Management), to manage the operations of applications or as part of dynamically or continuously built EA models.

Machine learning, in general, helps to solve repetitive problems. It is applicable if inputs vary in the nature of their contents [4]. Particularly for supervised learning (i.e. classification), a sufficient amount of labeled training data is required. The problem of identifying applications in an IT-landscape is challenging, because of the sheer amount of applications and because of the many possible smaller differences among individual installations such as installation directories and configurations. Supervised machine learning is a promising approach because of the repetitive characteristics, the large manual effort of the problem at hand and the varying nature of features. However, in contrast to typical problems solved by supervised machine learning, the problem at hand is a very challenging task for classifiers, because of the large number of different applications, resulting in a classification problem with many classes. However, parts of our experiments in Sect. 4 are sufficiently promising to merit investigating this approach more deeply.

Existing approaches detect running applications in an indirect way from the outside (i.e. without placing an agent on the server) for example with port scanners or by investigating traces that applications leave behind, for example network communication. Another, conventional approach to detect applications that are not executed is to create a knowledge base of rules that enables an agent installed on a server to find all (relevant) installed applications. The knowledge base can be either shipped with the agent or stored centrally and queried by agents. There are two challenges to this approach: one is the diversity of application characteristics and the other is the large manual effort to create and maintain rules for hundreds of different applications, even if central registries are available. However, there are commercial providers that maintain such knowledge-bases, for example Flexera[1].

The major difference between our approach and a conventional, strictly rule-based approach is to place an agent on a server that identifies all executables (which can be done efficiently and effectively) and classifies the executables as different applications. In our envisioned approach the result of the classification of executable binaries helps to identify applications present on a device or server. We believe that a rule-based refinement of the results will still be necessary. To our surprise, we observed that sometimes applications differ greatly in their binary strings even for equal versions across different devices, which imposes an additional challenge to our approach that we explore in Sect. 4. The benefit of our approach over the rule-based approach is that we identify all applications, even

---

[1] Flexera FlexNet, https://www.flexera.com, last accessed in November 2017.

when they are renamed or installed in non-standard directories, which is often the case on servers. Our evaluation dataset does not incorporate renamed files but the evaluation is still valid because the machine learning based approaches input are merely the binary strings of the applications executable files.

There are several design decisions that one has to make for a real-world application. For example, if the agent consumes a service that provides the classification functionality or if the agent ships with the trained model (and eventually needs to be updated often). A service-based solution might interfere with data protection requirements, but application binaries usually do not hold information worth high protection.

3   Literature Study and Related Work

In this Section publications related to the research are reviewed and summarized. The commonalities and differences to our approach are summarized in Table 1. Farwick et al. [7] automatically integrate various runtime information of the cloud infrastructure into the open-source EAM tool Iteraplan. The automatically integrated information is synchronized with a project management tool to distinguish between planned and unplanned changes of the cloud infrastructure.

Holm et al. [10] aims to map automatically collected information with the network scanner NeXpose to ArchiMate models. The approach collects IT infrastructure and application data. Buschle et al. [2] have the goal to evaluate the degree of coverage to which data of a productive system can be used for EA documentation. In order to do so, the database schema of SAP PI is reverse engineered based on its data model and conceptually mapped to the ArchiMate model and the CySeMol and planningIT tools.

Hauder et al. [9] aim to identify challenges for automated enterprise architecture documentation. They map the data model of SAP PI and Nagios to Iteraplan in order to extend Iteraplan models for identifying transformation challenges [9].

The goal of Välja et al. [15] is to automatically create enterprise IT architecture models by collecting, processing and combining data from more than one information sources, in particular from the NeXpose and Wireshark network scanners and by enriching the P^{2}CySeMoL security meta-model with the collected data. Farwick et al. [8] provide a context-specific approach for semi-automated enterprise architecture documentation. Farwick et al.'s approach consists of several configurable documentation techniques, a method assembly process, as well as an accompanying meta-model to store necessary meta-data for the process execution.

Johnson et al. [12] automatically create dynamic enterprise architecture models. The models leverage Dynamic Bayesian Networks to predict the presence of particular entities of an enterprise IT architecture over time.

Next, we investigate approaches for the automated population of EA models that have actually been implemented and evaluated. Using this inclusion

Table 1. Comparison of published approaches of automated EAD to our approach.

	Commonalities	Differences
Farwick (2010)	- Both approaches use agents in order to collect relevant data.	- The focus of Farwick (2010) lies on IT-infrastructure data, whereas we focus on standard software data from servers or clients. - Farwick (2010) focuses on collecting data from cloud specific information sources.
Holm (2014)	- Both approaches are using primary information sources for the automated collection of data. - Both approaches require access on the investigated devices to identify application components. - Both approaches can only identify a subset of application components.	- Holm (2014) can only collect data of applications that have an open interface to the outside of the server. - Holm (2014) supports multiple entities of all EA layers, whereas our approach supports only the collection of application component data. - Holm (2014) also uses an indirect way to collect data by using unauthenticated network scans (from the outside), but is not able to collect information about application components.
Buschle (2012)	- Both approaches collect data on application components (ArchiMate application layer)	- The proposed approach needs to formulate transformation rules in order to propagate data from SAP PI to other modelling tools. - The proposed approach needs a manual effort for creating data in SAP PI wheras our approach automatically collects installed software information from the running devices. - The proposed approach aims to maximize the model coverage of all ArchiMate layers. - The primary information source of our approach are is the automatically collected data from running devices, whereas the primary information source of Buschle (2012) is the ESB (SAP PI).
Hauder (2012)	- Both approaches collect data on application components (ArchiMate application layer).	- Hauder (2012) extends existing manually created EA models automatically with data from SAP PI and Nagios, whereas our approach uses a single source, namely the running devices themselves, to collect data. - Hauder (2012) classifies data with the help of transformation rules (manual task), whereas we use machine learning in order to automate the classification. - Hauder (2012) supports multiple EA layers, namely business, application and infrastructure layers, in contrast to our approach application components are collected manually or need to be configured in Nagios.
Välja (2015)	- Both approaches use automatically collected data. - Both approaches identify application components.	- Välja (2015) uses an indirect way to collect data by the use of NeXpose (network scanner) and Wireshark (network traffic analyzer), our approach places agents on devices in order to collect data. - Välja (2015) focuses on the infrastructure layer, whereas we focus on the application layer. - Välja (2015) also focuses on identifying relationships between entities of the infrastructure and application layers. - The main goal of Välja (2015) is to define a process for integrating data from different sources.
Farwick (2016)	-	- The approach by Farwick (2016) supports various types of information sources, e.g., CMDB, ESB, and Server Configurations, whereas our approach's primary information source is the running device itself. - Farwick (2016) manually maps the data import to the organization-specific information model. - The approach by Farwick (2016) supports the whole EA documentation, whereas our approach focuses only on the application components. - Farwick (2016) defines a process to adapt automated collection of data to specific organizational contexts.
Johnson (2016)	- Both approaches make the use of machine learning, however Johnson (2016) investigates the state estimation problem, in contrast our approach tackles a categorization problem.	- The focus of Johnson (2016) lies on the infrastructure layer, whereas we focus on the application components. - Johnson (2016) does not provide an implementation of the proposed approach, wheareas we evaluate the basic technical feasability. - Johnson (2016) uses a Dynamic Bayesian Network to account for insecurities in data collection.

criterion, we identified five[2] approaches [2,3,9,10,15]. Subsequently, we compared these approaches by contrasting which EA entities can be automatically retrieved from the different respective information sources.

Table 2. Comparison of approaches and respectively used information sources for automatically generating and populating EA models.

	Information Source	Buschle (2012)	Hauder (2012)	Buschle (2011) and Holm (2014)	Välja (2015)
		Excerpt of ArchiMate 3.0.1 entities, automatically extracted from information sources			
Business Layer	Business actor			NeXpose network scanner	
	Business interface	SAP PI (possibly)			
	Business process	SAP PI (possibly)			
	Business function		Iteraplan		
	Business service	SAP PI (possibly)			
	Business object	SAP PI (possibly)	SAP PI (depends on concrete instance)		
	Representation	SAP PI (possibly)			
	Product	SAP PI (possibly)			
Application Layer	Application component	SAP PI	Iteraplan, SAP PI	NeXpose network scanner	NeXpose and Wireshark network scanners
	Application collaboration	SAP PI	SAP PI		
	Application interface	SAP PI	Iteraplan, SAP PI	NeXpose network scanner	
	Application service	SAP PI (possibly)			
	Data object	SAP PI			
Infrastructure Layer	Node	SAP PI	Iteraplan, SAP PI, Nagios (possibly)		
	Device	SAP PI	Nagios (possibly)	NeXpose network scanner	
	System software	SAP PI		NeXpose network scanner	NeXpose and Wireshark network scanners
	Technology interface			NeXpose network scanner	NeXpose and Wireshark network scanners
	Path	SAP PI			
	Communication network			NeXpose network scanner	

To enable comparability between retrieved EA entities, we use the concepts defined in the ArchiMate 3.0.1[3] framework as a basis [14]. The ArchiMate framework defines a meta-model with generic EA entities and EA entity relationships across three different layers: the Business Layer, the Application Layer and the Technology Layer.

The detailed comparison of implemented approaches is depicted in Table 2. We excluded ArchiMate entities which could not be automatically populated in any of the identified approaches. On the Business Layer, the excluded entities are Business Role, Business Collaboration, Business Interaction, Business Event, and Contract. On the Application Layer, the Application Function, Application Interaction, Application Process and Application Event entities are excluded. Finally, on the Technology Layer the entities Technology Collaboration, Technology Function, Technology Process, Technology Interaction, Technology Event,

---

[2] Note that Holm et al. [10] is an extension of Buschle et al. [3].

[3] In most papers, the authors use an earlier version of the ArchiMate framework, e.g. ArchiMate 2.0. To allow comparability, the EA entities of earlier version versions have been carefully mapped to ArchiMate 3.0.

Technology Service, and Artifact could not be populated. This shows, that even though some approaches for automatic EA modeling have already been evaluated, they are far from capturing the whole EA model. One more approach that should be mentioned here is [12]. The authors provide a full list of all ArchiMate 2.0 entities and possible information sources for automated modeling. For example, to populate the entity Technology Service, information could be retrieved from network scanners, directory services, software asset inventory Tools and possibly network sniffers. Nevertheless, the use of these information sources for automatic modelling has not been implemented nor evaluated.

Summarizing, only a few approaches to automatic EA modelling have actually been evaluated and these approaches only cover limited parts of the EA model. This emphasizes the relevance of research in automated EAD.

4   Evaluation

We investigate the basic technical feasibility of our envisioned machine learning based approach to detect and identify applications in an IT landscape. Our approach identifies all binary executables on a device and then identifies the respective application through a machine learning classifier. We investigate the basic technical feasibility especially with respect to the major challenge of a many-label classification problem. To the best of our knowledge, there exists no (large-scale) dataset, yet. Therefore, we constructed a small dataset to conduct initial experiments.

Fig. 1. Leave-one-out training- and test-set splitting: inspired by k-fold cross-validation, we leave the binary executables for applications from one device as test-set out, while applications from all other devices constitute the training set. The test-set contains only applications where a record is present in the training set (shared applications), while the training set contains all records irrespective of the application's presence in the test-set.

A machine learning approach based on artificial neural networks requires a careful investigation of the neural network structure, the parameter selection, and regularization. In the following, we distinguish two viewpoints: from a machine learning point of view, we investigate the generalization capabilities of machine learning methods on such a dataset. Secondly, we also investigate the task from the perspective of practical applicability. In particular, we attempt to answer the following research questions regarding the technical feasibility of our approach by conducting experiments:

1. Do application binary executables hold discriminative information that allows to identify the applications? (RQ1)

2. Can machine learning algorithms tackle this multi-class problem? (RQ2)
3. Are machine learning algorithms capable of generalizing the classification task for different devices? (RQ3)

We created a dataset from seven different MacBook Pro devices from researchers of our research group. We used the python-magic library (a wrapper to libmagic) that allows us to identify executable binary files in the /app/ directory[4]. All experiments have been carried out on a MacBook Air (1.6 GHz Intel Core i5, 8GB RAM) with Keras[5] and Tensorflow[6]. The dataset consists of 3026 total records with the first 8096 bits of an executable binary as features (cf. Fig. 4) which is labeled with the application name (filename). The applications are, for example, labeled with *Dropbox* or *MS Word*, but also helper executables, for example, *CacheHelper* are contained. On the one hand, for an initial evaluation this leads to a high-quality, labeled dataset of standard software with low effort. On the other hand, the dataset is limited to applications from one operating system, few different versions of the same applications and predominantly non-server applications (Table 3).

Table 3. General dataset characteristics: the dataset consists of 3096 binary executables labeled with their filename collected from seven different Macbook Pro devices running Mac OS X from the applications folder. Note that the features differ for equal version applications on different devices. We use the Hamming distance as an indicator of the variation among the features for two applications and accumulate these for specific training- and test-set splittings with shared applications among training- and test-set, cf. Fig. 1.

#devices	7		Accum. Hamm. distance	# Shared appl.
OSX versions	10.12.5, 10.12.6	Max	1251.71	370
#total appl.	3026	Avg	1009.87	212.14
#unique appl.	1172	Min	923.13	370

In order to answer the research questions with experiments, we choose a train- and a test-set split of the dataset inspired by k-fold cross-validation. The records from all except one device serve as a training-set. The applications from the omitted device serve as test-set when there are corresponding records in the training set. I.e. the test set contains only applications that are present in the training set, while the training set contains applications that are not present in the test-set, cf. Fig. 1.

We use the Hamming distance (number of non-equal bits between a pair of binary executable strings) as a similarity measure between the features of two records. We use the Hamming distances as an indicator of how well a machine

---

[4] Executable binaries identified as *Mach-O 64-bit x86_64 executable* filetype.

[5] Keras, v. 2.0.4, https://keras.io/, last accessed in November 2017.

[6] Tensorflow v. 1.0.1, https://www.tensorflow.org/.

Table 4. Training- and test-set combinations and characteristics: For seven devices, seven different training- and test-set combinations can be formed using the leave-one-out approach. The total number of records in a leave-one-out dataset with shared applications in the test-set only is around 850 to 1550. The accumulated Hamming distance between all pairs of applications in the training- and test-set as well as the Hamming distance normalized using the number of pairs considered. Here, duplicates are included. Regarding these characteristics, the datasets appear very similar.

Test-set device	Total records	Accumulated Hamming distance	Normalized accumulated Hamming distance (including duplicates)	Normalized accumulated Hamming distance (duplicates removed
A	1100	1018971	926.3	1281.7
B	846	813668	961.7	1329.5
C	1055	1151599	1091.6	1258.5
D	1061	1021264	962.5	1289.4
E	1049	998913	952.2	1102.5
F	1569	1448398	923.1	1849.8
G	1155	1445735	1251.7	1897.2

learning algorithm could work to predict the application from its executable binaries, i.e. whether the binary strings contain discriminative information. From a machine learning point of view, the generalization capabilities can be only determined when exact duplicates of applications (Hamming distance equals zero) are removed, i.e. the test dataset does not contain exactly the same samples as in the training sets. We distinguish among training- and test-sets with and without duplicates. To create a dataset with no duplicates all instances of binary strings are removed from the training-set when they are equal to the test-set. Table 4 shows the Hamming distances for all dataset splittings. If no test-set instance remains, the test-set instance is removed. The datasets with duplicates contain all records. We assume that in a real-world setting duplicates occur often.

If not stated otherwise, all following experiments have been carried out with simple feed-forward neural networks (FFNN) with one dense hidden layer with 50 neurons, a batch size of 32, that are trained for 100 epochs. We choose the accuracy measure to evaluate classification performance. The precision/recall and derived F1 measure are not well suited for this evaluation, because we are interested solely if an application was classified correctly or not, i.e. there is no *relevance* criterion for this problem that is present, for example, in information retrieval tasks.

Experiment 1: Network Structure & Parameters for Classifier: In order to obtain credible results using a neural network classifier, one has to empirically determine a suitable network structure and reasonable values for hyperparameters. We ran experiments with more neurons in a hidden layer (25, 50, 100, 300,

Table 5. Prediction accuracy (train and test-set) for a FFNN (1 hidden layer with 50 neurons) after 100 epochs of training for all training-/test-set combinations where exact duplicates of binary executables have been included or removed. For the more real-world like case that exact duplicates of application binaries in the training-set also occur in the test-set, we achieve very good results with 98% accuracy. For the more scientifically interesting case that exact duplicates are removed we achieve reasonable results with up to 64 percent accuracy. However, two test-sets achieve very poor results of around eight percent accuracy and we investigate this in the remainder of the paper. The best results are indicated with *, the most relevant results are indicated in bold font.

Test set device	Normalized accumulated Hamming distance	With duplicates				Without duplicates			
		Train samples	Test samples	Train acc. (%)	Test acc. (%)	Train samples	Test samples	Train acc. (%)	Test acc. (%)
A	926.3	1081	159	99.07	94.34	795	159	99.12	**61.64***
B	961.7	846	100	98.83	**98.00***	612	100	99.02	58.00
C	1091.5	1035	159	94.30	55.97	915	159	94.10	44.65
D	962.5	1042	138	94.63	86.96	792	138	94.44	57.25
E	952.2	1033	162	98.84	81.48	906	162	99.23	59.26
F	923.1	1119	146	94.10	96.58	783	146	93.49	**8.22**
G	1251.7	930	146	94.19	97.26	762	146	93.70	**8.22**

500, 1000), but accuracy did not improve. We chose 50 neurons for one hidden layer. We experimented with two layers, but more layers did not improve the results significantly. We can conclude that there are no higher-order correlations among the positions of the bits. We also varied the batch size (25, 50, 64, 75) without a major difference in the results.

Experiment 2: Prediction Results with Neural Networks: The key result for a classification algorithm is the prediction performance on the task at hand. To answer the research questions (especially RQ1 and RQ2), we carried out experiments using the already identified network structure and parameters on all possible splittings of the dataset with duplicates and removed duplicates. The results after 100 epochs of training are displayed in Table 5. For five out of seven dataset splittings, we can report reasonably good performance on the test-set in the scientifically relevant case where exact duplicates have been removed and very good results for the more practically relevant case with duplicates included. However, two dataset splittings give very poor performance results (F and G). For the bad performing device test-set F, most applications are wrongly identified as the *autoupdate* application. Despite the fact, that this particular application occurs very often (but not most often) in the training set, we also investigated the Hamming distances for all applications in the test-set against this particular application. In contrast to the well-performing test device split A, the accumulated Hamming distance for *autoupdate* with the other applications in the test-set for test device split G was significantly lower (157249 versus 108933)

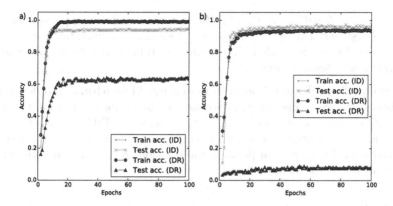

Fig. 2. Training- and test-set accuracy over 100 epochs for the best performing dataset A (a) and the worst performing dataset F (b) with a FFNN (1 hidden layer, 50 neurons). Despite around 3000 samples, our dataset is comparably small and the networks converge already after around 20 epochs which takes circa 1 min. (ID = Including duplictes, DR = Duplictes removed)

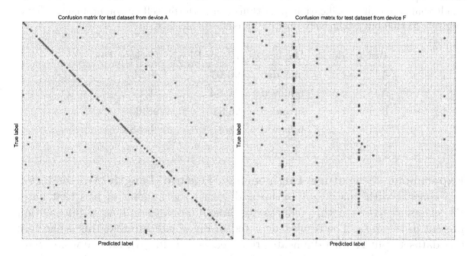

Fig. 3. The confusion matrices for datasets A and F (duplicates removed) reveal that in the well performing case (left), despite the challenge of a very large number of different classes, the majority of applications is classified correctly. On the other hand, for the bad performing dataset F, few applications are dominant and responsible for many wrongly classified records and we were able to identify a problem using Hamming distances, described in the remainder of this paper.

and also showed up in the top 10 in an ascending list of accumulated Hamming distances. We conclude that this very low accumulated Hamming distance can serve as an indicator for the poor prediction results. However, since five out of seven test device splittings perform well, we conclude that the many-label problem can be feasible for this classification task and our approach. For the best and worst performing dataset splittings we also examined the training over time, cf. Fig. 2 that shows that the training is stable and network convergence is reached after almost 20 epochs.

Experiment 3: Different Machine Learning Algorithms: In order to rule out a biased success using neural networks, we also trained a decision-tree classifier[7] with default parameters. The results displayed in Table 6 show that other machine learning algorithms can achieve similar results. As can be expected, our optimized neural networks outperform the decision-tree algorithm with default parameters in certain cases by 10%.

Table 6. Comparison of different machine learning algorithms: Tree-based classifier (with standard parameters) versus FFNN classifiers on the best-performing dataset splitting A as well as the worst-performing dataset split F (best-performing regarding the different dataset splittings with FFNN). On the best dataset-split the FFNN performs significantly better than the tree-based classifier. On the worst performing dataset-split the tree-based classifier performs slightly better than the FFNN. The result that different classification algorithms can perform well on the problem at hand helps us to rule out exclusively positive side-effects of FFNNs.

Test set device	Duplicates	1-layer FFNN	Decision tree
A	included	**99.07**	89.31
A	removed	**61.64**	53.45
F	included	96.58	**98.63**
F	removed	8.22	**9.58**

Experiment 4: Feature Engineering: Feature Length: We conducted experiments with our default setup and varied the number of bits that enter the classifier to see if this reduces the amount of discriminative information present in the data. The results, depicted in Fig. 4 indicate that this is the case (for dataset split A with duplicates removed and included), but we would have expected a much stronger drop in the classification performance for 100 bits. However, we assume for larger datasets an increasing number of features will help classifiers.

Experiment 5: Network Regularization: Over-fitting is a problem that occurs in any neural network application and is tied to RQ3. A standard way to tackle this problem is to use a regularization method, for example dropout, to prevent the networks during training from over-fitting. A randomly selected number of neurons is deactivated during training, e.g., 10% of the neurons corresponding to a dropout rate of *0.1*. However, several experiments with our standard network structure and also two layers with 50 neurons in each layer did

---

[7] Scikit-learn, v. 0.19.1, http://scikit-learn.org/stable/modules/tree.html, last accessed in November 2017.

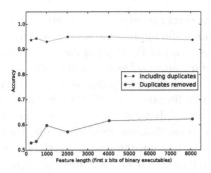

Fig. 4. The feature length, i.e. the amount of the first X bits of the binary executables, have a comparably small effect on the accuracy achieved on the test-set on the best performing dataset A for both cases: duplicates included or removed. However, a too small feature length performs poorly, because no discriminating information is left. We assume that for larger datasets also the number of features needs to be increased.

not significantly improve classification accuracy on the test-set for dataset split A. For the poor performing dataset split F, a low dropout rate (1.0 for the first layer, 0.08 for the second layer) can improve classification accuracy on the test set around one percent. For larger dropout rates, the classification performance gets, as expected, worse. We conclude that a carefully chosen small dropout rate is useful, but it does not significantly improve the classification results.

5   Limitations and Critical Reflection

We conducted a series of first experiments to evaluate the initial technical feasibility of our approach. Despite a dataset with roughly 3000 samples, the major drawbacks of our evaluation are the artificial setup and the small dataset. An evaluation of a much larger and real-world dataset is necessary. On the one hand, many-label classifications are technically difficult from a machine learning perspective and require a larger dataset, in general, but also specifically for the evaluation of this task. On the other hand, we neglected certain aspects of a real-world setup, for example the classification of applications installed on different operating systems, or the classification of different versions of the same application. Moreover, our dataset is restricted to desktop applications and does not fully reflect an IT-landscape with server applications. We also did not include custom-developed applications or applications within application servers. We identified the Hamming distance as a potential tool to identify and investigate poor classification performance results, however, so far we have not identified the reason why abnormal Hamming distances occur among applications.

6   Conclusion and Future Work

We envision a novel, machine learning based approach to discover and identify standard software in large IT-landscapes that can be used for software asset management or enterprise architecture documentation in an automated and continuous manner by framing the application detection and identification problem of applications as a classification problem of executable binaries. We identified related and complementary approaches in the domain of enterprise architecture documentation and evaluated the EA model coverage and the degree of automation in the form of a small literature study. We identified two major challenges for our approach: the many-label nature of the classification problem and the scarce occurrence of poor classification results. Despite the challenge of a many-label problem, we can report promising results for the technical feasibility of the approach evaluated with experiments on a dataset of applications collected from MacBooks from researchers at our research group. We can report that the hamming distance distributions among applications executable binaries are a good indicator to predict the quality of the results.

For the future, an evaluation on a larger, real-world dataset is necessary to examine the applicability of the approach under real-life conditions including applications from different operations systems and different versions of the same application. A deeper understanding of the causality between hamming distance distributions and classification results or other measures to predict the quality of classification results would be beneficial. An investigation of unsupervised methods to identify groups of related applications seems beneficial to us, e.g., to identify applications that have similar functionality, e.g., databases and application servers. Eventually, other machine learning approaches (e.g., Iyer et al. [11]) could be used to additionally identify and classify individually developed applications. We also see a strong benefit in combining entity detection and identification methods with dynamic models of an EA such as proposed by Johnson et al. ([12]).

Acknowledgment. This work is part of the TUM Living Lab Connected Mobility (TUM LLCM) project and has been funded by the Bavarian Ministry of Economic Affairs, Energy and Technology (StMWi) through the Center Digitisation.Bavaria, an initiative of the Bavarian State Government.

References

1. Brückmann, T., Gruhn, V., Pfeiffer, M.: Towards real-time monitoring and controlling of enterprise architectures using business software control centers. In: Crnkovic, I., Gruhn, V., Book, M. (eds.) ECSA 2011. LNCS, vol. 6903, pp. 287–294. Springer, Heidelberg (2011). https://doi.org/10.1007/978-3-642-23798-0_31
2. Buschle, M., Ekstedt, M., Grunow, S., Hauder, M., Matthes, F., Roth, S.: Automating enterprise architecture documentation using an enterprise service bus. In: AMCIS 2012 Proceedings. AIS Electronic Library (AISeL) (2012)
3. Buschle, M., Holm, H., Sommestad, T., Ekstedt, M., Shahzad, K.: A tool for automatic enterprise architecture modeling. In: Nurcan, S. (ed.) CAiSE Forum 2011. LNBIP, vol. 107, pp. 1–15. Springer, Heidelberg (2012). https://doi.org/10.1007/978-3-642-29749-6_1
4. Das, S., Dey, A., Pal, A., Roy, N.: Applications of artificial intelligence in machine learning: review and prospect. Int. J. Comput. Appl. **115**(9), 31–41 (2015). https://www.ijcaonline.org/archives/volume115/number9/20182-2402

5. Dijkman, R.M., Pires, L.F., Rinderle-Ma, S. (eds.): 20th IEEE International Enterprise Distributed Object Computing Workshop, EDOC Workshops 2016, Vienna, Austria, 5–9 September 2016. IEEE Computer Society (2016)
6. Farwick, M., Breu, R., Hauder, M., Roth, S., Matthes, F.: Enterprise architecture documentation: empirical analysis of information sources for automation. In: 2013 46th Hawaii International Conference on System Sciences, pp. 3868–3877 (2013)
7. Farwick, M., Agreiter, B., Breu, R., Häring, M., Voges, K., Hanschke, I.: Towards living landscape models: automated integration of infrastructure cloud in enterprise architecture management. In: 2010 IEEE 3rd International Conference on Cloud Computing (CLOUD), pp. 35–42. IEEE (2010)
8. Farwick, M., Schweda, C.M., Breu, R., Hanschke, I.: A situational method for semi-automated enterprise architecture documentation. Softw. Syst. Model. **15**(2), 397–426 (2016)
9. Hauder, M., Matthes, F., Roth, S.: Challenges for automated enterprise architecture documentation. In: Aier, S., Ekstedt, M., Matthes, F., Proper, E., Sanz, J.L. (eds.) PRET/TEAR -2012. LNBIP, vol. 131, pp. 21–39. Springer, Heidelberg (2012). https://doi.org/10.1007/978-3-642-34163-2_2
10. Holm, H., Buschle, M., Lagerström, R., Ekstedt, M.: Automatic data collection for enterprise architecture models. Softw. Syst. Model. **13**(2), 825–841 (2014)
11. Iyer, S., Konstas, I., Cheung, A., Zettlemoyer, L.: Summarizing source code using a neural attention model. In: Proceedings of the 54th Annual Meeting of the Association for Computational Linguistics, ACL 2016, 7–12 August 2016, Berlin, Germany. Long Papers, vol. 1. The Association for Computer Linguistics (2016)
12. Johnson, P., Ekstedt, M., Lagerström, R.: Automatic probabilistic enterprise IT architecture modeling: a dynamic bayesian networks approach. In: 20th IEEE International Enterprise Distributed Object Computing Workshop, EDOC Workshops 2016, Vienna, Austria, 5–9 September 2016, pp. 1–8 (2016)
13. Roth, S., Hauder, M., Farwick, M., Breu, R., Matthes, F.: Enterprise architecture documentation: current practices and future directions. In: Wirtschaftsinformatik, p. 58 (2013)
14. The Open Group: Archimate®3.0.1 specification, an open group standard (2016)
15. Välja, M., Lagerström, R., Ekstedt, M., Korman, M.: A requirements based approach for automating enterprise it architecture modeling using multiple data sources. In: 2015 IEEE 19th International Enterprise Distributed Object Computing Workshop (EDOCW), pp. 79–87. IEEE (2015)

Case and Activity Identification for Mining Process Models from Middleware

Saimir Bala[1]([⊠])[ID], Jan Mendling[1]([⊠])[ID], Martin Schimak[2], and Peter Queteschiner[3]

[1] Vienna University of Economics and Business, Vienna, Austria
{saimir.bala,jan.mendling}@wu.ac.at
[2] plexiti GmbH, Wien, Austria
martin.schimak@plexiti.com
[3] Phactum Softwareentwicklung GmbH, Wien, Austria
peter.queteschiner@phactum.at

Abstract. Process monitoring aims to provide transparency over operational aspects of a business process. In practice, it is a challenge that traces of business process executions span across a number of diverse systems. It is cumbersome manual engineering work to identify which attributes in unstructured event data can serve as case and activity identifiers for extracting and monitoring the business process. Approaches from literature assume that these identifiers are known a priori and data is readily available in formats like eXtensible Event Stream (XES). However, in practice this is hardly the case, specifically when event data from different sources are pooled together in event stores. In this paper, we address this research gap by inferring potential case and activity identifiers in a provenance agnostic way. More specifically, we propose a semi-automatic technique for discovering event relations that are semantically relevant for business process monitoring. The results are evaluated in an industry case study with an international telecommunication provider.

Keywords: Business process management · Process monitoring Process mining · Case identification

1 Introduction

Business process monitoring is a key step towards improvement. In practice, Business Process Management (BPM) solutions are implemented over multiple independent systems. While system integration is a common endeavor in this scenario, monitoring techniques are only available for the single systems and not for the entire system-landscape. For instance, in the telecommunications industry, a customer order request is typically processed through various systems

This work has been funded by the Austrian Research Promotion Agency (FFG) under grant 862950 (Business Process Optimization Toolkit).

for checking its contract conditions, available credit and promotions, several consents to the treatment of data, and finally activating the contract. Therefore, in order to monitor the business process, it must be taken into account that traces span over several systems and that identifiers for cases and activities are not known a priori.

This problem has been approached in two ways, namely *(i) manual integration* and *(ii) automatic matching*. Manual integration techniques are typically ad-hoc engineering solutions that exploit domain knowledge about events to be monitored. This class of techniques focuses on specific key events and often leave out interesting patterns that happen as a consequence of other events that were not manually selected as monitoring-relevant. Instead, automatic matching techniques aim to identify relevant events and relationships assuming no prior domain knowledge. Existing literature has addressed several challenges of automatic matching. Two main techniques are *case matching* [6,18] and *mapping* [3,7] of events to activities at different abstraction layers. Case matching approaches strive to reconstruct case identifiers compatible with eXtensible Event Stream (XES). Mapping approaches either assume the presence of a case identifier or make use of domain knowledge. These techniques help getting insights on extant relationships between events. However, they shortfall in practical situations where the event schema is not known a priori and events may have many possible case identifiers.

This paper addresses the problem of monitoring the business process using event data generated from independent systems. These events are available at different levels of granularity and more than one event can correspond to a business activity. Therefore, the first step towards process monitoring is the identification of event attributes that can serve as identifiers for cases and activities. We propose a semi-automatic approach for constructing system-spanning traces from a pool of events. Input to the approach is a set of *heterogeneous* events. We assume that these events contain data that are relevant for monitoring, but no prior knowledge of the event schema. Guided by these assumptions, the approach proposes identifiers for events and relations that are relevant for process monitoring. Thus, we position our contribution as a preprocessing technique to identify potentially interesting perspectives for the analysis of event logs. In particular, this research helps companies select attributes for creating event logs that can be analyzed with process mining techniques.

The rest of the paper is structured as follows. Section 2 illustrates the problem inspired from a real world telecommunications provides scenario, and elaborates on the state of the art. Section 3 introduces our approach to identify relevant events and attributes that can serve as identifiers. Section 4 evaluates our approach against an industry use case. Section 5 concludes the paper.

2   Background

In this section we elaborate on the addressed problem and related work.

2.1   Problem Illustration and Motivation

An international telecommunication provider has different *sales channels* to its customers. A sale channel defines a way in which customers can interact with the provider. There are two types of interactions: *(i)* direct interaction, when the customer contacts the provider directly, and *(ii)* indirect interaction, when the customer contacts the provider through partners or intermediaries. In order to handle these interactions, the company has developed a solution that relies on a middleware to connect systems from the provider and its partners. Figure 1 illustrates the architecture in the Fundamental Modeling Concepts (FMC) notation[1]. The middleware operates as a bridging layer that enables communication among IT systems from the different parties. Up to a limited period of time, it is possible to access historical events by means of queries. Given the different technologies involved, these queries usually return *heterogeneous* events.

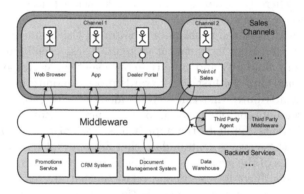

Fig. 1. Middleware bridging events from different systems

Let us illustrate the related challenges by the help of a simplified example. Figure 2 shows a typical *ordering process* from practice in the Business Process Model and Notation (BPMN). The process starts when an order is received by the order handling system and consists of two phases: *(i)* place order and *(ii)* confirm order. In the first phase an order is received from the client. A client is a software agent used by the customer, e.g., a web browser, a smartphone application or another third party system (cf. Figure 1). After a number of successful validity checks, the order is finally accepted. In the second phase, a confirmation

---

[1] http://www.fmc-modeling.org.

of the identity of the customer is expected. For instance, the identity confirmation can is carried out using web identification. Upon notification of successful customer identification, the order is further processed and confirmed. This concludes the ordering process.

Traces of the process are scattered across the systems that serve the different activities of the process. Because all the events are routed by the middleware, it is possible to collect these traces by querying the architecture and obtaining a set of middleware events. These middleware events are wrappers for other more fine granular events intended to reach the various systems connected. Given the different provenance of the events it is hard to have full knowledge on the database schemata of each of the source systems. Therefore, it is a challenge to understand whether an event is semantically meaningful for process monitoring.

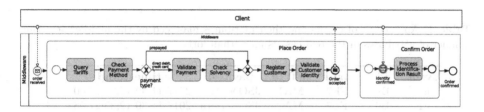

Fig. 2. A typical two step ordering process.

Table 1 shows a simplified excerpt of middleware events at a specific time interval. For illustration purposes we report only eleven attributes. In practice the number of attributes can grow up to more than forty attributes per event. In this case, we have the following: *(i) Event* is a friendly event name; *(ii) id* is a unique identifier given by the middleware; *(iii) mTrId* is transaction id representing a session in the middleware, i.e., a number of activities executed by the middleware for a specific request; *(iv) payload* carries data about the original event in different formats, e.g., JSON data from forms, SOAP XML from remote procedure calls, etc.; *(v) timestamp* reports the time the event appeared in the middleware; *(vi) sysId* may contain the name of the system that generated the event or the system that is intended to consume it; *(vii) inMethodName* contains the name of a specific method in one of the connected systems intended to consume this event; *(viii) outMethodName* contains the name of a specific method in one of the connected systems that produced this event; *(ix) uName* is an attribute that identifies the name of the user that is performing an action in the system, such as for instance requesting a new SIM card; *(x) oName* is the name of owner of the credit card requested for the payment.

As shown in Table 1, in practice events lack an explicit notion of case identifier and there might be multiple candidates that can be used. While it is true that some attributes can be checked in the documentation, it requires cumbersome coordination effort to obtain such documentation from all the partners. Moreover, in many practical settings documentation is often missing or outdated.

Although it is hard to automatically extract the business process from these data, yet, monitoring the business process is crucial. Therefore, it is useful to proceed in a schema agnostic way to support the engineer for a first classification of the attributes.

In the light of these considerations, we formulate the challenge as "**RQ:** *how to semi-automatically identify attributes that can serve as case or activity identifier?*". Note that the steps of a customer journey across the systems can be observed from different perspectives. For instance, depending on what attribute is chosen as a case identifier, it is possible to observe either the different journeys of a customer or the various customers for each journey in the systems landscape. In this sense, the problem of finding case identifiers is dual to the problem of selecting activity identifiers. Therefore, it can be assumed *orthogonality* between activities and cases in the way they partition the event space.

Table 1. An excerpt of events and their attributes managed by the middleware. The number of attributes in the real case is more than forty.

Event	id	trId	mTrId	payload	timestamp
e1	By	FE7	MA1	JSON Data	2017-11-30 12:35:27.003
e2	B0	FE7	MA2	JSON Data	2017-11-30 12:35:27.065
e3	u8	FE7	MA3	SOAP XML	2017-11-30 12:35:27.353
e4	vB	FE8	MA1	SOAP XML	2017-11-30 12:35:27.456
e5	vD	FE8	MA2	SOAP XML	2017-11-30 12:35:27.488
e6	vG	FE8	MA3	SOAP XML	2017-11-30 12:35:27.497
e7	Os	FE9	MA1	SOAP XML	2017-11-30 12:35:27.575
e8	Vi	FE9	MA2	SOAP XML	2017-11-30 12:35:27.575
e9	Ox	FE9	MA3	Text	2017-11-30 12:35:27.615
Event	**system**	**uName**	**oName**	**inMethod**	**outMethod**	**...**
e1	s1	Bob	Bob	/api/ordering		...
e2		Alice	Bob		/api2/ordering	...
e3	s2	Claire	Alice	ReqProms		...
e4	s2	Claire	Alice	ReqProms	ReqProms	...
e5	s2	Claire	Alice	CheckSolv		...
e6	s2	Claire	Alice		CheckSolv	...
e7	s3	Bob	Bob	QueryTarifs	QueryTarifs	...
e8	s3	Claire	Alice	RegCustomer		...
e9	s3	Claire	Alice	ProcIdRes	ProcIdRes	...

2.2 Related Literature

The problem has been addressed in the literature from different angles. Existing approaches can be classified into two main areas: *(i)* process mining research and *(ii)* database research. In the first category, a similar problem was tackled in [15,19]. Specifically, these two works consider the same problem setting but they only assume two attributes, namely id and message. In this work, we assume that it is possible to distinguish different attributes, although schema information is missing. Differently from the mentioned works, we abstract case and activity indicators. This provides a step beyond the simple identification of atomic, disjunctive and conjunctive correlation-conditions. Other approaches in this area rely on the use of process mining [2] techniques to reconstruct a process model from event logs [18,20]. Because these techniques work with "flat" event logs, i.e., unaware of the granularity and multidimensionality of the events, efforts were made on how to create flat event logs from multidimensional data. This case is supported by practical scenarios where business events are stored in several tables of relational databases. Often, these data are stored by humans and therefore the log quality is low. Work from [6] tackles this problem by finding correlations and case identifiers among events. The problem of event granularity has been especially tackled in [4,5,14]. As a result a many-to-many mapping technique was defined that is able to recognize business activities from groups of fine granular events based on time distance. In further work [3], event matching is tackled my mining declarative rules from the model and the log. The problem of discovering subprocesses has been treated in [9]. Here, the authors develop a technique to discover the process model including subprocesses, instead of flat model for as is analysis. The problem is also related to multi-instantiation of sub-processes. The work in [21] tackles such a problem for process discovery and conformance checking purposes.

Efforts from the database area also have links to processes. In [7], the authors propose an approach based on describing event logs with annotations of a conceptual model of the data. The technique takes as an input (i) an ontology in the Web Ontology Language (OWL) language; (ii) an Ontology-based Data Access (OBDA) mapping specification; (iii) and the schema annotations specifying cases and events [8]. The output consists of an event log in the XES format. This technique helps with automatic obtaining a customized view on the process. As a drawback, knowledge about the schema is necessary.

This paper is also related to foreign-key extraction. Work from [17] tackles this problem in the context of extracting the artifact lifecycle from multidimensional events. They identify table importance based on entropy of its attributes. However, the approach does not tackle event granularity issues. The last related stream of research regard the use of Natural Language Processing (NLP) to identify process cases and activities. Contributions in this group the have focused on process discovery. In [1] a model is discovered from group stories. Work from [11] reaches 77% of accuracy in reconstructing process models from text. In [16] legacy systems code is analyzed to infer business process rules and activities. The work of [10] uses NLP to aid the extraction of artful processes from knowledge workers emails. This body of contribution indeed suggests that valuable process insights can be obtained from unstructured data. In our setting, this is particularly useful when dealing with messages or payload of events. Differently from NLP works, we work with semi-structured data, i.e. our data can (roughly) be represented in tabular format, but the schema in unknown.

In light of the described literature, we focus on the gap of semi-automatically identifying case and activity candidates.

3   Engineering Approach for Process Monitoring

Next, we present the approach for addressing the problem.

3.1   Approach Overview

We devise a three step approach to produce flat event logs. Figure 3 illustrates this approach, which takes as input a pool of heterogeneous events and proceed as follows.

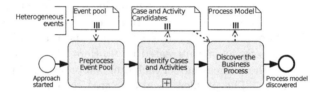

Fig. 3. Overview of the approach for extracting the business process

Step 1. Preprocess Event Pool. In this step, we extract the heterogeneous events from the middleware. Because these events contain diverse attributes, they need to be further processed and pooled together in such a way that they can be analyzed automatically. This includes enriching existing events with new attributes extracted from their payload data. A high number of events is generated in real-world scenarios. Therefore filtering techniques must be taken into account to rule out events that we do not want to monitor.

Step 2. Identify Cases and Activities. In this step, a mapping from events to activities is established. Note that business activities are not unequivocally represented in the event log. In fact, the problems of granularity and multiplicity between events and activity must be taken into account [5]. The input of this step is an enriched log with labeled cases. The output is a set of pairs that represents what can be considered as cases and activities.

Step 3. Discover the Business Process. In this step, the approach exploits the results of the previous steps to show a business process model. In particular, this step combines the case identifier, activity and timestamp for constructing an event log. The log is then converted to XES and a process mining algorithm is used for discovering the process.

3.2   Preliminaries

Next, we formalize the preliminary concepts required by our technique. We formally define heterogeneous events from multiple systems passing through the same channel as *pool of events*.

Definition 1 (Pool of Events, Attribute). Let $\mathcal{E}$ be the universe of all events. A pool of events $PL \subseteq \mathcal{E}$ is a set of recorded events in the process. Each event $e \in PL$ has attributes. Let AN be a set of attribute names. For any event $e \in PL$ and $n \in AN$, $\#_n(e)$ is the value of attribute n for event e. If an event e does not contain an attribute n, then $\#_n(e) = \bot$.

Events also contain data, which are referred to as *payload*. That is, for each event $e \in PL$, the payload is an attribute p such that $\#_p(e) \neq \bot$ where $p \in AN$, contains additional information about the event. Moreover, we assume that every event has a timestamp attribute $ts \in AN$ such that $\#_{ts}(e)$ marks the time e occurred in the middleware. Our definition of events pool does not have a notion of a case identifier. We assume that the data is recorded from different systems, and there is no unique case connected to events. Hence, the goal is to identify the most suitable case identifier among the attributes.

Every run of a process instance is a finite sequence of events, also known as trace $\sigma \in PL^*$, where PL^* is the set of arbitrary length traces. For example, $\sigma_1 = \langle e_1, e_2, e_3, e_4 \rangle$ is a trace constituted by a sequence of four events. In our problem setting there may be different ways in which events form a trace. We assume that events can be grouped into traces if there is a relation among them. Given that we have no prior knowledge on the data schema, we do not enforce the choice of any particular attribute for grouping events into traces.

Events in the middleware are produced as a result of activities that happen at business process level. An activity corresponds to the execution of a certain task that is business relevant. Examples of activities are *Query Tariffs*, *Check Payment*, *Register Customer*, and so on. We consider an N:1 mapping between the events and activities, i.e., for each business activity one or more events may occur in the middleware. Given this relation, it is possible to construct a log from activities by matching events onto activity traces. The challenge is to find a mapping $M : PL \to A$ from the pool of events to the set of activities A. That is, we aim to find a surjective function m as defined in Eq. 1 for that establishes this mapping.

$$\forall a \in A, \exists e \in PL : a = m(e) \tag{1}$$

Activities can be executed in many different orders. For process monitoring, we are interested into sequences of activities that may represent a full end-to-end execution of one process instance.

3.3   Approach

With the definitions presented above, we describe the steps for identifying case and activity attributes and extracting the business process.

Identifying Case and Activity Candidates. As discussed in Sect. 2.1, we assume that cases and activities almost partition the space of events orthogonally. Unquestionably, this assumption leaves out situations where activities appear multiple times within a case (e.g., rework loop). Nevertheless, we are interested at having a first characterization of process variants. Therefore we focus only on business processes where activities are unique within a case.

A characteristic of cases is that they uniquely identify traces (i.e., set of activities). At the same time, many activities usually belong to a case, i.e., many singular activities are labeled with the same case identifiers. Therefore, if we consider a sequence of attribute values in a trace of events $\#_\sigma = \langle \#_1, \ldots, \#_n \rangle$ then we must find at least i, j for which $\#_i = \#_j$. This condition states that case identifiers must be non unique. For an attribute A, we measure its *repetitiveness* as the fraction of unique values over the cardinality of all possible values of the attribute.

$$Rep(A) = 1 - \frac{|uniq(A)|}{|\#_A|}$$

For example, given $A = (1, 2)$ and $B = (b, b)$, then $Rep(A) = 1 - 2/2 = 0$ whereas $Rep(B) = 1 - 1/2 = 0.5$. This observation allows us to filter out attributes like the timestamp or other identifiers that are introduced by the middleware but do not represent business relevant information. For instance, timestamps present a low level of repetitiveness in a log.

Repetitiveness alone is not sufficient for determining case identifier attributes. In fact, attributes which do not have low level of repetitiveness are not necessarily case or activity candidates. We refer to these attributes as *noise*. One example is the attribute $score = None$ for all events, or attributes that only contain empty values. We can filter out these type of attributes by relying again on the almost orthogonality condition between case identifiers and activities. More specifically, to overcome erroneous inclusion of noise, we consider pairs of events which have high individual repetitiveness but a low pairwise repetitiveness, as follows.

Given a sequence of attributes, we compute the pairwise repetitiveness (a.k.a. co-repetitiveness) with Algorithm 1. The algorithm takes as input the whole set of attributes and returns the set PWR of all pairwise repetitiveness scores. Because the number of attributes in our problem setting is high, we use this measure to sort the attributes in increasing order of co-repetitiveness, namely $Sort(PWR)$. Candidate attributes A_c for case identifier are those who belong to a pair ranked on top $Sort(PWR)$ and score a high $Rep(A_c)$.

Algorithm 1. Computing pairwise repetitiveness

Input: An event pool PL, where AN is the set of its attribute names
Result: A set $PWR = \{(a_i, a_j, r)\}$ where a_i, a_j are attribute, r is their
  co-repetitiveness

1 $PWR \leftarrow 0$;
2 **forall the** e *in* PL **do**
3   **forall the** (i, j) *such that* $i \neq j$, *with* $a_i, a_j \in AN$ **do**
4           $V_i \leftarrow \#_{a_i}(e)$;   /* get all values for attribute name a_i */
5           $V_j \leftarrow \#_{a_j}(e)$;
6           $r \leftarrow 1 - \frac{|V_i \cap V_j|}{max(|V_i|,|V_j|)}$;
7           $PWR \leftarrow PWR \cup \{(a_i, a_j, r)\}$;
8   **end**
9 **end**

A corner case of this method is represented by attribute pairs that consistently assume the same values. For example, let us consider A, B with $\#_A = (a, a)$ and $\#_B = (a, a)$. Algorithm 1 would return as result $PWR = \{(A, B, 1)\}$, but A, B represent the same information. In order to overcome this problematic case, we restrict the search to those attributes which do not have extreme repetitiveness. Thus, we penalize the both high and low values by comparing the co-repetitiveness by computing the mean value between the individual repetitions of the attributes. Therefore, we select the pairs $r, \overline{r_{A,B}}$, where r was calculated by Algorithm 1 and $\overline{r_{A,B}} = \frac{Rep(A)+Rep(B)}{2}$. Ideally, the best candidate has a low value of r and a high value of $\overline{r_{A,B}}$. If we consider the couples in a Cartesian space, the optimal point has coordinates $Opt = (0, 1)$. This entails, that the best candidates for being case-activity identifier pairs are the geometrically closest to the optimum, i.e., they minimize the Euclidean distance $\delta^{Opt} = \|Opt - (r, \overline{r_{A,B}})\|$. The choice of one or another case identifier with similar low distance δ^{Opt} defines different perspectives on the business process.

Discovering the Process. In Sect. 3.3 we identified pairs that are candidate for being cases and activities. This final step is concerned with extracting a process model out of the event pool PL. This is performed by labeling which attributes of the event pool are cases and which are activities, and order them by timestamp. There are generally multiple candidate pairs returned by the aforementioned step. Thus, the challenge is to select the correct candidate. However, the set of possible candidates can be restricted to a small number of elements, through the usage of a customizable parameter κ, resulting in a set of pairs can be manually inspected. The κ attributes that were identified as *relevant* can contain other information that can be exploited by process mining algorithms, such as [12, 13]. At this point we have identified the cases, the activities, the timestamps and additional information. Thus, we can generate a log file and apply process discovery.

3.4   Example

Here, we see an example of how the method works in practice. For our purpose let us consider the subset of attributes $A = \{trId, mTrId, timestamp, uName, oName\}$ from Table 1.

First, we compute the case and activity candidates. For all the attributes $trId, mTrId, timestamp, uName, oName$ we compute $Rep(a)$, $a \in A$. The results are $Rep(trId) = 0.67$, $Rep(mTrId) = 0.67$, $Rep(timestamp) = 0$, $Rep(uName) = 0.67$, $Rep(oName) = 0.78$. Note, that attribute $timestamp$ as it was detected as $timestamp$ because it has no degree of repetitiveness. Thus, we can already exclude $timestamp$ from the case identifier candidates.

Table 2. Pairwise repetitiveness PWR (i.e. co-repetitiveness) and mean co-repetitiveness $\bar{r}$ computed for the example case

	trId	mTrId	timestamp	uName	oName
trId $PWR, \bar{r}$	- , -	$(0.00, 0.66)^*$	$(0.00, 0.33)$	$(0.33, 0.66)$	$(0.44, 0.72)$
mTrId $PWR, \bar{r}$	$(0.00, 0.67)^*$	- , -	$(0.00, 0.33)$	$(0.44, 0.66)$	$(0.44, 0.72)$
timestamp $PWR, \bar{r}$	$(0.00, 0.33)$	$(0.00, 0,33)$	- , -	$(0.00, 0.33)$	$(0.00, 0.38)$
uName $PWR, \bar{r}$	$(0.33, 0.66)$	$(0.44, 0.72)$	$(0.00, 0.33)$	- , -	$(0.66, 0.72)$
oName $PWR, \bar{r}$	$(0.44, 0.72)$	$(0.44, 0.72)$	$(0.00, 0.38)$	$(0.66, 0.72)$	- , -

The next step is to compute the co-repetitiveness set, as from Algorithm 1 and obtain the set PWR. We report the values $r \in PWR$ corresponding to each pair in the row PWR of Table 2. Likewise, we also compute the average co-repetitiveness $\bar{r}_{A_i, A_j}$ for all the pairs of attributes and report the result as $\bar{r}$ next to PWR in the same row of the table.

We have finally obtained a set of points $r, \bar{r}$ of the Cartesian space. For each point we compute the Euclidean distance δ^{Opt} to the optimum point $Opt = (0, 1)$. In our example, the couple $(trId, mTrId)$ scores the lowest distance from Opt, i.e., $\delta^{Opt}(trId, mTrId) = 0.33$ (cf. couple marked with an asterisk * in Table 2). This means that the attributes $trId, mTrId$ are candidates for being one the case identifier and the other the activity identifier.

4   Evaluation: Industry Use Case

In this section we evaluate our approach against real world data. In particular, we aim at showing the applicability and usefulness of our approach to support selection of case and activity identifiers.

4.1 Experimental Setup and Dataset

We used our approach on the ordering process scenario described in Sect. 2.1. The reference process model is the one shown in figure to Fig. 2, and it describes in a coarse-grained fashion how the process is supposed to be executed. Mechanisms to query events from the middleware were already in place. In particular, we retrieved the data exploiting the search engine Elaticsearch[2]. The output was presented in the JSON[3] format. Afterwards, the different events were grouped together and transformed as in Table 1.

Next, we describe the dataset used for in our evaluation. To extract the process data, we used knowledge about the start and end events. Then we proceeded by querying for all the start events in a specific day. For each start event, we followed several related events and made a new query in the middleware for each of them. This procedure led to systematically obtaining all related events, including several end events.

We extracted 8042 low-level event data concerning the ordering process. Note that this is already a considerable amount of data as we focus on the event attributes. In fact, similar results were obtained even with a smaller portion of data. After collecting all the events and building the event pool, we obtained a total number of 41 attributes. The data collection was stored in CSV files which were then also manually checked for parsing errors. Note that, despite their reference to a known start event, the events may and usually cover more than the ordering process. Also, due to the fact that some processes may take weeks before reaching the final state, we are aware that the traces may be incomplete. The aim is to show the applicability of our method and that we can identify meaningful candidates.

4.2 Results

In this section we show the results of applying our approach to the dataset. We proceed following the approach step by step. To this end, we implemented a proof-of-concept prototype[4] using Python and R.

Case and Activity Candidates. Fig. 4a shows the results of the repetitiveness computed for each attribute. Already at this stage events that are not case or activity candidates can be filtered out. In fact, time the attributes *timestamp* and *id* have a repetitiveness close to 0. Figure 4b plots the relation between pairwise mean repetitiveness and the co-repetitiveness of attribute pairs. The x-axis represents the repetitiveness of each pair, whereas the y-axis represents the mean value between the individual repetitiveness degree of each attribute of the pair. The optimal point $Opt = (1, 0)$ is colored in black, the points with a lower distance δ^{Opt} are colored with darker tonality, and the red ellipsis represents the top candidates that score the lowest δ^{Opt}.

---

[2] https://www.elastic.co/products/elasticsearch.

[3] https://www.json.org.

[4] open source in https://github.com/s41m1r/case-and-activity-identification.

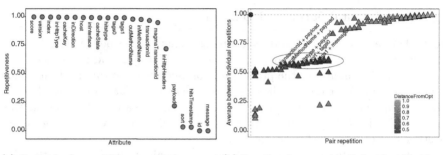

(a) Individual repetitiveness of the event attributes

(b) Results of case and activity identification on the real world data

Fig. 4. Results of the approach

We picked the top $\kappa = 10$ candidate for case and activity. These were the following couples: {(*trId*, *payload*), (*payload*, *host*), (*outMethodName*, *payload*), (*outMethodName*, *mTrId*), (*payload*, *cacheState*), (*cacheKey*, *payload*), (*cacheState*, *payload*), (*payload*, *inDirection*), (*payload*, *inInterface*), (*inDirection*, *payload*), (*inInterface*, *payload*)}. Because our approach is agnostic about the meaning of the attributes, we relied on domain knowledge to select attributes that are more meaningful. As a result, the couple (*outMethodName*, *mTrId*) was chosen as the best candidate, with *mTrId* being chosen as the case and *outMethodName* as the activity.

The company could confirm that *mTrId* and *outMethodName* were indeed key attributes representing respectively a transaction case (i.e., a sequence of actions taken by the customer) and a method called by a service task that implemented the activity. Therefore, the resulting business represents a user transaction perspective on the business process, with each activity being represented the action of the user.

Discovered Process Model. In this step we build an event log including the couple (*outMethodName*, *mTrId*). The timetamp that was identified in the previous phase in Sect. 3.3. In addition, we also included the top most relevant attributes that were connected to *outMethodName* and *mTrId*. In particular, we found other attributes like *inMethodName* and *sort* which were candidates for alternative activity and timestamp, respectively. More specifically, we analyzed the attribute ranges for the most relevant attributes that were identified previously. We report them in Table 3.

Figure 5 shows the resulting business process that was mined using the Celonis[5] process mining tool. The outcome showed that the process is similar to the one presented in Fig. 2, with the real process having a higher number of activities. In particular, Celonis showed that there were 13 cases in our event log and that happy path is constituted by the sequence of activities *ReqProms*, *QueryTarifs*, *ValidateAddress*, *RegCustomer*.

---

[5] https://www.celonis.com/.

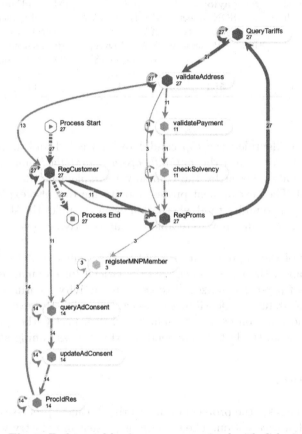

Fig. 5. End-to-end business process mined with Celonis

Table 3. Attribute ranges

Attribute	id	timestamp	trId	outMethodName	tags0
Range	20 digits	1511996925852	FE_1de0ea5d	qAdConsent	response
	unique	1511996925917	FE_213dc19d	checkSolv	backend
	values	1511996926244	FE_239bc992	RegCustomer	client
		1511996926335	FE_3039d556	/api/ordering	request
		[cont.]	[cont.]	[cont.]	[cont.]
Levels	**835**	**805**	**28**	**12**	**5**
Attribute	**host**	**payload**	**mTrId**	**inMethodName**	[cont.]
Range	ip address	29 JSON objects	MA_1ZBLJVV2	validatePayment	
		189 XML objects	MA_4YcwwtvU	checkSolv	
		346 SOAP messages	MA_75FDzegp	RegCustomer	
			MA_9USSsx8Y	/api2/ordering	
			[cont.]	[cont.]	
Levels	**4**	**564**	**31**	**12**	

Discussion. We identified the top candidate for case id and activity. In the top ranking there were also the *outMethodName*, *inMethodName* and *mTrId*. These one were also chosen by the company to implement their own process monitoring tool. The development process monitoring tool also exploits domain knowledge in order to understand whether an events signifies the start or an end of an activity. As a result they were able to map 8 activities over 9 for process monitoring.

Limitations of the approach are related to the quality of data. Given their diverse provenance, the preprocessing step is crucial for eliminating noise and further causes of parsing mistakes. The case and activity identification step of the approach is useful for identifying case-activity pairs. However, it supports no semantic and relies on expert domain knowledge. Lastly, the quality of the model resulting from the last step depends on the process mining algorithm.

5   Conclusion

In this work, we tackle the problem of monitoring business processes from event data which lack a *case* notion. The scenario is present in industry where events from different systems are pooled together. Process monitoring in these scenarios the discovery of the process. We proposed an approach to preprocess the data to solve the heterogeneity problem, and detect cases-activity candidate pairs. We use this information to build an event log and apply a process mining algorithm to obtain a process model. Our approach is suitable for real case scenarios where the event provenance is diverse and no event schema is know a priori. The approach is customizable by the domain engineer and can provide the top κ case-activity identifier candidates. In future work, we aim at improving the approach towards dealing with automatically detecting granularity between events and business activities, the discovery of causal dependencies, and the visualization of links between event pairs.

References

1. de A. R. Gonçalves, J.C., Santoro, F.M., Baião, F.A.: Business process mining from group stories. In: CSCWD. pp. 161–166. IEEE (2009)
2. van der Aalst, W.M.P.: Process Mining: Data Science in Action. Springer, Heidelberg (2016)
3. Baier, T., Di Ciccio, C., Mendling, J., Weske, M.: Matching events and activities by integrating behavioral aspects and label analysis. Softw. Syst, Model **17**(2), 573–598 (2017)
4. Baier, T., Mendling, J., Weske, M.: Bridging abstraction layers in process mining. Inf. Syst. **46**, 123–139 (2014)
5. Baier, T., Rogge-Solti, A., Mendling, J., Weske, M.: Matching of events and activities: an approach based on behavioral constraint satisfaction. In: SAC, pp. 1225–1230. ACM (2015)
6. Bayomie, D., Awad, A., Ezat, E.: Correlating unlabeled events from cyclic business processes execution. In: Nurcan, S., Soffer, P., Bajec, M., Eder, J. (eds.) CAiSE 2016. LNCS, vol. 9694, pp. 274–289. Springer, Cham (2016). https://doi.org/10.1007/978-3-319-39696-5_17
7. Calvanese, Diego, Kalayci, Tahir Emre, Montali, Marco, Tinella, Stefano: Ontology-based data access for extracting event logs from legacy data: the onprom tool and methodology. In: Abramowicz, Witold (ed.) BIS 2017. LNBIP, vol. 288, pp. 220–236. Springer, Cham (2017). https://doi.org/10.1007/978-3-319-59336-4_16
8. Calvanese, D., Montali, M., Syamsiyah, A., van der Aalst, W.M.P.: Ontology-driven extraction of event logs from relational databases. In: Reichert, M., Reijers, H.A. (eds.) BPM 2015. LNBIP, vol. 256, pp. 140–153. Springer, Cham (2016). https://doi.org/10.1007/978-3-319-42887-1_12
9. Conforti, R., Dumas, M., García-Bañuelos, L., Rosa, M.L.: BPMN miner: automated discovery of BPMN process models with hierarchical structure. Inf. Syst. **56**, 284–303 (2016)
10. Di Ciccio, C., Mecella, M.: Mining artful processes from knowledge workers' emails. IEEE Internet Comput. **17**(5), 10–20 (2013)
11. Friedrich, Fabian, Mendling, Jan, Puhlmann, Frank: Process model generation from natural language text. In: Mouratidis, Haralambos, Rolland, Colette (eds.) CAiSE 2011. LNCS, vol. 6741, pp. 482–496. Springer, Heidelberg (2011). https://doi.org/10.1007/978-3-642-21640-4_36
12. Günther, Christian W., van der Aalst, Wil M.P.: Fuzzy mining – adaptive process simplification based on multi-perspective metrics. In: Alonso, Gustavo, Dadam, Peter, Rosemann, Michael (eds.) BPM 2007. LNCS, vol. 4714, pp. 328–343. Springer, Heidelberg (2007). https://doi.org/10.1007/978-3-540-75183-0_24
13. Leemans, S.J.J., Fahland, D., van der Aalst, W.M.P.: Discovering block-structured process models from event logs containing infrequent behaviour. In: Lohmann, N., Song, M., Wohed, P. (eds.) BPM 2013. LNBIP, vol. 171, pp. 66–78. Springer, Cham (2014). https://doi.org/10.1007/978-3-319-06257-0_6
14. Mannhardt, F., de Leoni, M., Reijers, H.A., van der Aalst, W.M.P., Toussaint, P.J.: From low-level events to activities - a pattern-based approach. In: La Rosa, M., Loos, P., Pastor, O. (eds.) BPM 2016. LNCS, vol. 9850, pp. 125–141. Springer, Cham (2016). https://doi.org/10.1007/978-3-319-45348-4_8
15. Motahari-Nezhad, H.R., Saint-Paul, R., Casati, F., Benatallah, B.: Event correlation for process discovery from web service interaction logs. VLDB J. **20**(3), 417–444 (2011)

16. do Nascimento, G.S., Iochpe, C., Thom, L., Kalsing, A.C., Moreira, Á.: Identifying business rules to legacy systems reengineering based on BPM and SOA. In: Murgante, B., Gervasi, O., Misra, S., Nedjah, N., Rocha, A.M.A.C., Taniar, D., Apduhan, B.O. (eds.) ICCSA 2012. LNCS, vol. 7336, pp. 67–82. Springer, Heidelberg (2012). https://doi.org/10.1007/978-3-642-31128-4_6

17. Nooijen, E.H.J., van Dongen, B.F., Fahland, D.: Automatic discovery of data-centric and artifact-centric processes. In: La Rosa, M., Soffer, P. (eds.) BPM 2012. LNBIP, vol. 132, pp. 316–327. Springer, Heidelberg (2013). https://doi.org/10.1007/978-3-642-36285-9_36

18. Raichelson, L., Soffer, P., Verbeek, E.: Merging event logs: combining granularity levels for process flow analysis. Inf. Syst. **71**, 211–227 (2017)

19. Reguieg, H., Benatallah, B., Nezhad, H.R.M., Toumani, F.: Event correlation analytics: scaling process mining using mapreduce-aware event correlation discovery techniques. IEEE Trans. Serv. Comput. **8**(6), 847–860 (2015)

20. Senderovich, A., Di Francescomarino, C., Ghidini, C., Jorbina, K., Maggi, F.M.: Intra and inter-case features in predictive process monitoring: a tale of two dimensions. In: Carmona, J., Engels, G., Kumar, A. (eds.) BPM 2017. LNCS, vol. 10445, pp. 306–323. Springer, Cham (2017). https://doi.org/10.1007/978-3-319-65000-5_18

21. Weber, I., Farshchi, M., Mendling, J., Schneider, J.: Mining processes with multi-instantiation. In: SAC. pp. 1231–1237. ACM (2015)

Collaboration Modeling

Conceptualising Gamification Risks
to Teamwork within Enterprise

Abdullah Algashami[(⊠)], Sainabou Cham, Laura Vuillier,
Angelos Stefanidis, Keith Phalp, and Raian Ali

Bournemouth University, Poole, UK
{aalgashami, scham, lrenshawvuillier, astefanidis,
kphalp, rali}@bournemouth.ac.uk

Abstract. Gamification in businesses refers to the use of technology-assisted solutions to boost or change staff attitude, perception and behaviour, about the individual or collective goals and tasks. Previous research indicated that gamification techniques could introduce risks to the business environment, and not only fail to make a positive change, but also raise concerns about ethics, quality of work, and well-being in a workplace. Although the problem is already recognised in principle, there is still a need to clarify and concretise those risks, their factors and their relation to the gamification dynamics and mechanics. In this paper, we focus on gamification risks related to teamwork within the enterprise. To address this, we conducted three-stage empirical research in two large-scale businesses using gamification in their workplace, including two months' observation and interview study. We outline various risk mitigation strategies and map them to primary types of gamification risks. By accomplishing such conceptualisation, we pave the way towards methods to model, detect and predict gamification risks on teamwork and recommend design practices and strategies to tackle them.

Keywords: Gamification · Risk assessment · Human factors in computing

1 Introduction

Gamification is used in workplaces to increase staff desire toward implementing tasks and achieving certain goals. The set of rewarding and gaming mechanics used in gamification includes leaderboards, badges, points, avatars reflecting individual and collective performance, levels and status. An example of gamification techniques in a call centre may involve giving rewards to individual staff members or teams based on the amount and speed of answered calls and customer feedback. Despite the benefits, applying gamification in the enterprise has potential risks. For example, the way of calculating, assigning, and displaying rewards may increase the chance for adverse work ethics including free-riding, work intimidation, and lack of group cohesion [1, 2]. Despite the recognition of these risks, no reference models and systematic methods, to the best of our knowledge, have been developed to evaluate and mitigate these risks [39]. These risks have a peculiar nature due to their intermingled relation with human factors such as motivation, personality, enterprise culture and group dynamics.

© IFIP International Federation for Information Processing 2018
Published by Springer Nature Switzerland AG 2018. All Rights Reserved
R. A. Buchmann et al. (Eds.): PoEM 2018, LNBIP 335, pp. 105–120, 2018.
https://doi.org/10.1007/978-3-030-02302-7_7

Risk management is a subject of research in various areas, including information systems, business process management, and enterprise modelling [3–6]. Risks modelling has been studied in various settings, such as in small and medium enterprises where risks should be captured and represented alongside the various stages of the system analysis and design lifecycle [7]. Risk management has also been studied within the area of business process management for their effect on the flow of operation and its decisions [6]. It has also been argued that the concern for compliance risks and operational risks should be incorporated during the design-time and also run-time stages of business processes [8]. Risks considered in enterprise modelling literature are mainly related to mainstream requirements such as security, privacy, compliance and capability [8, 9]. Gamification engineering methods, reviewed in [10], are mainly focused on providing steps and techniques for designing the game mechanics in the first place and tend to overlook their risks.

Gamification risks have a unique nature in comparison to risks typically studied in information systems literature. Ethical concerns and negative connotations of gamification as being an exploitation tool are increasingly becoming a primary concern when deciding to adopt gamification solutions in enterprises. In [11] Kumar and Herger identified five steps towards the design of such motivational systems and their game elements and named the approach as "Player Centred Design". The emphasis is on the awareness of ethical considerations in the design process. In [12] Apter and Kerr highlighted the unwanted effects - such as stress and anxiety - resulting from pressures for efficiency through the application of gamification on staff daily tasks. Thiebes et al. [13] conducted a systematic literature review on design for motivation through gamification and found that research on the risks of these elements is still in its infancy and opens the way for more research in the area.

Risks of a gamification systems applied in an enterprise stem mainly from their usage or perceived usage as an appraisal and performance monitoring mechanism, as well as a pressure tool to perform better. Gamification elements can be used to motivate individuals via self-monitoring and self-comparison. For example, a progress bar can be used to encourage delivery staff to distribute a parcel within a specific time frame and following a specific process by showing them their current status and the remaining time and stages. Peer-comparison is another modality which can increase the perception of gamification as a pressure or intimidation tool. This includes elements like leaderboards, levels and badges assigned to individuals but visible to all team members and meant to motivate by reflecting and acknowledging individual metrics, such as customers' feedback on them.

Despite the recognition of potential side-effects of gamification, factors that contribute to these risks still need to be identified and conceptualised in a comprehensive and concretised style. In this paper, we conceptualise the main factors of risks in a gamification systems to the teamwork in an enterprise. Also, we sketch a mapping between a set of mitigation strategies which we proposed in [14] and our identified gamification risks. By doing that, we take the first step towards a systematic method for gamification risk elicitation, assessment, and mitigation within the enterprise.

2 Research Method

We conducted a three-stage empirical study employing multiple data collection methods from different sources aiming to increase the diversity and the credibility of the results. We adopt a multi-methods qualitative approach [15]. We summarise our method in Table 1.

Table 1. Research method stages

1st Stage		2nd Stage	3rd Stage	
Exploration		Confirmation	Clarification	
Secondary analysis & literature review	Interviews	Observation	Interviews	Focus group
– Review of the related literature on: Gamification ethics, Risk assessment in information systems, Game Mechanics, Group Dynamics – Secondary analysis of data gathered in previous work conducted in [1, 14, 22]	Interviews with ten experts in various related fields: – Two, experts in computing and social informatics – Four, experts in psychology and cyber-psychology – Two, practitioners – Two, managers	Two months in two call centres belonging to: – Tourism agency established for 40 years with over 50 call agents. – Telecommunication company has over 19 years of experience and more than 50 call agents.	Fifteen Interviews in two business companies: – Ten, call agents – Three, Supervisors – Two, Managers	Seven Participants from various backgrounds: – Two, Requirements Engineering – Two, Human-Computer Interaction – One, User Modelling – One, Cyber-Psychology – One, Business Management

In the exploration stage, we first identified a preliminary set of risks of digital motivation in its different versions, including gamification [16], game with purpose [17] and persuasive technology [18]. This was mainly informed by literature in risk assessment and management [19], value sensitive design [20], and group dynamics [21]. The identified risks were used as a template to guide a secondary analysis of data collected via interviews with experts, managers and end users in gamification related field. The primary analysis results were published in [1, 14, 22] and were meant for good engineering practices towards accountable design and ethics of gamification in general. We created a taxonomy of risks about gamification elements and used it as a basis for ten further interviews with specialists in computing, social informatics, and psychology, as well as practitioners and managers from selected business workplaces. From these interviews, we developed a more refined set of risks factors and mitigation strategies to be explored further in the second stage.

The second stage, the confirmation and enhancement stage, aimed to confirm the results of the first stage and to identify further gamification risk elements, as well as factors and situations which contribute to their emergence. To this end, an observational study was conducted in two gamified call centres in two large multinational businesses. The total duration of observations was two months, consisting of a month in each company. By observing two companies, we increased the chance of identifying different practices of gamification elements in different populations. Each of the call centres included over 50 staff. The first belonged to a tourism company, while the second to a telecommunication company. The setup in both call centres featured agents in their private cubicle offices, answering customer calls using headphone and a screen. Agents were distributed into teams on a self- constructed basis, motivated by their collective performance. A member of the research team interviewed an experienced supervisor in each centre to learn about the environment, the workflow, the gamification techniques used, real statistics, and qualitative analysis of achieved results. Gamification mechanics used in the first call centre included leaderboards for teams' collective performance and badges sent by the supervisors based on individual performance. The second call centre used a point system in which each team worked collectively to solve customer issues and gain points which lead to a 10% increase in salaries at the end of the month for the winning team. Also, the names and photos of staff in the winning team were displayed in an honour board visible to all. In both companies, the role played by the researcher was a *participant as observer* [23] to observe the actual work environment, collect data, and have discussions with both call agents and supervisors during the observation period.

The third stage was designed to (i) clarify the results of the first and the second stages and to (ii) map between the risks discovered through these stages and a set of 22 risk mitigation strategies which we proposed in [14] and meant to detect and manage the potential effects of gamification on teamwork. To achieve the first purpose, we conducted interviews with agents, supervisors and managers in the workplace, to clarify the results of the observation study which were themselves elaboration refinement and extension of the results of the exploratory phase. The interviews followed a semi-structured style. Fifteen interviews were conducted with ten agents, three supervisors and two managers. To achieve the second purpose of this stage, a focus group was conducted with seven participants from diverse backgrounds to map the 22 strategies to a set of identified risks of gamification to enterprise teamwork. At the start of the focus group, participants were given a presentation to familiarise them with the context. Also, they were given scenarios to immerse them in the problem and its context. They were asked to use card sorting and map the strategies given in cards with another set of cards containing the risks. The results are discussed in Sect. 4. Qualitative data collected in the studies were content analysed according to the six phases of thematic analysis proposed in [24]. All studies were reviewed and approved by the Bournemouth University Research Ethics Committee.

3   Gamification Risks and Risks Factors

We identified five main classes of risk factors, summarised in Fig. 1, which are related to performance, societal and personal, goals, tasks and gamification elements. Main risks associated with these factors are written in underline and *italic* text.

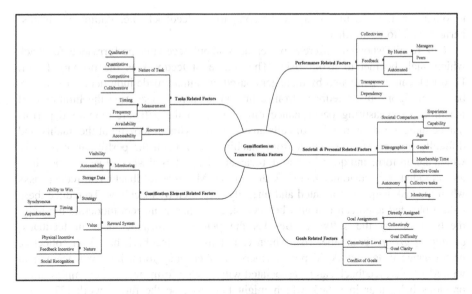

Fig. 1. Conceptualisation of Gamification risk factors to teamwork

3.1 Performance Related Risk Factors

Performance is defined as "scalable actions, behaviours and outcomes that employees engage in or bring about that are linked with and contribute to organisational goals" [25]. Performance monitoring is commonly used in organisations and has become widely pervasive with the aid of digital tools [26]. While a principal aim of gamification in an enterprise context is to increase staff performance, we found that this could lead to the following four main risk factors.

Performance Collectivism. Gamification elements, using rewards and feedback on the collective performance of staff, might have a negative influence on the level and quality of collaboration among them. Risks of *free riding* occur when some team members tend to perform less well as they receive rewards equal to others, regardless of their individual performance. Moreover, risks can be seen when some team members *work only to meet the minimum task requirements* without paying enough consideration to the level of quality of their work. Although the collective performance is needed for the sense of teamwork, these situations might affect the work collaboration and create a risk in the workplace. In other words, solving such issue requires mitigation techniques which support a sense of auditing and checking strategies, rather than just avoiding collective performance tasks.

Performance Feedback. Feedback related to staff performance is a vital element of motivation, but it may also contribute to risks related to the quality of teamwork environment. An example is a badge or an avatar representing the current status of work quality. The main risk here is the *misjudgement* of performance. In a teamwork environment, feedback can be based on self-comparison, i.e. comparing performance to one's own performance in the past, peer-comparison feedback, i.e. comparing a person to others in their team, or collective-comparison feedback, i.e. comparing teams' performance to each other.

Our results showed different preferences about receiving performance feedback which shall be met to avoid risks. The source of feedback is the primary factor. Feedback can be generated by managers based on human-made judgments or software based on algorithms. Feedback from a human is seen to overcome the limitation of machines of measuring performance only based on the software-monitored performance indicators, e.g. number of calls answered but without looking at the quality and difficulty of the issue. Feedback from machines would suit the performance of tasks which are uniform and quantity based. It can also be preferred when objective measures are provided, e.g. customer feedback and rating. Manager feedbacks can reduce risks when the task is quality oriented and uneasily measured by machines. To reduce these risk, a blended approach can also be needed, e.g. when managers moderate the judgments made by the software. Besides the perceived misjudgement in feedback, _clustering groups_ is another risk which can stem from feedback based on collective performance in teamwork. Top performers members may form their own teams and win. Moreover, feedback can be associated with past performance, e.g. examples of the previous behaviour in a task which might help to ease the future work [27]. In a teamwork environment, receiving such type of feedback may have a negative influence on staff that recently joins the team. It may _lower self-esteem_ or make them less motivated to engage with the team.

Performance Transparency. Transparency of a gamification system collected performance data, and judgments derived from processing such data, manifests itself in three ways; transparency to managers, transparency amongst acquaintances involved in or doing the same task and, finally, transparency with staff in the department or the organisation. Although performance transparency can mitigate risks about perceived unfairness and conspiracy, it seems that several ethical and moral concerns arise as a result of it [28]. There is a fine line between transparency as an enabler for trust in a gamification system and as a _counterproductive comparison_ and _pressure_ tool. For example, disclosing the number of calls answered and points earned by each agent can increase competition and improve performance but, at the same time, it may convert sales representatives to set their performance goals based on other staff performance rather than the company target. In the observed call centres, performance transparency causing staff to be featured on the leaderboard, did not appeal to those who "_did not like to be known as a top performer because others start to come to their desk and keep asking help_". Transparency can increase the chance of _anchoring bias_ among them by looking at each other's performance as a benchmark rather than realising their own strengths and skills and aiming to employ them in better-suited tasks.

Performance Dependency. The likelihood of risks in a teamwork environment increases when gamification techniques monitor and reward staff performing tasks which cannot be fully achieved independently. In the case of our call centre observations, risks of frustration and tension increased when an agent from the customer calls team needed support from a busy IT team to close a customer complaint. This can give rise to _bribes_, where a person may need to offer something in return to their dependees to get the gamification reward [1]. Addressing this issue, we should design gamification mechanics in a way that recognises potential deadlocks with the ultimate goal of not affecting the level of assistance required between staff.

3.2   Societal and Personal Related Risk Factors

Societal factors relate to the effects of a behaviour or a perception in relation to other staff, while personal factors relate to traits and inherent characteristics of staff.

Societal Comparison. Comparing staff with different capabilities and experiences, especially on a competitive basis, is a significant risk for a gamification system. _Lowering self-esteem_ and _intimidation_ are examples of such risks. Comparison is an essential game mechanics. Its design should seek to incorporate the differences between subjects, and measure their progress in a relative way.

Demographics. Age, gender and team membership duration influence acceptance and attitude towards games and gameplay applied to teamwork [29, 30]. It can be argued that: _"being with younger members in the same teamwork is frustrating, as they have better ability in digital techniques and their chance of winning the reward is higher"_. It can further be argued, that the appreciation of rewards of social benefits and collaborative nature, and those of competitive nature, can differ by gender [31]. The _novelty effect_ of gamification technology means it can be initially exciting for new members, but become less useful for those with more extended experience [32].

Autonomy. Being obliged or pressured to be part of a gamification system in a prescriptive way can be detrimental [28]. Self-determination theory states that autonomy is one of the human psychological needs [33]. Flexibility and freedom of choice in tasks and goal allocation, primarily when performed collectively within groups, can encourage better teamwork collaboration, and reduce the likelihood of conflicts. For example, as identified in the result of this study that, pre-defined steps in a gamification tunnelling based technique, e.g. progress bar with tasks and milestones, might be preferred by staff who prefer serialism. Alternatively, staff who have higher autonomy and prefer holism may experience such monitoring and feedback as negative reinforcement.

3.3   Goal Related Risk Factors

The results identified some risks which can be introduced to the teamwork environment can be related to the goals factors, either main gamification goals, e.g. increase staff performance or personal staff goals, e.g. winning rewards.

Goal Assignment. Goals in teamwork can be assigned directly such as by a manager, or collectively among team members. Assigning goals might affect the motivation to perform a task. For instance, _"the directly-assigned goals make staff working like a machine and affect their creativity in a task and the interest to perform it"_. On the other hand, in collective goal assignment, staff with high self-efficacy and confidence in their skills and ability to reach goals have more influence in setting goals for the team [34] and this result in _stress_ to others afterwards. Staff with high self-efficacy would prefer more challenging goals than staff with lower self-efficacy [34]. Hence, managing the participation in goal setting is a key to set participatory goals.

Commitment Level. Staff with higher self-efficacy tend to be committed more to assigned goals than those with lower self-efficacy [34]. In teamwork, lack of commitment to goals is strongly related to the level of performance in a task [35]. This is affected by two factors; goal difficulty and goal clarity.

Goal Difficulty. This indicates "*a significant drop-off in performance as goal commitment declined in response to increasingly difficult goals*" [36]. Moreover, there is a contradictory relationship between goal commitment and goal difficulty [36, 37]. Our study showed that in gamification teamwork where goals have been set collectively or via managers, the possibility of staff facing difficulties or discomfort in achieving goals is high. Consequently, such difficulties might affect their engagement with the team and create risks like *lowering self-esteem* and *deviation* from the primary goal.

Goal Clarity. It refers to the metrics and steps required to consider a goal achieved. Lack of clarity is another source of risk in gamification which might have an impact on staff's ability, intention or desire to commit to a goal. An example of this would be the case of adding a progress bar to motivate a call centre agent to help a client in completing an online registration form, but without clearly explaining why the client is given the help, or what system is used to evaluate the outcome.

Conflict of Goals. One of the primary reasons for having ethical and well-being issues in gamification systems is its potential conflict between stakeholders interests [38]. In a teamwork environment, conflict of goals can occur with a collectively assigned goal. This might affect the gamification system and cause staff to have a *lack of engagement* or a *lack of interest* in a task, failing to achieve the system goal. A participant stressed the conflict between being "*on probation and having to perform well to get the job permanently, and being with staff who already passed their probation and have different goals in the system*". This can have an effect on the performance, such as working extra hours and doing other staff tasks who are not under the same pressure, to appear on the leaderboard and prove efficiency.

3.4   Task Related Risk Factors

Engaging staff more successfully with a task is a key objective of a gamification system. The result of this study indicated gamification risks on team working stemming mainly from the characteristics of the task being subject to gamification techniques. For example, applying a gamification element such as a leaderboard - which follows a competitive ecology - to a collaborative task could have a negative impact on the intra-group relationships. In the following section, we explore three task-related risk factors about gamification in teamwork.

Nature of Task. A quantitative based task might introduce a risk such as *reduce the quality* of the work. For example, customer satisfaction may suffer if the reward is based on the number -rather than the quality - of customer calls. In quality tasks, the risk can be seen by the lack of clarity in setting task specification and requirements. In other words, one way to judge staff performance in quality based tasks is the systematic performance judgment based on electronic monitoring or feedback; this might increase the chance of *unfairly judge* staff performance, e.g. using predesigned automated measurements. Participants argued that: "*it is unfair to be judged only based on monitoring customer calls*", implying that the work required cannot be accurately reflected solely by the actual effort required. They added: "*the quality might be affected by a variety of elements like the level of difficulty and clarity in customers' requests as some are easier than others*".

Also, risks might also occur if the task is of a competitive nature. Our analysis of the observation notes suggested that adding a gamification element to a competitive task can still affect the required level of collaboration among staff in the work environment. For example in the call centre, staff may choose not to share a good solution for common customers issue with their colleagues to increase their chance to uniquely and efficiently solve more customers complains and win the reward. Similarly, risks also can occur when adding a gamification element to a collaborative task. Our study indicated that a situation like social loafing, where individuals reduce their effort when working with a group and rely on others, has a high chance to appear if a collective task is motivated using inter-group competition.

Measurement. Measuring staff performance is essential to decide on rewards and feedback provided through gamification elements. Failure or limitation in such measurement can lead to side-effect on the teamwork environment. Two main factors are duration and frequency.

Timing. The real-time ability in gamification elements to track staff performance and send real-time feedback makes the duration of the measurement a source of risk, e.g. unfair judgement. For instance, if the measurement of staff engagement in answering a call is based on real-time voice analysis, such as the level of comfort of the client and the friendliness of the call agent, this might lead to unfair judgments. The staff could be affected via various elements, e.g. difficult customer or inquiry during the performance measurement duration in such motivational technique which might cause *unfair judgment* of their engagement in a task. A participant argued that: "*judgment based on real-time observation of our performance might be affected by reasons like difficult customer or issue which could increase the possibility of bias*".

Frequency. Some staff may be more motivated by a daily performance report, while others would prefer it at the end of the task, as evidenced by one participant who stated: "*I prefer to be measured on a monthly basis to be motivated more as I might feel frustrated if I know the result before, like based on weekly or daily results*". Hence, having both kinds of staff on the same team might have adverse effects on the team.

Resources. The availability and accessibility of resources are essential factors which assist staff in performing tasks more effectively. For example, LiveOps, an application for online call centres, facilitates the real-time recording of customers' personal details. Hence, in competitive teamwork environments, where staff compete to win rewards, access to such resources plays a vital role in both individual and team performance. As a result, careful consideration is needed to avoid introducing *unwanted bias* which could affect staff motivation. In the call centre observed, it was noticed that some tasks required external resources, i.e., resources from another, potentially competing, team. This made the possibility of winning the gamification reward dependent on resources from others, which affected the gamification system and created risks. One participant in the call centre commented that *"some tasks required external resources from others which might affect the competition"*. Similarly, in such situations, where there are team metrics and team rewards, the likelihood of other negative behaviours such as <u>work intimidation</u> is increased.

3.5   Gamification Design Related Risk Factors

Gamification elements refer to those motivational techniques which can be added to the environment to engage, motivate, and monitor staff involvement in the workplace, to increase their engagement and achieve business goals. Commonly used examples of such elements are points, leaderboards, badges and missions. The digital nature of the motivational elements adds more effective features such as real-time monitoring and feedback, and tractability and traceability of staff's performance. However, the gamification element also introduces risks, especially around the lack of validation and implementation strategies. For example in the call centre observed, some staff continued to work without taking breaks, due to their perception that their performance - as shown on the leaderboard - was being scrutinised by other staff in the department. This might have a negative impact on the quality of their work or possibly their well-being. Below, we discuss the two main risk factors we identified about the gamification elements.

Monitoring. Monitoring is an essential mechanism of most gamification elements which support the enhancement of staff performance. It can help staff to engage more in a task by regulating their performance or behaviours. However, monitoring can also have negative consequences in a teamwork environment, due to the following factors.

Visibility. It was noticed in the call centre observed that some staff had concerns regarding what would be visible to colleagues, either in the same or other teams. For example, displaying the number of calls each team member has answered could impact <u>the coherence of the group</u> via dividing staff into new intra-groups based on their performance in a task [39]. Staff preferred their current performance to be visible to their managers or themselves only, with the choice to share it with others.

Accessibility. In a gamification system, decisions are made based on information gathered from the environment. In a teamwork setting, the accessibility of staff information in the monitoring technique might have a negative influence on the teamwork. For example, one agent in the call centre commented: *"I prefer to have the ability to decide what the system can access regarding my personal information and also what my team members are able to access"*. Risks like <u>infringe staff autonomy</u> can result from monitoring staff as they perform a task. For example, a supervisor in the call centre mentioned that they could access and monitor staff calls at any time. Some staff in the call centre agreed that they *"prefer to know the accessibility time and the sort of information that has been collected"*.

The Storage of the Data. The staff could have concerns about the type of information stored on the system and the access to such information. In a teamwork environment, a risk can be seen when performing competitive tasks, where teams might have access to data stored by other teams which might have a negative effect on the gamification system, i.e. *ineffective competition*. For example, in a fitness application where people are motivated by comparing their performance with peers, making the stored history available to others might affect the competition and *kill the joy* of the system.

Reward System. The primary motivator of most gamification elements is the reward mechanism. A reward system is another essential factor of the gamification that needs careful consideration to avoid adversely affecting the teamwork. Within the workplace, the gamification reward takes the form of physical rewards, feedback, or public recognition. The reward might be a source of risks in a gamification system due to the following factors.

The Strategy. Staff have a variety of preferences regarding how they want to be rewarded, which makes the strategy a potential risk factor in a teamwork environment. The strategy of the reward can be seen as a risk when the strategy introduces a sense of *perceived exploitation* in the workplace. Exploitation can occur when staff feel that their extra performance and quality of work are not rewarded. For example, this can happen when the reward strategy in place only rewards the best performance. It would be preferable, in such circumstances, to have a gamification strategy which recognised everyone's performance, and hence, supported teamwork.

The Ability to Win the Reward. Staff with low self-esteem might have difficulty to participate in tasks in teamwork when the ability to win the reward is high, which could have a negative effect on the coherence of the team. In the call centre observed, staff could be classified into two categories, those who preferred to be motivated to win the reward using a challenge, and those who found it a source of obstruction. Mixing both types of staff in the same team or same competition might affect the system and create a risk such as *lack of group cohesion* in the workplace.

The Timing. A reward in a gamification system can either be synchronous or asynchronous. In real-time, the system allows managers to provide synchronous rewards, such as real-time feedback. This can happen when the required goal of the task is achieved, even before the end of the task time. One example would be answering the target number of calls before the end of the week or month. In the call centre, some staff stated that they: *"prefer to be rewarded after finishing the task not to lose my motivation"*. However, a participant mentioned that *"I sometimes need extrinsic motivation while performing a task to increase my intrinsic motivation"*. In teamwork, especially in competitive tasks, receiving synchronous feedback might *affect the quality* of the work negatively, especially when staff feel they have little chance of winning the competition.

The Value. A low-value reward might demotivate staff, limiting their engagement with a task, and affecting their quality of work. The value of the reward should reflect the actual effort staff contribute to a task. In teamwork, for collaborative tasks, the collaboration might be affected when some staff are less motivated to participate in the task due to their perception of low-value rewards. The overall finding indicates that the value of the reward is recommended to be heavily connected to the level of performance staff required to win the reward, to avoid the risk of reducing motivation.

The Nature of the Reward. This can have different forms, e.g. physical reward, feedback, or public recognition. In the call centre observed, all of these rewards were used to motivate staff. The impact of the nature of the reward is heavily connected with the personality of individuals. The differences in staff preferences about the nature of reward might cause a risk in teamwork effectiveness, which can, in turn, affect the achievement of business goals. Some agents commented that *"we feel more motivated to participate in a task with physical rewards rather than other types of rewards".* Risks like *negative participation* might occur in the system applied in teamwork when some members are less motivated as a result of the nature of the reward.

4   Gamification Risks Vs Risk Management Strategies

The analysis in Sect. 3 demonstrated the need for careful consideration and design principles when applying gamification elements and managing their risks on teamwork. In this section, we link the risks discussed in Sect. 3 with a set of 22 strategies proposed

Table 2. Gamification Risks vs management strategies

Risk	Exemplar of mitigation strategy
Free-Riding	Auditing, member checking, random monitoring, get everyone involved, commitment, voting, common ground rules, reward individual contribution
Meet the minimum requirements	Get everyone involved, commitment, voting, common ground rules, norms
Performance Misjudgements	Auditing, peer-rating, member checking, self-assessment,
Clustering groups	Auditing, commitment, facilitator
Lowering self-esteem	Reward for of individual contribution, random monitoring
Counterproductive comparison	Auditing, Anonymity
Negative pressure	Auditing, reward for helping others, reward individual contribution
Anchoring bias	Common ground rules, commitment, transparency
Bribe for exchange	Get everyone involved, commitment, voting, common ground rules
Work Intimidation	Auditing, member checking, random monitoring, reward for helping others, norms
Novelty effect	Anonymity, rotations sensitivity
Deviation from goal	Reward for of individual contribution
Lack of engagement	Peer-rating, member checking, self-assessment
Reduce task quality	Reward for of individual contribution, random monitoring
Social loafing	Auditing, member checking, random monitoring, get everyone involved, commitment, voting, common ground rules
Infringe autonomy	Anonymity, managerial level monitoring, rotations sensitivity
Kill of the joy	Anonymity, rotations sensitivity, random monitoring
Exploitation	Common ground rules, commitment, peer-rating, member checking, self-assessment, transparency

in [14] to detect and manage the potential effects of the gamification system on teamwork. A focus group with seven participants from different professional and academic background was conducted to map identified risks to mitigation strategies. Table 2 gives a summary of the findings. Risk management strategies can be applied (i) to detect and identify risks, (ii) to prevent or reduce the chance of the risk, (iii) to resolve the risks or alleviate their effect when it happens.

Risks about staff performance when doing a job as a group, e.g. *free-riding, social loafing* and *work intimidation,* can be detected and alleviated using strategies which employ *auditing, member checking* and *random monitoring.* Gamification design strategies like a *reward for helping others* and *reward for of individual contribution* can be then applied as resolution strategies. Strategies revolving around setting rules and agreements like *common ground rules* and *commitment* can be used to prevent or reduce the likelihood of risks related to *misjudgement* and honesty like *anchoring bias* and *exploitation.*

The observation and interviews in the two call centres involved in this study showed that some risks need to be managed during the stage of gamification design and its introduction to a teamwork environment, whilst other risks might need to be managed when they or their indicators appear while the system is in operation. Some risks can benefit from being managed at both times. Management strategies that help setting up agreements and rules amongst multidiscipline staff involved in gamification would fit more at the design stage. Practitioners and managers interviewed agreed that strategies for collective agreement and participatory decision making like, *get everyone involved, commitment, voting* are best applied at the design stages to increase the intrinsic motivation and acceptance of a gamification system. This is due to taking part in its design process and hence reducing the chance of risks like *work to meet the minimum requirements, bribe for exchange, social loafing* and *free riding.* While the system is already in operation, surveillance strategies like *peer-rating, member checking and self-assessment* can help to detect and possibly resolve risks related to measurements and rewarding such as *misjudgements* of performance and *lack of engagement* in collective tasks or goals.

Finally, our strategies to manage risks raised a concern about the possibility of causing a domino effect, where a strategy might introduce or trigger more secondary unwanted risks and effects. For example, applying transparency strategy in staff performance as a risk management strategy could help to detect and alleviate risks in relation to misconception, conspiracy and unfairness such as, *anchoring bias, misjudgements* of performance and *perceived exploitation.* However, this strategy might introduce another risk like *infringe autonomy, negative pressure* and *lowering self-esteem* which might also trigger further risks such as *reduced task quality* and *deviation from goal.* Hence, this raises the need for a holistic method which utilises techniques like a participatory design, simulation and rehearsal for predicting scenarios, consensus building and catering for the multiple viewpoints.

5 Conclusion and Future Work

In this paper, we made the argument that gamification shall undertake a risk assessment and management process to cater for its potential side-effects on teamwork. As a first step towards proposing theory-informed methods for gamification risk management, the research we performed in this paper contributed with taxonomies of risks factors, exemplar risks and management strategies. In our future work, we will utilise this knowledge and develop a method for detecting gamification risks and assessing their mitigation strategies. This will add to the literature in risks assessment and augment approaches to risk management especially at the early stages of the systems development such as those proposed in [19, 40]. Given the human-intense nature of gamification, we speculate our method to have a participatory nature and employee techniques that help exploration and speculation such as role-playing, rehearsal, simulation and scenarios.

References

1. Shahri, A., Hosseini, M., Phalp, K., Taylor, J., Ali, R.: Towards a code of ethics for Gamification at enterprise. PoEM **197**, 235–245 (2014)
2. Forsyth, D.: An introduction to group dynamics (1992)
3. Barata, J., da Cunha, P.R., Abrantes, L.: Dealing with risks and workarounds - a guiding framework. PoEM **235**, 141–155 (2015)
4. Alter, S., Sherer, S.A.: A General, But Readily Adaptable Model of Information System Risk. CAIS (2004)
5. Muehlen, Zur, M., Rosemann, M.: Integrating risks in business process models. In: Presented at the ACIS 2005 Proceedings - 16th Australasian Conference on Information Systems December 1 (2005)
6. Suriadi, S. et al.: Current research in risk-aware business process management-overview, comparison, and gap analysis. CAIS **34**, 933–984 (2014)
7. Vilpola, I., Ojala, M., Kouri, I.: Risks and risk management in ERP project - cases in SME context. BIS, 179–186 (2006)
8. Zoet, M., Welke, R., Versendaal, J., Ravesteyn, P.: Aligning risk management and compliance considerations with business process development. E-Comm. Web Technol. **5692**, 157 (2009)
9. Stirna, J., Zdravkovic, J., Grabis, J., Sandkuhl, K.: Development of capability driven development methodology - experiences and recommendations. PoEM **305**, 251–266 (2017)
10. Morschheuser, B., Hassan, L., Werder, K., Hamari, J.: How to design gamification? A method for engineering gamified software. Inf. Softw. Technol (2018)
11. Kumar, J.: Gamification at work: designing engaging business software. In: Marcus, A. (ed.) DUXU 2013. LNCS, vol. 8013, pp. 528–537. Springer, Heidelberg (2013). https://doi.org/10.1007/978-3-642-39241-2_58
12. Apter, M.J., Kerr, J.H.: Adult Play. Garland Science (1991)
13. Thiebes, S., Lins, S., Basten, D.: Gamifying information systems - a synthesis of Gamification mechanics and dynamics. ECIS (2014)
14. Algashami, A., Shahri, A., McAlaney, J., Taylor, J., Phalp, K., Ali, R.: Strategies and Design principles to minimize negative side-effects of digital motivation on teamwork. Persuasive **10171**, 267–278 (2017)

15. Saunders, M., Lewis, P., Thornhill, A.: Research Methods for Business Students. Pearson Education (2009)
16. Deterding, S., Dixon, D., Khaled, R., Nacke, L.: From game design elements to gamefulness - defining "gamification". In: Presented at the The th International Academic MindTrek Conference Envisioning Future Media Environments (2011)
17. Ahn, von, L.: Games with a Purpose. IEEE Comput. **39**, 92–94 (2006)
18. Fogg, B.J.: Creating persuasive technologies - an eight-step design process. Persuasive **350**, 1 (2009)
19. Boehm, B.W.: Software risk management: principles and practices. IEEE Softw. **8**, 32–41 (1991)
20. Friedman, B., Kahn, Peter H., Borning, A., Huldtgren, A.: Value sensitive design and information systems. In: Doorn, N., Schuurbiers, D., van de Poel, I., Gorman, Michael E. (eds.) Early engagement and new technologies: Opening up the laboratory. PET, vol. 16, pp. 55–95. Springer, Dordrecht (2013). https://doi.org/10.1007/978-94-007-7844-3_4
21. Dion, K.L.: Group cohesion: from "field of forces" to multidimensional construct. Group Dyn. Theor. Res. Pract. **4**, 7–26 (2000)
22. Shahri, A., Hosseini, M., Phalp, K., Taylor, J., Ali, R.: Exploring and conceptualising software-based motivation within enterprise. PoEM **267**, 241–256 (2016)
23. Saunders, M., Lewis, P., Thornhill, A.: Research Methods for Business Students. Pearson Education (2009)
24. Braun, V., Clarke, V.: Using thematic analysis in psychology. Qual. Res. Psychol. **3**, 77–101 (2006)
25. Viswesvaran, C., Ones, D.S.: Perspectives on models of job performance. Int. J. Sel. Assess. **8**, 216–226 (2000)
26. Ball, K.S., Margulis, S.T.: Electronic monitoring and surveillance in call centres: a framework for investigation. New Technol. Work Employ. **26**, 113–126 (2011)
27. Liu, Y., Alexandrova, T., Nakajima, T.: Gamifying intelligent environments. In: Presented at the the 2011 International ACM workshop, New York, USA (2011)
28. Raftopoulos, M.: Towards gamification transparency: a conceptual framework for the development of responsible gamified enterprise systems. J. Gaming Virt. Worlds **6**, 159–178 (2014)
29. Greenberg, B.S., Sherry, J., Lachlan, K., Lucas, K., Holmstrom, A.: Orientations to video games among gender and age groups. Simul. Gaming **41**, 238–259 (2008)
30. Griffiths, M.D., Davies, M.N.O., Chappell, D.: Breaking the stereotype: the case of online gaming. Cyberpsychology Behav. **6**, 81–91 (2003)
31. Williams, D., Consalvo, M., Caplan, S., Yee, N.: Looking for gender: gender roles and behaviors among online gamers. J. Commun. **59**, 700–725 (2009)
32. Koivisto, J., Hamari, J.: Demographic differences in perceived benefits from gamification. Comput. Hum. Behav. **35**, 179–188 (2014)
33. Ryan, R.M., Deci, E.L.: Self-determination theory and the facilitation of intrinsic motivation, social development, and well-being. Am. Psychol. **55**, 68–78 (2000)
34. Locke, E.A., Latham, G.P.: Building a practically useful theory of goal setting and task motivation: a 35-year odyssey. Am. Psychol. **57**, 705–717 (2002)
35. Locke, E.A., Latham, G.P., Erez, M.: The determinants of goal commitment. Acad. Manag. Rev. **13**, 23–39 (1988)
36. Erez, M., Zidon, I.: Effect of goal acceptance on the relationship of goal difficulty to performance. J. Appl. Psychol. **69**, 69–78 (1984)
37. Locke, E.A.: Relation of goal level to performance with a short work period and multiple goal levels. J. Appl. Psychol. **67**, 512–514 (1982)

38. Kim, T.W., Werbach, K.: More than just a game: ethical issues in gamification. Ethics Inf. Technol. **18**, 157–173 (2016)
39. Shahri, A., Hosseini, M., Phalp, K., Taylor, J., Ali, R.: How to engineer Gamification: the consensus, the best practice and the grey areas. J. Organ. End User Comput. **31** (2019)
40. Asnar, Y., Giorgini, P., Mylopoulos, J.: Goal-driven risk assessment in requirements engineering. Requir. Eng. **16**, 101–116 (2010)

A Composition Method to Model Collective Behavior

Junsup Song and Moonkun Lee[✉]

Chonbuk National University, 567 Beakje-dearo Deokjin-gu,
54896 Jeonju-si Jeonbuk, Republic of Korea
moonkun@jbnu.ac.kr

Abstract. It is very important to understand system *behavior*s in collective pattern for each knowledge domain. However, there are structural limitations to represent collective behaviors due to the size of system components and the complexity of their interactions, causing the state explosion problem. Further composition with other systems is mostly impractical due to exponential growth of their size and complexity. This paper presents an abstraction method to model the collective behaviors, based on a new concept of domain engineering: *behavior ontology*. Firstly, the ontology defines each collective behavior of a system from *active ontology*. Secondly, the behaviors are formed in a quantifiably abstract lattice, called *n:2-Lattice*. Thirdly, a lattice can be composed with other lattices based on quantifiably common elements. The composition can be interpreted as behavioral composition, and can reduce all the unnecessary composition not related to the behaviors in the lattices. In order to demonstrate the feasibility of the method, two examples, Emergency Medical Service and Health Care Service systems, are selected and implemented on a Behavior Ontology tool, called PRISM, which has been developed on ADOxx Meta-Modelling Platform.

Keywords: Collective behavior · Behavior ontology · n:2-Lattice
Domain engineering · PRISM · ADOxx

1 Introduction

There are strong needs to represent system *behavior*s for each knowledge domain in some collective patterns. However, the needs cannot be easily satisfied due to the structural limitations caused by the considerable size of system components and the complexity of their interactions, generally known as *state explosion problem* [1]. Further composition with other systems seems to be impractical due to exponential growth of such explosion caused by their size and complexity [2].

In order to overcome these limitations, this paper presents an abstraction method to model the collective behaviors of systems, based on a new concept of domain engineering: *behavior ontology* [3]. The previous researches have been reported in the literatures [3]. However, the present research in this paper extended the previous researches with other domains and further made composition of the system behaviors

R. A. Buchmann et al. (Eds.): PoEM 2018, LNBIP 335, pp. 121–137, 2018.
https://doi.org/10.1007/978-3-030-02302-7_8

possible so that composite collective system behaviors can be constructed for larger and more complex domains. The approach is shown in Fig. 1, as follows:

(1) Firstly, a class hierarchy of a domain is constructed based on active ontology, where all the actors of a domain and their interactions are defined as classes.

(2) Secondly, each collective behavior of the domain is defined in *regular expression* [4], where each behavior is defined as a sequence of interactions among actors. The behaviors will be presented in a hierarchical order based on their inclusion relations, forming a special lattice, called *n:2-Lattice* [5].

(3) Thirdly, each behavior is quantifiably abstracted with a notion of cardinality and capacity for actors in behavior. This notion will be used to select appropriate behaviors and their relations from the lattice and to make quantitatively equivalent composition with other lattices.

(4) Fourthly, the abstract behavior lattice, *Abstract n:2-Lattice*, is constructed.

(5) Finally, two abstract behavior lattices can be composed for common actors with same cardinality and capacity between two lattices. It implies quantitatively equivalent composition of two types of collective behaviors.

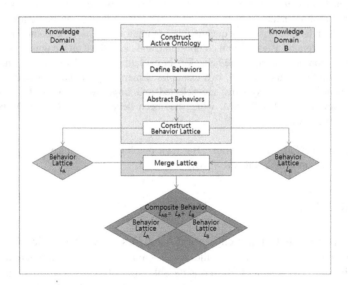

Fig. 1. An engineering and composite approach to model collective behaviors

In order to demonstrate the feasibility of the approach, *Emergency Medical Service* (EMS) [3] and *Health Care Service* (HCS) systems are presented for each steps. The examples show that the method is very effective and efficient to construct a hierarchy of collective behaviors in a lattice and that the composition of two collective behaviors is systematically performed by the composition operation of two lattices. Further, a tool, called PRISM, has been developed on ADOxx Meta-Modelling Platform [6] in order to demonstrate its feasibility and practicality.

This paper is organized as follows. Section 2 presents the approach in steps with an example for both EMS and HCS. Section 3 presents an application of an instance to EMS and HCS examples. Section 4 analyzes the approach and compares it with other approaches. Finally, conclusions and future research will be discussed in Sect. 5.

2 Approach

This section presents each steps of the approach to model collective behaviors for a system.

2.1 Step 1: Active Ontology (AO)

Definition 2.1. Actor (Ac). *Actor* is defined as a set of classes, that is, *Class* $C_1, \ldots, C_n \in Ac$. It implies a set of components in a system, and is represented as a set of classes in Active Ontology.

Definition 2.2. Interaction (It). *Interaction* is defined as a set of an ordered relation between two actors, that is, *Interaction* $a_1, \ldots, a_m \in It$, where for each interaction $a_i = \langle C_{i_s}, C_{i_t} \rangle_{in}$, *Class* $C_{i_s}, C_{i_t} \in Ac$. It implies that Ac C_{i_s} moves in Ac C_{i_t}, as an interaction between two actors, as defined in Definition 2.1.

Definition 2.3. Active Ontology (AO). Active Ontology is defined as $AO = \langle Ac, It \rangle$, based on Definitions 2.1 and 2.2. It consists of a set of system components as a set of classes and a set of interactions among the classes.

The first step is to design Active Ontology for EMS and HCS services. Active ontology consists of classes and subclasses in the domain, including their interactions.

A. Emergency Medical Service (EMS)

EMS service contains four classes: *Ambulance* (A), *Patient* (P), and *Place* (PL). Note that Place contains *Location* (L) and *Hospital* (H) as subclasses. Similarly, Hospital includes *Bill* (Bi) as subclass, too. The system's elements represent in the left side of Fig. 2.

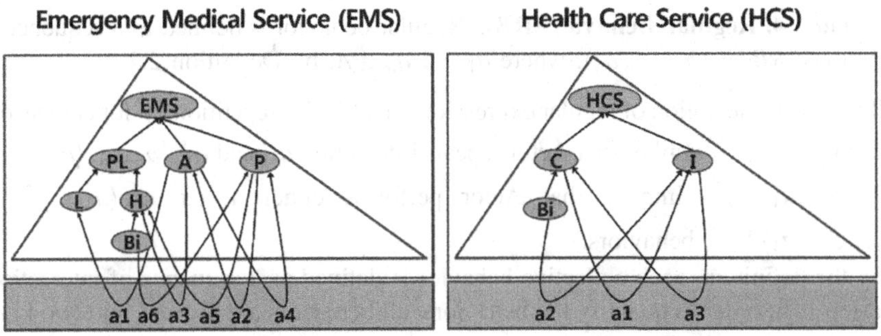

Fig. 2. Active Ontology for Emergency Medical Service (EMS) and Health Care Service (HCS)

- *Actors*: There are 5 different kinds of actors:

(1) Patient (*P*): Person to be transported.
(2) Ambulance (*A*): Actor to deliver object.
(3) Location (*L*): Place for Patient to be delivered from.
(4) Hospital (*H*): Place for Patient to be delivered to.
(5) Bill(*Bi*): Bill received by Patient from Hospital.

- *Interactions*: There are 6 kinds of interactions:

(1) $a_1 = \langle A, L \rangle_{in}$: Ambulance goes to Location
(2) $a_2 = \langle P, A \rangle_{in}$: Patient gets on Ambulance.
(3) $a_3 = \langle A, H \rangle_{in}$: Ambulance goes to Hospital.
(4) $a_4 = \langle P, A \rangle_{out}$: Patient gets off Ambulance.
(5) $a_5 = \langle P, H \rangle_{in}$: Patient goes to Hospital.
(6) $a_6 = \langle Bi, P \rangle_{in}$: Hospital sends Bill to Patient.

B.   Health Care Service (HCS)

This system contains two classes: *Customer* (C) and *Insurance Company* (I). And Customer has one subclass: *Bill* (B). The right side of Fig. 2 shows the relationship between classes and subclass.

- *Actors*: There are 3 different kinds of actors:

(1) Customer (*C*): Person to be insured.
(2) Insurance Company (*I*): Company to insure.
(3) Bill (*Bi*): Payment requested by Insurance Company to Customer.

- *Interactions*: There are 3 kinds of interactions:

(1) $a_1 = \langle C, I \rangle_{in}$: Customer contacts to Insurance Company.
(2) $a_2 = \langle Bi, I \rangle_{in}$: Customer sends a Bill to Insurance Company.
(3) $a_3 = \langle Bi, I \rangle_{out}$: Insurance Company pays the Bill for Customer.

2.2   Step 2: Regular Behaviors (RB)

Definition 2.4. Regular Behavior (RB). Regular behavior is defined as a sequence of interactions: $RB_i = \langle a_1, \ldots, a_n \rangle$, where $a_1, \ldots, a_n \in A$, by Definition 2.2.

It follows the basic notion of regular expression, i.e., '$+$' for repetition, '|' for choice, etc. For example, $\langle a_1 \rangle^+$ implies that Actor repeats Interaction a_1, and $a_1, \langle a_2, a_3, \langle a_4 \rangle^+ \rangle^+ |$ $\langle a_1, a_2, a_3, \langle a_4 \rangle^+ \rangle^+$ implies that Actor performs either $a_1, \langle a_2, a_3, \langle a_4 \rangle^+ \rangle^+$ or $\langle a_1, a_2, a_3, \langle a_4 \rangle^+ \rangle^+$ behaviors.

By the definition, each collective behavior is defined as a sequence of interactions from step 1. In order to quantify the behaviors, all behaviors are divided into two kinds

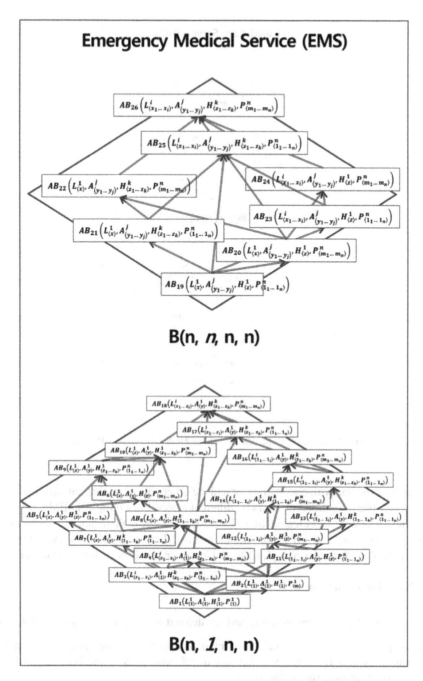

Fig. 3. Abstract Behavior lattice for EMS B(n, *1*, n, n) and B(n, *n*, n, n)

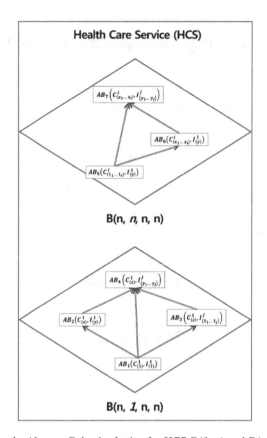

Fig. 4. Abstract Behavior lattice for HCS B(1, n) and B(n, n)

of behaviors: the one with one main actor and the other with more than one actors. In the other words, there are different views by different actors. For example, in EMS there are four kind of actors, represented as B(L, A, H, P). Then, there are two behaviors, represented as B(n, 1, n, n) for 1 Ambulance and B(n, n, n, n) for n Ambulances. Similarly to B(C, I) for HCS, B(1, n) for 1 Customer and B(n, n) for n Customer.

A.   EMS for B (n, 1, n, n)

There are total 18 behaviors possible and are defined in regular expression as follows:

(1) $RB_1 = \langle a_1, a_2, a_3, a_4, a_5, a_6 \rangle$: An Ambulance goes to a Location, gets a Patient on, goes to a Hospital, gets the patient off, who goes to the hospital, and the hospital sends a Bill to the patient.

(2) $RB_2 = \langle a_1, a_2, a_3, a_4, a_5, \langle a_6 \rangle^+ \rangle$: An Ambulance goes to a Location, gets a Patient on, goes to a Hospital, gets the patient off, who goes to the hospital, and the hospital sends number of Bills to the patient.

(3) $RB_3 = \langle a_1, a_2, a_3, a_4, a_5, a_6 \rangle^+$: A repeating behavior of B_1.

(4) $RB_4 = \langle a_1, a_2, a_3, a_4, a_5, \langle a_6 \rangle^+ \rangle^+$: A repeating behavior of B_2.

(5) $RB_5 = \langle a_1, \langle a_2 \rangle^+, a_3, \langle a_4, a_5, a_6 \rangle^+ \rangle^+$: An Ambulance goes to a Location, gets Patients on, goes to a Hospital, gets the patients off, who go to the hospital, and the hospital sends a Bill to each patient. And it repeats itself.

(6) $RB_6 = \langle a_1, \langle a_2 \rangle^+, a_3, \langle a_4, a_5, \langle a_6 \rangle^+ \rangle^+ \rangle^+$: An Ambulance goes to a Location, gets Patients on, goes to a Hospital, gets the patients off, which go to the hospital, and the hospital sends Bills to each patient. And it repeats itself.

(7) $RB_7 = \langle a_1, \langle a_2 \rangle^+, \langle a_3, a_4, a_5, a_6 \rangle^+ \rangle^+$: An Ambulance goes to a Location, gets Patients on, goes to Hospitals, to get some of the patients off until all the patients off, each of whose groups goes into its hospital, and the hospital sends Bill to each patient. And it repeats itself.

(8) $RB_8 = \langle a_1, \langle a_2 \rangle^+, \langle a_3, a_4, a_5, \langle a_6 \rangle^+ \rangle^+ \rangle^+$: An Ambulance goes to a Location, gets Patients on, goes to Hospitals, to get some of the patients off until all the patients off, each of whose groups goes into its hospital, and the hospital sends Bills to each Patient. And it repeats itself.

(9) $RB_9 = \left\langle \begin{array}{c} a_1, \langle a_2 \rangle^+, \\ a_3, \langle a_4, a_5, a_6 \rangle^+ | \langle a_3, a_4, a_5, a_6 \rangle^+ \end{array} \right\rangle^+$: A repeating behavior of B_5, B_7.

(10) $RB_{10} = \left\langle \begin{array}{c} a_1, \langle a_2 \rangle^+, \\ a_3, \langle a_4, a_5, \langle a_6 \rangle^+ \rangle^+ | \langle a_3, a_4, a_5, \langle a_6 \rangle^+ \rangle^+ \end{array} \right\rangle^+$: A repeating behavior of RB_6, RB_8.

(11) $RB_{11} = \langle \langle a_1, a_2 \rangle^+, \langle a_3, a_4, a_5, a \rangle_6^+ \rangle^+$: An Ambulance goes to Locations, gets Patients on, goes to a Hospital, gets the patients off, who go to the hospital, and the hospital sends Bill to each Patient. And it repeats itself.

(12) $RB_{12} = \langle \langle a_1, a_2 \rangle^+, \langle a_3, a_4, a_5, a_6 \rangle^+ \rangle^+$: An Ambulance goes to Locations, gets Patients on, goes to Hospitals, to get some of the patients off until all the patients off, each of whose groups goes into its hospital, and the hospital sends Bill to each patient. And it repeats itself.

(13) $RB_{13} = \langle \langle a_1, a_2 \rangle^+, a_3, \langle a_4, a_5, \langle a_6 \rangle^+ \rangle^+ \rangle^+$: An Ambulance goes to Locations, gets Patients on, goes to a Hospital, gets the patients off, which go to the hospital, and the hospital sends Bills to each Patient. And it repeats itself.

(14) $RB_{14} = \langle \langle a_1, a_2 \rangle^+, \langle a_3, a_4, a_5, \langle a_6 \rangle^+ \rangle^+ \rangle^+$: An Ambulance goes to Locations, gets Patients on, goes to Hospitals, to get some of the patients off until all the patients off, each of whose groups goes into its hospitals, and the hospital send Bills to each Patient. And it repeats itself.

(15) $RB_{15} = \left\langle \begin{array}{c} \langle a_1, a_2 \rangle^+, \\ a_3, \langle a_4, a_5, a_6 \rangle^+ | \langle a_3, a_4, a_5, a_6 \rangle^+ \end{array} \right\rangle^+$: A repeating behavior of B_{11}, B_{12}.

(16) $RB_{16} = \left\langle \begin{array}{c} \langle a_1, a_2 \rangle^+, \\ a_3, \langle a_4, a_5, \langle a_6 \rangle^+ \rangle^+ | \langle a_3, a_4, a_5, \langle a_6 \rangle^+ \rangle^+ \end{array} \right\rangle^+$: A repeating behavior of B_{13}, B_{14}.

(17) $RB_{17} = \left\langle \begin{array}{c} a_1, \langle a_2 \rangle^+ | \langle a_1, a_2 \rangle^+, \\ a_3, \langle a_4, a_5, a_6 \rangle^+ | \langle a_3, a_4, a_5, a_6 \rangle^+ \end{array} \right\rangle^+$: A repeating behavior of B_9, B_{15}.

(18) $RB_{18} = \left\langle \begin{array}{c} a_1, \langle a_2 \rangle^+ | \langle a_1, a_2 \rangle^+, \\ a_3, \langle a_4, a_5, \langle a_6 \rangle^+ \rangle^+ | \langle a_3, a_4, a_5, \langle a_6 \rangle^+ \rangle^+ \end{array} \right\rangle^+$: A repeating behavior of B_{10}, B_{16}.

B.   HCS for B (1, n)

There are total 4 behaviors possible and are defined in regular expression as follows:

(1) $RB_1 = \langle a_1, a_2, a_3 \rangle$: A customer calls to an Insurance Company, then sends a Bill to, and Insurance Company pays the Bill.

(2) $RB_2 = \langle a_1, \langle a_2, a_3 \rangle^+ \rangle^+$: A customer calls to an Insurance Company, then sends some Bills to, and Insurance Company pays the Bills.

(3) $RB_3 = \langle \langle a_1, a_2, a_3 \rangle^+ \rangle^+$: A customer calls to an Insurance Company, then sends a Bill to, and Insurance Company pays the Bill. And it repeats itself

(4) $RB_4 = \langle a_1, \langle a_2, a_3 \rangle^+ | \langle a_1, a_2, a_3 \rangle^+ \rangle^+$: A repeating behavior of B_2, B_3.

Note that regular behaviors for EMS B(n. 1, n, n) and HCS B(1, n) are presented here due to the size of the example. However similar approach can be made for n actors.

2.3   Step 3: Abstract Behaviors (AB)

In the second step, the regular behaviors from Step 2 are abstracted with respect to a number of actors and their capacity as follows:

- Cardinality: The number of actors in behavior.
- Capacity: The Capability of actor in behavior.

Definition 2.5. Abstract Behaviors (AB). Abstract behavior is defined as a tuple of actors with their cardinality and capacity: $AB_i \left(A_{\langle o_1, \ldots, o_n \rangle}^{\langle x \rangle}, B_{\langle o_1, \ldots, o_n \rangle}^{\langle x \rangle}, \ldots, Z_{\langle o_1, \ldots, o_n \rangle}^{\langle x \rangle} \right)$, where $A, B, \ldots, Z \in Ac$ by Definition 2.1, the cardinality and capacity of each actor are x and $\langle o_1, \ldots, o_n \rangle$, respectively. Further AB implies abstraction of these behaviors.

A.   EMS for B (n, 1, n, n)

18 regular behaviors are abstracted as shown in Fig. 3, by Definition 2.5. For example, the cardinality and capacity of $A_{\langle 1,2,2 \rangle}^{\langle 3 \rangle}$, $\langle 3 \rangle$ and $\langle 1, 2, 2 \rangle$ represent the number of Ambulances and the number of Patients for each Ambulance, respectively.

B.   HCS for B (1, n)

4 regular behaviors are abstracted in the lattice as shown in Fig. 4.

2.4 Step 4: Abstract Behavior Lattice (ABL)

Definition 2.6. Inclusion Relations. Inclusion Relations is defined as a relation two behaviors of Def 2.4: $RB_i \sqsubseteq RB_j$, where $RB_i = \langle a_{i_1}, \ldots, a_{i_n} \rangle$, $RB_j = \langle a_{j_1}, \ldots, a_{j_m} \rangle$, and $\langle a_{i_1}, \ldots, a_{i_n} \rangle$. is a sub-sequence of $\langle a_{j_1}, \ldots, a_{j_m} \rangle$. Further, if $RB_i \sqsubseteq RB_j$, then $AB_i \sqsubseteq AB_j$, where AB_i and AB_j are the abstract behaviors of RB_i and RB_j.

Definition 2.7. Abstract Behavior Lattice (ABL). Abstract Behavior Lattice is defined a lattice constructed by Definition 2.5 on abstract behaviors
Lattice can be constructed from Step 3, based on the inclusion relations among behaviors. Here we present the lattices for EMS and HSC examples.

A. EMS for B (n, 1, n, n) and HCS for B (1, n)

The Figs. 3 and 4 show the inclusion relations in EMS for B(n, 1, n, n) and HCS for B (1, n) with arrows, from which the abstract behavior lattices for EMS B(n, 1, n, n) and HCS B(1, n) are constructed as shown in Fig. 5. Note that the EMS lattices are shown in the left side of Fig. 5, and the HCS lattices in the right side of the figure.

2.5 Step 5: Composition

The last step is to make composition of two lattices for EMS and HCS. The steps of the composition are as follows:

(1) Firstly, the common actors between two abstract behavior lattices have to be selected. For the example, Patient from EMS is defined to be a common actor with Customer from HCS.
(2) Secondly, cardinality of the composition has to be selected for the common actors. For the example, there are two cases: one for the single cardinality and the other for the plural cardinality.

A. Composition for $EMS(L, A, H, P) \otimes_{EMS(P)=HCS(C)\&|P|=|C|=1} HCS(C, I)$

This is the first case of the composition for EMS and HCS with respect to Patient of Cardinality 1: $EMS(L, A, H, P) \otimes_{EMS(P)=HCS(C)\&|P|=|C|=1} HCS(C, I)$. $EMS(P) = HCS(C)$ implies that Patient from EMS is defined to be a common actor with Customer from HCS, and $|P| = |C| = 1$ implies that their cardinality is singular. The two top lattices of Fig. 5 shows the possible composition for EMS and HCS, and the top lattice of Fig. 6 shows that result of the composition: $(EMS(L, A, H, P) \otimes_{EMS(P)=HCS} (C)\&|P| = |C| = 1HCS(C, I))(L, A, H, P = C, I)_{|P|=|C|=1} = B(n, n, n, \mathbf{1}, n)$. There are total 4 possible collective behaviors, which is the half of the total composition with the same cardinality, that is, 8 behaviors, 2 from EMS by 4 from HCS, and is 1/18 of the total composition with the different cardinality, that is 72 behaviors, 18 from EMS by 4 from HCS.

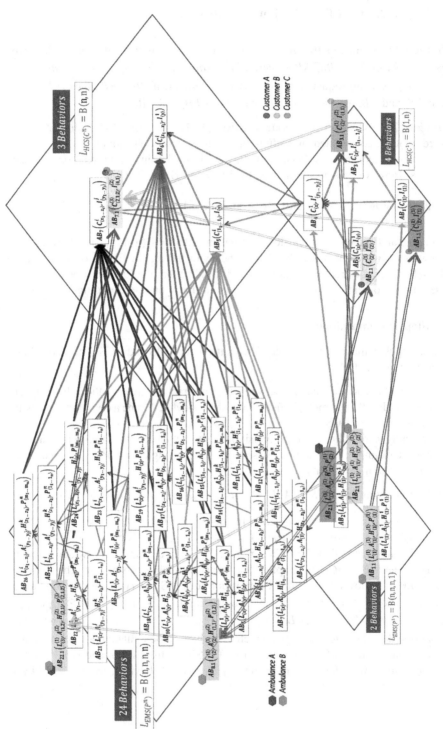

Fig. 5. Composition with plural cardinality for EMS and HCS

B.   Composition for $EMS(L,A,H,P) \otimes_{EMS(P)=HCS(C)\&|P|=|C|=n} HCS(C,I)$

This is the second case of the composition for EMS and HCS with respect to Patient of Cardinality n: $EMS(L,A,H,P) \otimes_{EMS(P)=HCS(C)\&|P|=|C|=n} HCS(C,I)$. $EMS(P) = HCS(C)$ implies that Patient from EMS is defined to be a common actor with Customer from HCS, and $|P| = |C| = n$ implies that their cardinality is plural. The two bottom lattices of Fig. 5 shows the possible composition for EMS and HCS, and the bottom lattice of Fig. 6 shows that result of the composition: $(EMS(L,A,H,P)\otimes_{EMS(P)=HCS}$ $(C)\&|P| = |C| = nHCS(C,I))(L,A,H,P = C,I)_{|P|=|C|=n} = B(n,n,n,\boldsymbol{n},n)$. There are total 36 possible collective behaviors, which is half of the total composition with the same cardinality, that is, 72 behaviors, 24 from EMS by 3 from HCS. Note that there are 8 more behaviors for EMS B(n, n, **n**, n) with n Ambulances and 3 more behaviors with HCS B(**n**, n) for n Customers. It is also 5.06% of the total composition with the different cardinality, that is, 189 behaviors, (18 + **8**) from EMS by (4 + **3**) from HCS.

3   Application

This section describes how the lattice can be used for specific instance of EMS and HCS occurrences. Figure 7 shows the case of $EMS\langle L_{\langle 3\rangle}^{\langle 1\rangle}, A_{\langle 1,2\rangle}^{\langle 2\rangle}, H_{\langle 2,1\rangle}^{\langle 2\rangle}, P_{\langle 2,1,2\rangle}^{\langle 3\rangle}\rangle$: 1 Location with 3 Patients, 2 Ambulances with seats of 1 and 2, 2 Hospitals with beds of 2 and 1, and 3 Patients with bills of 2, 1, and 2. The behaviors at Level 3 are omitted here, but contain detailed information about all the capabilities with IDs. Figure 7 shows the case of $HCS\langle C_{\langle 2,1,2\rangle}^{\langle 3\rangle}, I_{\langle 4,1\rangle}^{\langle 2\rangle}\rangle$: 3 Customers with bills of 2, 1 and 2, and 2 Insurance Companies with payments of 4 and 1. Other behaviors at Level 3 will contain detailed information about all the capabilities with IDs.

Figure 8 shows the composition of $EMS\langle L_{\langle 3\rangle}^{\langle 1\rangle}, A_{\langle 1,2\rangle}^{\langle 2\rangle}, H_{\langle 2,1\rangle}^{\langle 2\rangle}, P_{\langle 2,1,2\rangle}^{\langle 3\rangle}\rangle$ and $HCS\langle C_{\langle 2,1,2\rangle}^{\langle 3\rangle}, I_{\langle 4,1\rangle}^{\langle 2\rangle}\rangle$: $EMS \otimes_{P=C} HCS\langle L_{\langle 3\rangle}^{\langle 1\rangle}, A_{\langle 1,2\rangle}^{\langle 2\rangle}, H_{\langle 2,1\rangle}^{\langle 2\rangle}, P_{\langle 2,1,2\rangle}^{\langle 3\rangle}, I_{\langle 4,1\rangle}^{\langle 2\rangle}\rangle$. It represents that 3 Patients are transported to 2 Hospitals with 2 and 1 Beds by 2 Ambulance with 1 and 2 Seats for emergency treatments, received 2, 1, and 2 Bills from 2 Hospitals, respectively, and claimed the bills to 2 Insurance Companies for 4 and 1 Payments. This composition can be automatically generated between the abstract behavior lattices as shown in Figs. 5 and 6. The shaded behavior at the left top of Fig. 5 shows the behavior of $EMS\langle L_{\langle 3\rangle}^{\langle 1\rangle}, A_{\langle 1,2\rangle}^{\langle 2\rangle}, H_{\langle 2,1\rangle}^{\langle 2\rangle}, P_{\langle 2,1,2\rangle}^{\langle 3\rangle}\rangle$. The shaded behaviors below show each individual behavior in it. The shaded behavior at the right top of the figure shows the behavior of $HCS\langle C_{\langle 2,1,2\rangle}^{\langle 3\rangle}, I_{\langle 4,1\rangle}^{\langle 2\rangle}\rangle$. The lower ones show each individual behavior in it. The lines show the matching composition for both behaviors with respect to the same cardinality and capacity for the common actor, that is, EMS(P) = HCS(C). Finally, Fig. 6 shows the composite behavior for $EMS\langle L_{\langle 3\rangle}^{\langle 1\rangle}, A_{\langle 1,2\rangle}^{\langle 2\rangle}, H_{\langle 2,1\rangle}^{\langle 2\rangle}, P_{\langle 2,1,2\rangle}^{\langle 3\rangle}\rangle$.

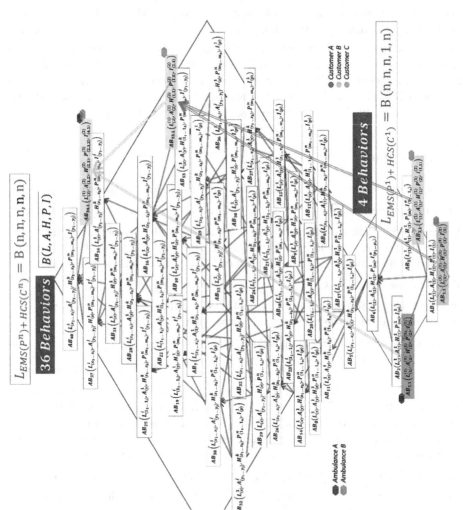

Fig. 6. The result of the composition in Fig. 7.

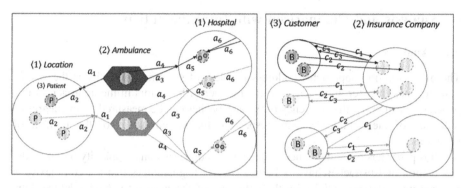

Fig. 7. Example of $EMS\,AB\left\langle L^{\langle 1\rangle}_{\langle 3\rangle}, A^{\langle 2\rangle}_{\langle 1,2\rangle}, H^{\langle 2\rangle}_{\langle 2,1\rangle}, P^{\langle 3\rangle}_{\langle 2,1,2\rangle}\right\rangle$ and $HCS\,AB\left\langle C^{\langle 3\rangle}_{\langle 2,1,2\rangle}, I^{\langle 2\rangle}_{\langle 4,1\rangle}\right\rangle$

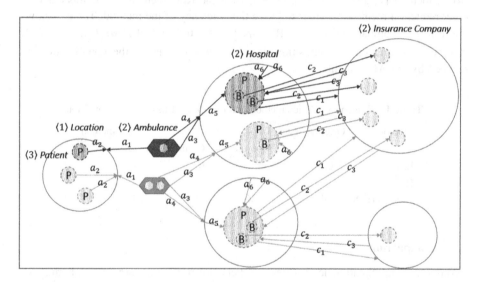

Fig. 8. Composition of EMS and HCS: $EMS\otimes_{P=C} HCS\left\langle L^{\langle 1\rangle}_{\langle 3\rangle}, A^{\langle 2\rangle}_{\langle 1,2\rangle}, H^{\langle 2\rangle}_{\langle 2,1\rangle}, P^{\langle 3\rangle}_{\langle 2,1,2\rangle}, I^{\langle 2\rangle}_{\langle 4,1\rangle}\right\rangle$

and $HCS\left\langle C^{\langle 3\rangle}_{\langle 2,1,2\rangle}, I^{\langle 2\rangle}_{\langle 4,1\rangle}\right\rangle$, that is, $EMS\otimes_{P=C} HCS\left\langle L^{\langle 1\rangle}_{\langle 3\rangle}, A^{\langle 2\rangle}_{\langle 1,2\rangle}, H^{\langle 2\rangle}_{\langle 2,1\rangle}, P^{\langle 3\rangle}_{\langle 2,1,2\rangle}, I^{\langle 2\rangle}_{\langle 4,1\rangle}\right\rangle$, on the lattice of $\left(EMS(L,A,H,P)\otimes_{EMS(P)=HCS(C)\,\&\,|P|=|C|=n} HCS(C,I)\right)(L,A,H,P=C,I)_{|P|=|C|=n}=B(n,n,n,\boldsymbol{n},n)$.

4 Analysis and Comparison with Implementation

4.1 Analysis

The most common approach to address problem of system complexity is the size of system states in other approaches, or the number of behaviors in the approach in this paper. Consequently, the efficiency of the approaches can be measured by the degree of reduction of the complexity with respect to the system states or the number of behaviors.

This paper has presented a new approach to reduce system complexity based on the new notion of Abstract Behaviors Lattice (ABL). It guarantees that the complexity is reduced inverse-exponentially by the definition of the *abstract behavior* lattice. Further, this method represents composition of two systems with common actors in the minimum states. Table 1 shows the comparing between the Reduction-by-Choice (RbC) method [7] and our approach. Note that the RbC method was compared with other reduction methods in order to prove the efficiency of the method. Table 1 shows the results of comparison with the RbC method for the case of $B_{EMS}(L_4^2, A_4^2, H_4^2, P_4^4)$, $B_{HCS}(C_4^4, I_4^1)$, and their composition. It shows how drastically the complexities are reduced by the ABL method.

Table 1. Comparing choice method and our method in the same condition

Methods	Original states	Choice		Our methods
		Conjunction	Complement	
EMS	746496	36	6	4
HCS	–	–	–	1
EMS ⊗ HCS	≥ 746496	≥ 36	≥ 6	4

4.2 Comparison

In order to comprehend general patterns of behavior of specific targets, i.e., humans or animals, large amount of data are collected by using various sensors, and the data can be used to extract useful information for analysis of the patterns and behavior, i.e., healthcare services based on human living patterns [8]. Such a data collection method using the sensors can increase degree of correctness of the patterns and behavior, but may require large amount of time and efforts to collect the data. Further the method only focuses on the patterns of the singular entities, but as a whole.

However, the method in the paper abstracts all the possible interactive behaviors among objects in the system based on system perspective, that is, as a whole, but as the singular entities. Therefore it is possible to comprehend all the bidirectional behavioral patterns of objects in the systems. In addition, it is possible to reduce the time and efforts to collect the data, including refinement, since the method models conceptually all the possible occurrence cases of the behaviors by limiting combinational conditions from the initial interactions to the target interactions among objects in the systems, not from collecting randomly unconditional data using sensors. For example, in the perspective of Ambulance from the example, an initial interaction can be the state before transport, a target interaction can be the state after transport, and a condition can be the capacity of Ambulance, that is, 1.

Table 2. Comparing between behavior ontology and general behavior modeling

	Behavior ontology	General
Target	System components (Multi-Target, Actors)	Single-Target
Data collection method	Conceptual modeling	Sensor collection
Amount of data	Limited state, constraint	Big data
Direction of behavior	Interactive	Unidirectional

Table 2 shows the summary of the comparison.

The advantages of the method in the paper can be further summarized as follows:

(1) The system behaviors are modeling quantitatively and abstracted based on normalization of their quantities in a mathematical structure, namely n:2-Lattice. And further the lattice provides a mathematical base to predict and analyze collective system behaviors.

(2) The lattice can be used to reorganize abstract system views with respect to main actor concepts and makes possible the analysis of the behaviors with respect to the individual or combinational actors, for example, Ambulance or Patient views from the example.

(3) The lattice can be used to define mathematical relations between collective behaviors of the collecting groups. For example, the group with 1 Ambulance and the group with n Ambulances. The relationship can be represented as a lattice for the lattices.

(4) Composition of two lattices is possible with respect to the common main actors. This is the main topic of the paper, and it gives general capability of the method to apply to the real example.

Most importantly, in the perspective of composition, the method provides one of the possible solutions to handle the state explosion problem. Generally the problem is known as one of the most fundamental problem in computer science, and there are a number approaches to handle complexity of the explosion. The best known ones can be summarized as follows:

• A compositional analysis of finite state systems to deal with state explosion due to process composition, they tried to reduce base on synchronous and asynchronous execution and showed the method by process algebra [9, 10].

• A technique to cluster states into equivalent classes which uses a graphical representation into text form [11]. It uses Communicating Real-Time State Machines (CRSMs) that works on automatic verification of finite state real-time systems.

• A technique to reduce possible infinite time space into finite time space which is developed for a compositional specification theory for components [12].

Compare to these approaches, the approach in the paper reduces the states with respect to the types of behaviors, that is, a sequence of interactions among actors. Further, it represents the composition of two system states with respect to the same cardinality and capacity of the common actors. In Sect. 4.1, the outstanding degree of reduction of the states has been demonstrated and compared with others quantitatively with the examples.

4.3   Implementation: PRISM

In order to demonstrate the feasibility of the approach in this paper, a tool, called PRISM, has been developed on ADOxx Meta-Modeling Platform [6], and reported as a Behavior Ontology tool [13].

5   Conclusion and Future Research

This paper presented a method for knowledge engineering and composition to model collective behaviors of systems. The method was based on a sequence of processes from constructing active ontology, defining regular behaviors, abstracting regular behaviors, constructing abstract behavior lattice, and finally generating a composite abstract behavior lattice from two abstract behavior lattices. The method was demonstrated with two examples: EMS and HCS systems. And the composite lattice for EMS $\otimes$ HCS was generated. Application of the examples was shown with the instance examples on these lattices. The efficiency of the method was shown with numbers for reduction of the system state. The method can be considered one of the most innovative approaches for collective representation of knowledge engineering and their composition, as well as state minimization.

The future research includes developing meta-modeling the method and its instantiation to target domains, as well as application to the real systems.

Acknowledgment. This work was supported by Basic Science Research Programs through Space Core Technology Development Program through the NRF (National Research Foundation of Korea) funded by the Ministry of Science, ICT and Future Planning (NRF-2014M1A3A3A02034792), and Basic Science Research Program through the National Research Foundation of Korea(NRF) funded by the Ministry of Education (NRF-2015R1D1A3A01019282).

References

1. Haxthausen, A.E., Peleska, J.: Formal development and verification of a distributed railway control system. IEEE Trans. Softw. Eng. **26**(8), 687–701 (2000)
2. Choe, Y., Lee, S., Lee, M.: SAVE: an environment for visual specification and verification of IoT. In: Enterprise Distributed Object Computing Workshop, pp. 1–8. IEEE Press, Vienna, Austria (2016)
3. Lee, M.: Composition model for cloud services with behavior ontology. In: ICServ2016, Tokyo, Japan, 6–9th September 2016

4. McNaughton, R., Yamada, H.: Regular expressions and state graphs for automata. In: IRE Transactions on Electronic Computers, vol. 9, no. 1, pp. 39–47. IEEE Press, (1960). https://doi.org/10.1109/tec.1960.5221603
5. Choe, Y., Lee, M.: A lattice model to verify behavioral equivalence. In: 2014 UKSim-AMSS 8th European Modelling Symposium (2014)
6. Fill, H.G., Karagiannis, D.: On the conceptualisation of modelling methods using the ADOxx meta modelling platform. Enterp. Model. Inf. Syst. Arch. 8(1), 4–25 (2013). https://doi.org/10.18417/emisa.8.1.1
7. Choe, Y., Lee, M.: A process algebra construct method for reduction of states in reachability graph: conjunctive and complement choices. J. KIISE 43(5), 541–552 (2016)
8. Yassine, A., Singh, S., Alamri, A.: Mining human activity patterns from smart home big data for health care applications. IEEE Access 5, 13131–13141 (2017)
9. Clarke, E.M., Emerson, E.A., Sifakis, J.: Model checking: algorithmic verification and debugging. Commun. ACM 52(11), 74–84 (2009)
10. Yeh, W.J., Young, M.: compositional reachability analysis using process algebra. In: Proceedings of the Symposium on Testing, Analysis, and Verification, pp. 49–59 (1992)
11. Chen, T., Chilton, C., Jonsson, B., Kwiatkowska, M.: A compositional specification theory for component behaviours. In: Seidl, H. (ed.) ESOP 2012. LNCS, vol. 7211, pp. 148–168. Springer, Heidelberg (2012). https://doi.org/10.1007/978-3-642-28869-2_8
12. Raju, S. C.: An automatic verification technique for communicating real-time state mechines. Technical report 93-07-08, Department of Computer science and Engineering, University of Washington (1993)
13. Rahmani, M., Song, J., Lee, M.: PRISM: a knowledge engineering tool to model collective behaviors of real-time IoT systems. In: 2017 Practicing Open Enterprise Modeling (2017)

DEMO and the Story-Card Method: Requirements Elicitation for Agile Software Development at Scale

Marné de Vries(✉)

Department of Industrial and Systems Engineering,
University of Pretoria, Pretoria, South Africa
Marne.devries@up.ac.za

Abstract. Enterprises of today are faced with rapidly changing technologies and customer needs within unpredictable environments that require a new mindset for creating an *agile enterprise*. Agile practices gained momentum within software development communities due to their speed-of-delivery and incremental value delivery. Yet, for software development projects *at scale*, theorists believe that stakeholders first need to have a *common understanding* of the *enterprise operational context*, sharing a common *big picture* as part of *requirements elicitation*. The *design and engineering methodology for organizations* (DEMO) encapsulates an organization construction diagram (OCD) that is useful for representing the *enterprise operational context*, i.e. removing unnecessary clutter of technology implementation detail. Theory indicates that abstract OCD concepts are *concise* and used in a *consistent* way. Yet, agile methodologies require models that *encourage collaboration*, are *easy to understand* and relate to a *concrete world*, rather than an *abstract world*. The main contribution of this article is to present a different means of introducing the OCD to software development stakeholders, relating *abstract concepts* of the OCD back to a *concrete world*. Using *design science research*, this study suggests and evaluates a *story-card method* that incorporates collaborative and easy-to-use technologies, i.e. *sticky notes* as *story cards*. Feedback from 21 research participants indicated that the *story-card method* indeed facilitated translation of a *concrete world* into more *abstract* (and concise) concepts of the OCD, also improving the possibility of adopting the OCD at an enterprise as a means to represent a *common understanding* of the *enterprise operational context*.

Keywords: Enterprise engineering · Requirements elicitation
Organization construction diagram · Agile methodologies · Agile at scale

1 Introduction

Most enterprises of today are faced with VUCA (volatility, uncertainty, complexity and ambiguity) and need to operate within unpredictable environments that require a new mindset for creating an *agile enterprise* [1]. Enterprises also need to ensure that they

© IFIP International Federation for Information Processing 2018
Published by Springer Nature Switzerland AG 2018. All Rights Reserved
R. A. Buchmann et al. (Eds.): PoEM 2018, LNBIP 335, pp. 138–153, 2018.
https://doi.org/10.1007/978-3-030-02302-7_9

expand their information system landscape in a *dynamic*, but *coherent and integrated way* [2].

Modern software development methodologies have already moved way from the autocratic, plan-driven approaches of the past towards light-weight and agile methodologies that are *iterative and incremental* [3, 4]. A study on agile methods and practices, performed in 2014 by VersionOne [5], inviting 3925 individuals from a broad range of industries in global software development, indicated that 53% of the respondents had *more than 1000 employees* at their enterprise. Since agile software development methods were originally intended for *small and individual teams*, several challenges emerged when agile practices were applied *at scale* [6].

Enterprise *size* is one of many *scaling factors* that need to be considered when adopting an agile methodology at an enterprise. Agile methods and practices may have to be tailored for contexts where *scaling factors apply*, especially regarding the *elicitation and management of requirements* [6, 7]. Since additional *requirements elicitation* practices should be incorporated when *scaling factors apply* [8], we believe that existing methods and practices, associated with the *design and engineering methodology for organizations* (DEMO), could be used to represent a *blue print* of enterprise operation, a foundation for *eliciting requirements* and developing supporting information systems.

In this article we argue that one of the DEMO constructs, called the organization construction diagram (OCD) is useful to communicate the *blue print of enterprise operation*. Yet, agile development stakeholders have different roles and therefor require methods and practices that *encourage collaboration*, are *easy to understand*, and relating to a *concrete world* rather than *abstract concepts* encapsulated in the OCD. Hence, we motivate the need to develop an additional method, called the *story-card method*, to facilitate cognitive understanding of the *abstract concepts* associated with the OCD. The purpose is not to demonstrate how the OCD solves all challenges associated with different kinds of *scaling factors*. Rather, we acknowledge that the OCD will only become useful within agile development contexts if one or more *scaling factors* apply, since more advanced *requirements elicitation and management* is needed when *scaling factors* apply.

Next, we briefly introduce the remaining sections of the article. Section 2 motivates the need to include additional *requirement elicitation practices* within agile methodologies when *scaling factors* apply, also introducing existing theory that may be useful for *requirements elicitation*. Section 3 introduces *design science research* (DSR) as an appropriate research methodology for developing an artefact, the *story-card method*, as a means to incorporate the OCD into agile methodologies when *scaling factors* apply. We present the *story-card method* in Sect. 4 and discuss evaluation results of the *story-card method* in Sect. 5. Finally, we summarize the results in Sect. 6 and suggest opportunities for future research.

2   Background Theory

Agile practices are currently applied to more complex environments than before, creating several challenges, including *requirements elicitation and management* challenges. The purpose of this section is to define the concept *agile at scale*, introducing some of the challenges associated with *agile at scale*. Section 2.1 provides a definition of *agile at scale* and *criteria* for addressing *requirements elicitation and management* challenges associated with projects where *scaling factors* apply. In Sect. 2.2 we present and critique current agile frameworks and practices in terms of the *requirements elicitation criteria*, whereas Sect. 2.3 presents an alternative modelling language, the *design and engineering methodology for organizations* (DEMO) that may be incorporated to address *requirements elicitation criteria*.

2.1   Agile at Scale and the Need for Requirements Engineering

Agile methodologies were originally intended for small teams with collocated team members, working face-to-face in team rooms. Application of agile methods within *scaled* contexts resulted in several challenges regarding coordination between teams (especially for distributed projects), lack of architecture, and *lack of requirement management* [8].

Definition of Agile at Scale and Requirements Elicitation. Different ideas exist on classifying an agile development as *large*, using *project cost, project duration, size of the software developed, number of people, number of teams involved* and *number of sites* [9]. Moe and Dingsøyr [10] believe that scaling should not only be defined in terms of *team size* or *number of teams*, since teams may be distributed across location and enterprise boundaries, creating additional complexity and challenges. Likewise, Ambler and Lines [11] elaborate on different *scaling factors* that may apply: *geographical distribution, team size, regulatory compliance, domain complexity, technical complexity, enterprise distribution, enterprise complexity* and *enterprise discipline*. In terms of regulatory compliance, regulatory requirements stipulated by Sarbanes-Oxley or BASEL II, may necessitate *documented evidence* for certain processes and *traceability* against relevant standards [12].

Robertson and Robertson [13, p. 9] believe that *requirements* "exist either because the type of product *demands* certain functions and qualities, or because the client justifiably *asks for the requirement* to be part of the delivered product". For a software development project, the *product* is a software application. In terms of a software development project, Leffingwell [14] distinguishes between *needs, features* and *software requirements*, i.e. different *requirements concepts* that elaborate on end user's operations within an enterprise and how end users expect support from information systems. Section 2.3 elaborates on the need to understand the *organization construction* (i.e. user's operational *needs*), prior to eliciting *features* and *software requirements* for a supporting software application. The *features* and *software requirements* translate *needs* into a software solution. According to Schön et al. [15] *agile* software development still incorporates *requirements elicitation and management*, but in a more iterative way, rather than at the start of the project. *High-level requirements* or operational *needs* should still be defined, but are expanded continuously throughout the project [15]. Yet, when *scaling factors* apply, software development teams need to reconsider the mechanisms and practices that are selected for *requirement elicitation and management* [8].

Understanding the Big Picture for Projects at Scale. According to Schön et al. [15], it is a challenge to keep sight of the *big picture* in terms of the *project vision* for projects where *scaling factors apply*. Schön et al. [15] define a project vision as: "an abstract description of the overarching goal that guides product development and aligns development, business people and other stakeholders". Ambler and Lines [11] believe that the *project vision* should be encapsulated in a number of abstract, *high-level requirements*. They propose several mechanisms for representing high-level requirements, such as a business process model, context diagram, mind map, UI flow diagram, storyboard, value stream maps and UML use case models.

In addition, the entire project team, which may consist of multiple smaller teams, should have a *shared understanding* of the *high-level requirements* [11], as discussed in the next paragraph.

Creating a Shared Understanding. Buchan [16] indicates that customers and software development teams need to develop a common understanding about a client's requirements, since inadequate *sharing and understanding* will have a negative impact on product quality and cost. Buchan [16] analyses the challenges involved in creating a *shared understanding of requirements* (SUR), applying principles from *cognition theory* to address the challenges of obtaining a SUR. He states that SUR is a specialized form of the *team mental model* (TMM) as discussed by Mohammed et al. [17], i.e. SUR is "viewed as structured mental representations of knowledge and understanding about relevant aspects of requirements, that are similar in each team member" [16]. The content of SUR is *shared knowledge structures* that include declarative (what), procedural (how) and strategic (why) knowledge about requirements [18]. Furthermore, the property *shared* indicates that team members have some common or overlapping (but not identical) knowledge structures that are *consistent* [19]. Lastly, SUR has the property of "accuracy", since it has to be aligned with the true state of the world [20]. A gap in SUR may indicate that relevant knowledge about a requirement is: (1) missing, or (2) lacks sufficient detail, or (3) is not adequately shared between team members, or (4) is inconsistent between team members, or (5) is an error, i.e. inconsistent with the *concrete world*. Project team members need to first *communicate* or *share* their ideas, making them explicit in the form of representations, such as *narratives or models*, before they could reach consensus on a *shared understanding* [21, 22].

Creating Traceability. Minimal documentation, as promoted by *agile methodologies*, creates problems in *tracing* requirements to their origin [23, 24]. Even though traceability may be perceived as a heavy-weight activity with little value, distributed projects still obtain more benefits than incurring costs [25]. Leffingwell [7] presents a traceability model to indicate how different kinds of models communicate requirements and how the models are related.

2.2   Existing Agile Frameworks and Embedded Mechanisms and Practices

Addressing *scaling* challenges, several *scaling frameworks* were developed, such as the Scaled Agile Framework (SAFe), Large-Scale Scrum (LeSS), Disciplined Agile Delivery (DAD), Scrum of Scrums (SoS) and LeanSAFE [26]. Two of the five frameworks addresses the *lack of requirements elicitation and management* challenge, identified by Paasivaara and Lassenius [8], a challenge that enterprises face, when they adopt *agile* within a context where *scaling factors apply*.

Leffingwell's [7] SAFe suggests *three levels of scaling*: (1) agile team level, (2) program level and (3) portfolio level. Each level suggests a *minimum number of artefacts, roles and practices* for effective software product delivery.

Ambler's [27] DAD provides a different means of *scaling*, already discussed in Sect. 2.1, and he provides a practice-based methodology that focuses on *effective modelling and documentation* of software products. DAD incorporates mechanisms from Scrum, Extreme Programming (XP), Agile Modelling (AM), Unified Process (UP), Agile Data (AD) and Kanban. DAD provides an Agile Scaling Model (ASM) as a foundation for scaling agile mechanisms according to the enterprise context, *without being too prescriptive* on the requirements modelling and documentation practices [27]. He also provides three scaling levels: (1) core agile development; (2) agile delivery; and (3) agile at scale. For all three levels, the level of detail of the *initial requirements* models and descriptions will differ depending on the type of project with the purpose of doing *just enough requirements elicitation* to gain agreement on the scope of the project [27]. Ambler [27] suggests that the development team uses modelling mechanisms that are inclusive, such as *drawing diagrams on white boards*.

Existing agile frameworks/methodologies follow a pragmatic approach, in suggesting *easy-to-use* modelling mechanisms and practices that are appropriate for the project context [21]. Patton and Economy [21] also indicate that agile practices, such as *user stories* and *user story mapping*, already address two of the three *requirements elicitation criteria*, discussed in Sect. 2.1. They argue that *user stories* and *user story mapping* can be used to (1) represent the *operational context* (i.e. the *big picture*) and (2) a *shared understanding* of requirements. The subsequent sections provide more detail about *user stories* and *user story mapping*, evaluating their ability to consolidate requirements *in a consistent way* into a *big picture*.

User Stories. User stories are the "general-purpose agile substitute for what traditionally has been referred to as *software requirements*" [7, p. 37].

User stories intend to relate to the *concrete world* of a user. Since a user story is framed as a goal, goals may encapsulate many sub-goals and the constructional complexity required to achieve a goal need not be stated when defining a goal. Patton and Economy [21] use the analogy of a rock (i.e. a goal) that is broken into pebbles (i.e. sub-goals). The problem is that there is no consistency in how the rock is broken into different-sized pebbles. Trkman et al. [28] warn against the use of user stories, since there may be a *lack of dependencies* between user stories and their relationship to the overall context. In dealing with the last-mentioned problem, Patton and Economy [21] suggests that user stories are *mapped*.

User Story Mapping. User story mapping seemingly satisfies the *requirements elicitation criteria* of providing a *shared understanding* and a *big picture* representation. The idea is that *user stories* are mapped on a large working space (e.g. office wall) to indicate relationships between stories, but also decide on priorities for software development [21]. The *user stories* are mapped as steps on *sticky notes*, sequencing from left to right, also discussing the software support that would be needed per step and placed vertically below the relevant step [21].

Even though *user stories* and *user story mapping* address two of the *requirements elicitation criteria*, namely a representation of the *big picture* and using easy-to-use *sticky notes* to create a *shared understanding*, requirements encapsulated in the user stories are not consolidated *in a consistent way* into higher-level stories. Although *use case models and narratives* provide more structure for software requirements detail than *user stories*, requirements detail encapsulated within use cases are also based on goal-decomposition [29]. In the next section, we present an alternative to *user stories* or *use cases*, namely the identification of *transaction kinds* that provide a consistent means for consolidating enterprise operational detail. In addition, we indicate how the *transaction kind* is used as part of an organization construction diagram (OCD).

2.3 The Organization Construction Diagram (OCD)

Background on the OCD. Similar to Leffingwell [7], Dietz (in Perinforma [30]) acknowledges that user's *needs* for information system support starts with an understanding of their *day-to-day operations*. He presents *four ontological aspect models* that are *coherent, comprehensive, consistent, and concise* and that are useful to represent the *essence of enterprise operation* [31]. The organization construction model (OCM) is the most essential model and consist of two representations, the *organization construction diagram* (OCD) and the *transaction product table* (TPT) [30].

The OCD provides a graphical representation of *actor roles* (implemented by human beings) that perform a number of *coordination acts* (e.g. requests and promises) with regards to *production acts*. The *production acts* may be either immaterial (e.g. devising, deciding or judging) or material (e.g. manufacturing or transporting) [30]. Furthermore, *production acts* may be classified as *original* (e.g. devising, deciding or judging), *informational* (e.g. recalling, deriving or calculating), or *documental* (e.g. saving, retrieving, copying, transmitting or destroying) [30]. Yet, *original* production acts are supported by *informational* production acts, which are in turn supported by *documental* production acts. Many software applications are developed as technologies to semi-automate or implement some of the *coordination acts* and the *production acts* [31].

Dietz [30] argues that software development stakeholders need to have a *common understanding* of the *original* production acts, since other acts (informational and documental) and implementation technologies (software applications) merely support the *original* production acts. Focusing on the *original* production acts, it is possible to compile a *concise* representation or *big picture* of the *operational context*.

Figure 1 provides a graphical representation of an OCD that consists of four *original production acts* and four *actor roles*, based on the following narrative: "Every year, in consultation with the CEO, the enterprise designer selects members for an enterprise governance committee, capturing the selected members on our *enterprise design application* (EDA). The selected members should also indicate their willingness to become members of the committee. Later, the enterprise designer refers back to the information about selected members to request from every selected member to participate at a workshop. The purpose of the workshop (a periodic event) is that the entire committee needs to evaluate enterprise governance concepts. When committee members arrive at the workshop, the enterprise designer first ensures that all members state their participation by signing an attendance register before the workshop can start. The workshop assistant also captures the attendance data on EDA. The selected committee members often become involved in other projects and then need to resign from the committee. In that case, the enterprise designer consults/communicates with the CEO to replace the committee member, i.e. re-select a member."

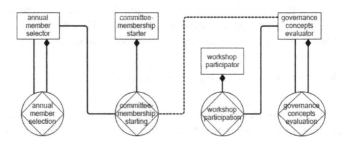

Fig. 1. Elementary OCD modelled with ABACUS

Partially explaining the constructs of Fig. 1, the actor role, *annual member selector*, initiates (via the solid link) *annual member selection*. The same actor role, *annual member selector*, is also the executor of *annual member selection* (represented via the solid link that ends in a solid diamond). Furthermore, the same actor role, *annual member selector*, also initiates *committee membership starting*. The combined diamond-disk constructs on Fig. 1 are called *transaction kinds*. Each *transaction kind* incorporates a *production act/fact* (represented via a diamond) as well as multiple *coordination acts/facts* (represented via a disc). Often, the generated *facts* need to be shared with other actor roles, since the facts may have an effect on the actor's behavior. Thus, additional information links (dotted links) are used to indicate access to particular coordination and production *facts*. For instance, the actor role in Fig. 1, *governance concepts evaluator*, needs to have access to the facts that are generated by *committee-membership starting*, since the *governance concept evaluator* has to involve members that already committed themselves to become members of the committee.

Addressing Requirements Elicitation Criteria with the OCD. In Sect. 2.1 we already indicated that additional *requirements elicitation* practices are only required within *agile methodologies*, if *scaling factors* apply. In addition, we presented *three criteria* for *requirements elicitation* practices. We now motivate that the OCD has the potential to address the *three criteria*, i.e. (1) representing the *big picture*, (2) creating a *shared understanding* of the big picture, and (3) providing sufficient structure to ensure *traceability of requirements.*

As discussed in the previous section, we believe that software development stakeholders (including enterprise stakeholders) need to have a *shared understanding* of the *original* production acts, since other production acts (informational and documental) and implementation technologies (software applications) merely support the *original* production acts. The OCD provides a *concise* representation or *big picture* of the *operational context* in a *consistent way,* i.e. every *transaction kind* (diamond-disc) on the OCD, represents an *entire transaction pattern* of an *original* production act and multiple coordination acts [30].

Regarding *traceability of requirements,* the structural composition of four *aspect models* (i.e. the organization construction model (OCM), the process model (PM), the action model (AM) and the fact model (FM), already ensure integration and traceability between the *four aspect models.* In accordance with Leffingwell's [14] distinction of requirements into *needs, features* and *software requirements,* we believe that the *four aspect models* provide sufficient structure to *trace software requirements* back to operation-supporting *needs.* As an example, the user may need software application support for the transaction kind *annual member selection* (see Fig. 1), i.e. to capture information about the selected members on a software application system called EDA. We acknowledge that other *features* may also be required from EDA, such as the ability *log onto the EDA system.* The stated *feature* will however not be traceable to a particular *transaction kind.*

Although the OCD has the potential to address the three *requirements elicitation criteria* that we identified in Sect. 2.1, *agile methodologies* require modelling techniques and tools that *encourage collaboration,* are *easy to understand* and the ability to relate back to a *concrete world* [21]. The next section presents a research methodology for designing a *story-card method* to facilitate reference to a *concrete world* and the *ease of understanding* OCD concepts.

3   Research Methodology

The study applied *design science research* (DSR), developing a new artefact, namely a *story-card method,* to enhance *ease-of-understanding* of OCD concepts when the OCD is used for requirements elicitation. According to Gregor and Hevner's [32] knowledge contribution framework, the *story-card method* can be considered as an improvement, since the *method* will be used for solving a known problem. Referring to the DSR steps of Peffers et al. [33], this article addresses the *five steps* of the DSR cycle in the following way:

Identify a problem: Previous research highlighted that agile methodologies are useful for small projects, but may require additional *requirements elicitation* practices for projects or enterprises where *scaling factors apply* [7]. As discussed in Sect. 2.3, the OCD has the ability to represent the *essence of enterprise operations* in a *consistent way* and the potential to convey a *shared understanding* of the enterprise *operation context,* also called the *big picture.* The *problem* is that agile development stakeholders have different roles and therefor require methods and practices that *encourage collaboration*, are *easy to understand*, and relating to a *concrete world* rather than *abstract concepts* encapsulated in the OCD.

Define objectives of the solution: Acknowledging the potential of the OCD to create a *shared understanding* of the enterprise *operation context*, whilst addressing the problem that agile team members require methods and practices that are *collaborative*, *easy to understand* and relate to a *concrete world*, an additional *method* is required to enhance understanding of the OCD concepts.

Design and development: In accordance with the solution objectives, a new method, i.e. the *story-card method*, was designed to introduce OCD concepts to *participants* from different backgrounds, i.e. addressing the need to create a *shared understanding* amongst stakeholders that fulfil *different roles*.

Demonstration: The *story-card method* was demonstrated to industry participants during an interactive session. During the demonstration, participants had the opportunity to criticize the *method*. The feedback was also used to refine the *story-card method*.

Evaluation: The industry participants evaluated the refined *story-card method* in practice by involving a colleague. A questionnaire, consisting of 18 questions/probes, was used to evaluate whether the *story-card method* addressed the solution objectives. In addition, the participants had to reflect whether modelling with *sticky notes* is preferred rather than using software modelling tools. Lastly, the participants had to obtain feedback from their colleague on whether the colleague would be confident to use the *story-card method* in future.

4 The Story Card Method

The *story-card method* specifies 5 *inputs* and 10 *method steps*.

Inputs: (1) flat working space, such as table or white board, (2) A1 paper, (3) sticky notes of 2 different colors (red and yellow), (4) a black pen, (5) a colleague's inputs.

Method steps:

- *Step 1:* Inquire from a colleague to explain a short process (about 10 to 15 activities) that s/he is involved with. Ensure that the process incorporates the use of information technology (e.g. the process followed from requesting vacation leave up to receiving notification about the approval of the request). Explain to your colleague that s/he needs to write the tasks (verb+noun) on yellow sticky notes and position the notes in sequence of occurrence, left to right on a flat working space (e.g. desk or white board).

- *Step 2:* Take a picture (photo) of the process. [Note that this step was only inserted to ensure that participants provided evidence about the initial process].

- *Step 3:* Discuss with your colleague all the actors that are involved and write down composite actors on yellow sticky notes, adding a smiley face, keeping actors aside.

- *Step 4:* Explain Dietz's red-green-blue triangle of production acts, also explaining the universal transaction pattern for actor-collaboration regarding production acts.

- *Step 5:* Have a discussion with your colleague as to identify *original* production acts from his/her process (as mapped out with sticky notes in Step 4).

- *Step 6:* Classify (in collaboration with your colleague) remaining acts as coordination acts vs. production acts.

- *Step 7:* Remove the *original* production act notes from the flat surface and phrase appropriate *transaction kind* descriptions (using adjective+noun) on red sticky notes that are positioned as diamonds on your A1 paper. Collapse initial production act notes underneath re-phrased *transaction kind* notes.

- *Step 8:* The remaining activities on your working space should be coordination acts or *informational/documental* production acts. Remove each of the remaining notes on your working surface and collapse them underneath the appropriate re-phrased *transaction kind* (red diamond notes) on your A1 paper.

- *Step 9:* Position the yellow actor role notes on the A1 paper, drawing in (with a black pen) the initiator actors (+initiating links) as well as the executing actors (+executing links) to the *transaction kinds*, completing a *composite OCD*.

- *Step 10:* Validate your *composite OCD* with your colleague.

The method steps were demonstrated to the participants. Figure 2 represents the result for performing *Steps 1 to 3*, whereas Fig. 3 resulted from performing *Steps 4 to 10*.

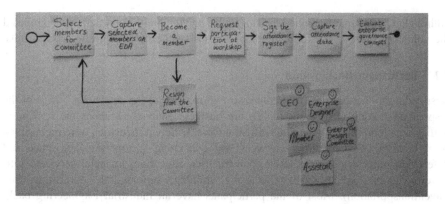

Fig. 2. Example of a process to demonstrate *method step 1* of the *story-card method*

The *OCD with composites* would require additional work as to be transformed into an *OCD withe elementary actor roles*. Thus, referring to Fig. 3, the yellow sticky notes at the bottom of the diamond-shaped *transaction kinds* need to be removed from the diagram, whereas the *composite actor roles* positioned above the diamond-shaped *transaction kinds* need to be replaced with *elementary actor roles*. An *elementary OCD* has been compiled using the software ABACUS, presented in Fig. 1.

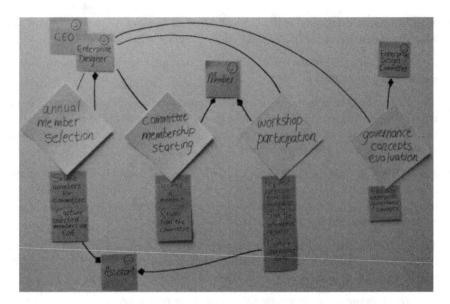

Fig. 3. An *OCD with composites* is the main deliverable of the *story-card method*

5 Results

Although 32 participants applied the *story-card method*, only 21 participants completed the voluntary survey. The following sub-sections synthesize the questionnaire results.

5.1 Participant Background

Responding to the question *"Indicate your existing role at the enterprise"*, 25% of the responding participants (4 out of 20) are business analysts, whereas the remaining participants represented 12 various different roles. Different industries were represented from both the manufacturing, services and consulting sectors (i.e. aerospace and defense manufacturing, automotive, construction, education, financial services, software vendors, industrial manufacturing, mining, agricultural, consulting and travel/transportation). Most of the participants have an Industrial Engineering background (i.e. 10 BEng and 3 BTech Industrial Engineering participants), whereas the remaining participants have an Engineering background (Mechanical Engineering, Metallurgical, Mining Engineering and Chemical) or a Science (BSc) background. The 10 BEng participants also have software development background, since a module (Information Systems Design) forms part of their undergraduate curriculum.

5.2 Feedback on the Story-Card Method

Participants had to indicate the time duration for completing the 10 *story-card method* steps. The average time to complete was 103 min, with a median of 105 min. Other descriptive statistics (the large standard deviation of 68 min, the minimum of 30 min and maximum of 300 min) indicate a huge variation when the *story-card method* is applied.

As motivated in Sect. 2.3, the OCD already has the ability to address three *requirements elicitation criteria* for scaled contexts, i.e. (1) understanding the *big picture*, (2) creating a *shared understanding* and (3) *traceability*. The *problem* is that agile team members require methods and practices that are *collaborative, easy to understand* and relate to a *concrete world* and the *story-card method* was developed to enhance understanding of OCD concepts. Thus, participants had to evaluate whether the solution artefact, i.e. the *story-card method*, was *useful* in relating to a *concrete world* when explaining abstract concepts of the OCD to a colleague. Feedback was positive. Participants (20 out of 21) that answered the question of whether *the story-card method helped to relate process steps to OCD constructs*, either agreed (14 out of 20) or strongly agreed (6 out of 20). In addition, participants either strongly agreed (7 out of 21), agreed (12 out of 21) or were neutral (2 out of 21) when they responded to the question on whether *the story-card method encouraged discussion with a colleague to classify appropriate activities as original production activities versus informational or documental production activities*. Participants were also positive to use the *story-card method* in future to explain OCD concepts, i.e. they either strongly agreed (9 out of 21), agreed (11 out of 21) or were neutral (1 out of 21) that *if I had to explain OCD concepts to another colleague in future, I would use the story-card method, rather than my own/another way of explanation*.

Evaluating whether participants *preferred to use sticky notes* (exemplified in Figs. 2 and 3) rather than using modelling software, such as ABACUS (exemplified in Fig. 1) for modelling, most participants (15 out of 21) *preferred manual modelling with sticky notes*, whereas some (6 out of 21) preferred to use *modelling software*. Participants had to motivate their preferred modelling method.

Themes extracted from those that *preferred manual modelling with sticky notes* include: Easy to understand (4 responses); encourages conversation/discussion (4 responses); less intimidating for the interviewee (1 response); less stressful to the modeler (1 response); allows for changes by moving sticky notes around (1 response); and sticky note modelling is useful for initial modelling (1 response). Yet, 2 responses indicate that the participants selected the manual option, since they never had exposure to software modelling tools before.

Themes extracted from those that preferred to use *software modelling* tools include: Easier to implement changes (3 responses); easier to draw the sequential process (1 response); sticky notes do not always stick (1 response); and diagram readability is improved (1 response).

Referring to Sect. 4 (i.e. the *method steps*) participants had to indicate whether they *experienced any difficulties in using the story-card method*. A number of themes emerged from the 8 responses:

- Step 3: Preferring a swim-lane diagram to assign actor roles to process steps (1 response).
- Step 5: Difficulty in deciding whether an activity is an *original* production activity (2 responses).

- Step 7: Difficulty in changing the sticky note descriptions from verb+noun to adjective+noun (2 responses).
- Step 9: Difficulty in explaining the purpose of the red diamond (1 response).
- Step 10: Difficult to validate and confirm the OCD with the company representative (1 response).
- Not step related: Difficulty in obtaining participation from Step 4 onwards, since non-technical staff "zoned out" when new concepts were introduced (1 response).

Evaluating whether participants *consider using the OCD within their own working environment*, rendered positive results, since 15 (out of 21) participants either strongly agreed (4 out of 21) or agreed (11 out of 21). Only one participant disagreed, providing the following rationale: *"I do not think it would add much value to my current working environment. The value that it would add is not worth the difficulty explaining to someone the technicalities of the OCD (personal opinion)."* Two participants that were neutral (neither agree nor disagree) indicated that *"Although it is not my preferred method of process modelling, it was still useful to map out the process in that manner. It provided a different aspect of the process"* and *"It's not used a lot in my work domain. However, if I had been in the enterprise engineering field, I would consider using it"*.

The *story-card method* had to ensure *ease-of-understanding*, relating *abstract concepts* of the OCD to a *concrete world*. In accordance, we evaluated whether the colleagues *would be confident to use the story-card method to model another process by him/herself to construct a composite OCD*. Almost half of the *colleagues* agreed (10 out of 21), some responded neutral (7 out of 21) and a few (4 out of 21) disagreed. Three of the *colleagues that disagreed* indicated that they would need another example prior to applying the *story-card method* with confidence. The other *colleague that disagreed* indicated that he/she did not understand the theory behind the story-card method and had difficulty in identifying the different type of acts.

Finally, participants had to present an *elementary OCD* (i.e. Fig. 5.2 from Perinforma [30, p. 74]) to their *colleagues* to inquire whether *a similar kind of diagram would be useful to represent a blue print of their enterprise operations*. The intension was to evaluate whether the OCD could be adopted as a means for representing a *big picture* for *essential enterprise operations*. The responses were overall positive, ranging from strongly agreeing (1 out of 21), agreeing (10 out of 21) and being neutral (10 out of 21).

6   Discussion and Future Research

For software development projects *at scale*, stakeholders first need to have a *common understanding* of the *enterprise operational context*, sharing a common *big picture* as part of *requirements elicitation*. The *design and engineering methodology for organizations* (DEMO) encapsulates an organization construction diagram (OCD) that is useful for representing the *enterprise operational context*, i.e. removing unnecessary clutter of technology implementation detail. Theory indicates that abstract OCD concepts are *concise* and used in a *consistent* way. Yet, agile methodologies require models that *encourage collaboration*, are *easy to understand* and relate to a *concrete world*, rather than an *abstract world*.

This article presented a different means of introducing the OCD to software development stakeholders, relating *abstract concepts* of the OCD back to a *concrete world*. Using DSR, this study suggested and evaluated a *story-card method* that incorporates *collaborative* and *easy-to-use* technologies, i.e. *sticky notes* as *story cards*. Feedback from 21 research participants indicated that the *story-card method* indeed facilitated *collaboration* and translation of a *concrete world* into more *abstract* (and concise) concepts of the OCD. The *story-card method* also improved the possibility of adopting the OCD at an enterprise as a means to represent a *common understanding* of the *enterprise operational context*. Since participants represented various different industries and roles, we believe that the *story-card method* would be useful within various different contexts, including context where *scaling factors* apply.

The qualitative feedback obtained from participants regarding difficulties experienced in applying some of the *method steps* provide the opportunity for further improvement of the *story-card method*. In addition, the *story-card method* may also need additional development to ensure its own scalability. We suggest that the *story-card method* is applied within real-world *agile at scale* projects where different scaling factors apply as to further validate the usefulness of the *story-card method* and the OCD within software development projects. Since this article did not expand too much on the *traceability* criterion, we suggest that Leffingwell's [7] meta-model for requirements concepts is adapted to demonstrate *traceability* of requirements when the *four aspect models* are included as part of the meta-model.

Acknowledgements. This work is based on the research supported wholly/in part by the National Research Foundation of South Africa (Grant Number 115089). We are also grateful towards the research participants for their valuable feedback.

References

1. Meyer, P.: Agility Shift: Creating Agile and Effective Leaders, Teams, and Organizations, 1st edn. Routledge, New York (2016)
2. Hoogervorst, J.A.P.: Practicing Enterprise Governance and Enterprise Engineering - Applying the Employee-Centric Theory of Organization. Springer, Heidelberg (2018)
3. West, D., Grant, T., Gerush, M., D'silva, D.: Agile development: mainstream adoption has changed agility. Forrest. Res. **2**(1), 41 (2010)
4. Zucker, A.: What we really know about successful projects. https://www.scrumalliance.org/community/articles/2016/october/what-we-really-know-about-successful-projects. Accessed 14 May 2018
5. VersionOne: 9th Annual State of Agile Survey 2015. https://www.watermarklearning.com/downloads/state-of-agile-development-survey.pdf. Accessed 6 June 2018
6. Dikert, K., Paasivaara, M., Lassenius, C.: Challenges and success factors for large-scale agile transformations: a systematic literature review. J. Syst. Softw. **119**, 87–108 (2016)
7. Leffingwell, D.: Agile Software Requirements: Lean Requirements Practices for Teams, Programs, and the Enterprise. Addison-Wesley, New Jersey (2011)

8. Paasivaara, M., Lassenius, C.: Scaling scrum in a large globally distributed organisation: a case study. In: IEEE 11th International Conference on Global Software Engineering. IEEE Computer Society (2016)

9. Dingsøyr, T., Moe, N.B.: Research challenges in large-scale agile software development. ACM SIGSOFT Softw. Eng. Notes **38**(5), 38–39 (2013)

10. Moe, N.B., Dingsøyr, T.: Emerging research themes and updated research agenda for large-scale agile development: a summary of the 5th international workshop at XP2017. In: Proceedings of the XP2017 Scientific Workshops, pp. 1–4. ACM, Cologne, Germany (2017)

11. Ambler, S.W., Lines, M.: Disciplined Agile Delivery: A Practitioner's Guide to Agile Software Delivery in the Enterprise. IBM Press, US (2012)

12. Ambler, Scott W.: Agile software development at scale. In: Meyer, B., Nawrocki, Jerzy R., Walter, B. (eds.) CEE-SET 2007. LNCS, vol. 5082, pp. 1–12. Springer, Heidelberg (2008). https://doi.org/10.1007/978-3-540-85279-7_1

13. Roberson, S., Roberson, J.: Mastering the Requirements Process: Getting Requirements Right, 3rd edn. Addison-Wesley, New York (2013)

14. Leffingwell, D.: Scaling Software Agility. Pearson Education, Boston (2007)

15. Schön, E., Thomaschewski, J., Escalona, M.J.: Agile requirements engineering: a systematic literature review. Comput. Stand. Interfaces **49**, 79–91 (2017)

16. Buchan, J.: An empirical cognitive model of the development of shared understanding of requirements. Requir. Eng. **432**, 165–179 (2014)

17. Mohammed, S., Ferzandi, L., Hamilton, K.: Metaphor no more: a 15-year review of the team mental model construct. J. Manag. **36**, 876–910 (2010)

18. Rouse, W.B., Cannon-Bowers, J.A., Salas, E.: The role of mental models in team performance in complex systems. IEEE Trans. Syst. Man Cybern. **22**, 1296–1308 (1992)

19. Cannon-Bowers, J.A., Salas, E., Converse, S.A.: Shared mental models in expert team decision making. In: Castellan, J. (ed.) Current Issues in Individual and Group Decision Making, pp. 221–246. Lawrence Erlbaum Associates Inc., Hillsdale, NJ (1993)

20. Edwards, B.D., Day, E.A., Arthur, W.J., Bell, S.T.: Relationships among team ability composition, team mental models, and team performance. J. Appl. Psychol. **91**, 727–736 (2006)

21. Patton, J., Economy, P.: User Story Mapping: Discover the Whole Story, Build the Right Product. O'Reilly Media Inc., Sebastopol (2014)

22. Kannan, V., Fish, J.C., Willett, D.L.: Agile model driven development of electronic health record-based specialty population registries. In: 2016 IEEE-EMBS International Conference on Biomedical and Health Informatics (BHI), pp. 465–468 (2016)

23. Inayat, I., Salim, S.S., Marczak, S., Daneva, M., Shamshirband, S.: A systematic literature review on agile requirements engineering practices and challenges. Comput. Hum. Bahav. **51**(PB), 915–929 (2015)

24. Heikkilä, V.T., Damian, D., Lassenius, C., Paasivaara, M.: A mapping study on requirements engineering in agile software development. In: 2015 41st Euromicro Conference on Software Engineering and Advanced Applications, pp. 199–207 (2015)

25. Cleland-Huang, J.: Traceability in agile projects. In: Cleland-Huang, J., et al. (eds.) Software and Systems Traceability, pp. 265–275. Springer, London (2012). https://doi.org/10.1007/978-1-4471-2239-5_12

26. Ebert, C., Paasivaara, M.: Scaling agile. IEEE Softw. **34**(6), 98–103 (2017)

27. Ambler, S.W.: The disciplined agile (DA) framework: a foundation for business agility. http://www.disciplinedagiledelivery.com/. Accessed 6 June 2018

28. Trkman, M., Mendling, J., Krisper, M.: Using business process models to better understand the dependencies among user stories. Inf. Softw. Technol. **71**, 58–76 (2016)

29. Cockburn, A.: Writing Effective Use Cases. Addison-Wesley, Indianapolis (2001)

30. Perinforma, A.P.C.: The essence of organisation, 3rd edn. Sapio (2017). www.sapio.nl
31. Dietz, J.L.G.: Enterprise ontology. Springer, Berlin (2006). https://doi.org/10.1007/3-540-33149-2
32. Gregor, S., Hevner, A.: Positioning and presenting design science research for maximum impact. MIS Q. **37**(2), 337–355 (2013)
33. Peffers, K., Tuunanen, T., Rothenberger, M., Chatterjee, S.: A design science research methodology for information systems research. J. MIS **24**(3), 45–77 (2008)

Reviews and Analyses of Modeling Methods

Adaptive Case Management - A Review of Method Support

Birger Lantow[✉]

University of Rostock, Albert-Einstein-Str. 22, 18059 Rostock, Germany
birger.lantow@uni-rostock.de
https://www.wirtschaftsinformatik.uni-rostock.de

Abstract. Knowledge-intensive Processes are difficult to support by traditional workflow oriented Business Process Management approaches. Reasons lie in in ad-hoc decisions and unpredictable workflows that come with them. Adaptive Case Management (ACM) is a paradigm for the management of knowledge-intensive processes that has recently drawn attention in industry and the scientific community. This development led to the standardization of CMMN as a notation for process models for the ACM implementation. This study assess the availability of method support for the use of ACM and the fitness of CMMN for fulfilling the modeling requirements in this context based on a systematic literature review. As a result missing method support, CMMN shortcomings as well as suggestions for the implementation of ACM in combination with CMMN are discussed.

Keywords: Adaptive Case Management
Systematic literature review · Knowledge-intensive processes
Method · CMMN

1 Introduction

Nowadays IT support for industrial production processes and well defined business processes has reached a certain maturity. Potentials for differentiation on the market stem from knowledge and the use of knowledge. Work processes in this area - so called knowledge-intensive processes - put some difficulties to the inclusion in Business Process Management (BPM) and thus the process support and control by IT systems. Knowledge-intensive processes are for example characterized by out of order task completion, a high autonomy of the so called knowledge workers, and a hardly predictable information demand. Adaptive Case Management (ACM) is a paradigm for the management of knowledge-intensive processes that has recently drawn attention in industry and the scientific community. Based on supporting IT systems, it allows a data or information centered process control, ad-hoc changes in process models, and execution at run-time [14]. The industrial interest in prospecting the potential of ACM led to a standardization process under the roof of the Open Management Group resulting in a standard notation for ACM process models called Case Management Model and Notation[1] (CMMN). Several tools for Business Process Management have evolved meanwhile that support this notation standard. Having a paradigm, a notation and certain tool support does not necessarily mean that there is also method support for the use of ACM and CMMN. Bider et al. [3] claimed in 2013 that there is a coherent theory required regarding ACM since it has not been more than a collection of practices so far.

The aim of this study is to asses the extent of method support for ACM that has been defined in the scientific community. Considering the prominence of CMMN a second goal is an assessment of the fitness of the standard to meet ACM requirements. This is done based on a systematic literature review.

In order to provide a frame for this literature review, Sect. 2 gives a short view on method theory. The following Sect. 3 describes the overall process of the literature review including a further specification of the research goals by defining research questions. Additionally, the process and results of paper selection are described. Section 4 deeply analyzes the literature. A summary and outlook is provided in Sect. 5.

2   Categories for the Assessment of Method Support

This study uses a meta-model based approach to assess the method support for the creation and handling of process models following the ACM paradigm. Scientific literature regarding method support mainly focuses on notation. This can also be found in the results of the systematic literature review in Sect. 3. However, a method does not consist of a notation and created models only. For example, there need to be procedures in order to extract the knowledge that can be found in the models. Depending on the purpose and the context of method application, a combination of different notations and procedures might be required [7]. In the discipline of method engineering, there are several approaches to describe a meta-model of methods for information system engineering. We take the models by Karagiannis and Khn [12] and by Goldkuhl et al. [7] as a base for our assessment. Both approaches together cover extensively what can be considered as required parts of a method in the information system engineering domain. Though, not all these parts might be defined in a method description.

According to Goldkuhl et al. [7] an important starting point for a method is the perspective which defines problems the method can be applied to and the scope. A method is described as a composition of so called method components that each addresses a sub-problem of the method application. Thus, different notations and procedures can be applied depending on the context. Furthermore, a distinction is made between the notation and the concepts used in a method component. Hence, there is a separation between notation symbols and

---

[1] https://www.omg.org/spec/CMMN.

the semantics. For example, different symbols in different notations can refer to the same concepts. In order control the use of method components, a framework is part of the method model. It helps to determine which method components are to be used when. As already mentioned, modeling procedures are used to acquire knowledge. Since the knowledge originates from the domain experts, cooperation forms are also to be defined as part of a method according to Goldkuhl et al.. This includes the definition of roles and interaction forms.

The method model by Karagiannis and Khn [12] has a stronger focus on Model Driven Development (MDD). While not explicitly considering perspective, framework and cooperation forms, the other method concepts from Goldkuhl et al. are represented more detailed in this model. Modeling procedures are further described by their steps and results. The modeling notation is described by syntax and symbols. As an addition from MDD, Karagiannis and Khn add mechanisms and algorithms to the method model. The latter address aspects of model transformation and analysis.

In order to derive a feasible mapping schema for the assessment of method support for ACM more coarse grained categories have been derived from the introduced method models. Furthermore, a common perspective - Creation and handling of process models for ACM - is assumed and thus not further investigated. The resulting categories are shown in Table 1. Approaches found in the literature review (Sect. 3) are analyzed with regard to them.

Table 1. Categories for method support assessment.

Category	Comment
Cooperation forms	Identified roles and collaboration settings for those who are involved in the system engineering process
Concepts and notation	Concepts that will be represented in the models and their representation in a certain notation considering symbols and syntax
Procedures and framework	Steps to be performed in the systems engineering process on different levels of abstraction
Tool support	Tools for model creation, analysis and transformation

3   Systematic Literature Review

A systematic literature review has been performed in order to assess the state of research regarding method support for the ACM paradigm. Specifically, the following research questions have been in focus.

- *RQ1:* To what extent are the required parts of a method considered in scientific literature on ACM?
- *RQ2:* What is suggested in scientific literature on ACM with regard to the required parts of a method?
- *RQ3:* How is the fitness of CMMN for ACM evaluated in scientific literature on ACM?
- *RQ4:* What solutions for possible shortcomings of CMMN with regard to ACM are suggested in scientific literature?

As described earlier, CMMN is seen as a broadly used and an accepted standard for process modeling in Adaptive Case Management. CMMN is supported by many commercial and research-based tools in the area. Thus, we set the focus on CMMN and possible CMMN adaptations when discussing ACM notations. The analysis process is oriented along the guidelines for a systematic literature analysis presented by Kitchenham [13] and Webster [19]. The review process is divided into four different parts (see Fig. 1). The first activity is to identify conference series, journals and catalogs that are likely to represent the state of the art of research on the topic of interest. Here, a base set of papers for review is extracted by keyword search. The second step is the exclusion/inclusion of papers based on title and abstract. Then, the remaining papers have to be classified and data has to be extracted with regard to the research questions. The classification is based on the categories for the assessment of method support that have been derived in Sect. 2. The fourth and last step is to analyze the extracted data. The next paragraphs describe the performance of these steps in detail.

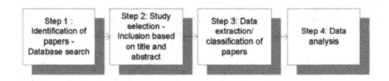

Fig. 1. Systematic literature review process [11].

3.1 Identification and Selection of Papers

The first step is the identification of papers dealing with ACM methods and CMMN in a selection of appropriate literature sources. The well-known portals for high quality scientific literature indexing Web of Science/Web of Knowledge and Scopus have been selected as literature sources. In order to include a publisher into the search too, the Elsevier portal has been selected as an additional source. The idea was to check whether a significant contribution to the analysis results can be expected from including publisher portals. Since ACM and CMMN are relatively new topics, the literature search has not been restricted to a specific time period. The following search terms have been applied to publication meta data (Title, Abstract, Keywords):

- "Adaptive Case Management" AND Method
- CMMN AND Method
- "Adaptive Case Management" AND CMMN

The combination of "Adaptive Case Management" and "Method" in the search terms can be directly derived from the research questions. The same is true for "CMMN" and "Method". The idea of searching for the combination of "Adaptive Case Management" and "CMMN" was that literature combining both should somehow address the use of CMMN in ACM and thus a method for CMMN model handling.

The initial search resulted in a combined set of 38 papers matching at least one of the search terms (see Table 2). First tries with different search terms resulted in a large amount of irrelevant papers. For example the combination "ACM" and "Method" had more than 48,000 hits because a lot of abstracts contained references to the Association of Computing Machinery (ACM). Therefore, only the described search terms have been used. Regarding the different portals that have been used for the search, there has been a high redundancy. Most of the results by Web of Science and Elsevier have also been found at Scopus. Only three added to the total number of candidate papers.

Paper selection singled out papers that did not deal with ACM at all. Furthermore, only those have been selected that considered at least one of the categories for method support assessment. If a paper was discussing an ACM related notation, a reference to CMMN was mandatory for inclusion. The selection process ended with 13 papers that have been used for further analysis.

Table 2. Paper identification and selection.

Source	# Identified	# Selected	Selected papers
Scopus	35	13	[1–6, 8–10, 14–16, 18]
Web of science	12	5	[1, 2, 4, 6, 16]
Elsevier	9	2	[14, 18]
Total (no duplicates)	38	13	[1–6, 8–10, 14–16, 18]

4 Data Extraction and Analysis

In the following, the findings with regard to the research questions formulated for the literature analysis are discussed. This analysis is based on the 13 papers found.

Table 3. Data collection results.

Source	Cooperation forms	Concepts and notation	Procedures and framework	Tool support
Benner-Wickner et al.: Supporting adaptive case management through semantic web technologies [1]		X		X
Bider: Towards Process Improvement for Case Management [2]		X		
Bider et al.: Adaptive Case Management as a Process of Construction of and Movement in a State Space [3]		X		X
Blaukopf and Mendling: An Organizational Routines Perspective on Process Requirements [4]		X		
Bukhsh et al.: Understanding modeling requirements of unstructured business processes [5]		X		
Cano et al.: An adaptive case management system to support integrated care services: Lessons learned from the NEXES project [6]		X	X	X
Hauder et al.: Empowering End-Users to Collaboratively Structure Processes for Knowledge Work [8]	X	X	X	X
Hinkelmann: Business process flexibility and decision-aware modeling- The knowledge work designer [9]		X		X
Hinkelmann et al.: The knowledge work designer-Modelling process logic and business logic [10]		X		X
Kurz et al.: Leveraging CMMN for ACM [14]		X		
Marin et al.: Data Centric BPM and the Emerging Case Management Standard: A Short Survey [15]		X		X
Routis et al.: Using CMMN to Model Social Processes [16]		X		
Wang and Traore: DEVS-based case management (WIP) [18]		X		X

4.1   RQ1: Extent of Method Support Consideration

The mapping of the found papers to the categories for method support assessment reveals a strong focus on "Notation and Concepts" in scientific literature when it comes to ACM methods. This can be seen in Table 3. All sources refer to notation or concepts while the categories "Cooperation Forms" and "Procedure and Framework" attract little interest. Many of the papers also refer to tool support for ACM.

4.2   RQ2: Suggestions for Method Support

With regard to "Cooperations Forms" there is a common understanding of a role "knowledge worker" who is the addressee of ACM solutions. However, how the knowledge worker is involved in the creation of process models that are the base for process execution in ACM systems is not addressed. Although Cano et al. [6] describe the process of model creation and adaption, they remain vague regarding the question who is doing what here. The most evident occurrence of cooperation between different roles can be found in Hauder et al.. Here an end-user (knowledge worker) enters data that can be used by modeling experts. However, while end-users work collaboratively in a wiki, cooperation of and with modeling experts is not further described.

The category "Notation and Concepts" will be evaluated thoroughly when *RQ3* and *RQ4* are discussed. In principle, four general suggestions can be derived from literature:

1. Using a reduced set of concepts in order to allow the end-user/knowledge worker to contribute to the modeling process [3,8]
2. Extending the CMMN notation with additional concepts [5]
3. Amending CMMN model by concepts from other standards like BPMN[2] and DMN[3] [9,10] or SBVR[4] [1]
4. Transforming CMMN models into other notations for further processing [2,18]

The other authors just emphasize on possible CMMN shortcomings without discussing solutions or naming CMMN compatible concepts that are used in their methods or tools.

There is also little information regarding "Procedures and Framework" in the literature. Hauder et al. roughly describe a framework and procedures as a two step process. In the first step, end-users enter process relevant information collaboratively in a wiki. They are using a textual representation in order to specify a process type, tasks to be performed and relevant attributes for task fulfillment. In a next step modeling experts create CMMN based process models (case plan models) as templates for process execution. Adaptation and Feedback is not further considered. Cano et al. [6] describe a general ACM process that also contains phases of process modeling and of model adaptation at run-time. However, concrete procedures to elicit model contents are not described. The process is depicted in Fig. 2. It shows the process of typical clinical case handling in combination with ACM. Starting with the "Case Identification", it is

---

[2] https://www.omg.org/spec/BPMN/.

[3] https://www.omg.org/spec/DMN.

[4] https://www.omg.org/spec/SBVR/.

determined whether a certain patient is eligible for a case management based treatment. In the next step the "Case Evaluation", parameters are assessed, providing information for the selection of possible work plans for further treatment. The work plan is determined in the "Work Plan Definition" step (shaded gray). This is the point where process models are created in form of work plan templates and instance (patient) based work plans. Precondition for this modeling step is a library of possible tasks that can be performed in the work plan and a library of work plan templates. The step of "Work Plan Definition" can be applied several times during work plan execution in order to allow situation based adaptations. This is triggered by events and follow-ups. The management of the case instance ends with the "Discharge" step - the patient leaves.

For the category "Tool Support", the literature can be divided into two groups: (1) sources describing workflow management systems that support ACM and (2) sources describing solutions for process model transformation and/or analysis. Several authors from the first group present systems that have been developed in their research groups: Bider et al. with the iPB-System [3], Cano et al. with the ICS-system developed in the NEXES project [6], and Hauder et al. with the Darwin Wiki [8]. Though not being exhaustive, Marin et al. give an overview of commercial ACM capable systems [15]: FLOWer from Pallas Athena, IBM Case Manager, Cordys Case Management. To the second group of authors belong Wang and Traore who discuss the transformation of CMMN models to DEVS models in order to allow simulation and formal verification. with the Knowledge Work Designer, Hinkelmann et al. provide a tool that allows the integration of CMMN, DMN, and BPMN [9,10]. Other authors that would have been assigned to this group did not refer to CMMN and aren't considered further.

Fig. 2. Case management process according to Cano et al. [6].

4.3   RQ3: Fitness of CMMN for ACM

Two general approaches exist in literature when evaluating CMMN for ACM. The first approach considers the method perspective on CMMN. Hence, roles in the modeling and the modeling process itself are taken into account. Thus, Bider et al. [3] , Hauder et al. [8], and Kurz et al. [14] see the problem of understandability of process models for end-users/knowledge workers that are involved. Furthermore, Kurz et al. address the use of CMMN in the ACM process similar to the process shown in Fig. 2, where the "Work Plan definition" step includes model changes at runtime and the usage as well as the improvement of model templates across cases. This reflects the ACM principle of adaption [14]. Since model adaption is primarily a matter of the modeling process, it is not further discussed with regard to notation.

The second approach for the evaluation of CMNN for ACM is to assess which concepts need to be considered and thus modeled when implementing ACM. The resulting concepts can be compared to those defined in CMMN. Hinkelmann [9], Bukhsh et al. [5], and Kurz et al. [14] take this approach. There is a general understanding, that ACM addresses mainly unstructured, knowledge-intensive processes. This implies, that there are also structured parts of the processes that need to modeled. Besides the so called process logic also the business logic hence data and the decision processes based on that data need to be considered [9]. This is also reflected by the ACM principles of data-centricity and goal-orientation as formulated by Kurz et al. [14]. Progress towards process goals should be somehow reflected in the process data. Hinkelmann [9] argues that business logic (data) in knowledge-intensive processes may be structured or unstructured as well, similar to the situation with the process logic. Further modeling requirements can be derived from the ACM principles of collaboration and integration of resources [14]. This requires a role concept and concepts for traceability. Summarizing the discussion, three fields of notation requirements for ACM can be derived: (1) Model support for process logic, (2) Model support for business logic, and (3) Model support for Collaboration. Table 4 collects the particular requirements from the literature sources and assigns them to the three fields. Furthermore, their fulfillment by CMMN is evaluated. The judgment is based on the analyzed sources and the current CMMN 1.1 standard definition. In the following detailed discussion, existing CMMN concepts are set in `typewriter` font.

Table 4 shows a good support for modeling the process logic of unstructured processes. CMMN does not allow a direct modeling of the temporal order of tasks. This can be done implicitly using the `Sentry` concept of CMMN which allows the definition of preconditions for task execution. Therefore, a partial support is indicated in Table 4 for requirement P1. There are three concepts defined in CMMN that allow different levels of task granularity (Requirement P2). The `Stage` concept may contain `Tasks` and `Stages` that are subject to `Stage`-specific process execution rules. Furthermore, the concept of a `CaseTask` refers to other CMMN process models while the concept of a `ProcessTask` refers to structured process models in BPMN, XPDL[5], or BPEL[6]. Thus, a more detailed specification of these tasks can be modeled. Requirement P2 is considered to be fulfilled. Out of order task execution (Requirement P3) is inherently supported by CMMN because the order of task execution is generally not prescribed by CMMN. Defining required and optional tasks as well as the possible re-execution of tasks (Requirements P4 and P5) is possible using the `PlanItemControl` concept of CMMN. Bukhsh et al. [5] suggest undo tasks as a special task type (Requirement P6). This concept is not available in CMMN. Furthermore, they suggest

---

[5] http://www.xpdl.org/.

[6] http://docs.oasis-open.org/wsbpel/2.0/.

to model an execution relation between tasks which implies a required parallel execution of tasks. This is justified by the collaborative nature of knowledge-intensive processes (Requirement P7). The parallel execution concept is not available in CMMN as well.

Discussing Business logic representation in CMMN covers several aspects. First, the principle of data-centricity requires the possibility to create a data or information model. With the `CaseFile` concept, this can be integrated in the process model. The `CaseFile` contains all information objects related to the process - it is a collection of `CaseFileItems` for a process model. A `CaseFileItem` can be any piece of information - structured or unstructured (Requirement B1). CMMN allows to define cardinalities of and simple relations between `CaseFileItems`. Each `CaseFileItem` comes with a predefined set of possible state-changes throughout the information life-cycle (`CaseFileItemTransitions`, Requirement B2). Similarly, there is a predefined set of transitions for processes and their elements (`PlanItemTransitions`). CMMN provides the `Property` concept which may be used to assign attributes and their types to `CaseFileItems`. A concept for data version control (Requirement B3) is absent. An alignment of information in the `CaseFile` to the executed tasks is provided by the `CaseParameters` concept which can be used to define `CaseFileItems` as in- and outputs of a task (Requirement B4). Generally, CMMN does not provide a graphical notation for information modeling. This can be seen as a drawback regarding understandability of the notation.

The CMMN information model forms the base for the definition of business rules an decisions. Taking the common definition of business rules to provide general guidelines for organizational behavior, decision models also form business rules (e.g. [1]). However, due to their importance in ACM according to the literature and their inherent complexity they will be handled separately. Different types of business rules can be distinguished. Sandkuhl et al. define the following types in [17]: (1) Derivation Rules, (2) Event-Action rules, and (3) Constraint rules. The first type – Derivation Rules – describes the derivation of new information from the existing information base. Hence, they describe information that is implicitly available by applying the business rules to existing information objects. Generally, CMMN does not provide concepts for information object manipulation. The `ParameterMapping` is an exception. It provides means to derive parameter values for sub-process execution from `CaseFileItems`. However, this is not an appropriate way to define business rules. Furthermore, CMMN allows the definition of `Decisions` within a `DecisionTask` using DMN. Thus, new information objects or information object values can be derived as decision results based on decision modeling. The second type of business rules – Event-action Rules – concerns the invocation of tasks. This purpose is fulfilled by the `Sentry` concept in CMMN. Pre- and post-conditions of task execution can be defined based on the predefined transitions of process elements in the information model, timer-events, and user-defined events. Whereas user-defined event specification is limited to event names, the `Sentry` may also contain complex expressions that include elements of the types `CaseFileItem` and `Property`.

Nevertheless, no expression language is specified for CMMN. The conditions defined by a `Sentry` are required to be fulfilled in order to allow task execution, but are only sufficient for task execution in the case of automated tasks. The third type of business rules – Constraint Rules – defines constraints for the integrity of the enterprise information and for the execution of tasks. While the execution of tasks can be constrained using the `Sentry` concept, no concept is available for information related constraints except for cardinalities. In summary, a partial support for business rule definition (Requirement B5) is seen for CMMN.

As already discussed, the concepts of `Decision` and `DecisionTask` allow the creation of decision models (Requirement B6). The results of decisions at runtime (Requirement B7) are not considered in the information model of CMMN. Case progress (Requirement B8) can partially be described using the CMMN concept of a `Milestone`. A `Milestone` stands for a desired state in the process execution and hence for progress and achieved objectives (Requirement B9). While the `Milestone` concept is available, it remains open how milestones can be connected to process information that allows the derivation of the current process state. Thus, these requirements are only partially supported.

Having a look into collaboration support, first the existence of a `Role` concept (Requirement C1) is mandatory. It is defined in CMMN. `Tasks` can be assigned to `Roles`. Nevertheless, this is not part of the visual notation of CMMN and an organizational model does not exist. An assignment of roles to individuals is not part of the notation as well. Thus, making individuals responsible for certain tasks (Requirement C2) is not supported. Due to CMMN's simple information model, there is no concept to specify authorizations for data access (Requirement C3).

4.4   RQ4: Notation Suggestions

The general suggestions for addressing the shortcomings of CMMN have already been introduced in the discussion of *RQ2*. The first group of suggestions – reducing the number of used concepts – stems from those authors that criticized the understandability of CMMN for end-users. Hauder et al. [8] reduce the concepts that end-users are required to use down to three: (1) Task, which is also present in CMMN, (2) Attributes, which correspond to `CaseFileItem` or `Property`, and (3) Type, which identifies the case and allows the generation of case templates. Further specification of process models is done by modeling experts based on the information obtained from end-users. Bider et al. [3] reduce the process model to a space of desired states on a given data structure. The data structure corresponds to the `caseFile` concept in CMMN. The closest CMMN concept to a State is a `Milestone`. In combining data structure and states, this approach addresses data-centricity better than CMMN.

Following the discussion of the CMMN limitations with regard to required CMMN concepts leads to suggestions 2 and 3 (see *RQ2*) which means the use of additional concepts either by own additions or by reference to other existing standards. Bukhsh et al. [5] decided to define own concepts and their notation.

Table 4. Requirements fulfillment of CMMN

Process logic		
ID	Requirement description	Fulfillment
P1	Temporal order of tasks [5,9,14]	Partially
P2	Different levels of task granularity [5,14]	Yes
P3	Tasks out of order [5,9,14]	Yes
P4	Optional and required tasks[5]	Yes
P5	Re-executable tasks[5]	Yes
P6	Undo tasks[5]	No
P7	Collaboration between tasks[5]	No
Business logic		
ID	Requirement description	Fulfillment
B1	Integrate unstructured documents and structured data [5,9,14]	Yes
B2	Model information life-cycle [5]	Yes
B3	Data version control [5]	No
B4	Align data with process [5]	Yes
B5	Define business rules [1,5,9]	Partially
B6	Model decisions [5]	Yes
B7	Capture decisions [5]	No
B8	Show Case Progress [14]	Partially
B9	Expression of case objectives [14]	Partially
Collaboration		
ID	Requirement description	Fulfillment
C1	Support a role concept [5,9,14]	Partially
C2	Show individual responsibilities [9,14]	No
C3	Data authorization[5]	No

In comparison with the existing elements of the current CMMN version, the following additions would be made:

- Concept and symbol of a Collaborative sub-process (Requirement P7)
- Concept and symbol of an Undo task (Requirement P6)
- Symbol of a Role (Requirement C1)
- Symbol and notation of a Business Rule (Requirement B5)

Hinkelmann et al. [9,10] use a combination of CMMN and BPMN for the description of process logic in their modeling approach. This results in BPCMN (Business Process and Case Management Notation) which allows an extended visualization of structured process parts using BPMN (Requirement P1) as well as of role assignments to tasks using the Lane concept from BPMN (Requirements C1 and partly C2). In the business logic domain, a graphical notation for information objects is provided.

Benner-Wickner et al. suggest to use SBVR for extended business rule support [1] (Requirement B5).

5   Conclusion and Outlook

the aim of this work was the assessment of the method support for ACM and the fitness of CMMN in this context. This has been further detailed to the four research questions that will shortly be answered in the following:

- *RQ1:* To what extent are the required parts of a method considered in scientific literature on ACM?
  Generally, a strong focus lies on notations and used concepts. This is considered in connection with process execution systems that use process models in the respective notations. In contrast, cooperation forms and modeling procedures receive little attention.
- *RQ2:* What is suggested in scientific literature on ACM with regard to the required parts of a method?
  Except for suggested notations in connection with tool support, there are two roles distinguished that need to be addressed differently in the modeling process - end-users and modeling experts. Furthermore, a rough modeling process with two steps specific to the two roles is described [8]. The paper of Cano et al. [6] suggests a general process for ACM implementation in a clinical context. This also includes the definition of tasks for run-time adaptation of the process model instance.
- *RQ3:* How is the fitness of CMMN for ACM evaluated in scientific literature?
  One key point mentioned in the analyzed papers is the lack of understandability of CMMN models for end-users. Another point are the limitations regarding the modeling of business logic and collaboration.
- *RQ4:* What solutions for possible shortcomings of CMMN with regard to ACM are suggested in scientific literature on ACM?
  As a solution for the first shortcoming of CMMN the reduction of used model concepts has been suggested. As a solution for the limited representation capabilities for important ACM concepts the extension by new concepts or concepts from other notations is discussed.

Overall, the current situation is characterized by a lack of method support for the modeling process. Most studies emphasize on the models and their usage in process execution but not on the model creation and adaption. Furthermore, it seems that collaboration aspects and data-centricity need to be addressed by future notation standards in the context of ACM. However, considering the mentioned problem of understandability, an extension of the available concepts for modeling will increase the demand for a method support regarding modeling procedures and frameworks. Different roles with different knowledge are likely to be involved in modeling.

The results of this study might be biased by the limited amount of analyzed papers. However, using the method of a systematic literature review, it is assumed that a representative cross section of scientific literature has been considered. Thus, there is a good possibility of generalization.

References

1. Benner-Wickner, M., Koop, W., Book, M., Gruhn, V.: Supporting adaptive case management through semantic web technologies. In: Reichert, M., Reijers, H. (eds.) BPM 2015. LNBIP, vol. 256, pp. 65–77. Springer, Cham (2016). https://doi.org/10.1007/978-3-319-42887-1_6
2. Bider, I.: Towards process improvement for case management. In: Reichert, M., Reijers, H. (eds.) BPM 2015. LNBIP, vol. 256, pp. 96–107. Springer, Cham (2016). https://doi.org/10.1007/978-3-319-42887-1_9
3. Bider, I., Jalali, A., Ohlsson, J.: Adaptive case management as a process of construction of and movement in a state space. In: Demey, Y.T., Panetto, H. (eds.) OTM 2013. LNCS, vol. 8186, pp. 155–165. Springer, Heidelberg (2013). https://doi.org/10.1007/978-3-642-41033-8_22
4. Blaukopf, S., Mendling, J.: An organizational routines perspective on process requirements. In: Teniente, E., Weidlich, M. (eds.) BPM 2017. LNBIP, vol. 308, pp. 617–622. Springer, Cham (2018). https://doi.org/10.1007/978-3-319-74030-0_48
5. Bukhsh, Z.A., van Sinderen, M., Klaas, N.S., Quartel, D.: Understanding modeling requirements of unstructured business processes. In: ICETE 2017 - Proceedings of the 14th International Joint Conference on e-Business and Telecommunications, vol. 2 (2017)
6. Cano, I., et al.: An adaptive case management system to support integrated care services: lessons learned from the NEXES project. J. Biomed. Inform. **55**, 11–22 (2015). https://doi.org/10.1016/j.jbi.2015.02.011
7. Goldkuhl, G., Lind, M., Seigerroth, U.: Method integration: the need for a learning perspective. IEE Proc. Softw. **145**(4), 113 (1998). https://doi.org/10.1049/ip-sen:19982197
8. Hauder, M., Kazman, R., Matthes, F.: Empowering end-users to collaboratively structure processes for knowledge work. In: Abramowicz, W. (ed.) BIS 2015. LNBIP, vol. 208, pp. 207–219. Springer, Cham (2015). https://doi.org/10.1007/978-3-319-19027-3_17
9. Hinkelmann, K.: Business Process flexibility and decision-aware modeling—the knowledge work designer. In: Karagiannis, D., Mayr, H., Mylopoulos, J. (eds.) Domain-Specific Conceptual Modeling, pp. 397–414. Springer, Cham (2016). https://doi.org/10.1007/978-3-319-39417-6_18
10. Hinkelmann, K., Pierfranceschi, A., Laurenzi, E.: The knowledge work designer-modelling process logic and business logic. In: Lecture Notes in Informatics (LNI). In: Proceedings - Series of the Gesellschaft fur Informatik (GI), p. 255 (2016)
11. Ivarsson, M., Gorschek, T.: Technology transfer decision support in requirements engineering research: a systematic review of REj. Requir. Eng. **14**(3), 155–175 (2009)
12. Karagiannis, D., Kühn, H.: Metamodelling platforms. In: Bauknecht, K., Tjoa, A.M., Quirchmayr, G. (eds.) EC-Web 2002. LNCS, vol. 2455, pp. 182–182. Springer, Heidelberg (2002). https://doi.org/10.1007/3-540-45705-4_19

13. Kitchenham, B.: Procedures for performing systematic reviews. Keele, UK, Keele University **33**(2004), 1–26 (2004)

14. Kurz, M., Schmidt, W., Fleischmann, A., Lederer, M.: Leveraging CMMN for ACM. In: Unknown (ed.) Proceedings of the 7th International Conference on Subject-Oriented Business Process Management - S-BPM ONE 2015, pp. 1–9. ACM Press, New York, New York, USA (2015). https://doi.org/10.1145/2723839. 2723843

15. Marin, M., Hull, R., Vaculín, R.: Data centric BPM and the emerging case management standard: a short survey. In: La Rosa, M., Soffer, P. (eds.) BPM 2012. LNBIP, vol. 132, pp. 24–30. Springer, Heidelberg (2013). https://doi.org/10.1007/978-3-642-36285-9_4

16. Routis, I., Nikolaidou, M., Anagnostopoulos, D.: Using CMMN to model social processes. In: Teniente, E., Weidlich, M. (eds.) BPM 2017. LNBIP, vol. 308, pp. 335–347. Springer, Cham (2018). https://doi.org/10.1007/978-3-319-74030-0_25

17. Sandkuhl, K., Stirna, J., Persson, A., Wißotzki, M.: Enterprise Modeling: Tackling Business Challenges with the 4EM Method. TEES. Springer, Heidelberg (2014). https://doi.org/10.1007/978-3-662-43725-4

18. Wang, S., Traoré, M.K.: DEVS-based case management (WIP). Simul. Ser. **46**(4) (2014)

19. Webster, J., Watson, R.T.: Analyzing the past to prepare for the future: writing a literature review. MIS q., xiii–xxiii (2002)

Metamodel-Based Analysis of Domain-Specific Conceptual Modeling Methods

Dominik Bork[(✉)] [iD]

Research Group Knowledge Engineering, University of Vienna,
Waehringer Street 29, 1090 Vienna, Austria
dominik.bork@univie.ac.at

Abstract. Metamodels play a pivotal role in conceptual modeling as they manifest the abstraction level applied when creating conceptual models. Consequently, design decisions made by the metamodel developer determine utility, capabilities, and expressiveness of the conceptual modeling language - and eventually the created models. However, only limited research defines and applies metrics for analyzing the structure and capabilities of a metamodel, and eventually support the development of new metamodels. This not only concerns general-purpose modeling languages, but also domain-specific ones, which usually undergo shorter update cycles. The paper at hand introduces a generic analysis framework to syntactically analyze modeling languages. The framework is applied to 40 metamodels of domain-specific conceptual modeling languages (DSML). This research establishes a foundation to support metamodel development in the future. The contribution of this paper is threefold: (i) an analysis framework for conceptual modeling method metamodels is proposed, (ii) results from applying this framework to 40 ADOxx-based DSML metamodels are presented, and (iii) a human-based reasoning after comparison of these results with Ecore-based metamodels is conducted.

Keywords: Domain-specific modeling · Conceptual modeling
Metamodel · Analysis · OMiLAB · Metrics

1 Introduction

Conceptual modeling historically plays an important role in information and computer science research. Numerous modeling approaches have been designed. Some of which aim for general applicability and wide adoption - general-purpose modeling languages like Unified Modeling Language (UML), and Business Process Modeling and Notation (BPMN) - whereas others aim to precisely address

R. A. Buchmann et al. (Eds.): PoEM 2018, LNBIP 335, pp. 172–187, 2018.
https://doi.org/10.1007/978-3-030-02302-7_11

the specific characteristics of a certain domain - domain-specific modeling languages (DSMLs). While the focus in early years was on the specification of general-purpose modeling languages, nowadays, researchers also emphasize the importance of creating DSMLs (cf. [29] for recently developer DSMLs). Such DSMLs employ an abstraction level that is aligned to the purposes of specific stakeholders in a specific application domain.

Metamodels are at the heart of any conceptual modeling language as they establish the abstraction level to be applied while creating models. This abstraction level is realized by means of the available concepts of a modeling language and the valid combinations thereof. Decisions taken by the metamodel developer determine quality, expressiveness, and utility of the modeling language (cf. [23]). A lot of research is focusing on the evaluation of modeling methods from a semantical point of view [18,19], from a notational point of view [7,37,41], or on methodological guidance in developing modeling languages [16,27] and methods [3,13,36]. By contrast, only limited research focuses on metamodels and their design. *"The rationale behind decisions made during the language/model specification are implicit so it is not possible to understand or justify why, for instance, a certain element of the language was created with that specific syntax or given that particular type."* [26] Thus, there is a research gap in analyzing existing and providing guidance for the development of new metamodels. Moreover, to the best of our knowledge, no comparative analysis has been performed targeting specifically DSML metamodels. The aim of this research is to derive empirical quantitative answers towards filling the identified research gap.

The aim of this paper is to assess current DSML metamodel designs and to derive ideas on how to improve metamodel design in the future. The contribution of this paper is aligned to two research questions (RQ): *RQ-1: How are domain-specific metamodels structured?*, and *RQ-2: Are there differences between ADOxx-based and Eclipse-based metamodels?*. The analysis reported in this paper used 40 openly available DSML metamodels of the Open Models Laboratory (OMiLAB) [8] that have been realized with the ADOxx metamodeling platform [15]. For the analysis we introduce a framework that adopts a set of metamodeling metrics [12,35]. The adoption of the metrics respects the idiosyncrasy of both, conceptual modeling generally and the ADOxx platform in particular. *"Similarly to software, metrics can be used to obtain objective, transparent, and reproducible measurements on metamodels too"* [12, p. 55]. Our work adds to the knowledge base by focusing on metrics rather than a qualitative evaluation of metamodels, and by focusing on ADOxx-based DSML metamodels.

This paper is structured as follows: Sect. 2 defines the foundations of this work by introducing domain-specific conceptual modeling, the Open Models Laboratory, as well as ADOxx and Eclipse as metamodel development platforms. An overview of related works is presented in Sect. 3 before Sect. 4 proposes the generic analysis framework. The results of applying this framework to 40 DSMLs are discussed in Sect. 5. Eventually, the paper closes with some concluding remarks and implications for research and practice in Sect. 6.

2   Foundations

2.1   Conceptual Modeling Methods

Conceptual modeling methods facilitate the reduction of complexity by applying abstraction for a specific purpose. Such methods are composed of *modeling language, modeling procedure,* and *mechanisms & algorithms* [28]. A vital part of a modeling method is the modeling language which can be further decomposed into *syntax,* i.e, the available syntactic elements, *notation,* and *semantics,* specifying the graphical representation and the meaning of the syntactic elements, respectively. The modeling procedure describes the steps to be applied by the modeler in order to create valid models. Mechanisms & algorithms define the model processing functionality provided by the modeling method, e.g., simulation, model transformation.

Based on the pragmatics and purpose, domain-specific modeling methods can be distinguished from general-purpose ones. The former has the potential to address domain-specificity in all aspects of a modeling method, while the latter aims for comparability, interoperability, and standardization across domains. A further differentiation can be drawn when considering the purpose of modeling methods. In computer science, most modeling methods are designed for model-driven systems engineering using the Eclipse Modeling Framework[1] which rely on Ecore metamodels (see Sect. 2.3). Such models often lack proper visualization and focus instead on the capabilities of model transformation and code generation. By contrast, conceptual modeling methods are used to create abstract representations of some part of the real world for *"human users, for purposes of understanding and communication"* [38]. In this perception, which is the one we apply in this paper, modeling of software systems and code generation is only one out of many possible purposes for conceptual modeling.

2.2   The Open Models Laboratory (OMiLAB)

OMiLAB, www.omilab.org is an open platform for the conceptualization of modeling methods, combining open source and open communities with the goal of fostering conceptual modeling [8]. Modeling tools realized as a project within the OMiLAB are based on the ADOxx metamodeling platform (see Sect. 2.3). Relevance of the OMiLAB is reflected in the high number of international contributors. 40 different DSMLs have been successfully conceptualized - addressing diverse domains like enterprise modeling [14], enterprise architecture management [4], design thinking [5,22], and knowledge acquisition [9,10]. A detailed description with sample conceptualizations is given in [29].

2.3   Metamodeling Platform

Metamodeling platforms are used for the development of modeling tools by raising the abstraction level to a more elaborate level that is adequate for

---

[1] Eclipse Modeling Framework [online], https://www.eclipse.org/modeling/emf/, last checked: 28.08.2018

method engineers to realize their modeling tools. The goal is to enable also non-programmers to realize modeling tools. This is achieved by providing a rich set of preconfigured functionality attached to a generic meta-metamodel. The method engineer then only needs to adapt this meta-metamodel to her domain. Moreover, engineers can benefit from existing tool developments and reuse/extend existing implementations.

ADOxx. ADOxx[2] has been successfully used in academia and industry for over two decades. The platform comes with a rich set of domain-independent functionality like model management, user management, and user interaction. What is left to be done for metamodel developers is to [2]: (1) configure the specific metamodel by referring its concepts to the meta-metamodel concepts of ADOxx; (2) provide a visualization for the concepts and combine them into logical chunks, i.e., ADOxx modeltypes; and (3) realize additional functionality like model transformations, queries, or simulations on top of the modeling language.

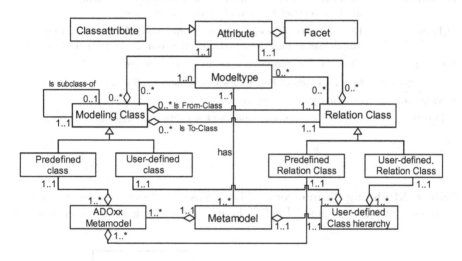

Fig. 1. Excerpt of the ADOxx meta-metamodel (adapted from [15])

A metamodel realized with ADOxx is composed of *modeltypes* which themselves comprise predefined and user-defined *modeling classes* and *relation classes* (Fig. 1). Following a graph-based structure, modeling classes refer to nodes and relation classes to edges between nodes. Attributes define the semantics of all ADOxx classes. Functionality in ADOxx is attached to predefined abstract meta classes of the ADOxx meta-metamodel (see Fig. 1). When defining an inheritance relationship between domain-specific concepts and predefined abstract meta classes, the functionality is inherited. Consequently, the metamodel design decisions determine the functionality of the resulting modeling tool.

---

[2] ADOxx platform [online], http://www.adoxx.org, last checked: 27.08.2018

Table 1 briefly introduces the most important ADOxx meta classes which are also part of the metrics introduced in Sect. 4. ADOxx meta classes are either static (prefix 'S') or dynamic (prefix 'D'). The former employ a tree-based structure for hierarchies between static classes while the latter employ a graph-based structure for realizing simulations. Furthermore, ADOxx modeling classes can be either *abstract*, thus not instantiable by the modeler, or *concrete*, thus can be instantiated thereby creating a conceptual model.

Table 1. Excerpt of ADOxx meta classes

Meta class	Description
D_Aggregation	Every modeled object 'a' having its x/y coordinates within the drawing area of any container 'b' has the relation *'a' is-inside 'b'*. Moreover, subclasses come with a self-defined "drawing area" by means of resizeable rectangles
D_Swimlane	Also provides the "is-inside" relation but the "drawing area" is limited to strict horizontal or vertical rectangles
D_Event	Encapsulates all nodes of a graph necessary for its simulation. Subclasses are e.g., D_Start, D_Subgraph, D_Activity, D_Decision
S_Group	This class represents a node in a tree structure
S_Aggregation	Special kinds of nodes in a tree structure. Similar semantics as
S_Swimlane	for the dynamic counterparts
S_Person	Implements person-dependent aspects like wages and working hours

Eclipse Modeling Framework. The Eclipse Modeling Framework (EMF) provides a generic metamodel called Ecore, one can inherit from in order to

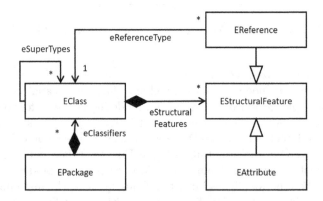

Fig. 2. Excerpt of the Ecore meta-metamodel [30]

develop metamodels. A dominant focus of using EMF is the generation of code from models in model-driven development. Thus, models are primarily perceived as "structured data models". EMF comes with a rich set of functionality that eases the generation of Java classes from EMF models.

The Ecore metamodel comes with a plethora of predefined meta classes necessary for code generation purposes and general model management. Relevant for conceptual modeling are particularly the classes visualized in Fig. 2. Ecore-based metamodels are clustered in *EPackages* which are comprised of *EClasses*. Every EClass itself is comprised of *EStructuralFeatures* like changeability or volatility. Two special kinds of features are further distinguished: *EReferences* relate two EClass instances to each other, whereas *EAttributes* define additional properties of EClasses.

3 Related Works

A lot of research can be found on the analysis of models, focusing for example on the usage of modeling concepts by modelers [33], the evaluation of modeling languages according to their notation [7,32,37], their semantics [19,42], their ontological completeness [18], their metamodels [34], their specification techniques [6], or their applicability in certain use cases [20] and domains [24,25]. These approaches however never investigate the syntactic metamodel backbone of the modeling language and the way metamodels are structured. Up to now, only limited research structurally assesses metamodels by applying metrics. The relevant works will be reviewed in the following sub-sections.

An approach for metamodel analysis was proposed in [43]. The authors introduced metrics for the syntactic analysis of metamodels. They distinguish between *metrics concerning meta-classes* and *metrics concerning meta-features*. The former comprises the number of (abstract) classes, and whether classes have features. Moreover, average numbers for *features*, *attributes*, and *references* are computed. The metrics for meta-features consider some of the class-level metrics, however, applied to the whole metamodel. The authors developed a script that automatically analyzed over 500 Ecore metamodels.

Di Rocco [12] proposed a set of metrics to analyze metamodels. A focus of their study was computing the correlations between different metrics toward the identification of structural characteristics of metamodels. The metrics have been applied to a corpus of Ecore metamodels. They identified e.g., that *the adoption of inheritance is proportional to the size of metamodels* [12, p. 59].

Ma et al. [35] proposed a quality model for metamodels. The aim of their work was to provide guidance for researchers and practitioners on how to design metamodels of "good quality" by introducing the following quality attributes: *syntactic, semantic, pragmatic, capability,* and *evolvability*. Their approach remains on a theoretical level, contributing a research model that, based on questionnaires with 15 metamodel developers, quantifies the relationships between the quality parameters and the quality properties of a metamodel. Eventually, the authors apply the quality model to evaluate a set of evolutionary UML metamodels.

Recently, Lopez et al. [34] proposed 30 quality properties for metamodels, comprising the categories *design*, *best practice*, *naming conventions*, and *metric*. The focus was on measuring ex post the quality of a given metamodel. The metrics introduced by the authors establish some threshold values, e.g., for the number of direct children (10-max as default), mostly related from object-oriented design. The five metrics focus on coupling and inheritance aspects. The metrics have been applied to EMF metamodels.

The reviewed approaches all analyze EMF metamodels. This is not surprising, as up until recently, no corpus of metamodels developed with any other metamodeling platform was available. Consequently, the introduced metrics are also designed for EMF metamodels, omitting aspects of DSMLs like relations and modeltypes. The paper at hand extends the knowledge base by: i) establishing a framework to comprehensively analyze DSMLs; and ii) applying this framework to 40 DSML metamodels.

4   Metamodel Analysis Metrics

In the following, a novel analysis metrics framework is proposed targeting the comprehensive analysis of syntactic and structural aspects of DSMLs. The framework includes generic metamodel metrics found in literature and extends them in two ways: First and foremost, generic metrics for conceptual modeling methods. Second, some metrics specifically for ADOxx metamodels.

Table 2. Metamodel analysis metrics

Metric	Description
Generic metamodel metrics	
Concrete classes	The number of concrete classes
Abstract classes	The number of abstract classes
Attributes	The number of attributes
References	Number of references between two concepts
Inheritance	Maximal inheritance level
Conceptual Modeling-specific metamodel metrics	
Modeltypes	The number of modeltypes
Relation classes	The number of relation classes
ADOxx-specific metamodel metrics	
Dynamic modeltypes	The number of dynamic modeltypes
Static modeltypes	The number of static modeltypes
Dynamic classes	The number of dynamic classes
Static classes	The number of static classes

Generic metamodel metrics Analyzing the relevant literature [12,34,35,43], a set of recurring metamodel metrics can be identified (see Table 2). For these metrics, average values, min-max values, and statistical measures like median, quartiles, and standard deviation can be computed.

Conceptual Modeling-specific metamodel metrics The set of metrics in literature does not consider important characteristics of conceptual modeling methods. Relation classes are not considered explicitly but subsumed in the classes metric. Moreover, the decomposition of a modeling language into modeltypes is neglected. Consequently, corresponding metrics are introduced in Table 2, particularly addressing these shortcomings.

ADOxx-specific metamodel metrics In addition to the metrics described previously, meta class-specific metrics are introduced in order to enable a deeper analysis of the realization of DSMLs by means of the inheritance relationships to the predefined ADOxx meta classes (see Table 1). These metrics indicate the functionality utilized by a DSML and contribute toward externalizing the implicit design decisions made by the metamodel developer. Thus revealing the rationale behind metamodel designs (cf. [26]).

5 Analyzing Domain-Specific Metamodels

In the following, the metrics will be applied to 40 DSML metamodels. All metamodels have been realized within the OMiLAB using the ADOxx platform. Section 5.1 will first describe the research procedure followed while Sect. 5.2 reports on the key findings. Eventually, Sect. 5.3 compares the results with metrics of Ecore-based metamodels.

5.1 Preparing the Analysis

The analysis was aligned to extensively used literature survey methodologies [31]. However, instead of surveying articles, we surveyed metamodels. Thus, we followed a three-phased approach, comprising: 1. Planning, 2. Conducting, and 3. Analyzing. In the *planning phase*, we defined the research objectives. We were interested in empirically analyzing metamodels of DSMLs. Besides, we were also interested in how our results differ from Ecore metamodels. As a consequence, we chose the openly available metamodel repository of the OMiLAB as a source.

In the *conducting phase*, we queried the OMiLAB and collected 44 DSMLs metamodels. We then applied two exclusion criteria: Ex-1: the metamodel combines several completely independent modeling languages; and Ex-2: metamodels realized on an old version of ADOxx, these methods are neither maintained nor used anymore. In total, 4 metamodels matched the exclusion criteria, resulting in 40 metamodels which were analyzed in the *analysis phase* by applying the metamodel analysis metrics introduced in Sect. 4.

5.2   Results of the Analysis

The average number of modeltypes for a DSML is 7.15, whereas dynamic modeltypes following a graph-based structure are dominant with 6.68 compared to static ones following a tree-based structure with 0.48. All investigated DSMLs have at least one dynamic modeltype whereas only 40% have at least one static modeltype. The maximum number of modeltypes was found for LearnPAD [11] with 23 (22 + 1), followed by CuTiDe [5] with 21 (20 + 1), HORUS [40] with 19 (19 + 0), and MEMO4ADO [1] with 18 (18 + 0) modeltypes (dynamic + static), respectively. Fig. 3 illustrates the dominance of dynamic modeltypes.

Heterogeneous results were derived by looking at the number of classes. The average number of concrete classes is 49.23, with a median of 36. The maximum number of classes was found in CuTiDe [5] with 180 whereas the minimal number was found in the SERM [17] metamodel containing five classes. Abstract classes are used in 57.5% of the DSMLs, whereas the average number of abstract classes per metamodel is only 3.45 with a median of 1. CuTiDe has the most abstract classes (24). We found an average number of 20.2 relation classes, the median was 15. The most relation classes were found for the MEMO4ADO method [1] with 81, whereas the lowest number was found for PGA [39] and JCS [21] which both only contain one relation class. Fig. 4 visualizes analysis results for concrete, abstract, and relation classes of the DSML metamodels.

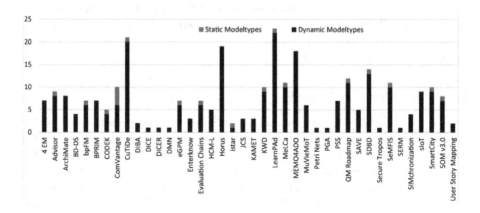

Fig. 3. Dynamic and static modeltypes per metamodel

In conceptual modeling, the majority of the semantics is encoded with the attributes of classes and relation classes. It is thus interesting to analyze, e.g., how many and which kind of attributes have been introduced as an indicator for the complexity of the domain to be addressed by the modeling method. Three kinds of attributes have been analyzed: *regular attributes*, e.g., of datatype string, integer, or boolean; *reference attributes*, enabling the creation of relationships between concepts within one or between different models; and *record table*

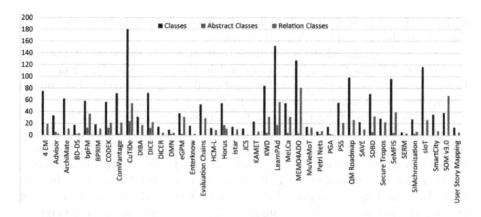

Fig. 4. Number of Concrete, Abstract, and Relation Classes per metamodel

attributes, used to create multi-dimensional attributes, i.e., tables. Finally, the DSMLs were analyzed for featureless classes - classes with no own attributes.

The average number of regular attributes is 11,76. The DICE method has the highest average amount of regular attributes per class (30.5), JCS has the lowest amount with 1.67. Reference attributes are used by 87.5% of the DSMLs with an average number of 45 per metamodel. By contrast, record table attributes are used by 67.5% of the DSMLs with an average number of only 8.75.

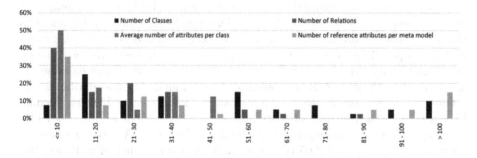

Fig. 5. Distribution of DSMLs based on classes, relations, attributes, and references

Besides the average and total numbers, it is also interesting to analyze the distribution of metrics criteria. We focus in the following on the most interesting ones due to limited space. Fig. 5 provides the results of grouping the DSMLs according to the total number of classes and relations, the average number of attributes per class, and the number of reference attributes per metamodel. It can be derived, that the biggest group of metamodels comprises 11 to 20 classes (25%), less than 10 relations (40%), and less than 10 references (35%). Moreover, in 50% of the metamodels, a class has in average less than 10 attributes. The majority of metamodels have less than 40 classes, less than 20 relations, less than 10 attributes, and less than 30 references.

Next, we investigated the inheritance relationships of the abstract and concrete classes. Within the analyzed metamodels, the abstract ADOxx meta class D_Aggregation was inherited from the most (in 67.5%), followed by D_Swimlane and S_Group from which was inherited from by 40% of the metamodels.

It can be derived from the complete analysis summarized in Table 3, that predefined abstract meta classes are more often used in the dynamic modeltypes compared to the static ones. Moreover, abstract classes for geographical containment (e.g., aggregation and swimlane) are used more frequently compared to simulation-specific classes like D_Event which was only inherited from by 10% of the DSMLs. Table 3 also provides for each applied metric, the total number of appearances in the 40 DSML metamodels and an average number, the maximal and minimal number of appearances, and the percentage of occurrences.

5.3   Comparison with Ecore-Based Metamodels

As mentioned in Sect. 3, related works exist that analyze Ecore-based metamodels. An assumption underlying both, Ecore and ADOxx metamodels is that the former primarily concentrates model-driven development and code generation whereas the latter primarily focuses on applying abstraction in order to create conceptual models for the purpose of communication and understanding by human beings [38]. Thus, we were interested in testing this hypothesis by comparing those metrics that are applicable to Ecore and ADOxx metamodels.

The results of this comparison are summarized in Table 4. The metamodel size is on average quite similar with 49.23 classes in ADOxx metamodels and 39.3 classes in Ecore. However, the median of ADOxx metamodels is almost 3 times higher compared to Ecore ones (36 compared to 13 classes). Abstract classes are almost equally used with 56% and 57.5%. Interestingly, Ecore metamodels differ significantly from ADOxx metamodels when analyzing the attributes and references. Ecore metamodels have a median of 13.5 references (ADOxx median is only 0.75), and a median of 8 attributes (ADOxx median is 7.5). They also differ with respect to the depth of the inheritance hierarchy. ADOxx metamodels have an average depth of 2.65 (Ecore: 5) and a maximal depth of 6 (Ecore: 10). The distribution of the size of the metamodels differs significantly. For ADOxx metamodels, only one third have less than 20 classes, whereas 69% of Ecore-based metamodels are this small.

It seems that the ADOxx based DSML metamodels are significantly larger compared to Ecore-based ones. This indicates, that the Ecore-based modeling languages are mostly designed for really narrow purposes which fits to the model-driven development domain. On the other hand, the usage of reference attributes is way more common in Ecore-based metamodels. This fact could be explained by the purpose of Ecore metamodels to act as structured data model. These references could solve referential integrity in the resulting data models.

Table 3. DSML metamodel metrics results

Metric	Total	Average per MM	Max	Min	Used by % of MM
Modeltype metrics					
Dynamic modeltypes	267	6.68	22	1	100 %
Static modeltypes	16	0.48	4	0	40 %
Classes and relation classes metrics					
Abstract classes	138	3.45	24	0	57.5 %
Concrete classes	1969	49.23	180	5	100 %
Dynamic classes	1782	44.55	169	5	100 %
Static classes	187	4.675	33	0	47.5 %
Relation Classes	808	20.2	81	1	100 %
Dynamic relation classes	655	16.38	81	1	100 %
Static relation classes	153	3.825	14	0	37.5 %
ADOxx-specific inheritance metrics					
D_Aggregation	80	2	8	0	67.5 %
D_Swimlane	41	1.03	8	0	40 %
D_Event	6	0.15	3	0	10 %
S_Group	44	1.1	4	0	40 %
S_Aggregation	15	0.38	2	0	35 %
S_Swimlane	22	0.55	2	0	27.5 %
S_Person	24	0.6	2	0	37.5 %
Attribute metrics					
Regular	27161	679.03	3411	14	100 %
References	1802	45.05	175	0	87.5 %
Record tables	350	8.75	59	0	67.5 %

Table 4. ADOxx vs. Ecore-based metamodel metrics

Metric	DSML metamodels	Ecore metamodels [43]
Average number of classes	49.23	39.3
Median number of classes	36	13
Max. number of classes	180	912
% metamodels using abstract classes	57.5 %	56 %
Median number of attributes per class	7.6	8
Median number of references per class	0.75	13.5
Average depth of inheritance	2.65	5
Max. depth of inheritance	6	10
Metamodels with <20 classes	33 %	69 %

6   Concluding Remarks and Future Work

To improve the development of new metamodels, analysis of existing ones seems promising. The paper at hand first introduced a generic metamodel analysis framework for analyzing conceptual modeling metamodels. This framework has then been applied to analyze 40 domain-specific conceptual modeling languages. Eventually, the results have been compared with Ecore-based metamodels.

It can be derived, that DSML metamodels are generally larger by nature considering the number of classes. When looking at the attributes, similarities and differences can be found. Ecore metamodels significantly more often use references, whereas the usage of regular attributes is almost equal. Moreover, Ecore metamodels have significantly deeper metamodel hierarchies.

As for any analysis, the results also have some threats to validity. All analyzed metamodels were realized with ADOxx. Thus, a platform bias is inevitable. Finally, it needs to be stated, that the Ecore metrics are based on a larger corpora of publicly available metamodels. Further application of the metrics need to verify completeness of the analysis framework and validity of the results.

From a practical perspective, the results indicate which concepts are actually used in DSMLs. It thus gives empirical insights into previously implicit metamodel design decisions and points metamodeling platform developers to aspects worthwhile for improvement - and others that can be lower prioritized.

We will prepare an open source webservice implementation of the metrics that will enable method engineers to apply the metrics to their metamodels by themselves. Moreover, we will now focus on identifying best practices and anti-patterns of metamodel design by investigating their quality impact. Moreover, research is left to be done in analyzing e.g., the metamodel domain, the communities developing the metamodels, and linguistic/semantic analysis of metamodels.

Acknowledgments. Part of this research has been funded through the South Africa / Austria Joint Scientific and Technological Cooperation program with the project number ZA 11/2017.

References

1. Bock, A., Frank, U.: Multi-perspective enterprise modeling—conceptual foundation and implementation with ADOxx. In: Karagiannis, D., Mayr, H.C., Mylopoulos, J. (eds.) Domain-Specific Conceptual Modeling, pp. 241–267. Springer, Cham (2016). https://doi.org/10.1007/978-3-319-39417-6_11
2. Bork, D., Sinz, E.J.: Design of a SOM business process modelling tool based on the ADOxx meta-modelling platform. In: Pre-proceedings of the 4th international workshop on graph-based tools. University of Twente, Enschede, pp. 90–101 (2010)
3. Bork, D.: Using conceptual modeling for designing multi-view modeling tools. In: 21st Americas Conference on Information Systems, AMCIS 2015, Puerto Rico, August 13–15 2015

4. Bork, D. et al.: Requirements engineering for model-based enterprise architecture management with ArchiMate. In: Enterprise and Organizational Modeling and Simulation, 14th International Workshop, EOMAS 2018, Held at CAiSE 2018, Tallinn, Estonia (2018), in press
5. Bork, D., Karagiannis, D., Hawryszkiewycz, I.T.: Supporting customized design thinking using a metamodel-based approach. In: Proceedings of the Australasian Conference on Information Systems (ACIS), Hobart, Australia (2017)
6. Bork, D., Karagiannis, D., Pittl, B.: How are Metamodels specified in practice? empirical insights and recommendations. In: Twenty-fourth Americas Conference on Information Systems, pp. 1–10 (2018)
7. Bork, D., Karagiannis, D., Pittl, B.: Systematic analysis and evaluation of visual conceptual modeling language notations In: 2018 12th International Conference on Research Challenges in Information Science (RCIS), pp. 1–11. IEEE (2018)
8. Bork, D., Miron, E.T.: OMiLAB - an open innovation community for modeling method engineering. In: Niculescu, A., Negoita, O.D., Tiganoaia, B. (eds.) 8th International Conference of Management and Industrial Engineering (ICMIE 2017), pp. 64–77 (2017). http://eprints.cs.univie.ac.at/5145/
9. Cairó, O., Guardati, S.: The KAMET II methodology: knowledge acquisition, knowledge modeling and knowledge generation. Expert Syst. Appl. **39**(9), 8108–8114 (2012)
10. Cairó Battistutti, O., Bork, D.: Tacit to explicit knowledge conversion. Cognit. Process. **18**(4), 461–477 (2017)
11. De Angelis, G., Pierantonio, A., Polini, A., Re, B., Thönssen, B., Woitsch, R.: Modeling for learning in public administrations—the learn PAd approach. In: Karagiannis, D., Mayr, H., Mylopoulos, J. (eds.) Domain-Specific Conceptual Modeling, pp. 575–594. Springer, Cham (2016). https://doi.org/10.1007/978-3-319-39417-6_26
12. Di Rocco, J., Di Ruscio, D., Iovino, L., Pierantonio, A.: Mining Metrics for understanding metamodel characteristics. In: Proceedings of the 6th International Workshop on Modeling in Software Engineering, pp. 55–60. MiSE 2014, ACM, New York, NY, USA (2014)
13. Efendioglu, N., Woitsch, R., Utz, W.: A toolbox supporting agile modelling method engineering: ADOxx.org modelling method conceptualization environment. In: Horkoff, J., Jeusfeld, M.A., Persson, A. (eds.) PoEM 2016. LNBIP, vol. 267, pp. 317–325. Springer, Cham (2016). https://doi.org/10.1007/978-3-319-48393-1_23
14. Ferstl, O.K., Sinz, E.J., Bork, D.: Tool support for the semantic object model. In: Karagiannis, D., Mayr, H., Mylopoulos, J. (eds.) Domain-Specific Conceptual Modeling, pp. 291–310. Springer, Cham (2016). https://doi.org/10.1007/978-3-319-39417-6_13
15. Fill, H.G., Karagiannis, D.: On the conceptualisation of modelling methods using the ADOxx meta modelling platform. Enterp. Modell. Inf. Syst. Architect. **8**(1), 4–25 (2013)
16. Frank, U.: Domain-specific modeling languages: requirements analysis and design guidelines. In: Reinhartz-Berger, I., Sturm, A., Clark, T., Cohen, S., Bettin, J. (eds.) Domain Engineering, pp. 133–157. Springer, Heidelberg (2013)
17. Glässner, T.M., Heumann, F., Keßler, L., Härer, F., Steffan, A., Fill, H.G.: Experiences from the implementation of a structured-entity-relationship modeling method in a student project. In: Bork, D., Karagiannis, D., Vanthienen, J. (eds.) Proceedings of the 1st International Workshop on Practicing Open Enterprise Modeling within OMiLAB (PrOse 2017). CEUR Proceedings (2017)
18. Guizzardi, G.: Ontological foundations for structural conceptual models. CTIT, Centre for Telematics and Information Technology (2005)

19. Guizzardi, G., Herre, H., Wagner, G.: On the general ontological foundations of conceptual modeling. In: Spaccapietra, S., March, S.T., Kambayashi, Y. (eds.) ER 2002. LNCS, vol. 2503, pp. 65–78. Springer, Heidelberg (2002). https://doi.org/10.1007/3-540-45816-6_15

20. Gupta, H.V., Clark, M.P., Vrugt, J.A., Abramowitz, G., Ye, M.: Towards a comprehensive assessment of model structural adequacy. Water Resour. Res. **48**(8) (2012)

21. Hara, Y., Masuda, H.: Global service enhancement for japanese creative services based on the early/late binding concepts. In: Karagiannis, D., Mayr, H., Mylopoulos, J. (eds.) Domain-Specific Conceptual Modeling, pp. 509–526. Springer, Cham (2016). https://doi.org/10.1007/978-3-319-39417-6_23

22. Hawryszkiewycz, I.T., Prackwieser, C.: MELCA—customizing visualizations for design thinking. In: Karagiannis, D., Mayr, H., Mylopoulos, J. (eds.) Domain-Specific Conceptual Modeling, pp. 383–396. Springer, Cham (2016). https://doi.org/10.1007/978-3-319-39417-6_17

23. Hinkel, G., Kramer, M., Burger, E., Strittmatter, M., Happe, L.: An empirical study on the perception of metamodel quality. In: 2016 4th International Conference on Model-Driven Engineering and Software Development (MODELSWARD), pp. 145–152. IEEE (2016)

24. Houy, C., Fettke, P., Loos, P.: Understanding understandability of conceptual models – what are we actually talking about? In: Atzeni, P., Cheung, D., Ram, S. (eds.) ER 2012. LNCS, vol. 7532, pp. 64–77. Springer, Heidelberg (2012). https://doi.org/10.1007/978-3-642-34002-4_5

25. Houy, C., Fettke, P., Loos, P.: On the theoretical foundations of research into the understandability of business process models. In: Avital, M., Leimeister, J.M., Schultze, U. (eds.) 22st European Conference on Information Systems, ECIS 2014, Tel Aviv, Israel, June 9–11, 2014 (2014). http://aisel.aisnet.org/ecis2014/proceedings/track06/7

26. Izquierdo, J.L.C., Cabot, J.: Collaboro: a collaborative (meta) modeling tool. Peer J. Computer. Sci. **2**, e84 (2016)

27. Karagiannis, D.: Agile modeling method engineering. In: Proceedings of the 19th Panhellenic Conference on Informatics, pp. 5–10. ACM (2015)

28. Karagiannis, D., Kühn, H.: Metamodelling platforms. In: Bauknecht, K., Tjoa, A.M., Quirchmayr, G. (eds.) EC-Web 2002. LNCS, vol. 2455, pp. 182–182. Springer, Heidelberg (2002). https://doi.org/10.1007/3-540-45705-4_19

29. Karagiannis, D., Mayr, H.C., Mylopoulos, J.: Domain-Specific Conceptual Modelling. Springer, Heidelberg (2016)

30. Kern, H., Hummel, A., Kühne, S.: Towards a comparative analysis of meta-metamodels. In: Proceedings of the Compilation of the Co-located Workshops on DSM'11, TMC'11, AGERE! 2011, AOOPES'11, NEAT'11, & VMIL 2011, pp. 7–12. ACM (2011)

31. Kitchenham, B., Brereton, P.: A systematic review of systematic review process research in software engineering. Inf. Softw. Technol. **55**(12), 2049–2075 (2013)

32. Koschmider, A., Figl, K., Schoknecht, A.: A comprehensive overview of visual design of process model element labels. In: Reichert, M., Reijers, H.A. (eds.) BPM 2015. LNBIP, vol. 256, pp. 571–582. Springer, Cham (2016). https://doi.org/10.1007/978-3-319-42887-1_46

33. Langer, P., Mayerhofer, T., Wimmer, M., Kappel, G.: On the usage of UML: initial results of analyzing open UML models. In: Fill, H., Karagiannis, D., Reimer, U. (eds.) Modellierung 2014, pp. 289–304. GI (2014)

34. López-Fernández, J.J., Guerra, E., de Lara, J.: Assessing the quality of meta-models. In: Boulanger, F., Famelis, M., Ratiu, D. (eds.) Proceedings of the 11th Workshop on Model-Driven Engineering, Verification and Validation, MoDeVVa@MODELS 2014, pp. 3–12 (2014)

35. Ma, Z., He, X., Liu, C.: Assessing the quality of metamodels. Front. Comput. Sci. **7**(4), 558–570 (2013)

36. Michael, J., Mayr, H.C.: the process of creating a domain specific modelling method (Extended Abstract). In: Mendling, J., Rinderle-Ma, S. (eds.) Proceedings of the 7th International Workshop on Enterprise Modeling and Information Systems Architectures, EMISA 2016. vol. 1701, pp. 40–43. CEUR-WS.org (2016)

37. Moody, D.: The "physics" of notations: toward a scientific basis for constructing visual notations in software engineering. IEEE Trans. Softw. Eng. **35**(6), 756–779 (2009)

38. Mylopoulos, J.: Conceptual modelling and Telos. In: Loucopoulos, P., Zicari, R. (eds.) Conceptual Modelling, Databases, and CASE: an Integrated View of Information System Development, pp. 49–68. Wiley, New York (1992)

39. Roelens, B., Steenacker, W., Poels, G.: Realizing strategic fit within the business architecture: the design of a process-goal alignment modeling and analysis technique. Softw. Syst. Model. (2017)

40. Schoknecht, A., Vetter, A., Fill, H.-G., Oberweis, A.: Using the horus method for succeeding in business process engineering projects. In: Karagiannis, D., Mayr, H., Mylopoulos, J. (eds.) Domain-Specific Conceptual Modeling, pp. 127–147. Springer, Cham (2016). https://doi.org/10.1007/978-3-319-39417-6_6

41. Stark, J., Braun, R., Esswein, W.: Systemizing colour for conceptual modeling. In: Leimeister, J.M., Brenner, W. (eds.) Proceedings der 13. Internationalen Tagung Wirtschaftsinformatik (WI 2017), St. Gallen, pp. 256–270 (2017)

42. Wand, Y., Weber, R.: On the ontological expressiveness of information systems analysis and design grammars. Inf. Syste. J. **3**(4), 217–237 (1993)

43. Williams, J.R. et al.: What do metamodels really look like? Eessmod@ Models **1078**, 55–60 (2013)

Towards a Framework for Shaping & Forming Enterprise Capabilities

Mohammad Hossein Danesh[1(✉)] and Eric Yu[1,2]

[1] Department of Computer Science, University of Toronto, Toronto, Canada
{danesh, eric}@cs.toronto.edu
[2] Faculty of Information, University of Toronto, Toronto, Canada

Abstract. In this era of rapid change and major technology-enabled transformations, information systems design needs to take into account the specific context of the organizational setting and the strategic direction of the enterprise. To this end, researchers and practitioners have built on the concept of *capability* to analyze what a business can and should do to manage its strategic trajectories. This paper describes four categories of modeling and analysis requirements to deal with capability formation. The requirements are identified through a review of the origins of the capability concept in the strategic management literature. A set of guidelines is proposed as part of a modeling framework based on the i* language. Enterprise Capabilities are modeled as a specialized type of intentional actor so that their socio-technical characteristics can be specified and analyzed. This approach to modeling capabilities enables reasoning about (1) why a capability is needed, (2) how it is achieved, (3) how it fits within the organizational and social setting of the enterprise, and (4) what relationships are required for its success. The applicability of the guidelines and associated viewpoints are demonstrated on a chatbot example.

Keywords: Enterprise capability · Dynamic capability · i*
Enterprise modeling · Capability modeling

1 Introduction

Enterprises compete in a fast-paced changing global environment that demands customer-driven innovation in which information technology and software systems play a key role [1]. Use of software systems in enterprises continues to transform businesses and plays a prominent role in their competitiveness [1, 2]. To achieve the transformative role and enable innovation in the organizational context, software systems need to be co-designed with the business [2, 3].

The concept of capability has been used by practitioners and researchers alike to conceptualize adoption and integration of new technologies and systems into existing organizational and technological fabric [4–7]. For example, capability maps and heatmaps have been used to communicate strengths and weaknesses and prioritize investments [6, 7]. Other formulations of the concept have been proposed to enable alignment of resources and capabilities to enterprise architecture [5], or to empower adaptation of business processes to changes in contextual parameters [4, 8].

© IFIP International Federation for Information Processing 2018
Published by Springer Nature Switzerland AG 2018. All Rights Reserved
R. A. Buchmann et al. (Eds.): PoEM 2018, LNBIP 335, pp. 188–202, 2018.
https://doi.org/10.1007/978-3-030-02302-7_12

In the field of strategic management, capabilities have long been studied to account for strengths and weaknesses in competitive positioning [9]. The literature views a capability as an enterprise-specific combination of resources and processes which has to be continuously renewed in order to attain and sustain competitive advantage [9–12].

In this paper we build on the theoretical foundations from strategic management to propose four aspects essential in understanding and analyzing the formation and evolution of an enterprise capability. These aspects result in modeling viewpoints and guidelines that (1) explicate why investments are made to develop and evolve a capability, (2) illustrate alternative couplings of resources and processes that can form the capability, (3) demonstrate how organizational and social setting shapes the capability, and (4) uncover capability relationships that enable co-creation of value.

The paper provides guidelines and examples on how to represent each of the mentioned aspects as part of a modeling framework. A meta-model was presented in an earlier publication [13] to provide an integrative view on capability and its related concepts. The meta-model serves as the conceptual foundation for modeling enterprise capabilities. Two analysis techniques that support reasoning on capability alternatives [14] and their flexibility [15] accompany the meta-model. The modeling notation of the framework builds on the i* modeling language [16] and involves a number of extensions, including the introduction of the capability concept as a specialized kind of strategic actor. While some of these extensions are explained through the examples, it is beyond the scope of this paper to present these extensions in any detail.

The expressiveness of the framework in representing and analyzing capability formation is demonstrated on an example. The context of the example deals with the strategy to adopt a chatbot agent as part of a customer interaction management capability. This example is inspired by the first author's experiences in applying the framework for designing and adopting a conversational (chatbot) platform in a Canadian company.

Section 2 of this paper briefly describes the illustrative example. In Sect. 3 of the paper, the four aspects of capability formation and their requirements are presented based on the review of the literature. Section 3 discusses four viewpoints to demonstrate how the i* framework is adopted and adapted to satisfy the requirements. In Sect. 4, the related work and their ability to model capability formation is reviewed. Finally, the paper is concluded in Sect. 5 with a discussion about components of the proposed framework and future work.

2   A Chatbot Example

To illustrate the use of the framework and its guidelines, an evolutionary scenario for a Customer Interaction (CI) capability is investigated that aims to add a chatbot agent to its communication channels. The capability is administered by the contact center department with the aim to effectively manage customer interactions on all channels.

To enable the evolution of the CI capability, one would need to (a) understand and justify investments on the technology and business processes required to support the new communication channel, (b) investigate what stakeholders need to be involved and what is needed to onboard them, (c) identify the required resources and information systems that should be acquired or developed to support the extended capability, (d) examine different sourcing options for major technical components, (e) recognize suitable organizational deployment configurations, and (f) plan for likely changes that are required in other domains and capabilities.

Without the ability to answer the above questions, a well-defined strategy and architecture that can support development and management of the new technology is not possible.

3   Modeling Specific Aspects of Capability Formation

Following the literature in strategic management [10, 17–20], Enterprise Capabilities are defined as *intentional combinations (orchestrations) of firm-specific assets, orga- nizational routines (business processes), and human knowledge (skillset/know-how) that take advantage of complementary relations and are created and evolved overtime through social collaboration and learning.* We use the term Enterprise Capability (EC) in this paper to distinguish the notion from other usages of the term, such as in capabilities of an individual or of a technology system.

To represent different aspects of the above definition, an agent-oriented modeling paradigm has proven to be useful [21]. Hence, the framework adopted in this paper represents enterprise capabilities as actors with strategic intent and social properties that co-evolve with organizational systems and norms.

Each of the sub-sections below elaborates on one aspect of capability formation and starts with a set of questions as requirements. The questions indicate what a modeling framework should address and serve as guidelines to steer the modeler in identifying and extracting the kinds of information required for decision making. Each sub-section discusses a review of the literature that explains the rationale and the origins of the questions. Once the theory is reviewed, the section illustrates how the modeling framework can be applied in the chatbot example to answer the questions.

3.1   Why Should We Invest in the Capability?

Requirements: To enable decision making and reasoning on capability development, the ability to explicate and analyze why a capability is needed and what strategic role it plays for the firm is necessary. For example, why is a chatbot agent that responds to customer inquiries and handles their interaction beneficial? More specifically a decision maker should be able to answer (a) Why should the enterprise invest in the EC? (b) How do different stakeholders with different responsibilities understand and breakdown the objectives? (c) Are there qualitative aspects about the objectives that require attention? (d) What competing objectives exist that are difficult to satisfy and require a compromise?

Theoretical Basis: the literature emphasizes the need to understand and analyze intentions for investing in ECs as they can account for differences in strength and weaknesses across firms [11, 12, 18]. ECs require co-design of IT and business as IT is playing a major role in differentiating enterprises in the market [1–3]. To this end, one needs to represent and reason on objectives that account for capability intentions from multiple perspectives such as technical, business, and organizational [3, 22]. Often qualitative aspects of intentions are responsible for differentiating ECs across firms resulting in different competitive positioning [23]. Hence, representing goals and their tradeoffs is crucial for steering capability development and evolution efforts.

Example: To model an EC, one should start by asking why the capability is beneficial while looking at multiple stakeholders and their viewpoints (focusing on questions (a) and (b)). For example, adding a chatbot agent to existing CI channels entails (1) a technical goal to ensure appropriate understanding and response to customer queries and intents, (2) a business goal to enhance response time and provide cost savings, and (3) an organizational goal to ensure policy enforcement with two distinct perspectives of addressing regulatory compliance, and maintaining and enhancing brand image.

The i* framework enforces separation of soft and hard goals to enable specification and refinement of quality attributes (answering question (c)). For example, in Fig. 1, the requirement of *"Enforce Organizational Policy"* is broken down to the softgoal of *"Enhance Brand Image"* and the hardgoal of *"Comply With Regulations"*. Furthermore, contribution of the chatbot goals to *"Effective Customer Interaction"* through *"Enhanced Response Time"* and *"Response to Customer Queries & Intents"* are explicated to elaborate the role of the new channel in satisfying the CI capability objectives. Enforcing the use of means-end relationships provokes the modeler and designer to investigate alternative breakdowns of the intentions. By illustrating different contribution levels of alternatives to softgoals, one can reason on tradeoffs among the strategic intents of an EC (responding to question (d)).

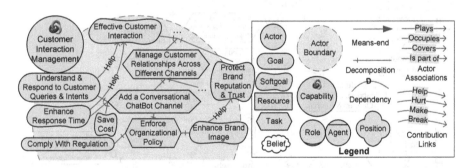

Fig. 1. Representing capability intentions for customer interaction

3.2 What Is the Right Combination of Processes and Resources

Requirements: ECs are formed by acquiring and coupling processes and resources. In the chatbot example, the software components of language processing and intent management must be coupled and coordinated with CRM processes and policies to ensure effective customer interactions. In this regard, a capability manager and designer should be able to answer (a) what resources are required to satisfy capability intentions? (b) What processes are needed to enable the capability? (c) What are the options available in coupling resources and processes? (d) Are there qualitative characteristics or enterprise-specific interests when coupling resources and processes? (e) How can one represent and reason on commitments of a given coupling option, e.g., how will outsourcing the intent management of the chatbot limit future choices for evolving the agent?

Theoretical Basis: Satisfying EC intentions require an intelligent coupling of enterprise-specific resources and processes [17, 24] that often entail long-lasting commitments (referred to as path dependency in the literature) [11, 20]. The esffort is twofold: (a) *Structuring* the portfolio of enterprise resources and processes i.e., what to invest in and what to retire, and (b) *Selecting and Bundling* a particular set of resources and processes within the portfolio to form ECs [17, 24]. The coupling alternatives have different impacts on the intentions and will be preferable under different circumstances.

Example: Aside from the interaction interface of a chatbot, any conversational agent has three main components: (1) Natural Language Processing (NLP) engine, (2) knowledge repository, and (3) intent identification engine (algorithms) [25]. Two approaches in sourcing and coupling such processes and resources are illustrated in Fig. 2, each relying on a specific way of coupling resources and processes (answering to question (c)). One can model decisions to acquire a resource/process using i* tasks

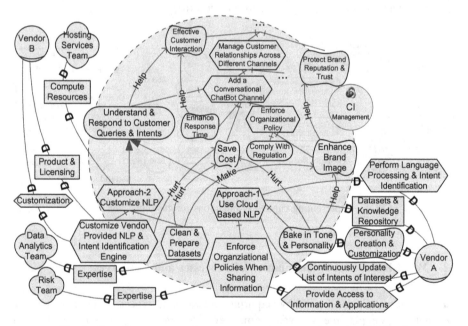

Fig. 2. Coupling resources & processes to shape ec – legend as in Fig. 1

and resources within the actor boundary, or to rely on others to provision the resource/process demonstrated by dependencies (responding to questions (a) and (b)). The impact of coupling alternatives on EC intentions is demonstrated through their contributions to softgoals (enabling answering to question (d)). For example, if an external data source is used to train a vendor-provided NLP engine, it is going to be much more expensive to incorporate enterprise-specific tone and personality compared to using an in-house dataset. To use an in-house dataset, one needs to clean and prepare the training and test data which requires data analysis expertise and will be costly. Figure 2 illustrates these tradeoffs using contribution links to softgoals of "*Save Cost*" and "*Enhance Brand Image*".

Aside from coupling of the three components, one needs to understand organizational processes and policies when accessing enterprise systems and integrating with them. Such integration requires technical, regulatory, and organizational expertise that is unique to the industry and often the enterprise. This is represented by the "*Expertise*" dependency to the "*Risk Team*" and the process of "*Enforce Organizational Policies When Sharing Information*" in Fig. 2. Such commitments have long-term consequences and can limit future options for evolving the EC. It is therefore important to analyze them when making decisions (relating to question (e)). An example of such a commitment is the involvement of the "*Risk Team*" and their best practices when interacting with "*Vendor A*".

3.3   Shaping the Capability to Fit the Organization

Requirements: As ECs reside and operate in the context of the enterprise, they are heavily impacted by organizational norms and values. In the chatbot example, the organization's experience in using vendors and sharing data with them while managing risk and regulatory compliance has a big impact on sourcing resources, employing processes, and choosing vendors. To enable understating of such context, one needs to answer: (a) Who is responsible for making decisions regarding the capability? (b) What social relationships are required to ensure effective collaboration and stakeholder on boarding? (c) What managerial decisions about incentive or organizational structures can impact the capability? (d) Are there organizational norms that enable or inhibit capability intentions and alternatives? (e) What are the domain-specific principles that a capability should build on? (f) What information systems does the EC rely on and how much influence and control does it have over them?

Theoretical Basis: ECs operate in the organizational context shaped by four interdependent kinds of systems - namely technical, human, managerial and value systems [20]. These systems co-evolve with ECs overtime, and have bi-directional impact on each other as they enable or inhibit decision alternatives [12, 20].

Technical systems refer to knowledge and domain-specific principles embedded in processes and information systems [20]. Hence, a modeling framework should be able to explicate the relationships of capabilities to such processes, systems and principles.

Human systems refer to the teams and their managers' social capital and relationships that enable stakeholder onboarding and resource acquisition [26]. Therefore, a capability modeling framework should enable representation of the human systems.

Managerial systems refer to the formal and informal ways of cascading goals throughout the organization. The formal aspect usually refers to the organizational structure and its means of enforcing goals while the informal aspect relates to incentive structures set in place [20].

Value systems include norms and values that emerge from accumulated organizational decisions, experiences, and policies. They are considered essential for attaining superior results by teams and managers [20]. Together, these four kinds of systems constitute important context that must be taken into account in EC decision-making.

Example: Responsibility for the CRM capability could be given to a central team with all necessary expertise, or alternatively to distinct teams with expertise in IT, business (e.g., marketing and sales), and organization development. The latter scenario is illustrated in Fig. 3. A new type of relationship titled "*Responsible-For*" (an extension to i*) is introduced to capture decision making rights for ECs, responding to questions (a) and (c).

Organizational norms can impact social relationships among stakeholders of a capability [13]. They are modeled as i* beliefs. The impact of norms that extend beyond an actor boundary are represented with dashed contribution links, following the work of Yu et al [27]. As an example, the belief that "*Build vs Buy Protects Our*

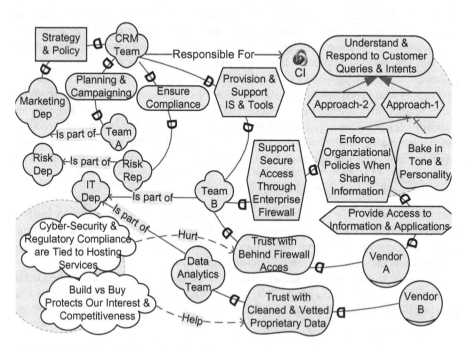

Fig. 3. Visualizing the Impact of organizational structure & norms – legend as in Fig. 1

Interest & Competitiveness" will positively impact the relationships with "*Vendor B*" as outlined in Fig. 3.

Social relationships of actors are modeled as softgoal dependencies. In Fig. 3, "*Vendor B*" depends on the "*Data Analytics Team*" for "*Trust with Cleaned & Vetted Proprietary Data*" to enable customization of their NLP engine. The representation of social relationships and the impact of organizational norms on such relationships enables addressing questions (b), (d) and (e).

Figure 3 demonstrates how the organization would favor "*Appraoch-2*" as its dependencies on "*Vendor B*" give the organization more control over how it shares data[1]. This becomes evident by representing organizational structure and norms of departments and teams.

Flexibility of the "*CRM Team*" in making decisions is significantly higher when they do not rely on teams of other departments and are centrally managed. This alternative was not presented in Fig. 3 in the interest of space.

The questions presented earlier in the requirements section serve as guidelines for the modeler to navigate the enterprise context and investigate its impact on capability alternatives. The final question in that list was not instantiated in the model as it overlaps with some of the requirements in the coming section and will be discussed in Sect. 3.4 and Fig. 4.

3.4 Making Capabilities Complement Each Other

Requirements: Network of ECs work together to serve customers. When designing and evolving ECs it is important to analyze and create complementary relationships among them. A capability modeling framework should enable answering (a) What does the capability have control over? What does it rely on others or share responsibilities with? (b) How do the relationships enable capability intentions and do they impose tradeoffs in achieving them? (c) What restrictions and limitations do the relationships entail and how do they impact strategic intentions? (d) How do changing (1) capability relationships, or (2) resource and process couplings supporting them, impact one another?

Theoretical Basis: ECs often form complementary and interlocking relationships in order to create superior value [10, 17, 24]. Some relationships can have a negative impact or pose constraints that inhibit evolution. Such relationships are referred to as suppressing relations [23]. With today's enterprises competing in global ecosystems, the requirement for complementary relationships and formation of co-creating networks is ever more pressing [1, 28]. On the other hand, due to the fast paced changes and highly dynamic environments, ECs need to operate in near autonomy in order to quickly respond to evolving requirements and foster innovation [10].

Aa a result, a modeling framework should be able to reason about the autonomy in making decisions and the interdependencies that enable or suppress capabilities. Such reasoning will allow a better understanding and alignment of the interdependent and localized intentions of capabilities.

---

[1] Dependencies for "Approach-2" are omitted from Fig. 3 to save space but are shown in Fig. 2.

Example: To achieve localization and faster decision making, the organization can decompose the *"CI"* capability into specialized sub-capabilities that manage different channels of communication. In the example given in Fig. 4, the *"CI Management"* capability is decomposed to *"Managing Telephone Services"* and *"Managing Chatbot Services"*. Decompositions are indicated by *"is-part-of"* associations and justified through dependencies, i.e., the intentions behind the decomposition should be explicated as dependencies. With explicit decomposition of intentions, one can answer what-if questions about distributing responsibilities and resources among capabilities and teams (answering questions (a) and (e)). For example, in Fig. 4 the decision to separate operation and management of the two main customer interaction channels, i.e., *Chat* and *Telephone,* is supported by the need to apply distinct principles and management mechanisms. The dependencies with numbers one to five in Fig. 4 outline the intentions behind the proposed decompositions.

Customers expect a seamless experience across multiple interaction channels (illustrated through dependencies 2 and 3 in Fig. 4), yet it can be challenging to orchestrate changes across chatbot and human phone services. For one, when renewing responses to customer queries, the update cycles and mechanisms differ between a team of human agents and chatbot software. The chatbot might go through update cycles every few weeks while the human agents retrain once or twice a year. In addition, changing the features and offerings of the *"CRM Software"* every few weeks will make it impossible for agents to keep up with all the changes in a big organization with multiple services/products. Surely a compromise is needed, but one needs to identify

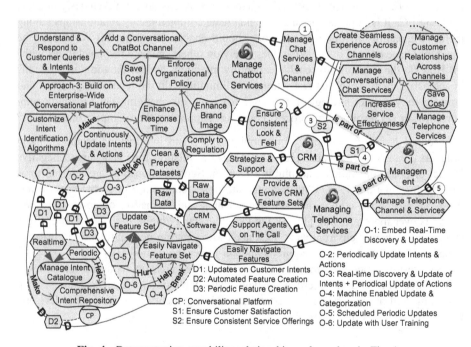

Fig. 4. Demonstrating capability relationships – legend as in Fig. 1

the right compromise that is acceptable to all parties and advances *"CI"*. Understanding the impacts of a capability choice on other capabilities, information systems, processes and actors is a pre-requisite in identifying such compromises.

In Fig. 4, the *"Easily Navigate Feature Set"* represents the interest of human agents supporting *"Telephone Services"*. The alternative mechanism in updating the *"CRM Software"* represented as *"O-4"*, *"O-5"*, and *"O-6"* contribute to *"Easily Navigate Feature Set"*. Furthermore, the choice among these three options will impact how *"Intents & Actions"* of the *"Chatbot Services"* is updated as it can be traced through dependencies *"D2"* and *"D3"* which impact alternatives *"O-1"*, *"O-2"*, and *"O-3"*. The impact and coordination needs do not end at the *"Chatbot Services"* capability as the choice on *"O-1"*, *"O-2"*, and *"O-3"* will impact the *"Comprehensiveness of Intent Repository"* which is a softgoal of the *"Conversational Platform (CP)"*. Depending on how crucial this softgoal is to the organization, one will have to prioritize and choose among the presented options. The dependency graph proposed in a related publication [15] can be used to trace the impacts of dependencies and ease the orchestration of choices.

Explication of alternatives for satisfying capabilities alongside their complementary relationships enables better decision making. It facilitates reasoning on how capabilities, actors and information systems should be orchestrated across the organization. Such representation and analysis enable answering questions (b), (c) and (d).

4   Discussion and Related Work

Many approaches have been built using the concept of capability to enable relating strategic intentions and operational choices of an enterprise [29]. Among these approaches, four ways of representing capability and its constituents are identified and will be evaluated against the proposed requirements of Sect. 3. The first one and the most popular representation is a capability map that illustrates what a capability does, and its only constituents are sub-capabilities. The map serves as a taxonomy of enterprise functions and is used to communicate and prioritize enterprise investments [6, 7, 29]. The second representation adds a strategic perspective to the ArchiMate language to enable better alignment of enterprise architectures to business trajectories [5, 30]. In this view, a capability may consist of both behavioral and structural elements of ArchiMate [5].

The third representation builds on the goal-oriented Enterprise Knowledge Development (EKD) and enables adaptation of software services and processes to the changing context of the capabilities. A capability in this view is created from one or more processes, fulfills a goal, and responds to a specific context. The approach provides a methodology for Capability Driven Development (CDD) to guide the modeling activities [4, 8]. The fourth representation as discussed in this paper focuses on a socio-technical representation of capabilities building on the i* language. The capability in this view is formed by coupling resources and processes to pursue a series of business goals. It heavily relies on organizational actors and norms, information systems, and other capabilities to perform.

4.1 Representing and Analyzing Strategic Intentions

Capability Maps: The representation of strategic intentions behind a capability in this view is through a textual description. Some approaches link capabilities to outcomes and value chains using multiple viewpoints. However, outcomes are the result achieved in pursuing a strategic goal and not the goal itself and hence do not help in capturing multiple perspectives. The maps are not well equipped to analyze and manage competing goals.

ArchiMate: The extended ArchiMate language enables association of capabilities to motivational elements including goals. As such, it can demonstrate the strategic intents and requirements that a capability satisfies. However, the notation does not differentiate qualitative goals and different levels of satisfaction, therefore limiting its ability to explicate compromises.

CDD: Business goals play a major role in defining capabilities in CDD. The goals help in defining measures that shape the context parameters of capability implementations. Such parameters will determine the adaptation criteria for capability delivery. Qualitative goals are not distinguished in this approach and a capability is developed in response to a single business goal. Capability evolution decisions depend on how one defines performance measures and contextual parameters i.e., they are not necessarily driven by the strategy but are related to the capability delivery mechanisms.

The i* Framework: The approach allows representation and reasoning on why a capability is needed from multiple perspectives while demonstrating how goals are refined and related to one another. Furthermore, softgoals in i* enable representation of qualitative goals and their satisfaction levels. This allows reasoning on tradeoffs and necessary compromises. The qualitative aspect of capabilities often accounts for unique and firm-specific characteristics that differentiate capabilities across enterprises.

4.2 Representing and Analyzing Resource and Process Coupling

Capability Maps: Depending on the approach, a capability map may be linked to business processes but is not actively investigated for options of coupling resources and processes. The linkages and multiple viewpoints are used to communicate priorities and do not empower reasoning about development, evolution or retirement choices.

ArchiMate: ArchiMate enables modeling how resources and processes are related to capabilities and represents their choices of coupling through the concept of "capability enabling bundle". The approach is capable of elaborating choices and their associations to goals. However, the language does not investigate qualitative contributions and no methodological support is provided to analyze commitments.

CDD: Business processes are the means to deliver a capability and therefore shape the capability delivery pattern (alternative). Resources are only used by processes and are indirectly related to capabilities. Qualitative goals are not a primary concern in the methodology unless they impact the contextual parameters and therefore cannot determine tradeoffs for capability design. Capability commitments in provisioning resources and processes are not modeled in this approach. The CDD approach has the appropriate tool support accompanying its meta-model to track changes in contextual parameters throughout the capability lifecycle.

The i* Framework: By representing capabilities as intentional actors, one can illustrate their strategy in sourcing required processes and resources. The coupling alternatives are demonstrated using means-end relationships. Contribution links empower understanding the impact of alternative couplings on qualitative goals. Internal and external commitments are shown through dependencies. However, the i* framework is only focused on point in time representation of commitments and cannot reason on their evolution. A solution would be to create a new/evolved instance of the model and enable tracking such instances throughout the capability lifecycle with tool support.

4.3   Representing and Analyzing Organizational Fit

Capability Maps: No representation of organizational actors and structure is present in capability maps. Suggestions have been made to link other viewpoints that represent organizational roles and their structure to capabilities [7]. However, the association does not empower and support the modeler to explore social relationships, organizational norms, and their impacts on one another. Therefore, it does not enable understanding of the fit between capability alternatives and organizational choices.

ArchiMate: The representation allows association of actors with capabilities, which is illustrative of an ownership relationship. Therefore, it does not help in understanding the social aspects of capabilities and their fit to enterprise context.

CDD: Actor, organizational situation and norms are not modeled.

The i* Framework: The approach focuses on representing and analyzing the organizational structure and its possible variations with respect to EC. It elaborates the tangible and intangible gains of teams and individuals in relation to a capability, and the norms and values impacting it. Such representation and reasoning are essential to manage social expectations and resistance to evolving strategies [20].

4.4   Representing and Analyzing Complementarities

Capability Maps: Capability relationships to one another and other entities such as actors and information systems are not investigated or represented. Mapping applications' contribution to capabilities are done through heatmaps but the nature and intentions behind the contributions are not specified. Hence, the heatmap cannot answer questions and analysis inquiries.

ArchiMate: Aggregation is the only capability relationship in this approach i.e., a series of capabilities and resources can be aggregated to form a new capability. The approach can express constraints imposed on capabilities but does not provide methodological support or guidance in identifying them.

CDD: Capabilities have no relationships with one another. Information systems impact capabilities through business processes. Constraints that limit capabilities can be explicated by contextual parameters, although the approach does not guide how one should identify such constraints.

The i* Framework: The framework uses dependencies to demonstrate relationships among capabilities, actors and information systems, enabling coordination of choices among them. Positive and negative impacts of relationships on strategic intents are depicted through contributions links to soft goal. However, the framework lacks the ability to explicate constraints imposed by dependencies.

5   Conclusion and Future Work

The notion of capability has gained attention as a concept to link and align operational decisions to strategic intents, and therefore plays an important role in modeling enterprises [29]. Building on the strategic management literature, this paper contributed to the field by (1) identifying a set of requirements for reasoning and analyzing on how capabilities are formed, (2) transforming the requirements into questions that guide modelers in gathering information about capability formation, and (3) illustrating how the i* language can be used to enable reasoning on different aspects of capability formation.

The contributions presented in this paper are part of an i* based capability modeling framework that consists of (1) an integrative meta-model [13] serving as a conceptual foundation, (2) the guidelines for representing and analyzing formation of capabilities (as presented in this paper), and (3) analysis techniques that enable reasoning on capability alternatives [14] and their flexibility [15]. The design of the framework follows a Design Science Research (DSR) methodology [31] and some of the framework's components have been tested in few cases [14, 15, 32, 33]. The guidelines presented in this paper were demonstrated in a case inspired by real world requirements. Additional empirical validations will be addressed in future publications.

The baseline i* framework presented in this paper needs to be formally described with clear specification of extensions and their conceptual justifications. The formalization should include a specification of how i* will represent concepts of the integrative meta-model. Tool support for the framework and its analysis techniques is essential to ease known scalability issues. Further guidelines on how and to what extent one should drill down when analyzing enterprise capabilities is needed to address possible impracticality of modeling full capability network(s).

References

1. Bosch, J.: Speed, data, and ecosystems: the future of software engineering. IEEE Softw. **33**, 82–88 (2016)
2. Ross, J.W., Sebastian, I.M., Beath, C.M., Jha, L.: Technology Advantage Practice of the Boston Consulting Group: Designing Digital Organizations - Summary of Survey Findings. MIT CISR, Boston, MA (2017)

3. Nevo, S., Wade, M.: The formation and value of IT-enabled resources: antecedents and consequences. Manag. Inf. Syst. Q. **34**, 163–183 (2010)
4. Bērziša, S., et al.: Capability driven development: an approach to designing digital enterprises. Bus. Inf. Syst. Eng. **57**, 15–25 (2015)
5. Azevedo, C.L.B., Iacob, M.-E., Almeida, J.P.A., van Sinderen, M., Pires, L.F., Guizzardi, G.: Modeling resources and capabilities in enterprise architecture: a well-founded ontology-based proposal for ArchiMate. Inf. Syst. **54**, 235–262 (2015)
6. Burton, B.: Eight Business Capability Modeling Best Practices. Gart. Res. ID (2012)
7. Business Architecture Guild: A Guide to the Business Architecture Body of Knowledge (2014)
8. Zdravkovic, J., Stirna, J., Henkel, M., Grabis, J.: Modeling business capabilities and context dependent delivery by cloud services. In: Salinesi, C., Norrie, M.C., Pastor, Ó. (eds.) Advanced Information Systems Engineering, pp. 369–383. Springer, Berlin Heidelberg (2013)
9. Teece, D.J., Pisano, G., Shuen, A.: Dynamic capability and strategic management. Strateg. Manag. J. **18**, 509–533 (1997)
10. Teece, D.J.: Explicating dynamic capabilities: the nature and microfoundations of (sustainable) enterprise performance. Strateg. Manag. J. **28**, 1319–1350 (2007)
11. Helfat, C.E., Peteraf, M.A.: The dynamic resource-based view: capability lifecycles. Strateg. Manag. J. **24**, 997–1010 (2003)
12. Winter, S.G.: Understanding dynamic capabilities. Strateg. Manag. J. **24**, 991–995 (2003)
13. Danesh, M.H., Loucopoulos, P., Yu, E.: Dynamic capabilities for sustainable enterprise IT – a modeling framework. In: Johannesson, P., Lee, M.L., Liddle, Stephen W., Opdahl, Andreas L., López, Ó.P. (eds.) ER 2015. LNCS, vol. 9381, pp. 358–366. Springer, Cham (2015). https://doi.org/10.1007/978-3-319-25264-3_26
14. Danesh, M.H., Yu, E.: Modeling enterprise capabilities with i*: reasoning on alternatives. In: Iliadis, L., Papazoglou, M., Pohl, K. (eds.) CAiSE 2014. LNBIP, vol. 178, pp. 112–123. Springer, Cham (2014). https://doi.org/10.1007/978-3-319-07869-4_10
15. Danesh, M.H., Yu, E.: Analyzing IT flexibility to enable dynamic capabilities. In: Persson, A., Stirna, J. (eds.) CAiSE 2015. LNBIP, vol. 215, pp. 53–65. Springer, Cham (2015). https://doi.org/10.1007/978-3-319-19243-7_5
16. Yu, E.: Modeling strategic relationships for process reengineering (1995). ftp://ftp.cs.toronto.edu/pub/eric/DKBS-TR-94–6.pdf
17. Helfat, C.E. et al.: Dynamic Capabilities: Understanding Strategic Change in Organizations. Wiley (2009)
18. McKelvie, A., Davidsson, P.: From resource base to dynamic capabilities: an investigation of new firms. Br. J. Manag. **20**, S63–S80 (2009)
19. Sirmon, D.G., Hitt, M.A., Ireland, R.D., Gilbert, B.A.: Resource orchestration to create competitive advantage breadth, depth, and life cycle effects. J. Manag. **37**, 1390–1412 (2011)
20. Leonard-Barton, D.: Core capabilities and core rigidities: a paradox in managing new product development. Strateg. Manag. J. **13**, 111–125 (1992)
21. Danesh, M.H., Yu, E.: Representing and analyzing enterprise capabilities as specialized actors - a BPM example. In: Advances in Conceptual Modeling Workshops. Springer International Publishing - To be published (2018)
22. Frank, U.: Multi-perspective enterprise modeling: foundational concepts, prospects and future research challenges. Softw. Syst. Model, pp. 1–22 (2012)
23. Sirmon, D.G., Hitt, M.A., Arregle, J.-L., Campbell, J.T.: The dynamic interplay of capability strengths and weaknesses: investigating the bases of temporary competitive advantage. Strateg. Manag. J. **31**, 1386–1409 (2010)

24. Sirmon, D.G., Hitt, M.A., Ireland, R.D.: Managing firm resources in dynamic environments to create value: looking inside the black box. Acad. Manage. Rev. **32**, 273–292 (2007)

25. Manusama, B., Karamouzis, F., Austin, T.: Seven Decision Points for Success With Virtual Customer Assistants. Gartner (2016)

26. Adner, R., Helfat, C.E.: Corporate effects and dynamic managerial capabilities. Strateg. Manag. J. **24**, 1011–1025 (2003)

27. Yu, E., Liu, L.: Modelling trust for system design using the i* strategic actors framework. In: Falcone, R., Singh, M., Tan, Y.-H. (eds.) Trust in Cyber-societies, pp. 175–194. Springer, Berlin Heidelberg (2001)

28. Augier, M., Teece, D.J.: Dynamic capabilities and the role of managers in business strategy and economic performance. Organ. Sci. **20**, 410–421 (2009)

29. Zdravkovic, J., Stirna, J., Grabis, J.: A comparative analysis of using the capability notion for congruent business and information systems engineering. Complex Syst. Inform. Model. Q., 1–20 (2017)

30. Iacob, M.-E., Quartel, D., Jonkers, H.: Capturing business strategy and value in enterprise architecture to support portfolio valuation. In: 16th International Enterprise Distributed Object Computing Conference (EDOC 2012), pp. 11–20. IEEE, Beijing, China (2012)

31. Gregor, S., Hevner, A.R.: Positioning and presenting design science research for maximum impact. MIS Q. **37**, 337–355 (2013)

32. Loucopoulos, P., Stratigaki, C., Danesh, M., Bravos, G., Dimitrakopoulos, G.: Enterprise capability modeling: concepts, method and application. In: Enterprise Systems Conference (ES) (2015)

33. Loucopoulos, P., Kavakli, E., Anagnostopoulos, D., Dimitrakopoulos, G.: Capability-oriented analysis and design for collaborative systems: an example from the doha 2022 world cup games. In: Proceedings of the 2018 10th International Conference on Computer and Automation Engineering, pp. 185–189. ACM, New York, NY, USA (2018)

Semantics and Reasoning

Reconciling Practice and Rigour in Ontology-Based Heterogeneous Information Systems Construction

Carme Quer[1]([✉]) [ID], Xavier Franch[1] [ID], Cristina Palomares[1] [ID],
Andreas Falkner[2], Alexander Felfernig[3] [ID], Davide Fucci[4],
Walid Maalej[4], Jennifer Nerlich[5], Mikko Raatikainen[6] [ID],
Gottfried Schenner[2], Martin Stettinger[3], and Juha Tiihonen[6]

[1] Universitat Politècnica de Catalunya (UPC), Barcelona, Spain
{cquer, franch, cpalomares}@essi.upc.edu
[2] Siemens AG Österreich, Vienna, Austria
{andreas.a.falkner, gottfried.schenner}@siemens.com
[3] Graz University of Technology, Graz, Austria
{felfernig, stettinger}@ist.tugraz.at
[4] University of Hamburg/HITeC, Hamburg, Germany
{fucci, maalej}@informatik.uni-hamburg.de
[5] Vogella GmbH, Hamburg, Germany
jennifer.nerlich@vogella.com
[6] University of Helsinki, Helsinki, Finland
{mikko.raatikainen, juha.tiihonen}@helsinki.fi

Abstract. Ontology integration addresses the problem of reconciling into one single semantic framework different knowledge chunks defined according to its own ontology. This field has been subject of analysis and many consolidated theoretical results are available. Still, in practice, ontology integration is difficult in heterogeneous information systems (HIS) that need to integrate assets already built and running which cannot be changed. Furthermore, in practice, the composed assets are usually not really defined according to an ontology but to a data model which is less rigorous but fit for the purpose of defining a data schema. In this paper, we propose a method for integrating assets participating in a HIS using a domain ontology, aimed at finding an optimal balance between semantic rigour and feasibility in terms of adoption in a real-world setting. The method proposes the use of data models describing the semantics of existing assets; their analysis in order to find commonalities and misalignments; the definition of the domain ontology, considering also other sources as standards, to express the main concepts in the HIS domain; the connection of the local models with this domain ontology; and its abstraction into a metamodel to facilitate further extensions. The method is an outcome of a collaborative software development project, OpenReq, aimed at delivering an ontology for requirements engineering (RE) designed to serve as baseline for the data model of an open platform offering methods and techniques to the RE community. The construction process of this ontology will be used to illustrate the method.

© IFIP International Federation for Information Processing 2018
Published by Springer Nature Switzerland AG 2018. All Rights Reserved
R. A. Buchmann et al. (Eds.): PoEM 2018, LNBIP 335, pp. 205–220, 2018.
https://doi.org/10.1007/978-3-030-02302-7_13

Keywords: Ontology integration · Heterogeneous information systems
Domain ontology · Requirements engineering ontology

1 Introduction

Modern information systems are rarely monolithic, but instead they are heterogeneous, composed of different subsystems that altogether provide the required functionality. Quite often, these subsystems follow their own rules and manage their own data schemas, which need to fit together at different levels, from conceptual (e.g., to provide a consolidated vocabulary) to operational (e.g., to allow their interoperability). This is especially true in collaborative software development projects, where different organizations bring some existing assets that need to be combined into a holistic system.

The reconciliation of the different data schemas can be implemented through ontology integration. An ontology defines an explicit specification of a conceptualization [1]. Ontologies are tightly related to other conceptual modelling artifacts as modelling languages and metamodels [2]. Ontology-based data model integration addresses the problem of building a new ontology for heterogeneous information systems (HIS) composed of subsystems that need to interoperate [3]. Methods for ontology integration have been proposed for more than 20 years (see Sect. 2), but integration in real settings remains a challenging problem due to several reasons. Among them, there is the need to find an adequate trade-off between rigour in the integration and feasibility in terms of return on investment for the organizations involved.

The need for such practical method became evident during the OpenReq collaborative software development project in which the authors are participating (www.openreq.eu). The main goal of OpenReq is to develop, evaluate, and transfer highly innovative methods, algorithms, and tools for community-driven RE in large and distributed software-intensive projects. To this end, four universities and five companies from Europe collaborate in the deployment of a platform providing services to the community. The platform will be built upon a data schema derived from a domain ontology for RE which should reconcile a global perspective to satisfy the requests of the community and a local perspective to integrate the current assets, techniques and needs from all the project partners. The purpose of the ontology is thus supporting the development and integration of techniques while serving as a reference framework for the community.

In this context, the present work addresses the following research goal:

Research Goal. To propose a method based on domain ontologies to integrate the data models of assets participating in a HIS with optimal trade-off of semantic rigour and feasibility in terms of implementation effort and adoption in a real setting.

The rest of the paper is organized as follows. Section 2 provides the background. Section 3 presents the context of our research. Section 4 shows the method proposed to construct the domain ontology applied in the OpenReq case, which is developed in details in Sects. 5–9. Finally, Sect. 10 conducts some discussion and identifies future work.

2 Background

The application of ontology integration in the context of HIS was claimed by Sowa [4], who also identified two possible ways to proceed: replace the original ontologies by the new one, or use the new one as an intermediary between the HIS. This second option seems more appropriate when integrating models with little room for changes, as it is the case for the context that we are addressing in this paper.

Calvanese et al. [5] formally defined the semantics of integration in this scenario. It is characterised by a mapping between the new ontology (called global ontology) and local ontologies (which are used as a starting point for the integration). This mapping can be defined adopting either a global-centric approach or a local-centric approach. In the global-centric approach, every term in the global ontology has associated a view (i.e., a query) over the local ontologies, while in the local-centric approach every term in a local ontology is mapped onto a view over the global ontology.

In our work, we follow this idea reviewed also in De Giacomo et al. [6]. In this kind of integration the ontology is a formal and conceptual view and constitutes the component to which the clients of the integrated information systems use to interact with them. In our case, we consider also as clients the own information systems integrated that use the ontology to interact with the rest of the system. Thus, the ontology provides the semantic data integration of the heterogeneous information systems.

3 The Context: The OpenReq Project

The OpenReq collaborative development project will support (see Fig. 1): (1) the automated identification of requirements from different knowledge sources (e.g., communities or natural language text documents); (2) the personal recommendation of requirements as well as requirement-related aspects (such as quality tips or requirement metadata fields) and stakeholders; (3) the support of group decision making (e.g., in release planning) by providing a solution that fulfills all users preferences or indicates the conflicts that need to be solved to provide a solution; (4) the automated identification of (hidden) dependencies between requirements. OpenReq will provide an open source tool and a set of APIs that will integrate these innovative technologies applied to RE.

OpenReq is a classic example of a collaborative software development project that needs to address contradicting challenges for producing a HIS, as defined in the introduction:

- Different partners bring to the project their own assets in the form of implemented software components. The partners developed these components for their own purposes and they do not want to change their data model and (underlying) ontology.

- These assets need to be reconciled because the project aims at delivering a single, unifying platform. Furthermore, given that the platform shall be open to the RE community, it is utterly important that the resulting domain model is cohesive and general-enough.

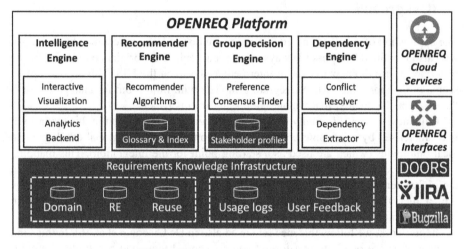

Fig. 1. The OpenReq approach to RE.

4   The Method

In this section, we briefly present the method proposed for ontology-based integration in the context stated above, emerging from our experience in the OpenReq project. The method is composed of five steps (see Fig. 2) briefly enumerated below and developed in detail in the next sections.

- **Step I:** *Creation of the Baseline.* Obtain (if they do not exist yet) the local data model of each of the existing assets to be reconciled.
- **Step II:** *Analysis of the Baseline.* Local data models are aligned to understand which are the core concepts and identify possible contradictions and variants.
- **Step III:** *Definition of the Domain Ontology.* From the previous analysis and considering conveniently standards and other reference models for the domain, the domain ontology is defined around the core concepts, integrating the different variants and solving all detected contradictions.
- **Step IV:** *Mapping among the Local Data Models and the Domain Ontology.* In order to support the semantic alignment of the existing assets, the mapping among the local data models and the domain ontology is defined.
- **Step V:** *Definition of the Metamodel.* With the purpose to better structure the domain ontology and to support easier maintainability, a metamodel is built abstracting the concepts appearing in the domain ontology.

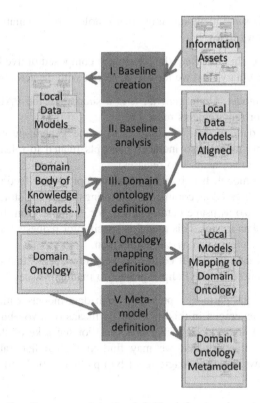

Fig. 2. The OpenReq approach to the definition of a domain ontology for RE.

5   Step I: Creation of the Baseline

In this first step, the goal is to represent in the same modelling paradigm the ontologies that the different partners participating in a collaborative development project are currently using as semantic framework for their assets. This way, we avoid two of the main types of ontology mismatches that could have make the integration process harder: paradigm heterogeneity and language heterogeneity [7].

As already stated, it will not be usual to have fully-fledged ontologies defining the assets to be integrated into the HIS. Therefore, we propose to use data models to describe such assets, as simplified representation of the (underlying) ontologies. More precisely, we propose UML class diagrams plus a vocabulary of terms for each input model, since the idea is to use UML for the domain ontology representation. The use of UML class diagrams in ontology representation is quite usual and well-established [8] and has two advantages. On the one hand, class diagrams for the assets may already exist or otherwise, they are easy to build from a database schema, which is a technical artefact that can be assumed to exist. On the other hand, class diagrams (particularly, in UML) are a widespread notation that usually will not require any kind of training. Working with UML instead of other more accurate formalisms has one drawback, namely the limitations in reasoning capabilities. If such capabilities were required, we could still apply this same method, using other ontology representation language, e.g., based on Description Logics.

The OpenReq Case. In OpenReq, the baseline is composed of five local data models (and associated vocabulary) that we identify hereafter with the acronym of the partner[1]:

- The UPC data model. Quite general, it is a subpart of the PABRE system conceptual model for requirements reuse [9].
- The TUGRAZ data model. In addition to some general-purpose concepts for requirements, this model also includes concepts related to release planning (i.e., distributing the requirements into releases).
- The HITEC data model. It is based on the concept of user feedback (as source of requirements), expressed as comments and ratings in an app stores [10] and social media [11], but also as usage data obtained, for example, from handheld devices.
- The SIEMENS data model. This model is specific for requests for proposal (RFPs) in an industrial context such as rail automation.
- The VOGELLA data model. It comprises very few classes that correspond to the Bugzilla system used by the Eclipse project to maintain issues.

In all the cases, the partners represented such data models with UML class diagrams, which were leveraged in this first step by means of a vocabulary including all the relevant concepts introduced in the diagram. For the sake of illustration, just to understand the big diversity that we may find in such collaborative development projects, Fig. 3 shows the class diagrams of two partners, UPC and VOGELLA.

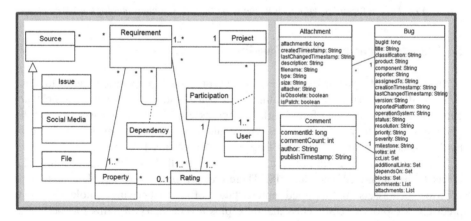

Fig. 3. Fig. 3 Class diagrams included in the baseline: UPC (up) and VOGELLA (down) (UPC data model does not include attributes due to space reasons).

---

[1] We refer to authors' affiliations in the first page.

6 Step II: Analysis of the Baseline

The main purpose of this step is to analyse the local models and vocabularies that compose the baseline for their later alignment. In a collaborative software project, we may expect different interests from all the partners, different contexts, scopes, etc. In addition, every domain may have its own additional challenges, e.g. heterogeneity of data sources. Therefore, it is utterly important to profoundly understand this variety to find alignments, overlapping, contradictions and differences, i.e., data heterogeneity.

In general, we may expect several data heterogeneity causes to emerge [12]: schematic (e.g., same concept with a different name), semantic (e.g., same name for different concepts) and intensional (e.g., fundamental differences in the domain).

The OpenReq Case. In OpenReq, the central concept around which all models revolve is that of requirement. This concept is represented explicitly in three models, and remarkably in two of them (UPC and TUGRAZ) its notion is quite similar. However, since the attributes are slightly different, it cannot be said that the concept is exactly the same. In the third case (i.e., SIEMENS) the concept of requirement is explicitly defined in the ontology, but in fact it is wider: in addition to requirements, pieces of text that are candidate to become requirements, and pieces of text that have been assessed and finally discarded as requirements, also are included in this concept. In the other models, the requirement concept as such does not exist. Instead, two related concepts appear, namely bug (VOGELLA) and users' feedback (HITEC). Both concepts are a potential source of requirements. Figure 4 summarizes these classes.

For the sake of illustration, Table 1 exemplifies the main causes of data heterogeneity at the level of attributes for the requirement concept considering three of the local data models. Note that it may be the case that more than one heterogeneity cause occurs for a given attribute. An extended version of this table including all the models and all the causes could be considered the outcome of this step.

Table 1. Examples of the main causes of data heterogeneity at the level of attributes in three of the local data models with respect to the notion of requirement.

SIEMENS	TUGRAZ	UPC	Data heterogeneity
id: long	---	ID: Integer	*Semantic*: different scale for the same attribute *Intensional*: attribute is not considered in all the models
text: Text	description: String	Description: String	*Schematic*: different data type and name for the same attribute
type: {DEF, Prose, Not Classified}	---	---	*Intensional*: attribute is not considered in all the models
---	status: Enum	---	*Intensional*: attribute is not considered in all the models
---	creationDate: DateTime	CreatedAt: DateTime	*Schematic*: different name for the same attribute *Intensional*: attribute is not considered in all the models
---	priority: Float	Priority: Integer	*Schematic*: different name for the same attribute *Semantic*: different scale for the same attribute *Intensional*: attribute is not considered in all the models

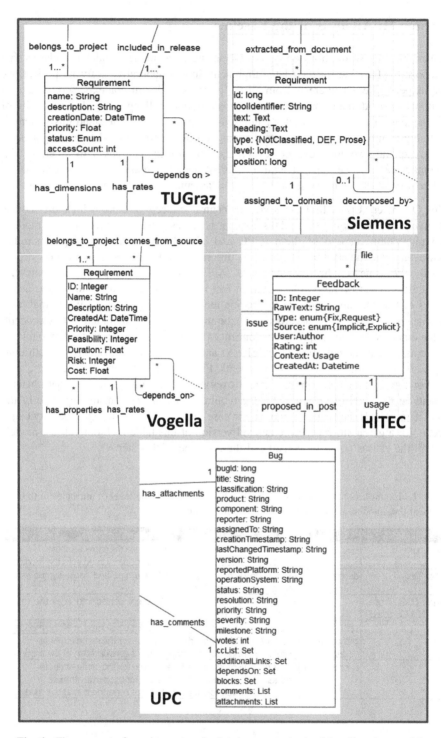

Fig. 4. The concept of requirement and related concepts in the 5 baseline data models.

7 Step III: Definition of the Domain Ontology (M1)

In the third step, the analysis made in the previous step is consolidated into a domain ontology, again considering the needs outlined in Sect. 3: it is required to satisfy the needs of the different project participants (i.e., asset providers), while opening the space to accommodate new, sometimes unforeseen evolutionary paths. The domain ontology will be represented through a UML class diagram plus associated glossary to define all the classes, attributes and associations appearing therein.

The main task in this process is to solve the heterogeneity causes identified in Step II. Schematic causes are the easiest to solve, while intensional causes are the most difficult and require a strong decision based on the purposes of the domain ontology. The use of bodies of knowledge pertaining to the domain, e.g. in the form of standards, can help to make decisions in this process.

The OpenReq Case. From the analysis above, it is clear that the `Requirement` class is central to the domain ontology. We present in detail the consolidation of this concept from the analysis carried out in Step II (for the rest of the ontology, due to space limitations, not all details are reported):

- The most fundamental intensional heterogeneity is agreeing on the concept of requirement itself. We decided to define requirement according to the IEEE standard glossary of software engineering terminology [13]: "A condition or capability that must be met or possessed by a system or system component to satisfy a contract, standard, specification, or other formally imposed document". This means that all definitions need to fit this referential framework. As an additional advantage, adhering to a well-known standard paves the way for dissemination and evolution.

- The rest of intensional heterogeneities refer to attributes that are not included in all the local models (*modulo* other heterogeneities). The selection of the attributes to include is based on expert judgement and, in a project of this nature, requires the consensus from all partners, who evaluate them in terms of the impact on their assets and their goal for evolution.

- Similarly, schematic and semantic heterogeneities are solved by expert criteria. In general, they are not fundamental for the final result.

As for the rest of information conveyed in the domain ontology, requirements are structured into a hierarchy by means of a `decomposition` association. Two other relationships, namely `conflict` and `synergy`, are mentioned in several local data models, therefore we introduce two associations with the same name.

Since the ultimate concept of OpenReq is the planning of requirements into releases, we introduce the `Release` class. Releases exist in the scope of `Projects`. Requirements bound to a release are bound to the project that defined such release, made explicit with a derived association, `belongs-to`. `TeamMembers` are members of a `Project` in which they participate (i.e., `Participant`) playing a given role. `TeamMembers` may have requirements assigned.

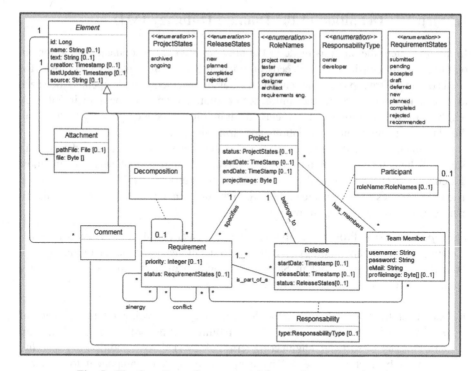

Fig. 5. The OpenReq reference model for requirements engineering.

Last, for practical reasons, we introduce one abstract class, Element. It is the most generic in the model and encapsulates attributes that are shared by virtually all the classes: identifier, name, description, creation date, last update date and their source. Also the associations to Comment and Attachment are related to Element, to allow for adding these explanatory elements to all type of elements. This generalization serves to exemplify the need of adding non-graphical integrity constraints to the model, e.g., an attachment cannot be attached to another attachment.

Figure 5 shows the OpenReq domain ontology for requirements engineering. The domain ontology includes also the vocabulary, not reported due to space limitations.

8   Step IV: Mapping Among the Local Data Models and the Domain Ontology (M1)

As mentioned in Sect. 2.2, mappings are a central element in the integration of HIS through ontologies [5].

The concrete definition of the mapping ultimately depends on the purpose for building the domain ontology. In some contexts, the ontology has the purpose of mediating among the local data models, e.g., interconnecting software components or data bases, or providing a single access point to a distributed data base, in which case an implementation in the form of, for instance, SPARQL queries is required [14]. In other cases, the domain ontology is conceived as a semantic framework to provide an intermediate layer to the consumers and providers of a heterogeneous information system, facilitating the development of services on top of this layer. In this situation, a more conceptual implementation of the mapping is convenient.

We propose to implement the mapping at the level of the UML class diagrams used to represent the global ontology and local data models. In particular, we bind concepts in the local models to the domain ontology through specialization. At the end, all those concepts in the local data models which are related to the domain ontology will have their correspondence to the domain ontology, which could eventually be expressed through OCL expressions if needed. In some cases, they will be subclasses of a class in the domain ontology, in other cases there will be necessary to create a new class in the local data model that will be subclass of the domain ontology. Elements in the local ontologies not clearly related to the domain will remain independent of the domain ontology.

The OpenReq Case. For the sake of space, we illustrate this step with two representative situations. First, we focus on how the different local data models connect with the `Requirement` class introduced in the domain ontology. Given that the definition of requirement in the domain ontology has been kept generic enough to accommodate the semantics of that concept in all the local models, we define a specialization from the local class (renamed into `XX-Requirement`, being `XX` the name of the partner) to the domain ontology class. The declaration of this specialization implies removing from `XX-Requirement` all the attributes and associations that are inherited from the domain ontology, e.g., id, name and text. This way, schematic and semantic heterogeneities are automatically fixed. Figure 6(a) shows the details for one of the OpenReq cases.

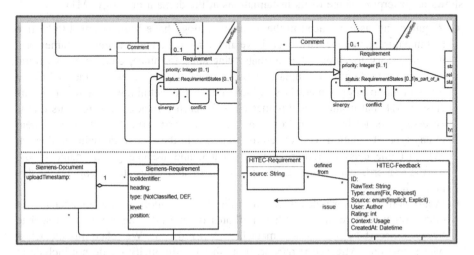

Fig. 6. Mappings with the OpenReq RE domain ontology: (a) mapping SIEMENS requirements; (b) Mapping HITEC user feedback.

Second, there are several concepts in the local data models that do not specialize any class in the domain ontology but are related. For instance, this is the case of HITEC's Feedback class. User feedback is not a type of requirement but one possible source of requirements; therefore, a subclass has been added to the HITEC ontology that specializes Requirement and a new association definedFrom so that a requirement may have its origin after an undetermined number of feedback instances (see Fig. 6(b)).

9   Step V: Definition of the Metamodel (M2)

Finally, we aim at consolidating the core concepts of the domain ontology into a metamodel. This allows a more compact view of the concepts at hand and support future evolution and extension of the domain ontology as new business cases and opportunities arise. Some points worth to remark are:

- The metamodel shall be such that most concepts of the domain ontology are instances of metaclasses. However, it may be the case that some concepts are not, if they are not considered in the backbone of the domain ontology. In addition, the classes introduced as abstract for convenience (in the case of OpenReq, the class Element, see Sect. 7) are not intended to be instances of any metaclass.
- The definition of the metamodel can require slight adjustments in the domain ontology. The mappings defined in the former step need to be adjusted accordingly.

The OpenReq Case. We consider as starting point a metamodel for requirements proposed by UH based in the metamodel presented in [15] for the area of variability modelling. The upper part of Fig. 7 shows the metamodel (M2), and the lower part shows an excerpt of some of its instantiations at the domain ontology (M1).

- Requirements as introduced in the domain ontology have been assumed to be free text in natural language. However, if we aim at having a comprehensive framework, it is necessary to allow other formats: diagrams, formulae, etc., or even natural language according to a template or user stories. Therefore, we define in M2 the RequirementType metaclass, which allows the definition of a requirements class in M1 that instantiates this metaclass for each format of requirements that is necessary. As attribute, apart from the name, the contents (i.e., the requirement in any type of notation) is declared as Object. In the current domain ontology at M1, just one class of requirement is needed, and we change the name of the Requirement class into NL-Requirement and adjust the mappings to this name change.
- In addition to the attributes included in the domain ontology, we consider that in other contexts there can be other attributes of interest. Therefore, we associate RequirementType to a new metaclass, Attribute. We relate this metaclass with a new one, AttributeType (note that for simplicity we do not include in Fig. 7 the metaclasses corresponding to enumerates or sets). Names as identifiers are the only attributes in these two metaclasses.

- Similarly, we can think that eventually other type of relationships over requirements could be stated; therefore, we introduce a metaclass `RelationshipType` where the name of the relationship (synergy, conflict, ...) is declared as attribute.

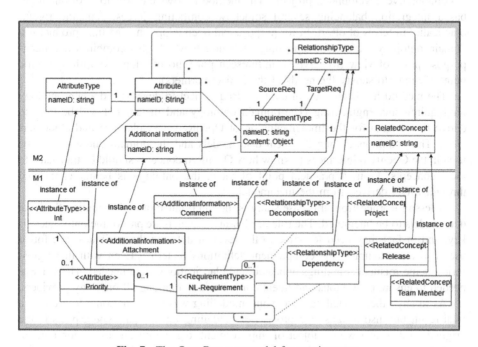

Fig. 7. The OpenReq metamodel for requirements.

On the other hand, we realize that there are two types of classes with respect to their relationship with Requirements:

- Classes extending requirements to provide richer information. These are `Comment` and `Attachment`. Note that they are optional (i.e., a requirement does not need a comment or attachment to exist). We define a metaclass `AdditionalInformation` to capture this concept.
- Classes defining elements that describe some context of the requirement. These are `Release`, `Project` and `TeamMember`. Note that they may be mandatory (i.e., a requirements needs to be defined in the context of a project) or optional (i.e., a requirement may be temporarily not assigned to any release). We define a metaclass `RelatedConcept` to capture these types of elements.

10 Discussion and Future Work

In this paper, we have presented a method to be used in the context of HIS construction in collaborative development projects. The method follows the principles of ontology-based integration balancing several somehow conflicting forces: semantic rigour, practicality in terms of effort, fit for purpose and open adoption. The final product is a domain ontology with a corresponding metamodel, which also combines a general-purpose point of view (to serve an unforeseen portfolio of adopters) with a specific point of view (to satisfy the needs of the project partners).

The method has been used in the OpenReq project to develop a domain ontology for requirements engineering. The domain ontology and metamodel will be used to derive the schema for the implementation of OpenReq, i.e., platform and cloud services. The mappings among the local data models and the domain ontology will be used in the OpenReq interfaces to know how OpenReq concepts should be translated to local concepts. From a practical point of view, the ontology is being represented through JSON derived from the metamodel.

A lesson learned from this case study is the importance of understanding the local data models to be integrated. The role of glossaries (which are part of the ontologies) is key, and in fact they need to arrive to the level of defining the attributes. We found useful to use examples that complement definitions of terms. Even with these glossaries, some misunderstandings appeared and clarifications were needed. Thus, it was needed to ensure continuous and fluent communication among all ontology providers.

As in any other modelling endeavour, modelling was useful not only to produce a final result but also because the process of modelling uncovered some aspects in the original models that were subject of improvement, e.g. redundancies or non-optimal modelling solutions. We fixed these problems before defining the mapping.

The domain ontology obtained through our method should not be seen as a final product. For instance, we foresee that the OpenReq ontology will continue evolving as the OpenReq project does, including new elements that did not appear in the local data models. Candidate concepts at the moment are Classifiers (to allow grouping requirements by concepts, e.g. to organize a requirements document) and External Elements (such as code or tests cases) to be linked with requirements. Also new concepts may be necessary in local models of partners working on contributing to OpenReq new functionalities (see Sect. 3). In all the cases, the changes will be considered in order to evolve the domain ontology, and if it is necessary the metamodel.

Despite our effort to ensure validity, some threats could impact the results [16]. For instance, internal validity concerns are covered by the fact that we restrain ourselves to the retrieved evidence and expert knowledge. As for reducing reliability threats, we departed from a set of RE data models from different domains (usually with characteristics that are domain-dependent), some of them being already used by the industrial partners (i.e., SIEMENS and VOGELLA). Last, concerning external validity, we have produced a method with the aim to be general, but we need to be aware that it comes from a single experience in one particular domain, therefore further cases are needed.

Our future work spreads along several directions. First, as mentioned above, we envisage changes in the domain ontology due to evolution in the platform as the project progresses and also at the end of the project, as new local ontologies implementing additional functionalities will join the OpenReq platform.

Acknowledgments. This work is a result of the OpenReq project, which has received funding from the European Union's Horizon 2020 research and innovation programme under grant agreement No 732463.

References

1. Gruber, T.R.: A translation approach to portable ontologies. Knowl. Acquis. **5**(2), 199–229 (1993)
2. Guizzardi, G.: On ontology, ontologies, conceptualizations, modeling languages, and (meta) models. Front. Artif. Intell. Appl. **155**, 18 (2007)
3. Wache, H., Voegele, T., Visser, U., Stuckenschmidt, H., Schuster, G., Neumann, H., & Hübner, S.: Ontology-based integration of information-a survey of existing approaches. In: IJCAI-01 Workshop: Ontologies and Information Sharing (2001)
4. Sowa, J.F.: Building, Sharing, and Merging Ontologies (2001). http://users.bestweb.net/~sowa/ontology/ontoshar.htm
5. Calvanese, D., de Giacomo, G., Lenzerini, M.: Ontology of integration and integration of ontologies. In: DL Workshop 2001 – CEUR 49 (2001)
6. De Giacomo, G., Lembo, D., Lenzerini, M., Poggi, A., Rosati, R.: Using ontologies for semantic data integration. In: Flesca, S., Greco, S., Masciari, E., Saccà, D. (eds.) A Comprehensive Guide Through the Italian Database Research Over the Last 25 Years. SBD, vol. 31, pp. 187–202. Springer, Cham (2018). https://doi.org/10.1007/978-3-319-61893-7_11
7. Visser, P.R.S., Jones, D.M., Bench-Capon, T.J.M., Shave, M.J.R.: An analysis of ontology mismatches; heterogeneity versus interoperability. In: AAAI Spring Symposium on Ontological Engineering, Stanford University, California, USA (1997)
8. Cranefield, S., Purvis, M.: UML as an ontology modelling language. In: IJCAI (1999)
9. Franch, X., Palomares, C., Quer, C., Renault, S., De Lazzer, F.: A metamodel for software requirement patterns. In: Wieringa, R., Persson, A. (eds.) REFSQ 2010. LNCS, vol. 6182, pp. 85–90. Springer, Heidelberg (2010). https://doi.org/10.1007/978-3-642-14192-8_10
10. Gómez, M., Adams, B., Maalej, W., Monperrus, M., Rouvoy, R.: App Store 2.0: from crowdsourced information to actionable feedback in mobile ecosystems. IEEE Softw. **34**(2), 81–89 (2017)
11. Kurtanović, Z., Maalej, M.: Mining User Rationale from Software Reviews. In: RE 2017 (2017)
12. Goh, C.H.: Representing and reasoning about semantic conflicts in heterogeneous information sources. Ph.D. thesis, MIT (1996)
13. IEEE Std 610.12-1990 - IEEE Standard Glossary of Software Engineering Terminology (1990)
14. Schenner, G., Bischof, S., Polleres, A., Steyskal, S.: Integrating distributed configurations with RDFS and SPARQL. In: confWS 2014 (2014)

15. Asikainen, T., Männistö, T., Soininen. T.: Kumbang: A Domain Ontology for Modelling Variability in Software Product Families. Adv. Eng. Inform. **21**(1), 23–40 (2007)
16. Wohlin, C., Runeson, P., Host, M., Ohlsson, M.C., Regnell, B., Wesslen, A.: Experimentation in Software Engineering: An Introduction. Kluwer Academic Publishers Norwell, MA, USA (2012)

An Agile and Ontology-Aided Modeling Environment

Emanuele Laurenzi[1,2,3]([✉]), Knut Hinkelmann[1,3], and Alta van der Merwe[3]

[1] FHNW University of Applied Sciences and Arts Northwestern Switzerland,
Riggenbachstrasse 16, 4600 Olten, Switzerland
{emanuele.laurenzi,knut.hinkelmann}@fhnw.ch
[2] University of Applied Sciences St. Gallen, IPM-FHSG,
Institute of Information and Process Management,
Rosenbergstrasse, 59, 9001 St., Gallen, Switzerland
[3] University of Pretoria, Department of Informatics,
Lynnwood Rd, 0083 Pretoria, South Africa
alta.vdm@up.ac.za

Abstract. Enterprise knowledge is currently subject to ever-changing, complex and domain-specific modeling requirements. Assimilating these requirements in modeling languages brings the benefits associated to both domain-specific modeling languages (DSMLs) and a baseline of well-established concepts. However, there are two problems that hamper the speed and efficiency of this activity: (1) the separation between the two key expertise: language engineering and domain knowledge, and (2) the sequential modeling language engineering life-cycles. In this work, we tackle these two challenges by introducing an Agile and Ontology-Aided approach implemented in our Modeling Environment - the AOAME. The approach seamlessly integrates meta-modeling and modeling in the same modeling environment, thus cooperation between language engineers and domain experts is fostered. Sequential engineering phases are avoided as the adaptation of the language is done on-the-fly. To this end, a modeling language is grounded with an ontology language providing a clear, unambiguous and machine-interpretable semantics. Mechanisms implemented in the AOAME ensure the propagation of changes from the modeling environment to the graph-based database containing the ontology.

Keywords: Agile and ontology-aided modeling environment
Domain-specific adaptation · Domain-specific modeling language

1 Introduction

Today's enterprises are subject to a continuous digital business evolution. Many different complex aspects of enterprises are affected such as processes, organization and product structures, IT-systems as well as different degree of domain

© IFIP International Federation for Information Processing 2018
Published by Springer Nature Switzerland AG 2018. All Rights Reserved
R. A. Buchmann et al. (Eds.): PoEM 2018, LNBIP 335, pp. 221–237, 2018.
https://doi.org/10.1007/978-3-030-02302-7_14

specificity, i.e. an entire industry or an application area or a single case in an enterprise. Complex and domain-specific aspects take place within an increasingly challenging environment for enterprises characterized by high competition, cross-organization cooperation, and continuous and unexpected change [1,2]. As a consequence, modern enterprises should have the ability to continuously, quickly and efficiently capture relevant ever-changing, complex and domain-specific aspects and represent them in enterprise knowledge. Burlton at al. [3] call this ability "Business Agility", which creates competitive advantage and enables to thrive in innovative environments.

Enterprise models' main purpose is to capture enterprise knowledge. Due to the frequent change of the latter, models have to be re-designed continuously as they become outdated. Ideally, modeling approaches and tools should enable modelers to continuously adapt enterprise models by accommodating new modeling requirements quickly and efficiently. Assimilating modeling requirements directly in modeling languages has many benefits that are typically associated to domain-specific modeling languages (DSMLs) built by adapting existing modeling languages. Conversely to DSMLs built from scratch, a set of concepts and well-established semantics already foster the dissemination of a DSML within the modeling community. Also, the latter provide a baseline of lessons learned in the field and a set of well-known concepts that can be borrowed. This "domain-specific adaptation" of one or more modeling languages has the ultimate goal of facilitating modeler's task in creating meaningful models as well as increasing understanding of models by domain experts. This goal should be achieved by the language engineer (developer and adapter of the modeling language), who is required to continuously, quickly and efficiently adapt modeling languages. This activity, in contrast, is a time-consuming engineering effort. This is mainly due to the lack of agility in the domain-specific adaptation life-cycles and in the way these are implemented in modeling tools.

This paper elaborates an agile and ontology-aided approach for a domain-specific adaptation of modeling languages. The approach is implemented in the modeling environment called AOAME (Agile and Ontology-Aided Modeling Environment). Section 2 presents the theoretical background upon which AOAME is built. Next, Sect. 3 emphasizes the two main challenges addressed in this work and introduces the related works that strive to address them. Section 4 describes our AOAME solution, including the architecture, the ontologies and the mechanisms that support the solution. The paper ends with Sect. 5, where a validation of the AOAME is presented with respect to a use case derived from a research project.

2   Background

This section introduces the theoretical foundations of this work. In the following sub-sections we first define a modeling language. Next, notions on the modeling language developing technique "meta-modeling" are provided. Finally, the term domain-specific adaptation is introduced.

2.1 Modeling Language Specification

A modeling language is specified by notation, abstract syntax and semantics [4]. Abstract syntax refers to the class hierarchy of modeling elements together with their relations and attributes, through which the language terminology is defined. Modeling constructs are typically expressed through graphical or textual notation (also known as concrete syntax), which should be cognitively adequate to ensure users' understanding of models [5]. The semantics define the meaning of the syntactic elements of a modeling language. Harel and Rumpe [6] claim that the semantics of a modeling language is described in two parts: the semantic domain and the semantic mapping. "The semantic domain can be defined independently of the syntax: in fact, we can use completely different languages for describing the same kinds of systems, so that these languages might all use the same semantic domain" [6]. Whilst concrete syntax (e.g. graphical notation) is used to create models, abstract syntax specifies what kind of knowledge a model is allowed to contain. Hence, the semantic mapping takes place from concepts in the abstract syntax to the domain semantics.

In some cases, however, not all semantics can be expressed through this mapping [7]. In order to govern how the language constructs can be combined to produce valid models, constraints (or rules or restrictions) should be inserted over concepts. Thus, the semantics of a modeling language can be defined by (a) abstract syntax, including constraints or restrictions on concepts, (b) domain semantics and (c) the mapping between concepts from the abstract syntax to those of the domain. The mapping can be seen as a relation between the linguistic view and the domain of discourse view. The differentiation between the two views is consistent with the work in [8], which regards fundamental to have both the linguistic definition and the domain definition in a modeling language.

Semantics can be expressed formally (i.e. through mathematics or ontologies) or informally (i.e. through natural language). Formality of the semantics depends on the formalism of the abstract syntax, the domain semantics and the semantic mapping. The latter should be made explicit (according to Harel and Rumpe [6]) as it is not satisfactory to define the semantic mapping by examples, as it does not allow analysis through which insights can be gained. Therefore the semantic mapping also must be formally defined. Section 4.2 describes how the semantic language, including the semantic mapping, is made explicit and formal.

2.2 Meta-modeling for Enterprise Modeling Languages

Enterprise Modeling Languages (EML) such as ArchiMate[1] and BPMN[2] are typically specified in UML class diagrams. Concepts of an EML reside at Level 2 of the meta-modeling hierarchy introduced by Strahringer [9]. Abstract syntax and constraints of an EML are specified in the meta-model and elements of the abstract syntax are furnished with graphical notations such that modelers can

---

[1] http://pubs.opengroup.org/architecture/archimate3-doc/.

[2] https://www.omg.org/spec/BPMN/2.0/About-BPMN/.

then create models in the lower level, i.e. Level 1. That means graphical notations are not just shaped boxes that rely on the human-interpretation. Instead, each notation is instantiated from a higher abstraction concept with explicitly defined semantics, which is based on a concept taxonomy and descriptive properties. This leads to the definition of the language terminology, thus a vocabulary for modeling constructs in the considered domain is made available. As a consequence, the semantics of a modeling language emerges as a tangible artifact that may be exchanged, inspected, and discussed. Hence, an understanding of the problem domain increases together with a better comprehensibility of the modeling language. As an example, concepts like *Sequence Flow* or *Task* in BPMN are part of a taxonomy that reflects the semantics of the language. These concepts are associated with correspondent graphical notations in order for the modeler to use them.

Karagiannis at al. [10] introduce the notion of *domain-specificity degree*, where an higher specificity degree means assimilating concepts in the meta-model that target a more specific domain. Meta-models of EMLs capture aspects that target a particular degree of a domain. BPMN targets process modeling, whereas Archimate targets enterprise architecture modeling. Their particular degree of a domain can serve as a baseline to build modeling languages with higher domain-specificity degree [10–12], which in literature are also known as domain-specific modeling languages (DSMLs) [7]. The baseline provides many advantages. For instance, established experience, lessons learned and best practices can be taken into account. Also, EMLs provide concepts with well-known notations and a widely accepted semantic, which foster the dissemination of the DSML within the modeling community [13].

2.3   Domain-Specific Adaptation

The activity of adapting a modeling language to add more domain-specificity degree is commonly known as modeling language adaptation or extensibility [14–16]. Jablonski at al. [14] define the latter as an "extension or extensibility so that domain specific requirements can be integrated or domain specific semantics are better reflected". However, the term extensibility is limited only to add new concepts or restricting value types or values, e.g. profiling mechanisms from UML like stereotype and tagged values [17]. Additionally, the term modeling language adaptation is commonly limited to one modeling language, excluding the integration of different modeling languages [13].

Another emerging term for this activity is "domain-specific adaptation" [5,11,13]. As shown in [11], domain-specific adaptation also includes integration of different modeling languages and simplification of these by removing unnecessary concepts. In this work, we define a "domain-specific adaptation" as the adaptation of one or more modeling languages. It can comprise the following actions: (1) removal of unnecessary concepts, (2) specialization of concepts, (3) integration of concepts from different modeling languages, (4) restrictions on attribute types and values.

3   Problems and Related Work

Most of current meta-modeling approaches and the way these are implemented in modeling workbenches (e.g. EMF, ADOxx, TextEdit, Eugenia, MetaEdit, Kaos, ATL) address different expertise. Namely, the conceptualization and implementation of the meta-model (Level 2) target language engineers, whereas the domain expert (Level 1) would use the concrete syntax to create models. Noteworthy is the fact that the most significant feedback and amendments for the language originate at the early stage as soon as the first version of the language is being used. Pitfalls related to inappropriate constraints, abstraction issues, or ambiguity of modeling constructs are likely to arise [7]. Also, decisions on whether to promote productivity at the expenses of re-usability (or vice versa) of the modeling language are subject to continuous changes. Unless domain experts have language engineering skills, new requirements cannot be accommodated by modelers or domain experts. Instead they have to be properly communicated to the language engineer, who adapts the modeling language at the meta-level. In turn, changes should be propagated in the modeling tool, which implements the new language specifications. If feedback or amendments are not properly communicated (e.g. due to a lack of cooperation), misinterpretations can arise, which hamper the adaptation process and the quality of the released DSML [18].

Ideally, conditions to foster the cooperation between language engineers and domain experts should be created. This sets the *first challenge* of this work. It goes in line with the recent research agenda of Enterprise Modeling proposed in [19], where with the slogan "modeling for the masses" emphasizes the need to welcome non-experts in the field of modeling for an inter-disciplinary benefit. Research work addressing this challenge, however, is still in its infancy. Izquierdo at al. [18] were first to propose a collaborative approach to create DSMLs. Namely, an example-driven and collaborative supported tool was developed to engage end-users in the construction of DSMLs. With a similar end, Barisic at al. [20] propose the USE-ME as a methodological approach that covers the language development process, along which domain experts are involved in the assessment through user interface experimental techniques. While on one hand these solutions improve the quality of the final DSML, on the other hand they do not solve the problem of the time-consuming engineering effort. This is mainly due to the sequential engineering approach that characterizes the life-cycle of domain-specific adaptations.

Avoiding this sequential life-cycles sets the *second challenge* addressed in this work. Typically, such a life-cycle follows the iterative phases of (1) first eliciting relevant domain knowledge. Then, (2) the language engineer conceptualizes the meta-model. Subsequently, (3) the meta-model is implemented in a meta-modeling tool, allowing the modeler or domain expert to use the intermediate modeling language, and thus (4) evaluating it. The latter generates feedback and determines language amendments. Hence, the process iterates until a stable enough version of the language is achieved. Some examples of such life-cycle can be found in [20–22]. To foster agility, the AMME framework is proposed in [23] and instantiated by the OMiLab Lifecycle. The latter foresees feedback channels along different engineering phases to promote agility in the evolution of modeling requirements.

In domain-specific adaptation, however, each time a new modeling requirement is to be embedded in the modeling language, it has to go through the all above-mentioned engineering phases, sequentially [24]. This does not just result in a time-consuming engineering effort as in the case of a lack of cooperation. A sequential approach also becomes problematic with the long duration of each phase as the longer they take the higher is the risk of having outdated requirements. This would lead to a mismatch between the created DSML and the actual needs of end-users.

4   The Agile and Ontology-Aided Modeling Environment

The Agile and Ontology-Aided Modeling Environment (AOAME) was conceived through the design science research (DSR) approach [25], which provided guidance throughout the construction of the artifact. In particular, the awareness of problem was initially raised by use cases and lessons learned from three research projects targeting three different domains: (1) a patient discharging process among sites of care within the health-care sector [11,26]; (2) business process requirements and cloud service specification for the Business-IT matchmaking in the Cloud [27,28]; (3) workplace learning in public administrations [29]. Each project presented a model-driven solution and domain-specific adaptation activities were performed adopting current engineering life-cycles. As a result, the main challenges introduced in the previous section raised together with the first set of requirements for the conceptualization of AOAME (listed in [24]).

Differently from the work described in [24], this paper elaborates on the AOAME architecture. To this end, we first describe the main idea for addressing the two above-mentioned problems (Sect. 4.1). Next, Sect. 4.2 introduces the AOAME architecture that builds upon an ontology-based approach. Thus, the ontology architecture is also presented together with the motivation of the adopted ontology language. This section ends with mechanisms that allows the automatic propagation of domain-specific adaptations (Sect. 4.3).

4.1   Seamless Integration of Meta-modeling and Modeling

To address the two main challenges introduced in Sect. 3, we found inspiration in UML mechanisms such as *stereotype* and *tagged values*, which allow customizing modeling constructs on-the-fly. These mechanisms are typically implemented in modeling tools and both the customization and modeling take place in the same modeling environment (e.g. Visual Paradigm[3]).

Similarly, we conceptualized a unique modeling environment that seamlessly integrates meta-modeling and modeling for an on-the-fly domain-specific adaptation. That means, the sequential engineering phases are avoided as adaptations

---

[3] https://www.visual-paradigm.com/.

can (a) occur on-the-spot as they are needed and (b) be tested right away in the same modeling environment. Thus, both expertise language engineering and domain knowledge can be employed at the same time. This enables a tight and synchronized cooperation between the language engineer and the domain expert. Obviously, in case where someone has expertise in both fields would anyway benefit from the agile approach.

However, on-the-fly adaptations may lead to new modeling constructs for which semantics need to be made explicit. If not, the meaning of the new modeling constructs may be ambiguous or not understood by the users. To overcome this issue our solution makes use of ontologies. Namely, abstract syntax and additional semantics of a modeling language are made explicit by grounding them with an ontology formalism.

Making use of ontologies for a formal representation of models or modeling language constructs is an established practice within the research community, e.g. [29–31]. An ontology has not just the benefit of providing clear and unambiguous understanding of the meaning of language constructs and model concepts. Also, ontologies are interpretable by and interchangeable among machines and enable automated reasoning. Additionally, compared to approaches adopting standard data-bases, the ontology-based ones are more powerful in terms of query results. However, current ontology-based approaches mainly refer to semantic annotation, where ontology concepts (i.e. machine-interpretable concepts) are annotated to concepts of the meta-model or models (i.e. human-interpretable models). This approach has the drawback of the manual or semi-automatic alignment between meta-model concepts and ontology concepts, which can be error-prone and time-consuming. On one hand, mechanisms for the automatic generation of ontologies from models overcome this drawback. Examples for such mechanisms range from the creation of knowledge graphs [30] to more expressive ontologies (e.g. OWL - Ontology Web Language[4]) like in [29]. On the other hand, this solution may cause inconsistency issues that originate from the separation between human-interpretable models and machine-interpretable concepts [32]. For instance, if a change occurs in the ontology, the human-interpretable model has to be adapted, accordingly. Also, if changes occur in the meta-model, transformation patterns for the ontology generation might need to be adapted. This is the case in [29], where XSLT[5] templates are created for the automatic generation of ontology instances from XML models.

To avoid these problems we build upon the ontology-based meta-modeling approach introduced in [5]. This approach foresees an ontology as a meta-model, where ontology concepts are furnished with human-interpretable modeling constructs, i.e. graphical notations. This approach is implemented in our solution so that changes that occur in ontology concepts (e.g. adding a data type property to a class) are automatically reflected in the human-interpretable modeling constructs. Additionally, we took a step further by implementing the automatic propagation of changes that occur in the human-interpretable

---

4 https://www.w3.org/OWL/.
5 https://www.w3.org/TR/xslt-10/.

modeling constructs back to the ontology. This enables language engineers who are non-ontology experts to adapt a modeling language while the reflecting ontology is adapted automatically. Hence, a symbiosis is achieved between human-interpretale modeling constructs and related machine-interpretable concepts. To this end, a new architecture was introduced and is described in the next section.

4.2   AOAME Architecture

The AOAME architecture (see Fig. 1) foresees the support not just of the propagation from ontology concepts to modeling constructs, which ensures that all the displayed graphical notations in the modeling environment are grounded by ontology concepts (see arrow 1 and 2 in Fig. 1) but also, as mentioned above, it supports the propagation of changes (on modeling constructs) from the modeling environment back to the ontology (see arrows 3 and 4 in Fig. 1).

The architecture consists of three main components: a web-based modeling environment (ME) developed in AngularJS[6] (see left-hand side of Fig. 1). This has two sub-components: (a) the "Palette" where graphical notations of modeling constructs are displayed and (b) the "Canvas" where models are designed. In this work we focus on the "Palette" sub-component as it is the one enabling a domain-specific adaptation. The second main component is the Java-based web-service (WS) - at the center of Fig. 1 - which implements algorithms and mechanisms for the automatic propagation of changes from and to the Palette sub-component. The third component is a graph-based database (a.k.a. triple store - TS) implemented in Apache Jena Fuseki[7], which contains the three main ontologies of AOAME: the Palette Ontology (PO), the Modeling Language Ontology (MLO) and the Domain Ontology (DO).

Ontology Architecture. Figure 2 shows the three main ontologies of AOAME. Namely, the MLO reflects the abstract syntax, while the DO reflects the semantic domain. Concepts from the MLO are mapped with concepts of the DO (see Sect. 2.1 for the theoretical foundation that motivates the mapping). Concepts in the PO reflect the graphical notations of the language, and are directly linked to the concepts in the abstract syntax.

In more detail, the PO contains concepts and relations about graphical notations of the modeling language as well as knowledge for positioning the graphical notations over the palette. Thus, the palette in the ME is populated by the PO concepts. In particular, the class $po:$ $PaletteConnector$ contains instances reflecting connectors of one or more modeling languages (e.g. message flow and sequence flow for BPMN), while the class $po:$ $PaletteElement$ contains instances reflecting modeling elements of one or more modeling languages (e.g. task, data object for BPMN). Instances from both classes are meant to contain knowledge regarding the graphical notation, e.g. the name of the image extension, the size, whether it should be visible or hidden from the palette. These are all in the

---

[6] https://angularjs.org/.
[7] https://jena.apache.org/documentation/fuseki2/.

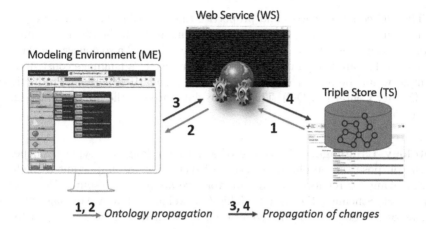

Fig. 1. AOAME architecture

form of data type properties. Also, they contain object properties, where the most relevant are *po: hasParent* and *po: isRelatedTo*. The former determine the hierarchy among modeling constructs that will then be shown in the Palette sub-component. The latter specifies which class of *MLO* the instance relates to. This relation reflects the link that connects notation with (abstract) syntax as described in [4]. In terms of ontology architecture, this implies that the *PO* includes the *MLO* (see Fig. 2).

Fig. 2. Ontology architecture

The *MLO* contains classes and properties describing the abstract syntax elements of a modeling language, i.e. modeling elements and modeling relations with respective taxonomy and object properties. MLO includes one or more modeling languages, which are separate from each other or integrated. Each *MLO* concept gets the prefix of the language it belongs to, e.g. Task in BPMN is shown as a class bpmn:Task. The object property *lo:is Mapped With* reflects the formal explication of the semantic mapping introduced in Sect. 2.1. This connects concepts from the *MLO* to those from the *DO*. Hence, the former includes the latter in the architecture shown in Fig. 2. In case there is the need to use a concept of a modeling language, the related ontologies (*MLO* and *PO*) need to be loaded in the *TS*.

The *DO* contains classes and properties that describe the semantic domain. As introduced in Sect. 2.1, the latter is independent from the abstract syntax of a language and describes a domain of discourse. The *DO* also consists of existing ontologies that are loaded in the *TS* to further specify a language construct. An example would be an ontology reflecting the standard American Productivity and Quality Center (APQC). This will be elaborated in the use case introduced in Sect. 5.

Ontology Language. The choice of a ontology language typically depends on the purpose the ontology, i.e. types of facts that are important to deduce, represent and/or retrieve [33]. In our work we adopt the Resource Description Framework Schema (RDFS) 1.1[8]. This lightweight ontology language fits the actions of the domain-specific adaptation as defined in Sect. 2.3, e.g. create a sub-class, attribute, relations etc. Moreover, it allows to have classes as instances of other classes, on the contrary to the more expressive above-mentioned OWL. The latter is limited to the knowledge representation of two levels: the TBox (i.e. classes) and the ABox (i.e. instances). This representation makes OWL unable to support a multi-layer representation that characterizes meta-model representations [34].

Instead, by adopting RDFS in AOAME we are able to further instantiate modeling elements from the *PO* to create models. Also, multilayer representation at design phase is supported, e.g., by modeling execution data as instances of process activities. Semantic rules (e.g. SPIN[9]) and the SPARQL[10] query language can be performed against the ontologies. The former are used to infer new knowledge while the latter provides powerful query constructions. The research works described in [28,29,35] show the validity of this approach.

An initial set of ontologies reflecting modeling languages should be provided by an ontology engineer. Next, actions allowed by the user in the *ME* are such that the expressivity power of the ontology does not increase. Hence, the risk of entering axioms that might be contradicting is avoided, and the ontology quality is not harmed over time. A way to allow expressive statements (e.g. in BPMN, a start event is not allowed to have an incoming sequence flow) while keeping the current ontology expressivness is by adopting the recent W3C recommendation language constraint SHACL[11]. This topic is, however, out of scope in this work but currently under investigation for its user-friendly applicability on the AOAME.

4.3   Mechanisms for an On-the-Fly Domain-Specific Adaptation

To enable the on-the-fly domain-specific adaptation from the modeling environment, we first derived operators from possible action on the ontologies. The

---

[8] https://www.w3.org/TR/rdf-schema/.

[9] http://spinrdf.org/.

[10] https://www.w3.org/TR/rdf-sparql-query/.

[11] https://www.w3.org/TR/shacl/.

list of operators is introduced in [24] and was implemented in the Palette sub-component. These, mainly consists of creating, updating and deleting of (i) sub-class relations, (ii) object properties and (iii) data type properties. Concrete types and values can also be assigned to the latter. To ensure the automatic propagation of changes from *ME* to the *TS*, mechanisms were conceptualized in terms of semantic rules and subsequently implemented for each operator. Semantic rules always impact both the PO and the MLO. Depending on the user actions over the operator semantic rules might also impact the DO. This is following explained through the description of mechanisms that are applied to a concrete operator: the "create sub-class". This leads to two possible results: (1) integration of modeling constructs from different modeling languages, i.e. a modeling construct is extended with a modeling construct of another modeling language; (2) extension of a modeling construct with a new modeling construct. Both generate different semantic rules. The former leads to the following seman-tic rules that are described in natural language:

1. Create a relation *po:hasParent* in the *PO* between the instance that is being extended and the selected instance.
2. Create a relation *rdfs:subClassOf* in the *MLO*, between the class that relates to the selected instance and the class that relates to the instance that is being extended.

The second possible result generates the following semantic rules:

1. Create a new class and a new relation *rdfs:subClassOf* in the *MLO*, where the new class is sub-class of the modeling construct that is being extended.
2. Create a new instance in the *PO*, containing two new relations *po: isRelatedTo* pointing to the class created in rule 1, *po:hasParent* pointing to the instance of parent class of the class created in rule 1.
3. If concepts from the *DO* are selected, create as many relations *po: isMapped-With* as the number of the selected concepts pointing to the selected concepts. In case concepts from the *DO* are not selected, this semantic rule is not generated.
4. If attributes are inserted, create as many data type properties as the number of the attributes pointing to the specified type, e.g. string, integer, boolean etc. In case attributes are not inserted, this semantic rule is not generated.

Generating the semantic rules and subsequently firing them against the *TS* enable the insertion of the new data from the modeling environment (*ME*) to the ontology. Semantic rules are created in the *WS* component and algorithms are implemented to feed them automatically with data coming from the *ME*.

5   Validation

The validation of the approach is based on a use case extracted from the Euro-pean research project CloudSocket[12]. For space reasons we only show one imple-mented scenario of the use case. This is motivated by the need for a cloud broker

---

[12] https://site.cloudsocket.eu/.

(i.e. domain expert) of specifying predefined functional requirements of parts of a business process (BP) that reflects a send invoice scenario. The aim is to facilitate the requirement annotation of BP models. This enables the ontology-based business matchmaking between BP requirements and specifications of existing BPs residing in a cloud marketplace. Hence, the most suitable BPs are retrieved for the given BP requirements by means of a SPARQL query. In this scenario we describe the actions needed to adapt the BPMN language such that a requirement annotation of BPs is made possible. Language adaptations would then be propagated to the ontologies. Also, models built with such language are grounded with an ontology language. Thus, the SPARQL query for the matchmaking can be performed straight without intermediate transformations (e.g. from models to ontologies) or semantic annotation steps. For a comprehensive description on how a SPARQL query and semantic rules are implemented for the matchmaking we suggest to have a look at the research work in [28].

We assume that the cloud broker cooperates with a language engineer to analyse the problem and sketch an appropriate solution. The latter includes a predefined requirement annotation regarding the activities of customer relationship management. For this, the BPMN modeling construct "Group" should be extended with the new "Managing Customer Relationship" construct. The latter should be further specified with semantic domain elements such as predefined values of APQC category, an Action and an Object. For instance, APQC category *3.5.2.4. ManageCustomerRelationship*, Action *Manage*, and Object *Customer* would suite the annotation of an activity called *Manage Customer Relationship* of a BP. The language engineer selects the BPMN construct to extend (from the *ME*), which in this case is "Group". This leads to the pop-up window pointed by arrow 1, shown in Fig. 3. The tab shown in the pop-up enables the extension of modeling constructs with new ones (the second-right tab enables the integration of existing constructs but it is out of scope in this use case). Hence, information related to the abstract syntax concept of the new modeling construct are to be added. These will be the name of the new concept, the semantic relation pointing to the Domain Ontology concepts and the graphical notations to associate them with. The latter should be uploaded beforehand on a dedicated folder before it can be selected. Additional information like attributes and further relations are omitted for space reasons. In this use case we assume that concrete values for *3.5.2.4 Manage Customer Relationship* (as APQC category), *Manage* (as an action) and *Customer* (as an object) are already loaded in the *TS* as part of the *DO*. Thus, the language engineer can select them from the drop-down menu entitled Semantic Domain Element (see it in Fig. 3 with the value already selected). In case a semantic element does not exist yet, the language engineer can create it on the spot. This is then inserted in the *TS* as a *DO* concept.

After saving the new modeling construct *bpmn: ManagingCustomerRelationship*, a SPARQL INSERT DATA query is generated, and Fig. 4 shows an excerpt of it. This reflects the implementation of the second set of semantic rules introduced in Sect. 4.3. Namely, the new class Managing Customer Relationship is inserted as a sub-class of the BPMN Group construct and labelled with the

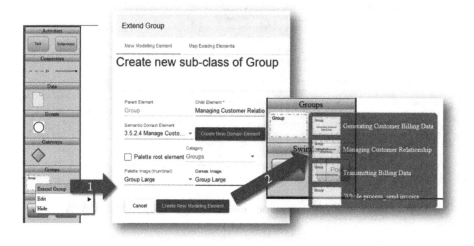

Fig. 3. Extending the BPMN construct "Group" in AOAME

inserted name. Also, the class is mapped to the three semantic elements (see rows with relations *po:is Mapped With* shown in Fig. 4). A new instance *po:Managing Customer Relationship* is created in the class *po:Palette Element* (see third last row of the figure). An object property *po:hasParent* is added pointing from the created instance *po:Managing Customer Relationship* to the instance that corresponds to the parent class of the created class, i.e. *po:Group*. An object property *po:is Related To* is created pointing from the created instance *po:Managing Customer Relationship* to the created class *bpmn:Managing Customer Relationship* (see last row of Fig. 4).

The SPARQL INSERT DATA in this case would contain additional data types and object properties, e.g., the *po: hasGraphicalNotation* containing the URI of the graphical notation of *po: ManagingCustomerRelationship* as well as the value for the data type property *po: hiddenfromPalette*, which is set to false by default to show the related graphical notation in the palette. This value then can be changed from the palette (see the Hide feature in the small window on the top-left quadrant of Fig. 3). If additional attributes or relations would be added by the user, these would be attached to the SPARQL INSERT DATA in the form of data types and object properties, respectively. Next, algorithms implemented in the *WS* fetch the new changes made in the ontology and propagate them back in the palette sub-component of the *ME*. Thus, the new graphical notation of the modeling construct "Managing Customer Relationship" will be displayed in the palette as a sub-element of "Group" (see far right screen-shot pointed to by the second arrow in Fig. 3). Hence, the new modeling construct is now ready to be used to annotate existing BP models by the domain expert. In case he or she needs to modify the modeling construct, the change can be performed on-the-fly with the help of the language engineer.

```
 1 ▼ PREFIX rdf: <http://www.w3.org/1999/02/22-rdf-syntax-ns#>
 2   PREFIX rdfs: <http://www.w3.org/2000/01/rdf-schema#>
 3   PREFIX bpmn: <http://ikm-group.ch/archiMEO/BPMN#>
 4   PREFIX apqc: <http://ikm-group.ch/archimeo/apqc#>
 5   PREFIX fbpdo: <http://ikm-group.ch/archimeo/fbpdo#>
 6   PREFIX po: <http://fhnw.ch/modelingEnvironment/PaletteOntology#>
 7 ▼ INSERT DATA {
 8   bpmn:ManagingCustomerRelationship rdf:type rdfs:Class .
 9   bpmn:ManagingCustomerRelationship rdfs:subClassOf bpmn:Group .
10   bpmn:ManagingCustomerRelationship rdfs:label "Managing Customer Relationship" .
11   bpmn:ManagingCustomerRelationship po:isMappedWith apqc:3.5.2.4_Manage_Customer_Relationship .
12   bpmn:ManagingCustomerRelationship po:isMappedWith fbpdo:Customer .
13   bpmn:ManagingCustomerRelationship po:isMappedWith fbpdo:Manage .
14   po:ManagingCustomerRelationsip rdf:type po:PaletteElement .
15   po:ManagingCustomerRelationsip po:hasParent po:Group .
16   po:ManagingCustomerRelationsip po:isRelatedTo bpmn:ManagingCustomerRelationsip .
17   }
```

Fig. 4. Excerpt of the automatic generated SPARQL INSERT DATA

6 Conclusion

This paper introduces the Agile and Ontology-Aided Modeling Environment (AOAME) with two main objectives: (1) fostering cooperation between language engineers and domain experts while performing a domain-specific adaptation on modeling languages, and (2) avoiding sequential engineering phases in the modeling language engineering life-cycle. These are pillars of agile approaches. To achieve these two goals an architecture has been conceptualized that is built upon the ontology-based meta-modeling. Hence, while language engineers and domain experts cooperate in adapting one or more modeling languages, mechanisms in the background allow the propagation of changes to the ontologies. Also the propagation of ontologies to the modeling environment are made possible. Namely, algorithms implement the ontology-based meta-modeling approach by showing the graphical notations of ontology concepts in the palette of the modeling environment. The ontology architecture supporting the AOAME is also introduced, with three main ontologies: the Palette Ontology, Modeling Language Ontology and the Domain Ontology. These reflect the notation, abstract syntax and semantics of a modeling language, respectively. The AOAME also implements the concept of semantic mapping between the abstract syntax and language-independent concepts. The latter can be contextualized within the LinkedData, which increasingly contain world-wide standards and vocabularies. Thus, we regard the AOAME as a concrete step to address the challenge of not just making semantics of enterprise modeling languages explicit but also linking them to the bottom-up web of semantically annotated data, as introduced in the research agenda for Enterprise Modeling [19]. Future work goes in the direction of enhancing the AOAME prototype based on projects addressing different industry applications. Also, a user-friendly way to insert constraints among modeling concepts (e.g. prohibiting the connection between two specific modeling constructs) is being investigated.

References

1. Horkoff, J., Jeusfeld, M.A., Ralyté, J., Karagiannis, D.: Enterprise modeling for business agility. Bus. Inf. Syst. Eng. **60**(1), 1–2 (2018)
2. Hinkelmann, K., Gerber, A., Karagiannis, D., Thoenssen, B., van der Merwe, A., Woitsch, R.: A new paradigm for the continuous alignment of business and IT: combining enterprise architecture modelling and enterprise ontology. Comput. Ind. **79**, 77–86 (2016)
3. Burlton, R.T., Ross, R.G., Zachman, J.A.: The Business Agility Manifesto (2013). https://busagilitymanifesto.org
4. Karagiannis, D., Kühn, H.: Metamodelling platforms. In: Bauknecht, K., Tjoa, A.M., Quirchmayr, G. (eds.) EC-Web 2002. LNCS, vol. 2455, pp. 182–182. Springer, Heidelberg (2002). https://doi.org/10.1007/3-540-45705-4_19
5. Hinkelmann, K., Laurenzi, E., Martin, A., Thönssen, B.: Ontology-based meta-modeling. In: Dornberger, R. (ed.) Business Information Systems and Technology 4.0. SSDC, vol. 141, pp. 177–194. Springer, Cham (2018). https://doi.org/10.1007/978-3-319-74322-6_12
6. Harel, D., Rumpe, B.: Modeling Languages: Syntax, Semantics and All That Stuff, Part I: The Basic Stuff. Technical report (2000)
7. Frank U.: Domain-Specific Modeling Languages: Requirements Analysis and Design Guidelines. In: Reinhartz-Berger I., Sturm A., Clark T., Cohen S., Bettin J. (eds.) Domain Engineering, pp. 133–157. Springer, Berlin (2013). https://doi.org/10.1007/978-3-642-36654-3_6
8. Atkinson, C., Kuhne, T.: Model-driven development: a metamodeling foundation. IEEE Softw. **20**(5), 36–41 (2003)
9. Strahringer, S.: Metamodellierung als Instrument des Methodenvergleichs: Eine Evaluierung am Beispiel objektorientierter Analysenmethoden. Publications of Darmstadt Technical University, Institute for Business Studies (BWL) (1996)
10. Karagiannis, D., Buchmann, R.A., Burzynski, P., Reimer, U., Walch, M.: Fundamental conceptual modeling languages in OMiLAB. In: Domain-Specific Conceptual Modeling, pp. 3–30. Springer International Publishing, Cham (2016)
11. Laurenzi, E., Hinkelmann, K., Reimer, U., van der Merwe, A., Sibold, P., Endl, R.: DSML4PTM - A domain-specific modelling language for patient transferal management. In: ICEIS 2017 - Proceedings of the 19th International Conference on Enterprise Information Systems, Porto, Portugal, pp. 520–531 (2017)
12. Braun, R.: Extensibility of Enterprise Modelling Languages. Ph.D. thesis, Technischen Universitaet Dresden (2016)
13. Braun, R.: Towards the state of the art of extending enterprise modeling languages. In: 3rd International Conference on Model-Driven Engineering and Software Development, Angers, France. IEEE (2015)
14. Jablonski, S., Volz, B., Dornstauder, S.: A meta modeling framework for domain specific process management. In: 32nd Annual IEEE International Computer Software and Applications Conference, vol. 2008, pp. 1011–1016. IEEE (2008)
15. Chiprianov, V., Kermarrec, Y., Rouvrais, S.: Extending enterprise architecture modeling languages. In: Proceedings of the 27th Annual ACM Symposium on Applied Computing - SAC 2012, vol. 1661. ACM Press, New York, USA (2012)
16. Atkinson, C., Gerbig, R., Fritzsche, M.: Modeling language extension in the enterprise systems domain. In: 2013 17th IEEE International Enterprise Distributed Object Computing Conference, pp. 49–58. IEEE (2013)

17. Fuentes, L., Vallecillo, A.: An Introduction to UML Profiles, UPGRADE. Eur. J. Inf. Prof. **5**(2), 5–13 (2004)

18. Izquierdo, J.L.C., Cabot, J., López-Fernández, J.J., Cuadrado, J.S., Guerra, E., de Lara, J.: Engaging end-users in the collaborative development of domain-specific modelling languages. In: Luo, Y. (ed.) CDVE 2013. LNCS, vol. 8091, pp. 101–110. Springer, Heidelberg (2013). https://doi.org/10.1007/978-3-642-40840-3_16

19. Sandkuhl, K., et al.: From expert discipline to common practice: a vision and research agenda for extending the reach of enterprise modeling. Bus. Inf. Syst. Eng. **60**(1), 69–80 (2018)

20. Barišić, A., Amaral, V., Goulão, M.: Usability driven DSL development with USE-ME. Comput. Lang. Syst. Struct. **51**, 118–157 (2018)

21. Cho, H., Gray, J., Syriani, E.: Creating visual Domain-Specific Modeling Languages from end-user demonstration. In: 2012 4th International Workshop on Modeling in Software Engineering (MISE), pp. 22–28. IEEE (2012)

22. Ceh, I., Crepinsek, M., Kosar, T., Mernik, M.: Ontology driven development of domain-specific languages. Comput. Sci. Inf. Syst. **8**(2), 317–342 (2011)

23. Karagiannis, D.: Conceptual modelling methods: the AMME agile engineering approach. In: Silaghi, G.C., Buchmann, R.A., Boja, C. (eds.) IE 2016. LNBIP, vol. 273, pp. 3–19. Springer, Cham (2018). https://doi.org/10.1007/978-3-319-73459-0_1

24. Laurenzi, E., Hinkelmann, K., Izzo, S., Reimer, U., van der Merwe, A.: Towards an agile and ontology-aided modeling environment for DSML adaptation. In: Matulevičius, R., Dijkman, R. (eds.) CAiSE 2018. LNBIP, vol. 316, pp. 222–234. Springer, Cham (2018). https://doi.org/10.1007/978-3-319-92898-2_19

25. Vaishnavi, V., Kuechler, B.: Design science research in information systems. J. MIS Q. **28**(1), 75–105 (2004)

26. Reimer, U., Laurenzi, E.: Creating and maintaining a collaboration platform via domain-specific reference modelling. In: EChallenges e-2014 Conference : 29–30 October 2014, Belfast, Ireland, pp. 1–9. IEEE (2014)

27. Hinkelmann, K., Laurenzi, E., Lammel, B., Kurjakovic, S., Woitsch, R.: A semantically-enhanced modelling environment for business process as a service. In: 2016 4th International Conference on Enterprise Systems (ES), pp. 143–152. IEEE (2016)

28. Kritikos, K., Laurenzi, E., Hinkelmann, K.: Towards business-to-IT alignment in the cloud. In: Mann, Z.Á., Stolz, V. (eds.) ESOCC 2017. CCIS, vol. 824, pp. 35–52. Springer, Cham (2018). https://doi.org/10.1007/978-3-319-79090-9_3

29. Emmenegger, S., Hinkelmann, K., Laurenzi, E., Martin, A., Thönssen, B., Witschel, H.F., Zhang, C.: An ontology-based and case-based reasoning supported workplace learning approach. In: Hammoudi, S., Pires, L.F., Selic, B., Desfray, P. (eds.) MODELSWARD 2016. CCIS, vol. 692, pp. 333–354. Springer, Cham (2017). https://doi.org/10.1007/978-3-319-66302-9_17

30. Karagiannis, D., Buchmann, R.A.: A proposal for deploying hybrid knowledge bases: the ADOxx-to-GraphDB interoperability case. In: Proceedings of HICSS 2018, University of Hawaii, pp. 4055–4064 (2018)

31. Fill, H.G., Schremser, D., Karagiannis, D.: A generic approach for the semantic annotation of conceptual models using a service-oriented architecture. Int. J. Knowl. Manag. **9**(1), 76–88 (2013)

32. Hinkelmann, K.: Business process flexibility and decision-aware modeling—the knowledge work designer. Domain-Specific Conceptual Modeling, pp. 397–414. Springer, Cham (2016). https://doi.org/10.1007/978-3-319-39417-6_18

33. Brachman, R.J.: The Basics of Knowledge Representation and Reasoning. AT&T Tech. J. **67**(1), 7–24 (1988)
34. Fanesi, D., Cacciagrano, D.R., Hinkelmann, K.: Semantic business process representation to enhance the degree of BPM mechanization - an ontology. In: 2015 International Conference on Enterprise Systems (ES), pp. 21–32. IEEE (2015)
35. Emmenegger, S., Hinkelmann, K., Laurenzi, E., Thönssen, B.: Towards a procedure for assessing supply chain risks using semantic technologies. In: Fred, A., Dietz, J.L.G., Liu, K., Filipe, J. (eds.) IC3K 2012. CCIS, vol. 415, pp. 393–409. Springer, Heidelberg (2013). https://doi.org/10.1007/978-3-642-54105-6_26

Modeling and Reasoning About Privacy-Consent Requirements

Marco Robol[1], Elda Paja[1], Mattia Salnitri[2], and Paolo Giorgini[1(✉)]

[1] University of Trento, Trento, Italy
{marco.robol,elda.paja,paolo.giorgini}@unitn.it
[2] Politecnico di Milano, Milan, Italy
mattia.salnitri@polimi.it

Abstract. Since the origin of the web, up to social networks, and now to the internet of things, the quantity of personal information produced and shared is uncontrollably increasing. Privacy regulations protect our right to have the control on our personal data. According to the recent General Data Protection Regulation (GDPR), entered into force in May 2018, infringements can be very costly to organizations, ranging from 10s to 100s of thousands of Euros. In order to ensure compliance with such regulations, privacy should be taken into consideration as early as at requirements time, so to avoid expensive after-the-fact fixes. Modeling frameworks have been proposed to support the analysis of requirements in complex socio-technical systems, however, even if a primary role is given to security, for privacy more work need to be done. In this paper, starting from the social concept of consent, we propose a modeling language and define the formal framework for the analysis of privacy-consent requirements. We report on our experience in the analysis of privacy in the medical domain, in the context of a research project with the Trentino health-care provider (APSS).

Keywords: Privacy · Regulations · Consent
Socio-technical systems · Requirements · Modeling
Automated reasoning

1 Introduction

The European General Data Protection Regulation (GDPR) [12] has entered into force on May 2018. Compliance is of utmost importance for organizations, in order to avoid monetary penalties which can be up to 20 million Euros. Moreover, public debates on privacy, such as the recent one about personal data being sold away by a well known social network [8], have a strong impact on people, with consequences for organizations that can be even worst than actual fines.

The way how companies do their business is shifting from a traditional closed one, to an approach more open to collaborations with external parties. This way

R. A. Buchmann et al. (Eds.): PoEM 2018, LNBIP 335, pp. 238–254, 2018.
https://doi.org/10.1007/978-3-030-02302-7_15

of doing business is supported by *consent*, a key element in privacy regulations that allows the processing and sharing of personal data among organizations, yet it gives users control over their own data. Personal data are stored and shared among organizations by humans through information system. In such complex socio-technical systems, compliance with privacy regulations should be considered starting from social components, down to technical ones.

Compliance with privacy regulations should be handled as soon as possible, considering it as an early requirement, so to avoid unexpected costs of re-engineering [22]. Most importantly, given the relevance of humans in organization activities, the analysis of privacy requirements must carefully represent the social context, the actors involved, their interactions, as well as their expectation and responsibilities in light of privacy regulations.

Methods for the analysis of privacy requirements has been often discussed [3,6,18], however, most of these works either does not put social aspects first, or does not take into consideration regulations. Nómos [29,30] propose a solution for regulatory compliance of software specifications, while other works analyze requirements under a social perspective, such as, i^* [36] or Tropos [7], and focus on security as Secure Tropos [14] or STS [11]. In previous work [27], we have presented preliminary results of a framework for privacy requirements, which includes a modeling language based on STS and automated reasoning capabilities.

In this paper, we propose a method, based on STS, for the analysis of privacy and *consent* requirements, to support compliance with regulations. It is based on (i) the modeling of the domain, (ii) the specification of privacy and *consent* requirements, and (iii) automated reasoning to support compliance with regulations.

The contributions of the paper are as follows:

- a modeling language, goal-oriented, focused on privacy and consent;
- A reasoning framework to automate the detection of conflicts between system operations and consent provided by users;
- A validation of the modeling language and the reasoning framework in collaboration with privacy experts in the medical domain, including legal experts, experts in the organization processes, and technical people.

The paper is structured as follows. Section 2 presents the problem of privacy and consent requirements, followed by a motivating case study in Sect. 3 and the baseline in Sect. 4. Section 5 introduces the modeling language for privacy and consent requirements. Section 6 discusses the formal framework for automated reasoning. Section 7 presents the results of the validation, with experts from APSS. Section 8 discusses related work, and Sect. 9 concludes.

2   From Regulations to Privacy and Consent Requirements

Regulations are composed of a set of principles that impact on interactions between organizations and users. Compliance with regulations is not straightforward and should be reached throughout a careful analysis of the regulations with respect to the organization.

The European Union (EU) has developed a new privacy law, the General Data Protection Regulation (GDPR)[12], to improve privacy safeguard of all European citizens. The GDPR is based on general principles which include privacy-by-default, transparency, data minimization, storage limitations, accuracy, and integrity. **Privacy-by-default** prevent the collection, processing, or use of personal data if it is not the case that the user has previously agreed on such operation. **Transparency** imposes organizations to inform the user on the performed processing operations. **Data minimization** is on the minimal set of personal data that are necessary for the provision of a service. **Storage limitation** impose constraints on the storage of the data, such as, time constraints or the right to be forgotten. **Accuracy** and **integrity** require for reliable and non corrupted data and adequate security measures.

Consent is a key element adopted by the majority of privacy regulations, including EU GDPR [12] and US HIPAA [2], to put the user in control of his own personal data. In relation with consent, the GDPR provides a set of principles, such as, purpose limitation, free, informed and explicit consent. For the **purpose limitation** principle, consent must have a well-defined purpose, clearly stated in the privacy notice, no general consent is allowed. **Free consent** is the freedom of deciding whether to consent or not on personal data processing, without being forced by the organization. **Informed consent** imposes organizations to provide users with a privacy notice with clear and understandable details on the processing. **Explicit consent** requires companies to demonstrate a legally compliant acquisition of consent from each user. For example, this can be enforced by asking the user to sign a paper version of the consent.

3   Motivating Case Study: Trentino Health-Care Provider

For what concerns privacy regulations, the medical domain is one of the most critical, because of the big quantity of highly confidential clinical data involved. Here, a trade-off between privacy and accessibility of data is fundamental. If on one hand there is the need for privacy of patients, on the other, availability of data can be of vital interest. For this reason, the traditional management of user consent, paper-based and not integrated in the organization processes, is not a viable solution. This makes the analysis of requirements related to consent not straightforward, also considering that the health-care system is an evolving complex socio-technical system, where requirements identified at social and organizational level impact on operational processes, such as, accountability of the transmission of medical reports between doctors, impacts on the processes and on technical components.

We report on the analysis of privacy that we have conducted on the Trentino health-care provider of the province of Trento (Italy), the APSS (Azienda Provinciale Servizi Sanitari). The APSS, not only directly provides health care services, but also collaborates with external organizations so to integrate them in the national health-care system. We focus on the newborn Italian national register of citizens' medical data (FSE), which is going to become operative in the near future, and for which, the APPS is working toward the implementation for what concern the province of Trento. With the FSE, public and private Italian medical service providers will be all interconnected, giving the possibility to doctors to access patient medical and administrative data from everywhere.

4   Baseline

The work presented in this paper is based on STS [11], a security requirement engineering method to support the design of secure systems. STS focuses on social aspects as the main causes of security problems in complex systems. It includes (i) modeling languages to represent the system both at a socio-technical level and at the business process (procedural) level, (ii) an automated reasoning framework, (iii) a supporting tool. STS-ml is the formally defined goal-based modeling language provided by the STS method. It is used to model socio-technical systems as a composition of intentional actors, which represent either a single instance (agent) or a class (role) of either technical components or humans. Such overall representation of the system allows to focus on actor interactions, i.e. goal delegations and document transmissions. The language is multi-view, so to capture and focus on different aspects of the same system separately.

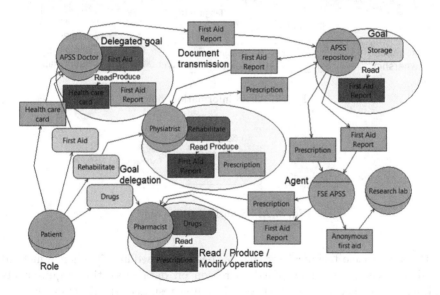

Fig. 1. APSS social view

Figure 1 shows an excerpt of the **social view**, representing the dependencies between actors, from a model of the case study [1], where a patient interacts

---

[1] The complete model can be found at disi.unitn.it/marco.robol/

with a doctor of the APSS, who provides the first aid, collects his personal data, produces a report, and uploads it to the FSE system, then the patient interacts with a physiatrist for the rehabilitation, who reads the first aid report and produces a prescription, and with a pharmacist, who reads the prescription to provide drugs. A research lab obtains an anonymous version of the first aid report.

Figure 2 shows an excerpt of the **information view**, representing the structure of documents and their informative content, from the model of the case study. Patient first aid data are made tangible by the first aid report document possessed by the APSS doctor. Prescription data are made tangible in the document possessed by the physiatrist. Last information is the health care identifier of the patient, which is made tangible in the health care card.

Figure 3 shows an excerpt of the **authorization view**, representing the operations permitted by owners of information. In this example, *Pharmacist* is authorized by the *Physiatrist* to read the *Prescription data* in the context of *providing drugs*, while he is not authorized to modify or produce these.

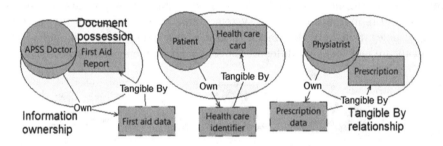

Fig. 2. APSS information view

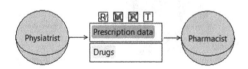

Fig. 3. APSS authorization view

Privacy in socio-technical systems has been discussed in [27], where a method based on STS has been proposed to reason on data protection requirements and normative aspects. The work describes first results of the development of a method to support the design of complex systems with the principle of privacy-by-design. Here we compliment the method with a support for consent, which is crucial to comply with GDPR.

5   Modeling Consent Requirements

Graphical models can be used to ease the analysis of requirements both in the design of a new system or in the re-engineering of an existing one. In the analysis of privacy and consent requirements, it is important to model the system so to represent (i) personal data, (ii) data operations, and (iii) privacy consent. We propose a modeling language, based on STS-ml, for the analysis of privacy and consent requirements in complex and evolving socio-technical systems. The new modeling language includes the concepts of (i) *personal data*, based on linkability, (ii) *privacy operations*, based on a taxonomy that includes collection, processing, and disclosure, and (iii) *consent*, based on authorizations. In the rest of the section we go into more details on these aspects, for each of them we present how they are supported by the modeling language.

Our definition of **personal data** is aligned with the one provided in the GDPR [12]. Here an excerpt from Article 4(1): "personal data means any information relating to an ... identifiable natural person (data subject); ... one who can be identified, directly or indirectly ..." [12]. The idea behind this definition is in the identifiability of the person in the information. Spiekermann and Cranor, in [33], relate the identifiability of users to **linkability** of data, they talk of personal data in case of linkability and anonymous data in the case of unlinkability. Information is not always linkable by its own, but could became such depending on how it is made tangible. Therefore, we define personal data as an information that is made tangible in a form so that it can be linked to an identifiable user. We are aware that linkability is actually a very discussed and controversial topic. Deciding and demonstrating the linkability or unlinkability of data is not straightforward and several studies have been done on this, starting from k-anonymity [34] to l-diversity [23] and t-closeness [21]. The process of de-identification of personal information is critical and if not approached correctly, could lead to unwanted and malicious data breaches [13]. We suggest that the lack of linkability, is a property that must be carefully verified. The eventuality that an information could be linkable to the user should be always taken into consideration. In our modeling language, we introduce the *Linkable To* relationship to represent the potential linkability to a *Data Subject* actor, of a *Document*, our tangible form of *Information*.

We investigate on **data operations** that are relevant for privacy, and we propose a classification based on our interpretation of the privacy taxonomy presented in [31]. The taxonomy, in addition to the concept of personal data and data subject [27], is based on the concept of data holder, who is the performer of the following operations: (i) *information collection*, related with the means by which information is gathered from the user by the data holder, (ii) *information processing*, related with the consolidation and use of information and its transfer between information systems by the data holder, (iii) *information dissemination*, related with the disclosure to the public or to another person, (iv) *invasion*, related with intrusion in the private life of the user and interference with his decisions. In our modeling language we include three privacy-relevant operations, namely collection, processing, and dissemination, while we not included invasion since it does not necessary involve information and it is therefore not relevant to information analysis. We speak of *Collection* of personal data in the case of transmission of a document from the data subject, the actor to which the document can be linked to, to another actor. *Processing* of personal data is in the case of any of the operations of reading, modification or production, and also in the case of transmission of documents between actors that are part of the data holder. While *Dissemination* is any transmission made by the data holder, to any other actor that differs from the data holder, and the data subject.

To support **consent** requirements analysis we adopt the definition of consent given in Article 4(11) of the GDPR: "Consent of the data subject means any freely given, specific, informed and unambiguous indication of the data subject's wishes by which he or she, by a statement or by a clear affirmative action, signifies agreement to the processing of personal data relating to him or her". In our interpretation consent in an agreement between two actors, the data subject and the data holder, that consists in the permission for operating on personal data for a specific purpose. For the consent on the processing of personal data, defined in the GDPR, we propose a classification based on [32], that includes consent on the collection, processing (use), and dissemination. In our language we support the modeling of *Consent* as a social relationship between two actors, the *Data Subject* and the *Data Holder*, in terms of authorizations for operating over personal data. The set of actors authorized within a consent defines the *Scope* of the consent, with respect to which we speak of *consent to the collection* in case of authorizations for the transmission of personal data from the data subject to any actor part of the consent scope, *consent to the processing* in case of authorizations to read, modify, produce, or transmit, personal data between actors in the scope, and *consent to the dissemination* in case of authorizations for the transmission of personal data to actors outside consent scope.

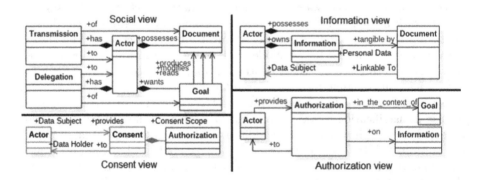

Fig. 4. Meta-model of the proposed modeling language

Figure 4 shows the **meta-model** of the modeling language, in red the elements related to privacy and consent. The meta-model is organized in four diagrams, each representing one of the views proposed in the modeling language.

Concepts of the language shared between views are here represented separately in each of the respective meta-model diagrams. The replication of such concepts between the views can be automated by the supporting tool, so to help the modelers in creating consistent diagrams. The modeling language splits across a total of four different views. With respect to STS-ml we added a fourth one, the consent view, to model consent and analyze its requirements. Consent is represented as a relationship between a data subject and a data holder, and consists in a set of authorizations. Permissions specified in this view differs from the ones in the authorization view because: (i) they includes the operations of collection and dissemination and (ii) such permissions are related to a specific consent.

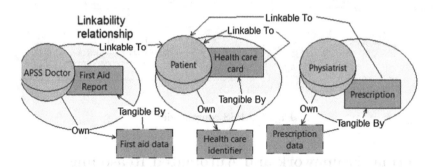

Fig. 5. APSS information view modified

Figure 5 shows an excerpt of the **information view** from the model of the case study, modified with respect to its STS version presented in Figure 2. Patient first aid report is represented as a document, possessed by the actor APSS doctor, such document is *linkable to* the patient himself, meaning that the patient is identifiable. Similarly, the prescription document, that is possessed by the physiatrist, is also linkable to the patient, and the same is for the health care card, also linkable to the patient.

Figure 6 shows an excerpt of the consent view from the model of the case study, that includes the details of the three consents provided by the patient to APSS. On the top, details of the processing consent provided to the APSS, which includes in its scope physiatrist, APSS doctor and APSS repository. Letters C, R, M, P, T, and D stands respectively for Collect, Read, Modify, Produce, Transmit, and Disseminate. The APSS doctor is authorized to read, produce and transmit information of the patient within the scope of the consent. Physiatrist is authorized to read and modify first aid data, and read produce and transmit prescription data. On the right, details of the collection consent provided to the APSS, where the APSS doctor is authorized to collect information from the patient. On the bottom, details of the dissemination consent provided to the APSS, which consists in authorizing the FSE in disseminating first aid data and prescription data of the patient to actors outside the scope of this consent.

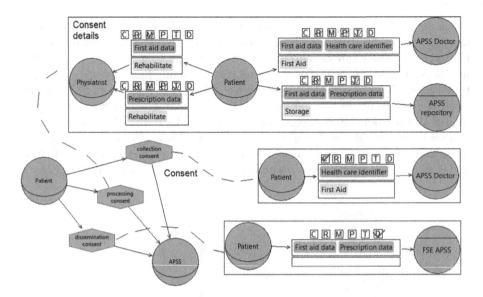

Fig. 6. APSS consent view

6   Formal Framework and Automated Reasoning

Modeling languages should be simple enough to easily identify inconsistencies but, as the models start growing, to adequately represent real world cases, this could became harder [35]. Automated reasoning, based on formal languages, can support users in the identification of potential inconsistencies in the models. The formalization we propose relies on [11,27], for further supporting consent requirements for privacy.

6.1   Formalizing the Modeling Language

This section provides a formalization of the language based on the formalization of STS-ml provided in [11]. We use set theory and we define atomic variables with strings in typewriter with a leading capital letter (e.g., G, I); sets are defined with strings in the calligraphic font for mathematical expressions (e.g., $\mathcal{G}$, $\mathcal{I}$); relationship are defined in italics style with a leading non-capital letter (e.g.,*wants*, *possesses*). Table 1 lists the predicates used to represent concepts and relationships. We focused on the formalization of concepts related to privacy, such as, consent and personal data. See the information relationship of *linkableTo*(D, A) and the social relationship of *consents*(A, A', S) and authorization.

Definition 1 (Intentional actor). An intentional actor is any agent or role that commits himself in the achievement of a set of goals. An intentional actor model AM is a tuple $\langle \mathsf{A}, \mathcal{G}, \mathcal{D}, \mathcal{IRL} \rangle$, where A is an actor, $\mathcal{G}$ is a set of goals, $\mathcal{D}$ is a set of documents, and $\mathcal{IRL}$ is a set of intentional relationships. An actor model

Table 1. Predicates

Concepts:
$actor(A)$, $agent(Ag)$, $role(R)$, $goal(G)$, $document(D)$, $information(I)$
Intentional relationships ($\mathcal{IRL}$):
$wants(A, G)$, $possesses(A, D)$, $decomposes(A, G, S, DecT)$, where $DecT \in \{and, or\}$, $reads/modifies/produces(A, G, D, OpT)$, where $OpT \in \{R, M, P\}$
Social relationships ($\mathcal{SRL}$):
$plays(Ag, R)$, $delegates(A, A', G)$, $transmits(A, A', D)$, $authorizes(A, A', J, G, OP, Tr)$, $consents(A, A', A'', \mathcal{AUTH})$, where $OP = (\{C, R, M, P, T, D\} \cup \{\overline{C}, \overline{R}, \overline{M}, \overline{P}, \overline{T}, \overline{D}\})$ and $Tr \in \{true, false\}$
Information relationships ($\mathcal{I_{RL}}$):
$owns(A, I)$, $partOfI(I_1, I_2)$, $partOfD(D_1, D_2)$, $tangibleBy(I, D)$, $linkableTo(D, A)$

$AM = \langle A, G, D, \mathcal{IRL} \rangle$ is well-formed if all intentional relationships are defined over actor A, goals in G, and documents in D.

For example, considering the actors in Figure 1, the *APSS Doctor* commit himself in the achievement of the goal *First aid provided to the patient*, goal delegated to him by the *Patient*. The model of actor *APSS Doctor* is composed by the goal *First Aid* and the documents *Health Care Card* and *First Aid Report* and the intentional relationships *Read* and *Produce* on the documents.

Definition 2 (Consent). $consents(A, A', A'', \mathcal{AUTH})$ is a social relationship defined between a data subject A, a data holder A', and a set of actors representing the consent scope A''. Consent consists in a set of authorizations $\mathcal{AUTH}$ provided to actors in the consent scope. A $consents(A, A', A'', \mathcal{AUTH})$ is well-formed only authorizations in the consent are provided only to actors in the consent scope, represented by the set of actors A''.

For example, considering the Figure 6, the *patient*, as data subject, provides the *consent for the collection* of his personal data to the *APSS actor*, the data holder. Such consent consists in permitting the *APSS doctor* to collect from the *patient* the information *health care identifier* in the context of achieving the goal *first aid*.

Definition 3 (Social model). We bind together actors models and social relationships to compose a social model of the system. A social model SM is a tuple $\langle AM, \mathcal{SRL}, \mathcal{I_{RL}} \rangle$ where AM is a set of intentional actor models, $\mathcal{SRL}$ is a set of social relationships, and $\mathcal{I_{RL}}$ is a set of information relationships.

Definition 4 (Authorization closure). We define a closure over authorizations so that if no explicit authorization is provided, any operation on any information is implicitly forbidden. Let SM be a well-formed social model, the authorization closure over $\mathcal{SRL}$ in SM, denoted as $\triangle_{\mathcal{SRL}}$, is a super-set of $\mathcal{SRL}$ that makes prohibitions explicit, when no authorization is granted by any actor.

Definition 5 (Consent closure). We define a closure over consents so that if no consent provide an explicit permission to operate on linkable documents, then operating on linkable documents is implicitly forbidden.

6.2 Reasoning About Privacy and Consent

In this section, we present our contribution in the automated reasoning, proposed to support analysis related to privacy and consent.

First example of automated reasoning is related to violated authorizations.

Definition 6 (Violated authorization). An authorization is violated when, even if it makes prohibition to an actor A to operate on an information I, the actor A actually operates on a document D that makes tangible the information I, also considering the operating context G. Formally, for each provided authorization $authorizes(A, A', \mathcal{I}, \mathcal{G}, \mathcal{OP}, TrAuth)$, a violation is detected if exists an operation $reads/modifies/produces(A', G, D, OpT)$ s.t. $G \in \mathcal{G}$, OpT is negated in $\mathcal{OP}$, and exists a $tangibleBy(I, D)$ s.t. $I \in \mathcal{I}$.

In the example of Figure 1, considering only the authorizations specified in Figure 3, different authorizations are violated. The *APSS Doctor* can not read the *Health care card* of the *Patient*, the Physiatrist can not read the *First air report* of the *APSS Doctor*, and also the the *FSE repository* agent and the *FSE APSS* can not read the *First air report*, and they can not transmit any documents.

Consent requirement specifies the need of assessing user decision on the collection, processing, and disclosure of his personal data. We can automatically detect violation of consent reasoning on operations performed on document, and linkability of documents.

Definition 7 (Violated collection consent). Violation of collection consent is automatically detectable in the case of transmission of a document D, from actor A owner of some information I tangible in D, if it is the case that the document is linkable to A.

Definition 8 (Violated processing consent). Violation of processing consent is automatically detectable in the case of any processing operation on a document D, executed by an actor A', including the transmission toward an actor A'', whether it is the case that the document is linkable to another actor A, owner of some information I tangible in D, and both actors A' and A'' are part of the consent scope.

Definition 9 (Violated dissemination consent). Violation of dissemination consent is automatically detectable in the case of transmission of a document D, from an actor A' to an actor A'', if it is the case that the document is linkable to another actor A, owner of some information I tangible in D, and that the transmission is not authorized within the scope of any consent.

In the example of Figure 1, considering the consent view in Figure 6, some consent are violated. For example, the transmissions of *First Aid data* and *Prescription data*, from the *APSS repository* to the *FSE APSS*, raise a violation of the dissemination consent, because dissemination consent is provided only to the agent *FSE APSS*.

We provide automated reasoning for the minimization of personal data, based on the analysis of information used in the achievement of goals and consent. Excessive permissions are provided by consent in the case no such operations are performed.

Definition 10 (Excessive consent). A consent is excessive when the provided actor A, in the context of achieving any of the goals G in the authorization, does not perform any of the allowed operations on any document D that makes tangible any of the information in the authorization. Formally, an authorization *authorizes*(A, A', $\mathcal{I}$, $\mathcal{G}$, $\mathcal{OP}$, TrAuth) is excessive if given I $\in$ $\mathcal{I}$, G $\in$ $\mathcal{G}$, OpT $\in$ $\mathcal{OP}$, do not exists any *reads/modifies/produces*(A', G, D, OpT), s.t *tangibleBy*(I, D).

For example, in the *processing consent*, represented in Figure 6, *APSS doctor* is authorized to transmit the *Health care identifier*, while this is not necessary in the achievement of any goal, as in Figure 1.

Core Logic Implementation. In STS [11], automated reasoning has been implemented in DLV [1], and integrated in the graphical modeling editor tool. Different types of automated analysis are provided with the tool, such as, well-formedness and security analysis. We present here an excerpt of the core logic implementation, while the integration in the modeling tool is still under development.

Table 2. DLV rules for consent

(i) *violatedCollectionConsent*(A, I, D) :-   not *canCollect*(A, I, G), *transmits*(A', A, D), *tangibleBy*(I, D), *linkableTo*(D, A')
(ii) *violatedProcessingConsent*(A, I, G, D) :-   not *canProcess*(A, I, G), *reads/mod./prod./tx.*(A, G, D), *tangibleBy*(I, D),   *linkableTo*(D, A')
(iii) *violatedDisseminationConsent*(A, I, D) :-   not *canDisseminate*(A, I, G), *transmits*(A, A″, D), *tangibleBy*(I, D), *linkableTo*(D, A')
(iv) *excessiveConsent*(A, I, G, OP) :-   (*canCollect*(A, I, G), not *transmits*(A', A, D)) $\vee$ (*canProcess*(A, I, G), not *reads/mod./prod./tx.*(A, D)) $\vee$ (*canDisseminate*(A, I, G), not *transmits*(A, A″, D)),   *tangibleBy*(I, D), *linkableTo*(D, A')

In Table 2 the rules implementing in DLV the following reasoning: (i), (ii), and (iii) identification of violation of consent for the collection, processing, and disclosure, (iv) excessive consent.

7   Evaluation

This section discusses the results of evaluating the method with domain practitioners. Research questions that we wanted to address are about the usability and completeness of the modeling language and the utility of the reasoning framework.

The evaluation has been done in a real case study provided by the Trentino health-care provider (APSS), in the context of a research project consisting in the experimentation of the STS method for the certification of processes with the GDPR. The experiment design consists in an iterative process on the activities of refinement and validation of the modeling language and the reasoning framework. This required several interactions with domain experts. People involved had different backgrounds, different perspectives on privacy, and different levels of expertise in modeling languages. They included legal, business, and technical people from the APSS, such as, privacy and legal experts, organization experts, experts in the processes, and APSS system experts.

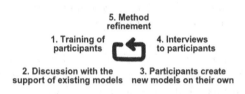

Fig. 7. User-centred evaluation process

Figure 7 shows the steps of each iteration. We first provided a quick introduction on the modeling language, then we discussed with participants with the support of models provided by us, then we let them use the language on their own to produce new models, finally we collected their opinions with respect to the research questions.

The first research question is related to the usability of the language, and how much it can be understand by non experts. Second research question is related to the completeness of the modeling language, and the missing concepts in representing the system and constraints imposed by regulations. Third research question is related to the utility of the automated reasoning framework in identifying privacy criticalities and problems. In the following, we discuss the results of the evaluation.

Usability. Opinion of the participants was positive with respect to the usability of the modeling language. They were all able to understand the models, that have been successfully used to support the discussions. Some of the participants were also able to modify existing models and produce new ones. The continuous interactions provided us with new ideas on how to refine and improve the language, on the basis of feedback, comments, and suggestions. For example, the consent relationship between actors, and its detailed view in terms of authorizations, was initially spread among the social and authorization view. After some interaction with experiment participants, we have been able to improved the graphical aspects of the language, by introducing the consent view.

Completeness. In the evaluation of completeness of the language, we focused on its ability to represent privacy and consent. In the fist iterations, opinion of the participants was a lack of the language in representing consent. It was not clear if consent was a goal, a document, or an authorization, even if last one seems to be the more similar concept. There was a lack in the language in covering the concepts of collection, processing, and dissemination. We modified the language so to support consent, defined as an agreement between two actors consisting in a set of authorizations, and we also introduces the operations of collection, processing, and dissemination.

Utility of the reasoning framework. We evaluate the utility of the reasoning framework in supporting humans in the analysis of privacy and consent. Models produced in the experimentation are composed by many organizations, departments, and technical systems, with a lot of dependencies, a complex structure of information and documents, and a not straightforward specification of security requirements, such as authorizations. It turned out that models were so complex to be as nearly as impossible for non expert users, and still difficult for experts like us, to analyze and reason on them by hands. For this reason, we improved some automated reasoning, in particular for the identification of violated consent on collection, processing, and dissemination. Opinion of the participants was positive with respect to the utility of the newly integrated automated reasoning on consent.

8   Related Work

Several description languages for authorizations and access control rules are available in the literature [4,5,24,26], most of which are based on allow/deny rules, These can be used to protect personal data, as a good privacy practice, however, alone, they does not provide compliance with privacy regulations. A different use of authorization language, specific for controlling privacy in the web, is proposed in the P3P platform [9,10], where users, surfing the web, are allowed to express their privacy preferences.

Frameworks for the analysis of privacy and security requirements are available in the literature. Qingfeng et al. in [18] presents a privacy goal-driven requirements modeling framework to support the design of a Role-Based Access Control (RBAC) system. Kalloniatis et al. in [3] present PriS, a requirement engineering method for security and privacy, for the analysis of the impact of privacy requirements on organizational processes, with the use of privacy-process patterns.

The use of automated reasoning to support analysis in requirements frameworks, is first proposed by Van Lamsweerde et al. in [35]. Giorgini et al. in [15], introduce automated reasoning in the Tropos method [7] to support the identification of conflicts. Giorgini et al. in [14,25] present Secure Tropos, a security requirement engineering framework that extends Tropos. Breaux et al. in [6] propose a privacy requirements specification language, called Eddy, with automated reasoning feature. The language provides a set of privacy requirements, on which automated reasoning allows for the detection of conflicts between requirements. Nómos, a software requirement framework, is proposed by Siena et al. in [29,30] and in its revisited versions [28] and [20], to tackle the problem of regulatory compliance of software. It includes a tool-supported modeling language that can detect conflicts between requirements. Privacy is not directly supported, but the framework can also be applied to privacy regulations.

Different designing frameworks, specific for privacy, have been proposed in the literature. Guarda et al. in [16] present an overview of legal aspects of privacy, which are considered of primary importance, in a technological interpretation. Spiekermann et al. in [33] propose an introduction to the privacy domain for engineers, by proposing two privacy design approaches: (i) privacy-by-policy, based on fair information practices; and (ii) privacy-by-architecture, based on data minimization. Gurses et al. in [17], provide an overview of privacy-by-design practices. The work focuses on data minimization and its importance in privacy-by-design. Hoepman et al. in [19] review mains PETs and patterns and propose privacy design strategies to integrate privacy-by-design in the software development life cycle.

9   Conclusion

We have proposed a modeling language and a reasoning framework for the analysis of consent and privacy requirements. Challenges were in the interpretation of the regulation, for example in the formalization of the concepts of personal data and consent, and in the definition of a language to support the analysis of compliance. We proposed a goal-oriented modeling language, a reasoning framework and a first evaluation based on a real case study in the medical domain. Future work includes (i) a detailed analysis and formalization of the requirements of privacy and consent and their integration in the modeling language and in the reasoning framework, (ii) the development of a supporting tool for the modeling and the automation of the analysis and (iii) the inclusion in the modeling language of other concepts related to privacy.

References

1. DLVSYSTEM S.r.l. — DLV. http://www.dlvsystem.com/dlv/
2. The Health Insurance Portability and Accountability Act (HIPAA). U.S. Department of Labor, Employee Benefits Security Administration, Washington, D.C. (2004)
3. Kalloniatis, C., Kavakli, E., Gritzalis, S.: Addressing privacy requirements in system design: the PriS method. Requir. Eng. 13(3), 241–255 (2008)

4. Ashley, P., Hada, S., Karjoth, G., Powers, C., Schunter, M.: Enterprise privacy authorization language (epal). IBM Res. (2003)
5. Ashley, P., Hada, S., Karjoth, G., Schunter, M.: E-p3p privacy policies and privacy authorization. In: Workshop on Privacy in the Electronic Society, pp. 103–109. ACM (2002)
6. Breaux, T.D., Hibshi, H., Rao, A.: Eddy, a formal language for specifying and analyzing data flow specifications for conflicting privacy requirements. J. Requir. Eng. 19(3), 281–307 (2014)
7. Bresciani, P., Giorgini, P., Giunchiglia, F., Mylopoulos, J., Perini, A.: Tropos: an Agent-Oriented Software Development Methodology. JAAMAS 8(3), 203–236 (2004)
8. Cadwalladr, C., Graham-Harrison, E.: Revealed: 50 million Facebook profiles harvested for Cambridge Analytica in major data breach. The Guardian 17 (2018)
9. Cranor, L., Langheinrich, M., Marchiori, M., Presler-Marshall, M., Reagle, J.: The platform for privacy preferences 1.0 (p3p1. 0) specification. W3C recommendation 16 (2002)
10. Cranor, L.F.: Platform for privacy preferences (P3P). In: Encyclopedia of Cryptography and Security, pp. 940–941. Springer, Boston (2011). https://doi.org/10.1007/978-1-4419-5906-5
11. Dalpiaz, F., Paja, E., Giorgini, P.: Security requirements engineering: designing secure socio-technical systems. MIT Press, Cambridge (2016)
12. Regulation (EU) 2016/679 of the European Parliament and of the Council of 27 April 2016 on the protection of natural persons with regard to the processing of personal data and on the free movement of such data, and repealing Directive 95/46/EC (General Data Protection Regulation). Official Journal of the European Union L119/59 (May 2016)
13. Garfinkel, S.L.: De-Identification of Personal Information. Technical report (2015)
14. Giorgini, P., Massacci, F., Mylopoulos, J., Zannone, N.: Modeling security requirements through ownership, permission and delegation. In: Proceedings of 13th IEEE International Conference on Requirements Engineering, pp. 167–176. IEEE (2005)
15. Giorgini, P., Mylopoulos, J., Sebastiani, R.: Goal-oriented requirements analysis and reasoning in the tropos methodology. Eng. Appl. Artif. Intell. 18(2), 159–171 (2005)
16. Guarda, P., Zannone, N.: Towards the development of privacy-aware systems. Inf. Softw. Technol. 51(2), 337–350 (2009)
17. Gürses, S., Troncoso, C., Diaz, C.: Engineering privacy by design (2011)
18. He, Q., Antón, A.I., et al.: A framework for modeling privacy requirements in role engineering. Proc. REFSQ. 3, 137–146 (2003)
19. Hoepman, J.-H.: Privacy design strategies. In: Cuppens-Boulahia, N., Cuppens, F., Jajodia, S., Abou El Kalam, A., Sans, T. (eds.) SEC 2014. IAICT, vol. 428, pp. 446–459. Springer, Heidelberg (2014). https://doi.org/10.1007/978-3-642-55415-5_38
20. Ingolfo, S., Siena, A., Mylopoulos, J.: Goals and compliance in Nomos 3. In: International Conference on Conceptual Modeling, pp. 275–288 (2014)
21. Li, N., Li, T., Venkatasubramanian, S.: t-closeness: privacy beyond k-anonymity and l-diversity. In: IEEE 23rd International Conference on Data Engineering, pp. 106–115 (2007)
22. Liu, L., Yu, E., Mylopoulos, J.: Security and privacy requirements analysis within a social setting. In: 11th International Requirements Engineering Conference, pp. 151–161. IEEE (2003)

23. Machanavajjhala, A., Kifer, D., Gehrke, J.: l-Diversity: privacy beyond k-anonymity. ACM Trans. Knowl. Discov. Data **1**(52) (2007)
24. Moses, T., et al.: Extensible access control markup language (xacml) version 2.0. Oasis Standard 200502 (2005)
25. Mouratidis, H., Giorgini, P.: Secure Tropos: A security-oriented extension of the tropos methodology. Int. J. Soft. Eng. Knowl. Eng. **17**(2), 285–309 (2007)
26. Park, J., Sandhu, R.: The ucon abc usage control model. ACM Trans. Inf. Syst. Secur. (TISSEC) **7**(1), 128–174 (2004)
27. Robol, M., Salnitri, M., Giorgini, P.: Toward GDPR-Compliant Socio-Technical Systems: modeling language and reasoning framework. Leuven (2017)
28. Siena, A., Jureta, I., Ingolfo, S., Susi, A., Perini, A., Mylopoulos, J.: Capturing variability of law with nómos 2. ER 7532, pp. 383–396 (2012)
29. Siena, A., Mylopoulos, J., Perini, A., Susi, A.: Designing law-compliant software requirements. In: Laender, A.H.F., Castano, S., Dayal, U., Casati, F., de Oliveira, J.P.M. (eds.) ER 2009. LNCS, vol. 5829, pp. 472–486. Springer, Heidelberg (2009). https://doi.org/10.1007/978-3-642-04840-1_35
30. Siena, A., Susi, A.: Engineering Law-Compliant Requirements - The Nomos Framework. Ph.D. thesis, University Of Trento (2010)
31. Solove, D.J.: A Taxonomy of Privacy (2005)
32. Solove, D.J.: Introduction: Privacy self-management and the consent dilemma. Harv. L. Rev. **126**(7), 1880 (2012)
33. Spiekermann, S., Cranor, L.: Engineering privacy. IEEE Trans. Softw. Eng. **35**(1), 67–82 (2009)
34. Sweeney, L.: k-anonymity: a model for protecting privacy. Int. J. Uncertain. Fuzziness Knowl. Based Syst.**10**(5), 557–570 (2002)
35. Van Lamsweerde, A., Darimont, R., Letier, E.: Managing conflicts in goal-driven requirements engineering. IEEE Trans. Softw. Eng. **24**(11), 908–926 (1998)
36. Yu, E.: Modelling strategic relationships for process reengineering. Soc'. Model. Requir. Eng. **11** (2011)

Experience Reports

Enterprise Modelling in the Age of Digital Transformation

Bas van Gils[1] and Henderik A. Proper[2,3](✉)(iD)

[1] Strategy Alliance, Lelystad, The Netherlands
bas.vangils@strategy-alliance.com
[2] Luxembourg Institute of Science and Technology, Esch-sur-Alzette, Luxembourg
e.proper@acm.org
[3] University of Luxembourg, Esch-sur-Alzette, Luxembourg

Abstract. The digital transformation forces enterprises to change. In addition, the notion of economic exchange, core to the economy, has shifted from following a goods-dominant logic to a service-dominant logic, putting the focus on continuous *value co-creation* between providers and consumers. These trends drive enterprises to transform continuously.

During enterprise transformations, *coordination* among the stakeholders involved is key. Shared understanding, agreement, and commitment, is needed on topics such as: the overall strategy of the enterprise, the current affairs of the enterprise and its context, as well as the ideal future affairs.Models, and ultimately enterprise modelling languages and frameworks, are generally seen as an effective way to *enable* such (informed) coordination. To this end, different languages and frameworks have been developed, including ArchiMate.

ArchiMate, which has evolved to become a widely accepted industry standard, was developed at a time where the digital transformation was not yet that noticeable. At that time, the focus was more on consolidation and optimisation. As such, it is logical to expect that the existing ArchiMate language may require some "updates" to be ready for digital transformations. The objective of this paper is therefore threefold: (1) posit, based on practical experiences and insights, key challenges which the digital transformation puts on enterprise (architecture) modelling languages, (2) assess to what extent ArchiMate meets these challenges, and (3) provide suggestions on how to possibly improve ArchiMate to better meet these challenges.

Keywords: Enterprise modelling · Digital transformation · ArchiMate

1 Introduction

Most modern day enterprises find themselves confronted with the challenge of dealing with digital transformations. Where IT originally was a mere supportive tool for administrative purposes, it is safe to say that nowadays IT has become

R. A. Buchmann et al. (Eds.): PoEM 2018, LNBIP 335, pp. 257–273, 2018.
https://doi.org/10.1007/978-3-030-02302-7_16

an integral part of an organisation's primary processes. Merely considering the *alignment* of *business* and *IT* [21] no longer suffices. The difference between business and IT is increasingly fading; they have been "fused" into one. Companies such as Amazon, AirBnB, Uber, Netflix, Spotify, Bitcoin, etcetera, illustrate how IT and business have indeed become fused. The CEO of a major bank can even be quoted as stating *We want to be a tech company with a banking license* [20].

In addition, marketing sciences [16,25,51,52] suggest that the notion of economic exchange, core to the economy, has shifted from following a goods-dominant logic to a service-dominant logic. While the former focuses on tangible resources to produce goods and embeds value in the transactions of goods, the latter concentrates on intangible resources and the creation of value in relation with customers. Service-dominance puts the continuous *value co-creation* between providers and consumers at the core. For instance, in the airline industry, jet turbine manufacturers used to follow a classical goods-dominant logic by selling turbines to airlines. However, since airlines are not interested in *owning* turbines, but rather in the realisation of *airtime*, manufacturers nowadays sell airtime to airlines instead of jet turbines. *Value co-creation* is shaping up as a key design concern for modern day enterprises.

We consider the trends of *business-IT fusion* and the *shift to value co-creation*, as being the key challenges to enterprises (be they companies, governmental agencies, or organisations) which aim to thrive (or at least survive) in the digital transformation of society. As a result of these intertwined, and mutually amplifying, trends, enterprises are more than ever confronted with a need to transform.

During any enterprise transformation, *coordination* among the key stakeholders and the projects/activities that drive the transformations is essential [40]. A shared understanding, agreement, and commitment, is needed on (1) what the overall strategy of the enterprise is, (2) the current affairs of the enterprise, i.e. the current situation, as well as the relevant history leading up to it, and possible trends towards the future, (3) the current affairs of the context of the enterprise, and (4) what (given the latter) the ideal future affairs of the enterprise are. Borrowing the terminology from architecture frameworks such as TOGAF [48], this refers to the development of a shared vision, a baseline architecture, and a target architecture, respectively.

Models, and ultimately enterprise (architecture) modelling languages and framework, are generally considered as an effective way to support such (informed) coordination. Many languages and frameworks have indeed been suggested as a way to create and capture a shared understanding of the desired future affairs. Examples, include BPMN [14], UML [28], ArchiMate [4,24], 4EM [46], and MERODE [47]. It appears[1] that ArchiMate [4,24] is rapidly

---

[1] The support for this claim lies in the steady growth of the number of certified professionals http://archimate-cert.opengroup.org/certified-individuals as well as the popularity of the ArchiMate topic on Google trends https://trends.google.com/trends/explore?date=all&q=archimate.

becoming a the leading industry standard for enterprise architecture modelling and has, as such, a key role to play in the coordination of [40] enterprise transformations.

When ArchiMate was developed, the digital transformation challenges were not yet that noticeable. At that time, the focus was more on consolidation and optimisation. As such, it is logical to expect that the existing ArchiMate language may require some "updates" to be truly ready for the digital transformation, and the emerging focus on value co-creation. The objective of this paper is therefore threefold: (1) define some of the challenges that the digital transformation puts on enterprise architecture modelling languages, (2) assess to what extent ArchiMate meets these challenges, and (3) provide suggestions on how to possibly improve ArchiMate to better meet the challenges of digital transformations. These topics will be covered in Sects. 2, 3 and 4 respectively.

2   Challenges for Enterprise Modelling

In this section, we identify some of the key challenges on enterprise (architecture) modelling in the context of digital transformations. These challenges are also based on our own experience in using ArchiMate in practice[2], as well as teaching the language to practitioners and University students[3].

In this paper, we consider the *digital transformation of an enterprise* to be any *enterprise transformation* which has a major impact on the digital resources and capabilities of the enterprise, where we define *enterprise transformation* to be a coordinated effort that changes the architecture of an enterprise.

The identified challenges have been grouped in three classes. First, we discuss challenges pertaining to the general expressiveness of the modelling language used. Since the digital transformation and value co-creation trends push for further specialisation and domain specificity of modelling languages, the second class of challenges concerns the need to be able to manage the resulting spectrum of modelling concepts. Finally, the third class concerns the earlier made observation that the digital transformation fuels the speed of change in organisations and their enterprises.

Expressiveness of the Modelling Language. In traditional views on enterprise architecture, it was more or less assumed that objects were either passive (operand) or active (operant), but not both, for their entire life. This simplification might indeed have worked in former times. However, in the context of the digital transformation, this simplification becomes increasingly difficult to uphold, especially since digital objects may (aid to) create other digital objects.

Key is, that it is natural for the same objects to play different roles in the course of time, or even in parallel. An enterprise architecture modelling language

---

[2] Involving Dutch public institutions, international fund management institutions, banks and lease companies, as well as retail organisations.

[3] Typically involving groups of full-time and/or part-time (i.e. practitioners) MSc students from e.g. Antwerp Management School, TIAS business school, Radboud University, Technical University of Vienna, and the University of Luxembourg.

used in digital transformations should therefore support this plurality of the roles played by objects:

Challenge 1: *Objects should be allowed to play operand and operant roles.*

Digital transformations also result in an increased reliance on the quality of information in terms of being *aware* of the level of (in)correctness at which it represents the world around us. This makes it increasingly important to remain aware of, and explicitly capture, the distinction between elements *in* the real world and the information that (is assumed to) *refer to* those real world elements. For example, in terms of a clear distinction between *business objects* as they exist in the real world, and *business information objects* that represent information *about* the former. Enterprise (architecture) modelling languages should, therefore, also clearly reflect such a distinction:

Challenge 2: *Clear separation between objects that represent "things" in the real world, and objects representing information about the real world.*

A consequence of the digital transformation [8] is that we should prepare for new forms of diversity in the work-force, where humans should learn to collaborate closely with digital actors (e.g. agents, robots, etcetera). Modern day enterprise modelling languages should, therefore, have the:

Challenge 3: *Ability to deal naturally with the duality of human and digital actors.*

A key aspect in traditional (conceptual) data modelling is the notion of *unique identification*; i.e. the ability to specify how objects in the real world can be distinguished from one another. The need to be able to model this depends on the situation at hand. Not all applications will need it, while in some cases it might even be illegal, e.g. due to privacy considerations. Even when a unique identification mechanism is available there may be limits regarding its precision. In a business network involving multiple partners, one may have to use multiple, partially overlapping, identification mechanisms. Even more, one may not have control over the creation of objects, which may (accidentally or maliciously) end up having the same properties as used in the identification. For enterprise modelling languages, this leads to the following challenge:

Challenge 4: *Ability to specify if objects can, should, and/or are allowed, to be uniquely identified, and what the expected reliability is.*

Most enterprise modelling languages do not allow for detailed modalities (mandatory, optional, one-to-one, one-to-many, exclusion, etcetera) on relationships. In general, this has been a deliberate choice by the language designers. In practice, however, this decision becomes increasingly challenged. It has been debated extensively among practitioners – for example in the LinkedIn group for ArchiMate as well as during training and coaching sessions – how useful it would be to be able to specify modalities, in particular in e.g. the context of privacy and security. A typical example would be the four-eyes principle, where two roles must be fulfilled when performing a certain task.

We suggest that, although one should not categorically require architecture models to use modalities on relationships, this should be addable when needed:

Challenge 5: *Ability to specify modalities on relationships.*

Several studies [16,26,51] observe a fundamental shift from, what they call, a goods-dominant logic to a service-dominant logic. While the former focuses on the production of goods, the latter concentrates on the delivery of services using resources and/or goods in doing so. These studies motivate this shift by observing that it is ultimately the customer who attributes value to a good or a service. Goods and services, "at rest", only have a potential value to a customer. The actual value is experienced when the resources/goods are actually *used* by the customer to some purpose.

The *digital transformation* not only brings about a new wave of digital services, it also acts as an enabler that allows providers of goods and service to better optimise the co-creation of value with their customers. Leading to the challenge for enterprise (architecture) modelling languages:

Challenge 6: *Ability to capture (potential) value(s) of products and services, and how this results in value co-creation between providers and consumers of services by way of resource integration.*

Given the speed of technological developments that drive digital transformations, it is increasingly important for organisations to be aware of the design choices that shape the essence of their activities, as well as choices with regards to their implementation in terms of e.g. different platforms, (business process) outsourcing, and technologies.

For enterprise modelling languages, this means that one should be able to express the design of the enterprise (including its use of information technology) at different levels of specificity with regards to implementation decisions, as well as enable the capturing of the associated design decisions and their motivation [33,34].

Challenge 7: *Capture design decisions and their motivation, at different levels of specificity with regards to implementation decisions.*

Managing the Spectrum of Modelling Concepts. An enterprise modelling language typically features a rich set of modelling concepts. As a natural consequence of the use of such a language, and as a corollary to the law of increasing entropy, there is a tendency to continue adding concepts to modelling languages without cleaning up concepts and relations that are infrequently used [5].

The digital transformation, due to its deep impact and multi-facetness, is likely to further fuel the entropic forces. Some of the challenges listed above, already point towards a desire to extend existing modelling languages. At the same time, an ever increasing set of modelling concepts will lead to a modelling language that will be hard to learn and master [22,27]. This leads to the following challenge:

Challenge 8: *A way to manage the set of modelling concepts, balancing the needs of domain, and purpose, specificity, the need for standardisation, and comprehensibility of the modelling language.*

Enterprise modelling languages typically involve different abstraction layers. Examples include the business, application and technology layer as used in ArchiMate [24], the business, information systems and technology layer from TOGAF [48], the business, information, information systems, and technology infrastructure columns from IAF [53], as well as the conceptual, logical, and physical layers of the same.

We observe in practice (both in using such frameworks, as well as teaching about them) that confusion about the precise scoping of the used abstractions exists. In this regard, one can even distinguish changes in the interpretation of the business, application, and technology layer, from the earlier version(s) of ArchiMate, where the technology layer was purely intended as the (IT) technological *infrastructure*, to the current interpretation, where it has evolved to include the entire (IT) technological implementation.

In general, one could say that abstraction layers result from the *design philosophy* underlying the specific framework. In this paper, we do not aim to take a specific position on which *design philosophy* would be best. However, we do argue that it is important that modelling frameworks must provide clear and consistent abstractions:

Challenge 9: *Provide a structure that allows for a consistent use of abstractions across relevant aspects of the enterprise.*

Enterprise (architecture) models play an increasingly important role. When changing an enterprise, models are used to capture the current affairs, as well as articulate different possible future affairs. Even more, nowadays it is quite common that models are even part of the "running system", in the sense that they are an artefact that drives/guides day-to-day activities. This includes e.g. work-flow models and business rules.

This makes it important that enterprise models also capture their meaning in a way that is understandible to the model's audience. We therefore posit that a conceptual model should be grounded in the terminology as it is actually *used* (naturally) by the people involved in/with the modelled domain. We also see this as a key enabler for the transferability of models across time and among people, in particular in situations where the model needs to act as a *boundary object* [3].

Most existing enterprise modelling languages (e.g. process models, goal models, value models, architectural models, etcetera), only offer a "boxes and lines" based representation, which, by its very nature only provide a limited linkage to the (natural) language as used by the model's audience. In general, the only link in this regard are the names used to label the "boxes". Relationships are replaced by generic graphical representations in terms of arrows and lines capturing relations such as "assigned to", "part of", "realises", "aggregates", "triggers". While these notational styles enable a more compact representation of models, they offer no means to provide a "drill down", or "mouse over", to an underlying grounding in terms of well verbalised fact types that capture, and honour, the original natural (language) nuances. They leave no room for situation specific nuance, or more explicit capturing of the meaning of the models a way that is understandible to the model's audience (beyond engineers). The challenge therefore is:

Challenge 10: *How to ground enterprise models in terms of natural language like verbalisations, without loosing the advantages of having compact notations (as well).*

Enterprises are in Motion. Modern day enterprises, and their context, are in a constant state of change; they are continuously in motion. As argued before, the digital transformation of society further increases the speed at which enterprises change. As such, it is doubtful, if not unrealistic, to use traditional notions such as "baseline" architecture and "target" architecture. For instance, an enterprise's baseline can not simply be thought of "structural state", but should rather be thought of as a "structural vector" [35, 38]. The rate of change in modern day enterprises is so high, that maintaining models that sufficiently capture the architecture (i.e. the fundamental organisation and the principles guiding design and evolution) from the perspective of involved stakeholders does not seem to be feasible. Hence, it is better to speak about capturing "current affairs", which includes past, and present, change trends, of the enterprise and its environment. This allows one to reason both about "what is" as well as "what was before" and therefore take the history into account when making decisions. This results in the challenge:

Challenge 11: *How to capture the motion of an enterprise, it terms of its current and desired affairs.*

3 ArchiMate's Readiness for the New Modelling Challenges

In section, we discuss to what extent the current version of ArchiMate meets the challenges of digital transformations, as identified in the "challenges".

ArchiMate[4] is a dedicated language for the representation of (enterprise) architecture models that was originally developed by a research consortium involving industrial and academic partners from the Netherlands. Later, it was adopted by The Open Group as a standard [4, 24]. Its adoption has grown rapidly, both in terms of the *users* of the language, and the *vendors* that deliver software solutions based on this language.

The current version covers six layers (strategy, business, application, technology, physical, as well as implementation & migration) and four aspects (active structure, passive structure, behaviour, and motivation). The core consists of the business/application/technology layers. Services are a key modelling construct

---

[4] At the time of writing, ArchiMate 3.0.1 is available online.

in ArchiMate, and are used as a decoupling mechanism between the layers. They are used to specify what an active structure element exposes to its environment and hides the complexity of how the service is actually realised. Services can be used within a layer or across layers.

A second abstraction mechanism in the language is the *specialisation relation*, which is to be interpreted as "is a kind off". Some languages, such as ORM [19] and UML [28], distinguish between (a) specialisation, (b) generalisation, and (c) type/instance relations. In ArchiMate, these are all captured by the same specialisation relation. Using this relation, it is possible to relate generic architecture constructs (e.g. a process pattern) to more specific manifestations (e.g. distinguishing between the regular manifestation of the process, or the one that is followed during times of crisis).

An abstraction mechanism that was introduced in version 3 of the ArchiMate language is the use of *grouping*. Previously, the grouping was a visual construct only, which was intended to show on a view which concepts "belong together" for some reason. Since ArchiMate version 3, the intended meaning is more rigourous: the grouping is said to aggregate the concepts that are in it, and thus functions as a semantic whole. Groupings may be related to other concepts (including other groupings). This makes it particularly well suited to use the grouping as a form of *building blocks* along the lines of the TOGAF standard (e.g. [48, Chapter 37]).

The last mechanism that is relevant to our discussion here is the notion of *cross layer dependencies* [4, Chap. 12]. This has changed significantly between version 2 and 3 of the language. The general idea is that behavioural elements from one layer may be *realised* by (more concrete) behavioural elements in other layers, which appears to express that the more abstract concept is *instantiated* by the more concrete one. Along the same lines, it allows us to specify that a group of elements (i.e. a building block) is realised by another group of elements (another building block).

In the remainder of Section, we briefly assess ArchiMate in the light of the challenges brought forward by the digital transformation.

Challenge 1: *Objects should be allowed to play operand and operant roles.*

The current ArchiMate language does not deal with this at all, due to the strict distinction between *active* and *passive* structure elements. This challenge lies at the heart of the ArchiMate language and has its origin in the fundamental choice to use a linguistic (subject-object-verb) base for modelling.

Challenge 2: *Clear separation between objects that represent "things" in the real world, and objects representing information about the real world.*

Currently, there is no clear distinction between the two types of objects, other than the observation that data objects/artefact presumably are about the bits and bytes that represent information. The ArchiMate specification does suggest that the *business object* concept can be specialised but in the default language this has not been done. What the specification does not mention is that additional relations may also be required in order to present that a *business information object A* is about real world *business object B*.

Challenge 3: *Ability to deal naturally with the duality of human and digital actors.*

Here, the ArchiMate language, through its layering, does provide a fair attempt at tackling this challenge since there are different concepts for e.g. actor, information system, and node. Some interesting challenges remain, however. First of all, only (business) actors can be assigned a role in behaviour, other structure elements cannot. A second mismatch lies in the fact that *collaborations* in ArchiMate can only be composed of structure elements from the same layer. This prevents us from specifying, for example, that a human actor and computer actor collaborate to achieve a certain task.

Challenge 4: *Ability to specify if objects can, should, and/or are allowed, to be uniquely identified, and what the expected reliability is.*

In ArchiMate, (most) concepts are essentially "types", representing "instances" in the real world. The ArchiMate concepts, representing "things in the real world" have a name to tell one apart from the other. There is no mechanism to specify how the "instances" should be told apart.

Challenge 5: *Ability to specify modalities on relationships.*

For this challenge we can be short. ArchiMate has no support for this. Objects are either related, or they are not.

Challenge 6: *Ability to capture (potential) value(s) of products and services, and how this results in value co-creation between providers and consumers of services by way of resource integration.*

The ArchiMate language does feature the *value* concept, and it seems possible to model value cocreation by using the collaboration/interaction concepts. However, value, or even a value stream, is not yet value *co-creation*. As discussed in e.g. [42, 43], representing value co-creation [16] scenarios requires more dedicated modelling constructs.

Challenge 7: *Capture design decisions and their motivation, at different levels of specificity with regards to implementation decisions.*

There is limited support in ArchiMate to address this. The actual level of detail at which design decisions remains rather crude. For example, it excludes explicit trade-offs between design alternatives, nor does it capture the actual decision making process and (compensatory and/or non-compensatory [44]) criteria used to make decisions.

Challenge 8: *A way to manage the set of modelling concepts, balancing the needs of domain, and purpose, specificity, the need for standardisation, and comprehensibility of the modelling language.*

This challenge is addressed partially by the *extension mechanisms* to tailor the language to local needs, while keeping the core of the language compact. This can be done by specialising existing concepts, or adding properties to existing concepts. Additions to the original version of the language have also been positioned as so-called "extensions", such as the *motivation* extension, and the *implementation & migration* extension.

While it is good that the language indeed supports this, being able to re-use extensions across toolsets of different vendors is not straightforward. Even more, the actual extension mechanism is not really positioned as a key feature in the standard either.

Challenge 9: *Provide a structure that allows for a consistent use of abstractions across relevant aspects of the enterprise.*

The latest version of ArchiMate does indeed provide some rudimentary support to tackle these challenges through the *grouping* mechanism. It is now possible to express the fact that one group of concepts (together) realises another group of concepts. This allows the modeller to work from a big picture level to a more detailed level, as well as from a functional level to a more construction-oriented level.

Challenge 10: *How to ground enterprise models in terms of natural language like verbalisations, without loosing the advantages of having compact notations (as well).*

ArchiMate has no support for this; neither in the language nor the modelling process (which is non existent). Even more, there is no pre-defined modelling procedure such as ORM's CSDP [19], leaving (in particular novice modellers) to guess how to master ArchiMate's elaborate set of modelling concepts [37].

Challenge 11: *How to capture the motion of an enterprise, it terms of its current and desired affairs.*

Support for this challenge is limited. TOGAF and ArchiMate have indeed extended the concepts of "baseline" and "target" architecture into a multi-stage version in terms of "plateaus" towards the future. They allow the modeller to specify multiple points in time as well as capture "alternate realities" (i.e. different potential futures) through the use of *plateaus*. Even more, ArchiMate allows the modeller to link concepts to motivational elements of key stakeholders.

Building a modelling language that supports modellers to consistently solve challenges, and solve them well while keeping in the return on modelling effort (RoME) in mind, is a difficult task indeed. After listing the modelling challenges for digital transformations, and evaluating the current version of ArchiMate against these challenges, we conclude that, even though ArchiMate has been around for a while, and has a strong conceptual framework, its support for digital transformations can be improved.

4   Recommendations for Next Generation EA Modelling

Below, we provide (motivated) recommendations that could overcome (some of) the challenges as discussed above.

Modular language design – The set of modelling constructs within the ArchiMate language has grown considerably since its first version, thus fuelling Challenge 8. In meeting this challenge, we suggest that modelling language standards in general should focus primarily on providing a generic core of well-defined modelling concepts. On top of this core, one could then define refinement mechanisms, that can be used to extend/tailor the core to the needs at hand. This may involve both specialisations of the core concepts, as well as e.g. the introduction of (purpose specific/user defined) layers.

As discussed in the Section, the use of ArchiMate's *extension mechanism* indeed provides a potential starting point to better manage the resulting set of concepts. The positioning of recent additions to the language as *extensions*, such as the *motivation* extension, and the *implementation & migration* extension, indeed underlines this. When looking at the original architecture of the ArchiMate language [23], there are ample opportunities for further modularisation. Following [23], the core of the language is formed by five key generic "active systems" modelling concepts: *objects, service, internal behaviour, interface* and *internal structure*. All other concepts (including the layers) are explicitly derived from these in terms of specialisations [23]. In our view this specialisation hierarchy has been left too implicit for far too long. An explicit re-factoring of the current ArchiMate language based on this hierarchy seems long overdue.

In addition, a library of (meta-model) *modules* can be defined, which could potentially even be (re)used across different language cores. For example, a generic *motivation* module could be shared between ArchiMate, 4EM [46] and UML [28].

Grounding enterprise modelling – As suggested by Challenge 10, enterprise models should (unless they only serve a temporary "throw away" purpose) include a precise (enough) definition of the meaning of the concepts used in the model.

We posit that, to ensure that a model is understandable to its audience, it should be grounded on an (underlying) model involving verbalisations using the terminology as it is actually *used* (naturally) by the people involved in/with the modelled domain. As exemplified in [6,7,37,50], fact-based models can be used to ground enterprise models expressed in languages such as ArchiMate, system dynamics [45] and BPMN [29], and architecture principles [15]. Fact-based models [19] are created by verbalising the domain to be modelled in terms of elementary facts as structured sentences in natural language. These elementary facts express (unsplittable) properties of, and relationships between, the objects in the modelled domain. Based on these elementary facts, the conceptual model is then created in terms of fact-types and object-types. An added advantage of using fact-based models is that it also leads to an evidence (in terms of example facts) based approach to modelling.

Grounding ArchiMate on fact-based models would also result in a natural solution to Challenge 1, i.e. the need for objects to be able to play operand and operant roles. When observing objects and expressing their engagements in activities in terms of fact types, one can easily observe objects mixing *passive structure/active structure/behaviour* roles. Even though we strongly suggest to remain close to the terminology as it is actually *used* by the people involved in/with the modelled domain, we do see the potential benefits of providing guidance in structuring/refining this terminology based on e.g. foundational ontologies [18].

Adding more semantic precision – Both Challenges 4 and 5 require the ability to specify more semantic details regarding objects and relations. It would be logical to "import" such mechanisms from these existing languages into ArchiMate. When, grounding enterprise models (e.g., using a fact-based approach as discussed above), then this will also come as a direct consequence. Even though it is not required for architects to specify such constraints in all situations, it is key to provide the ability to do so when required.

Abstraction layers – Challenges 2 and 9, are essentially all concerned with the need to "separate concerns", albeit in different ways. As argued before, it is important to ensure a clear and consistent structure of abstraction layers. When looking across different frameworks (e.g. ArchiMate [24], Enterprise Ontology [11], TOGAF [48], IAF [53], and Zachman [54]), we posit that these frameworks use four key mechanisms in creating abstractions (in different dimensions, possibly combining these mechanisms).

1: Function-construction – This abstraction mechanism involves making a distinction between, *function* referring to the way a system is intended to function in light of what users, clients, and other stakeholders might deem useful, and *construction* pertaining to the way a system actually functions/is constructed to realise the provided functions.

2: Informational functioning – This pertains to different levels of *functioning* [10,30,39] of an enterprise in terms of informational support, e.g. leading to a *business* level (the activities conducted that have a direct impact in the socio-economical world), an *informational* level (the information needed/created in the business activities) and a *documental* level (how this information may be laid down in documental concepts). A clear distinction between *business* and *informational* activities, also results in a natural way to deal with Challenge 2; i.e. separating the real world and the informational world.

3: Infrastructural usage – This concerns the fact that one system (of systems) can *use* the functions of another system (of systems), where the actual construction of the latter is of no interest to the (designers) of the former, except to the extent of defining service-level agreements.

4: Implementation abstraction – This concerns the gradual/stepwise introduction of details of the socio-technical implementation. For example, in IAF [53] this corresponds to the distinction between a conceptual, logical, and physical level, while in TOGAF [48], this corresponds to the level of architectural and logical building blocks.

Making a clear implementation abstraction, also provides a natural way to deal with Challenge 3 pertaining to the duality of human and digital actors. At the highest level of implementation abstraction, one would need to describe the workings of the enterprise independent of the question if it will be implemented with human actors or computerised actors. The immediate next level of implementation abstraction, might then make choices with regards to human/computerised actors explicit, even allowing for mixed scenarios.

Each of the above discussed abstraction mechanisms has a potential added value, also in the context of digital transformation. It is important to note that these abstraction mechanisms should not be thought of as a set of orthogonal dimensions. On the contrary. The *function-construction* mechanism and *information functioning*, or *function-construction* and *infrastructural usage* can easily be mixed. We also do not want to suggest to "prescribe" a specific set of dimensions. We do, however, argue that an enterprise modelling language (framework) should ensure a consistent use of the above mechanisms within one dimension. As discussed in Sect. 3, ArchiMate seems to have been mixing some of these dimensions in an inconsistent way.

Accommodate value co-creation – The increasing focus on value co-creation, resulting from the shift from a goods-dominant logic to a service-dominant logic [16,25,51,52], results in Challenge 6, i.e. how to capture (potential) value(s) of products and services, and how this results in value co-creation between providers and consumers of services by way of resource integration.

ArchiMate already provides *value* concept, and it seems possible to model value *co*creation by using the collaboration/interaction concepts. However, as mentioned before, value, or even a value stream, is not the same as value *co-creation*. How to best express this, is still largely an open question. Some initial work/suggestions, has been presented in [12,13,41,42].

The very nature of value co-creation also requires a shift from (only) architecting the "internals" an enterprise, to co-architecting the collaboration (including e.g. needed inter-organisational IT platforms) between multiple network partners [9].

In further elaborating the set of needed concepts for value co-creation, our recommendation [36] is to (1) use the provider/customer roles as identified in [17], specialised to more specific co-creation activities taking place within the *provider sphere*, the *joint sphere*, or the *customer sphere*, as a reference model, while (2) using the foundational premises as articulated in [52] as design/architecture principles [15] that will guide the design of service systems for value co-creation, and (3) apply this in the context of real world cases, to gain insight into the actually needed modelling concepts.

Capturing design motivations – The current version of ArchiMate does provide a motivation extension. However, as discussed in the Section, it does not meet Challenge 7 in a satisfactory way. Separate from the fact that, as suggested above, it would be good if such an extension could be shared between e.g. Archi-Mate, 4EM [46] and BPMN [29], the level at which design decisions are captured remains rather crude.

The work as reported in e.g. [31,32] provides suggestions on how to remedy this. This includes the ability to e.g. capture trade-offs between design alternatives, as well the actual decision making process and the criteria used to make decisions (including e.g. the identification of compensatory and/or non-compensatory [44] criteria).

Managing constant change – As discussed in Sect. 2, the digital transformation requires enterprises to change constantly. This makes it less realistic to capture an enterprise's *current affairs* and/or *desired affairs* in terms of traditional notions such as "baseline" architecture and "target" architecture, or even *plateaux/transition* architectures. Even though we observe some ingredients towards solutions for this challenge, we would argue that more research is certainly needed.

In an ideal world, the description of the *current affairs*, would be maintained continuously, preferably in an automated way [35]. Approaches such as e.g. process mining [1], and enterprise cartography [49], indeed provide good starting points.

Architectures capturing the *desired affairs*, also tend to be specified using a rather "instructive" of typical "boxes and lines" diagrams. This does not really invite architects to reflect on what the more *endurable* elements and assumptions, and what the less stable elements and assumptions are. This has also triggered the development of the concept of multi-speed enterprise (IT) architectures [2]. It also resulted in a stronger positioning of e.g. (normative) architecture principles [15] as a way to complement the "instructive" style (the "boxes and lines" diagrams) by a more directional/"regulative" perspective.

5   Conclusion and Further Research

In this paper, we presented key challenges which the digital transformation puts on enterprise (architecture) modelling languages. These challenges are based on practical experiences and insights from the field of enterprise architecture.

We then assessed the extent to which the current version of ArchiMate meets these challenges. The conclusion was that ArchiMate does not yet fully cover all of the identified challenges. This can be explained by the fact that ArchiMate was developed at a time when the digital transformation was not yet that dominant.

We then provided suggestions on how to possibly improve ArchiMate to better meet the challenges of digital transformations. In further research, we intend to further elaborate these suggestions, in particular with the aim of finding strategies that work in real world practice.

References

1. van der Aalst, W.M.P.: Process Mining: Discovery, Conformance and Enhancement of Business Processes. Springer, Heidelberg (2011)
2. Abraham, R., Aier, S., Winter, R.: Two speeds of EAM—A dynamic capabilities perspective. In: Aier, S., Ekstedt, M., Matthes, F., Proper, E., Sanz, J.L. (eds.) PRET/TEAR -2012. LNBIP, vol. 131, pp. 111–128. Springer, Heidelberg (2012). https://doi.org/10.1007/978-3-642-34163-2_7

3. Abraham, R., Niemietz, H., de Kinderen, S., Aier, S.: Can boundary objects mitigate communication defects in enterprise transformation? Findings from expert interviews. In: Jung, R., Reichert, M. (eds.) Proceedings of the 5th International Workshop on Enterprise Modelling and Information Systems Architectures (EMISA 2013), St. Gallen, Switzerland. LNI, vol. 222, pp. 27–40. Gesellschaft für Informatik (2013)

4. Band, I., et al.: ArchiMate 3.0 Specification. The Open Group (2016)

5. Bjeković, M., Proper, H.A., Sottet, J.-S.: Enterprise modelling languages. In: Shishkov, B. (ed.) BMSD 2013. LNBIP, vol. 173, pp. 1–23. Springer, Cham (2014). https://doi.org/10.1007/978-3-319-06671-4_1

6. van Bommel, P., Buitenhuis, P.G., Hoppenbrouwers, S.J.B.A., Proper, H.A.: Architecture Principles - a regulative perspective on enterprise architecture. In: Reichert, M., Strecker, S., Turowski, K. (eds.) Proceedings of the 2nd International Workshop on Enterprise Modelling and Information Systems Architectures (EMISA 2007), St. Goar am Rhein, Germany, pp. 47–60, vol. 119 in LNI, Gesellschaft für Informatik (2007)

7. van Bommel, P., Hoppenbrouwers, S.J.B.A., Proper, H.A., van der Weide, T.P.: On the use of object-role modeling for modeling active domains. In: Research Issues in System Analysis and Design, Databases and Software Development, pp. 123–145. IGI Publishing (2007)

8. Brown, S.: The new diversity: working with Nonhumans. IEEE Computer 50(3), 90–95 (2017)

9. Chew, E.K.: iSIM: an integrated design method for commercializing service innovation. Inf. Syst. Front. 18(3), 457–478 (2016)

10. Dietz, J.L.G.: Enterprise Ontology - Theory and Methodology. Springer, Heidelberg (2006)

11. Dietz, J.L.G., Hoogervorst, J.A.P.: Enterprise ontology and enterprise architecture - how to let them evolve into effective complementary notions. GEAO J. Enterp. Arch. 2(1), 121–149 (2007)

12. Feltus, C., Proper, H.A.: Conceptualization of an abstract language to support value co-creation. In: 12th Conference on Information Systems Management (ISM 2017), Federated Conference on Computer Science and Information Systems. Prague, Czech Republic (2017)

13. Feltus, C., Proper, H.A.: Towards a security and privacy co-creation method. In: IEEE International Conference for Internet Technology and Secured Transactions (ICITST-2017) (2017)

14. Freund, J., Rücker, B.: Real Life BPMN. Camunda (2012)

15. Greefhorst, D., Proper, H.A.: Architecture Principles - The Cornerstones of Enterprise Architecture. Enterprise Engineering Series. Springer, Heidelberg (2011)

16. Grönroos, C., Ravald, A.: Service as business logic: implications for value creation and marketing. J. Serv. Man. 22(1), 5–22 (2011)

17. Grönroos, C., Voima, P.J.: Critical service logic: making sense of value creation and co-creation. J. Acad. Mark. Sci. 41(2), 133–150 (2013)

18. Guizzardi, G.: On ontology, ontologies, conceptualizations, modeling languages, and (meta)models. In: Vasilecas, O., Eder, J., Caplinskas, A. (eds.) Databases and Information Systems IV - Selected Papers from the Seventh International Baltic Conference, DB&IS 2006, 3–6 July 2006, Vilnius, Lithuania. Frontiers in Artificial Intelligence and Applications, vol. 155, pp. 18–39. IOS Press (2006)

19. Halpin, T.A., Morgan, T.: Information Modeling and Relational Databases. Data Management Systems, 2nd edn. Morgan Kaufman, San Francisco (2008)

20. Hamers, R.: We want to be a tech company with a banking license (2017). https://tinyurl.com/ycn8l2kh. Accessed 25 Jan 2018

21. Henderson, J.C., Venkatraman, N.: Strategic alignment: leveraging information technology for transforming organizations. IBM Syst. J. **32**(1), 4–16 (1993)

22. Krogstie, J., Lindland, O.I., Sindre, G.: Defining quality aspects for conceptual models. In: Falkenberg, E.D., Hesse, W., Olivé, A. (eds.) Information System Concepts: Towards a Consolidation of Views - Proceedings of the third IFIP WG8.1 Conference (ISCO-3), pp. 216–231. Chapman & Hall/IFIP WG8.1, London, UK, Marburg, Germany, March 1995

23. Lankhorst, M.M., Proper, H.A., Jonkers, H.: The anatomy of the ArchiMate language. Int. J. Inf. Syst. Model. Des. **1**(1), 1–32 (2010)

24. Lankhorst, et al., M.M.: Enterprise Architecture at Work: modelling, Communication and Analysis, 4th edn. Enterprise Engineering Series. Springer, Heidelberg (2017)

25. Lusch, R.F., Nambisan, S.: Service innovation: a service-dominant logic perspective. MIS Q. **39**(1), 155–175 (2015)

26. Maglio, P.P., Vargo, S.L., Caswel, N., Spohrer, J.: The service system is the basic abstraction of service science. Inf. Syst. E-Bus. Manag. **7**(4), 395–406 (2009)

27. Moody, D.L.: The "physics" of notations: toward a scientific basis for constructing visual notations in software engineering. IEEE Trans. Softw. Eng. **35**(6), 756–779 (2009)

28. Object Management Group: Unified Modeling Language - Superstructure. Technical report version 2.4.1, OMG (2010)

29. OMG: Business Process Modeling Notation, V2.0. Technical Report OMG Document Number: formal/2011-01-03, Object Management Group (2011)

30. Op 't Land, M., Proper, H.A.: Impact of principles on enterprise engineering. In: Österle, H., Schelp, J., Winter, R. (eds.) Proceedings of the 15th European Conference on Information Systems, pp. 1965–1976. University of St. Gallen, St. Gallen, Switzerland (2007)

31. Plataniotis, G., de Kinderen, S., Ma, Q., Proper, H.A.: A conceptual model for compliance checking support of enterprise architecture decisions. In: Proceedings of the 17th IEEE Conference on Business Informatics (CBI 2015), Lisbon, Portugal, vol. 1, pp. 191–198 (2015)

32. Plataniotis, G., de Kinderen, S., Proper, H.A.: Capturing design rationales in enterprise architecture: a case study. In: Proceedings of the 7th IFIP WG 8.1 Working Conference on the Practice of Enterprise Modeling (PoEM 2014) (2014)

33. Plataniotis, G., de Kinderen, S., Proper, H.A.: EA anamnesis: an approach for decision making analysis in enterprise architecture. Int. J. Inf. Syst. Model. Design **5**(3), 75–95 (2014)

34. Plataniotis, G., Ma, Q., Proper, H.A., de Kinderen, S.: Traceability and modeling of requirements in enterprise architecture from a design rationale perspective. In: Proceedings of the 9th IEEE Internaltional Conference on Research Challenges in Information Science (RCIS 2015), Athens, Greece, pp. 518–519 (2015)

35. Proper, H.A.: Enterprise architecture - informed steering of enterprises in motion. In: Proceedings of the 15th International Conference (ICEIS 2013), Angers, France - Revised Selected Papers. LNBIP, vol. 190, pp. 16–34. Springer, Cham (2014)

36. Proper, H.A., Bjeković, M., Feltus, C., Razo-Zapata, I.S.: On the development of a modelling framework for value co-creation. In: Proceedings of the 12th International Workshop on Value Modelling and Business Ontologies (VMBO) (2018)

37. Proper, H.A., Bjeković, M., van Gils, B., Hoppenbrouwers, S.J.B.A.: Towards grounded enterprise modelling. In: Debruyne, C., Panetto, H., Weichhart, G., Bollen, P., Ciuciu, I., Vidal, M.-E., Meersman, R. (eds.) OTM 2017. LNCS, vol. 10697, pp. 141–151. Springer, Cham (2018). https://doi.org/10.1007/978-3-319-73805-5_15
38. Proper, H.A., Lankhorst, M.M.: Enterprise architecture - towards essential sensemaking. Enterp. Model. Inf. Syst. Arch. (EMISA) 9(1), 5–21 (2014)
39. Proper, H.A., Op't Land, M.: Lines in the water. In: Harmsen, F., Proper, E., Schalkwijk, F., Barjis, J., Overbeek, S. (eds.) PRET 2010. LNBIP, vol. 69, pp. 193–216. Springer, Heidelberg (2010). https://doi.org/10.1007/978-3-642-16770-6_9
40. Proper, H.A., Winter, R., Aier, S., de Kinderen, S. (eds.): Architectural Coordination of Enterprise Transformation. Enterprise Engineering Series. Springer, Heidelberg (2018)
41. Razo-Zapata, I.S., Chew, E., Proper, H.A.: Visual modeling for value (Co-)creation. In: Proceedings of the 10th International Workshop on Value Modelling and Business Ontologies (VMBO) (2016)
42. Razo-Zapata, I.S., Chew, E., Proper, H.A.: Towards VIVA: A Visual language to model VAlue co-creation. In: The 5th International Conference on Serviceology (2017)
43. Razo-Zapata, I.S., Chew, E., Proper, H.A.: VIVA: A VIsual Language to Design VAlue Co-creation. In: The 20th IEEE International Conference on Business Informatics (CBI 2018) (2018)
44. Rothrock, L., Yin, J.: Integrating compensatory and noncompensatory decision-making strategies in dynamic task environments. In: Kugler, T., Smith, J.C., Connolly, T., Son, Y.J. (eds.) Decision Modeling and Behavior in Complex and Uncertain Environments, Springer Optimization and Its Applications, vol. 21, pp. 125–141. Springer, New York (2008)
45. Rouwette, E.A.J.A., Vennix, J.A.M.: System dynamics and organizational interventions. Syst. Res. Behav. Sci. 23, 451–466 (2006)
46. Sandkuhl, K., Stirna, J., Persson, A., Wißotzki, M.: Enterprise Modeling: Tackling Business Challenges with the 4EM Method. Springer, Heidelberg (2014)
47. Snoeck, M.: Enterprise Information Systems Engineering - The MERODE Approach. Enterprise Engineering Series. Springer, Heidelberg (2014)
48. The Open Group: TOGAF Version 9.1, 10th edn. Van Haren Publishing (2011)
49. Tribolet, J., Sousa, P., Caetano, A.: the role of enterprise governance and cartography in enterprise engineering. Enterp. Model. Inf. Syst. Arch. (EMISA) 9(1), 38–49 (2014)
50. Tulinayo, F.P., van Bommel, P., Proper, H.A.: Enhancing the system dynamics modeling process with a domain modeling method. Int. J. Coop. Inf. Syst. 22(02), 1350011 (2013)
51. Vargo, S.L., Lusch, R.F.: Service-dominant logic: continuing the evolution. J. Acad. Mark. Sci. 36, 1–10 (2008)
52. Vargo, S.L., Lusch, R.F.: Institutions and axioms: an extension and update of service-dominant logic. J. Acad. Mark. Sci. 44(1), 5–23 (2016)
53. Wout, J.v., Waage, M., Hartman, H., Stahlecker, M., Hofman, A.: The Integrated Architecture Framework Explained. Springer, Heidelberg (2010)
54. Zachman, J.A.: A framework for information systems architecture. IBM Syst. J. 26(3), 276–292 (1987)

Organizational Value Creation by IT in Industry 4.0

Domonkos Gaspar[(⊠)] [ID]

Corvinus University of Budapest, Budapest 1093, Hungary
dgaspar@gmx.de

Abstract. At the doorstep of the 4th industrial revolution, standardization and digitalization are high on the agenda of many management boards. With technology having already outpaced organizational development, IT departments may become the engines of the current revolutionary sentiment if they master the transformation of their role and position in the corporate Operations Excellence efforts. CIOs are finding themselves between multiple disrupting fronts: the expectation to be a key driving force in the corporate transformation, while needing to transform their own organization to meet today's challenges, at times when information technology solutions is becoming "everyone's" business in the companies. In this journey the key success factor is the right approach to managing the demand from their customer: the business. This practitioner paper offers a response by reflecting on relevant models, describing an integrated approach and validates certain assumptions based on the experience of a pilot implementation of the Integrated Change Management model.

Keywords: Industry 4.0 · Digitalization · Change management
Standardization · Transformation · Operations Excellence · Integration

1 Introduction and Problem Statement

Standardization and digitalization are high on the agenda of many management boards. This processes and tools related challenge demands a corporate strategic approach and ownership. It can be argued that the successful management of change is crucial to any organization in order to survive and succeed in the present highly competitive and continuously evolving business environment. However, theories and approaches to change management currently available to academics and practitioners are often contradictory, mostly lacking empirical evidence and supported by unchallenged hypotheses concerning the nature of contemporary organizational change management.

At the doorstep of the 4th industrial revolution, where technology already outpaced organizational development, IT departments may become the engine room of the corporate transformation if they master the transformation of their own role and position in the Operation Excellence efforts. At times where "disruption" is a preferred state of mind, any past models may be questioned on a basic level, and information technology solutions become "everyone's" business, should IT departments reinvent themselves, or it is possible to capitalize on past robust practices and still deliver their contribution?

© IFIP International Federation for Information Processing 2018
Published by Springer Nature Switzerland AG 2018. All Rights Reserved
R. A. Buchmann et al. (Eds.): PoEM 2018, LNBIP 335, pp. 274–287, 2018.
https://doi.org/10.1007/978-3-030-02302-7_17

This document provides a possible response from the IT department by reflecting on existing models, further developing them based on experience, to come to the description of a model that had proven itself against the challenges Industry 4.0 put on IT and on the entire organization.

2 IT in the Lead of the Transformation

Organizations and processes change dynamically, simultaneously in multiple parts of the organizations, often without coordination, in response to external influence and/or internal needs. These changes almost without exception have a change demand on IT capabilities often impact the same tool/feature(s), eventually causing contradicting requirements. These changes also often join one unified space only in information technology, making the volume and extent of the diverse changes in the organization visible in IT.

In the age of the 4th industrial revolution, organizational units are targeted directly by providers with appealing, sophisticated solutions or look out for new digital capabilities themselves, increasing the demand on the IT organizations twofold: on one hand demand for IT resources internal or external are exceeding capacity/budget, making it necessary for periodization, on the other hand IT organizations struggle to keep structure and harmonized evolution of the IT landscape, for the operation which they will be responsible, at least to a certain degree (even Software as a Service and cloud- based models require safe and multi-faceted connection between the own IT infrastructure and the external solution).

While IT assets often seen only as "enablers" of business, organizational anomalies often manifest firstly in insufficient use of the needed IT tools. More often than justified, the messengers are shot on executive levels, making the inappropriate IT assets and capabilities the reason for those anomalies. While much of the costs, too, for a change are realized in the IT space, the benefits (tangible or intangible) of a successful implementation of a change or a new tool are regularly realized on other parts of the organization.

In response to these challenges CIOs are out on the search for integrative and effective ways to steer requests arriving from their clients, the business. It had been recognized already in the emergence of the reliance on information technology tools, that IT need to align with internal and external domains [1] while remaining/becoming compliant to an ever-increasing number of internal and external regulations and guidelines (eg ISO TS, ISO 17001, external audit, internal audit, COBIT 5, local legal requirements).

We argue that in this circumstance the best defense is to be proactive: the IT organization should learn the motivations and operating systems of its business, reach out and provide it with a commonly recognizable approach to manage changes in an integrated way. Many IT focused change management models (e.g. ITIL [2]) are well performing in technology related change management but come to their limit in practical use when functional transactional aspects ("business" side) need to be intensively dealt with.

Assumptions. In our work we took certain assumptions which we intended to reflect on following our project:

1. Majority of the IT deliverables fail to perform due to improperly prepared organization (users) or changing requirements.

2. It is possible to develop a model which manages all elements of a successful organizational change implementation. Such a model can be lead out of the IT Department.

3. An integrated approach to change management assures operational sustainability and potentially reduces cost of change.

4. An integrated approach of Systems, Data and Organization should be robust enough to carry business transformation initiatives.

In our article we will elaborate on the context of this initiative. We will also introduce an example for such a structure which relies on theories and methodologies, but tailored and completed for best fit the needs of a globally present mid-size enterprise.

3   Principles of the Integrated IT Change Management

3.1   Background and Relevance

Background. In order to be successful in finding a common denominator for change management with business stakeholders, IT needs to critically review its own approach and it must reflect on the key models and approaches driving the way of thinking and acting in operations in manufacturing.

The second half of the 20th century changed significantly the landscape of manufacturing management. In the search of more efficient production models, Toyota Motors developed in the '50s and '60s a model [3] that combines attitudes, themes and specific techniques into an integrated socio-technical system for manufacturing. It is commonly referred to as the Toyota Production System (TPS). The LEAN methodology [4] is an evolution of TPS. TPS and LEAN are today the industrial reference in the manufacturing space. It is without exaggeration to state, that every production company developed its own manufacturing system based on the principles of TPS and LEAN. A key common point of these approaches is the establishment of the Continuous Improvement (CI) process as operational initiator of changes. The CI process seeks to progress through "incremental" improvement over time or "breakthrough" improvement all at once by developing and maintaining a self-learning organization.

Among the most widely used tools for CI is a four-step quality model – the plan-do-check-act (PDCA) developed by Shewhart [5] and enhanced by Deming to the PDSA cycle (plan-do-study-act) [6] through incorporating the idea of deductive and inductive (organizational) learning throughout the process. The PDCA cycle has inspired other, broadly recognized industrial approaches [7] and it keeps evolving [8] to adapt to other industries and organizational maturity levels as well.

In order to address the imminent need of strategic alignment between IT and other departments, the Business Process Management (BPM) approach was developed [9] to control software related process changes. BPM focuses on business operations, as well as key value adding and supporting activities of organizations. BPM integrates several methods and techniques for modelling, analyzing, reorganizing, operating and monitoring the processes of an organization. The BPM lifecycle is widely used in IT related projects and it has a potential to be utilized for process improvement as well [10]. Its stages can well be put in relation with the PDCA cycle, providing a potential for common denominator in projects approach with industrial stakeholders (Table 1).

Table 1. Alignment between the process steps of the business process management lifecycle and the Shewhart cycle

Business process management life cycle	Shewhart cycle
Process documentation	Plan
Process and system analysis	
Implementation and change management	Do
Process operation	
Process controlling and monitoring	Check
Business process strategy	Act

ITIL provides a set of detailed practices for IT service management and focuses on aligning IT services with business needs. Project- and Program management principles commonly used in IT environment, such as PRINCE2 [11] and MSP [12] also provide orientation for change management handling. There is argumentation though, that while they define processes for most relevant information technology related aspects, their governance processes lack the right strategic view for achieving the objectives of the business in the organizations [13, 14]. IT organizational structures, which are tendentially defined by these IT service management frameworks [15] can be an obstacle in efficient engagement with the business stakeholders.

Relevance. To respond adequately to Industry 4.0 challenges, a cross departmental evaluation of opportunities and rethinking of processes is necessary in the enterprises – and beyond. Larger integration of production machinery and other systems requires collaboration between IT and other departments even on areas, which were previously no common domains. While striving for more efficient collaboration within departments should be a constant effort, the current momentum created by Industry 4.0 could be leveraged by the IT departments to rethink their approach for better alignment and conclusively more value add collaboration with the business stakeholders. When successful, IT departments will not only be able to co-create the transition of production operations into the new era while keeping their services structured on high level and quality, but more generally, they will be able to maintain their position as key value creator in the organizations. Establishing an improved way for Change Request management may just be the right first step.

3.2 Integration with Business Process Management

As mentioned above, the BPM life cycle approach aligned with the company's CI structure is sufficient for a common denominator with the business stakeholders on change management. In this chapter we will expand the theoretic basis with IT change relevant aspects to define a conceptual model which will be referred to later.

We use the model described by Gabor et al. [16] to demonstrate the integration of the IT Change Request processing in an overall BPM model. Our key statement is that an IT change can only be successful, if the related organizational, process and data changes are handled simultaneously in an integrated way. This way the automatism delivered is embedded and can be operated on the required quality level. Many actual cases demonstrate the devastating consequence of not developing to enable the IT technology change when it is delivered (Fig. 1).

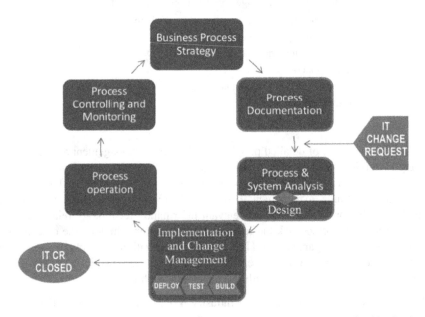

Fig. 1. Business process management circle by Gabor et al [16], enhanced with IT change management components based on ITIL [2]

In general, we argue, that the BPM model needs to be completed by a decision making point, since in an organization not all alteration to the process are approved consciously or practically. We locate the decision making point between analysis of the change requirement and detailed design. The decision making point is the final approving authority for the Change Requests (a.k.a Change Advisory Board, CAB). Should the CAB decline the realization of a Change Request, so it's processing will be aborted and the Change Request either reassigned for further Analysis or it will be closed altogether.

Furthermore, we made the following extensions to the model to assure an integrated approach:

- Process description must include description of the used IT tools. Appropriate documentation of processes and system use are prerequisites for integrated IT Change Request management. This point will be further discussed in Chap. 5.2.
- IT Change Requests will be included in the loop before the Analyze and Design stage so that they can be included in the following stage.
- Analysis and Design must be made in an integrated way. The decision making point contains the total cost of the Implementation and Change Management: Processes, Data and (IT) Systems.
- Implementation and Change Management will contain the process and data related changes, but this phase also covers (IT) System activities. These are commonly broken up into Build, Test & Accept and Deploy phases.
- Upon successful implementation of the IT CR, it is closed and the process is lived with standard level of supports on Process as well as IT side

3.3 Knowledge Management

Knowledge management is a key element in assuring the sustainability of the implemented process. Experience shows, that processes and related benefits do not get fully realized and/or erode if knowledge management is left to the software training only. Knowledge management drives organizational learning which takes place during the entire Business Process Management lifecycle. A conscious approach to knowledge management improves efficiency of implementation of a change and the maintenance of the result of the change. Our integrated Change Management approach is addressing knowledge management on multiple layers:

- It assumes the existence of a base line: a complete operational map, organizational template and enablement infrastructure (including continuous improvement and lessons learned initiatives) to perform the tasks as defined
- By analyzing the complete impact of a change, adjustment in knowledge is also mapped out and addressed in trainings
- It places the Change Request process into the company's process map, assuring that also this process would benefit from the organizational learning's the company develops.

3.4 Integrated Approach to the Change Elements

IT Change Management is often understood purely in IT context: build new functionality, test, train and deploy. I argue that the approach needs to distinguish between the following domains, and involve impacted business domains. Changes in any of these domains need to be planned and followed up individually in an integrated way. Although they might be achieved in common steps (eg training new process and system usage), they have their specifics. The below categorization distinguishes among those key elements (Table 2).

Table 2. Overview of the change elements

Element	Purpose	Typical content
Organization and process	Definition of business processes and the organizational aspects (e.g. organization structure, roles, skills) to perform the process Embedment of the Change Request process into the process landscape of the organization	• Business process design • Organization hierarchy • Roles and responsibilities • Execution capacity considerations
Data	Data used, referred to, processed or created while performing the process	• Data flow map • Master data, transactional data record • Data taxonomy • Data standards (as applicable)
System	(Information) Technology enablers to perform the process in the designed way. Technology Systems may support or completely take over performing of process steps	• Enterprise architecture • Information Technology architecture • Software functionality • Access rights • Information Security

Our experience shows that the above view is simple yet complete in identifying and combining the key domains impacted by a change in the current digital era and that in its simplicity it helps communicating the approach to any stakeholder organization. The domains may be further broken down though (e.g. People, Organization, Processes within Organization and process; Information Technology, Controls Technology within Systems) if scaling requires. The integrated nature assures a maximization of the benefits expected from the change by (i) reducing collateral damage caused by omitted aspects of interrelated processes; (ii) securing ROI through good control of total cost of the Change implementation; (iii) potentially reducing Systems changes by enabling a business side solution.

4 Description of the Integrated IT Change Request Process

The described integrated IT change request management process model was developed as a trial and implemented in a globally active Tier 1 Automotive supplier.

During the development of the model the frequent scenario was considered, where a new process, task, or data flow is often not possible to test without the readiness of the supporting system. Therefore, from the Phase "Build" onwards the model merges the three elements into one course of action (Fig. 2).

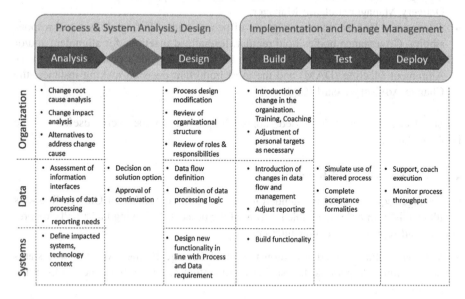

Fig. 2. Integrated IT change request process (own work)

Workshops during the implementation phase indicated that the defined approach is useable with "agile" and with "waterfall" delivery models alike, with little adaptation, although hereto further studies are needed. Due to its role based approach companies of different size and management models can find it applicable.

4.1   Roles and Responsibilities, Governance Bodies

Key enabler of process efficiency as well as knowledge management is the clear and transparent allocation of the roles and responsibilities among the stakeholders. The above Change Request process contains new tasks and assumes new responsibilities, which need to be allocated to assure process sustainability. Due to its integrated nature, there is a broad range of stakeholders needing to input in the process, however their contribution may be timely and content-wise limited. This makes the justification of the creation of new jobs for the purpose of a Change Request challenging and partially disproportional.

Well known management approaches [8] as well as new disciplines [17] suggest to define roles that can be sized and assigned to people (one person can have multiple roles) rather than jobs, in order to make the model universally applicable in different delivery and management methodologies.

- To assure scalability for the implementing organizations, the model uses the role-based approach. In that sense it distinguishes between

- Individual contributor roles, which are embodied by one person or a group of persons with the same skillset, such as Change Requester, Business Relationship Manager, Change Manager, Release Manager, Competence Center (CC) Leader, Delivery Manager, Release Manager.
- Governance Bodies, which are group of people with differing skillset and responsibility. Governance bodies hold regular, formalized meetings for alignment and/or decision making. Governance bodies in the Changer Request process are: Delivery Alignment Meeting (DAM) and the most important decision making instance: the Change Advisory Board (CAB)

These decisions for role based approach proved to be very useful in the implementation.

4.2 Process KPIs and Reporting

Our change request model is intended to manage a large number of Change Requests simultaneously. In order to enable steering of the process, following basic KPIs are predefined and reported in regular intervals:

- Volume evolution trend – demonstration of Change Request volumes per status through multiple periods. It visualizes momentum and identifies bottlenecks in the process
- On Time Delivery (OTD) - The % of changes that are delivered to Test and Acceptance according per plan or earlier. This KPI monitors the throughput reliability of the domains building the solution (process, data, and systems). Bottlenecks can be identified.
- On Time Release (OTR) - process flow KPI demonstrating the reliability of the planning and robustness of all participating organizations in realizing the Change
- First Time Right (FTR) - KPI for quality monitoring of the technical components: % of changes whose technical release was successful for the first attempt

5 Implementing and Maintaining the IT CR Process

The Company, a global Tier 1 automotive supplier headquartered in Winterthur, Switzerland, with worldwide 50+ plants, and more than 12 thousand employees. It operates in four highly independent business units. Information Technology (IT) is a centrally located function, supporting 150+ applications locally, regionally and globally. It services all business groups as well as promotes standardization, in Technology and beyond. In 2015 the Company's management requested IT to expedite standardization both in IT assets as well as in the "way of working". The Company's IT Department decided to implement the here described integrated IT Change Request management model.

5.1 Preparation

After initiation of the project, the model was introduced and the scope and context of the IT Change Request management process was defined. The process was to be up-and-running in 6 months' time.

- Scope: As per management intention, the process had to cover all IT assets, and needed to integrate with the existing Business Process Governance Body.
- Context: the initial study showed that although 100+ people belonged to the global IT organization, there was neither central information for the Change Request volumes and costs, nor structured decision making and planning. Due to lack of prioritization globally, it was uncertain if the IT organization is spending its resources efficiently.

Once the integrated change request model was introduced and approved by the leadership team in the IT community, the concept was carried to the major stakeholders, influencers, and members of the Business Process Governance Body. The IT CR process was strategically placed within the service offering of IT (Fig. 3).

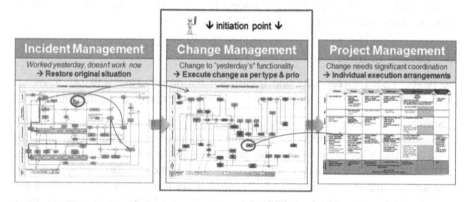

Fig. 3. Service architecture of the IT department (own work)

A Workgroup was created to define the needed categorizations and groupings (e.g. Software-wise, Process categories), define schedule and agenda of the recurrent events and allocate process roles formally. The job of the Workgroup was completed in 12 weeks.

5.2 Implementation

Following positive decision from all stakeholders, the implementation work focused on 3 major tracks:

- Process definition and training of stakeholders. User group focused training courses were developed and delivered to small groups. Trainings were interactive classroom trainings provided in person or on line. Altogether, until the end of the implementation, 67 units of trainings were delivered.

- Establishment of legacy – we intended to start the process with all open Change Requests in one database. This required a large amount of data scouting (finding all registers of change requests, if any existed) and data cleansing to bring the information into the same format. The process started with 138 Change Requests, and by the end of the first 8 weeks the number of CRs were 271.
- Set up the Change Request Management software. Following successful functional tests, agreed categorizations needed to be entered, legacy Change Requests migrated, users created and user rights assigned. The team decided to utilize the already existing, but only partially used Change Management tool.

September 2015 marked the start of the IT Change Request process. In order to manage expectations a 2 months "grace" period was introduced, since it was impossible to simulate organizational reactions to the new process and initial adjustments could have been necessary. Finally, 3 months after the start of use of the Integrated Change Request process, the implementation project was closed with general satisfaction of stakeholders and the management team alike.

As of 2018, the Change Request process is still in use in the Company, with a history of more than 500 open and closed change requests.

5.3   Lessons Learned

The project ended successfully and it enriched the organization with key learnings which can be used to improve the model and the implementation recommendations:

1. Stakeholders provided a very positive feedback on the structure of the Change Request process. It had met a long existing need – this is one of the explanations for the "explosion" of the numbers of the change requests especially in the first months.
2. The role based responsibility approach prove to be the only feasible approach to make sure that the broad range of stakeholders are formally engaged, without the need of new recruitment on those positions. It also helped to engage the most adequate persons for each task – if it was necessary we split roles for this purpose.
3. Training of the user groups revealed that certain underlying clarifications with line management needed to be made. Resistance for change was also a hurdle that the trainers needed to overcome with special skills and support from management.
4. Positive feedback was countered by lack of free capacity on long term during the learning phase, therefore c.a. 60% of the training units needed to be repeated.
5. Process KPIs were very useful to steer the process velocity, as bottlenecks became visible, fact-based countermeasures could be introduced. Due to their similarity with manufacturing operational KPIs, they could be easily understood by non-IT stakeholders as well.
6. CRs implemented according to the model had tendentially a smoother acceptance in the organization. Rework on implemented CR remained low (no historic data from before the model, the statement is based on feedback from the requestors).

7. The actual CRs brought to light that the assumed process base-line in the company is incomplete. A recovery plan was launched outside the IT CR implementation project.
8. Multiple Change Requests did not reach realization phase. The process responsible persons stopped them (in defense of standards) and/or provided a process based solution without need for Software change.
9. The CR process proved to be a good initial filter for Industry 4.0 related projects. It facilitated common thinking and evaluations of the actual value add of a new technology in the organization.

In recognition of the strength of the backbone that the ITCR process provides, and due to the increasing volumes, in 2017 the IT leadership decided to orientate its teams according to the structures of the IT CR process, and created the role of Service Deliver Responsible in each IT sub-department.

5.4 Applicability for Managing Industry 4.0 Related Changes

The same Company initiated its Industry 4.0 thought process in 2016, and as a consequence, in early 2017 the first Industry 4.0 related change requests were registered. Many of the process stakeholders were not aware that the actual change requests were related to Industry 4.0 – their bare recognition was that the requests were not ordinary and they needed a large amount of conceptual considerations as well as process impact was larger than usual.

In case the impact assessment could not be done within a reasonable effort, or the necessary anticipations could not be done as expected, under the phase of Analysis, Proof of Concepts (PoC) were conducted and the result of these were integrated back into the Analysis considerations.

All change requests had been processed according to the process. Change requests with large efforts were categorized projects thus moved outside the Change request process. The remaining Change requests, as of 2018 these were over 20, were processed and delivered in good quality and under control.

In an Industry 4.0 context the IT Change Request process leveraged its thorough integration of organizational and data aspects, and prove to be a solid mean to address the special needs of Industry 4.0 initiatives.

The robust handling model of IT had been recognized by high management of the company, and as a result, IT became a driving force in the Industry 4.0 transformation initiative.

6 Conclusion

A single case study is not sufficient for quantitative conclusions, yet it allows qualitative conclusions that can be indicative for organizational change practitioners and IT departments seeking for improvement in their engagement with the operational stakeholders.

The development of our integrated IT Change Request process started with some basic assumptions, as described in Chap. 2. These assumptions could be validated during the piloting use of the model. Herewith we refer to them:

1. **ASSUMPTION:** Majority of the IT deliverables fail to perform due to improperly prepared organization (users) or changing requirements.
   FINDING: Confirmative. The inclusion of Organizational and Data aspects in the Change Request model, Change Request delivery became more successful and appreciated.
2. **ASSUMPTION:** It is possible to develop a model which manages all elements of a successful organizational change implementation. Such a model can be lead out of the IT Department.
   FINDING: Confirmative. The integrated IT Change Request process covers all domains of organizational change. The model is recognized by all stakeholders. Most important constraint for the Leadership of the model is understanding of requirements of all stakeholders, and seeing the Change Requests as part of a business change. It is even well positioned to build up and lead such a cross-functional model.
3. **ASSUMPTION:** An integrated approach to change management assures operational sustainability and potentially reduces cost of change.
   FINDING: Partially confirmative. The change request process covers all important elements to assure seamless integration. Cost of change went through a perceived reduction, although the total effort the organization needs to invest into Change Management had increased due to the more intensive involvement of other domains ("business side stakeholders"). Through the provided transparency stakeholders and managers see resources spent on Change Requests as "good investment"
4. **ASSUMPTION:** An integrated approach of Systems, Data and Organization should be robust enough to carry business transformation initiatives.
   FINDING: Confirmed. The recent use of the IT Change Request process for Industry 4.0 related initiatives confirmed that the model is capable to manage any kind of organizational changes regardless the proportion of system changed associated. Through this it had also been confirmed, that with the right approach, an IT organization can be a central driving force for Industry 4.0 or Digitalization transformations

The current attention to Industry 4.0 might historically prove to have been a hype. Nevertheless, it is currently reshaping the landscape of intra-organizational collaboration. Some of those changes will institutionalize, especially the impact made by stronger collaboration among traditionally separated specialist domains such as IT, CT (Control Technology of machines) and Production Systems. Conclusively, highly integrated approach to change management, such as the example described in this paper, will remain a key vehicle for sustainable organizational value creation. It also bears the opportunity for IT departments to remain, independently of the respective current trend, in the center of gravity for value creation in operations.

References

1. Henderson, J.C., Venkatraman, N.: Strategic alignment: leveraging information technology for transforming organisations. IBM Syst. J. **32**(1), 4–16 (1993)
2. SMME: ITIL V3 foundation – student manual; Ver 5, pp. 234–272. Leuven (2009)
3. Ohno, T.: Toyota Production System: Beyond Large-Scale Production (English translation ed.), pp. 75–76. Productivity Press, Portland, Oregon (1988). ISBN 0-915299-14-3
4. Womack, J.P., Jones, D.T., Roos, D.: The Machine That Changed the World (1990). ISBN 978-0-7432-9979-4
5. Shewhart, W.A.: Statistical Method from the Viewpoint of Quality Control. Dover Publ., New York (1986). ISBN 0-486-65232-7, S. 45
6. Deming, W.E.: The New Economics for Industry, Government, and Education, p. 132. MIT Press, Boston, Ma (1993). ISBN 0262541165
7. Tennant, G.: SIX SIGMA: SPC and TQM in Manufacturing and Services. Gower Publishing, Ltd, p. 3–4 (2001). ISBN 0-566-08374-4
8. Moen, R., Clifford, N.: Evolution of the PDCA Cycle (PDF). Accessed 12 Feb 2017
9. Scheer, A.-W., Abolhassan, F., Jost, W., Kirchmer, M.: Business Process Excellence - ARIS in Practice. Springer, Heidelberg (2002). http://dx.doi.org/10.1007/978-3-540-24705-0
10. Josic, D.: Kritische Analyse der Prozessoptimierung als wesentliches Element des Change Managements. GRIN Verlag, München (2016)
11. Berry, D., Atkins, W.S., Allen, P.: Managing Successful Projects, pp. 251–291. TSO Publishing, London (1996)
12. Sowden, R. et al.: Managing Successful Programmes, pp. 47–75. TSO Publishing. London (2007)
13. Alonso, I.A., Verdún, J.C., Caro, E.T.: Description of the structure of the IT demand management process framework. Int. J. Inf. Manag. **37**(1), Part A, 1461–1473 (2017)
14. Rahimi, F., Møller, C., Hvam, L.: Business process management and IT management: The missing integration. Int. J. Inf. Manag. **36**(1), 142–154 (2016)
15. Marrone, M., Kolbe, L.: Einfluss von IT-Service-Management-Frameworks auf die IT-Organisation. Wirtschaftsinformatik **53**(1), 5–19 (2011)
16. Gabor, A., Szabo, K.A.: Corporate Knowledge Discovery and Organizational Learning, pp. 6–23. Springer, Heidelberg (2015)
17. Robertson, B., Thomison, T.: "Holacracy – discover a better way of working. White Paper, HolacracyOne, LLC, Spring City, PA, pp. 1–10 (2015)

A Case Study on Modeling and Validating Financial Regulations Using (Semi-) Automated Compliance Framework

Suman Roychoudhury[(⊠)], Sagar Sunkle, Namrata Choudhary,
Deepali Kholkar, and Vinay Kulkarni

Tata Consultancy Services Research, 54B Hadapsar Industrial Estate, Pune, India
{suman.roychoudhury, sagar.sunkle, namrata.choudhary,
deepali.kholkar, vinay.kulkarni}@tcs.com

Abstract. Modern enterprises operate in an unprecedented regulatory environment where increasing regulation and heavy penalties on non-compliance have placed regulatory compliance among the topmost concerns of enterprises worldwide. Previous research in the field of compliance has established that the manual specification/tagging of the regulations not only fails to ensure their proper coverage but also negatively affects the turnaround time both in proving and maintaining the compliance. Our contribution in this paper is a case study using a subset of European Union Regulation in the financial markets, namely, Money Market Statistical Reporting (MMSR) and that we validated it in the context of our model-driven semi-automated compliance framework. The novelty of the framework is the key participation of domain experts to author regulatory rules in a controlled natural language to enable compliance checking. We demonstrate transformation of regulations present in legal natural language text (English) to a model form via authoring of Structured English rules in the context of MMSR regulations for a large European bank. This generated regulatory model is eventually translated to formal logic that enables formal compliance checking contrary to current industry practice, that provides content management-based, document-driven and expert-dependent ways of managing regulatory compliance.

Keywords: Regulatory compliance · Money Market Statistical Reporting
Structured English · Compliance checking

1 Introduction

Modern Enterprises are regulated by stricter norms and regulations that are often present in the form of legal documents, compliance process descriptions and audit reports. A major concern for enterprises arise due to heavy penalties imposed on them due to non-compliance. This has compelled enterprises to place regulatory compliance as a top priority among other challenges. Therefore, to avoid unnecessary penalties and remain compliant with respect to newer regulations, enterprises are increasingly looking towards technologies that may assist them in their overall compliance checking process.

As legal documents captures a major chunk of the regulations that should be processed to facilitate compliance checking, enterprises spent considerable effort to

© IFIP International Federation for Information Processing 2018
Published by Springer Nature Switzerland AG 2018. All Rights Reserved
R. A. Buchmann et al. (Eds.): PoEM 2018, LNBIP 335, pp. 288–302, 2018.
https://doi.org/10.1007/978-3-030-02302-7_18

decipher such enormous volume of legal text, and subsequently build software systems that can assist them in compliance checking. However, the cost of building such systems from scratch is both effort intensive and time consuming. Typical solutions that are prevalent in the industry, known as the governance, risk, and compliance (GRC) offerings, rely on taxonomies, which are collection of predefined tags that can be affixed to data [1] pertinent to the regulations. Taxonomy tagging tools used separately or from within the GRC frameworks, enables auto-population of, and in some cases, user definition of taxonomies [6, 9, 14, 15]. However, GRC based offerings do not provide support for formal compliance checking [20].

On the contrary, significant research literature by academia focuses on checking compliance of business processes and/or enterprise data using a formal specification of the regulatory rules [3, 7, 10]. Such formal representation and subsequent checking of legal rules offers significant merit over existing GRC based frameworks [8]. Therefore our approach towards automated regulatory compliance checking emphasizes on using formal methods and rules specified in formal languages like DR-Prolog [8, 22] and/or DROOLs [13]. However, formal languages have their own drawbacks and it is almost impossible for legal or domain experts to write rules using low-level logic based languages. Therefore, a high-level representation of such rules in a domain-specific language is more desirable, where participation of domain experts is of paramount interest [16]. Therefore, we provide a high-level controlled natural language (CNL) as an abstraction layer on top of the formal specifications to hide the underlying complexities and provide a business friendly English like notation to express regulations. This language is adapted from Structured English [16] and compliant to OMG's Semantic of Business Vocabulary and Rules (SBVR) [12]. However, legal text of regulations that exists in plain English is subject to scrutiny and interpretation by legal/domain experts and may require significant effort on their part to extract out the applicable legal clauses from large volume of English language sentences. Therefore to aid domain experts in authoring regulatory rules using our CNL seamlessly, we provide a machine-learning/natural-language processing (ML-NLP) based front-end engine that extracts the domain model and dictionary (i.e., various terms and concepts) from the regulatory text and provide suggestions to domain experts in their authoring process [17].

Figure 1 motivates the above hypothesis and describes our end-to-end semi-automated compliance framework that has specific human touchpoints (i.e., manual intervention) with tool support (M+T) at certain parts, while others being fully automated (T). The framework assumes precise interpretation of regulations already available with enterprise in the form of natural language (NL) legal text. Using machine-learning/distributional semantics techniques a domain model (refer to number [1] in Fig. 1) is first obtained by processing the given text with active participation by the domain expert [19]. The domain model primarily captures the keys concepts, relations and their mentions (i.e., ontology) in the given domain and serves as a core artefact for model authoring. For model authoring, the domain expert expresses the desired regulations in a controlled natural language (refer to number [2] in Fig. 1) using the domain model/dictionary and rule suggestions originating from the ML-NLP engine [16, 17]. In our case, this language was built from scratch using the XTexT language engineering workbench [4] and adapted from OMG's SBVR Structured English (SE) specification [16]. Once regulatory rules are authored in SE, a model of the regulation in SBVR is

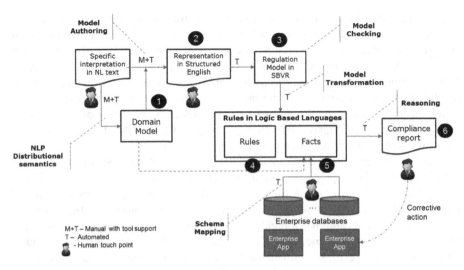

Fig. 1. Overview of automated compliance framework

automatically generated (refer to number [3] in Fig. 1) that serves as an intermediate representation for translating to low-level logical specifications (e.g., DROOLs, refer to number [4] in Fig. 1). The SBVR model is also used for obtaining suitable data facts (refer to number [5] in Fig. 1) from the enterprise databases (DBs), necessary for compliance checking [8]. A DB expert maps the suitable data model obtained from SBVR with the database schema already available with the enterprise. Finally, rules are applied to the populated fact base to generate a compliance report (refer to number [6] in Fig. 1) amenable for human understanding and suitable corrective action, if any.

The remaining parts of the paper is organized as follows. Section II of the paper describes our case study in detail with respect to a regulation from the financial domain, while section III discusses the results from the case study. Section III also provides valuable feedback and comparison of our framework with prevalent industry practice, before we conclude in section IV.

2   Case Study – Financial Regulations

In this section we introduce Money Market Statistical Reporting (MMSR) as our base case and describe in detail each of steps as outlined in Fig. 1. MMSR is a reporting regulation in the European Union involving the money markets and is regulated by the European Central Bank (ECB). All financial institutions, namely banks are mandated to report their daily transactions to ECB as prescribed by the MMSR regulatory document [11]. A leading European bank (one of our customers) was interested in validating our framework using MMSR, as test data[1] for MMSR was already available. In addition, the regulation was well understood by the bank, hence validation would be precise.

---

[1] Sample data is currently used due to GDPR restrictions.

Therefore, it was mutually agreed to do a pilot case study using MMSR as a litmus test of our framework.

A MMSR regulation typically consists of four different sections pertinent to money market, namely, secured market, unsecured market, FX swaps and overnight index swaps [11]. The structure and nature of regulations in all the four sections are similar, therefore modeling and validating one section will give a fairly good idea about validating other sections as well. For our case study, we chose secured market (Sect. 3) of MMSR, which captures the conceptual and field definitions of various variables that must be reported by individual banks to ECB. Overall, there are 24 such variables defined in Sect. 3 of MMSR [11], with each variable having their own conceptual definition and field definition. Conceptual definition pertains to the underlying semantics of the variable, while field definition pertains to how the variable should be constructed structurally. With this background, we would demonstrate how our auto-compliance framework can be used to model and validate regulations referring to secured market by traversing each of the six steps (numbered 1–6) as described in Fig. 1. We begin with Step 1, domain model construction.

2.1 Domain Model Construction

This is a human assisted step with tool support [19] (refer to number [1] in Fig. 1). Figure 2 shows a snapshot of the domain model generator (DMG). The input to the DMG is the set of MMSR regulations as defined in natural language text. Here, the toolset helps the domain expert to unearth the important concepts, relationships and their mentions in the underlying text. The domain expert provides the seed concept, i.e., entity types and relations immediately available from the definitions section of the legal NL text. The DMG uses two techniques to retrieve other mentions of seed entity types as well as relations between all entity types [21].

The first technique that the generator uses is based on context-based clustering. The idea behind this technique is that the contexts, i.e., spans of texts, around the mentions of various domain entities (e.g., *central bank, maturity date, transaction status, currency*) are important and could be clustered to extract useful information from the text. We cluster the contexts, i.e., n characters to the left and right of mentions of each entity type so far known and then cluster these to suggest to the domain expert, what looks like other possible mentions [21].

The second technique that the generator uses is based on open information extraction to discover relations between the known entity types. We input Ollie with sentences and extract relations. We try to match mentions of known entity types in the subject and object of each relation (see top half of Fig. 2). The dictionary is automatically build as shown in the bottom half of Fig. 2, while the domain model captures the complete set of concepts and their relationship (RHS of Fig. 2).For MMSR Sect. 3, the DMG captured 55 core concepts, 201 mentions (i.e., 4 mention on an average for every concept) and 49 relations. Thus, the domain model serves as an ontology for the domain expert and aids her to author rules in Structured English as described in the following step.

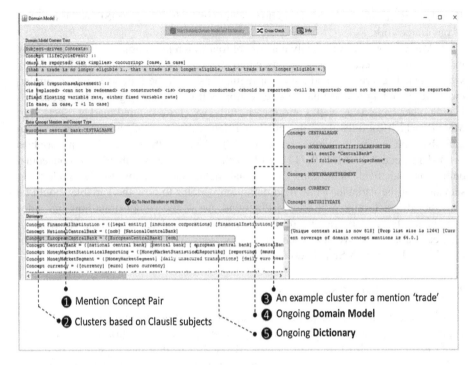

Fig. 2. Domain model generation

2.2 Rule Authoring Phase

This is a human assisted step with appropriate language support [16] (refer to number [2] in Fig. 1). In this phase the domain expert authors regulations using one form of Controlled Natural Language (CNL), which is called Structured English (SE) whose initial description appeared in OMG SBVR specification (Appendix C) [12]. The main motive behind OMG SE is to provide a business vocabulary for capturing business rules in simplified natural English in textual format. We had to adapt the language to remove some of the ambiguities from SE whose detail description is available in [16]. SE contains concepts like *general terms, individual terms, facts, verbs, quantification, modality, quantifiers* and *rules*. The English like semantics of SE makes it amenable for domain experts to specify rules at a level of abstraction appropriate to them (described in Fig. 3).

The SE editor is divided into 4 parts – *vocabulary editor* for capturing concepts, definitions, synonyms etc., the *fact editor* for relating terms or concepts in the underlying domain using verbs [16]. We use two kinds of verbs - *object* verbs for relating binary terms and *data* verbs for relating unary terms (also known as characteristics). Finally, facts are expanded by adding *implications, modality, quantification* and *qualification* to form rules. Rules are the final product that domain experts author in the *rules editor* from their natural language representations (see Fig. 3). Rules can contain any number of valid facts that are checked and validated by the error handler.

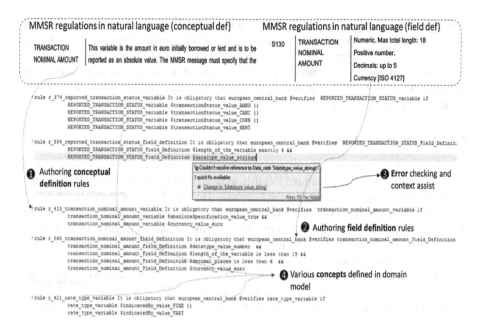

Fig. 3. Rule authoring phase

For our MMSR case study, 48 rules in Structured English were authored for each of the 24 variables belonging to either of the two categories from secured market segment, namely conceptual definition and field definition. A snapshot of the authored rules is shown in Fig. 3. The NL text of regulations for a given variable (e.g., *transaction nominal amount*) as present in MMSR specification [11] is shown the top half of the figure. The SE *rule editor* shows how the given NL text is correspondingly authored (see rule *r_415*, etc.) by the domain expert using the domain model already obtained in step 1. The SE rules are self- explanatory and easy to comprehend and author.

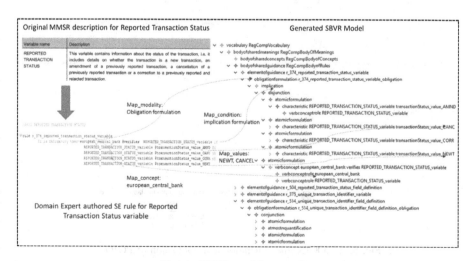

Fig. 4. SBVR model generation

Typically, rules are conjuncted and/or disjuncted by facts in an implication (conditional) statement and contains an antecedent and a consequent. Rules could be further quantified using quantifiers (e.g., *is less than 6*) as shown in Fig. 3. The SE language editor also supports error handling capabilities in the form of syntactic and/or consistency checks that may occur during the authoring phase and provides assistance for context-assist as shown in Fig. 3.

2.3   SBVR Model Generation

This is a complete automated step (refer to number [3] in Fig. 1). As domain experts author regulatory rules in Structured English, a corresponding SBVR model of the textual representation is generated in the background. This model is an instance of SBVR metamodel as given by OMG specification [12, 17]. This intermediate regulatory model is language and platform independent and can be translated to any target formal language (i.e., not tied to a particular one), which provides the execution platform. Further, domain experts are completely oblivious of this intermediate step, which is primarily used for various purposes, like consistency/model checking and also translating SE to DROOLs and/or DR-Prolog executable specifications. We chose SBVR as our desired choice of intermediate modelling language, specifically because SBVR is an "industry" standard

Fig. 5. DROOLs rule generation and population of POJOs

and comes with rich semantics for capturing business vocabularies and rules [11], which is ideally suited for capturing the semantics and vocabulary of regulations.

Figure 4 describes how this translation to SBVR model is realized from SE. The figure shows the original regulation information about a particular variable (i.e., *reported transaction status*) in its natural language form as present in MMSR specification [11]. Corresponding authored rule in SE is shown in bottom right of the figure. Generated SBVR model (snippet) is shown in the RHS of the figure and the dotted arrows depicts how the mapping from SE to SBVR is realized in the translator. For example, *modality* in SE is realized as *obligationformulation* in SBVR, *concepts* are realized as *verbconceptrole*, condition ("if" statement) is mapped to *implication*, *data verbs* are mapped to *characteristics*, and their *values* are mapped to *characteristic values*. Creating this SBVR model by hand is an enormous effort and statistics revealed for 48 rules authored for 24 secured market segment variables in SE, 1076 model elements were generated. This again proves the usefulness of SE, as domain experts can work at a higher level of abstraction instead of being knowledgeable about the low level details of underlying SBVR model, which is primarily required for translation to executable logical specification, inter-operability with other SBVR based tools and internal consistency or model checking of the authored rules etc.

2.4   Rules and Fact Generation

This is a fully automated step, except for schema mapping which is human assisted (see steps 4 and 5 in Fig. 1). The generated SBVR model serves as an intermediary representation that is translated to low-level logical specifications for reasoning by inferencing engines like DROOLs [13] or DR-Prolog [22]. Our framework currently supports translation to both DROOLs and DR-Prolog but can be easily extended to

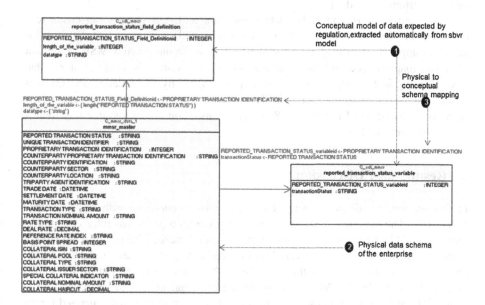

Fig. 6. Conceptual to enterprise schema mapping

support any other reasoning engine. The choice of which execution engine to be used is based on the nature of reasoning/computation required. For example, if defeasible reasoning is required to resolve conflict in modalities among rules (e.g., *obligation* vs *necessity*), then DR-Prolog is a superior choice, while DROOLs provides more fine grained Java API support for regulations that require computation. Since MMSR regulations generally require procedural computation, we chose DROOLs as our primary execution engine. As seen in Fig. 4, each SBVR model rule element (i.e., *elementofguidance*) is formed of an expression of type *implication* having an antecedent and a consequent part. At a generic level, we translate a SBVR rule to a corresponding DROOLs rule specification by mapping each antecedent with the *when* clause and each consequent with the *then* clause in DROOLs. For example, in Fig. 5, one can observe how a generated DROOLs rule for a given MMSR variable (i.e., *reported transaction status*) is translated with suitable evaluation operators. The antecedent for the *reported transaction status* variable is evaluated in the *when* part of the rule while the consequent is evaluated in the *then* part.

In addition to rule generation, one also needs data to check against the generated rules. Data typically resides in multiple physical databases (DBs) or data warehouses in an enterprise. Therefore data required for compliance checking against a particular regulation needs to be extracted from the enterprise DBs. The intermediate SBVR model here also aids the DB expert to derive a conceptual data model (i.e., data required for checking) which is then mapped against the enterprise schema. The source conceptual data model is automatically derived by inferring the leaf level nodes from the SBVR model [8]. For MMSR regulation, 49 tables were derived from the SVBR model as part of the conceptual schema. Each table typically pertains to a MMSR variable definition or field definition as seen in Fig. 6. Note, there are 24 variable definitions and 24 field definitions that corresponds to 48 derived tables and 1 master table containing ECB data.

Using our in-house enterprise data integration tool, DB experts can create relationship and mappings between the source (conceptual) and target (enterprise) schemas. A snippet of such mapping is shown in Fig. 6 for the given MMSR regulation. Once this mapping is established, suitable *select* queries are generated to pull out data from the physical enterprise DBs and populate facts by instantiating POJOs with suitable values as present in each MMSR transactions (sample dataset). An example of such an instantiation of POJOs for *Reported Transaction Status* variable is shown in the bottom right of Fig. 5.

3 Results and Discussion

In this section, we discuss the results of compliance checking with respect to our framework. The sample dataset used for testing the auto generated rules contains 90 records of MMSR transaction with respect to secured market. Each of this 90 records contains values pertaining to 24 variables of secured market segment that needed to be checked for compliance with the regulations that were authored during the earlier phases. An example of a MMSR message can be found in [11] in pg. 63 and 65 of Annex VII. We begin with describing the compliance report that was generated for the given regulation (Sect. 3 of MMSR) and dataset.

3.1 Compliance Report

Figures 7 and 8 shows the output of compliance checking with respect to the given dataset (refer to number [6] in Fig. 1). As explained in Section II, we had already obtained the rules in DROOLs executable specification and data facts in the form of POJOs (Fig. 5). The generated DROOLs rules are stored in the *Production Memory* and the facts that the Reasoning Engine matches against are stored in the *Working Memory*. The process begins by propagating facts from the working memory and asserting their values against all rules in production memory. Therefore each of the 90 facts were asserted against the 48 rules that were generated earlier and their result is shown in the form of a graphical output (snippet) as seen in Figs. 7 and 8. The graph of Fig. 7 shows the number of rule/fact pair that were successfully fired by the DROOLs engine while the graph of Fig. 8 shows the rule/fact pair that were not fired. For example out of the 90 given facts *rule r_440* was successfully fired 85 times, while it failed to fire 5 times. Similarly all the facts relating to variable *deal rate* (rule ID: r_422) were successfully fired. For unsuccessful facts (i.e. facts that did not satisfy the regulation), one can navigate through the graph down to the exact cause of error. The rule IDs that are preserved from rule authoring stage (Fig. 3) to SVBR model generation (Fig. 4) to DROOLs code generation (Fig. 5) stage help us to realize traceability

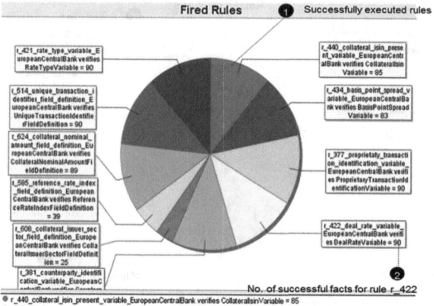

- r_440_collateral_isin_present_variable_EuropeanCentralBank verifies CollateralsinVariable = 85
- r_434_basis_point_spread_variable_EuropeanCentralBank verifies BasisPointSpreadVariable = 83
- r_377_proprietaty_transaction_identification_variable_EuropeanCentralBank verifies ProprietaryTransactionIdentificationVariable = 90
- r_422_deal_rate_variable_EuropeanCentralBank verifies DealRateVariable = 90
- r_381_counterparty_identification_variable_EuropeanCentralBank verifies CounterpartyIdentificationVariable = 90
- r_608_collateral_issuer_sector_field_definition_EuropeanCentralBank verifies CollateralIssuerSectorFieldDefinition = 25
- r_585_reference_rate_index_field_definition_EuropeanCentralBank verifies ReferenceRateIndexFieldDefinition = 39
- r_624_collateral_nominal_amount_field_definition_EuropeanCentralBank verifies CollateralNominalAmountFieldDefinition = 89
- r_514_unique_transaction_identifier_field_definition_EuropeanCentralBank verifies UniqueTransactionIdentifierFieldDefinition = 90
- r_421_rate_type_variable_EuropeanCentralBank verifies RateTypeVariable = 90

Fig. 7. Compliance report (Success rules)

in case of errors. Therefore whenever a fact is not fired, one can traverse back to SE or to the actual text of regulation in NL and obtain a formal proof of compliance or non-compliance. For our case study with 90 sample facts and 48 rules for secured market segment, the results thus obtained were 100% accurate.

3.2   MMSR Statistics

As shown in Fig. 1 the entire process of compliance checking began by processing NL text of MMSR regulations (*secured market*) [11], thereby obtaining the domain model, followed by rule authoring in Structured English followed by a series of text-to-model/model-to-text transformations along with fact population and compliance report generation. In each of these steps there have been a significant automation involved that raises the level of abstraction from low-level formal rule specification to a high-level Controlled Natural Language based rule authoring without losing traceability or specificity. However the approach is firmly grounded in formal methods and provides accurate, sound and consistent results. The following statistics will highlight some of the benefits of our approach against pure manual or tagging based implementation. In order to model secured market segment regulations in MMSR, we encountered 24 variables that either captured their conceptual or field definitions.

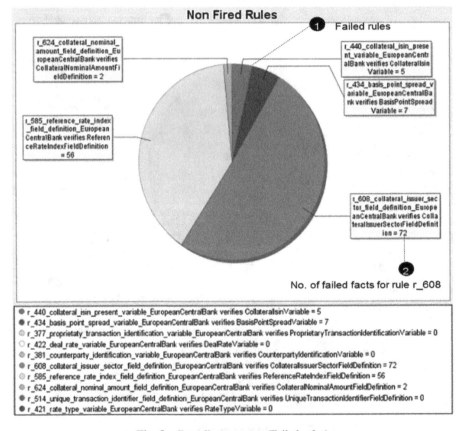

Fig. 8. Compliance report (Failed rules)

We authored 48 rules in Structured English covering all the 24 variables with the help of the domain model that captured mentions and relationships pertaining to these variables. From here on, the next chain of transformations were fully automated. We generated the SBVR model from SE rules that consisted of 582 *Terms*, 112 *Atomic Formulations*, 184 *verb concept roles*, 43 *conjunctions/disjunctions* and 62 *characteristics*. Overall, the SVBR model consisted of more than 1000 model elements which would have taken a considerable amount of time and effort to create manually, yet difficult to comprehend by a domain (human) expert. Thus, abstracting SE over SBVR gave domain experts sufficient gain in comprehensibility, yet they remained oblivious to the underlying modelling details.

Next, we automatically generated the conceptual data model (DDL) from SBVR, that consisted of 49 *tables* with 181 columns and 97 *select* queries. This served as a basis of mapping enterprise schema to the conceptual schema by a DB expert, which is required to populate the 90 data facts into suitable POJOs. Finally, using the SBVR model and mapped schemas, the framework automatically generated the DROOLs code base consisting of 497 LOC of rules specification, 2757 LOC of POJO classes and 25758 LOC of populated java objects. Quite clearly, as DROOLs code base generation was fully automated except schema mapping, it gave an order of magnitude savings in both time and effort w.r.t constructing them manually. Instead, using the compliance framework, all that the domain expert had to do was to author those 48 MMSR rules in Structured English, which was anyway much easier to comprehend and author. Nevertheless, without compromising on accuracy, the framework preserved complete traceability from any part of the tool chain to another to locate exact cause of error or inconsistency in case of non-compliance of data facts. The compliance report thus generated against the sample test dataset were accurate to the extent of 100%.

3.3   Comparison with Current State-of-Practice

The current state-of-practice in compliance checking can be categorized along three dimensions. The first dimension offers solutions in the form of governance, risk and compliance frameworks (GRC) [9]. However GRC based offerings mostly provide content management-based, document-driven and expert-dependent ways of managing regulatory compliance. They are usually semi-formal and are not as rigorous as formal approaches to compliance checking. Such techniques typically rely on tagging important concepts present in the regulations to data available in the enterprise. Such tags are generally incomplete, expert driven and lack in providing formal proof of compliance. On the contrary our approach towards compliance checking is built on the basis of formal compliance checking that offers several analysis benefits as described in [3, 7, 10], thereby reducing the burden on domain experts towards accurately covering all aspects of a regulation. Nevertheless, the domain experts are oblivious of the underlying formal techniques and operates at a level of abstraction that is closer to natural language (i.e., in the form of Structured English).

The second category of industry practice solutions is based on ETL-based queries [18] that are typically data-driven leveraging IT experts to encode SQL queries specific to regulations directly in the enterprise schemas. These queries are then executed on the enterprise data and suitable compliance reports are generated. However, such an approach fails to leverage the knowledge of domain experts in encoding regulations, instead heavily relies on IT experts to acquire the knowledge from domain experts and fill the gap to accurately encode all parts of the regulation. This gap in knowledge between the domain and IT/DB experts can often lead to incorrectly interpreting or encoding the regulations into undesired queries resulting in inaccurate reporting. Our framework on the other hand is *non-intrusive* and provides human touch points for both domain experts in rule authoring and IT experts in schema mapping, thereby bridging the gap between them but still leveraging their respective knowledge.

The third category of industry based practice do employs NLP/ML techniques to process legal NL text [5], but do not derive SE rules (as in our approach), or an SBVR model or formal logical specification like DROOLs or DR-Prolog. These machine learning based approaches on the other hand have primarily focused on classifying the sentences/paragraphs from the legal texts into different kinds of provisions as in [2, 5], with underlying learning techniques that require training sets labelled by the domain expert, which is a cost and time intensive effort. These approaches stand in contrast to our own use of active learning, a semi-supervised machine learning technique, for rule identification based on the features engineered from the domain model and the dictionary, which we detailed in [19].

4 Conclusion

In this paper, we described a model-driven framework for semi-automatic compliance checking through a series of transformations (i.e., NL → SE → SBVR → DROOLs) involving interactive human touch points. We provided a detailed case study in validating the framework using a subset of European Union Regulation in the financial markets, namely, Money Market Statistical Reporting. The novelty of the framework was the key involvement and participation of domain-experts to author regulations in a Controlled Natural Language at an appropriate level of abstraction, while the generated formal specifications and mapping to enterprise data were managed by IT experts. This allowed better coordination for enacting compliance between domain and IT experts. In comparison to other industry based practices, our framework is built on the foundation of formal compliance checking and considerably reduced time and effort (via automation and as observed in the pilot case study) required by an enterprise to accomplish compliance checking without losing soundness, consistency or accuracy in terms of the desired result. As part of future work, we would be exploring how the framework can cater to rule changes and how to manage scalability issues with respect to validating high volume of regulatory data more effectively.

References

1. AvePoint: AvePoint compliance guardian product brochure (2014). http://www.avepoint.com/assets/pdf/Compliance_Guardian_product_brochure.pdf
2. Awad, A., Decker, G., Weske, M.: Efficient compliance checking using BPMN-Q and temporal logic. In: Dumas, M., Reichert, M., Shan, M.-C. (eds.) BPM 2008. LNCS, vol.

5240, pp. 326–341. Springer, Heidelberg (2008). https://doi.org/10.1007/978-3-540-85758-7_24

3. Becker, J., Delfmann, P., Eggert, M., Schwittay, S.: Generalizability and applicability of model based business process compliance-checking approaches—a state-of-the-art analysis and research roadmap. BuR—Bus. Res. **5**(2), 221–247 (2012)

4. Bettini, L.: Implementing Domain-Specific Languages with Xtext and Xtend. Packt Publishing (2013). ISBN: 1782160302 9781782160304

5. Boella, G., Janssen, M., Hulstijn, J., Humphreys, L., van der Torre, L.: Managing legal interpretation in regulatory compliance. In: Francesconi, E., Verheij, B. (eds.) International Conference on Artificial Intelligence and Law, ICAIL 2013, Rome, Italy, June 10–14, 2013, pp. 23–32. ACM (2013). https://doi.org/10.1145/2514601:2514605

6. Cau, D.: Governance, risk and compliance software business needs and market trends (2014)

7. Kharbili, M.E., de Medeiros, A.K.A., Stein, S., van der Aalst, W.M.P.: Business process compliance checking: current state and future challenges. MobIS. LNI, **141**, 107–113. GI (2008)

8. Kholkar, D., Sunkle, S., Kulkarni, V.: Towards Automated Generation of Regulation Rule Bases Using mda. In: MODELSWARD, pp. 617–628 (2017)

9. KPMG: A good offense is the best defense: managing regulatory compliance with GRC whitepaper (2012)

10. Ly, L.T., Maggi, F.M., Montali, M., Rinderle-Ma, S., van der Aalst, W.M.P.: A framework for the systematic comparison and evaluation of compliance monitoring approaches. In: Gasevic, D., Hatala, M., Nezhad, H.R.M., Reichert, M. (eds.) 17th IEEE International Enterprise Distributed Object Computing Conference, EDOC 2013, Vancouver, BC, Canada, September 9–13, pp. 7–16 (2013)

11. Money Market Statistical Reporting - ECB - Europa EU. https://www.ecb.europa.eu/stats/money/mmss/shared/files/MMSR-Reporting_instructions.pdf

12. OMG: Semantics of business vocabulary and business rules (SBVR), v1.3 (2015)

13. Proctor, M.: Drools: a rule engine for complex event processing. In: Schürr, A., Varró, D., Varró, G. (eds.) AGTIVE 2011. LNCS, vol. 7233, p. 2. Springer, Heidelberg (2012). https://doi.org/10.1007/978-3-642-34176-2_2

14. Racz, N., Weippl, E., Seufert, A.: Governance, risk & compliance (GRC) software - an exploratory study of software vendor and market research perspectives. In: 44th Hawaii International Conference on System Sciences, pp. 1–10. IEEE Computer Society, Washington, DC, USA (2011)

15. Racz, N., Weippl, E.R., Bonazzi, R.: IT Governance, risk & compliance (GRC) status quo and integration: an explorative industry case study. In: SERVICES 2011, USA, July 4–9, 2011, pp. 429–436. IEEE Computer Society (2011)

16. Roychoudhury, S., Sunkle, S., Kholkar, D., Kulkarni, V.: A domain-specific controlled english language for automated regulatory compliance (Industrial Paper). In: Proceedings of 2017 ACM SIGPLAN International Conference on Software Language Engineering (SLE 2017), Vancouver, BC, Canada. https://doi.org/10.1145/3136014.3136018

17. Roychoudhury, S., Sunkle, S., Kholkar, D., Kulkarni, V.: From natural language to SBVR model authoring using structured english for compliance checking. In: Proceedings IEEE Enterprise Distributed Object Computing (EDOC 2017), Quebec, Canada (2017)

18. Simitsis, A., Vassiliadis, P., Sellis, T.: Optimizing ETL processes in data warehouses. In: 21st International Conference on Data Engineering (ICDE 2005), pp. 564–575 (2005). https://doi.org/10.1109/icde.2005.103

19. Sunkle, S., Kholkar, D., Kulkarni, V.: Informed active learning to aid domain experts in modeling compliance. In: 2017 IEEE Enterprise Distributed Object Computing (EDOC) 2016, pp. 1–10, Vienna, Austria (2016)

20. Sunkle, S., Kholkar, D., Kulkarni, V.: Toward better mapping between regulations and operations of enterprises using vocabularies and semantic similarity. CSIMQ **5**, 39–60 (2015)
21. Sunkle, S., Kholkar, D., Kulkarni, V.: Comparison and synergy between fact-orientation and relation extraction for domain model generation in regulatory compliance. In: Comyn-Wattiau, I., Tanaka, K., Song, I.-Y., Yamamoto, S., Saeki, M. (eds.) ER 2016. LNCS, vol. 9974, pp. 381–395. Springer, Cham (2016). https://doi.org/10.1007/978-3-319-46397-1_29
22. Antoniou, G., Bikakis, A.: DR-Prolog: a system for defeasible reasoning with rules and ontologies on the semantic web. IEEE Trans. Knowl. Data Eng. **19**(2) (2007). https://doi.org/10.1109/tkde.2007.29

Enterprise Modeling at the Work System Level: Evidence from Four Cases at DHL Express Europe

Thomas Köhler[1](✉), Steven Alter[2], and Brian H. Cameron[3]

[1] DHL Global Management GmbH, Fritz-Erler-Str. 5, 53113 Bonn, Germany
thomas.koehler@dhl.com
[2] University of San Francisco, 2130 Fulton Street, San Francisco,
CA 94117, USA
[3] The Pennsylvania State University, University Park, PA 16802, USA

Abstract. Enterprise Architecture is the process of translating business vision into strategy. Hence, Enterprise Modeling is the process of translating an organization's strategic intent into mandated socio-technological innovation projects required to reach an agreed future state of the firm's operation.

This paper uses four longitudinal case studies at DHL Express Europe to introduce a significant paradigm shift to modeling of the enterprise at the work system level as an abstract representation of the desired future state of the enterprise. This representation specifies in full the business capabilities serving current and future customer needs and the work system configuration enhancements needed to satisfy the customer needs. The associated project has four p steps: (1) Assessment of Status Quo, (2) Agreeing on the desired End-State, (3) Evolution of legacy work-systems, (4) Removal of Obsolete components. This process model explicitly includes the necessity to search for, address and remove all strategic, financial, operational and technical legacy issues identified during the baseline of the status quo. Enterprise Architects should be embedded in each implementation project for Project Assurance purposes in order to monitor the delivery of the agreed end-state.

Keywords: Enterprise modeling · Work system · Work system framework

1 Need for New Approaches to Enterprise Modeling

EM methods and tools are like lenses in that they focus on and clarify some topics and issues while downplaying or ignoring others. A general challenge for any lens for EM is apparent from the range of topics and issues often associated with enterprise models and enterprise modelling: rigour AND agility AND business architecture AND IT architecture AND information AND systematic and integrated change AND sense making AND communication between stakeholders AND model deployment and activation AND standardization AND documentation.

Adding a further challenge, a recent article in BISE by widely recognized leaders in the enterprise modeling (EM) community (Sandkuhl et al. 2018) proposes a vision for extending the reach of EM, saying that "EM addresses the systematic analysis and

© IFIP International Federation for Information Processing 2018
Published by Springer Nature Switzerland AG 2018. All Rights Reserved
R. A. Buchmann et al. (Eds.): PoEM 2018, LNBIP 335, pp. 303–318, 2018.
https://doi.org/10.1007/978-3-030-02302-7_19

modeling of processes, organization and product structures, IT-systems and any other perspective relevant for the modeling purpose (Vernadat 1996)." ... "EM is driven primarily by architects and is valued primarily by IT people so that its effects are often limited to these groups. EM thus appears to be an elitist discipline." A straightforward remedy would be lightweight EM approaches that do not focus on traditional EM qualities like completeness and coherence but on usefulness and impact. "Such approaches would need to support not only architects and corporate IT, but also organizational stakeholders that might benefit from improved models". (p. 71)

An Existing Lightweight Approach. Many aspects of Sandkuhl et al. (2018) call for something like an existing lightweight approach whose initial version was described over two decades ago in a paper called "How should business professionals analyze information systems for themselves?" (Alter 1995). Applications of that approach were reported in a paper (Truex et al. 2010) called "Systems Analysis for Everyone Else: Empowering Business Professionals through a Systems Analysis Method that Fits Their Needs." That paper describes how 75 working business professionals with extensive business experience used a systems analysis template in MBA assignments that called for analyzing IT-reliant work systems in their organizations and recommending improvements. This paper explains the successful practice of EM based worksystem theory and method (WST, WSM respectively). The paper further provides a stepwise approach as proposed by by Sandkuhl et al. (2018). Similar abitions prevailed during the history of WST and WSM. These ambitions intended on providing an organized approach that helps business professionals analyse and understand work systems across enterprises.

The Rational of Linking WST/WSM and Enterprise Modeling. Although Bock et al. (2014) included WST along with Archimate, DEMO, and MEMO in its comparison of four enterprise modeling approaches, to date WST/WSM generally has not been viewed as part of the EM discourse because WST/WSM focuses explicitly on analyzing and designing work systems, a conceptual lens that is not widely recognized in the EM community. It could be used for EM, however, because any given enterprise can be viewed as consisting of multiple work systems that can be analyzed and designed using WST/WSM. Models created to date by using WST/WSM have been more informal than models produced by using more formalized EM approaches such as BPMN, Archimate, MEMO, and DEMO. In contrast with the fundamentals of formal modeling languages in Karagiannis and Kühn (2002) and Bork and Fill (2014), (e.g. modeling language, modeling procedure, and mechanisms and algorithms), WST/WSM defines many terms carefully but currently does not have a formal language with defined syntax and notation.

Goal and Organization. This practice-oriented paper uses four examples from DHL to illustrate how WST/WSM has been used as an enterprise modelling approach. Illustrating its use in practice demonstrates that an approach that has been used in academic settings by many hundreds of MBA and Executive MBA students producing management briefings about improving work systems also can be incorporated into enterprise level projects. The next section summarizes a work system approach to enterprise modelling. Four cases from DHL Express Europe illustrate how ideas from

WST/WSM proved effective in enterprise modelling efforts that played important roles in major projects. A final section on conclusions and implications for practice shows how

2 A Work System Approach to Enterprise Modeling

The core of WST/WSM is the assumption that the topic at hand is a work system and that work systems can be understood, analysed, and designed using WST. The three comonents of WST – the definition of work system, the work system framework, and work system life cycle model were designed to be straightforward enough to avoid seeming overwhelming to business professionals and researchers who need to think about a work system in an organization but do not need level of detail approaching detailed requirements for software development. This section provides summarizes WST and WSM, both of which have been presented many ties. The next section explains how those ideas were applied in four EM case examples at DHL.

Definition of Work System. A work system is defined as a system in which human participants and machines perform processes and activities using information, technology, and other resources to produce product/services for internal and external customers. A work system operates within an environment that matters (e.g., national and organizational cultures, policies, history, competitive situation, demographics, technological change, other stakeholders, and so on). Work systems rely on human, informational, and technical infrastructure that is shared with other work systems. Work systems should support enterprise and departmental strategies. The definition of work system was crafted to make it clear that work system is a very general case that includes many special cases such as information systems, supply chains, service systems, projects, and totally automated work systems. An information system is a working system all of whose activities are devoted to capturing, storing, retrieving, transmitting, manipulating, and displaying information.

   The work system framework outlines elements of even a rudimentary understanding of a work system's form, function, and environment as the work system exists during a time interval when its structure is basically stable. In other words the work system is retaining its identity even as minor incremental changes may occur, such as inconsequential personnel substitutions or minor technology upgrades. Placing emphasis on business rather than IT concerns, the work system framework covers situations that might not have a well-defined business process and might not be IT-intensive. Processes and activities, participants, information, and technologies are viewed as completely within the work system. Customers and product/services may be partially inside and partially outside because customers often participate in work systems. Figure 1 presents a version of the work system framework that was modified to incorporate DHL terminology.

Work System Method. WSM is a flexible systems analysis and design method that was developed over several decades to help business professionals visualize work systems in their organizations and collaborate more effectively with IT professionals. To date, almost all students who used WSM did so through work system analysis templates that outlined an organized way to proceed from describing aspects of a work system's structure and performance toward producing a preliminary recommendation about how to improve the work system. Applications of WST in teaching have used various versions of WSM that all embody the same "way of working" individually or in collaboration with business stakeholders and IT professionals:

(1) identify the smallest work system that has the problem or opportunity;
(2) summarize the "as-is" work system using a work system snapshot, a stylized one page summary;
(3) evaluate the work system's operation using measures of performance, key incidents, social relations, and other factors;
(4) drill down further as necessary;
(5) propose changes by producing a work system snapshot of a proposed "to be" work system that will probably perform better;
(6) describe likely performance improvements.

The following discussion of enterprise modelling at the work system level at DHL explains how the above ideas were adapted to make them as effective as possible for the enterprise modelling challenges that DHL faced in those cases.

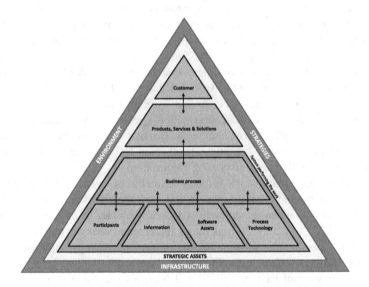

Fig. 1. A logistics works system (Köhler and Alter 2017)

3   The Context: DHL Express

DHL Express[1]. The Deutsche Post DHL Group is the leading global brand in the logistics industry, with about 100,000 employees in over 220 countries and territories

---

[1] Extracts from the DHL Express – GLOBAL Fact Sheet March 2018.

worldwide. Its family of divisions provides a portfolio of logistics services including national and international parcel delivery, international express, and road, air, and ocean transport for industrial supply chain management. Deutsche Post DHL's Express division provides specialized solutions for many growth markets and industries. DHL connects people and businesses and serves an important role in global trade. DHL Express serves its customers through more than 500 airports via three main global hubs in Cincinnati, Hong Kong and Leipzig. The airports in its hub and spoke system serve as country gateways linked to over 38,500 service points that serve approximately 1.4 million customers around the world.

DHL Express Europe[2]. In 2018 the DHL Express Region Europe 36,000 employees operated roughly 740 daily flights and transported more than 150 million shipments in over 60 countries and territories. Those countries and territories are served from the main hubs in Leipzig (Global Hub), Amsterdam, Bergamo, Brussels, Copenhagen, East Midlands (UK), Frankfurt, London, Madrid, Marseilles, Paris and Vitoria (Spain).

Enterprise Architecture at DHL Express. As DHL grew through mergers and acquisitions, it started to experience redundancy and low-value variation in significant parts of its application system landscape. It became increasingly important to implement an enterprise architecture process that would avoid reinventing existing solutions and would reduce waste due to unnecessary inconsistency across different applications and business units.

DHL Express treats Enterprise Architecture as the process of translating business vision into technology strategy. Supporting this process requires embedding an Enterprise Architect in the cross-functional team managing the translation from an organization's business vision and strategic intent to a road map of the required technological change. This strategic alignment helps exploit technology-supported processes that deliver the outputs needed to create product and service offerings for customers. DHL's enterprise architecture process aims at creating agile work systems that can react quickly to ever-changing market conditions. In other words, enterprise architecture focuses on how the business intends to address threats and opportunities and how to evolve technology as the business environment changes.

Enterprise Modeling at the Logistics Work System Level. Logistics services are processes by nature (Johne and Storey 1997) and almost always IT-reliant (Davenport 1993). In DHL Express' approach to enterprise architecture, service providers' product, service and solutions portfolio can be be understood as work systems rather than software or IT systems. Enterprise Architecture thus becomes strategic socio-technological decision making about how to leverage the system performing the work in support of a predefined set of business capabilities serving customers. The current and future customer needs, the product, service and solution offering have to be aligned. This stance treats Enterprise Modeling as the process of understanding current and future customer needs and specifying in full the desired end-state. This desired end-state is then the basis for all associated socio-technological change needed to serve those needs. The associated socio-technological change process has four project-based steps, is an assessment

---

[2] Extracts from the DHL Express – EUROPE Fact Sheet March 2018.

of the status quo, agreeing the desired end-state and the evolution of current legacy work systems in use (Köhler and Alter 2017). This process model explicitly includes the necessity to search for and address all strategic, financial, operation and technical legacy issues identified during the baseline of the status quo. An important issue in logistics is that sender, payer and recipient benefit from the process with the sender being the contracting party. Hence, implying the term customer in logistics may address up to three parties. Products (e.g. Same Day, Time Definite or Day Definite) and services (e.g. Customers or global trade services) or dedicated solutions (e.g. break bulk cargo or medical express) a works system produces for customers.

Those products, services and solutions need to be understood as the business capabilities delivered by a system performing the work. A "business capability" in logistics is a logistics service provider's ability to execute a defined and repeatable portfolio of standardized business processes to produce the desired outcome (e.g. a Time Definite International service) by deploying specific participants, information, software assets and processing technology in a logistics system performing the work. Thus, customers pay for a business capability which is the output of a system performing the work. This makes the system performing the work the key differentiator (Fig. 2).

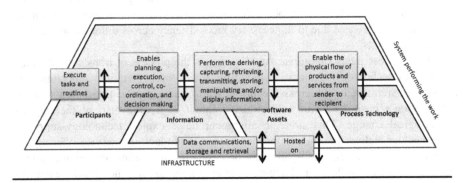

Fig. 2. The system performing the work in a logistics work system (Köhler and Alter 2017)

All business processes in a logistics work system need to be archetypes and associated phases, steps, activities, tasks and routines within the work systems and thus have to be standardized within a logistics network. DHL Express has codified its standards in the Global Standard Operating Procedure. Process technology is used as the label for all tools that increase participant efficiency which is not associated with software assets, like a sorter, plane, lorry or forklift. Participants are people or machines performing at least some of the work in the business process.

Enterprise Modeling at DHL Express. This paper's main contribution is demonstrating that WST/WSM has been used for enterprise modelling in four significant projects at DHL Express. All four projects were managed as four stand-alone projects.

The first leg of all projects involved taking stock of all capabilities in use and their legacy status. Clustering all capabilities in use by their strategic, financial, operational and technical legacy is the key decision making asset for EAs to achieve business alignment when addressing current and future customer needs. Future customer needs are usually those capabilities DHL's customer had on their roadmap triggering a co-evolution of the capability portfolio at DHL.

The second leg involved designing, aligning and agreeing on the desired end-state. Work system proposals addressed this end-state. Each proposal ensured a simultaneous 'clean sweep' of all legacies and innovation of the product, service and solution offering. The key output of this exercise is the framing of socio-technical changes needed in all associated work systems. The aligned and agreed work system evolution proposals will then be forwarded to all suppliers for quotation purposes (i.e. an offer which include costs and timelines). Modeling at the work system level occurred in this second leg. The modelling was based on the portfolio of business capability require-ments voiced by the customer. The accountable Senior User acted as the customer's representative. Based on a joint gap analysis (mostly in workshops) Senior Users listed their capability needs. Then the accountable Domain EA modeled the work system to perform the work and codified all necessary changes.

Every capability addressed in the process was scrutinized regarding added value and cash margin generation. Any capability which did not have a defensible business benefit or cash margin was removed from service. In this review, modelling sometimes became controversial when a capability required an architecture change where the cost-case out-weighed the benefits. Two noticeable exceptions were those capabilities which are con-tractually agreed with customers (usually in sales agreements) or legally required. The content of the model included the agreement on the capability definition the system per-forming the work has to offer (aligned with the global process and capability office and the Senior User) and architecture diagrams (aligned with the global domain EA) to identify all affected vendors. This model was then translated into a project and all documentation by Prince2. Once all work system evolution projects have their Project Briefs, costs and timelines finalized, they were submitted for endorsement in the capability roadmap. This endorsement process at DHL Express included three stage gates. (1) A Project Review Team meeting with all Domain Heads at Vice President level (Finance, HR, Customer Service and so forth). This team conducts quality and feasibility health check, (2) European Project Portfolio Review Board which is the final regional endorsement at C-level (CEO, CFO, COO and so forth), and (3) the Global Project Portfolio Board which is about the final endorsement of resource allocation and all socio-technical changes needed.

At this point, EA modelling was complete from a planning perspective. Nonetheless, certain information provisioning which was contractually agreed with customers could not be handled well existing work systems, especially when those customers used outdated technology. Justified non-compliance or exceptions were addressed through dedicated Architecture Concession Agreements that specified why a capability was needed and could be provided by a dedicated stand-alone software asset.

Enterprise Architecture Assurance at DHL Express. From then on, EA was about monitoring the project and gaining awareness of all game changers during imple-mentation in leg three. After project approval, all four projects followed a chain of process innovation landscaping. First, all associated business processes were updated in the Global Standard Operating Procedure. Derived from those updates, the requirements for the evolution of the system performing the work were finalized and defined in manageable and traceable work packages.

Those work packages had three strategic dimensions. The first was the updating of process technology. The second was the augmentation of how participants receive all information when using software assets in a process. These changes fan out into the managed evolution of software in use by corrective, perfective, or adaptive patches of software assets or by new system developments of generic or bespoke software. The third and most important one is participant readying (i.e. training courses) for the to-be process. This includes all alignments with social partners such as work councils or the representative body for disabled employees.

Once all changes were deployed and confirmed by the Senior User, the final clean-up project was started to remove all process technology or software assets that became outdated or obsolete. This included building back all code, decommissioning all hardware, and returning all licenses in use in leg four. The innovation cycle ended with suspending all financial flows to run and host removed legacy items.

A new Architecture Assurance role which currently does not exist in Prince2 (Hedeman and Seegers 2010) is a direct consequence derived from enterprise modelling in legs three and four. EA modelling is not about an Enterprise Architect producing slide decks and specifications. Rather, it is about supporting Project Board members in four ways:

1. The Executive is supported in all four Business Assurance issues, especially those of performing the work using the agreed to-be business capabilities.
2. The Senior User is supported in all User Assurance matters. All components need to be in alignment, all landscaping activities need to deliver the pre-aligned socio-technical changes, and those changes need to meet the expected business capabilities serving the current and future customer needs. Therefore, the Enterprise Architect is a permanent member of a project's Change Authority aligning and agreeing on requests for change.
3. The Senior Supplier in his Supplier Assurance role including making sure that all software assets and process technology are delivered as agreed and that the committed resources are in place to do the work.
4. Finally, EA Assurance needs to measure how well the landscaping of the system performing the work delivers the aspired customer promise. This is a key sign-off prerequisite for the removal of obsolete legacy systems.

This overall stance implies that (using a Prince2 analogy) the accountable Domain Enterprise Architect consults the Program Board and guides the Project Manager in an Architecture Assurance role in all four legs of the innovation cycle.

4   Four Case Examples from DHL

Example 1 "Exploratory Case Study"[3]. The first case was the first hypothesis testing case of the Clean Sweep approach. Part from this being the exploratory case, it was

---

[3] The in extensor publication of this longitudinal case study can be found under Köhler et al. (2013).

Table 1. Case 1 summary

Leg	Timeline	Key Task	Scope	Main Output
Project 1	Q3/2012	Review of the 9 legacy components in use in 17 countries in one region	28 capabilities found	Baseline of the capabilities in use and assessment of their legacy status (including the assessment of opportunities and limiting factors based on their status)
Project 2	Q4/2013	Design, align and agree on a legacy strategy for each capability and component found	18 capabilities (almost all of them workarounds) were made globally available 10 capabilities classified as obsolete, outdated or rejected as no longer adding value	Agreed joint course of action and decisive points to get the system performing the work in the pre-defined desired end-state
Project 3	Q1/2014	Evolution of the system performing the work	6 stand-alone implementation projects for the 18 capabilities agreed to be retained	Landscaping the agreed end-state and go-live
Project 4	Q2/2014	Final and conclusive removal of components having become obsolete	Code removal, hardware decommissioning, Solution Support contract termination, hosting contract termination and license cancellation	Final and conclusive removal of all strategic, financial, operational and technical legacy AFTER operational acceptance of all landscaping

sufficiently complex as the six implementation quotations addressed various capability enhancements in the current system performing the work (Table 1). DHL replaced

(1) two internal Customer Service reports,
(2) two reports for country authorities (Shipment information for drug enforcement authorities and shipment information for Customs Investigation and Intelligence),
(3) shipments monitoring for various key accounts, real-time reports based on checkpoints raised same day,
(4) an interface that allows security staff to search for various shipment details for country authorities (usually requested in relation to a court decision),
(5) one local software asset sending invoices to customers via email,
(6) a legally required report for a country security bureau,
(7) 52 automated interfaces to other data sources or data target systems,
(8) a new ad-hoc track and trace queries capability and
(9) 51 contractually agreed on customer reports.

Example 2 **"Hypothesis Testing at Regional level"**(see Footnote 3). The second case was the first hypothesis testing case of the Clean Sweep approach. It was the most multinational and most consequential case because it involved 308 capabilities used in 28 countries and took three years to complete. Some model users were hesitant to get involved, but after acknowledging that the exploratory case "SIS" was unsuccessfully attempted seven times and using the Clean Sweep approach delivered (Table 2).

The biggest insight from this clean sweep was that local capabilities (i.e. workarounds) in use could be grouped regarding demonstrated best practices, redundant or obsolete. When modelling the to-be system performing the work Enterprise Architects

Table 2. Case 2 summary

Leg	Timeline	Key task	Scope	Main output
Project 1	Q4/2012 Q1/2013	Review of the 220 legacy components in use in 17 countries in one region	308 capabilities found	Baseline of the capabilities in use and assessment of their legacy status (including the assessment of opportunities and limiting factors based on their status)
Project 2	Q1/2013 Q3/2013	Design, align and agree on a legacy strategy for each capability and component found	44 capabilities (almost all of them workarounds) were perceived as demonstrated best practices and were made globally available 11 capabilities were already available in global operations systems elsewhere 253 capabilities classified as obsolete, outdated or rejected as no longer adding value	Agreed joint course of action and decisive points to get the system performing the work in the pre-defined desired end-state
Project 3	Q4/2013 Q4/2014	Evolution of the system performing the work	26 stand-alone implementation projects for the 44 capabilities agreed to be retained	Landscaping the agreed end-state and go-live
Project 4	Q3/2014 Q1/2015	Final and conclusive removal of components having become obsolete	Code removal, hardware decommissioning, Solution Support contract termination, hosting contract termination and license cancellation	Final and conclusive removal of all strategic, financial, operational and technical legacy AFTER operational acceptance of all landscaping

add severe value by addressing all three variants. Demonstrated best practices are opportunities to innovate, while redundant and obsolete capabilities are limiting factors tying resources (both brain power and budget) which should be used to add value to customers. Retaining redundant and obsolete business capabilities is a costly burden and thus competitive disadvantage.

Example 3 "Hypothesis Testing at the Global Level". This case was used to test the clean sweep approach at a truly global level in over 220 countries and territories. This case was the archetype of what happens if Enterprise Architecture focuses on the new only. "WorldNet" was superseded in 2005 and was still fully operational. Six of the capabilities found were hardly used, not updated since 2005 and the associated capabilities were not part of any DHL Express roadmap. The entire infrastructure had several security risks (e.g. code injection into the DHL network) which had to be removed as part of the sunset. Hence, Enterprise Modeling is also about designing, aligning and agreeing a security risk minimization strategy is addressing the security risks found on the work systems infrastructure. This scope enhancement was managed as part of a Change Request at the project level (Table 3).

Example 4 "Hypothesis Testing at Country Level". In this example, we addressed a legacy landscape after delineating a country cluster (Benelux) setup at work system

Table 3. Case 3 summary

Leg	Timeline	Key task	Scope	Main output
Project 1	Q1/2014	Review of the 3 legacy components in use globally in over 220 countries and territories	10 capabilities found	Baseline of the capabilities in use and assessment of their legacy status (including the assessment of opportunities and limiting factors based on their status)
Project 2	Q2 and Q3/2013	Design, align and agree on a legacy strategy for each capability and component found	3 capabilities (all of them globally used workarounds) were retained in a secure environment 7 capabilities classified as obsolete, outdated or rejected as no longer adding value	Agreed joint course of action and decisive points to get the system performing the work in the pre-defined desired end-state
Project 3	Q4/2014	Evolution of the system performing the work	1 stand-alone implementation project for the 3 capabilities agreed to be retained	Landscaping the agreed end-state and go- live
Project 4	Q1/2015	Final and conclusive removal of components having become obsolete	Code removal, hardware decommissioning, Solution Support contract termination, hosting contract termination and license cancellation	Final and conclusive removal of all strategic, financial, operational and technical legacy AFTER operational acceptance of all landscaping

Table 4. Case 4 summary

Leg	Timeline	Key task	Scope	Main output
Project 1	Q4/2015 and Q1/2016	Review of the 16 legacy components in use in Belgium and Netherlands	734 capabilities found	Baseline of the capabilities in use and assessment of their legacy status (including the assessment of opportunities and limiting factors based on their status)
Project 2	Q2/2016	Design, align and agree on a legacy strategy for each capability and component found	99 capabilities were retained globally (of which 6 were "Specialist" components) 606 capabilities were classified as obsolete, outdated or were rejected as no longer adding value 29 capabilities were redundant	Agreed joint course of action and decisive points to get the system performing the work in the pre-defined desired end-state
Project 3	Q3/2016	Evolution of the system performing the work	1 stand-alone implementation project for the 99 capabilities agreed to be retained	Landscaping the agreed end-state and go-live
Project 4	Q3/2016	Final and conclusive removal of components having become obsolete	Code removal, hardware decommissioning, Solution Support contract termination, hosting contract termination and license cancellation	Final and conclusive removal of all strategic, financial, operational and technical legacy AFTER operational acceptance of all landscaping

level into three country-specific work systems for Belgium, Netherlands and Luxemburg (Table 4).

Country delineation defined of the 734 capabilities discovered 497 outdated or obsolete. Further capabilities were rejected by Senior Users of which 109 capabilities were deemed not adding value and 29 capabilities were redundant and available in other systems. Those 29 capabilities implied user is readying (i.e. training on the job with the new systems) without any work system components changed.

As this project was about delineation, it was not about innovation in Controlling (42 capabilities), Sales (41 capabilities), Finance (15 capabilities) and Key Account management (1 capability) rather than updating the product, service and solution portfolio itself. Sales, Finance and Key Account management, have an impact on how and organization interacts with customers and how it is perceived by the outside world. Hence, modelling customer interaction is classified as being part of the product, service and solution portfolio.

Five of the capabilities to be retained had to be retained outside the global standard application portfolio. Those five were retained as "specialist" components or under an Architecture Concession Agreement.

5 Conclusions and Implications for Practice

5.1 Conclusion 1: Maximizing the Value of Enterprise Architecture Calls for Bringing It to the Work System Level

Enterprise Architecture adds the most value when applied not only at the entire enterprise level but also at the work system level. All four cases at DHL Express share the common work system theory feature that prior Enterprise Modeling an organization it is recommended to the first trawl for current, and future customer needs and then plan their product, service and solution portfolio accordingly. That updated solution portfolio, as well as the legacy status of work systems components in use, are the impetus for Enterprise Architects to design, align, agree and ultimately guide the joint course of action to implement the agreed strategy. In that context, Enterprise Modeling is about how to innovate best the system performing the work to serve a customer.

Enterprise Modeling draws on input from the environment, business strategy, the legacy status of infrastructure, current and future customer needs as well as the aspired product, service and solution portfolio. This stance views Enterprise Architecture as a process to facilitate the execution of a business strategy that includes understanding future and current states of different aspects of the organization in different layers of detail and abstraction. Understanding the work system level becomes key to this organizational understanding.

5.2 Conclusion 2: Emphasis on Customer Needs and Wishes Is Essential for Maximizing the Value of Enterprise Architecture

The evidence in the four cases supports the view that Enterprise Architecture is preferred to be managed as part of a customer-centric culture and at work system level. All key decision makers (senior users, senior suppliers, and enterprise architects) need to collaborate fully in a joint iterative endeavour of evaluating existing capabilities and deciding how to move to better work system capabilities and greater value for customers.

5.3 Conclusion 3: The Final and Conclusive Removal of Work System Components Have Become Obsolete Is also in Scope Every Time

We conclude that Enterprise Modeling needs to address the final and conclusive removal of components having become

- strategic legacy work system components which support business processes which have been deliberately abandoned and

- financial legacy works system components as they are more expensive to maintain than their profit contribution and
- operational legacy work system components which require a planned evolution to address changes in the work system's environment or infrastructure and
- technical legacy work system components having become End of Life or End of Service are no longer supported.

The final and conclusive removal of components is managed in line with current, and future customer needs as well as their internal added value. This internal added value explicitly includes axing capabilities which do not deliver or are forecasted not to deliver a justifiable cash margin.

5.4   Conclusion 4: Enterprise Architecture Is a Key Source of Competitive Advantage

Enterprise Architecture is a key source of competitive advantage for it facilitates business strategy execution and work system innovation by providing the multi-layered organizational understanding, the process for strategy execution and the ongoing evaluation and alignment of projects to the ongoing evolution of the business strategy. Updating Probert et al. (1999) and Köhler et al. (2013) we propose that the alignment of work system in use and current and future customer needs are achieved as depicted below (Fig. 3).

Key activities in this end-to-end process are to

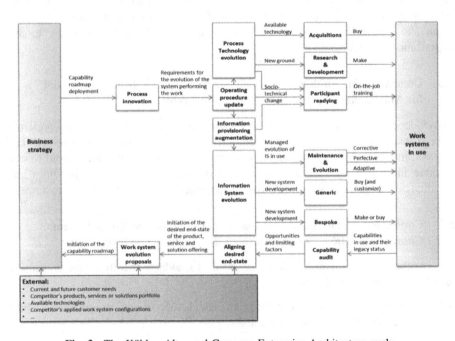

Fig. 3. The Köhler, Alter and Cameron Enterprise Architecture cycle

(1) analyze, select and successfully implement work system level innovations to gain and sustain a competitive advantage and

(2) plan the further development of existing technological capabilities to create a new and improved product, service or solution offerings and

(3) model new or upgrade work systems in use in a way to ensure them being as adaptable as possible to future changes in the business environment and

(4) remove all of work system components which have become obsolete.

5.5   Conclusion 5: A Four-Leg Approach of Four Stand-Alone Projects Is the Preferred Way to Address Current, and Future Customer Needs

The four legs are stage gates which start with the baseline of a status quo. The baseline of the status quo is the most important information source when modelling a to-be work system, as it surfaces all opportunities and limiting factors to be considered when addressing current and future customer needs within the life cycles of all third-party products, services, and partnerships associated with a working system. Based on the findings which are always unique, the second leg is about Enterprise Modeling. Enterprise Modeling is viewed as designing, aligning and agreeing to the desired end-state of a system performing the work. This System performing the work delivers a product, service and solution offering which serves customer needs. The desired-end state includes the final product, service and solution portfolio and the agreed config-uration of the system performing the work as well as the portfolio of projects needed to get to that end-state. The third leg is about implementing the agreed course of action. In this third leg, Enterprise Architects are recommended to assure continuous monitoring and adjustments of the project portfolio as changes in business strategy arise. Enterprise architects need to stay with major projects to make sure that the systems produced fit with the enterprise model developed by the key decision makers. The final leg is the clean-up by removing all strategic, operational, financial and technical legacies.

5.6   Conclusion 6: Enterprise Architecture Assurance Is a Key Follow-up Activity of Enterprise Modeling

Enterprise architects need to stay with major projects to make sure that the systems produced fit with the enterprise model developed by the key decision makers. This new Enterprise Architecture Assurance role was perceived as valuable addition to all four leg three and for projects reviewed. Enterprise Architecture Assurance is proposed to be a new standard role in implementation projects. This role is about ensuring that the model delivers the aspired customer promise and also trigger the removal of obsolete legacy systems.

References

Alter, S.L.: How should business professionals analyze information systems for themselves? In: Falkenberg, E.D., Hesse, W., Olivé, A. (eds.) Information System Concepts. IAICT, pp. 284–299. Springer, Boston, MA (1995). https://doi.org/10.1007/978-0-387-34870-4_29

Bock, A., Kaczmarek, M., Overbeek, S., Heß, M.: A comparative analysis of selected enterprise modeling approaches. In: Frank, U., Loucopoulos, P., Pastor, Ó., Petrounias, I. (eds.) PoEM 2014. LNBIP, vol. 197, pp. 148–163. Springer, Heidelberg (2014). https://doi.org/10.1007/978-3-662-45501-2_11

Bork, D., Fill, H.G.: Formal aspects of enterprise modeling methods: a comparison framework. In: 2014 47th Hawaii International Conference on System Sciences (HICSS), pp. 3400–3409. IEEE (2014)

Davenport, T.H.: Process Innovation. Harvard Business School Press, Boston (1993)

Johne, A., Storey, C.: New Service Development: A Review Of the Literature and Annotated Bibliography. Management Working Paper: B97/2 (1997)

Hedeman, B., Seegers, R.: Learn PRINCE2 – PRINCE2 2009 Edition – Das Taschenbuch. Van Haren Publishing, Zaltbommel (2010)

Karagiannis, D., Kühn, H.: Metamodelling platforms. In: Bauknecht, K., Tjoa, A.M., Quirchmayr, G. (eds.) EC-Web 2002. LNCS, vol. 2455, p. 182. Springer, Heidelberg (2002). https://doi.org/10.1007/3-540-45705-4_19

Köhler, T., Alter, S.: Using enterprise architecture to attain full benefits from corporate big data while refurbishing legacy work systems. In: Proceedings of the 18th IEEE Conference on Business Informatics, Paris, France (2017)

Köhler, T., Cameron, B.H., Sweeney, M., Harrison, A.S.: Strategic market-technology linking in Logistics Work Systems – Evidence from two longitudinal Enterprise Architecture case studies at Deutsche Post DHL. In: Proceedings of the British Academy of Management Conference, Liverpool, UK (2013)

Probert, D., Farrukh, C., Gregory, M.: Linking technology to business planning: theory and practice. Int. J. Technol. Manag. 18(1/2), 11–30 (1999)

Sandkuhl, K., Fill, H.G., Hoppenbrouwers, S., Krogstie, J., Leue, A., Matthes, F., Opdahl, A.L., Schwabe, G., Uludag, Ö., Winter, R.: From expert discipline to common practice: a vision and research agenda for extending the reach of enterprise modeling. Bus. Inf. Syst. Eng. 60(1), 69–80 (2018)

Truex, D., Alter, S., Long, C.: Systems analysis for everyone else: empowering business professionals through a systems analysis method that fits their needs. In: European Conference on Information Systems (2010)

Vernadat, F.B.: Enterprise Modelling and Integration. Chapman & Hall, London (1996)

Teaching Challenges

Learning from Errors: Error-based Exercises in Domain Modelling Pedagogy

Daria Bogdanova$^{(\boxtimes)}$ and Monique Snoeck

Research Center for Management Informatics, KU Leuven, Naamsestraat 69,
3000 Louvain, Belgium
{daria.bogdanova,monique.snoeck}@kuleuven.be

Abstract. Conceptual modelling remains a challenging topic for educators, as it concerns ill-defined problems and requires substantial amount of practice for reaching even the initial level of proficiency. Year after year, novice modellers tend to make similar errors when learning to design models and some of those errors become persistent even at the higher level of proficiency. Are these errors the unavoidable "necessary evil" or there is a possibility to address them at the very early stage of a modeller's education? In this work, we examine a novel approach to teaching conceptual modelling by identifying the most frequent errors in students' models and introducing error-based step-by-step exercises in the framework of a Small Private Online Course for university students.

Keywords: Conceptual modelling · Domain modelling · Enterprise modelling
Education · Error-based learning · Adaptive expertise · UML · Class diagrams

1 Introduction

The question of properly addressing students' errors in the subjects rich with ill-defined problems is one of the substantial challenges arising before educators. In conceptual modelling pedagogy, this question is of a particular significance, as the novice modelers should not only reach the "routine"-level expertise that implies knowledge of a repertoire of tools or procedures, but also become adaptive experts that are able to promptly grasp the core of provided requirements, identify the changes in the previously learned task, and adapt the procedures accordingly.

Although numerous guidelines, reusable patterns and other materials on conceptual modelling (and, specifically, on UML class diagrams) are available, novice modelers tend to struggle with grasping the gist of the subject. Moreover, the extensive amount of materials may even hinder the development of a novice – "typical novice analysts fail to derive maximum benefit from such assistance due to the cognitive overload involved in the recommendations and guidelines" [1:108].

In addition to the challenge of the "cognitive overload", novice modellers are often provided with unbalanced learning material, which is focused either on the lowest-level cognitive skills (e.g. "understand" level, according to the revised Bloom's taxonomy [2]), or the highest, such as the very creation of a model "from scratch", while the intermediate levels necessary for a constructive skill acquisition involving learning to

R. A. Buchmann et al. (Eds.): PoEM 2018, LNBIP 335, pp. 321–334, 2018.
https://doi.org/10.1007/978-3-030-02302-7_20

apply procedures, analyse and evaluate models and their parts, remain underrepresented in the pedagogical materials [3].

The abovementioned difficulties require thorough reflection and action at least at a level of a particular university course, and ask for rethinking of conceptual modelling curriculum fieldwide.

In this paper, we will take a closer look particularly at domain modelling errors that students tend to make, propose an error-based approach to creating step-by-step modelling exercises and evaluate the preliminary result of its implementation in the context of a master-level course of Architecture and Modelling of Management Information Systems at KU Leuven. We will examine the effectiveness of targeted step-by-step online exercises for preventing the most common student errors in simple UML models design at a task level and identify the content areas and concepts, which cause most difficulties.

2 Background

2.1 Knowledge Evaluation Criteria

The quality of a model designed by a student can be considered the most important indication of mastery of the subject. One of the most commonly accepted modelling quality frameworks is the three dimensional framework proposed by Lindland et al. [4]. The framework proposes to evaluate a conceptual model from three quality perspectives: syntactic (formal syntax of the model), semantic (relevance of the model to the domain it describes) and pragmatic (readability/understandability of the model). Thus, errors in modelling can be classified according to the quality dimensions they belong to, both in the professional and educational settings. However, in an educational setting dedicated to the initial stages of training and design of simple models, more narrow evaluation criteria can be applied, so that students could reflect not only on the final modelling solution, but also on the flaws in the various stages of modelling, and/or be informed on the specific content area that requires revising. As an example, in [5], a simplified set of criteria suitable for novice learners of simple class diagrams is proposed, including the syntactic, class-related, attribute-related and association-related errors. If classified according to [4], these types are part of only syntactic and semantic quality dimensions, with no pragmatic dimension involved. However, those two dimensions of quality are considered the most important at the initial stage of learning, when the students must grasp the core principles of modelling. Afterwards, students should be able to refine the semantically and syntactically valid model according to the pragmatic quality standards.

2.2 Novices' Errors in Domain Modelling

Identification of typical modelling errors has been subject of a number of studies in the last two decades. Novice modelers tend to struggle with similar types of tasks and notions throughout time. In 1994, an experimental study on novice errors in conceptual database design showed that the typical errors included literal translation of requirements, bias related to incomplete knowledge, errors in relationship degree, as well as incorrect connectivity ("one" or "many") [6]. Similar errors were found in 2005 by Leung and Bolloju, who performed a detailed analysis of the quality of domain models developed by novice systems analysts [7] based on the Lindland et al. [4] model quality framework and studied the interrelations between the pairs of commonly occurring errors. According to their findings, the most common errors were related to semantic and pragmatic quality, with the most popular error in the category "unexpected is presented", which means that the novice modelers tend to overload the model with unnecessary entities or attributes. The most frequent semantic error was placing the wrong cardinality or multiplicity. The syntactic errors were also quite common (about the quarter of the errors, overall), despite the fact that an automated tool was checking the model syntax for the students prior to submission.

Although the solutions and recommendations proposed by researchers and educators regarding common and recurring errors differ in detail, there is a consensus on the very need for modification of modelling pedagogy regarding those errors, as every paper found had a suggestion regarding such modification. Several successful attempts to employ teaching methods based on common modeling errors have been reported. For instance, a quantitative error analysis of class diagrams created by university freshmen and subsequent modification of the teaching method with greater focus on most common errors (syntactic, attribute-related, association-related and class-related), led to the "improved performance related to syntactic errors and relation errors in fundamental tasks" [7:621]. An analogical use of a "prophylactic approach" to teaching UML provided improved results in summative quizzes developed to test the competences of students in modelling relationships between classes, requirements identification and creating a simple class diagram [9].

2.3   Technology-Enhanced Learning Support

Another approach to dealing with novice errors is providing immediate feedback on the simple models designed by students. The ability to create simple class diagrams (by "simple" we imply those consisting of up to five classes) without errors can be considered a fundamental first step for mastering conceptual modelling. On the level of a simple model, where the variety of possible valid solutions is still much more limited and the model solution is easily available, the use of intelligent tutoring systems (ITS) or other educational software becomes possible. In [10], an implementation of a sample solution-based ITS for teaching UML skills, with a pre-built set of possible error messages, resulted in no worse result than a traditional learning setting, while providing a more enjoyable experience for students and reducing teacher's time on correcting students' solutions. In [11], the use of technology-enhanced support with implementation of immediate automated feedback in a conceptual modelling course resulted in improvement of students' performance, as well as the positive student perception of the course.

In modelling pedagogy, technology is employed not only at the task level, but also throughout the whole modelling curriculum – for example, by means of MOOCs (Massive Open Online Courses) or SPOCs (Small Private Online Courses). MOOCs on conceptual data modelling remain not numerous, with just a few available for the wide audience [3]. Typically, such courses consist of a number of modules that include videos with theoretical and practical materials and practice exercises at the end of each module – in a form of a multiple-choice quiz or other formative or summative task with automated assessment. Such a variety in types of materials and sequencing of tasks and theory lessons provides additional educational opportunities both for the students and for the educators and could be leveraged to provide error-based support. However, none of the currently available online courses on modelling provides students with gradual step-by-step exercises specifically on conceptual modelling, and UML diagram design, in particular.

3   Methodology

3.1   General Approach

The course Architecture and Modelling of Management Information Systems is taught to the master students of the faculty of Business and Economics at KU Leuven. The course has been successfully taught for over a decade, evaluated and improved after each iteration. A thorough evaluation of student mistakes was made in 2017 to propose a targeted improvement the next year. The targeted improvement was performed in 2018 by introduction of step-by-step error-based formative exercises in an online course. The improvement was set up according to an experimental design, such as to be able to evaluate the effectiveness of the proposed improvement by comparing students' performance in 2018 to the performance of the 2017 cohort. In particular, care was taken to isolate the treatment and keep the rest of the course similar to the 2017 setting as much as possible.

3.2   Subjects and General Setting

Two similar groups of master students (39 students in 2017 and 32 in 2018) from the same trajectories and following the same set of mandatory courses followed the course of Architecture and Modelling of Management Information Systems. The course includes an extensive module on UML class diagram design following the MERODE approach [12] and employs the JMermaid modelling software that provides students with immediate automated feedback. As part of the course, students are required to complete a series of exercise sessions and submit the solution of provided cases.

Student groups are very similar across the successive academic years, in particular concerning variables that might influence their modelling skills. In terms of language skills, the course is taught in English, which is a second language for the very large majority of the students. To be accepted to the master program and, subsequently, to the particular course, the international students have to pass a unified English proficiency exam, thus, we assume that the students in both groups possess sufficient mastery of English language to understand the tasks and the requirements provided in the course equally. In terms of prior education on modelling or other IT skills, all students have very limited experience in these matters as the master program is intended for academic bachelors with a non-IT background.

The course materials on theory were identical for both groups of students, however, in 2018 a Small Private Online Course was introduced to provide formative exercises and ensure better understanding of the subject.

3.3   Instructional Design

Throughout the course, 4C/ID instructional design model was applied. 4C/ID is a model developed specifically to design training programs aimed at complex skills [13]. The key parts of the model are: a sequence of learning tasks (whole-task practice – authentic learning experience), supportive information, just-in-time information (including examples and corrective feedback) and part-task practice (practice for a selected skill with tasks of a narrower focus). In the Architecture and Modelling of Management Information System course, the learning tasks (whole-tasks) are represented by complete cases, where students have to build a model based on textual requirements. Supportive information is provided in the textbook, presentations or in the online course: the information is doubled throughout different resources, so the students could choose the most convenient one. Just-in-time information is provided by means of automated feedback in the modelling software and/or by means of automated feedback in the SPOC exercises, while part-task practice is provided during the exercise sessions either by means of the modelling software during a collective exercise or in the SPOC.

In 2017, after the presentation of theoretical material and examples, the students solved two cases during a lab sessions. The two exercises had an identical set-up: in the course of the session, the students were given automated feedback of two types by the modelling software – a reminder to simulate the model after certain amount of actions, and a multiple choice question provoking the reflection on an association just created by the student.

In 2018, the "treatment" constituted of using the identical cases as in 2017, but providing part-task practice for the first case by means of step-by-step online exercises in a SPOC. The second case was (similarly as in 2017) given "as a whole", without subdividing it into part-tasks. This allows to assess to what extent the students were able to extrapolate the practical experience received in the first case to the second one. The effectiveness of the treatment can then be assessed by measuring the improvement on the second exercise in 2018, compared to the 2017 performance.

3.4   The Cases

The students were asked to solve two cases provided requirements documents. The cases were designed to test the ability of students to understand and apply the following concepts and elements:

- Correct identification of classes and associations from the requirements document
- Inheritance and the notion of roles
- Correct multiplicities of associations.

Each of the model solutions included: five or six classes, with one central element connected with a chain of two or three classes, a single class and a class with a recursive association. The multiplicities in the two cases differed according to the specific requirements given in the task.

The model solutions of the two cases are provided in Figs. 1 and 2.

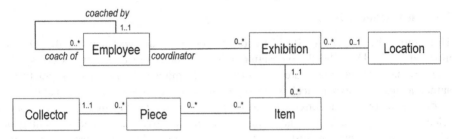

Fig. 1. Model solution for Case 1, central class being exhibition

The full description of the cases can be found in Appendix A.

3.5 Frequent Errors Identification

The student solutions of the exercise session cases became the source for a frequent errors collection. The error identification resulted in the following error types related to classes and associations (the corresponding quality dimension according to the Lindland et al. [4] is mentioned in parentheses):

Class-level errors:

1. No meaningful name is given to a class (Pragmatic)
2. Missing classes (Semantic)
3. Superfluous classes (Semantic)

Association-level errors:

4. No meaningful name is given to an association (Pragmatic)
5. Missing association (Semantic)
6. Superfluous association (Semantic) – see Fig. 3
7. Name-concept mismatch (Semantic)
8. Wrong multiplicity (Semantic)
9. Unnecessary reification (Semantic)
10. Role inversion/Degree (Semantic)
11. Wrongly linked association (Semantic).

When modelling associations, students are requested to think about the relationships between the life cycles of the objects, and in particular to reflect about which objects need to exist first, whether associations ends are frozen or not, and what objects need to be deleted first. For example, when modelling the association between AirlineCompany and Contract, the student should realize that before a Contract can be registered, there needs to be a AirlineCompany (or the AirlineCompany needs to be registered simultaneously), that the contract cannot "change" AirlineCompany throughout its life and

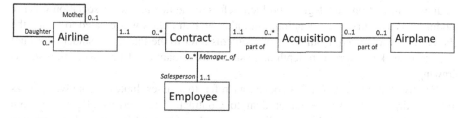

Fig. 2. Model solution for Case 2, central class being contract.

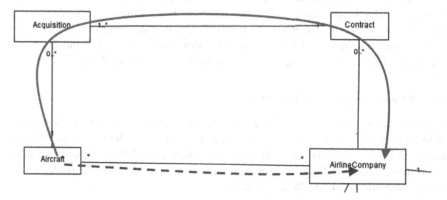

Fig. 3. An example of a superfluous association (dashed arrow) from a student solution: the airline company that owns the aircraft (yellow dashed path) is the airline company that placed the contract for the acquisition of the aircraft (green path).

that it cannot exist any longer than the AirlineCompany-object it refers to (meaning that the association end is frozen). In ER-terms, the weak entity (Contract) will need the strong entity (AirlineCompany) to exist first, and cannot outlive it.

Some clarification is necessary for error types 7, 9, 10 and 11:

"Name-concept mismatch" refers to the problems where an association has been reified to an association class, and the name of the association class does not convey the meaning of the association. A typical example is the unary "partnership" association between airlines. If reified to an association class, its name should reflect the fact that the class represents a partnership. If the association class is named e.g. "daughter_airline", this represents a name-concept mismatch.

"Reified too often" refers to an association that has been reified to an association class, and whereby one of the resulting new associations has been reified again. A typical example is the association between employee and contract, giving rise to an association class "SalesManagerDuty" (with attributes such as start date, end date, etc.). If then an association between "SalesManagerDuty" and "Contract" is reified again, such reification is excessive. Weak associations that express existence dependency should not be reified.

"Inverted roles" refers to the fact that the student made a wrong analysis, and indicated the wrong class as the "strong" vs "weak" entity in the association. For

recursive associations, a "degree" problem refers to the fact that the association was not modelled as a recursive association, but rather an extra class was created to which the class airline was linked. Both types of problems refer to the fact that a student does not manage to make a correct in-depth analysis of the semantics of the association s/he is drawing.

Finally, "*wrongly linked*" associations refer to classes linked wrongly, such as linking Airplane to Airline rather than to Contract. These errors also result from missing classes (e.g. the Airplane directly linked to Contract because of the missing Acquisition class).

As it can be seen from the list, most of the errors are related to the semantic quality dimension. The small amount of syntactic errors is explained by the fact that the JMermaid tool prevents the input of models with syntactical errors.

The student solutions of Case 2 from both academic years (2017 and 2018) were checked and marked according to the list of errors identified in 2017.

3.6   Step-by-Step Online Exercises

A set of step-by-step online exercises was designed for the iteration of the course in 2018 to prevent most of the commonly occurring errors in class diagram design, as identified in the previous academic year. The steps provided in the online learning platform as case-related guided exercises, had to be reproduced by the students in the second case afterwards, without guidance.

The exercises included the following:

1. Identifying enterprise object types – students could choose several options that they believed were object types according to the requirements document. This exercise aimed to address error types 1, 2 and 3.
2. Modelling associations – multiple-choice test based on given case requirements to address error types 5, 6 and 11.
3. "People and their roles" – and multiple choice exercise aimed at differentiation between a base concept and a role, to address error types 3 and 10.

No specific treatment was given for error type 4, as the semantic quality of the models was given a higher priority. Errors 7 and 9 (name-concept mismatch and reification problems) were not addressed in the online course due to the complex nature of the problems related to those errors, which is hard to address in an entirely automated way. Error 8 (multiplicity error) was not treated specifically for these tasks, as the theoretical material as well as a number of exercises related to the topic of multiplicity were presented to the students previously in the course.

Immediate automated feedback on the answers was provided to the students. An example of and exercise with feedback can be seen in Fig. 4.

4   Results

This part presents the summary of student solutions analysis for Case 2 and the comparison of the solution quality to the model solution (see Fig. 2).

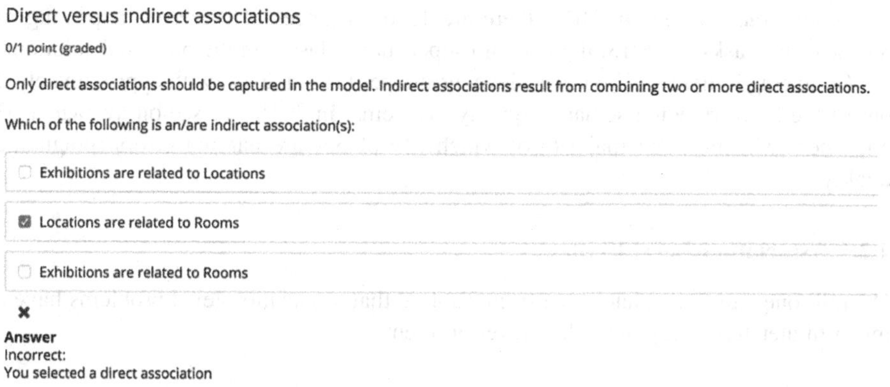

Direct versus indirect associations

0/1 point (graded)

Only direct associations should be captured in the model. Indirect associations result from combining two or more direct associations.

Which of the following is an/are indirect association(s):

☐ Exhibitions are related to Locations

☑ Locations are related to Rooms

☐ Exhibitions are related to Rooms

✗

Answer
Incorrect:
You selected a direct association

Fig. 4. Part of a guided exercise with feedback.

4.1 Class-Level Errors

Table 1 gives an overview of the class-level errors found in student solutions. The total count of error occurrence is listed in the "Total" column for each error type. The "Task frequency" column indicates the percentage of tasks where the errors of certain type occurred (one or several times). The columns with class names indicate the relative frequency of an error: the number of times the error occurred divided by the total number of tasks (student solutions).

Table 1. Summary of the class-level errors

Class-Level	2017								2018							
	Contract	Airline	Employee	Acquisition	Airplane	General	Total	Task Frequency	Contract	Airline	Employee	Acquisition	Airplane	General	Total	Task Frequency
Pragmatic Quality																
Problem with name			0,36	0,08			17	44%		0,06	0,66	0,19			29	78%
Semantic Quality																
Missing class		0,10		0,31	0,18		23	59%				0,13			4	13%
Superfluous class(es)						0,31	12	31%							0	0%
Relative frequency/totals	0,00	0,10	0,33	0,38	0,18	0,31	51	1,308	0,00	0,06	0,66	0,31	0,00	0,00	33	1,03

Name problems. Whereas in 2017 there is an average of 44% of the tasks showing name problems, the frequency in the 2018 solutions is much higher. This increased frequency is mostly due to students using the role name "SalesPerson" as a name for the class "Employee", and subsequently using "Assignment" or "Management" as role names.

Missing classes. In the 2017 solutions, this error occurs 23 times, and in 59,0% of the tasks, whereas in 2018, this error appears only 4 times and in 13% of the tasks.

Superfluous classes. In 2017, there are 12 occurrences of the error, appearing in 30.8% of the tasks. In 2018, there are no superfluous classes in the proposed solutions.

On average, there are 1.31 class-level errors per task in 2017, with approximately 2 out of the 3 errors being semantic quality problems. In 2018, we see on average 1,03 error per task, the large majority of which (29 of 33) are naming errors (pragmatic quality).

4.2   Association-Level Errors

Overall, one can immediately see from Table 2 that association-level problems have a much higher frequency than class-level problems.

Table 2. Summary of the association-level errors

Association-Level	2017								2018							
	Contract-Airline	Airline-Unary	Contract Employee	Contract-Acquisition	Acquisition-Airplane	General	Total	Task Frequency	Contract-Airline	Airline-Unary	Contract Employee	Contract-Acquisition	Acquisition-Airplane	General	Total	Task Frequency
Pragmatic Quality																
Problem with name		0,05	0,21				10	26%		0,09	0,31				13	41%
Semantic Quality																
Missing association		0,08					3	8%		0,03					1	3%
Superfluous association							0	-								
Name-concept mismatch		0,13	0,03				6	15%		0,34					11	34%
Multiplicity problem	0,13	0,18	0,26	0,03	0,56		45	95%	0,06		0,09	0,06	0,81		33	94%
Reified too often	0,03		0,08	0,05			6	15%	0,03						1	3%
Role inversion/Degree	0,08	0,21	0,31	0,03	0,05		26	54%	0,03	0,06	0,06	0,06	0,06		9	28%
Wrongly linked	0,13	0,08	0,08		0,38		26	51%	0,06		0,06	0,03	0,19		11	22%
Relative frequency/totals	0,31	0,59	0,69	0,10	0,79		122	3,13	0,15	0,41	0,33	0,08	0,82		79	2,469

Missing associations. Obviously, when a class is missing, any association that would involve this class is missing as well. Therefore, we only counted the additional missing associations when the required class(es) were present, but the association was missing. In 2017, in three solutions the recursive association representing airline partnership was missing. In 2018, this happened only once.

Superfluous associations were always the result of superfluous classes, so these errors were not counted separately. There were no solutions where an additional association was added on top of the required associations between two correctly captured classes.

Name-concept mismatch. In 2017, we find this problem occurring mainly for the recursive association on Airlines, and three times for the Contract-Employee association. In 2018, the relative frequency is higher, especially for the recursive association on Airlines.

Multiplicity seems to be the most complicated concept to get right, as more than 90% of the tasks suffer from this problem in both years.

Reified too often error appears 6 times and in 15,4% distinct tasks in 2017, and only once in 2018.

Inverted role/degree problems occurred 26 times in more than a half (54%) of the distinct tasks, as opposed to only 9 times in 28% distinct tasks in 2018.

Wrongly linked associations occurred 26 times in more than half (51%) of the distinct tasks, as opposed to only 11 times in 22% distinct tasks in 2018.

In total, the overall amount of association-level errors decreased – from 122 errors in total (3,13 errors per task) in 2017 to 79 (2,47 errors per task) in 2018.

5 Discussion

There are a number of limitations that should be considered regarding this study. First of all, it should be viewed as a small-scale exploratory analysis, as the groups of students were relatively small ($\sim$30 to 40 persons in each group). However, such group size is typical for university exercise session setting. Nevertheless, larger population of students should be addressed and treated with step-by-step exercises in the future research, e.g. by means of a MOOC. Second, the focus of this study is narrowed to a specific type of modelling tasks, in order to capture the granular view of the learning process. In the future, it may be beneficial to "zoom out" to the level of the entire course and check the impact of step-by-step exercises for modelling on student performance throughout the course. Third, the error detection was done for the exercise that followed the previous one immediately (Case 2 was given in the same exercise session as Case 1 for both years). Thus, the long-term effectiveness of the step-by-step exercises is yet to be determined. Also, more focus could be given to improving the pragmatic quality of student models, as in the current version of the course, semantic quality was considered the key problem to tackle, with no specific exercises for improving the pragmatic quality.

As it can be seen from the preliminary results, the group that was treated by step-by-step exercises showed improved results in comparison with the group of the previous years in all types of errors, except for pragmatic (name-concept mismatch).

Class-level errors are less numerous than association-level errors in both years, which is consistent with the findings of previous studies [1, 8]. The name problems were more common in 2018 than in 2017, though compensated by much less semantic errors. The increased number of wrongly named classes in 2018 is mostly located at the level of the class employee. This may have been induced by the part-task training on roles, as many students named the class "Employee" as "SalesManager" instead. This calls for a revision of the corresponding exercise to better emphasize the need for a correct name for the base class. The number of missing classes in 2018 dropped significantly in comparison with 2017, while the superfluous classes error was completely eliminated in 2018, which might be the result of the targeted exercise in the online course that provided students with an opportunity to reflect on the choice of classes from the textual description. In average, there are less class-level errors in 2018 than in 2017.

On association level, the group of 2018 also outperforms the group of 2017. The most common error in the association level was wrong choice of multiplicity, which in both years occurred in the vast majority of the tasks. Multiplicity errors are common in various types of modelling exercises reported in other sources [6, 7]. Missing recursive associations, as well as unnecessary reification, were several times less common in 2018 than in 2017, which can suggest that the targeted exercise showed its effectiveness in training the association-level skills. However, since the missing associations were, obviously, not counted for the classes that were missing, this implies an underrepresentation of association errors for 2017 compared to 2018, as in 2018 there were a few missing classes, while there were much more missing classes in 2017.

Overall, concerning task-specific errors, from the totals in each column of Table 2, it is easy to see that the recursive association on "airplane", the "acquisition"-to-"contract" and the "sales representative" association between employee and contract are the most difficult ones to capture correctly. This calls for an additional part-task training on recursive associations. At the same time, the error frequencies also demonstrate that the "part-task" exercise, in which the students were requested to analyze in detail three potential associations, can be viewed as a way of substantial improvement for the course. Errors that indicate shortcomings in understanding the semantics of an association and the roles classes play in the association as witnessed by name-concept mismatches, inverted roles, degree problems and wrongly linked associations, are much less frequent in 2018 than in 2017.

6   Conclusion and Future Research

In this work, we have implemented a series of step-by-step exercises based on known common errors to teach a specific part of the modelling course – building a simple UML model with a recursive association and a chain of associations based on textual case description. Summing the results presented above, we can make a preliminary conclusion that the step-by-step exercises implemented in a Small Private Online Course in the framework of 4C/ID instructional design model have shown to be effective, at least when it concerns the immediately following exercise. Nevertheless, while the majority of errors (semantic) both on class and association levels seem to be tackled successfully in the latter group of students, there were two error types – name-concept mismatch (pragmatic) and multiplicity errors – that require thorough investigation and targeted training.

We are planning to continue the implementation of 4C/ID model and introduction of more step-by-step online exercises in the course, and to check whether the improvement on the task level will extrapolate to the course level, as well. In addition, the current SPOC on enterprise information systems modelling will be expanded into a MOOC to address larger groups of students, so it will be possible to investigate and improve this type of pedagogical approach further, and make a larger and more representative collection of student errors.

Appendix A. Cases Descriptions

Case 1. Mouvre Museum

The Mouvre Museum in Paris is a huge museum with quite a large number of rooms, so that many exhibitions can be organised in parallel in the Museum. Also, the planning phase of an exhibition starts at least two years before the actual opening date of an exhibition, so that even for a single room, several exhibitions in different stages of advancement need to be followed up simultaneously. Therefore, a little management system is required to make sure all these exhibitions run smoothly.

The museum has identified a set of locations inside the museum that can hold exhibitions. The locations can be considered as museums inside the museum. So, for each location a series of exhibitions is developed. For each exhibition, first a series of desired exhibition items is defined. For example, for an exhibition on Vincent Van Gogh, it is defined that one item of his early period is desired, one pencil drawing with the corresponding painting, one sunflower painting, etc. For each desired item, a suitable piece is sourced from the collectors that possess candidate pieces. For some items, only one unique piece is available, but some exhibition items several potential pieces are available from different collectors. (There are for example several "Sunflower" paintings from Vincent Van Gogh). For each exhibition item, the system will keep track of what pieces are requested from which collector.

Each exhibition is assigned an employee of the museum as coordinator. To foster knowledge transfer, junior employees are assigned a senior employee as coach.

Case 2. Boncardier

Boncardier sells aircrafts to airline companies. As aircrafts are very expensive to build, they are only built "on demand", meaning that first a sales agreement is made with a customer, before the airplane is actually built. (An exception are demo versions of airplanes, but these are out of scope for this case). The sales are regulated by means of contracts with the airline companies, whereby a single contract may consist of several acquisitions of airplanes. The global contract stipulates common elements across all acquisitions such as delivery conditions, legal aspects, etc. Each acquisition of an airplane has further specific details, such as the chosen model of airplane, the negotiated price for that airplane, chosen options & customizations, delivery date, etc. Each contract is managed by a Boncardier salesperson. An employee can act as salesperson for several contracts. Given the long term of contracts, the assigned salesperson may change over time, but Boncardier ensures there is always a salesperson available for the client.

Some airlines are related to each other: for example, main airlines often have a low cost daughter airline company. Boncardier therefore keep track as much as possible of the mother-daughter relationships between airline companies, to be able to track whether to sold aircrafts are shifted to partner airlines of the original buyer.

References

1. Bolloju, N., Leung, F.S.K.: Assisting novice analysts in developing quality conceptual models with UML. Commun. ACM **49**, 108–112 (2006)
2. Krathwohl, D.R.: A Revision of Bloom's Taxonomy. Theory Into Pract. (2002)
3. Bogdanova, D., Snoeck, M.: Domain modelling in bloom: deciphering how we teach it (2017)
4. Lindland, O.I., Sindre, G., Solvberg, A.: Understanding quality in conceptual modeling. IEEE Softw. **11**, 42–49 (1994)
5. Kayama, M., Ogata, S., Asano, D.K., Hashimoto, M.: Educational criteria for evaluating simple class diagrams made by novices for conceptual modeling. Int. Assoc. Dev. Inf. Soc. (2016)
6. Batra, D., Antony, S.R.: Novice errors in conceptual database design. Eur. J. Inf. Syst. **3**, 57–69 (1994)
7. Leung, F., Bolloju, N.: Analyzing the quality of domain models developed by novice systems analysts. In: Proceedings of the 38th Annual Hawaii International Conference on System Sciences, p. 188b. IEEE
8. Kayama, M., Ogata, S., Masymoto, K., Hashimoto, M., Otani, M.: A practical conceptual modeling teaching method based on quantitative error analyses for novices learning to create error-free simple class diagrams. In: 2014 IIAI 3rd International Conference on Advanced Applied Informatics, pp. 616–622. IEEE (2014)
9. Elva, R., Workman, D.: A prophylactic approach to teaching UML in undergraduate computer science courses. In: The Fifteenth International Conference on Learning (2008)
10. Schramm, J., Strickroth, S., Le, N.-T., Pinkwart, N.: Teaching UML skills to novice programmers using a sample solution based intelligent tutoring system. In: Flairs 2012 (2012)
11. Sedrakyan, G., Snoeck, M.: Technology-enhanced support for learning conceptual modeling. In: Bider, I., et al. (eds.) BPMDS/EMMSAD -2012. LNBIP, vol. 113, pp. 435–449. Springer, Heidelberg (2012). https://doi.org/10.1007/978-3-642-31072-0_30
12. Snoeck, M.: Enterprise Information Systems Engineering: The MERODE Approach. Springer Publishing Company, Incorporated (2014)
13. Merriënboer, J.J.G., Jelsma, O., Paas, F.G.W.C.: Training for reflective expertise: a four-component instructional design model for complex cognitive skills (1992)

Discovering the Impact of Students' Modeling Behavior on their Final Performance

Galina Deeva[✉], Monique Snoeck, and Jochen De Weerdt

Research Center for Management Informatics, KU Leuven,
Naamsestraat 69, 3000 Leuven, Belgium
galina.deeva@kuleuven.be

Abstract. Conceptual modeling is an important part of Enterprise Modeling, which is a challenging field for both teachers and learners. Creating conceptual models is a so-called 'ill-structured' task, i.e. multiple good solutions are possible, and thus students can follow very distinct modeling processes to achieve successful learning outcomes. Nevertheless, it is possible that some principles of modeling behavior are more typical for high-performing rather than low-performing students, and vice versa. In this study, we aimed to discover those patterns by analyzing logged student modeling behavior with process mining, a set of tools for dealing with event-based data. We analyzed data from two individual conceptual modeling assignments in the JMermaid modeling environment based on the MERODE method. The study identified the presence of behavioral patterns in the modeling process that are indicative for better/worse learning outcomes, and showed what these patterns are. Another important finding is that students' performance in intermediate assignments is as well indicative of their performance in the whole course. Thus, predicting these problems as early as possible can help teachers to support students and change their final outcomes to better ones.

Keywords: Conceptual modeling · Domain modeling
Process mining · Education · Learning analytics

1 Introduction

Recently, learning analytics and educational data mining have provided teachers with new tools to facilitate learning. Some of the important objectives of learning analytics are to understand and predict student performance and behavior, and to improve teaching support. With growing availability and accessibility of learners' data, it became possible to analyze students' behavior, and even provide them with feedback automatically and in real-time.

© IFIP International Federation for Information Processing 2018
Published by Springer Nature Switzerland AG 2018. All Rights Reserved
R. A. Buchmann et al. (Eds.): PoEM 2018, LNBIP 335, pp. 335–350, 2018.
https://doi.org/10.1007/978-3-030-02302-7_21

Nevertheless, performing such behavior analyses is not always a straightforward task, especially for so-called 'ill-structured' domains with multiple good solutions. One of such domains, conceptual modeling is challenging for both teachers and learners. While creating a conceptual model, students can follow very different modeling processes to achieve successful learning outcomes. However, some principles of modeling behavior may be more typical for high-performing rather than low-performing students, and vice versa. In this paper, we approach conceptual modeling from a process-oriented perspective and aim to discover behavioral patterns by analyzing logged modeling behavior with process mining.

Process mining enables the creation of process models based on event log data that are captured in an information system [1]. In this research, process mining is used to gain more insight into student behavior in the context of an individual course on conceptual modeling. Specifically, students enrolled in the course of 'Architecture and Modeling of Information Systems' are given two individual assignments. These assignments require students to create a conceptual model in the JMermaid modeling environment, which logs all student modeling activities. We analyze these log data to find patterns that are indicative of better or worse learning outcomes, as well as to discover the correlation between the scores on each individual assignment and the final score.

1.1 Research Questions

The main goal of this study is to improve the understanding of how certain sequences of modeling activities correlate with better/worse learning outcomes. As such, we aim to address the following research questions:

1. Is there a correlation between the performance in intermediate assignments and the final score of the course?
2. Are there any recognizable patterns of a modeling process that can be correlated with better or worse learning outcomes?
3. What are these patterns, if they exist?

The paper is organized as follows. In Sect. 2, we present an overview of recent literature on conceptual modeling education and educational process mining. Next, the methodology of the study, including the data collection process, is given in Sect. 3. The results of the analysis are presented in Sect. 4. Subsequently, the main findings and limitations of the study are discussed in Sect. 5. Finally, Sect. 6 summarizes the findings and gives directions for future work.

2 Related Work

2.1 Conceptual Modeling

A conceptual model (also known as domain model) is a complete and holistic view of a system based on conceptual but precise qualitative assumptions about its concepts (entities), their interrelationships, and their behavior [2]. A conceptual model of an information system provides an abstract model of an enterprise and enables the design of an information system [2,3].

Conceptual modeling requires problem analysis and solving, which are by nature inexact skills. As a consequence, teaching such skills to novice modelers is a difficult task: novice modelers produce incomplete, inaccurate, ambiguous and/or incorrect models in their early careers [4]. There are many reasons that make teaching and learning conceptual modeling difficult. First, the quality of a conceptual model depends on a variety of knowledge factors: the knowledge of modeling concepts, of the modeling language and of the domain to be modeled are key factors affecting the quality of a model [5]. These issues can be addressed by providing students with the proper amount of supportive information about required knowledge [6]. Second, different procedural factors also affect the outcome of a modeling effort. Observations of the modeling process of novices indicate that they follow a linear problem-solving pattern, thereby focusing on one task at a time rather than switching between modeling activities [7]. Furthermore, novice modelers show poorly adapted cognitive schemata with regards to the identification of relevant triggers for verifying the quality of models [4], a problem that is exacerbated by the absence of established validation procedures [8]. These factors pertain to the process of modeling, which is why in this study we try to tackle a process-oriented view on conceptual modeling.

2.2   Educational Process Mining

Many studies applied process mining within the field of education, in which case it is often referred to as educational process mining (EPM). Recently, there was an increasing number of studies that exploited EPM in different real-life scenarios. For example, Weerapong et al. [9] analyzed the control flow perspective of student registration at the university. Juhaňák et al. [10] studied students' quiz-taking behavior patterns in a learning management system Moodle.

A common goal in EPM is to find behavioral patterns that are typical for certain groups of learners. For example, van der Aalst et al. [11] compared different student groups with comparative process mining using process cubes, discriminating between the learning behavior of successful vs. unsuccessful, male and female, local and foreign subgroups, as well as the behavior of students within different chapters of the course. Similarly, Papamitsiou and Economides [12] exploited comprehensive process models with concurrency patterns in order to detect and model guessing behavior in computer-based testing, revealing common patterns for students with different goal-orientation levels.

In the field of business process models, there is a recent research stream that studies the process of process modeling (PPM). For instance, Pinggera et al. [13] performed a cluster analysis on the log data from large-scale modeling sessions and identified three distinct styles of modeling. Claes et al. [14] introduced a way to visualize different steps that modelers conduct to create a process model. These and similar studies on PPM give useful examples of insights into business process modeling process that can be obtained with process mining. The main difference of our study is its focus on the process of conceptual modeling with the MERODE method, since typical behavioral patterns of modelers in different domains and different modeling languages may as well differ.

Previous research involving the JMermaid learning environment can be found in [15,16], where process mining was used for revealing modeling behavior patterns that can be related to certain learning outcomes. Event log data captured in JMermaid was used to analyze student performance in a group assignment. The main difference between the current study and [16] is that we analyze student behavior and performance at the individual level instead of a group level, and thus aim to provide recommendations for improving modeling skills of the individual learners, as well as investigate how the scores obtained in individual assignments are correlated with the final scores of the course.

3   Methodology

3.1   The JMermaid Modeling Environment

We analyze behavioral data from the JMermaid modeling environment, developed in our Management Informatics Research Group at the Faculty of Business and Economics, KU Leuven for teaching Information Systems modeling. It is based on MERODE, a method for Enterprise Systems development [17], and used in the Architecture and Modeling of Management Information Systems (AMMIS) course[1]. The main objective of the AMMIS course is to introduce the learners to the latest techniques for object-oriented analysis and enterprise information system modeling. Students have to learn how to create an information system's conceptual model, which includes three modeling perspectives: the structural properties (domain object types and their associations) are captured by means of a class diagram (called Existence Dependency Graph (EDG)), the behavioral aspects of domain object types are described by means of Finite State Machines (FSM), and the interactions between domain objects are captured by means of an object-event table. The JMermaid tool allows drawing these different types of diagrams, and offers the students support for the verification and simulation of their models.

3.2   Logging Functionality in JMermaid

JMermaid is capable to log student activities in the format shown in Fig. 1. The log file contains each activity that a student conducted or triggered in the system, timestamped to milliseconds. There is a total of 60 possible *Activities*, and they are further abstracted into eight *Categories*, which can be seen as higher level activities. The *View* indicates which of the three parts of the model, i.e. EDG, OET or FSM, is being currently worked on, and *Model aspect* can be structural (S, i.e. working on the class diagram) or behavioral (B, i.e. working on the FSMs or OET).

---

[1] http://onderwijsaanbod.kuleuven.be/syllabi/e/D0I71AE.htm.

Timestamp	Student	View	Model aspect	Category	Activity
2017-03-05 17:33:31.180	Student1	EDG	S	ERROR	Error: Illegal name
2017-03-05 17:33:40.237	Student1	EDG	S	CREATE	Create object
2017-03-05 17:35:15.253	Student1	EDG	S	CUSTOMIZE	Move object
2017-03-05 17:37:16.782	Student1	EDG	S	CREATE	Create dependency
2017-03-05 17:37:16.780	Student1	EDG	S	FEEDBACK	Dependency feedback
2017-03-05 17:37:39.911	Student1	EDG	S	FEEDBACK	Correct answer
2017-03-05 17:37:41.200	Student1	EDG	S	FEEDBACK	Dependency feedback
2017-03-05 17:37:41.201	Student1	EDG	S	CREATE	Create dependency

Fig. 1. An example of an event log from JMermaid

3.3 Data Collection

During the semester, students enrolled in the course are required to complete two individual take-home assignments. Both assignments include a specification document that states all the requirements. Students have to transform the requirements to a semantically correct conceptual model using the JMermaid modeling environment, which captures student data to event logs.

For the first assignment, students were given a case description on a problem related to a gas station company, for which they were instructed to create a class diagram (EDG). The second assignment included a given class diagram and a description of behavioral aspects, based on which students created FSMs for domain object types with non-default behavior and define interaction aspects in the OET. Population and other data statistics are provided in the next section.

4 Results

4.1 Data Description

We use the data of students who participated in two assignments (referred to as *HW1* and *HW2*) during two academic years (2017 and 2018). The first assignment is focused on modeling structural aspects of the model, while the second one involves modeling the behavioral part for a given class diagram. The models of the students are evaluated on a scale from 1 (fail) to 5 (excellent). Based on these marks, we identified two groups: low-performing students, who received 1 (fail), and high performing students, who received 4 (very good) or 5 (excellent). For this analysis, we don't take into account the students whose assignments were ranked as 2 and 3, since the goal of this study is to find the differences in behavior of worse vs. best scoring students (for the assignment). An overview of the data is given in Table 1, including the number of students and the total number of activities performed in each subgroup.

4.2 Correlation between the Assignment Scores and the Final Score

The distributions of exam scores for each assignment score for the years 2017 and 2018 are shown in Figs. 2 and 3, respectively. The exam scores from 1 to

Table 1. An overview of the data

Dataset	Assignment score	# of students	# of activities	Average # of activities per student
hw1-17-h	4 or 5	13	1609	123.8
hw1-17-l	1	19	2765	145.5
hw1-18-h	4 or 5	7	809	115.6
hw1-18-l	1	12	1386	115.5
hw2-17-h	4 or 5	11	3146	286
hw2-17-l	1	6	1226	204.3
hw2-18-h	4 or 5	3	1067	355.7
hw2-18-l	1	6	1476	246

20 are subdivided into 3 categories: fail (below 10), satisfactory (from 10 to 13) and good (14 and more). As previously explained, the assignments are evaluated with a score from 1 to 5; it is also possible that the student didn't hand in the assignment (shown as "no assignment" in the graphs).

For all the four cases, the students who obtained 4 and 5 for the assignments have performed with distinction (score 14 or more) in the exam. In fact, for the HW1 in 2017 HW2 in 2018, 100% of the students who scored 4 and 5 have obtained good exam scores. Additionally, in 2017, it is easy to see that students who scored at least 2 for both assignments were capable to pass the course with

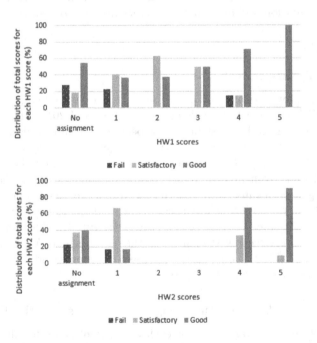

Fig. 2. Distribution of total scores for each HW1 and HW2 scores (2017)

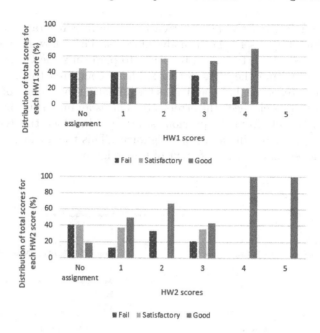

Fig. 3. Distribution of total scores for each HW1 and HW2 scores (2018)

a satisfactory or good mark. In 2018, some students who scored 2 or higher still failed the course, but it was in most cases a minority within the group.

Interestingly, in 2017 no students received marks 2 or 3 for the second assignments. This means that for the second task most students have either improved the quality of their models and received a better score (and have passed the course successfully, as seen in Fig. 2), or this quality decreased and they failed the second assignment, which made it more likely for them to fail the course as well. In 2018 this trend of the second assignment to be more predictive of final performance is not as strong, however, there is a clear tendency for the better scoring students to also perform much better in the exam.

For the students who didn't hand in the assignments, it can be observed that while there is still a chance they will pass the course, their chances to fail the course are the highest from all the groups, and even higher than for the students who made the assignments and failed it. This is especially observed for 2018, in which 40% of the "no assignment" group failed the exam. While the scores of the assignments are found to be predictive for the exam score, it would be interesting to be able to provide students with feedback already while they make their assignment. We therefore analyze the modeling processes in Sects. 4.3 and 4.4.

4.3 Analysis of the Activity Frequencies

Categories of Activities. Before discovering process models, we analyzed the frequency of activities of students with the Disco process mining tool. First, we looked into categories of activities. Figure 4 (HW1) and Fig. 5 (HW2) give an overview of relative activities occurrences (given in percentage) for high and low performing students for both analyzed years. The following patterns can be observed. First of all, there is a tendency to perform some CHECK activity more frequently within the high-scoring students compared to the low-scoring students. This category includes activities for validating the quality of the model, e.g. simulate the model, check the errors, etc. This is an important finding, since it confirms the results from the previous study [16], in which this tendency has been reported in performing a group assignment. This trend can be seen for all the cases, independently of the context of the assignment.

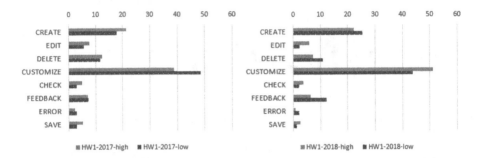

Fig. 4. Frequency of activity categories in HW1 in 2017 and 2018. The values are given as percentage of the total number of activities

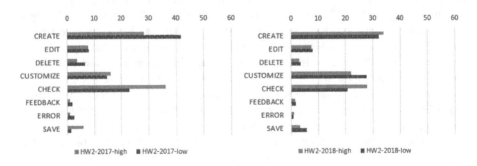

Fig. 5. Frequency of activity categories in HW2 in 2017 and 2018. The values are given as percentage of the total number of activities

Secondly, in three out of four graphs, it is observed that low-scoring students have more ERROR activities than their better scoring peers. This result might seem intuitive, nevertheless it is an important step towards predicting the performance of students using their event-based data. We can assume that low-scoring students make more errors while modeling, and it can be captured by the modeling tool.

Similarly, for both assignments in 2017 and for the first assignment in 2018, there is a pattern of performing the SAVE activity, i.e. save the model, more frequently for high-scoring students. A possible explanation could be that high-performing students save more often in view of simulating their model, but also that they are in general more careful about the modeling process.

Next, independently of the context of the task, there is no clear correlation between frequencies of CREATE, DELETE and CUSTOMIZE activities and better performance. There is a tendency for EDIT activity to be more frequent for students who scored well in the first assignment, but it doesn't hold for the second task. CREATE, EDIT and DELETE activities are used to build the model, while the CUSTOMIZE category contains activities which help the modeling process, but don't affect the quality of the model, e.g. show grid in the tool or move the object. An overall conclusion for these categories could be that the "quality" of performed activities matters more than the quantity. Creating more objects, events or FSMs won't necessarily result in a better quality model.

Finally, there is a slight tendency of low-scoring students to receive more feedback (FEEDBACK category) than high-scoring students do. This can be due to the fact that, first, by making more errors or waiting too long before simulating their model, low-scoring students trigger more automated feedback. Second, low-scoring students might feel that they need more help from the system, and thus don't switch off learning dialogs or actively request learning reports. Although currently JMermaid has a limited amount of feedback implemented, this finding might give a direction for further research in this area.

Fine-Granular Level of Activities. Next, we analyze frequencies of occurrence of student activities on a more fine-granular level. Figure 6 (assignment 1) and Fig. 7 (assignment 2) provide an overview of the most frequent activities. Note that the set of activities is different for the two assignments. Similarly to the analysis of the activity categories, we can see that successful students simulate their model significantly more often than less successful students. "Simulate model" is one of the possible actions in the CHECK category, which provides students with the most insights about the quality of their model. Thus, it might be concluded that model simulation could potentially enhance model quality.

For HW1, we observe that the better students switch much more frequently between views than the low-scoring ones. When performing behavioral modeling,

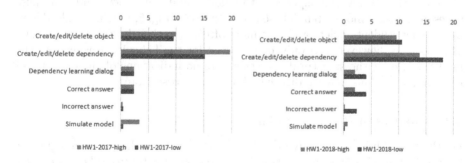

Fig. 6. Most frequent activities in HW1 in 2017 and 2018. The values are given as percentage of the total number of activities

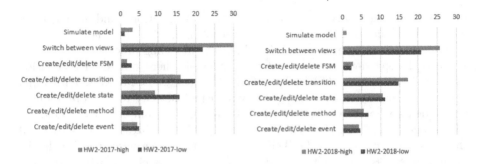

Fig. 7. Most frequent activities in HW2 in 2017 and 2018. The values are given as percentage of the total number of activities

this switch can be considered as a validation activity used to verify the behavioral model against the default behavior implied by the data model [18,19].

Next, for the first assignment, it can be observed that low-scoring students give more incorrect answers to the learning dialogs (Fig. 6). Interestingly, it seems that low-scoring students give more or at least the same number of correct answers compared to the high-scoring students. The reason for this could be that these students are simply asked more questions because of their actions. Nevertheless, the number of incorrect answers can serve as a predictive feature of future problems with the model.

This time we look into CREATE, EDIT and DELETE activities from another angle. Instead of looking at the number of CREATE actions, independently of the created entity, we compare possible activities for each distinct entity, such as object, dependency, FSM, and so on. In general, the conclusion is similar to the one previously obtained: it seems there is no strong correlation between the quantity of building model activities, but it is quality that matters. This finding generally holds for both assignments, except for create/edit/delete actions on methods, events and states. These activities (which all belong to OET or FSM view) are being performed slightly more frequently by the low-scoring students. This correlation might indicate that low-scoring students might be less sure while creating behavioral aspects of the model, and thus delete and edit these types of elements more often. These is confirmed by Fig. 5, in which indeed low-performing students delete and edit more often than their better scoring peers. This pattern, however, can only be observed for the behavioral aspects of the model, while for the structural ones there are no indications of the quantity of the building actions being indicative of a better/worse score.

4.4   Analysis of Process Models

For the sake of brevity, we only provide process models for the second assignment for the high level of activity abstraction (category of activity). The reasons for this choice are that, first, as described in Sect. 4.3, HW2 seems to be more predictive of the final score. Second, HW2 is slightly bigger, and as such, the log files contain more student actions on average (see Table 1). However, similar patterns are observed in the process models for the first assignment as well.

The process models are given in Figs. 8 (high-scoring students, 2017), Fig. 9 (low-scoring students, 2017), Fig. 10 (high-scoring students, 2018) and Fig. 11 (low-scoring students, 2018). As modeling is a complex task, there is inherently a very large variation of possible process paths. The visual inspection of the models seems to indicate the absence of clearly dominant patterns for good or

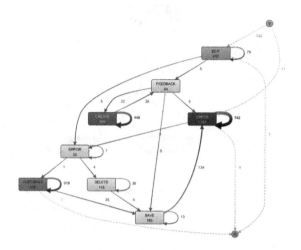

Fig. 8. Process model created in Disco for HW2, high-scoring students, 2017

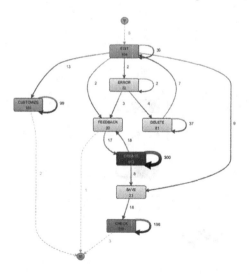

Fig. 9. Process model created in Disco for HW2, low-scoring students, 2017

bad processes for modeling a single perspective. It is nevertheless interesting to see the reaction of students to FEEDBACK events. Low-performing students tend to react to feedback with CREATE (2017) or CUSTOMIZE (2018) events, while better scoring students often CHECK their model after receiving feedback.

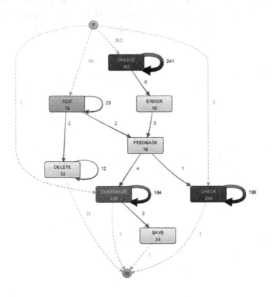

Fig. 10. Process model created in Disco for HW2, high-scoring students, 2018

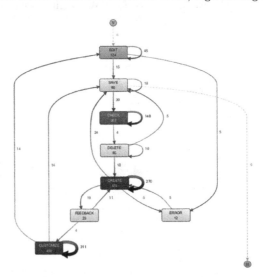

Fig. 11. Process model created in Disco for HW2, low-scoring students, 2018

5 Discussion

This study addresses the question of how the modeling process can be correlated with learning outcomes. In particular, we investigated the modeling process for "part-tasks" where students address a single perspective of a modeling task: data modeling only, or behavioral modeling only for a given data model. The analysis of the scores clearly indicates that the outcome of the process of these part-tasks are indicative for the final achievement of the course, yet the goal of the research is to find features of the modeling process that are indicative for the quality of the outcome, thus allowing to give process-oriented feedback, rather than outcome feedback only. The seemingly absence of dominant patterns indicative for good or bad results in the process models shown in Sect. 4.4, can easily be explained by the large variety of possible paths a student can follow when elaborating models, and the fact that in this case we investigated only part-task modeling behavior for fairly simple assignments and for a small sample. Previous research investigated modeling behavior for a large and complex whole-task assignment. There we more clearly witnessed a series of dominant patterns, such as the iterative modeling as opposed to linear modeling, a pattern also revealed in [7].

Yet the analysis of the frequency of the activities in Sect. 4.3 also revealed that better students switch views much more frequently than their low-scoring peers. This confirms the superiority of the iterative modeling, also at the part-task level. Furthermore, novices' inability to identify triggers for verifying the quality of models identified in [4] is also confirmed as being experienced more by low-scoring students than by high-scoring students as evidenced by their lower number of 'check' activities.

In general, the results of this research illustrate that there are some patterns that can influence the model quality. These patterns are summarized below.

1. Better performing students validate their model more often while modeling. More specifically, simulating the model and cross-checking with the data model when doing behavioral modeling can significantly improve its quality.
2. Low-scoring students tend to make more errors, such as entering illegal name or connecting wrong types of objects. This could be attributed to a better knowledge background of higher scoring students. Most importantly, this can be captured by the modeling tool and used as a feature in a predictive algorithm.
3. In general, execution of more CREATE, EDIT or DELETE activities does not lead to a better conceptual model. Nevertheless, for behavioral aspects the low-scoring students execute more EDIT and DELETE activities, probably due to the fact of struggling with complex parts of the model.
4. Better students tended to save their model much more frequently than worse-scoring students did.
5. High-scoring students tended to respond to feedback with validating model activities, while low-scoring students often perform creating or customizing activities instead.
6. The scores of intermediate assignments are indicative of the final score.

It is interesting to see that pattern 1 indicates that the pattern observed in group work for complete models [16] also holds at the level of part-tasks. Despite the positive results, there are certain limitations to the study. One of the limitations is the limited sample size. Since the assignments were not graded, not all the students made them, and some of the students might not have put a sufficient effort into making the tasks. This could mean that some of the observed behavior might not fully represent the modeling ability of the person. Furthermore, collecting data across academic years induces the limitation that the conditions under which the tasks have been performed as well as their grading may be subject to slight variations. Yet at the same time, the research clearly shows that findings from a single year cannot be easily generalized: the pattern of worse students creating and deleting substantially more than better students in 2017 for HW2 is not fully present for students in 2018 for the same homework. The collection of data in consecutive years thus allows to identify persistent patterns that are more likely to be generalizable. Finally, working with the JMermaid tool has certain limitations as well. For example, some of the log files have been lost or corrupted because some students used the old version of the tool.

6   Conclusion and Future Work

Creating conceptual models is a challenging task to acquire, especially for novices, due to its 'ill-structured' nature. Building better models requires not only a better knowledge background, but also a certain order of actions in which such model is created. Given this, in this study we employed a process-oriented view on modeling to explore potential behavioral patterns and indicative features correlated with better learning outcomes. We exploit process mining, as well as descriptive statistics and activity counts, and show behavioral patterns that occur for the students with different performance in the assignments. These patterns are listed in previous sections; most importantly, we show that they exist and could be implemented as features in a predictive algorithm. As such, potential problems in the performance of the students can be spotted in advance, providing an opportunity to help those students and provide them with needed feedback in an automated way [20]. Another important finding is that problems in the intermediate assignments are indicative of the performance in the whole course. Thus, predicting these problems as early as possible can help teachers to support the students and change their final outcomes to better ones.

The main contributions of this work was to provide an empirical approach for studying learners behavior by applying process mining techniques. The goal is to find features that are predictive for better or worse outcome, so that students can be given process-oriented feedback while modeling, rather than only outcome feedback. Further research needs to deepen the current results by repeating the analysis for similar task, in order to confirm the detected patterns. Furthermore, these first results can already be used to expand the tool's current feedback functionalities. These implemented features can then be used in the future to study the students' reaction to process-oriented feedback.

References

1. Van der Aalst, W.M.: Process Mining: Data Science in Action. Springer, Heidelberg (2016)
2. Embley, D.W., Thalheim, B.: Handbook of Conceptual Modeling: Theory, Practice, and Research Challenges. Springer, Heidelberg (2012)
3. Wand, Y., Monarchi, D.E., Parsons, J., Woo, C.C.: Theoretical foundations for conceptual modelling in information systems development. Decis. Support Syst. 15(4), 285–304 (1995)
4. Schenk, K.D., Vitalari, N.P., Davis, K.S.: Differences between novice and expert systems analysts: what do we know and what do we do? J. Manag. Inf. Syst. 15(1), 9–50 (1998)
5. Nelson, H.J., Poels, G., Genero, M., Piattini, M.: A conceptual modeling quality framework. Softw. Qual. J. 20(1), 201–228 (2012)
6. Van Merriënboer, J.J., Kirschner, P.A.: Ten Steps to Complex Learning: A Systematic Approach to Four-Component Instructional Design. Routledge (2017)
7. Wang, W., Brooks, R.J.: Empirical investigations of conceptual modeling and the modeling process. In: Proceedings of the 39th Conference on Winter Simulation: 40 Years! The Best is Yet to Come, pp. 762–770. IEEE Press (2007)
8. Shanks, G., Tansley, E., Weber, R.: Using ontology to validate conceptual models. Commun. ACM 46(10), 85–89 (2003)
9. Weerapong, S., Porouhan, P., Premchaiswadi, W.: Process mining using α-algorithm as a tool (a case study of student registration). In: 2012 10th International Conference on ICT and Knowledge Engineering (ICT & Knowledge Engineering), pp. 213–220. IEEE (2012)
10. Juhaňák, L., Zounek, J., Rohlíková, L.: Using process mining to analyze students' quiz-taking behavior patterns in a learning management system. Comput. Hum. Behav. (2017)
11. van der Aalst, W.M.P., Guo, S., Gorissen, P.: Comparative process mining in education: an approach based on process cubes. In: Ceravolo, P., Accorsi, R., Cudre-Mauroux, P. (eds.) SIMPDA 2013. LNBIP, vol. 203, pp. 110–134. Springer, Heidelberg (2015). https://doi.org/10.1007/978-3-662-46436-6_6
12. Papamitsiou, Z., Economides, A.A.: Process mining of interactions during computer-based testing for detecting and modelling guessing behavior. In: Zaphiris, P., Ioannou, A. (eds.) LCT 2016. LNCS, vol. 9753, pp. 437–449. Springer, Cham (2016). https://doi.org/10.1007/978-3-319-39483-1_40
13. Pinggera, J., et al.: Styles in business process modeling: an exploration and a model. Softw. Syst. Model. 14(3), 1055–1080 (2015)
14. Claes, J., Vanderfeesten, I., Pinggera, J., Reijers, H.A., Weber, B., Poels, G.: A visual analysis of the process of process modeling. Inf. Syst. e-Bus. Manag. 13(1), 147–190 (2015)
15. Sedrakyan, G., Snoeck, M., De Weerdt, J.: Process mining analysis of conceptual modeling behavior of novices-empirical study using jmermaid modeling and experimental logging environment. Comput. Hum. Behav. 41, 486–503 (2014)
16. Sedrakyan, G., De Weerdt, J., Snoeck, M.: Process-mining enabled feedback: tell me what i did wrong vs.tell me how to do it right. Comput. Hum. Behav. 57, 352–376 (2016)
17. Snoeck, M.: Enterprise Information Systems Engineering: The MERODE Approach. Springer Publishing Company, Incorporated, Switzerland (2014)

18. Haesen, R., Snoeck, M., Lemahieu, W., Poelmans, S.: Existence dependency-based domain modeling for improving stateless process enactment. In: 2009 World Conference on Services-I, pp. 515–521. IEEE (2009)
19. Snoeck, M., Dedene, G.: Existence dependency: the key to semantic integrity between structural and behavioral aspects of object types. IEEE Trans. Softw. Eng. **24**(4), 233–251 (1998)
20. Serral, E., De Weerdt, J., Sedrakyan, G., Snoeck, M.: Automating immediate and personalized feedback taking conceptual modelling education to a next level. In: 2016 IEEE Tenth International Conference on Research Challenges in Information Science (RCIS), pp. 1–6. IEEE (2016)

Towards Assessing the Multi-view Modeling Capability of Enterprise Modeling Methods

Afef Awadid[1(⊠)], Dominik Bork[2], and Selmin Nurcan[1]

[1] University of Paris 1 Pantheon-Sorbonne, Paris, France
afef.awadid@malix.univ-paris1.fr,
nurcan@univ-paris1.fr
[2] University of Vienna, Vienna, Austria
dominik.bork@univie.ac.at

Abstract. Today's enterprises and their underlying information systems ask for Multi-view Enterprise Modeling Methods (MVMMs) toward a comprehensive model representation. MVMMs capture the required aspects of complex systems using multiple views – the Multi-view Modeling (MVM) capability. However, not all modeling methods are endowed with a MVM capability. Means for assessing and improving such capability are therefore needed. Based on a comparative analysis of three MVMMs, we define the notion of MVM capability. Drawing on these criteria, an EBNF-based description is proposed, serving as a basis for MVM capability assessment. The strengths of the approach go beyond offering a common understanding of the MVM capability notion by (i) assessing the MVM capability, and (ii) identifying requirements to achieve this capability. Consequently, this approach primarily addresses method engineers aiming to employ MVM capability to a modeling method.

Keywords: Multi-view modeling · Capability · Assessment
Business process modeling · Enterprise modeling · Comparative analysis
EBNF rules

1 Introduction

In light of the complexity of today's enterprise and information systems owing to globalization and fierce competition amongst businesses, the need for Multi-view Modeling (MVM) to cope with such complexity in enterprise modeling is undisputed. MVM captures different aspects of the modelled system (e.g. its structure and its behavior) by different views (models) [1]. Each view (i) sheds light on certain aspects of the system, and (ii) is specified by a viewpoint which depicts the concepts considered by the view and the valid combinations (e.g. specified by a metamodel) [2].

MVM capability refers to how well an enterprise modeling method supports MVM [3]. This capability is embraced by what is commonly known as multi-view modeling methods (MVMMs). Enterprise Knowledge Development (EKD) [4], Function, Information, Dynamics, and Organization (FIDO) [5], and the Semantic Object Model (SOM) [6] are sample MVMMs from the enterprise modeling domain. All of them represent an enterprise by several interrelated views. However, when focusing the business process, not all are endowed with MVM capability.

© IFIP International Federation for Information Processing 2018
Published by Springer Nature Switzerland AG 2018. All Rights Reserved
R. A. Buchmann et al. (Eds.): PoEM 2018, LNBIP 335, pp. 351–361, 2018.
https://doi.org/10.1007/978-3-030-02302-7_22

Extant approaches focus on improving the MVM capability of a given method, usually eluding the question of assessment. This observation spawned the research that culminated in this paper. The overall question addressed in the present work is: *How to assess the MVM capability of a modeling method?* As a step towards an answer, we perceive the MVM capability as a quality criterion and decompose it into more fine-grained criteria. This idea has emerged from our previous work on the quality of business process modeling methods [7]. To identify the criteria, a comparative analysis of three MVMMs has been performed. Based on the analysis results, a formalized description for the MVM capability is presented that enables assessing the MVM capability of any modeling method.

Our approach can (i) assess the MVM capability of a modeling method, and (ii) identify requirements for adopting it in the context of method engineering. Method engineers aiming to introduce MVM capability benefit from this research in two ways: First, the formalized description enables the assessment of the MVM capability of a method. Second, our analysis reveals different ways of realizing MVM.

This paper is structured as follows: Sect. 2 provides the terminology used in the paper and briefly presents related works. Section 3 puts emphasis on the analysis of three MVMMs. In Sect. 4, a formalized description for assessing the MVM capability of modeling methods is defined and applied. Finally, we conclude the paper with an outlook on future work.

2   Terminological Foundations and Related Works

2.1   Multi-view Modeling: Key Terms

The viewpoint refers to the modelling language used to specify a view. A modeling language is syntactically defined by a meta model. Each view is represented by a conceptual model, and is specified by a viewpoint. The relationship between view and viewpoint is thus analogous to that between model and meta model [8]. A view allows capturing perspective(s). A perspective refers to certain aspect(s) from which the system under study can be viewed [9] (e.g., behavior and structure). These definitions given to the terms "viewpoint", "view" and "perspective" are respectively in line with the terms "viewpoint", "view" and "concern" as provided by ISO/IEC/IEEE 42010 [10]. The latter defines these three terms as follows: A viewpoint: is a work product establishing the conventions for the construction, interpretation, and use of architecture views to frame specific system concerns. A view is a work product expressing the architecture of a system with respect to specific system concerns. A concern is "any interest in the system". The term "concern" is usually associated with the notion of "separation of concerns". Separation of concerns means dealing with different aspects of a system individually. A separation of concerns is of type "horizontal" if the considered concerns belong to the same level of abstraction/phase of development, or otherwise of type "vertical" [11].

The notion of "capability" gains quite a lot of attraction in conceptual modeling (e.g., "capability-oriented information systems", "capability-driven development"). A comprehensive paper on the variety of interpretations of this notion is [12]. In this paper, we introduce the notion of "MVM capability". The latter is an instance of a more generic notion: "modeling method capability". In its broad sense, "modeling method capability" refers to the degree to which a method is able to achieve the goal(s) of modeling. A "modeling method capability" is therefore a quality criterion that is related to "Goals of modeling G": one of the main parts of the generic quality framework defined by [13]. When the modeling goal is to reduce the complexity of the system under study and hence to foster a better understanding of it, a specific notion is employed: "MVM capability". Based on this, MVM capability is defined *as the ability of a method to support MVM in order to curtail the complexity of the system under study.*

In MVM, viewpoints and hence views are not independent from each other since they all depict the same system under study. Consequently, inter-viewpoint relationships should be identified in order to manage consistency. Six types of inter-viewpoint relationships have been stressed in [14]. These types are useful in the management of inter-view consistency. By inter-view consistency, we refer to the extent to which information contained in multiple views is not contradicting [14].

2.2   Related Work

Most emphasis of the literature dealing with MVM in enterprise and business process modeling, is put on how to improve the MVM capability of a given modeling method. Broadly, each work uses either a unified or an hybrid approach to improve such capability. The former extends an existing unified overarching meta model to cover additional aspects. By contrast, the latter combines distinct modeling languages with separate meta models.

[15, 16] are example works adopting the unified approach. In [15], the emphasis was set on extending the UML Statechart language with security aspects. The focus in [16] was on extending BPMN to cover resource management and planning aspects. Additionally, literature yields works pursuing the hybrid approach. In [17], an integrative approach combines distinct modelling languages like BPMN and ER. The work in [18] illustrates the combination of I-STAR and BPMN.

In recent years, several works also aimed at the comprehensive analysis and comparison of enterprise modeling methods. The work presented in [19] analyses six enterprise modeling methods based on the formality of their specifications and enabled capabilities thereof. The authors in [9] performed a comparative assessment of three modeling methods with regard to criteria like completeness and simplicity. [20] proposed an analysis framework for assessing the explanatory capabilities of enterprise modeling methods. The authors in [21] analyzed four enterprise modeling methods with respect to background and goals of the methods in order to contribute to the elucidation of their overlaps, conceptual differences, and focal points. The work presented in [22] systematically evaluates enterprise modeling methods according to their capability of automatically generating ERP software.

In this paper, we build on these existing works and perform a comparative analysis that targets the MVM capability of enterprise modeling methods in order to contribute to a more comprehensive understanding on the design principles of such methods.

3   Analysis of Enterprise Modeling Methods

In this section, we start by defining a MVM analysis framework based on which a comparative analysis of enterprise modeling methods is performed

3.1   A Multi-view Modeling Analysis Framework

Guided by the terminological foundations presented in Sect. 2, an analysis framework is proposed (see Table 1) that accounts for the main particularities of MVM. This framework will steer the comparative analysis that follows. Table 1 points out the analysis criteria along with questions clarifying their intended scopes.

Table 1. Analysis framework.

Criterion	Explanation
System subject to multi-view modeling	What is/are the system(s) subject to multi-view modeling?
	What views are being specified by the method?
Viewpoints	What are the different modeling languages employed by the views?
Perspectives	What are the perspectives [9, 23] covered by the viewpoints?
	Which kind of separation of concerns [11] is employed?
Inter-viewpoint relationships	What kinds of relationships [14] exist between the viewpoints?
Inter-view consistency	Is inter-view consistency specified by the modeling method [14]?
	By which mechanisms is it realized [8]?

3.2   Comparative Analysis

In this subsection, the analysis framework is applied to comparatively analyze the EKD [4], FIDO [5] and SOM [6] enterprise modeling methods. These methods are selected as representative of MVMMs. Note that in our analysis, we are referring to the first version of the EKD method, which is significantly different from its successors. Moreover, for the sake of brevity and due to limited space, the analysis concentrates on the process-related aspects of these methods. In other words, considering a representation of an enterprise structure in terms of layers, our analysis targets only the layer "business processes". The comparative analysis is presented in Table 2.

The results show the heterogeneity of the methods regarding the MVM (e.g. heterogeneity in terms of the perspectives supported and the type of separation of concerns adopted). Hence, different ways of realizing MVM and therefore of managing complexity are possible. At the same time, common characteristics of the investigated methods with respect to MVM can be identified:

- All methods hold at least two modeling languages (viewpoints).
- Different perspectives are covered by the methods.

- Viewpoints and hence views are overlapping.
- A given perspective can be covered by more than one modeling language.
- Each modeling language can capture one or more perspectives.
- Horizontal and/or vertical separation of concerns is employed.
- Inter-view consistency management is a recurring aspect, but treated differently.

Table 2. Comparative analysis.

Criterion	EKD [4]	FIDO [5]	SOM [6]
System subject to multi-view modeling	Enterprise	Enterprise	Enterprise
	Intra-enterprise business processes	Inter-enterprise business processes	Enterprise business processes
Viewpoints	Actor-role Role-activity Business objects	FIDO 1 FIDO 4	Interaction schema Task-event schema Transaction decomposition Object decomposition
Perspectives	Behavioral Functional Informational Intentional Organizational	Behavioral Functional Informational Organizational Operational	Informational Behavioral Structural
	Horizontal separation of concerns	Vertical separation of concerns	Horizontal and vertical separation of concerns
Inter-viewpoint relationships	Semantic overlaps Syntactic overlaps	Semantic overlaps Syntactic overlaps Refinement/abstraction	Semantic overlaps Syntactic overlaps Refinement/abstraction
Inter-view consistency	Consistency rules on overarching metamodel	Shared concepts in distinct metamodels	Consistency rules on overarching metamodel
	Modeling guidelines	Conversion mechanisms	Automatic consistency mechanisms

In light of these results, the comparative analysis highlighted in Table 2 can be beneficial for any stakeholder whose purpose is to reduce the complexity of a given system. It indeed helps him in choosing between different ways of managing complexity the one that better meets his specific requirements.

4   An EBNF-Based Description to Assess the MVM Capability

This section introduces an Extended Backus Naur Form (EBNF)-based description of the MVM capability. It then shows how this description can be used to assess the MVM capability of modeling methods. Finally, a sample application evaluates the feasibility and shows its application with the EKD modeling method.

4.1   A Formalized Description of the Multi-view Modeling Capability

Compared to informal assessment, a formal assessment promotes an unambiguous understanding of the notion of MVM capability. To derive such description, we proceeded in two steps: First, we delineate the notion of MVM capability by separating it into its constitutive parts. Second, we used this notion to create a formalized description for assessing the MVM capability based on EBNF.

To delineate the notion of MVM capability (step 1), we chiefly relied on two aspects: On the one hand, the common characteristics of MVMMs drawn from the comparative analysis. On the other hand, we relied on our previous work [7] in which we performed a systematic literature review on the quality of business process modeling methods. Apart from perceiving the MVM capability as a quality criterion, the findings of such review showed that the expressiveness of a modeling method with respect to each required perspective is a basic quality criterion. Based on these two aspects, we define the MVM capability criterion in terms of three complementary sub criteria viz., *the support of separation of concerns principle*, *the support of multi-perspective modeling*, and *the expressiveness with respect to each required perspective*. The support of separation of concerns principle is defined as the ability of a modeling method to separate the covered perspectives into multiple views. The support of multi-perspective modeling refers to the ability of a modeling method to capture all required perspectives. Lastly, the expressiveness criterion refers to the extent to which a modeling method provides all required modeling constructs for each perspective.

Bearing in mind the output of step 1, assessing the MVM capability (step 2) amounts to combining means for assessing all the three sub criteria. As to 'separation of concerns principle', the assessment of this criterion can be based on the analysis results, and particularly on one of the identified characteristics: "A MVMM holds at least two modeling languages (viewpoints)". To assess the criterion "support of multi-perspective modeling', we will use the Giaglis' framework [24], as it matches the breadth (the modelling goals) with the depth (the required modeling perspectives). For the assessment of 'expressiveness with respect to each perspective', one can refer to one of the several frameworks in the literature. We choose the framework defined in [25] since it is generic, i.e., applicable independently of the modeling goal and because it covers multiple perspectives.

The EBNF description presented in Fig. 1 is a way of coupling the aforementioned means for assessing the three sub criteria. EBNF has the advantages of being simple, formal, and rule-based. The proposed description takes then the form of six EBNF rules that are mainly derived from our comparative analysis. Each rule comprises a Left Hand Side (LHS) and a Right Hand Side (RHS). The LHS refers to the name of the symbol which has to be non-terminal (i.e. non-atomic) and can be replaced by the RHS. The RHS represents the definition of the symbol. It can include terminal symbols, non-terminal symbols, or a combination of both.

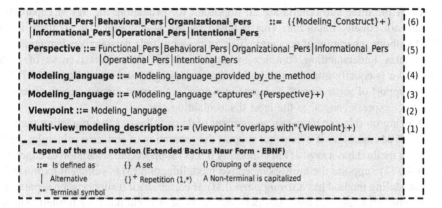

Fig. 1. A formalized description of MVM capability using EBNF.

4.2 Assessing the Multi-view Modeling Capability

Based on a construction of a proof tree (graphical demonstration), an assessment determines not only whether or not a modeling method is endowed with a MVM capability, but also graphically reveals the criterion (criteria) that establish(es) requirements for improving MVM capability. Considering the proposed EBNF description (Fig. 1), the tree is built in depth-first left-first order. At the root appears the LHS of the rule (1) (i.e. 'Multi-view_modeing_description'). By referring to the root level as level 0, each new tree level is derived from the previous one by following the procedure below:

- If the current node is 'Modeling_language_provided_by_the_method', replace the node by the actual modeling language provided by the assessed method.
- If the current node is a terminal, keep the node and move to the adjacent node.
- If the current node is a repetition (marked with the ' + ' sign) of a non-terminal, replace the node n times by this non-terminal. As for {Perspective} +, n and the required perspectives are determined using the Giaglis framework [24]. "Ø" is assigned to each not supported perspective. Regarding {Modeling_Construct} +, n and the required modeling constructs are determined using the metamodel defined in [25]. With respect to {Viewpoint} +, (n = total number of viewpoints provided by the method − 1). In case n is equal to zero, replace the node by "Ø".
- If the current node is 'Modeling_Construct', x is the level of this node. Using the aforementioned metamodel, replace the node by the actual required modeling construct at the tree level x + 1. Then, replace each required modeling construct by its corresponding modeling construct provided by the assessed method at the level x + 2. If no corresponding construct exists, replace the required construct by "Ø".
- If the current node is any other non-terminal, replace the node by its RHS using the EBNF rule number: (level of the current node + 1) if its root node at the level 1 is 'Viewpoint' and using the rule number: (level of the current node) if its root node is '{Viewpoint} +'. Repeat until the current node becomes a terminal.
- The construction terminates when all leaves are terminals.

Albeit the three sub criteria are all important for evaluating the MVM capability, they are not equally important. This is based on our assumption that: (i) there is no MVM without separation of concerns, (ii) capturing multiple perspectives is relevant as it facilitates understanding complex systems, and (iii) the expressiveness of each perspective is equally important to both customary (single view) modeling and MVM. Thus, 'support of separation of concerns principle' is the most discriminating criterion. Whereas, 'expressiveness' is the least discriminating one.

Drawing on this, we define an assessment scale as follows: (a) A modeling method has *no MVM capability* if it does not support the separation of concerns principle; (b) A modeling method has a *total MVM capability* if it (1) supports the separation of concerns principle, (2) supports the multi-perspective modeling, and (3) is sufficient expressive; (c) A modeling method has a *strong partial MVM capability* if it supports the separation of concerns principle and the multi-perspective modeling, but has only limited expressiveness; and (d) Otherwise, a modeling method has a *weak partial MVM capability*.

An assessed method requires improvement in terms of (i) 'Support of separation of concerns principle', if the symbol "∅" is assigned at least to one 'Viewpoint' node; (ii) 'Support of multi-perspective modeling', in case the symbol "∅" is assigned to all the occurrences of at least one 'Perspective' node, and (iii) 'Expressiveness, if the symbol "∅" is assigned to all the occurrences of at least one 'Modeling_Construct' node.

4.3   Assessing the Multi-view Modeling Capability of EKD

To evaluate the MVM capability of EKD, we opted for an advanced level of assessment by constructing a proof tree. Since the tree is too large to show in the paper, only the part that reveals deficiencies of the method is visualized (Fig. 2). By referring to the Giaglis framework, four perspectives are required to grasp the wider system picture: functional, organizational, behavioral, and informational.

As highlighted in blue in Fig. 2, the Role Activity Language does not support all the required modeling constructs for the functional and the behavioral perspectives. As to the organizational and the informational perspectives, their required modeling constructs are fully supported by respectively the Actor Role Language and the Business Objects Language (the two other parts of the tree). Hence, following the

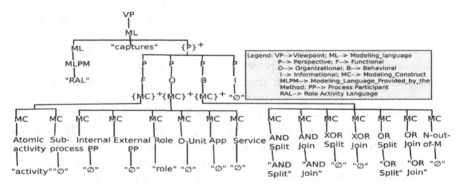

Fig. 2. A part of the constructed tree for assessing the MVM capability of EKD.

assessment scale defined in the previous section, EKD possesses a *strong partial MVM capability*, as only the criterion 'expressiveness' needs improvement. The deficiency in expressiveness has also appeared in the part of the tree pertaining to the Actor Role Language, where only one modeling construct (Actor) is provided to represent all types of process participants (internal, external and organizational unit).

5 Concluding Remarks

Based on a systematic analysis of three enterprise modeling methods with respect to how they realize multi-view modeling, this paper (1) describes the main characteristics of realizations of multi-view enterprise modeling; and (2) defines the notion of MVM capability in terms of support of separation of concerns principle, support of multi-perspective modeling, and expressiveness. These findings have been used to develop a set of EBNF rules that enable the formalized description of the MVM capability. An application of the rules to the EKD method showed, how they enable the assessment of the MVM capability of modeling methods.

This research establishes a first step towards a common understanding of the MVM capability notion. The results of this research are of primary interest for the assessment of existing methods and method engineers, designing a new multi-view modeling method. Future research will apply the rule base to evaluate more modeling methods in order to improve the EBNF description and to cover also individual aspects that have, for now, been neglected by aiming at general applicability.

References

1. Reineke, J., Tripakis, S.: Basic problems in multi-view modeling. In: Ábrahám, E., Havelund, K. (eds.) TACAS 2014. LNCS, vol. 8413, pp. 217–232. Springer, Heidelberg (2014). https://doi.org/10.1007/978-3-642-54862-8_15
2. Bork, D., Karagiannis, D.: Model-driven development of multi-view modelling tools the MUVIEMOT approach. In: 9th International Conference on Software Paradigm Trends, p. IS-11. IEEE (2014)
3. Awadid, A.: Supporting the consistency in multi-perspective business process modeling: a mapping approach. In: 11th International Conference on Research Challenges in Information Science, pp. 414–419. IEEE (2017)
4. Loucopoulos, P., Kavakli, V., Prekas, N., Rolland, C., Grosz, G., Nurcan, S.: Using the EKD approach: the modelling component, Paris (1997). https://hal.archives-ouvertes.fr/hal-00707997. Accessed 19 May 2018
5. Shunk, D.L., Kim, J.I., Nam, H.Y.: The application of an integrated enterprise modeling methodology—FIDO—to supply chain integration modeling. Comput. Ind. Eng. **45**(1), 167–193 (2003)
6. Ferstl, O.K., Sinz, E.J.: Grundlagen der Wirtschaftsinformatik, 7th edn. Oldenbourg, München (2013)
7. Awadid, A., Nurcan, S., Ghannouchi, S.A.: Towards a decision-support system for selecting the appropriate business process modeling formalism: a context-aware roadmap. In: Enterprise, Business-Process, and Information Systems Modeling, pp. 239–256. Springer (2017)

8. Bork, D., Buchmann, R., Karagiannis, D.: Preserving multi-view consistency in diagrammatic knowledge representation. In: Zhang, S., Wirsing, M., Zhang, Z. (eds.) KSEM 2015. LNCS (LNAI), vol. 9403, pp. 177–182. Springer, Cham (2015). https://doi.org/10.1007/978-3-319-25159-2_16

9. Daoudi, F., Nurcan, S.: A benchmarking framework for methods to design flexible business processes. Softw. Process. Improv. Pract. **12**(1), 51–63 (2007)

10. Systems and software engineering—architecture description: ISO/IEC/IEEE 42010. http://www.iso-architecture.org/ieee-1471/cm/. Accessed 19 May 2018

11. Solberg, A., Simmonds, D., Reddy, R., Ghosh, S., France, R.: Using aspect oriented techniques to support separation of concerns in model driven development. In: 29th International Conference on Computer Software and Applications, vol. 1, pp. 121–126. IEEE (2005)

12. Zdravkovic, J., Stirna, J., Grabis, J.: A comparative analysis of using the capability notion for congruent business and information systems engineering. Complex Syst. Inform. Model. Q. **10**, 1–20 (2017)

13. Nysetvold, A.G., Krogstie, J.: Assessing business process modeling languages using a generic quality framework. In: Advanced Topics in Database Research, pp. 79–93. IGI Global (2006)

14. Persson, M., et al.: A characterization of integrated multi-view modeling in the context of embedded and cyber-physical systems. In: Proceedings of the Eleventh ACM International Conference on Em-bedded Software, p. 10. IEEE Press (2013)

15. El-Attar, M., Luqman, H., Karpati, P., Sindre, G., Opdahl, A.L.: Extending the UML statecharts notation to model security aspects. IEEE Trans. Software Eng. **41**(7), 661–690 (2015)

16. Meyer, A.: Resource perspective in BPMN: extending BPMN to support resource management and planning. Master's thesis, Hasso Plattner Institute, University of Potsdam (2009)

17. Letsholo, K.J., Chioasca, E.V., Zhao, L.: An integrative approach to support multi-perspective business process modeling. Int. J. Serv. Comput. **2**(1), 11–24 (2014)

18. Koliadis, G., Vranesevic, A., Bhuiyan, M., Krishna, A., Ghose, A.: Combining *i** and BPMN for business process model lifecycle management. In: Eder, J., Dustdar, S. (eds.) BPM 2006. LNCS, vol. 4103, pp. 416–427. Springer, Heidelberg (2006). https://doi.org/10.1007/11837862_39

19. Bork, D., Fill, H.G.: Formal aspects of enterprise modeling methods: a comparison framework. In: 47th Hawaii International Conference on System Sciences, pp. 3400–3409. IEEE (2014)

20. Kaczmarek, M., Bock, A., Heß, M.: On the explanatory capabilities of enterprise modeling approaches. In: Aveiro, D., Pergl, R., Valenta, M. (eds.) EEWC 2015. LNBIP, vol. 211, pp. 128–143. Springer, Cham (2015). https://doi.org/10.1007/978-3-319-19297-0_9

21. Bock, A., Kaczmarek, M., Overbeek, S., Heß, M.: A comparative analysis of selected enterprise modeling approaches. In: Frank, U., Loucopoulos, P., Pastor, Ó., Petrounias, I. (eds.) PoEM 2014. LNBIP, vol. 197, pp. 148–163. Springer, Heidelberg (2014). https://doi.org/10.1007/978-3-662-45501-2_11

22. Schunselaar, D.M., Gulden, J., van der Schuur, H., Reijers, H.A.: A Systematic evaluation of enterprise modelling approaches on their applicability to automatically generate ERP software. In: 18th Conference on Business Informatics, pp. 290–299. IEEE (2016)

23. Awadid, A., Nurcan, S.: Softw. Syst. Model (2017). https://doi.org/10.1007/s10270-017-0629-2

24. Giaglis, G.M.: A taxonomy of business process modeling and information systems modeling techniques. J. Flex. Manuf. Syst. **13**(2), 209–228 (2001)
25. List, B., Korherr, B.: An evaluation of conceptual business process modelling languages. In: Proceedings of the symposium on applied computing, pp. 1532–1539. ACM (2006)

Toward an Adaptive Enterprise Modelling Platform

Amjad Fayoumi[(✉)]

Management Science, Lancaster University, Lancaster LA1 4YX, UK
a.fayoumi@lancaster.ac.uk

Abstract. For the past three decades, enterprise modelling (EM) has been emerging as a significant yet complex paradigm to tackle holistic systematic enterprise analysis and design. With a high fluctuation in the global economy, industrial stability and technology shift, the necessity of such paradigms becomes crucial in determining the decisions that an enterprise can make for surviving in such a highly dynamic business ecosystem. EM practices have focused for a long time, on the design-time of enterprise systems. Recently, there has been a rapid development in data analytics, machine learning and intelligent systems from which an EM platform can benefit. EM needs to cope with the new changes in both business and technology; it should also help architects to determine optimum decisions and reduce complexity in technical infrastructure. In this paper, the author discusses several challenges facing enterprise modelling practices and offers an architectural notion for future development focusing on the requirements of a platform that can be called intelligent and adaptive.

Keywords: Enterprise modelling · Enterprise modelling challenges
Enterprise modelling adaptive platform

1   Introduction

In recent years, we have seen a rapid advancement in practices and technologies that aid enterprise development and their ability to support informed and timely decisions. Enterprise Modelling (EM) has seen much interest and development, and in fact, has proved useful for many enterprises in the industry. Although EM has developed significantly in the last three decades and helped organisations in their business and IT (Information Technology) transformation efforts, it still needs to incorporate the paradigm shift in technology. Recent researches in the area of EM have highlighted the need to increase the sophistication and capabilities of both their practices and tools as they are still far from their maximum potential [1]. For instance, previous researches have acknowledged the issues of integration and interoperability of enterprise models, and organizations' need to be able to exchange and integrate their enterprise models easily [2]. In addition, specific research has suggested further consideration of assistive technology [1]. EM has for a long time been concerned with the enterprise design-time; the focus should also cover the run-time. Previous researches almost neglected the paradigm shift but now organisations are moving towards more shared service models

R. A. Buchmann et al. (Eds.): PoEM 2018, LNBIP 335, pp. 362–371, 2018.
https://doi.org/10.1007/978-3-030-02302-7_23

that heavily use APIs and micro-services towards more data analytics and more automation that reduces human errors and minimises their involvement in the Cyber-Physical Systems (CPS) [3]. EM practices should demonstrate how enterprises can be designed for future demand, increased resilience, agility and be able to respond to emergent changes rapidly.

This paper argues that future EM can support this notion through the use of intelligent and knowledge-based systems toward an adaptive enterprise modelling platform. What is meant by adaptive EM platform is bringing together the two notions of automated design, and run-times enterprise models intertwined, thus enabling the design, governance and validation of enterprise models within the same platform. I propose using advanced analytics and AI (Artificial Intelligence), to enable self-healing or the correction mechanism enterprise systems that are performed by systems instead of humans [4, 5]. In this case, the role of the enterprise designer is limited to monitoring the dashboards to check the enterprise status and to recreate only if adjustment is required for any part of the enterprise models due to the limitation in information. With a versioning mechanism, we can also track the evolution of the enterprise models, how it was and what it became with the help of intelligent systems. This paper focuses on the following research questions:

1. What are the current themes of EM and the focus of current research?
2. What are the limitations and challenges of EM research and practices?
3. What are the requirements for an adaptive enterprise modelling platform?
4. How possible is it to implement this platform through utilising available tools?

The rest of the paper is structured accordingly: Sect. 2 offers a brief review on EM practices and illustrates the current themes and capabilities of contemporary EM frameworks. There is then discussion of the current challenges of these practices from an IT paradigm shift perspective toward more adaptive and intelligent platforms. Section 3 identifies future EM platform requirements for an intelligent and adaptive EM platform, and offers a notion on how it can be implemented in Sect. 4. Finally, the paperconcludes with Sect. 5, which discusses the next steps of this research.

2 Current Themes and Capabilities in EM Research

One of the focuses of a recent development was the domain-specific modelling languages [6, 7], which can offer models (syntax, semantic, and notations) embedded in modelling tools for specific business or system domains. Loucopoulos et al. [8] introduced capability oriented enterprise modelling, focusing on the concept of capability and how it responds to an enterprise and changing need. Fill [9] developed a modelling framework from semantic annotation called SeMFIS (Semantic-based Modelling Framework for Information Systems). Multi-perspective Enterprise Modelling (MEMO) also shows a sophisticated development in terms of metamodel, notations and enterprise aspects integration. These frameworks were implemented using the ADOxx framework [10]. Boissier et al. [11] proposed an extension of the EM practices for a decentralised enterprise, e.g. corporate and holding companies, with the model containing a metamodel and practices for tackling enterprise efforts in a similar environment. Hinkelmann et al. [12] also proposed an approach using the metamodelling framework ADOxx [13] and integration ontology to align business with IT. The same framework was used for creating domain-specific modelling languages [14]. Many of these initiatives were part of OMiLAB [13] – the Open Model initiative Laboratory. Two other important EM frameworks are DEMO (e.g. Dietz [15]) and 4EM (e.g. Sandkuhl et al. [16]) were proposed. Another area which has also received attention is that which is relevant to architecture patterns [17], whereby an analyst can orchestrate enterprise models from previously defined patterns, and thus speed up the modelling process and deployment [18]. These patterns can be used and re-used in different scenarios within different organizations.

Another line of recent research focuses on simulation. One interesting implementation is related to the effort made to map business-process modelling notations to simulation-executable specifications. The Workflow Management Coalition (WfMC) has developed a standard, called BPSim, to respond to the need to support interoperability between modelling standards and simulation engines. BPSim can interchange and parameterize business-process analysis data to apply KPIs better, predict business performance, validate process design, allocate resources, and reduce overall operational risk [19]. Simulation can cover both discrete-event and continuous dynamic [18] simulations. Other recent researches have also made a considerable contribution in linking both Business Process Modelling and Notation (BPMN) and process mining [20, 21]. A summary describing the capabilities of current enterprise modelling platforms and frameworks are presented as the following:

- Modelling notation: A graphical representation that has sound syntax, sometimes it is supported by a procedural approach to guide the designer through the modelling steps. It is used to model and simulate both the current enterprise state ('as is') and the future design goal state ('to be'). The design stage may also involve testing, evaluation of the designed model, and the measure of scalability, robustness, agility, and security. Modelling notations can be developed using modelling frameworks such as ADOxx, and EMF.

- Interoperability semantic metamodel: This consists of two parts – model integration and model transformation. The integration will allow models from different enterprise perspectives to be linked together semantically; while transformation, with the support of ontology, can help to map model artefacts to another form, which can be used in another model that has a different level of granularity, mathematical formulation, or software code. The metamodel layer should be agile in a way that allows practitioners to change some of its parameters without affecting the entire metamodel semantic. Metamodels can be developed using metamodels editors like MetaEdit, ADOxx, and EMF.

- Simulation and logical formulation: To enable simulation and optimization, the model artefacts need to be calibrated to formal logic and mathematical equations. The formal logic describes how the model artefacts are connected to the simulation constructs, and the impact they have on each other. Moreover, depending on the simulation technique used, it might allow for simulating and testing different 'what-if' scenarios and the values-flow between model elements.

- Implementation and code-generating: A typical model-driven development mechanism translates models to code. Here, some of the models should be translated to some sort of software enabler form; from the high-level abstract domain notations rather than building a large number of Unified Modelling Language (UML) analysis and design models. Typically, many of the model-driven development tools can generate code out of software models e.g. Eclipse, Papyrus, and many others. One of the main challenges here is related to the ability of mapping to serve different levels of implementation scenarios. Pattern orchestration among different levels of model granularity can help to streamline the process of scenario change in order to generate different sets of software-dependent components or code. It is important to mention that not all of the enterprise models are developed for this purpose, rather they capture enterprise holistic knowledge for various purposes.

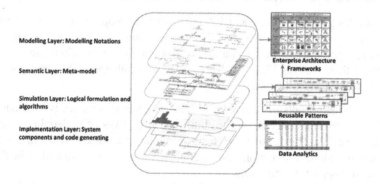

Fig. 1. Enterprise modelling and simulation capabilities layers

With reference to Fig. 1, the capabilities are recognised as layers of design interface (syntax), design interoperability (semantic), simulation, and implementation. There is feedback from the simulation layer to the design layer, where the simulation of business activities beside advanced data analytics can offer an insight to how enterprise aspects can be designed better to continuously move from 'as is' to 'to be'. Also, it helps in evaluating the current business activities based on performance metrics, and against the design objectives. This, with the support of enterprise simulation and optimization, will feed into rethinking and evolving the architecture and the design models. In the same way, technology and information systems will feed back to business activities in terms of potential new capabilities that can lead to innovation in the applicable business model, and can also provide information about the challenges and limitations that technology imposes on the enterprise's business activities. Thus, technology and information systems might also require a new design, modernization, or optimization. Therefore, feedback regarding modelling, design and simulation is necessary to support appropriate rethinking of the technical design and architecture.

The semantic layer will support the interoperability between modelling notations and simulation engines. Two solutions were proposed in the literature [2] to address models' interoperability: (1) building a unified semantic metamodel that can be used by every tool and every model, and (2) model transformation by building transformation rules to translate between two models, which also requires the use of ontology to map concepts from two different models. The model integration can also take place by both mapping and unifying the model artefacts' semantics. Also, current literature describing the state-of-the-art in the modelling domain has acknowledged that using design and architecture patterns will certainly make the modelling easier. Analysts will be able to orchestrate their enterprise models from previously defined patterns, and thus speed up the modelling process and deployment. Patterns can be structural, behavioural, constraining, or values. Business and IS design models should be available in a repository to cut the design and development time significantly. Also, these patterns can be used and re-used in different scenarios within different organizations. Further, the analyst/architect experience plays a role that impacts the quality of the analysis and design as noticed.

2.1   Challenges to Current Enterprise Modelling Practices

Despite the long time that EM and EA have been developing, the level of maturity reached in some cases has not met the expectations of some current enterprises. Many EM projects are subject to failure, or sometimes organizations are not able to fully realize their benefits [22]. To overcome these challenges, EM practices need to address the following limitations:

- Most of the effort falls on the analyst/designer to decide what needs to be addressed in the enterprise's concerns and to fulfil their objectives of undertaking the entire modelling effort. This needs to be changed to minimise human error and any lack of judgement. More automation and intelligence need to be embedded in the EM system to support decision-making.
- The difficulty of managing and coordinating knowledge among stakeholders from one side and the systems' ever-increasing complexity from the other. It should enable acquiring and exposing information whenever it is required in rigid visualization [23].
- Although EM was presented with the aim of reducing analysis and design complexity, the maintenance and manual updating of enterprise knowledge is still the main theme of how EM is conducted. The current techniques and models have only mitigated this by building domain-specific modelling languages (DSML) [6, 7] which can simplify manual updating for non-expert users. Nevertheless, building domain graphical notations is still an important aspect, but the future development should focus on building an adaptive and intelligent platform that minimises human involvement and relies more on automated decision-making. The EM platform should have the ability to sense and reconfigure enterprise models according to any changes in the environment.

3   Requirements for Adaptive Enterprise Modelling Platform

Recently, new research has focused on the reverse design that focuses on understanding the enterprise design from the data, e.g. the process mining approach presented in [24]. This work focuses on visualising the process model from a log-events analysis, with an aim to understand what is actually happening when the process is executed and helps to identify any bottlenecks in the process. It also helps in identifying the gap between the actual processes (in run-time) and the designed ones (in design-time). A similar notion is fairly well-developed in tools like 'IBM business process management'; this tool has a workflow engine underlying the process model that is supporting service-oriented architecture (SOA) and allows tracking of all the activities and outputs during the run-time with sophisticated dashboards. Such a notion is not widely developed in the mainstream enterprise modelling tools. Some other researches have explored the link between business processes and intelligent systems [25], showing how a role activity diagram (RAD) can be implemented using multi-agent systems.

The adaptive EM platform allows enterprises to intertwine between the design-time and run-time configuration in a semi-automated manner. The platform will enable reconfiguration of the enterprise models according to a set of high-level rules that use advance data analytics and machine learning to visualise models from run-time, and consequently govern, identify gaps, alert and rebuild enterprise models to achieve the goals in the highest enterprise level. To fulfil this aim I identified the set of requirements listed below:

REQ1: Modelling Decision-Support: The EM platform should offer decision-support capabilities for enterprise analysts and designers. For instance, designers will select the enterprise business domain, then the reference architecture will be automatically selected to match the selected business domain. The EM platform will ask for the size of the enterprise, number of employees, customers types and segments, products and services. Then the platform will be able to reconfigure the architecture accordingly and suggest core and secondary operational processes with the industrial best practices (e.g. industrial practices listed in [18]) that are required to ensure operational process quality. The system will notify designers about what happens if either a core or secondary process is neglected and thus determines the impact on the enterprise. The system then will suggest what underlying IS services and components are required to execute the processes; offering alternative implementations where possible.

REQ2: The Use of Data Analytics: Data analysis and pattern recognition: Modern enterprise modelling should respond to changes in the enterprise environment. Nowadays, the means of external and internal data collection are increasing. Capturing data and events from numerous enterprise activities and sources such as social, economic, organizational, and financial data can be invaluable to inform the enterprise modelling design. The data can also help in evaluating the efficiency and effectiveness of the designed enterprise models for better optimization (using the simulation models). Finally, the data can be used to create predictive analysis and should support the design of future enterprise models.

REQ3: Intelligent Adaptive System: EM must be more intelligent and proactive. A large number of activities and decisions can be automated to improve responsiveness and minimise errors. Insight from other artificial intelligence (AI) research areas is required (e.g. multi-agent systems, machine learning, knowledge query, and reasoning and rule-based systems) to enhance the responsiveness and adaptability of the enterprise information systems. For example, machine and deep learning can be used for predictive analysis and inform the designer when some aspects of the design need to be changed. Other methods can also be used to support automatic configuration such as game theory, goal-orientated multi-agent systems, and swarm intelligence. Methods inspired by self-healing systems can be used to ensure the stability of the enterprise system.

4 EM for Adaptive Enterprise Systems – Future Scope

The main goal of developing adaptive systems is to create an autonomic heterogeneous system that can sustainably design and reconfigure itself to handle different types of change and new knowledge [26]. It should consider different types of knowledge that the enterprise ecosystem can offer. It is strongly influenced by evolutionary theory and sees the enterprise as a self-organising entity. To realise this modelling ecosystem, the proposal in this paper focuses on four main components of the adaptive enterprise modelling platform as proposed in Fig. 2.

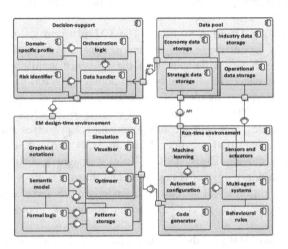

Fig. 2. Components for adaptive enterprise modelling platform (future scope)

1. The design-time: this contains the basic elements of EM, modelling notation, semantic-metamodel, the logical formulation of the models and the simulation engine. The simulation engine can optimise and confirm simulation results toward some specific configuration. Lessons can be learned from process mining methods [24] which extract and visualise processes from operating systems in real time, which in turn helps to support decision-making and perform enterprise transformation or change. The optimiser should be connected to the process-mining visualiser to import real-time data/event-logs to support the design process. The platform will take into consideration the transformation of: (a) the current enterprise business design to a ubiquitous architecture, and (b) the involvement of stakeholders and their impact on the evolution of the entire enterprise. Also, it should be supported by a repository of enterprise models' patterns for quicker deployment and

adaptation. The repository will offer the means to extract enterprise systems patterns from legacy systems 'bottom up' which answers the question of what an enterprise can do with its current IS capabilities, and will be able to suggest alternative enterprise systems patterns in a lower level of granularity to implement higher-level enterprise goals 'top down'. At the execution level, the patterns will be executed using a workflow engine, business rule management systems (rule engines), an events handler, and with the service's code generating in the run-time environment.

2. Decision-support: to offer the logical and automated rules that help designers in constructing enterprise models in responding to Req. 1. The models should correspond to standard practices in industry – this is referred to as domain-specific profiles, and these can be industry-based, e.g. manufacturing or public services, or functional-based, e.g. IT services delivery. When models in a high-level of enterprise granularity are constructed, the platform will suggest what models are required in the lower-level of granularity and which ones are best used with the constructed models. Also, it will support some sort of data analytics and visualisation to analyse the risk associated with deploying one or more enterprise models. This is also supported by real-time data analysis which is required to identify the nature, level and impact of changes and offer feedback to the designer. This is particularly important when information/knowledge is limited, a human must intervene to make a decision as human-in-the-loop.

3. Data pool: data sources are required to address Req. 2, where an organisation gathers all the relevant data or has access to external data which is useful for their business. Both structured and non-structured data is currently stored, and enterprises start to make better decisions by analysing this data using different mechanisms. It is recommended to ingrate the data pipeline with the enterprise design either for direct analysis and visualisation for human decision-making, or to reconfigure and re-link enterprise models, or to change the configuration of the enterprise systems according to a set of predefined rules.

4. The run-time: intelligent systems are required to build an intelligent information system infrastructure that addresses Req. 3. The run-time of the suggested adaptive platform could help in automating the knowledge or data acquisition into the enterprise information systems' architecture. The run-time will also use techniques of machine learning to handle the acquired data. Therefore, it will adjust the deployment of the run-time using a classifier to classify the acquired knowledge classes and their potential impacts. A synthesizer will work to match the classified data with their relevant enterprise systems and behavioural rules to enable the automatic configuration of one or more parts of the enterprise system. The required change can support: (a) optimisation, (b) a change in execution rules, events or workflow, and (c) a change in the APIs or the software service architecture. Any required change in the IS infrastructure will need an involvement from the designer. Furthermore, agents can learn and make decisions towards the optimal goal set by managers using AI techniques which enables agents to evolve, adapt and change their behaviour according to the new situation, in order to achieve the assigned goal (e.g. using human cognitive BDI agent structure (belief, desire, intention, and action)) [25]. It will make enterprises adaptable according to the environment changes towards the realisation of the dynamic information systems' architecture.

The software agents will interact with each other in a multi-agent system framework. The software agents will also interact with the human actors to audit and control the human behaviour to ensure quality and achievement of the goal. Also, agents will bridge the knowledge from the environment with both the design and run-time platforms. Figure 2 depicts the future adaptive platform components.

5 Conclusions

In this paper, I offered a brief discussion on the current state-of-the-art in EM and discussed the limitations and challenges of EM practices. I then presented what is needed for the future EM platform; a list of requirements has been identified. A notion to move forward towards adaptive EM for implementing a next-generation EM platform was also presented. The platform contains components of advanced data analytics, process mining, machine learning and multi-agent systems as additional elements that extend EM capabilities. The research-in-progress presented in this paper follows the design science approach for information systems research [27] by identifying the problem, objectives of the solution and designing the solution. The research will continue in the development, evaluating and communicating of the suggested platform. Future research can focus on developing and implementing the suggested platform by exploiting the successful ADOxx [28] and create an extension of the current ADOxx metamodel. The extension will consider creating a metamodel for both the decision-support components and the intelligent adaptive components.

References

1. Sandkuhl, K., et al.: From expert discipline to common practice: a vision and research agenda for extending the reach of enterprise modeling. Bus. Inf. Syst. Eng. 60(1), 69–80 (2018)
2. Karagiannis, D., Fill, H.-G., Höfferer, P., Nemetz, M.: Metamodeling: some application areas in information systems. In: Kaschek, R., Kop, C., Steinberger, C., Fliedl, G. (eds.) UNISCON 2008. LNBIP, vol. 5, pp. 175–188. Springer, Heidelberg (2008). https://doi.org/10.1007/978-3-540-78942-0_19
3. Hehenberger, P., Vogel-Heuser, B., Bradley, D., Eynard, B., Tomiyama, T., Achiche, S.: Design, modelling, simulation and integration of cyber physical systems: Methods and applications. Comput. Ind. 82, 273–289 (2016)
4. Seiger, R, Huber, S, Schlegel, T: Toward an execution system for self-healing workflows in cyber-physical systems. Softw. Syst. Model. 17, 1–22 (2016)
5. Schneider, C., Barker, A., Dobson, S.: A survey of self-healing systems frameworks. Softw. Pract. Exp. 45(10), 1375–1398 (2015)
6. Frank, U.: Domain-specific modeling languages: requirements analysis and design guidelines. In: Reinhartz-Berger, I., Sturm, A., Clark, T., Cohen, S., Bettin, J. (eds.) Domain Engineering. Springer, Heidelberg (2013). https://doi.org/10.1007/978-3-642-36654-3_6
7. Laforcade, P.: A Domain-Specific Modeling approach for supporting the specification of Visual Instructional Design Languages and the building of dedicated editors. J. Vis. Lang. Comput. 21(6), 347–358 (2010)

8. Loucopoulos, P., Stratigaki, C., Danesh, M.H., Bravos, G., Anagnostopoulos, D., Dimitrakopoulos, G.: Enterprise capability modeling: concepts, method, and application. In: 2015 International Conference on Enterprise Systems (ES), pp. 66–77. IEEE (2015)
9. Fill, H.-G.: SeMFIS: a flexible engineering platform for semantic annotations of conceptual models. Semant. Web, 1–17 (2017, Preprint)
10. Bock, A., Frank, U.: Multi-perspective enterprise modeling—conceptual foundation and implementation with ADOxx. In: Karagiannis, D., Mayr, H., Mylopoulos, J. (eds.) Domain-Specific Conceptual Modeling, pp. 241–267. Springer, Cham (2016). https://doi.org/10.1007/978-3-319-39417-6_11
11. Boissier, F., Rychkova, I., Zdravkovic, J.: Extending enterprise modeling for decentralized organizations. Université Paris 1-Panthéon Sorbonne, Stockholm University (2016)
12. Hinkelmann, K., Gerber, A., Karagiannis, D., Thoenssen, B., van der Merwe, A., Woitsch, R.: A new paradigm for the continuous alignment of business and IT: combining enterprise architecture modelling and enterprise ontology. Comput. Ind. **79** (2015). https://doi.org/10.1016/j.compind.2015.07.009
13. OMiLAB Open Model Lab. http://www.OMiLAB.org/. Accessed 20 Mar 2017
14. Karagiannis, D., Buchmann, R.A., Burzynski, P., Reimer, U., Walch, M.: Fundamental conceptual modeling languages in OMiLAB. In: Karagiannis, D., Mayr, H., Mylopoulos, J. (eds.) Domain-Specific Conceptual Modeling, pp. 3–30. Springer, Cham (2016). https://doi.org/10.1007/978-3-319-39417-6_1
15. Dietz, J.L: Enterprise Ontology: Theory and Methodology. Springer, Heidelberg (2006). https://doi.org/10.1007/3-540-33149-2
16. Sandkuhl, K., Stirna, J., Persson, A., Wißotzki, M.: Enterprise Modeling. Tackling Business Challenges with the 4EM Method, p. 309. Springer, Heidelberg (2014). https://doi.org/10.1007/978-3-662-43725-4
17. Stirna, J., Persson, A., Aggestam, L: Building knowledge repositories with enterprise modelling and patterns-from theory to practice. In: Proceedings of the ECIS 2006 (2006)
18. Fayoumi, A., Loucopoulos, P.: Conceptual modeling for the design of intelligent and emergent information systems. Expert Syst. Appl. **59**, 174–194 (2016)
19. Workflow Management Coalition: BPSim standard (2012). http://www.bpsim.org
20. Kalenkova, A.A., van der Aalst, W.M., Lomazova, I.A., Rubin, V.A.: Process mining using BPMN: relating event logs and process models. Softw. Syst. Model. **16**(4), 1019–1048 (2017)
21. Fayoumi, A.: Ecosystem-inspired enterprise modelling framework for collaborative and networked manufacturing systems. Comput. Ind. **80**, 54–68 (2016)
22. Stirna, J., Zdravkovic, J.: Interview with Sladjan Maras on "Challenges and Needs in Enterprise Modeling". Bus. Inf. Syst. Eng. **57**(1), 79 (2015)
23. Goul, M., Corral, K.: Enterprise model management and next generation decision support. Decis. Support Syst. **43**(3), 915–932 (2007)
24. Van Der Aalst, W.M.P.: Process Mining: Discovery, Conformance and Enhancement of Business Processes, vol. 8, p. 18. Springer, Heidelberg (2011). https://doi.org/10.1007/978-3-642-19345-3
25. Bădică, A., Bădică, C., Leon, F., Buligiu, I.: Modeling and enactment of business agents using Jason. In: Proceedings of the 9th Hellenic Conference on Artificial Intelligence, pp. 10:1–10.10 ACM (2016)
26. Dalpiaz, F., Giorgini, P., Mylopoulos, J.: Adaptive socio-technical systems: a requirements-based approach. Requir. Eng. **18**(1), 1–24 (2013)
27. Peffers, K., Tuunanen, T., Rothenberger, M.A., Chatterjee, S.: A design science research methodology for information systems research. J. Manag. Inf. Syst. **24**(3), 45–77 (2007)
28. Fill, H.-G., Karagiannis, D.: On the conceptualisation of modelling methods using the ADOxx meta modelling platform. Enterp. Model. Inf. Syst. Arch. Int. J. **8**(1), 4–25 (2013)

OntoREA© Accounting and Finance Model: Hedge Portfolio Representation of Derivatives

Christian Fischer-Pauzenberger[ID] and Walter S. A. Schwaiger[(✉)][ID]

Institute of Management Science, Technische Universität Wien,
Theresianumgasse 27, 1040 Vienna, Austria
{christian.fischer-pauzenberger,
walter.schwaiger}@tuwien.ac.at

Abstract. OntoREA© is a specification of the Accounting and Finance domain in the OntoUML language [1]. In a previous article [2] the authors use a forward contract financial derivative instrument to demonstrate the validity of the OntoREA© model within the design science research methodology (DSRM) [3]. A forward contract does not change over time and therefore can be modelled as *static* hedge portfolio composition. However, it is of interest if the OntoREA© model can also hold true for *dynamic* hedge portfolio compositions, as induced by option contract financial derivative instruments. This article investigates on that and delivers proof that the OntoREA© model is suitable for option contracts as well. Through adequately refining the platform specific database model (PSM) the policy's dynamic nature can be demonstrated. Moreover, including a Plan/Do/Check/Act (PDCA) process model for the specification of the option contract replication also demonstrates the information processing in the REA accounting infrastructure. The proposed approach is implemented into an R/Shiny software prototype where the 3-tier-architecture is used to integrate the database and the PDCA process model at the R/Shiny implementation specific model (ISM) level. The presented hedge portfolio representation of derivatives can be useful for business analysts in the finance and accounting domain as well as for teaching financial derivative instruments.

Keywords: OntoREA© Accounting and Finance model
Design science research methodology DSRM
Model driven development MDD · Conceptual modeling
Derivative instruments · Dynamic hedge portfolio

1 Introduction

In a preceding article contributing to the OntoREA© Finance and Accounting model research, a forward contract is used to demonstrate validity of the OntoREA© Accounting and Finance Model by specifying a static hedge portfolio representation [2]. The OntoREA© model act as conceptual platform independent model (PIM) for the development of a platform specific PostgreSQL relational database model (PSM) within the model-driven software development context (MDD). The composition of the forward contract does not change over time and that's why it is called a *static hedge portfolio*. Modelling option contracts however result in *dynamic hedge*

© IFIP International Federation for Information Processing 2018
Published by Springer Nature Switzerland AG 2018. All Rights Reserved
R. A. Buchmann et al. (Eds.): PoEM 2018, LNBIP 335, pp. 372–382, 2018.
https://doi.org/10.1007/978-3-030-02302-7_24

portfolio, which comprise the generic research interest of this article: Can the OntoREA© model can also hold true for dynamic hedge portfolio compositions?

The hedge portfolio representation of derivative instruments is one of the core features of the OntoREA© model and it is expressed in the upper left part of Fig. 1 in form of the *Collective* class Derivative Instrument and its *MemberOf* relationship to the *Kind* class Economic Resource. In simple terms the meta-physical stereotypes of the OntoUML language have the following meaning: A derivative instrument is represented as a rigid and identity-providing portfolio *collective* that *consists of* two economic resources that are themselves rigid and identity providing *kinds*.

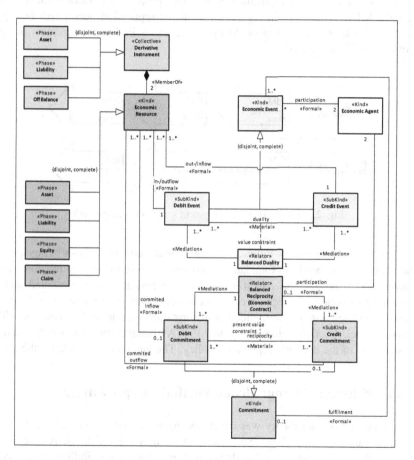

Fig. 1. OntoREA© Accounting and Finance model - conceptual PIM level

The hedge portfolio [4] representation of derivative instruments was originated by the Nobel laureates Black/Scholes [5] and Merton [6] who developed to the *no-arbitrage pricing theory*. This representation holds true for *unconditional derivatives* (e.g. forward contracts) as well as for *conditional derivatives* (e.g. option contracts). Unconditional derivatives include the obligation for the buyer of the contract to buy the underlying asset in the future. Due to this obligation the hedge portfolio composition does not change over time. Conditional derivatives include the right for the buyer of the contract to buy the asset in the future. As the probability of executing the option is changing over time, the hedge portfolio composition changes as well.

The primary research objective of this article lies in delivering the proof that the conceptual OntoREA© PIM model incorporates not only the static but also the dynamic hedge portfolio representation of derivative instruments. The traditional data layer transformation (PIM-PSM-ISM) is enhanced by the inclusion of an additional process model at the PIM and the ISM level to adequately specify the dynamic peculiarities of the dynamic replication policy. This process model extension is shown within the MDD framework in Fig. 2: the dynamic replication policy will be represented as Plan/Do/Check/Act (PDCA) cycle [7] and a PDCA management activity diagram (Fig. 5), respectively.

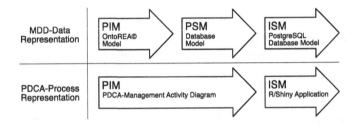

Fig. 2. Model driven development – extended framework

This paper is organized as follows: The next section covers the no-arbitrage pricing theory and its hedge portfolio foundation is presented. Next, the refined relational PSM database model for un- and conditional derivative instruments is presented and its applicability to conditional option contracts is demonstrated for a stock call option. Section 4 outlines the software-aided transformation of the PSM- into the ISM-database model. Section 5 introduces the PDCA management activity diagram as representation of the dynamic replication policy. The last section concludes the paper.

2   No-Arbitrage Pricing: Hedge Portfolio Representation

The no-arbitrage pricing theory was developed by the Nobel laureates Black/Scholes [5] and Merton [6]. They show that there is only one price for the derivative instruments, i.e. the no-arbitrage price that does not allow arbitrage possibilities. They derive the no-arbitrage price for European stock call options. European stock calls have the peculiarity that the right to buy refers to a stock asset, which is the underlying of the contract, and that the right can be exercised by the buyer of the contract only at expiration date (European style). The no-arbitrage price for the European stock call is given by the Black/Scholes formula:

$$\text{Fair Value}_{Call,t} = \overbrace{+P_{A,t} \cdot \underbrace{N(d_{1,t})}_{asset\ weight}}^{\substack{value \\ (asset/left\ leg)}} \overbrace{-X_{0,T} \cdot N(d_{2,t}) \cdot e^{\left(-ln(1+R_{0,T})\cdot T_{t,T}\right)}}^{\substack{present\ value \\ (liability/right\ leg)}} \qquad (1)$$

The no-arbitrage price, which is called *fair value*, corresponds according to the hedge portfolio of two parts: The value of the asset (*asset value*) on the left side (left leg) and the present value of the liability (*loan liability*) on the right side.

The *asset weight*, i.e. $N(d_{1,t})$ gives the fraction of the underlying stock that is hold in the hedge portfolio. It is calculated by evaluating the standard normal distribution function $N()$ at the value of $d_{1,t}$. The $d_{1,t}$-value (for further details see [5]) is a function of the stock *Price* $P_{A,t}$ and the time to maturity $T_{t,T}$. Consequently this value changes over the life cycle of the call option. The asset weight is a probabilistic term that expresses the probability of a stock option execution. It ranges between zero and 100%.

The present value of the loan liability is calculated by weighting the exercise price $X_{0,T}$ with the weighting factor $N(d_{2,t})$ and discounting the resulting product by multiplying it with the discount factor $exp(-ln(1+R_{0,T}) * T_{t,T})$. The discount factor is calculated in form of a continuous compounding by inserting the interest rate $R_{0,T}$ over the whole life time of the option, i.e. from 0 to T, and the time to maturity $T_{t,T}$ into the Euler exponential.

Finally, by using the t variable for the pricing date, the Black/Scholes formula is generically defined so that it can be applied for the initial (i.e. $t = 0$) and the subsequent (i.e. $t > 0$) pricing.

Table 1. European stock call (running example) – specification and pricing

Contracting date:	01.01.	Initial interest rate:	5%
Expiration date:	31.12.	Asset weight N(d1):	63.68%
Exercise price:	100	Liability weight N(d2):	55.96%
Initial stock price:	100	Stock Asset:	63.68
Volatility:	20%	Loan Liability:	53.23
		Fair value: = A - L	10.45 (A)

Table 1 contains the specification of a European stock call and its initial pricing at the beginning of the year (01.01.) according to the Black/Scholes formula, which is evaluated at the contracting date, i.e. $t = 0$. The *fair value* of the stock option, i.e. its no-arbitrage price, amounts to 10.45 and it is calculated by subtracting the present value of the *loan liability* (53.23) from the value of the *stock asset* (63.68).

The composition information is of special importance in the case of a *dynamic call replication policy*, where the call is not bought initially but instead it is synthetically created by implementing and rebalancing the dynamic hedge portfolio over time. In this case the asset weights $N(d_{1,t})$ are of special importance. They indicate the fractions of the underlying stock assets in the hedge portfolio.

For demonstrative purposes a pricing after each quarter is assumed. Furthermore, it is assumed that the stock price from initially 100 does not change after the first and second quarter and then increases to 120. In this constellation – as can be seen in the first column of Table 2 – the asset weights start decreasing from 63.68% (01.01.: 100) to 61.91% (31.03.: 100) and to 59.77% (30.06.: 100) and consequently increase to 97.72% (30.09.: 120). The initial decrease at the stable price of 100 indicates a decreasing execution probability and consequently a smaller stock position is hold in the hedge portfolio. The stock price increase increases the execution probability and consequently the stock position in the hedge portfolio. The changing asset weights over the call's life time demonstrate what is meant by saying that the composition of the option's hedge portfolio is changing over time. This changing composition in the dynamic hedge portfolio is contrasted to the stable composition in the static hedge portfolio of stock forwards where at each point in time exactly one unit of the underlying stock is held in the hedge portfolio.

3   Hedge Portfolio: From PIM- to PSM-Database Models

After having a deeper understanding of the hedge portfolio in the Black/Scholes formula, the transformation of its conceptualization in the OntoREA© Accounting and Finance model – as the *Collective* class Derivative Instrument with a *MemberOf* relationship to the *Kind* class Economic Resource – into a PostgreSQL database model can be addressed. In the MDD context this transformation corresponds to the switch from an abstract conceptual PIM model into a specific database PSM model. Associated with this concretization step is an informational extension that is accomplished by adding additional attributes and tables in the PSM model to capture the more detailed contents at the PSM model level.

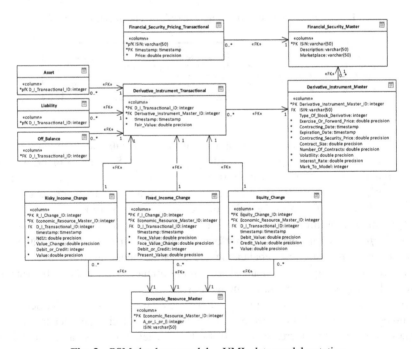

Fig. 3. PSM database model – UML data model notation

Figure 3 contains the refined PSM database model in the UML data model profile that concretizes the OntoREA© conceptualization of the derivative instruments' hedge portfolio representation. It covers not only unconditional but also conditional derivative instruments. Compared to the development of the PostgreSQL database (PSM) model related to the static hedge portfolio representation in [2], the dynamic hedge portfolio peculiarities for the stock options are now explicitly incorporated for the:

1. *Collective* class Derivative Instrument,
2. *MemberOf* relationship between *Collective* class Derivative Instrument and *Kind* class Economic Resource and
3. *Formal* relationship in-/outflow (out-/inflow) between *Kind* class Economic Resource and *SubKind* class Debit Event (Credit Event).

Ad 1) The *Collective* class Derivative Instrument is transformed via the four tables in the right upper corner of Fig. 3. The splitting into four tables allows a clear distinction of information that is stable over time (*master information*) and information that changes (*transactional information*).

- The table Derivative_Instrument_Master contains the stable information which specifies the derivative instruments. Its attribute Type_Of_Stock_Derivative is of INTEGER type so that un- and conditional derivatives are covered in the PostgreSQL database model.
- The table Derivative_Instrument_Transactional contains the pricing information which is associated to the initial and subsequent pricing dates measured with the Attribut timestamp. In the case of a dynamic replication policy the hedge portfolio composition adjustments are connected with capital market transactions.
- The two tables Financial_Security_Pricing_Master and Financial_Security_Pricing_Transactional are included in order to allow the separate specification of the derivative's underlying asset (i.e. financial security) which is fully defined by its international security identification number (ISIN).

Ad 2) The *MemberOf* relationship is transformed via the three tables in the lower left part of Fig. 3 according to the financial categorization of financial instruments into risky income, fixed income and equity resources. All three tables have a foreign key to the table Derivative_Instrument_Transactional. The inclusion of the tables specifies the different financial resource types of the hedge portfolio constituents, i.e. the stock asset (risky income) and the loan liability (fixed income).

Ad 3) The *Formal* relationship in-/outflows (out-/inflows) between the *Kind* class Economic Resource and the *SubKind* class Debit Event (Credit Event) is transformed by introducing change classes for the asset (A), liability (L) and equity (E) resource types. Furthermore the asset and liability related classes are each equipped with the attribute Debit_Or_Credit in order to get the connection with the debit and credit entries in the REA accounting infrastructure of the OntoREA© model.

The introduction of the equity resource type is needed for capturing the revenues and expenses that occur by executing the dynamic replication policy over time.

In Table 2 the calculations for the stock call can be seen in the first column. It is interesting to note the last fair value at the end of the year (31.12.) amounting to 19.23 is close to the intrinsic value of the stock call amounting to 20 which is calculated as difference between the stock asset value of 120 and the exercise price of 100. The resulting fair value at the option's expiration date is connected to a self-financing policy. According to this policy the changing asset fractions are either used for redemption of the loan if they decrease or financed by increasing the loan if the increase.

Table 2. European stock call – specification and subsequent pricing

	Dynamic Hedging		Attribute	Table
				PSM Relational Schema
Contracting date:		01.01.	Contracting_Date	Derivative_Instrument_Master
Expiration date:		31.12.	Expiration_Date	Derivative_Instrument_Master
Exercise price:		100	Exercise_Or_Forward_Price	Derivative_Instrument_Master
Initial stock price:		100	Contracting_Security_Price	Derivative_Instrument_Master
Volatility:		20%	Volatility	Derivative_Instrument_Master
Initial interest rate:		5%	Interest_Rate	Derivative_Instrument_Master
Asset weight N(d1):		63.68%	Nd1t	Economic_Resource_Risky_Income
Liability weight N(d2):		55.96%	-	-
Stock Asset:		63.68	Value	Risky_Income_Change
Loan Liability:		53.23	Present_Value	Fixed_Income_Change
Fair value: = A - L		10.45 (A)	Fair_Value	Derivative_Instrument_Transactional
Pricing date #1:		31.03.	timestamp	Financial_Security_Pricing_Transactional
Actual stock price:		100	Price	Financial_Security_Pricing_Transactional
Actual time to maturity: 9 months			-	-
Asset weight N(d1):		61.91%	Nd1t	Risky_Income_Change
Stock Asset:		61.91	Value	Risky_Income_Change
Loan Liability:		52.13	Present_Value	Fixed_Income_Change
Fair value: = A - L		9.78 (A)	Fair_Value	Derivative_Instrument_Transactional
Pricing date #2:		30.06.	timestamp	Financial_Security_Pricing_Transactional
Actual stock price:		100	Price	Financial_Security_Pricing_Transactional
Actual time to maturity: 6 months			-	-
Asset weight N(d1):		59.77%	Nd1t	Risky_Income_Change
Stock Asset:		59.77	Value	Risky_Income_Change
Loan Liability:		50.65	Present_Value	Fixed_Income_Change
Fair value: = A - L		9.12 (A)	Fair_Value	Derivative_Instrument_Transactional
Pricing date #3:		30.09.	timestamp	Financial_Security_Pricing_Transactional
Actual stock price:		120	Price	Financial_Security_Pricing_Transactional
Actual time to maturity: 3 months			-	-
Asset weight N(d1):		97.72%	Nd1t	Risky_Income_Change
Stock Asset:		117.26	Value	Risky_Income_Change
Loan Liability:		96.82	Present_Value	Fixed_Income_Change
Fair value: = A - L		20.44 (A)	Fair_Value	Derivative_Instrument_Transactional
Pricing date #4:		31.12.	timestamp	Financial_Security_Pricing_Transactional
Actual stock price:		120	Price	Financial_Security_Pricing_Transactional
Actual time to maturity: 0 months			-	-
Stock Asset:		117.26	Value	Risky_Income_Change
Loan Liability:		98.03	Present_Value	Fixed_Income_Change
Fair value: = A - L		19.23 (A)	Fair_Value	Derivative_Instrument_Transactional

(Left margin row labels: Initial Pricing/Static Data; Subsequent Pricing/Dynamic Data)

4   Hedge Portfolio: From PSM- to ISM-Database Models

After translating the OntoREA© PIM model into the PSM database model the second MDD transformation is performed, i.e. the transformation from the PostgreSQL PSM database model into the Shiny ISM database model. The ISM database model represents the physical database schema of the PostgreSQL relational database.

This second transformation step is partly automated and supported by the UML modeling software *Enterprise Architect*. With this automated transformation all data storage requirements of the dynamic hedge portfolio are covered in the ISM database model. But the ISM data model does not consider the information of the dynamic replication policy which is modeled in the PDCA management activity diagram (Fig. 5). To include the policy's PDCA representation in the R/Shiny application a generic 3-tier-architecture is chosen.

The left side of Fig. 4 shows the 3-tier-architecture and the right side relates to its implementation in the R/Shiny technology. The 3-tier-architecture is built upon a modular layer concept. In R/Shiny the modularity between Tier 3 and Tier 2 is achieved by using R/DBI database interface.

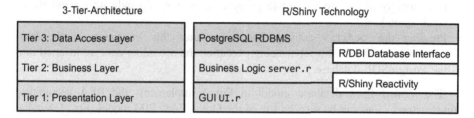

Fig. 4. 3-Tier-architecture – implementation in R/Shiny

The traditional data transformation in the extended MDD framework (Fig. 2) relates to Tier 3, i.e. to the Data Access Layer. The PDCA management process representation of the dynamic replication policy relates to Tier 2 and Tier 1. This transformation from the PSM process model into the Shiny PIM process model is given now.

5   Hedge Portfolio: PDCA-Process Representation

The R/Shiny Reactivity technology is the key for implementing the PDCA management process representation of the dynamic replication policy.

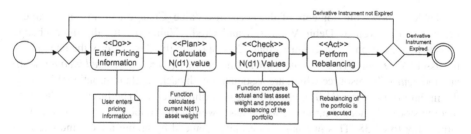

Fig. 5. PDCA management activity diagram

The repeating (iterating) nature of the dynamic replication policy can be seen in Fig. 5 by the arrow that links the gateway before the termination node to the gateway after the starting node. After having specified the PIM process model for the dynamic replication policy in form of the PDCA management activity diagram it can be translated into the R/Shiny ISM process model.

- The <<Do>> prompts the user to enter the present pricing information (stock price and timestamp). The information gets stored in the table Financial_Security_-Pricing_Transactional (see Fig. 3).
- After pressing the <<Plan>> activity button the current asset weight $N(d_1)$ is calculated and displayed.
- The <<Check>> activity activation compares the actual $N(d_1)$ value with the one of the last pricing observations and calculates the difference. The difference indicates the required change in asset weights. The negative value of $-0,0177$ indicates to sell this quantity of the stock asset (a positive amount would indicate a purchase of stock assets).
- Pressing the <<Act>> activity button executes this indication in the final step. Connected with this rebalancing execution the according data are inserted into the PostgreSQL database.

The refined PSM database model in Fig. 3 implements the REA accounting infrastructure – that can be seen on top of the OntoREA© PIM model (Fig. 1) via the three *Kind* classes Economic Resource, Economic Event and Economic Agent – in a special, somehow hidden way.

Table 3. Showing resource chances in T-accounts

Date	Risky Income Change (A) Value Change		Fixed Income Change (L) Present Value Change		Equity Change (E)	
	Debit	Credit	Debit	Credit	Debit Value	Credit Value
01.01.	63.68			53.23		10.45
31.03.		1.77	1.10		0.67	
30.06.		2.14	1.48		0.66	
30.09.	57.49			46.17	0.63	11.95
31.12.	0.00			1.21	1.21	

Table 3 shows the contents of the attributes Value_Change (A), Present_Value_-Change (L) as well as Debit_Value (E) and Credit_Value (E) for the three change classes in a traditional T-account format. Correspondingly, they specify the changes of the asset (A) resource *risky income* (stock), the liability (L) resource *fixed income* (loan) and the *equity* (E) resource which are associated with each single transactional loop. At the initial pricing date (01.01.) the hedging portfolio is set up. The buying of the risky income stock (A) according to the initial asset weight of 0.6368 causes the debit entry amounting to 63.38. This purchase is partially financed by taking a fixed income loan (L) amounting to 53.23. As the purchase price is higher than the loan the difference has to be covered by cash. In order to fund the needed cash amount (10.45) an equity position is established by booking a corresponding Credit_Value entry.

At the subsequent pricing date (31.03.) the stock asset weight declines according to the Black/Scholes formula. The negative difference of the asset weight (-0.0177) is sold in the stock market at the stock price of 100 (Credit entry of 1.77 in the stock asset). The cash earned (+1.77) is used to pay the interest (Debit_Value entry of 0.67) and to pay back part of the loan's face value (Debit entry of 1.10). At the following to the next pricing date (10.09.) the same procedure applies. The only difference is the inclusion of a capital gain that results from the stock price increase from 100 to 120. The capital gain (Credit_Value entry) is calculated by multiplying the asset weight of the previous pricing date (0.5977) with the stock price change (20).

Finally, the balanced duality of the different debit and credit entries can be shown: They correspond to the equal sums of the debit and credit entries at each pricing date.

6 Conclusion

The primary research objective of this article is the delivery of the proof that the hedge portfolio representation of derivative instruments specified in the OntoREA© PIM model covers not only unconditional (forward contracts) but conditional (option contracts) as well. This proof is delivered in the MDD-context by translating the OntoREA© PIM model into a PSM database model which is refined compared to [2]. The refinement refers especially to the separation of master and transactional data, which allows the adequate inclusion of the hedge portfolio data representation.

To include the conditional derivatives' dynamic management processes the MDD framework was extended by including the process representation next to the traditional data representation. Equipped with this view the dynamic replication policy is represented as a PDCA management process model at the PIM level that can be directly transformed into a ISM process model. For demonstrative purposes a European stock call is synthetically constructed by executing the dynamic replication policy. Its software implementation is demonstrated in an R/Shiny application where the 3-tier-architecture is used to integrate the database and the PDCA process model at the R/Shiny ISM level.

The hedge portfolio representation of (un-)conditional derivative instruments in the extended MDD framework can be useful for business analysts in the finance and accounting domain as well as for software engineers by not only explaining derivatives in form of PIM, PSM and ISM data and process models but also by implementing the derivatives' hedge portfolio representation models in real software application.

References

1. Fischer-Pauzenberger, C., Schwaiger, W.S.A.: The OntoREA© Accounting and Finance model: ontological conceptualization of the accounting and finance domain. In: Mayr, H.C., Guizzardi, G., Ma, H., Pastor, O. (eds.) ER 2017. LNCS, vol. 10650, pp. 506–519. Springer, Cham (2017). https://doi.org/10.1007/978-3-319-69904-2_38
2. Fischer-Pauzenberger, C., Schwaiger, W.S.A.: The OntoREA© Accounting and Finance model: a retroactive DSRM demonstration evaluation. In: Poels, G., Gailly, F., Serral Asensio, E., Snoeck, M. (eds.) PoEM 2017. LNBIP, vol. 305, pp. 81–95. Springer, Cham (2017). https://doi.org/10.1007/978-3-319-70241-4_6
3. Geerts, G.L.: International journal of accounting information systems a design science research methodology and its application to accounting information systems research. Int. J. Account. Inf. Syst. 12, 142–151 (2011)

4. Cox, J.C., Ross, S.A., Rubinstein, M.: Option pricing: a simplified approach. J. Financ. Econ. **7**, 229–263 (1979)
5. Black, F., Scholes, M.: The pricing of options and corporate liabilities. J. Polit. Econ. **81**, 637 (1973)
6. Merton, R.C.: Theory of rational theory option pricing. Bell J. Econ. **4**, 141–183 (1973)
7. Schwaiger, W.S.A., Abmayer, M.: Accounting and management information systems. In: Proceedings of International Conference on Information Integration Web-based Application Services - IIWAS 2013, pp. 346–352 (2013)

Reflections on Using an Architecture Model for Matching Existing Applications to a Radical Business Requirements Change: A Case Study

Debbie Tarenskeen[1(✉)] [iD], Stijn Hoppenbrouwers[1,2] [iD],
and Rogier van de Wetering[3] [iD]

[1] HAN University of Applied Sciences Arnhem and Nijmegen,
Arnhem, The Netherlands
debbie.tarenskeen@han.nl
[2] Radboud University, Nijmegen, The Netherlands
[3] Open University, Heerlen, The Netherlands

Abstract. In this practice paper, we report the outcomes of a case study in a new Dutch hospital, where enterprise architects are working toward a 'lean' and 'simplified' EA model to align existing IT systems to new requirements. The objective of the case study was to examine if the developed EA model could support architects in selecting components of an existing IT infrastructure for re-use, with regard to radically new requirements. We have developed an EA model in close collaboration with enterprise architects. This study reflects on the use of this model in the hospital. The approach combines analysis of the content in the model, a study of documents in the organization, and communication with the architects. We signal that the existence of an integrated suite for an Electronic Health Record system largely determined how the model was used. Reflection disclosed that a lack of information on requirements and applications, as well as low adaptability of existing systems, negatively affected the flexibility of IT in the organization.

Keywords: Enterprise Architecture · Conceptual model · Healthcare
Strategic alignment · IT Flexibility

1 Introduction

Extant literature describes Enterprise Architecture (EA) as a promising approach to bridge the gap between Business and IT. In this paper we focus on aspects encountered in the practice of EA modeling. We explain the state-of-the-art concerning EA, at that time, by referring to a study from 2013 that gives an overview of the literature about EA in the period between 2003 and 2009 [1]. In the literature, frameworks of EA are essential in research. TOGAF has been a de facto guideline for practitioners. TOGAF is relevant for the case study, because it can be applied as a roadmap for the transformation of a Base Architecture (AS-IS) to a Target Architecture (TO-BE) as described in [2]. We refer to recent research, where new concerns for IT Flexibility on a strategical level have been described [3–5].

© IFIP International Federation for Information Processing 2018
Published by Springer Nature Switzerland AG 2018. All Rights Reserved
R. A. Buchmann et al. (Eds.): PoEM 2018, LNBIP 335, pp. 383–393, 2018.
https://doi.org/10.1007/978-3-030-02302-7_25

This case study introduces a new specialized Dutch hospital (H1) in 2012, planning 600 beds. The hospital required the design of an EA with emphasis on the IT perspectives (Application Architecture, Information Architecture, Technical Architecture). As a guiding principle, the management decided that H1 should reuse the existing IT systems of a nearby academic hospital (H2). The development of the EA would be done by an Enterprise architect and an IT project manager (henceforth called "the architects"). H1 differs from H2 because it specializes in pediatric oncology. Also, H1 aspires to realize a vision in which child and family are positioned in the center of the care processes. Consequently, IT systems needed to be re-evaluated based on this basic assumption.

The case can be characterized as an exception in healthcare in the Netherlands, i.e., the possibility to start a new hospital (from scratch) is rare. However, the hospital builds on the existing infrastructure of a nearby hospital. Therefore, it will not really be built from scratch. The in-use IT systems are not typically legacy systems but are state-of-the-art systems currently (2018) in operation. The specific Dutch "Electronisch Patient Dossier" (Electronic Health Record System; EHR) solution is in use in more than half of all Dutch hospitals. The number of implementations of EHR-systems was growing in 2014, so EHR-systems can be expected to play a dominant role in the IT of other hospitals as well [6]. The new hospital will be the central node in a network of hospitals. They will be working with "shared care hospitals" in the Netherlands.

We followed the design science research method [7] in designing a model for the EA in close collaboration with the architects. In a first paper, we have presented the resulting model [8]. In the current paper, we reflect on the use of the model, and define the question for our research: *Does the developed model support architects in selecting the suitable applications for re-use?*

To answer this question, we analyzed the model and studied the decision-making process of the Board of Directors, informed by the internal advice reports and evaluations in the follow-up period. Hence, we reflect on the way the model is applied in practice.

2   Reflection on Model in Use

We evaluated two underlying purposes of the model. First, the model had to assist the architects with structuring all the information they collected concerning requirements and functionality of existing applications. Secondly, the model should give an overview of the relations between applications and requirements, in such a way that it helps architects decide on applications for re-use. Two sub research questions were formulated (SRQ1 and SRQ2):

- SRQ1: Is the model suitable for structuring the information collected by the enterprise architects?
- SRQ2: How does the model assist the architects with selecting applications for re-use?

We reflected on the model during development with the architects (development phase) and afterwards by studying documentation (reflection phase).

2.1 Development Phase

In the development phase the architects determined new requirements of the organization and the relations of the requirements to the existing IT infrastructure (in H2) by consulting 12 focus groups, the vendors of software, and the IT department in the organization. Examples of focus groups consulted are: Care Unit, Radiology and Radiotherapy, Education, Lab, Enterprise Principles, LATER (concerning health and complications after therapy). Architects provided the mapping of requirements to applications, based on the information they collected in the organization.

The EA model has been developed in iterations. In every iteration the researcher proposed a model and the enterprise architects evaluated the proposal and accepted or changed the model. We registered all drafts and discussed every adaptation with the architects. During development, insertion of data (instance pairs) was a regular activity. Examples of changes were: Adding, deleting or editing concept types names or relations. After the final model had been decided upon, all data considered important by the architects had been successfully inserted into the model. Inserting the data in the model was performed as a check for completeness of the model, and for suitability for structuring information provided by the model.

2.2 Reflection Phase

After the development phase, an in-depth analysis was performed in the form of frequency distributions and content analysis of relations between requirements and applications. The objective of the analysis was to answer SRQ2, how the model could assist the architects with the task of selecting applications for re-use.

Also, we studied documentation, the reports of meetings of the steering group and architects, and reports of the 12 focus groups that formulated requirements. The results of the documentation study were discussed with the architects for answering SRQ2.

3 Description of the EA Model

We selected the Ampersand business rules approach for modeling the EA because it can be applied to produce simplified models that have a mathematical foundation [9, 10]. The conceptual model for the EA is flexible and is defined in a separate script; the business rules can be declaratively defined separately in relation algebra, in the same script.

Ampersand is based on relation algebra and defines business information in a meta model. The meta model consists of descriptions of CONCEPTS, RELATIONS, PROCESSES and RULES [8]. A model is defined within a CONTEXT. All information is formulated in text, in the language of the stakeholders. There are no constraints on language for names, as long as the names are 'text'. Names have been used as identifiers. In this paper it is sufficient for the reader to interpret the Ampersand concepts and relations as similar to the entity and relationship names in an ER (Entity-

Relationship) model. The business rules in the model allow us to check the degree to which existing systems could fulfill new requirements. See page 5.

3.1   EA Model Overview

Figure 1 presents the final model of the EA. The final model is the result of 12 iterations.

An explicit goal in designing the model was to include only the concepts needed by the architects for the specific (and somewhat unusual) architecture job at hand. We recognized: strategic goals (named Enterprise Principles by the architects), healthcare and business processes, and the services that are expected from the organization for supporting the processes. The services in the model were primarily application services (information technology services). The model has similarities with TOGAF architecture models. However, it is a simplified model because TOGAF models consist of separate extended models for Business Architecture, Information Architecture and Technology Architecture. In Fig. 1 the concept types and named relations are shown. The model includes both applications and requirements in one view.

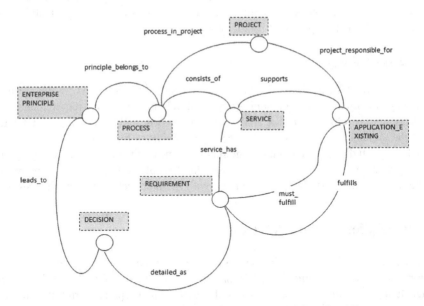

Fig. 1. Concepts and relations in the EA model (Version 12)

Details of Concepts. In this section, all concepts in the Ampersand model are described.

Enterprise_Principle. An Enterprise principle is a principle that must be met according to the architects in the project (30 instances). Principles are derived from the healthcare vision of the hospital and can be compared to the strategic business goals of the hospital. Examples are "Intensive collaboration with medical staff and nursing care personnel and scientific research," "Child and family will influence the care process where ever possible," "Child and family will have the possibility to participate in education when in treatment."

Process. A Process is a primary process in the healthcare organization (11 instances). Examples are typical healthcare processes, such as Laboratory and Images, and Medication.

Decision. A Decision is an Action or Goal that is based on an Enterprise Principle (43). Examples of Decisions: Visits must be planned, Reports of Anesthesia and Surgery must be made. It seemed that Decisions are sort of a dead end in the model because only relations to Enterprise principles exist.

Service. A Service can be described as a composite service that delivers services for care processes in the healthcare organization (159 instances). Examples are the support for care processes, such as Diagnosis, but also Catering service or the Communication platform.

Requirement (or Question). Requirements are specific demands on an application or a combination of applications (132 instances). A large part of the Requirements have been marked Questions by the architects (75 of them). Some examples of Requirements (the remaining 57) are: "Formulate specific learning objective for every child", "Functionality of patient portal is available through a website, a column in the building with electronic card, and via an app", "The new and existing scheduling data from application X have to be transferred to another financial salary application", "E-consultation". Architects marked 75 requirements as "questions" that needed an answer before a requirement could be mapped to an application. That has resulted in two types of requirements, requirements and questions.

Application_Existing. This Ampersand concept concerns an application module or another component of the Information System (88 instances). An existing application is a software system that supports the care processes in the healthcare organization. A specific set of applications is the EHR, where all information about patients and treatment is stored and can be edited, or retrieved. The EHR System accounted for a significant part of the applications that were defined. In the model, the EHR-system consisted of 39 modules, a ratio of 44% of all defined applications.

Project. A project stands for a main EA project in the healthcare organization (1 instance). The architects have not reached the stage of formulating Projects.

Relations and Rules. Relations are sets of tuples, instances of two concepts. A total of 2756 instance pairs have been formulated. Some relations were filled with only one, fake pair (1 pair).

When analyzing the Rules, we can conclude there are two kinds of rules. Rules for achieving the goals of selecting applications and rules for consistency of data in the model. For instance, all *must_fulfill* instance pairs have a similar *fulfills* pair. In Table 1 the relations[1] can be overviewed.

---

[1] Relations are defined in Ampersand with two Concepts and a set of instance pairs.

Table 1. Overview relations and a number of pairs.

Relation	Concept1	Concept2	Number of instance pairs
fulfills	Application_Existing	Requirement	0
detailed-in	Decision	Requirement	1
relates-to	Process	Project	1
responsible-for	Project	Application_Existing	1
belongs-with	Enterprise_Principle	Process	109
consists-of	Process	Service	225
supports	Application_Existing	Service	249
leads-to	Enterprise_Principle	Decision	251
must-fulfill	Application_Existing	Requirement	793
has	Service	Requirement	1126

3.2   Analysis of Requirements and Applications

The researchers have performed an analysis after collected data had been inserted into the final model by architects. It was part of the Reflection phase. For this phase, we concentrated on the *must-fulfill*-relation since the *fulfills*-relation is empty.

To deepen our understanding and insights, we counted the number of requirements coupled to application modules and vice versa. We aimed to find the mapping relation, as a 1:1, 1:many, or many:many relation. The type of relation enabled us to see whether it is feasible to map requirements unambiguously to applications. For instance if every requirement only concerned one application and vice versa (1:1 relation) then the requirements were unambiguously related to one application and vice versa. First, we have checked if every requirement had been linked to only one application. This relationship demonstrates traceability of every requirement to an application. We could further investigate the degree in which the application did support the requirement. See Fig. 2.

When categorizing the *must-fulfill*-relation, we find a many:many relation between requirements and applications. Questions of architects also concern many applications each. Combining results of all counted pairs leads to the conclusion, that the requirements and applications are not structured in the same way, and that requirements cannot be mapped unambiguously to a specific application.

In related research, a framework has been developed that describes how to detect Business-IT misalignment symptoms [11]. When analyzing the misalignment of the TO-BE and AS-IS architecture with that framework, important indications concern organization and responsibilities, such as "S.01 Undefined organizational mission, strategy and goals", "S.02 Undefined business process goals, business process owners", "S.03 Lack of relation between process goals and organizational goals". These symptoms of misalignment have not been found in the case study EA model. However, other symptoms regarding misalignment of Business process tasks and Applications are present in the model. For instance, "S.06 Application does not support at least one Business process" is signaled in the form of missing *fulfills*-relation in the EA model.

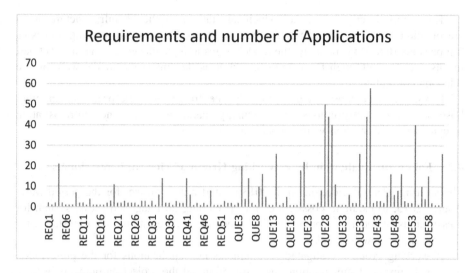

Fig. 2. Number of applications with each requirement, final model

Also, the indication "S.07 Business process task supported by more than one application" is signaled. The *must-fulfill*-relation shows S.07 in the case study. We conclude, based on this analysis, that the simplified EA model signals misalignment of business requirements and applications.

4 Using the Model

4.1 The Role the Model Played in the Decision Process

In the follow-up after the model had been completed with data, we could observe the role the model played in decision making. It was decided by the Board of Directors and architects, that in the startup period (planned in 2014) the components of the IT systems were considered sufficient, unless medical professionals objected to specific components or applications. For their evaluation of the existing IT systems, the scope of the requirements had been restricted. Requirements related to many strategic goals were declared outside of evaluation scope, only working processes would be considered. The evaluation report stated that the IT infrastructure had sufficient capabilities to support the short time requirements for opening of the new hospital. Citation from Evaluation end report May 2013:

"The current, existing IT infrastructure is to a large extent sufficiently capable of supporting the working processes in the startup period. Some adaptations of application X are necessary for the adequate support of specific healthcare processes. These adaptations have to be realized in the period preceding startup period."[2]

---

[2] Internal Evaluation end report, May 2013.

The report describes in detail which adaptations in the IT infrastructure are a precondition for the new hospital. The bottom line is that standard working processes can be supported. Unfortunately, the model seems to have played only an indirect part in this decision, although the enterprise architects that made the model were on the selection committee.

However, healthcare processes that deviate from the work processes in other hospitals, such as prescriptions for medicine, preparation of medicine and registration of cytostatics for children were considered a risk.

4.2 Follow up Evaluation by a Working Group of Medical Professionals

The steering group decided in April 2013 to start a new project for the period May-August 2013, to examine possibilities for developing an integrated (new) system for prescriptions of medicine, preparation of medicine and registration of cytostatics for children in the new hospital.

A working group investigated requirements and applications for the prescription process. From the documentation, the assumptions of the project participants became apparent. The working group set out with the following assignment[3]:

1. Describe the processes of working with protocols;
2. Define essential components in the current IT infrastructure that have to be included in the new IT systems;
3. Define criteria for scenarios;
4. Work out scenarios in detail to combine the functionality of different existing applications;
5. Evaluate the scenarios;
6. Advice the steering group of the most suitable combination of applications.

The working group reported a scenario that combined three existing applications, including applications that were not used in the existing IT architecture.

We can read in the report of the follow-up project[3] that a mismatch was found in the existing application landscape to support care processes for prescription of medicine. The medical professionals observed the same misalignment as was disclosed by the EA model.

Since the enterprise architects were part of the steering group, we assume the model played a role in the decision-making process, because we know that the model did provide an overview for the involved architects, though possibly an indirect one.

---

[3] Internal report Research of working with Protocols - cytostatica v03, June 2013.

5   Conclusion and Discussion

5.1   Research Questions Revisited

We answer the sub research questions in this paragraph. For SRQ1, we conclude that the model served the purpose of structuring information sufficiently, based on the test of inserting information in the model and discussions with architects. See Sect. 2.1.

The mapping of new requirements to existing application proved a challenge. The architects concluded that the mapping of requirements to applications could not be performed unambiguously, such that applications or modules could be selected for re-use. However, the model did provide the possibility for indicating that an application fulfilled the new requirements. See Sect. 3.2.

Therefore, for SRQ2, we conclude that the information that was collected by the architects was incomplete for selecting applications for re-use with the model.

5.2   Reflection and Discussion

We observed that a large number of applications are part of a EHR-suite, or other integrated/interwoven application systems. Consequently, it was difficult to map requirements separately to each application module in the EA model.

We found numerous questions of architects about functionality, hence an indication that the documentation of functionality for specific hospitals is insufficiently accessible (if at all). As a further consequence, one cannot see how new requirements compare with the old ones.

Our study does confirm the findings in the study [12], that a radical renovation of existing EA has to overcome the traditional structure of working and supporting IT. Our study adds new information by showing in some detail how the current IT architecture made up of integrated applications has obstructed innovation. It describes how lack of transparency and a modular structure that does not offer required flexibility, can obstruct innovation.

Our findings suggest that the core assumptions of architects: 1. insight in a fine-grained functionality in the applications, 2. flexibility of functionality for re-use and 3. transparency of the IT infrastructure, have been disproved.

It is too early to say that similar projects in other hospitals might lead to similar impasses because of similarity like IT systems. More research of EA in changing environments (of various kinds) is needed to extend the knowledge domain of EA to include adaptability, especially of the Application Architecture.

5.3   Recommendations & Future Research

We suggest that elaborate and costly efforts like the one in our case (business requirements, 12 focus groups, model), should lead to actual and explicit use of the model in the decision process (Return on Modelling Effort). Fortunately, it does seem to have been used indirectly, through the involvement of the architects in the decision process and steering group.

In a new study, we will perform a follow-up on this research by investigating how a separation of the data structure from the application layer can add to IT Flexibility. This research is likely to result in an expansion of the model of the EA model.

5.4   Limitations of Validity of the Research

This case study demonstrates clearly how architects struggle with many unknowns in the situation of modeling the EA for selecting applications for re-use. Since the case describes the situation of an organization startup, this could (partly) have caused some of the unknowns. However, the value of this case study lies in calling into question the core assumptions of architects and EA frameworks, such as the possibility of adapting existing IT systems and having complete access to information about IT systems and integrated application suites. If these core assumptions are not confirmed then IT Flexibility cannot be achieved by applying this EA model.

References

1. Simon, D., Fischbach, K., Schoder, D.: An exploration of enterprise architecture research. Commun. Assoc. Inf. Syst. CAIS 32(1), 1–72 (2013)
2. TheOpenGroup: TOGAF Version 9.1 Evaluation Copy. The Open Group (2011)
3. Van de Wetering, R., Mikalef, P., Pateli, A.: How strategic alignment of IT flexibility, a firm's networking capability, and absorptive capacity influences firm innovation. In: The 11th Mediterranean Conference on Information Systems (2017)
4. Van de Wetering, R., Mikalef, P., Helms, R.: Driving organizational sustainability-oriented innovation capabilities: a complex adaptive systems perspective. Curr. Opin. Environ. Sustain. 28, 71–79 (2017)
5. Van de Wetering, R., Versendaal, J., Walraven, P.: Examining the relationship between a hospital's IT infrastructure capability and digital capabilities: a resource-based perspective. In: Twenty-Fourth Americas Conference on Information Systems (AMCIS) (2018)
6. Boonstra, A., Versluis, A., Vos, J.F.: Implementing electronic health records in hospitals: a systematic literature review. BMC Health Serv. Res. 14(1), 370 (2014)
7. Hevner, A.R., March, S.T., Park, J., Ram, S.: Design science in information systems research. MIS Q. 28(1), 75–105 (2004)
8. Tarenskeen, D., Bakker, R., Joosten, S.: Using ampersand in IT architecture. In: 7th International Conference on Research and Practical Issues of Enterprise Information Systems CONFENIS2013, pp. 206–214 (2013)
9. Michels, G., Joosten, S., van der Woude, J., Joosten, S.: Ampersand. In: de Swart, H. (ed.) RAMICS 2011. LNCS, vol. 6663, pp. 280–293. Springer, Heidelberg (2011). https://doi.org/10.1007/978-3-642-21070-9_21
10. Joosten, S.: Deriving functional specification from business requirements with ampersand. Citeseer (2007)

11. Őri, D.: An artifact-based framework for Business-IT misalignment symptom detection. In: Horkoff, J., Jeusfeld, M.A., Persson, A. (eds.) PoEM 2016. LNBIP, vol. 267, pp. 148–163. Springer, Cham (2016). https://doi.org/10.1007/978-3-319-48393-1_11

12. Labusch, N., Koebele, F., Aier, S., Winter, R.: The architects' perspective on enterprise transformation: an explorative study. In: Harmsen, F., Proper, Henderik A. (eds.) PRET 2013. LNBIP, vol. 151, pp. 106–124. Springer, Heidelberg (2013). https://doi.org/10.1007/978-3-642-38774-6_8

Conceptual Modeling to Support the "Larger Goal" Pivot – An Example from Netflix

Vik Pant[1(✉)] and Eric Yu[1,2]

[1] Faculty of Information, University of Toronto, Toronto, Canada
vik.pant@mail.utoronto.ca, eric.yu@utoronto.ca
[2] Department of Computer Science, University of Toronto, Toronto, Canada

Abstract. Many organizations mistakenly or inadvertently focus on tactical aims rather than on strategic goals. "Strategy" commonly denotes long-term objectives and high-level policies while "tactic" refers to deployment concerns and implementation considerations. By focusing on lower-level objectives an organization can potentially overlook or neglect better ways of achieving higher-level goals. Shifting from a short-term to a long-run orientation can be considered a type of pivoting, as the structure and relationships of an organization are substantially reconfigured. The Larger Goal pivot is essential when lower-level options for achieving a higher-level organizational goal are either unavailable or insufficient. It entails shifting focus to a larger or higher goal and exploring strategic alternatives to satisfy that goal. In this paper we present conceptual models of the Larger Goal pivot based on a historic example from Netflix – a movie streaming service.

Keywords: Pivoting · Design · Analysis · Modeling · Strategy
Tactic

1 Introduction

The distinction between strategy and tactic is studied by researchers in many disciplines including economics and business management [1]. The term "strategy" denotes long term objectives and high level policies while the term "tactic" refers to deployment concerns and implementation considerations [2]. It is argued that ideally tactics should support the achievement of their associated strategies [3]. However, in the business world, this is not always observed to be the case. Many organizations, startups and large enterprises alike, mistakenly or inadvertently center their plans and actions around tactics rather than around strategy. This is problematical for them because even if they can meet their short-term targets – the fulfilment of their long-term goals is far from guaranteed.

Organizations can pivot and shift focus from a short-term to a long-run orientation. For example, Microsoft pivoted away from defending the market share of Windows operating system (OS) from threats by rival Linux to building application software that could run on multiple operating systems [4, 5]. This pivot allowed Microsoft to access the Linux installed base and increase the addressable market for its applications at the cost of losing some OS market share. eBay pivoted away from being an online

R. A. Buchmann et al. (Eds.): PoEM 2018, LNBIP 335, pp. 394–403, 2018.
https://doi.org/10.1007/978-3-030-02302-7_26

auctioneer to becoming a diversified e-Commerce platform on the Internet [6, 7]. This pivot positioned eBay to compete in many new markets including those served by Amazon while moving away from rivals in its original market. In spite of many success stories associated with pivoting – it is a nontrivial undertaking that requires foresight and insight about the nature and scope of the intended change.

The notion of pivoting was popularized among entrepreneurs, startup founders, and venture owners by a book titled "Lean Startup" where the author, Ries, proposed a catalog of ten pivot archetypes [8–10]. Ries' [8] catalog of ten pivot archetypes is not exhaustive and researchers have proposed additional archetypes [9] after the publication of Ries' book. These new pivot archetypes include market zoom-in, complete and side project pivots [10]. Our work is related to this line of research as we also propose a new pivot archetype in this paper – i.e., the Larger Goal pivot.

The Larger Goal pivot represents a situation in which an organization generates new lower-level alternatives (e.g., tactics) to achieve some higher-level objective (e.g., strategy). Casadesus-Masanell and Ricart [2, 3] note that strategy refers to how a firm competes in the marketplace, through its choice of business model, while tactics refer to the residual choices open to a firm by virtue of the business model that it employs. A Larger Goal pivot is necessary in an organization if existing tactical options are inadequate or unsatisfactory for achieving its strategic goals. Larger Goal pivot indicates navigation along a goal hierarchy from existing lower-level goals to higher level-goals and the generation of new lower-level goals from higher-level goals. This approach can be applied to any scenario of business goal change however when a goal hierarchy is involved then it involves Larger Goal rethinking. In this context, the term "Larger" refers only to relative positions of goals in a hierarchy.

In an earlier paper [11], we proposed a goal-modeling based technique using the $i*$ modeling language for articulating and analyzing pivot archetypes proposed by Ries [8]. In that work [11], we had argued that various types of pivoting follow specific patterns of reasoning. These patterns of reasoning can be abstracted and expressed as conceptual models. We illustrated the application of that technique by instantiating a multi-actor model of a real-world startup in Toronto that undertook pivoting. In that work [11] we proposed strategic patterns and decontextualized representations of Ries' pivot archetypes [8] using the $i*$ modeling language. For instance, for zoom-in and zoom-out pivots – we needed to represent a hierarchy of needs for narrowing and enlarging the scope of the customer value proposition; and for customer segment pivot – we needed to represent target groups of customers as strategic actors [11]. In [27] we use a retrospective case of Twitter to illustrate the application of conceptual modeling to support pivoting.

In this paper, we propose the Larger Goal pivot as a new type of organizational pivot relative to the archetypes proposed by Ries [8]. We use a retrospective case of Netflix to illustrate the application of conceptual modeling to support pivoting. In a historic case the solution space (i.e., To-Be options) is already known to the modeler. In the real-world, domain specialists and subject matter experts (SMEs) would apply their situational awareness and contextual knowledge to generate a solution space with new alternatives iteratively, creatively, and incrementally.

2   Case Example: Customer Segment Retargeting by Netflix to Achieve Larger Goal

The following summary of this Netflix case is based on published details that were co-authored by the Vice President of Edge Engineering at Netflix in [12]. Netflix operates a streaming video-on-demand platform that allows its subscribers to access its content on a variety of devices including smartphones, tablets, laptops, and desktop computers. It was founded as a postal-mail based DVD rental service in 1997 and transformed into an Internet based video streaming service between 2005 and 2007. Coupled with its international expansion, its transformation contributed to a tenfold growth in Netflix's annual revenues between 2005 and 2016.

A key enabler of Netflix's transformation into a video streaming service was its public Application Programming Interface (API). Netflix had built up an ecosystem of mashup apps over nearly ten years of running a video streaming business. These mashup apps were created by third party developers and combined Netflix assets (e.g., content, catalog) with third Party resources (e.g., forums, feeds) that added value to Netflix services. App developers were either software vendors that created mashups or hardware manufactures that developed device-specific viewer apps.

Netflix cultivated this ecosystem by offering its public API to third party developers because its complementors built synergistic offerings for its subscribers that were outside the core business of Netflix (i.e., video streaming). Examples of such mashups included apps for video recommendations, ratings, rankings, and referrals. Netflix encouraged the proliferation of such mashups because the usage of any mashup necessitated a Netflix subscription which was central to its strategy. Netflix absorbed the costs of maintaining and provisioning its API over time (i.e., to upgrade interfaces, sustain adequate capacity, etc.) as well as of supporting members of its ecosystem (e.g., by updating documentation, performing code reviews, etc.).

In 2014, Netflix decided to shut down its public API and thereby close this ecosystem [13, 14]. Netflix's ecosystem was vibrant at that time however, after being in existence for almost ten years, Netflix's ecosystem had started to return diminishing returns. Specifically, Netflix's approach of growing its revenues from its existing subscribers via its ecosystem stopped contributing substantially to its strategic objective of overall revenue growth. Therefore, Netflix decided to pivot its revenue model to focus on revenue growth from prospective subscribers via its core business to grow its overall revenue. This case example analyzes this pivot that was undertaken by Netflix in 2014 and resulted in the shuttering of its public API.

3   Modeling the Pre-pivot and Pivot Scenarios

3.1   Pre-pivot Scenario: Cultivation of Ecosystem via Public API

Following [11, 27] we use the $i*$ modeling language to express and analyze pivoting scenarios. We acknowledge that other types of goal modeling languages may also work if they support multiple actors. The $i*$ language was originally developed to support early stage requirements engineering [15] but has been applied to many other areas involving complex socio-technical phenomena [16] including business model analysis [17], pivoting [11, 27], and strategic coopetition [23–26, 28]. Figure 1 presents an *i** diagram showing the pre-pivot scenario in the Netflix case study.

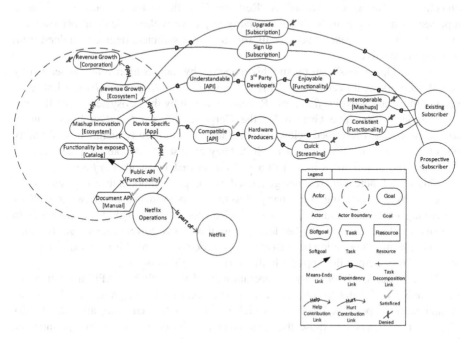

Fig. 1. *i** Strategic Rationale (SR) diagram showing pre-pivot scenario in the Netflix API case

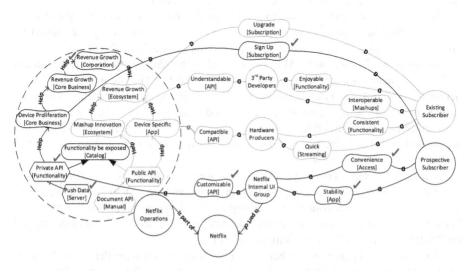

Fig. 2. *i** Strategic Rationale (SR) diagram showing pivot scenario in the Netflix API case

"Netflix Operations" is a business unit within the "Netflix" organization. This is depicted by associating the *actors* "Netflix Operations" and "Netflix" with an *is-part-of* link, which is used to show aggregation. An *actor* is an autonomous, reflective, self-interest seeking, and social agent with a contingent boundary [18]. The primary objective of "Netflix Operations" is "Revenue Growth for the Corporation". This is represented as a *softgoal*, which is a quality objective without clear-cut achievement criteria. Each *actor* seeks to achieve its *softgoals* to a sufficient degree as judged from its own perspective.

"Netflix Operations" can pursue this objective by increasing revenue generated by complementors in its ecosystem. This is depicted by a *Help contribution* link connecting the second-level *softgoal* of "Revenue Growth by the Ecosystem" with the top-level *softgoal* "Revenue Growth for the Corporation". *Contribution* links connect *softgoals* or *tasks* (described below) to other *softgoals* to portray hierarchies of quality objectives and their effects on each other. They are used to denote the positive, negative, neutral, or unknown impact of a *softgoal* or *task* on another *softgoal*.

This aim of increasing revenue generated by complementors in its ecosystem can be achieved by encouraging third party developers to innovate mashups as well as motivating hardware producers to build device specific apps. This is shown by *Help contribution* links linking a higher-level *softgoal* with two lower-level *softgoals* which are: (1) "Mashup Innovation be performed in the Ecosystem by third party developers", and (2) "Device Specific Apps be built by Hardware Producers".

These lower-level *softgoals* are operationalized via a "Public API" that offers the functionality of Netflix to third party developers and hardware producers. This operationalization is portrayed as a *task* which is a means for achieving an end. "Netflix Operations" intends to expose the functionality of its catalog to its complementors. This intention is depicted as a *goal* which is a state of affairs in the world that an *actor* wishes to achieve. Therefore, the *task* "Public API" is connected to the *goal* "Functionality be exposed of the Netflix catalog" via a *means-ends* link.

Means-ends links connect *tasks* to *goals* such that the completion of any *task* leads to the satisfaction of its associated *goal*. A *goal* describes something that should be done while a *task* specifies a particular way in which something should be done.

Netflix must "Document its API" in a manual so that third party developers can use it. This is depicted as a subordinate *task* of the superior *task* "Public API" using a *task-decomposition* link. A *task-decomposition* link connects *tasks* to their subordinate entities which can be *tasks*, *resources*, *goals*, and *softgoals*. Each subordinate entity of a *task* must be accomplished for that *task* to be completed. Therefore, *means-ends* links are treated as logical OR while *task-decomposition* links are treated as AND when evaluating goal achievement.

Actors in *i** may depend on other actors for *goals* to be achieved, *tasks* to be completed, *resources* (i.e., a physical or informational entity) to be obtained, and *softgoals* to be accomplished. For example, "third party developers" depend on "Netflix Operations" for an "Understandable API" while "Hardware Producers" depend on "Netflix Operations" for a "Compatible API".

An *actor* that depends on another *actor* is referred to as a depender while the *actor* on which the depender depends is referred to as a dependee. The depender depends on the dependee for a dependum. While a dependency can be beneficial for a depender it can also be deleterious since any dependum can make a depender vulnerable to exploitation and opportunism by its dependee. The curved side of the character 'D' in the *Dependency* link points towards the dependee while the flat side points towards the depender.

In the Netflix case, "Existing Customers" of Netflix depend on "third party developers" for mashups that are "Enjoyable" as well as "Interoperable" with each other and they also depend on "Hardware Producers" for device specific apps that offer "Quick Streaming" as well as "Consistent Functionality". "Netflix Operations" depends on "Existing Subscribers" to "Upgrade" their Subscriptions due to the beneficial value propositions of mashups by "third party developers" as well as device specific apps by "Hardware Producers".

After a model has been developed it can be used to assess the viability and desirability of alternative means for achieving an end. The goal graph is crucial for performing trade-off analysis in *i** models. A technique for forward propagation of *contribution* links is described in [19]. In this technique, propagation rules are applied to attach current values (i.e., satisfied, denied, etc.) from offspring to their parents and the resolution of the *softgoal* labels is performed at the parent level [20]. Viability of a particular *task* is evaluated by checking whether it satisfies or denies certain *softgoals*. The selection of an unviable alternative at a lower-level can lead to the denial of an important objective at the higher-level.

Alternative means (i.e., *tasks*) for achieving an end (i.e., *goal*) can be compared on the basis of the impact of each *task* on relevant quality objectives (i.e., *softgoals*). Desirability of a particular *task* is examined by comparing the *softgoals* that are satisfied or denied by that *task* with the *softgoals* that are satisfied or denied by other *tasks*. The selection of an undesirable alternative at the lower-level means that better alternatives for achieving an objective at the higher-level are not selected.

Forward propagating satisfaction labels via *contribution* links reveals that "Netflix Operations" published an API that was "Understandable" by "third party developers" and "Compatible" for "Hardware Producers". These dependencies are denoted with ✓. Nonetheless, "third party developers" were unable to offer mashups to "Existing Subscribers" of Netflix that were "Enjoyable" or "Interoperable". Similarly, "Hardware Producers" were unable to offer device specific apps to "Existing Subscribers" of Netflix that supported "Quick Streaming" or "Consistent Functionality". As a result, "Existing Subscribers" of Netflix did not "Upgrade" their Subscriptions.

This led to the denial of the Larger Goal for "Netflix Operations" which was "Revenue Growth for the Corporation". Therefore, each of these dependencies are denoted with ✗. This means that "Netflix Operations" was bearing the cost of supporting a public API for its partners but was not benefiting from that public API in terms of substantial contributions to its strategic objective.

Subsequently, "Netflix Operations" decided to pivot away from its approach of "Revenue Growth by the Ecosystem" to achieve its Larger Goal of "Revenue Growth for the Corporation". It switched to an approach of "Revenue Growth from its Core Business" to achieve its Larger Goal of "Revenue Growth for the Corporation". This pivot is discussed in the next sub-section.

3.2   Pivot Scenario: Service Proliferation on Devices via Private API

The first step of the Larger Goal pivot of "Netflix Operations" starts with identifying the highest level strategic objective that it needs to achieve. This is done by tracing the links from the pre-pivot low-level operationalization (i.e., *task*) upwards to the highest-level objective (i.e., *softgoal*). The operationalization that "Netflix Operations" was pivoting away from entailed offering a "Public API" and the highest level strategic objective that this operationalization was related to was "Revenue Growth for the Corporation". This strategic objective was not satisfied via the low-level operationalization of offering a "Public API".

Therefore, in the second step of the Larger Goal pivot, "Netflix Operations" needs to create a new way to satisfy this strategic objective. Domain Specialists and Subject Matter Experts (SMEs) in "Netflix Operations" decided to abandon the approach of "Revenue Growth by the Ecosystem" since it was related to the low-level opera-tionalization that entailed offering a "Public API". Instead they adopted the approach of "Revenue Growth from its Core Business" which entailed shifting the revenue growth focus away from its "Existing Subscribers" and onto its "Prospective Customers". This shift represents a Customer Segment pivot per the pivot archetypes of Ries [8].

The pre-pivot scenario lacked an operationalization for encouraging "Prospective Subscribers" to "Sign Up" for new Subscriptions. Therefore, in Fig. 1, the dependum "Sign Up" for new Subscriptions is connected to the highest level strategic objective of "Netflix Operations". In the third step of the Larger Goal pivot, SMEs in "Netflix Operations" designed and explored new alternatives for satisfying the strategic objective in a systematic and structured manner. This step extended the goal graph from the pre-pivot scenario to include new model elements in the pivot scenario. The pivot scenario is depicted in Fig. 2. For ease of interpretation in the visual presentation of Fig. 2, existing model elements from Fig. 1 are greyed-out and new model elements are depicted in black color.

In the pivot scenario, the highest-level objective of "Revenue Growth from Core Business" is refined into a new approach of "Device Proliferation". This lower-level aim entailed the creation of a standardized app for watching videos on Netflix that works across a wide range of device families (not shown*). A standardized app offers consistent features as well as uniform functionality across device families (not shown*). Moreover, it is less costly to build and maintain a single app that is stable than many apps that are stable (not shown*[1]).

In the pivot scenario, "Prospective Customers" depended on Netflix for a "Stable App" that afforded them "Convenient Access" to the Netflix catalog and content. "Netflix Operations" depended on "Prospective Customers" to "Sign Up" for new Subscriptions. However, "Netflix Operations" was not experienced in designing user interfaces (UIs). In the pre-pivot scenario, "third party developers" and "Hardware Producers" designed mashups and apps for watching Netflix videos.

In the pivot scenario, "Netflix Operations" needed to find a different way to build a standardized app for watching videos on Netflix. For this purpose, "Netflix Operations"

---

[1] *In this instance, and in the remainder of this paper, certain aspects of the relationship between *actors* are not shown due to page limitations.

established the "Netflix Internal UI Group" which was comprised of staff members on the Netflix payroll. The "Netflix Internal UI Group" depended on "Netflix Operations" for a "Customizable API". Since the "Netflix Internal UI Group" was a part of "Netflix" then "Netflix Operations" only needed to offer a "Private API" to it. "Netflix Internal UI Group" could leverage a "Customizable" "Private API" to build a standardized app for watching Netflix videos. "Netflix Operations" merely needed to "Push Data" onto a Server that was accessible to "Netflix Internal UI Group" via this "Private API".

"Netflix Internal UI Group" used this "Private API" to design and distribute a "Stable App" to "Prospective Subscribers". These "Prospective Subscribers" were able to use this app to "Conveniently Access" Netflix services. This incentivized "Prospective Subscribers" to "Sign Up" for a Netflix subscription and helped "Netflix Operations" to achieve its aim of "Device Proliferation". Consequently, "Device Proliferation" allowed "Netflix Operations" to satisfy its higher-level objective of "Revenue Growth for the Core Business" and ultimately satisfy its highest-level objective of "Revenue Growth for the Corporation".

4 Related Work

This paper contributes to the body of research literature pertaining to Enterprise Modeling (EM) of organizational pivots. Currently, EM research that is exclusively focused on pivoting in organizations is relatively scarce. However, the body of research literature on EM of organizational strategy (of which pivoting is one part) is comparatively richer. We [11] adopt *i** to model various types of pivots in startups and large enterprises. We also [27] present conceptual models of pivoting based on a retrospective case example of Twitter. Giannoulis et al. [21] offer a language for modeling strategy maps. Kim et al. [22] propose a modeling technique to depict a value chain of a virtual enterprise. We introduced a technique for modeling and analyzing strategic coopetition between organizations [23, 24] as well as its characteristics of complementarity [25] and reciprocity [26].

5 Conclusion and Future Work

We utilized a strategic modeling approach to systematically search for and create viable approaches for implementing a Larger Goal pivot. The approach available in the pre-pivot scenario was shown to be inadequate for meeting the strategic objective of the focal organization. Therefore, a pivot scenario was generated that encompassed the design of a new approach for meeting the Larger Goal of the focal organization. An abstract pattern and decontextualized representation of Larger Goal pivot has been developed and future work includes validating this model in real world organizational settings. Future work also includes developing a catalog of pivoting goals to serve as a knowledge base for SMEs and domain specialists.

Future work also seeks to address certain limitations of *i** modeling that were encountered during the expression and analysis of the Netflix case. *i** models have limited visual scalability in terms of human interpretability. Goal graphs with multiple actors and multiple goal structures can become inscrutable for humans. $i*$ models do not support the depiction of temporality and therefore pre-pivot and pivot configurations are depicted in separate diagrams. This requires a model analyst to switch back and forth between the models to compare them. $i*$ models lack support for depiction of negative dependencies and therefore it is not possible to perform counterfactual reasoning.

Some of these limitations can be partially addressed with tool support. A tool for $i*$ modeling can help to make $i*$ models more explainable to humans. Features and functions of such a tool might include expanding/collapsing, revealing/hiding, enlarging/shrinking, and coloring/discoloring parts of the $i*$ model. A tool for $i*$ modeling can also help with model evaluation by calculating satisfaction of goals in a model. It can do so by propagating satisfaction labels across elements over contribution links and then applying rules to resolve a single label for each goal from contributions to it.

References

1. Ghemawat, P.: Competition and business strategy in historical perspective. Bus. Hist. Rev. **76**(1), 37–74 (2002)
2. Casadesus-Masanell, R., Ricart, J.E.: From strategy to business models and onto tactics. Long Range Plann. **43**(2–3), 195–215 (2010)
3. Casadesus-Masanell, R., Ricart, J.E.: How to design a winning business model. Harv. Bus. Rev. **89**(1/2), 100–107 (2011)
4. Stanton, P.: Microsoft's pivot and the importance of windows containers (2016). Accessed from https://www.infoworld.com/article/3113161/it-management/microsofts-pivot-and-the-importance-of-windows-containers.html
5. Townsend, K.: Why microsoft's Linux Lovefest goes hand-in-hand with its azure cloud strategy (2016). Accessed from https://www.techrepublic.com/article/why-microsofts-linux-lovefest-goes-hand-in-hand-with-its-azure-cloud-strategy/
6. Baribeau, S.: Pivoting from Auctioneers to online Sellers–eBay takes on amazon (2013). Accessed from https://www.fastcompany.com/3004125/pivoting-auctioneers-online-sellers-ebay-takes-amazon
7. Weissbrot, A.: Inside eBay's repositioning as a modern e-Commerce platform (2017). Accessed from https://adexchanger.com/advertiser/inside-ebays-repositioning-modern-ecommerce-platform/
8. Ries, E.: The Lean Startup: How Today's Entrepreneurs Use Continuous Innovation to Create Radically Successful Businesses. Crown Publishing Group, New York (2011)
9. Edison, H., Smørsgård, N.M., Wang, X., Abrahamsson, P.: Lean internal startups for software product innovation in large companies: enablers and inhibitors. J. Syst. Softw. **135**, 69–87 (2018)
10. Bajwa, S.S., Wang, X., Duc, A.N., Abrahamsson, P.: "Failures" to be celebrated: an analysis of major pivots of software startups. Empir. Softw. Eng. **22**(5), 2373–2408 (2017)
11. Pant, V., Yu, E., Tai, A.: Towards reasoning about pivoting in startups and large enterprises with i*. In: Poels, G., Gailly, F., Serral Asensio, E., Snoeck, M. (eds.) PoEM 2017. LNBIP, vol. 305, pp. 203–220. Springer, Cham (2017). https://doi.org/10.1007/978-3-319-70241-4_14

12. Jacobson, D., Woods, D., Brail, G.: APIs: A Strategy Guide. O'Reilly Media, Inc. (2011)
13. Jacobson, D.: Why you probably don't need an API strategy (2014). Accessed from https:// thenextweb.com/entrepreneur/2013/09/15/why-you-probably-dont-need-an-api-strategy/
14. Lawler, R.: Netflix will shut down public API support for third-party developers on November 14 (2014). Accessed from https://techcrunch.com/2014/06/13/netflix-api-shutdown/
15. Yu, E.S.: Towards modelling and reasoning support for early-phase requirements engineering. In: Proceedings of the Third IEEE International Symposium on Requirements Engineering, pp. 226–235. IEEE (1997)
16. Yu, E., Giorgini, P., Maiden, N., Mylopoulos, J.: Social Modeling for Requirements Engineering. MIT Press, Cambridge (2011)
17. Samavi, R., Yu, E., Topaloglou, T.: Strategic reasoning about business models: a conceptual modeling approach. Inf. Syst. e-Bus. Manag. 7(2), 171–198 (2009)
18. Yu, E.: Agent orientation as a modelling paradigm. Wirtschaftsinformatik 43(2), 123–132 (2001)
19. Horkoff, J., Yu, E.: Comparison and evaluation of goal-oriented satisfaction analysis techniques. Requir. Eng. 18(3), 199–222 (2013)
20. Horkoff, J., Yu, E.: Analyzing goal models: different approaches and how to choose among them. In: Proceedings of the 2011 ACM Symposium on Applied Computing, pp. 675–682 (2011)
21. Giannoulis, C., Petit, M., Zdravkovic, J.: Towards a unified business strategy language: a meta-model of strategy maps. In: van Bommel, P., Hoppenbrouwers, S., Overbeek, S., Proper, E., Barjis, J. (eds.) PoEM 2010. LNBIP, vol. 68, pp. 205–216. Springer, Heidelberg (2010). https://doi.org/10.1007/978-3-642-16782-9_15
22. Kim, C.H., Son, Y.J., Kim, T.Y., Kim, K., Baik, K.: A modeling approach for designing a value chain of virtual enterprise. Int. J. Adv. Manuf. Technol. 28(9–10), 1025–1030 (2006)
23. Pant, V., Yu, E.: Modeling simultaneous cooperation and competition among enterprises. Bus. Inf. Syst. Eng. 60(1), 39–54 (2018)
24. Pant, V., Yu, E.: Coopetition with frenemies: towards modeling of simultaneous cooperation and competition among enterprises. In: Horkoff, J., Jeusfeld, Manfred A., Persson, A. (eds.) PoEM 2016. LNBIP, vol. 267, pp. 164–178. Springer, Cham (2016). https://doi.org/10. 1007/978-3-319-48393-1_12
25. Pant, V., Yu, E.: Modeling strategic complementarity and synergistic value creation in coopetitive relationships. In: Ojala, A., Holmström Olsson, H., Werder, K. (eds.) ICSOB 2017. LNBIP, vol. 304, pp. 82–98. Springer, Cham (2017). https://doi.org/10.1007/978-3-319-69191-6_6
26. Pant, V., Yu, E.: Generating Win-Win strategies for software businesses under coopetition: a strategic modeling approach. In: International Conference of Software Business. Springer, Cham (2018)
27. Pant, V., Yu, E.: Conceptual modeling to support pivoting – an example from twitter. In: Proceedings on Advances in Conceptual Modeling - ER 2018 Workshops AHA, MoBiD, MREBA, OntoCom, and QMMQ, Lecture Notes in Computer Science. Springer, Verlag (2018)
28. Pant, V., Yu, E.: Getting to Win-Win in industrial collaboration under coopetition: a strategic modeling approach. In: Zdravkovic, J., Grabis, J., Nurcan, S., Stirna, J. (eds.) International Conference on Business Informatics Research. Springer, Cham (2018)

Author Index

Printed in the United States
By Bookmasters